PAUL D. SANSONE, O.F.M.

NEW TESTAMENT APOCRYPHA

I

NEW TESTAMENT APOCRYPHA

Revised Edition
edited by
Wilhelm Schneemelcher

English translation edited by
R. McL. Wilson

I

GOSPELS
AND RELATED WRITINGS

James Clarke & Co
Westminster/John Knox Press

Published in Great Britain by
James Clarke & Co. Ltd
P.O. Box 60
Cambridge CB1 2NT

Published in the United States by
Westminster/John Knox Press
Louisville, Kentucky 40202-1396

British Library Cataloguing in Publication Data
[Bible. N.T. Apocryphal books. English, 1991] New
  Testament Apocrypha. - 2nd. ed.
  I. Schneemelcher, Wilhelm
  229.9
  ISBN 0-227-67915-6

Library of Congress Cataloging-in-Publication Data
Neutestamentliche Apokryphen. English.
    New Testament apocrypha / edited by Wilhelm Schneemelcher ;
English translation edited by R. McL. Wilson. — Rev. ed.
      p.   cm.
Translation of: Neutestamentliche Apokryphen.
Includes bibliographical references.
Contents: v. 1. Gospels and related writings.
ISBN 0-664-21878-4

    I. Schneemelcher, Wilhelm, 1914- . II. Wilson, R. McL. (Robert
McLachlan) III. Title.
BS2832.S3 1991
229' .92052—dc20   90-23504

Printed in the United States of America
2 4 6 8 9 7 5 3 1

Preface to the English Edition

For many years the standard work in English in this field, indeed for practical purposes the only work, was *The Apocryphal New Testament* edited by M.R. James and first published in 1924. By the late fifties, however, for all its unquestioned merits, it could be said to suffer from two defects: it was then more than thirty years old, and consequently took no account of the discoveries made in that period; and it provided but little in the way of guidance to the literature devoted to these apocryphal writings. Both these deficiencies were made good in the third edition of its German counterpart, the *Neutestamentliche Apokryphen*, originally edited by Edgar Hennecke and directed in its latest form by Wilhelm Schneemelcher. An English edition (vol. I, 1963; vol. II, 1965) met with a cordial reception, and went into a second impression some ten years later.

'Hennecke-Schneemelcher' is now, however, some thirty years old, and much has happened in these three decades. For one thing, the Nag Hammadi library is now accessible, and can be evaluated; for another, there has been a considerable accession to the literature in this whole area. A new edition is therefore very welcome, and it is appropriate that the English version also should be revised and updated (some German works have gone through six or seven editions, but their English versions have remained unchanged from the first!).

The policy adopted is that which governed the previous English edition: to present an English version, checked and corrected to make it in every way possible an adequate tool for the use of the English-speaking reader. Some parts are completely new, and these have been translated from scratch. At other points much of the earlier edition has been retained, and here use has been made of the contributions of my colleagues in that earlier volume, Dr George Ogg and Prof. A.J.B. Higgins, both now deceased, and Dr R.E. Taylor. The whole has, however, been rigorously checked and revised against the new German edition, and the translation editor must assume the full responsibility. Dr Einar Thomassen has kindly undertaken the translation of three sections: VIII 1, the Book of Thomas; VIII 4, the Apocryphon of James; and VIII 5, the Dialogue of the Saviour.

One point should be made, to avoid possible misunderstanding (such as afflicted one reviewer of the earlier first volume!): the several introductions are straight translations from the German, except for the 'residue' of the section contributed by H.C. Puech, for which a copy of the original French was also made available. The texts, however, presented something of a problem, which was envisaged from the outset in the earlier edition: merely to translate the German here would have produced something at some remove from the originals, whereas completely new translations could scarcely have been put under the names of the German contributors. The solution adopted then as now was to check the translations against the originals in Latin, Greek or Coptic, to ensure that they were English versions of the original and not merely versions at third hand. Some things go more easily into English than into German!

It is hoped that the second volume will follow at not too great an interval after the first.

R. McL. Wilson

Preface to Sixth German Edition

The first volume of the *Neutestamentliche Apokryphen in deutscher Übersetzung*, founded in 1904 by Edgar Hennecke († 1951), appeared in a third edition in 1959. A fourth edition which came out in 1968 was simply a corrected reprint of the third edition. The present sixth edition is a corrected reprint of the fifth edition, in which printing errors have been removed; at one point only some supplementary material has been introduced.

The complete recasting of the third (fourth) edition was necessary because in recent years there has been a considerable amount of work in the area of research into the apocrypha.

In recent years there has been so much research in this area that a completely new recasting of the work seemed appropriate. In particular the texts of the Coptic gnostic library of Nag Hammadi, which in 1959 could not yet be comprehensively evaluated, have in the interval been opened up and made generally accessible. A number of works from this find belong beyond doubt to the kinds of text the extant witnesses of which are assembled in this volume. In deciding which texts from Nag Hammadi ought to be included in our collection, I have profited from the advice of C. Colpe, H.-M. Schenke and H.J. Klimkeit, to whom I would express my cordial thanks.

Through the inclusion of texts from Nag Hammadi the book has become more voluminous than in the previous edition. The remaining sections had in part to be completely remodelled, but in part the drafting of the previous edition could be taken over in a revised form. I have to thank all the collaborators who have shared in this edition. We may also remember with gratitude those who through their work contributed to the success of the previous edition, but in the interval have been called from this life.

R. Kassel, R. Merkelbach and R. Stichel have advised me in many questions of detail. A. de Santos Otero has frequently helped with his special knowledge. K. Schäferdiek, who already in the previous edition rendered great service, has been a true helper this time also. G. Ahn has assisted me in correcting the proofs. To all those named I would express my hearty thanks.

Finally I must also thank the publisher G. Siebeck and his colleagues (especially R. Pflug) for their understanding collaboration. For over eighty years this work has been taken care of by the Tübingen publishing house - a notable testimony to the solid continuity of this house.

The second volume "Apostolisches. Apokalyptik und Verwandtes" appeared in 1989.

Wilhelm Schneemelcher

Table of Contents

Abbreviations

For abbreviations of journals and series, the lists of Schwertner (*Theologische Realenzyklopädie, Abkürzungsverzeichnis*, 1976) and RGG³ (1957) have in general been used. For the texts from Nag Hammadi (apart from the Book of Thomas) reference may be made to the list of abbreviations in James M. Robinson's introductory volume to the Facsimile Edition of the Nag Hammadi Codices (Leiden 1984), pp. 96ff., which provides a comparative table of the forms used in English, French and German. See also *The Nag Hammadi Library in English*, 3rd rev. ed., 1988, pp. xiii-xiv. A few abbreviations frequently employed are listed below.

Aa	*Acta apostolorum apocrypha* I, ed. Lipisius, 1891; II 1 and 2, ed. Bonnet, 1898 and 1903 (reprint 1959)
ANRW	*Aufstieg und Niedergang der Römischen Welt*
Apa	*Apocalypses apocryphae*, ed. C.Tischendorf, 1866
BHG	Bibliotheca hagiographica Graeca, ³1957
BHL	Bibliotheca hagiographica Latina, ²1949
BHO	Bibliotheca hagiographica orientalis, 1910
CChrSL	Corpus Christianorum, Series Latina, 1953ff.
CChrSG	Corpus Christianorum, Series Graeca, 1976ff.
CChrSA	Corpus Christianorum, Series Apocryphorum, 1983ff.
CSCO	Corpus scriptorum Christianorum orientalium
CSEL	Corpus scriptorum ecclesiasticorum Latinorum, Vienna
Ea	*Evangelia apocrypha*, ed. C. von Tischendorf, ²1876
Erbetta	Mario Erbetta, *Gli Apocrifi del Nuovo Testament, I-III*, 1966-1981
FS	Festschrift
GCS	Die griechischen christlichen Schriftsteller der ersten drei Jahrhunderte, Berlin
James	M.R.James, *The Apocryphal New Testament*
KIT	Kleine Texte für Vorlesungen und Übungen
Moraldi	Luigi Moraldi, *Apocrifi del Nuovo Testamento*, 2 vols., 1971
NHC	Nag Hammadi Codex
NHLE	*The Nag Hammadi Library in English, ed. James M. Robinson* Leiden 1977 (3rd revised ed. 1988)
NHS	Nag Hammadi Studies
NTApo¹	*Neuetestamentliche Apokryphen in deutscher Überzetzung*, ed. Edgar Hennecke, 1904
NTApo²	id., 2nd edition, 1924
NTApo³	id., 3rd edition, ed. E. Hennecke and W. Schneemelcher, 1959/1964 (reprint ⁴1968; ET 1963, 1965; 2nd impression 1973, 1974)
NTApoHandb	*Handbuch zu den Neuetestamentlichen Apokryphen*, ed. Edgar Hennecke, 1904
PG	Patrologiae cursus completus. Accurante J.-P. Migne, Series Graeca

RGG[3]	*Die Religion in Geschichte und Gegenwart,* [3]1956ff.
de Santos	*Los Evangelios apocrifos* (BAC 148), [4]1984, [6]1988
Starowieyski	*Apokryphy Nowego Testamentu, Pod redakcja ks. Marka Starowieyskiego,* vol. I, Lublin 1980
TDNT	*Theological Dictionary of the NT, tr. G.W. Bromiley* (ET of *Theologisches Wörterbuch zum NT,* 1933ff.)
TRE	*Theologische Realenzyklopädie,*1976ff.
TU	Texte und Untersuchungen zur Geschichte der altchristlichen Literatur
Vielhauer, Lit. gesch.	Philipp Vielhauer, *Geschichte der urchristlichen Literatur,* 1975

I

GOSPELS
AND RELATED WRITINGS

General Introduction

Wilhelm Schneemelcher

The concept 'New Testament apocrypha' is probably formed on the analogy of that of the 'Old Testament apocrypha'. The latter designation is generally given to the writings of which Luther says that 'while they are not regarded as being on an equality with Holy Writ, they yet make useful and good reading'. But even for the Old Testament apocrypha this definition is by no means adequate to cover the complex situation with which we are concerned.[1] For the so-called 'New Testament apocrypha' it is quite unserviceable, since here it is not a question of writings the canonicity of which was for a long time canvassed. Rather we have to do with writings which were excluded from ecclesiastical usage very early, to a small extent even before the completion of the canon at the end of the 2nd century and in the course of the 3rd, and which then continued to have a separate existence among groups outside the Great Church, or again with works which for various motives availed themselves of the forms and *Gattungen* of the New Testament, for didactic purposes, for propaganda or for entertainment.

An exact definition of this general concept is certainly difficult, and will have to take very diverse aspects into consideration (see below, pp.50ff.). A necessary pre-condition for any attempt to characterise the mass of diverse writings under a uniform concept, and thereby distinguish them from other forms and *Gattungen* as a special kind of literature in terms of form and content, is a clarification of certain terms often inexactly used, and a knowledge of the main features of the history of the New Testament canon.

1. The concepts: canon, testament, apocrypha

Literature: Th. Zahn, *Grundriß der Geschichte des ntl. Kanons*, ²1904; G. Quell and J. Behm, Art. διατίθημι, διαθήκη , in TDNT II, 1964, 104-134; H. Oppel, ΚΑΝΩΝ. *Zur Bedeutungsgeschichte des Wortes und seiner lateinische Entsprechungen*, 1937; H.W.Beyer, Art. κανών, in TDNT, 1965, pp. 596-602; R.Meyer and A.Oepke, Art., κρύπτω κτλ.'Supplement on the Canon and the Apocrypha', in TDNT III, 1965, 978-1000; H. von Campenhausen, *The Formation of the Christian Bible*, ET 1972; P. Vielhauer, *Geschichte der urchristlichen Literatur*, 1975, pp. 774ff.; W.Schneemelcher, Art. Bibel III, in TRE VI, 1980, 22ff. (Lit.); E. Grässer, *Der Alte Bund im Neuen*, 1985, pp. 1-134.

1. The term 'canon' as a designation for the Bible is first attested in the middle of the 4th century: Canon LIX of the Council of Laodicea (middle of the 4th cent.) decrees that 'books not canonised' (ἀκανόνιστα βιβλία) are not to be read in the Church; only the canonical writings of the Old and New Testaments are allowed. These canonical writings are then enumerated in Canon LX.[1]

In his 39th Festal Letter in 367, Athanasius of Alexandria defined his position on the question of the books recognised in the Church, and gave a list of the acknowledged books of the Old and New Testaments (for text, see below pp.49f.). Athanasius here speaks of the writings which have been 'canonised, handed down and confirmed as divine', but sets the lists of the books of the Old and New Testaments under the concept of 'testament'(διαθήκη). We may deduce from this that in the middle of the 4th century the concepts 'canon' and 'testament' (or 'covenant') still marched side by side, although probably in the sense that 'canon' was used as a designation for the whole Bible, i.e. for the collection of the holy scriptures recognised by the Church, and that the two parts of the Bible are occasionally described by 'testament'.[2]

The Greek word κανών is formed from κάνη, a loan-word from the Semitic with the basic meaning 'reed'; the Greek form κάννα is also attested.[3] The Hebrew קָנֶה is used with the meanings 'reed, corn-stalk', then also in the further sense of 'measuring-reed, measuring-rod, measuring-stick'. The Septuagint however never translates this קָנֶה by the Greek κανών, which in it appears only in three places: Judith 13:6 (here 'bed-post'), Micah 7:4 ('an inexplicable flaw in translation', Beyer, p.596) and 4 Macc. 7:21. In the last-mentioned passage it is said: 'Should not a man πρὸς ὅλον τὸν τῆς φιλοσοφίας κανόνα φιλοσοφῶν (who philosophises according to the whole canon of philosophy) have control over desire?' Here κανών is used (as also in Philo) in the general Greek sense: κανών is the rule, the precept, indeed almost the law. The word is transferred to various spheres of life. κανών becomes a description for the norm, the completed shape, the standard or criterion. The application of this term to the ethical or philosophical domain was certainly important. The moral law is described as κανών, and specific ideals are exalted into κανόνες. It can be shown from Epicurus and Epictetus how important this idea became for philosophy. ' To philosophise means nothing other than to investigate and establish standards, κανόνες' (Epict. *Diss.* II 11. 24). 'The κανόνες are then the basic rules for the right use of free will' (Beyer, p. 598).

It has been thought that the lists of exemplary authors drawn up by the Alexandrian grammarians (e.g. Aristophanes of Byzantium) were described by this term. But this is only 'a modern catachresis that originated in the 18th century' (David Ruhnken, 1768). 'From its frequent use in ethics, κανών always retained the meaning of rule or model.'[4] The lists of the Alexandrians were called πίνακες and not κανόνες. This should be borne in mind in the discussion of the taking over of the concept by the Church.

In the NT κανών occurs four times (Gal. 6:16; 2 Cor. 10:13, 15, 16). Here too the word is probably used with the meaning of 'norm, rule of conduct, standard', even though in the difficult passage 2 Cor. 10:13-16 the sense is not quite so unambiguous as in Gal 6:16.[5]

The word is widely used in the Church with the meaning 'norm, standard' (1 Clem. 1.3; 41.1, here with an ethical aspect). In the second half of the 2nd century it is then more frequently employed, and especially in the phrases κανὼν τῆς ἀληθείας and κανὼν τῆς πίστεως.[6]

These formulae belong in the context of the development of Church history in the 2nd century, which has often been placed under the catchword 'birth of early Catholicism'. This description is not entirely false, but we must beware of unduly stereotyped ideas. It is correct that in this period the manifold variety of Christian doctrine and expressions of the faith begins to become unified. The struggle against Gnosticism and the syncretistic dissolution of the Christian message which it entailed made it necessary to seek for uniform norms for life and doctrine and for the constitution of the Church, and so secure the unity of the *ecclesia catholica* and the purity of its proclamation.

The word κανών presented itself as a designation that could express unmistakably what ecclesiastically was now obligatory. It served in the first place quite generally to set in relief what the binding ecclesiastical norm was to be, and was used in this sense above all in a threefold connection: Rule of Truth (κανὼν τῆς ἀληθείας), Rule of Faith (κανὼν τῆς πίστεως) and Rule of the Church (or Ecclesiastical Rule, κανὼν τῆς ἐκκλησίας). The Rule of Truth is the obligatory truth as the Church proclaims it. It takes shape in the Rule of Faith, the *regula fidei*. However, in this idea of a κανὼν τῆς πίστεως or *regula fidei* we ought not to think prematurely of fixed and unalterable formulae of belief, a baptismal confession or the like. 'Rule of Faith' in the texts of the 2nd and 3rd centuries rather means 'a definite objective summary of Christian doctrinal truth and in this sense of the faith'.[7] It should further be noted that in the course of time κανονιζόμενος and ἐκκλησιαζόμενος become synonymous designations, and that thus the Church was regarded as the creator of the norm. From the 4th century on the general use of the word 'canon' was supplemented or delimited: certain parts were extracted from the total teaching of the Church and the total content of its life, and then designated as κανών or κανονικός.[8] But above all from the middle of the 4th century the collection of the recognised writings of the Old and New Testaments was so described (see above, Canons of Laodicea and Athanasius).

How did it come about that a term already long used in the Church was transferred to the collection of the recognised writings?

As already mentioned, we cannot assume a taking over of the description from the lists of the Alexandrian grammarians, for these were called πίνακες and not κανόνες. Now there is a use of κανών the origin of which is not clear and which also is not so frequently attested: 'canon' as a list, catalogue or table. This description occurs in the pre-Christian and non-Christian area for astronomical (astrological) and chronological tables. Eusebius of Caesarea describes his tables for the Synoptics in this way (Nestle-Aland[26], pp.73ff.).

Zahn maintained (and Vielhauer agreed with him) that from the derivative verb κανονίζειν we must conclude that the transference of κανών to the collection of writings recognised by the Church was determined by the meaning 'catalogue'.[9]

On the other hand Beyer, like Jülicher before him, held to the view that the idea of a norm was decisive for this description of the Holy Scriptures. With this I concurred in NTApo[10].

Now we have no evidence as to why in the 4th century the Bible was described as canon. It is however very improbable that a purely formal concept ('catalogue') was attached to the collection, about the final consolidation of which people were concerned, especially since the concept of 'canon' from the 2nd century played a considerable role in the Church, but not as a statement of any formal function, rather as a designation for a comprehensive formula for what in that period was vital to the life of the Church: a norm of doctrine and of faith.

At any rate there is everything to be said for the view that the term canon as a designation for the Church's Bible was suggested by the history of its meaning within the Church (and its pre-Christian stages). 'The canon is the norm to which everything in the Church accommodates itself; to canonise means to recognise as part of this norm.'[11]

2. Another term appeared very much earlier than 'canon' as a description of the books recognised by the Church: Διαθήκη. This word, which occurs frequently in the NT, originally described a testament, but can also be understood as a disposition, enactment or declaration of will (so in LXX).'Διαθήκη is from first to last the 'disposition' of God, the mighty declaration of the sovereign will of God in history, by which he orders the relation between himself and men according to his own saving purpose, and which carries with it the authoritative divine ordering, the one order of things which is in accordance with it'.[12]

The literary use of this term, which sounds for the first time in Paul (2 Cor. 3:14: the reading of the Old Testament), made its way only gradually, in parallel with the consolidation of the collection of the NT writings. We can, however, no longer say when and where this usage came into full effect. Irenaeus, who knows as a theological term, did not apply the word to the Bible.

On the other hand Melito of Sardis, in a letter preserved by Eusebius (H.E. IV 26.13f.), reports on a journey to Palestine on which he obtained information about τὰ τῆς παλαιᾶς διαθήκης βιβλία. The result he sets out in a list of the OT books. The term διαθήκη as a description for books is thus attested at least for the OT. Whether Melito also spoke of books of the 'New Covenant', we do not know. In Clement of Alexandria (Strom. I 5; V 85) and Origen (Comm. in Joh. X 28; de Princ. IV 11) the usage appears to be already quite familiar, even though Origen notes a certain inaccuracy in the Church use of a biblical concept.[13] Canon LIX of Laodicea, already mentioned, shows that this use of an important theological term as the formal designation of the two parts of the Bible is firmly established.

From διαθήκη the adjective ἐνδιάθηκος was derived (e.g. Origen, *Or.* 14.4; Euseb. H.E. III 3.1 etc.), which indicated belonging to the canon. Whether we can explain from this the usage of ἐνδιάθητος for the same situation, which occurs in the 4th century (e.g. Epiphanius, *Haer.* 55.2), remains questionable.

Even if the transition from the meaning 'covenant, testament' to that of 'documents of the covenant' can no longer be explained in detail, we can yet establish that even with the technical use of the term it always remained possible in the Greek area 'to discern the connection between the two and make it directly understood theologically'.[14] The Latin translation of διαθήκη had far-reaching consequences in so far as *testamentum*, by which the Greek word was rendered, has persisted as a designation even to today. In Tertullian *instrumentum* also occasionally occurs alongside *testamentum*, but *instrumentum* (probably taken over from 'earlier Jewish terminology for the Old Testament'[15]) was supplanted by *testamentum*.

The description of the two 'Testaments' by διαθήκη thus probably came into use in the period when the NT canon was in formation and there was concern for the consolidation of the OT writings. As already stated, people in this period still did not speak of the canon when they meant the Bible, but they had to take thought for a designation. Διαθήκη or *testamentum* met the most important requirements: 'each part of the Scripture has acquired a new name which simultaneously unites the two and distinguishes between them. It is no longer possible to divorce the New Testament from the Old, as Marcion had tried to do; but it is even less possible simply to put the two collections on the same level, as if there were no difference beween them. At least, this is the consequence which is bound to follow constantly from the predicates 'Old' and 'New', so long as these are not completely ignored.'[16]

Behind the name for the documents of the divine will to salvation stands the theology of Irenaeus and his forefathers in Asia Minor, 'who in their turn drew upon the ancient prophets and Paul'.[17] In other words, the history of the term διαθήκη is only correctly understood when it is set in the context of the history of theology.

3. Writings which were not accepted into the canon of the Old or New Testament, and thus do not rank as 'canonical', but are in some way or other connected with Old or New Testament writings, are commonly described as *Apocrypha*. This usage is relatively late. The old canon catalogues[18] know the writings with which we are concerned for the most part only as 'extra-canonical', 'disputed', 'writings which are not read in the Church, but before catechumens'. However, the description of such writings as 'apocrypha' also appears (cf. the canon catalogues printed below), and here the uncertainty in usage becomes clear from the fact that alongside what we describe as apocrypha other writings (e.g. the Letters of Barnabas and Ignatius, etc.) are placed under the same head. For the usage familiar to us today, the use of the term by Karlstadt in his work *De canonicis scripturis* (1520) was important;[19] it was probably from there that it came into the Luther Bible (as a description for the disputed Old Testament books).

In the early Church the designation ἀπόκρυφα appears from the time of Irenaeus onwards, but has a different meaning and also in the early centuries had a history which is far from easy to survey.

What did ἀπόκρυφος originally mean?[20] It has been thought that ἀπόκρυφος was a translation of the Hebrew גנוז, therefore of an expression by which were designated the books which were banned from reading in public worship, although their secular use was not thereby ruled out. That could be brought into accord with certain statements of the rabbis regarding such writings. But this opinion, advocated above all by Th. Zahn,[21] cannot be maintained. It must rather be emphasised that גנז in its basic significance means 'to gather' or 'to preserve' and only in a derived sense 'to hide, withdraw from the clutches of publicity', whereas ἀπόκρυφος means in the first place 'kept hidden because of its costliness or because of the objectionable nature of its content' and then 'of hidden origin'. In any case the use of ἀπόκρυφος for certain writings cannot be explained from Judaism; rather we must turn to the gentile-gnostic terminology for the root of this usage. Gnosticism favoured esoteric and secret doctrines, used cryptograms, and kept its writings secret. Thus the great Leiden magical papyrus prefaces the revelation of the Uphôr-charm with the instruction: ἔχε ἐν ἀποκρύφῳ ὡς μεγαλομυστήριον. κρύβε, κρύβε (Preisendanz, *Pap. gr. mag.* XII 321), and similar instructions are a constant element in gnostic gospels (cf. below, pp.372ff.). In this context belongs also the concern to trace back Greek philosophy to oriental secret books which were described as ἀπόκρυφα βιβλία (Suda IV 713.16 Adler). This terminology was decisive for the introduction of the notion 'apocryphal' into the Church. This is already shown by the fact that the word 'apocryphal' first comes before us not in connection with the history of the canon, but in the Church's conflict with Gnosticism and other heresies. Thus according to Clement of Alexandria (*Strom.* I.69.6) certain gnostics appealed to βίβλοι ἀπόκρυφοι, and a famous gnostic work bears the title 'Apocryphon Johannis'. Now these were certainly not books that had been removed from a Jewish or Christian lectionary, but secret books that were peculiarly precious to the gnostics.[22] The ecclesiastical writers took over this use of the word, but since they rejected the occult sciences of the gnostics they gave to it a pejorative connotation. Thus Irenaeus sets ἀπόκρυφος alongside νόθος (forged), and Tertullian uses *apocrypha* and *falsa* as synonymous.[23] Writings used by the Church - whether books read in public or books for private reading - are at any rate fundamentally not 'apocryphal'. For a time, admittedly, another usage became current, when over against the gnostic 'apocrypha' the Church set as early secret books those Jewish books which the synagogue had rejected, but which enjoyed in it an extensive popularity. It is in this sense at all events that Origen speaks of such works as 'apocrypha'.[24] As the valuation of these Old Testament 'apocrypha' declined, the expression also fell into disrepute. About 400 the depreciatory meaning of the word ἀπόκρυφος, applied now to the Jewish apocrypha as well, finally prevailed, as is clear from the following quotation from Augustine: *de his qui appellantur apocryphi - non quod habendi sint in aliqua auctoritate secreta, sed quia nulla testificationis luce declarati de nescio quo secreto nescio quorum praesumptione prolati sunt* (*c. Faust.* 11.2: CSEL 25, 314.25-315.3).

The withdrawal of the abundant apocryphal literature from ecclesiastical use set the term 'apocryphal' free for the writings which were not withdrawn, but were included only in the Septuagint. This use of the word, however, prevailed only in Protestantism. In the later canon catalogues these texts (in themselves permitted, but not set on an equality with the canonical writings) are still differentiated from those that were rejected. And in the catalogues only the latter are called ἀπόκρυφοι or also νόθοι καὶ ἀπόβλητοι, *libri apocryphi, qui nullatenus a nobis recipi debeant* (Decr. Gelasianum). At the same time the selection is still somewhat fluctuating. The Jewish pseudepigrapha and the gospels and Acts of Apostles that did not attain to the canon are certainly rejected. But when 1 Clement, the so-called 2 Clement, the Didache, the writings of Ignatius and the Shepherd of Hermas are also designated ἀπόκρυφοι, the usage is inexact, and the notion of ἀπόκρυφος is blended with that of the ἀντιλεγόμενα; these writings do not belong to the canon, but the reading of them is permitted.

2. On the history of the New Testament canon

Literature: Th. Zahn, *Geschichte des ntl. Kanons* I II, 1888-92; id., *Grundriß der Geschichte des ntl. Kanons*, [2]1904; H. Lietzmann, *Wie wurden die Bücher des NT heilige Schrift? 5 Vorträge*, 1907 (= Kleine Schriften II, TU 68, 1958, 15-98; quotations from the 1907 edition); A.von Harnack, *The Origins of the New Testament*, 1925; H. von Campenhausen, *The Formation of the Christian Bible*, ET 1972; W. Schneemelcher, Art. Bibel III. 'Die Entstehung des Kanons des NT und der christlichen Bibel', in TRE VI, 1980, 22-48 (Lit.); William R. Farmer and Denis M. Farkasfalvy, O.Cist, *The Formation of the New Testament Canon. An Ecumenical Approach*, New York 1983. There is also a short sketch of the history of the canon in many introductions to the NT, e.g. A. Jülicher - E. Fascher, *Einleitung in das NT*, [7]1931, pp. 450-558; P. Vielhauer, *Geschichte der urchristlichen Literatur*, 1975, pp. 774-786; W.G. Kümmel, *Introduction to the NT*, ET 1966, pp. 334-358 (20th German edition 1980, pp. 420-451 [Lit.]).

1. The 'New Testament Apocrypha' assembled in this book are not a unity which one may simply set over against the canon of the New Testament. They also never formed a self-contained corpus.[1] Rather, very diverse early Christian writings are here presented, chosen according to specific criteria, which all in some way show some relation to the content or the forms of the NT writings. This relation must be separately determined for each individual text, and here naturally the time of origin merits special attention (before the composition of a particular NT writing, before or after the completion of the canon), even though for many apocrypha the date of origin can be stated only approximately.

The question whether, despite the considerable differences between the texts assembled in this work, an appropriate definition of the concept 'New Testament apocrypha' can be formulated, covering all aspects, has still to be examined (see below, pp.50ff.). Here in the first place it should simply be established that all these writings have some relation to the writings united in the canon, and that therefore for the understanding of this complex material attention must be paid not only to the origin of the different *Gattungen* of NT writings (Gospels, Letters, Acts, Apocalypses) but also to the formation of a binding collection of writings recognised by the Church.[2]

Despite many labours in its investigation, the history of the canon remains as ever 'one of the most complicated parts of the study of Church History' (Lietzmann, p. 3). To be sure, a certain consensus has taken shape in regard to many questions of detail. But precisely the most important problems are still controversial: When and how did a New Testament come to be a recognised authority alongside the writings of the OT? What theological driving forces were operative in the process? How are we to assess the position of Marcion in the history of the canon? These uncertainties naturally hang together with the question of sources. Above all for the beginnings in the 2nd century we are often reduced to hypotheses and conjectures, which ought not to be put forward as solid facts, as often happens.[3]

For a proper grasp of the process of the formation of the canon, some points are of fundamental importance:

a) The brief survey of the concept 'canon' (see above) has shown that this designation for the collection of the books recognised in the Church only came into use at a late date. The history of the canon thus cannot start out from this concept, but must take account of the fact that it is a question of the complicated history of the fixation and assembling together of many older and by no means uniform traditions, the result of which was then - very late - described by the word 'canon'.

b) Primitive Christianity had a holy 'scripture', the Old Testament. It must, however, be observed that in the period in which the infant Christianity made use of it the range of the OT was not yet finally settled.[4] The putting into literary form of the Jesus traditions (Gospels) and the collection of apostolic writings signifies that a new 'scripture' took its place beside the old. Since the oral tradition was still very much alive alongside that fixed in writing - as becomes clear from the early 'apocrypha' - the problem of how 'scripture' and 'tradition' are related to one another was from the beginning an aspect of the process of the formation of the canon (cf., e.g., Papias).

c) The history of the NT canon cannot be mastered by establishing when, where and how a document which later belongs to the canon is quoted. Naturally investigations of this kind are necessary, and useful for the early history. But use of a document, or a special value given to it, does not yet mean canonisation. Even a possible demonstration of its use in public worship does not say much for the beginnings of the canon.

d) The history of the NT canon is a part of Church history and the history of theology, and can only be correctly evaluated when it is set in the total context of the development of the Church in the 2nd and 3rd centuries. Here it is scarcely enough to proclaim the canon alongside Church office and the regula fidei as the decisive 'norms' of the early Catholic Church. The historical processes in their complexity elude any stereotyped characterisation. The rise of the canon - like the formation of the regula fidei - was largely determined by the concern to separate off the 'genuine' tradition from false traditions.

2. The process of the formation of the canon is on the one hand determined by the collection, sifting and delimitation of the Jesus tradition and the apostolic tradition, but on the other hand it is also a part of the struggle regarding the

authoritative norm for the Church's faith and proclamation. This concern about a norm for Christian existence can already be identified in the earliest Christianity. We may therefore probably say that the roots of the canon as a collection of normative documents reach back into the 1st century, although naturally we must pay due heed to the history of the concept presented above, and may not combine any anachronistic ideas with the statement.

Primitive Christianity took over 'the scriptures' (Mk. 12:24) as normative, evidently without reflecting on their number (which in Judaism also was in this period not yet firmly fixed). Only in the second half of the 2nd century did people concern themselves with the question of what writings belonged to the canon of the OT (Melito of Sardis in Euseb. H.E. IV 26.13f.). When Melito there speaks of ἐκλογαί (extracts), this might refer to a testimony-collection or *florilegium*. This would mean that in early Christianity (down to Melito) people did indeed recognise 'the scriptures' as normative, but that they did not regard the whole OT (as a book) as important, but selected what corresponded with the norm, which was the Lord. For it may be concluded from all the witnesses of the early Christian period that the Lord and not any writing was the supreme norm.

With the collection of sayings and speeches of Jesus (the document Q) and the rise of Gospels the way was opened up for putting the Jesus tradition into literary form. Here it is not a question of the authority of a document. Rather the Lord remains the authority working through and in the Spirit, which takes priority over all other norms (cf. 2 Cor. 3: 14ff.). Thus even the Gospels were not written as 'canonical' books, which were intended to be a norm as a 'new scripture' or to claim authority (otherwise Luke and Matthew could not have expanded and recast Mark). Rather it is a question of an interpretative summary of the Jesus tradition, to safeguard it and to hand it on in the proclamation of the message of salvation. But this guaranteed for the following generation also that the Lord and not a new 'scripture' remained the norm and the authority within the community. However, it should not be overlooked that the handing on of the tradition to the next generations, which had to be done in writing if people were not to become petrified in esoteric secret circles, contained in itself the impulse for the process of the formation of a canon.

It is not surprising that special attention and respect was accorded to the original messengers of the Gospel. Some of them had known the earthly Jesus and they had jointly determined the path of the message of salvation in the world, and their authority was conceded. This authority, however, was not dependent on their writings, since it was not the dominant personality that was the decisive factor. Rather it was the primitive Christian conviction that the Holy Spirit worked through these first witnesses, and their testimony might therefore claim authority. Above all, the authority of the Lord was not thereby called in question.

With the collection of the Pauline letters, their reading in public worship (Col. 4:16) and their subsequent imitation (Deutero-Paulines) the process of putting the apostolic preaching also into literary form began, and this was then further advanced through a theological interpretation of the apostolic office (Luke; 1 Clement).

In sum we may say that the norm in primitive Christianity is the Lord alone, and that in the sense that he is 'a living authority which becomes actual in preaching' (Kümmel, p. 336). Alongside him the early witnesses of the Gospel (the apostles) are accorded a derivative authority. 'Scripture' also, i.e. the OT, is subordinated to the Lord. In the course of the 1st century we then find the fixation in writing of the Jesus tradition and the collection of apostolic testimonies, so that 'a new, living norm was developing in the Church, a norm which from the first included the Lord and the apostles who witnessed to the message from the Lord' (Kümmel, p. 336). This is naturally not yet a canon of the NT; but the way to it is prepared for in the 1st century.

3. Even if no final conclusion of the canon was yet attained in the 2nd century, considerable significance still attaches to this period. For, on the one hand, in these decades the process of the consolidation of the Jesus tradition was completed by the formation of the Four-Gospel canon (and connected with it: the exclusion of the apocryphal gospels), as was the process of the fixation of the 'apostolic tradition' through the formation of the 'Apostolos'. On the other hand there was also recognition in the last decades of the 2nd century of the problem posed by the collections of the Old and New Testament writings, which differed in compass and content; that is, reflection about problems of canon now begins.

A survey of the sources clearly shows that we can treat the development down to the Apologist Justin (middle of 2nd century) only as *pre*-history. For the result of such a survey is that before Justin we cannot speak of 'canonical' status for individual books of the NT. Certainly there is evidence for knowledge of, and even citations from, individual books of the later NT. But these facts simply show that the process of the putting into literary form and fixation of the Jesus tradition and of the 'apostolic teaching', begun in the 1st century, has continued.

The question of the existence of the NT canon before the middle of the 2nd century was in their day discussed with astonishing vehemence between Zahn and Harnack. The positions of that time are on particular points still influential even today. Zahn wanted to place the origin of the NT very early. He thought that 'some considerable time before 140, in the whole sphere of the Catholic Church, the collection of the four Gospels and that of the 13 Pauline epistles were already read alongside the scriptures of the OT, and that several other writings, such as Revelation, Acts and in some parts of the Church probably also Hebrews, 1 Peter, James and the letters of John, and perhaps even the Didache, were held worthy of the same honour' (*Grundriß*, p. 35). (It should be noted that for Zahn reading in public worship is tantamount to 'canonical').

Against this Harnack affirmed that the formation of the canon - like the origin of church office and the *regula fidei* - belongs in the context of the rise of the 'early Catholic' Church. For Harnack it is accordingly clear that about 150 there was still no NT. The NT canon rather first came into being in the second half of the 2nd century, and that through the elimination of books which did not agree with the early Catholic doctrine. 'The collection and canonising of Christian writings, resting upon a process of elimination, was so to speak an involuntary undertaking by the Church in the conflict with Marcion and the Gnostics.'[5]

The researches of recent decades have made it clear that the development of Church and theology in the 2nd century took a much more complex course than Harnack and Zahn thought. Above all, the schematic categories of the 19th century are scarcely adequate for the understanding of this period.[6]

Nevertheless the discussion between Zahn and Harnack is instructive even today. On the one hand, the two scholars presented an abundance of material and pointed out many important aspects, so that - as the literature shows - we must again and again reach back to their works. On the other, this controversy makes it clear that we can scarcely do justice to the process of the formation of the canon on the basis of preconceived categories.

Here it must be specially emphasised that in the investigation of the history of the New Testament canon we must not overlook the connection between the rise of the NT and the canonising of the OT. The origins of the two-part Christian Bible and the formation of a New Testament canon hang closely together. At any rate the 'crisis of the OT canon' (von Campenhausen, *Formation*, pp. 62ff.) must be kept in view if we are to answer the central question of the history of the canon: 'How did it happen, or what happened, that out of the abundance of the early Christian literature a number of particular writings was selected, elevated in rank above the rest, and set beside the received 'scripture' of the OT as on the same level?' (Vielhauer, *Lit. gesch.*, pp. 780ff.).

In the first half of the 2nd century there was still no NT as a canonical collection. The sources of this period can only be examined in regard to the question whether and how they cite writings which later belong to the canon, whether the quotations are adduced as γραφή (scripture), and what indications for the further development follow from the results of our inquiry. This investigation of the literature of the period from the point of view of the questions mentioned has often been undertaken, and very thoroughly, but with very divergent results.[7] This, however, cannot be discussed here in detail. It must suffice to sketch the most important points in summary fashion. Here it will be appropriate to separate the question of the position of the Gospels from that of the value set on the 'Apostolos'. Since the role of Gnosticism, of Marcion and of Montanism in the formation of the canon is still debated, some brief consideration must also be given to these questions.

a) **Gospels:** In some of the writings from the first half of the 2nd century included under the misleading name of 'Apostolic Fathers' there are quotations which belong in the context of the Jesus tradition (oral or written), but whose derivation from a Gospel is improbable (e.g. 1 Clem. 13.1-4; 46.7-8; Barn. 4.14; 5.9). In others, knowledge of one of the four Gospels is a natural assumption, even if we cannot prove literal quotation (e.g. Ign. *Philad.* 5.1, 2; 8.9; 9.2; *Sm.* 5.1; 7.2). More important than this conclusion, based on a scrupulous examination of the material, is the fact that there is no trace of any canonical significance for the Gospels alongside the OT. Only in so-called 2 Clement (middle of the 2nd century) can we identify the first indications that the authority of the Lord and of his words is being transferred to writings in which these words are contained (2 Clem. 2.4; 5.2; 8.5 etc).[8]

Of interest is the venture of bishop *Papias* of Hierapolis, who (probably between 120 and 140) composed five books of an 'interpretation of the Lord's words' (λογίων κυριακῶν ἐξηγήσεως συγγράμματα πέντε), of which however only fragments have survived.[9] From the remains which have come down to us, it is clear that Papias did not write a commentary on a Gospel, but collected and expounded reports of diverse origin about the words and deeds of Jesus. Papias did know Gospels (at least Mark and Matthew), but he nevertheless undertook to attempt a new compilation of the Jesus tradition, keeping to the oral tradition which he had learned from the 'elders' and preserved. 'That which comes from books seems to me not to be of such service as that which begins as living speech and remains so' (in Eus. H.E. III 39.4; translation from H. von Campenhausen, *Formation*, p. 130). This means, however, that Papias does not accord any authoritative status to the four Gospels (or even fewer), but adheres to the free oral tradition.[10] The position of the Gospels as 'scripture' was thus at this period still very uncertain (which says nothing as to their diffusion, the value placed upon them, or their use in public worship; here we are concerned only with the process of the formation of the canon).

The apologist *Justin*, who can well be adduced as a witness for the situation in Rome in the middle of the 2nd century, not only knows several Gospels but attests their use in public worship (*Apol.* I 65ff.). He speaks of the ἀπομνημονεύματα , the memoirs,[11] which were composed by the apostles and those who followed them (*Dial.* 103.8). Examination of the quotations and allusions shows that Justin probably knew all three Synoptics, and that as writings which were read in public worship as of equal value beside the OT. His knowledge of the Gospel of John is disputed.[12]

Justin is so important for the history of the canon, because on the one hand, like the witnesses before him, he still shows a certain freedom over against the text of the Gospels (harmonisation; use of texts outside the Gospels). But on the other hand there appears in Justin the development to a fixed position for the Gospels (three or four) as normative writings, of equal value with the OT. It seems to be equally clear from Justin that these writings received their standing in the Church above all from the tradition of the words of the Lord. The way forward to the canon is also heralded in Justin's statement that this Jesus tradition was recorded by apostles and disciples of apostles.

This is not the place to enter further into details. A few summary notes must suffice:

The extant sources from the first half of the 2nd century attest in very diverse ways acquaintance with individual Gospels. In addition it can be established that people also used traditions which are indeed in some way connected with the synoptic tradition, but did not in this form find entry into the first three Gospels. Similar observations can also be made with regard to the earliest apocryphal gospels (e.g. P.Egerton 2, see below, pp.96ff.).

So far as Gospels are known and used, that of Matthew appears to have enjoyed especial popularity, while there is hardly any evidence for the Gospel of John, although it was yet used in particular areas (cf. P[52] from the first quarter of the 2nd century). Most communities in that period will in any case have had only one Gospel. The Gospels are largely used as sources for the tradition of the words of the Lord, but not as 'holy scripture' like the OT. This is just as clear from the free method of citation as from the presumable existence of logia collections, testimony books and similar epitomes. All this, however, shows that it is a question here of a usage determined by the authority of the Lord as the norm of Christian faith and utterance. In other words, 'Gospel' is still to a large extent not a literary concept, but describes the content of the proclamation.[13] Only so indeed is Papias' undertaking comprehensible.

In this period, however, we can also identify the first signs of a consolidation, which means a putting into literary form. The authority of the Lord passes over to the writings in which the words of the Lord are handed down (Justin). The reasons for this change are certainly very complex: we must pay attention just as much to the growing awareness of the increasing distance in time as to the growth of gnostic traditions and their fixation in writing (Gospel of the Egyptians, Gospel of Thomas, etc. On these gospels see below, pp. 110ff.; 209ff.;354ff.).

b) **Apostolic writings:**In this part of the later NT canon also we cannot for the first half of the 2nd century start out from any 'canonical' validity, but may simply ask whether quotations can be identified, or evidence of knowledge. This will not be undertaken here in detail, but a few indications will reveal the problem. Knowledge of Acts cannot be affirmed before Justin, and even for him it scarcely has a normative character (cf. *Apol.* I 39.3; 41.5 etc.).[14] The Apocalypse of John is likewise largely unknown before Justin (*Dial.* 81.4). Knowledge and use of the Letter of James cannot be demonstrated in the 2nd century. For the rest of the so-called Catholic epistles also the results are very meagre. On the other hand the Letter to the Hebrews appears to have been known in Rome at the end of the 1st century (1 Clem. 17.1; 36.2-5).

The case of the Pauline epistles is somewhat different - and more difficult. For in the texts of this period there are many indications of a knowledge of Paul's letters (cf. 1 Clem. 47.1-3; 49.5 etc.; Ignatius, see below; Polycarp 11.2). It is striking that *Papias* - so far as we can see - does not mention Paul. But even in *Justin* Paul 'does not get a word in'.[15] Naturally Justin knew something of Paul, and also probably knew some letters. For we must probably reckon with a collection of Paul's letters about A.D. 100, even if we cannot reach any clarity with regard to its extent, the sequence of the letters, its place of origin and other details. Possibly Justin renounced any use of Paul because he had been completely taken over by Marcion and the gnostics.[16]

At all events the fact remains that only very few witnesses can be brought forward for the knowledge and use of the 'apostolic' part of the later NT in the first half of the 2nd century. These texts did not have any normative significance in this period. On the other hand the 'apostolic' authority is so strongly emphasised in various texts that even the controversial Paul must profit thereby. When Ignatius speaks of the δόγματα τοῦ κυρίου καὶ τῶν ἀποστόλων (*Magn.* 13.1), he means the living tradition of instruction by the Lord and his apostles. Since, however, on the other hand he refers directly to Paul's letters (*Eph.* 12.2), the basis is provided for the later fixing of the apostolic instruction in written documents of the 'apostles'. Finally we may refer once again to the collection of the Pauline letters.[17] Even if we cannot say anything as to the manner of its origin, and also there can be no talk of any 'canonical' validity of the collection in this period, yet it may probably be presumed that it contributed to the consolidation of the 'apostolic tradition', in that it attracted to itself other 'apostolic' texts.

c) **The significance of Gnosticism, Marcion and Montanism for the history of the canon:** So far we have spoken only of those witnesses for the history of the NT canon which can be claimed as belonging to the Church. Beside these in the 2nd century there are phenomena which in their time or in a later phase were designated 'heretical', even though they themselves understood themselves as Christians and the boundaries between 'orthodoxy' and 'heresy' were still very fluid in the 2nd century.[18] The written word, i.e. what later became canonical, soon played a certain role in the discussions with these phenomena.

The importance of *Gnosticism* for the rise of the NT canon and of the Christian Bible is certainly not to be overlooked. In particular it is probably the case that the debate with Gnosticism compelled the Church to reflect upon the 'true' and 'genuine' tradition. This does not mean that the process of the formation of the canon is to be understood merely as a defence against the gnostic threat. But in this conflict the Church recognised the safeguarding of the tradition as a problem.

Here we must refer once again to the connection between the acceptance of the OT and the formation of the NT canon. The various attempts to deal with the problem of the OT (e.g. the Letter of Barnabas) show that in the 2nd century people in the Church were no longer so unbiassed towards these writings as in the 1st century. The gnostics did not conjure up 'the crisis of the Old Testament Canon in the 2nd century' (von Campenhausen, *Formation*, pp. 62ff.), but they made people aware of it and sharpened it. They also represented very varied positions in this matter, but probably all of them - so far as we can establish - accorded a certain authority to the OT. Certainly they departed from the Church in their exposition, in that they drew in pagan literature also and their own revelation documents, and so relativised the authority of 'scripture'. Again, the 'dismembering of the sacred text among a number of different beings who were held to have inspired it or acted as mediators of revelation' (von Campenhausen, p. 87) scarcely strengthened the position of the OT in these circles.

The gnostics also, like the theologians of the Church, measured the OT in various ways by the standard of the words of Christ - whatever was understood by that.[19] Since in the period in which a 'Christian Gnosticism' was in formation there were still no 'canonical' Gospels (in the later sense of normative writings), the older gnostics were not bound to any text of the kind. New works were produced which professed to present old revelations and traditions. The gnostic 'gospels' and related works presented in this volume give an impression of the abundance of this production, which is governed above all by the concern to impart true and genuine teachings of the Revealer.

This literature probably did not arise so much in opposition to the Gospels of the Church, so far as they were known, as rather in analogy to the free handling of the Jesus tradition which in the first half of the 2nd century was still usual in the Church as well. We cannot say with certainty whether the reports of the creation of their own gospels by Basilides and Valentinus are accurate (cf. von Campenhausen, *Formation*, pp. 139ff.). The Coptic Gospel of Thomas (see below, pp.110ff) shows how in gnostic circles old Jesus traditions were handed on, but at the same time transmuted and expanded. In other circles people were even more free in the modification of the tradition and in the invention of new 'traditions'. It is striking how many names from older tradition were used by people wishing to propagate their own ideas as 'genuine', 'old' and reliable statements of revelation.

These brief remarks are simply intended to indicate that in the 2nd century the process of the consolidation in writing and delimitation of the Jesus tradition and the apostolic tradition had its counterpart in the gnostic area in the rise of texts of their own. How far this was in conscious opposition or unconscious analogy to writings of the Church has to be established in the case of each individual text, and this is certainly not a simple task.

We cannot deny a certain influence on the formation of the canon to the debate between the Church and Gnosticism with its literary products, even if this confrontation was not the decisive factor. At any rate we cannot overlook the fact that a gnostic NT could be put together from the Christian gnostic texts from Nag Hammadi.[20] Here we find Gospels (some writings describe themselves as gospels: the Gospel of Philip, the Gospel of Thomas, the Gospel of Truth, etc.), Acts (of Peter), Epistles and Apocalypses (of James, Paul and Peter).[21]

There was, as is well known, no gnostic NT. But the fact that the material for one actually lay ready to hand is just as important for the problem of the formation of the canon as for the question of the origin of the apocryphal literature.

The significance of *Marcion* for the history of the Christian Bible is still debated.[22] While some affirm that Marcion was 'the creator of the Christian Holy Scripture' (so Harnack and von Campenhausen), others emphasise that Marcion's canon only expedited but did not occasion the formation of a canon by the Church (so Kümmel).[23] The state of our sources scarcely allows of any stringent proof for either of the two positions. Yet there is much to be said against any overemphasis on the 'great personality' Marcion. On the other hand there is no question that Marcion's attempt, after rejecting the OT, to create a New Testament for himself (consisting of an expurgated Luke and ten likewise expurgated Pauline letters) hastened the development of a Church canon.

It should also be noted that Marcion was certainly not the creator of the Christian Bible, as Harnack thought, but at most of the New Testament. For the Church both before and after Marcion recognised the OT as a book of the Church. Marcion also was certainly not the first to collect the Pauline letters, but found them already together. His high regard for Paul, which however rested upon a magnificent misunderstanding, was imparted to him through this collection. The collection did not have any 'canonical' status, but its authoritative character is demonstrated precisely through Marcion's theology. Marcion probably found no collection of the four Gospels in existence, but only individual Gospels. He employs the word 'gospel' as a literary designation,[24] i.e. the Jesus tradition set down in writing in a Gospel was known to him, and that as a norm.

It is striking that Marcion's New Testament was not treated as closed by his adherents (cf. the Epistle to the Laodiceans).[25] This too speaks against any undue emphasis on Marcion's significance for the history of the canon. We may well ask whether what we today call Marcion's NT did not form along with the Antitheses *one* great work, with which Marcion intended to operate in a Marcionite sense, through the bringing together and interpretation of the genuine and unadulterated documents of the 'Gospel'. But this question can scarcely be answered.

The significance of *Montanism* for the history of the canon was in their day hotly debated between Zahn and Harnack,[26] but here also it has proved in the interval that the positions then adopted are in that form not tenable.[27]

In the first place it must be emphasised that for anyone concerned with this phenomenon Montanism presents many hitherto unresolved problems. Thus for example the chronology, which is important precisely for the position of Montanism in relation to the canon, is just as disputed as the interpretation of the various phases of the movement. We must here distinguish very carefully between hypotheses and demonstrable facts.

It is only a conjecture, although there is much to be said for it, that the question of the canon played no very great role for the Montanists, whether it was that at the time of the rise of the 'Phrygian prophecy' the formation of the canon was not yet very far advanced, or that the Montanists simply accepted the development. Even in the later phase (Tertullian) there appear to have been no fundamental discussions on this point. On the other hand we can establish that in the debate between the Church and Montanism what was at stake was 'over and above the problem of the canon, the much more fundamental question of the function and significance of historical tradition, its completeness, and its relation to present revelation' (Paulsen, p. 34). Thus Montanism also, like the Church, was affected by the problems of the consolidation of the normative tradition.

We therefore cannot indeed say that Montanism was 'the factor which brought about the concentration of the Canon' (von Campenhausen, p. 221). But through it the questions of the normative character of the tradition, its exclusiveness and also its correct interpretation were brought nearer to a solution in the Church. Here the Johannine writings, and above all the Apocalypse, stood at the centre of the discussion.

4. In the second half of the 2nd century, not only did the collection of writings develop into a firmly circumscribed New Testament, but also the two-part Christian Bible of the Old and New Testaments was formed. As already emphasised, this connection must be taken into account in a history of the New Testament canon. It is, moreover, not unimportant for the origin of 'apocryphal' literature also. Part of this literature links up with Old Testament personages or events (cf. e.g. the Ascension of Isaiah; 5 and 6 Ezra). In the gnostic texts which can be reckoned among the apocrypha, Old Testament personages in part also play a role.

We cannot here take up a position in any detail with regard to the problem of the Old Testament in the Church of the 2nd century. A few remarks must suffice.

The re-interpretation of the OT by the gnostics and its rejection by Marcion made no difference to the attitude of the churches. In the scriptures of the Old Covenant people found Christ, and naturally also the command of God. The theologians certainly had to concern themselves with defending the OT against Marcion. Here Justin above all rendered great service. The question of the extent of the OT which the Church possessed cannot be answered quite unambiguously.[28] There seem also to have been differences between the individual churches and the provinces. *Melito of Sardis* was the first to concern himself about an exact list (Euseb. H.E. IV 26.13f.). His enumeration corresponds to the Hebrew canon (without Esther). The question was then brought to a positive conclusion in the 4th century. Melito's list shows that people in the Church were evidently concerned about agreement with the Hebrew canon. The influence of LXX was, however, also ever-present, and finally gained the upper hand. The learned discussion was considerably interested in the relation of the Hebrew text to LXX and to other translations. All these concerns about the OT are closely connected with the contemporary effort to establish the extent of the Jesus tradition and the apostolic preaching.

The phase of the pre-history of the NT canon came to an end in the middle of the 2nd century. The process of consolidation now began. Here the tendencies which make their appearance in the period before Justin emerge ever more clearly. Marcion's attempt to achieve a normative Gospel and a binding collection of the Pauline letters (both 'expurgated', i.e. falsified) strengthened the tendencies towards a firmly closed canon.

As already mentioned, this becomes clear in Justin. For him (three or four) Gospels have the same rank as 'scripture' as the OT. As for the Pauline letters, such a valuation cannot yet be established (cf. above, p.20f).

Tatian's Diatessaron, a 'harmony' from the four Gospels, shows that on the one hand these writings occupy an authoritative position, but on the other that their text is not inviolable and can be supplemented by extra-canonical material. This Diatessaron was recognised as holy scripture in Syria right down to the 5th century. That makes it clear that Tatian's undertaking was regarded as legitimate in the 2nd century. Paul's letters were probably not regarded as 'scripture' by Tatian.[29] Theophilus of Antioch (second half of 2nd century) knows Gospels and letters of Paul as authoritative scripture (*Autol.* II 22; III 14).[30]

It is interesting that in the letter of the churches of Vienne and Lyons, from the year 177, Rev. 22:11 is cited as 'scripture' (Euseb. H.E. V 1.58). This shows that in the early period of Irenaeus in Gaul at least this NT book, if not also other parts of the 'Apostolos', was set on the same level as the OT.

We have already spoken of Melito's concern about the canon of the OT (see above, p.12). There is much to be said for the view that the term 'Old Testament (διαθήκη)' used by him implies that he also knew the term 'New Testament'. But this cannot be proved.

From these witnesses it can be seen how in this period there is a growing consciousness in the different areas that in the Church there are normative 'scriptures' besides the OT. However, people are probably still not everywhere clear as to the exclusive character of the NT canon. Thus the martyrs of Scilli in North Africa in 188 do not seem to have set Paul's letters on the same level as the

Gospels (*Passio* 12: Krüger-Ruhbach, p. 29.18f.). As a further example we may name bishop *Serapion of Antioch*, who about 200 at first permitted to the congregation of Rhossus the reading of the Gospel of Peter (see below, pp.216ff.), but later, after he had convinced himself of the heretical character of the work, prohibited its use (Euseb. H.E. VI 12.2ff.). Uncertainties and differences which still exist in this period can also be appraised as indications that the NT canon is not to be understood as a deliberate reaction against Marcion and Gnosticism, but took shape in the various regions of the Church (at first in different ways) on the basis of old deposits. In addition it is clear from the conduct of Serapion that the process of the formation of the canon was not only one of the collection (or exclusion) of traditions and of their fixing in writing, but also belongs in the context of the formation of the Church's doctrine.[31] This naturally was of considerable importance for the relation of the Church to the 'apocrypha'.

5. About the turn from the 2nd to the 3rd century we can see a certain stabilisation. Even if there are still local differences in the assessment of individual writings, and the limits of the canon are not yet firmly fixed, it is yet clear that the Church possesses a two-part Bible of the Old and New Testaments. For the NT the content is widely acknowledged: the four Gospels belong to the writings recognised by the Church (the Gospel of John may here and there be still in dispute). The apostolic writings, of which Paul's letters form the core, are still undecided in regard to their number and also their sequence, but are predominantly a recognised part of the canon.

Irenaeus can already be adduced as a witness for this state of affairs. Rightly described as 'the first catholic theologian, the first man to know and acknowledge a New Testament both in theory and in practice' (von Campenhausen, *Formation*, p. 203), he reckons to 'scripture' the four Gospels, Acts and thirteen letters of Paul. 1 Peter and the two Johannine letters (1 and 2) are appraised like the Pauline letters, while James and Hebrews are probably not so highly esteemed. The Apocalypse is known to Irenaeus, but is not particularly prominent. It is worthy of note that the Shepherd of Hermas is quoted as 'scripture'.[32]

Even if the limits of the canon appear still fluid, yet the tendency towards a firm delimitation cannot be overlooked. This is connected with Irenaeus' concern for a theological penetration of the problem of 'scripture and tradition'. This cannot be set out here in detail.[33] We need only refer to the fact that Irenaeus is at pains to justify the 'four-fold Gospel' (*Haer.* III 11.8), a problem which must have been of considerable significance for the question of the canon.[34]

In controversy with Marcion and the gnostics Irenaeus used a catholic New Testament alongside the OT for his scriptural proof - an indication of the state of the development of the canon. Here he uses the *regula fidei* as the standard for assessing the recognised writings, which is not surprising. Irenaeus is not only a witness to 'the transition from the earlier period of belief in tradition to the new age of deliberate canonical standardisation' (von Campenhausen, p. 182), but above all he inaugurated, and for a long time determined, the theological work on the problem of the canon. This holds also for the assessment of 'apocryphal' works (e.g. the Gospel of Truth, *Haer.* III 11.9).

For *Tertullian* also the Bible as *totum instrumentum utriusque testamenti* (*Prax.* 20) is a fixed entity, even if the Apostolos is not yet defined with certainty.[35]

The situation is similar with *Clement of Alexandria*. He does indeed use the Gospel of the Hebrews and that of the Egyptians, but normative authority is accorded only to 'the four Gospels handed down to us' (*Strom.* III 93.1). For Clement, Acts, the Apocalypse, fourteen Pauline letters (thus including Hebrews), 1 Peter and 1 John belong to the canon. On the question of the remaining catholic epistles his judgment vacillates.

It must, however, be added that with these statements we have not yet grasped the core of Clement's conception. His understanding of scripture, with which we shall not deal further here, is beyond doubt determined by other points of view than the statements of Irenaeus or Tertullian. One must concur with von Campenhausen: 'It is . . . no accident that he got no further than he did in developing and creating a rationale for the new Canon - he was unable to provide a theological solution to the problem of the normativeness of Scripture.' Hence he remains 'of no significance for the history of the concept of the Canon' (*Formation*, p. 307).

A particularly interesting document, and beyond doubt important for the history of the canon, is the so-called *Canon Muratori*. This is a fragmentary canon catalogue, handed down in a manuscript of the 8th century (for translation see below, pp.34ff.). Owing to its barbarous Latin the text, probably a translation of a Greek original, presents many difficulties for its understanding.

It is generally assumed that this catalogue originated about the year 200 in the West, probably in Rome.[36] Against the prevailing opinion, A.C. Sundberg has attempted to produce the proof that the Canon Muratori originated in the 4th century in the East. Despite the erudition displayed and the extensive material worked over, one can probably not assent to this attempt, which is governed by too narrow a conception of the idea of a canon, but must adhere to the traditional definition of the time and place of the document: the Canon Muratori is a text which reflects the state of the canon question in the West (Rome?) about A.D. 200.[37] In view of its fragmentary character (the beginning is missing) we cannot say whether the document had any 'official' character or was a private work. It is to be assumed that with his list the author intends to establish which of the Church's writings are permitted for use and which are refused.

The range of the NT, as it emerges from the Canon Muratori, presents no particular surprises: four Gospels, Acts, thirteen letters of Paul, Jude, 1 and 2 John (here, curious to relate, Wisdom is also listed), and the Apocalypse - these are the recognised documents of the Church. The Apocalypse of Peter is rejected by 'some of our people'. The Shepherd of Hermas is only allowed for private use. The letters to the Laodiceans and the Alexandrians are rejected, as are all kinds of heretical writings which are named at the end of the fragment.

The Canon Muratori thus gives us a picture of the extent of the NT about the year 200. In addition we can also read off from it some tendencies which determined the development towards the completed canon.

It must, however, be emphasised that in this much-discussed question of the 'principles' of the text it must never be overlooked that this is not a matter of a theological tractate, and that the few hints as to the motives for acceptance or rejection of a writing which we can draw from the Muratorianum are probably indeed later reflection. However important and portentous such theological reflections may be (we may recall Irenaeus), they do not precede the acceptance of writings in the churches, but are later interpretations of the process, intended to provide the reasons for the delimitation and the exclusiveness of the recognised collection.

What criteria for this delimitation emerge from the Canon Muratori? It is widely held that the author of the text adhered to the 'prophetic-apostolic principle'. 'The Old Testament was written by prophets, the New by apostles. Fundamentally, what does not derive from the apostles does not belong in the New Testament - that is the theoretical standpoint' (Lietzmann, p. 63, linking up with Harnack). This conception is based above all on the statements about the Shepherd of Hermas (lines 73ff.).[38]

Against this thesis Hans von Campenhausen has affirmed that the Canon Muratori 'is merely asking for documents which are ancient and reliable', i.e. the critical principle is 'determined by historical or, if preferred, dogmatic-salvation-history considerations' (*Formation*, p. 254). Von Campenhausen also finds his support above all in the notice about Hermas. He thinks that this writing was excluded from the canon because its author was no longer a representative of the classical era. Hermas - such is the view of the Muratorianum - 'does not belong in a canon which collects and gives binding force to documents of this primitive period. 'Primitive Christianity' finally belongs to the past, and may not be extended. This is the determining and delimiting principle behind the new Canon' (*Formation*, p. 259).[39]

Apart from the questionable character of so far-reaching an interpretation of the fragment, it seems very doubtful whether one can so speak of a historical interest as a 'principle'. On the other hand it is in fact not to be overlooked that for the author the reliability of the tradition which is now brought together in the canon in a certain fashion depends on the age of the writings. But this is not 'historical' interest (in the modern sense). Rather the legitimation of a writing ensues through the demonstration of its origin from the first witnesses, i.e. the apostles. (The connection of the OT writings with the prophets corresponds to this).

This recourse to the reliable witnesses is not a 'principle' which was decisive for the collection, but an interpretation of the facts. Here the significance of the *regula fidei*, both for the process of the collecting and for the interpretation, is certainly to be assessed very high. In the Canon Muratori this rings out in the rejection of the 'heretical writings'. In the canonised writings it is a matter of texts which correspond to the κανὼν τῆς ἀληθείας. But the truth which is proclaimed through these writings does not rest upon the statements of teachers

28

who have recently come forward (like Marcion), but on the witnesses of the earliest period, i.e. on the apostles called by the Lord.

To sum up: the Canon Muratori presents a statement of the books which in his time were recognised by the Church as a 'New Testament'. The author thus does not make the selection himself, but describes the actual stock. In so doing he sets up no 'principle' for selection or rejection. That would be contrary to his intention. Rather he explains the actual range of the canon, or the exclusion of other writings. The motives which are to be recognised in this explanation are secondary reflections, and allow us to conjecture parallels in the theology of the time (e.g. Irenaeus), without the author developing them in detail. Here the exclusiveness of the canon (over against Marcionite and other heretical writings) is just as important as its apostolic anchoring. The apostolic tradition, as it comes to expression in the κανὼν τῆς πίστεως, is to be found in these writings and only in them.

These remarks about the Canon Muratori perhaps go somewhat beyond what the text itself says. But they do more justice to it than the identification of 'principles' or the reading-in of modern ideas of historicity.

It was necessary to speak here in such detail of the Canon Muratori. It is not only the oldest canon catalogue which has come down to us, but from the interpretation of the text certain insights follow for the 'apocryphal' literature.

Of the motives and the factors which led to the origin of 'apocrypha' something will be said later (see below, pp. 55ff.). Here it need only be remarked that parallel with the process of the formation of the canon there runs the production of apocryphal writings, that is of works in which also an attempt is made to fix normative tradition. This holds at least for many of the older writings, but quite specially for the gnostic apocrypha. In the later apocryphal literature, which arose after the completion of the canon, other motives and tendencies were influential.

While in the churches the received and recognised writings gradually grew together into a New Testament, 'heretical' writings, i.e. writings which did not correspond with the *regula fidei*, also staked their claims to communicate 'true' and 'genuine' tradition. Against these the Church defended itself by establishing the exclusiveness and finality of its canon. The Canon Muratori confirms this view of things.

6. About the turn from the 2nd century to the 3rd, the development has reached a certain conclusion, in so far as it is now established that alongside the OT the Church also has a New Testament, the authority of which indeed is more highly rated, because it represents the norm for the interpretation of the older part of the Bible. The extent of the NT is fixed for the four Gospels, Acts and the letters of Paul (without Hebrews), while the Apocalypse, the 'catholic' epistles and Hebrews are variously assessed in the different regions of the Church. There was no change in this situation down to the 4th century.

It can be readily understood that in the 3rd and 4th centuries we find all sorts of efforts towards a final settlement of the canon, and in particular a clear delimitation over against the 'apocrypha'. For even if the basic decision has been taken in the sense outlined above, the differences with regard to the extent of the NT must have been felt disturbing in the Church, which was steadily spreading throughout the entire empire.

Origen, the great exegete, also concerned himself with this question. Eusebius has gathered together from the writings of Origen the statements relating to the canon and its range (H.E. VI 25; translation below, pp.43ff.). We cannot deduce from these a canon catalogue in the technical sense (like the table in the Codex Claromontanus, for example; see below, p.37). Rather it is a matter of a discussion of the literature which in the various areas of the Church is recognised, disputed or rejected, and here Origen's own theological reflection is naturally of special significance.[40]

Origen distinguishes three categories of writings:

1. ὁμολογούμενα , i.e. the generally acknowledged writings;

2. ψευδῆ , i.e. false writings forged by heretics (e.g. the Gospel of the Egyptians, the Gospel of the Twelve);

3. ἀμφιβαλλόμενα , i.e. writings about whose authenticity there is doubt (e.g. 2 Peter, Hermas).[41]

This classification, which Eusebius later takes over (see below, pp. 47f.), is probably to be interpreted as meaning that Origen actually wished 'to fix the situation statistically' (Jülicher, *Einleitung*, p. 514). The judgments about individual writings in different churches ought not to be suppressed. This has the consequence that for a part of the writings the judgment as to whether they belong in the canon remains open or uncertain. Unambiguously canonical according to Origen are: four Gospels, Acts, thirteen Pauline letters, 1 Peter, 1 John and the Apocalypse. The remaining 'catholic' epistles are indeed frequently cited by him, but according to his statements are not generally recognised. Other works treasured and quoted by Origen (Hermas, the Didache, Barnabas) are not regarded as holy scripture.

His attitude towards the Apocalypse is interesting. Origen reckons it to the canon, but has little sympathy for it (Euseb. H.E. VI 25.9). This NT book then remains disputed right down to the 4th century.[42] This can be seen in the attitude adopted by Dionysius of Alexandria in the middle of the 3rd century.[43] In the West, in contrast, it belongs firmly to the canon from the end of the 2nd century.

Hebrews, on the other hand, was early recognised as a Pauline letter in the East, while the West rejected it down to the 4th century (cf. Jerome, *Ep.* 129.3). With regard to some 'catholic' epistles also the uncertainty seems to have lasted a long time. Only gradually did a seven-letter canon develop out of an original three-letter canon (James, 1 Peter, 1 John), and that very differently in the various areas.[44]

In the canon catalogue of the *Codex Claromontanus* (see below, p. 37) the seven 'catholic' epistles and the Apocalypse are reckoned to the canon, but not Hebrews. It is striking that Hermas, the Acts of Paul and the Apocalypse of Peter are named in this catalogue - and probably as recognised writings. This speaks for a relatively early dating of the text. When and where it originated is, however, disputed. It is widely assumed that here we have a Latin version of a Greek text of the 3rd century;[45] but this cannot be proved.

In the 4th century the tendency towards unification grew stronger in every sphere of the Church's life (liturgy, organisation, Church order, etc.). The canon also was affected by this.

Eusebius of Caesarea, who in his *Church History* devoted a chapter of its own to the problem of the canon (H.E. III 25; see below, p.47f.), certainly still reflects the situation of the 3rd century, but tends strongly towards delimitation. Following the example of Origen, he divides the Church's literature into three categories:

1. ὁμολογούμενα, the generally recognised writings (four Gospels, Acts, fourteen Pauline letters - thus despite reservations including Hebrews - 1 John and 1 Peter);

2. ἀντιλεγόμενα, the writings which in some churches are recognised, in others disputed (the remaining 'catholic' epistles);

3. νόθα, the spurious and therefore rejected writings (Acts of Paul, Hermas, Apocalypse of Peter, Barnabas and the Didache).

It is interesting that Eusebius names the Apocalypse twice. On the one hand he mentions it among the recognised writings ('provided it is considered proper'); on the other it is named among the spurious ('which some, as has been mentioned, reject but which others reckon among the recognised writings': H.E. III 25.4). This uncertainty with regard to the Apocalypse leads to certain contradictions in Eusebius' enumeration. But apart from the vacillation on this question it is clear that in the Eastern Church in that period there was a NT extending to twenty-one books (i.e. without the four smaller 'catholic' epistles and the Apocalypse) or twenty-six Books (i.e. without the Apocalypse).

Finally it is to be observed that Eusebius knows some apocryphal writings (like the Acts of Paul and the Apocalypse of Peter) as works to be rejected. This indicates that, despite the stabilisation of the canon which appears in him, the 'inauthentic' writings were still read and used.

Later writers of the 4th century confirm that the canon of twenty-six books has largely prevailed (Cyril of Jerusalem, *Catech.* IV 36; Gregory of Nazianzus, *Carm.* I 12), while in others the old suspicions against Hebrews, the smaller 'catholic' epistles and naturally the Apocalypse are repeated (Amphilochius of Iconium, *Iambi ad Seleucum* 289ff., pp. 38f. Oberg).

A clear acknowledgement of the NT canon of twenty-seven books appears in the 39th Festal Letter of *Athanasius of Alexandria* for the year 367 (translation below, pp. 49f.). Here the threefold division of Origen or Eusebius is abandoned. As 'springs of salvation' there are only the twenty-seven writings in which 'the doctrine of piety is proclaimed'. Over against them are set the apocrypha fabricated by the heretics. Only the Didache and Hermas - beside a few OT apocrypha - are permitted for reading by those newly received into the Church, since the Fathers have so appointed. But these writings are not κανονιζόμενα. We may however infer from the concession that the two writings mentioned still enjoyed very great esteem.

There is no question that the emphasis on the exclusiveness and finality of the canon is closely connected with Athanasius' total theological conception, anti-heretical and Bible-related.[46] Over and above that it has to be observed that precisely in the years after 362 the Alexandrian's concern was directed towards the unity of the 'orthodox' Church, and hence that for him a uniform canon was also a necessity.

It is important that Athanasius turns sharply against all apocrypha, and that too under appeal to the 'Fathers': 'And although, beloved, the former [the recognised writings] are in the canon and the latter [Hermas and the Didache] serve as reading matter, yet mention is nowhere made of the apocrypha; rather they are a fabrication of the heretics, who write them down when it pleases them and generously assign to them an early date of composition in order that they may be able to draw upon them as supposedly ancient writings and have in them occasion to deceive the guileless.'

With this the lines are drawn as sharply as possible between canonical and apocryphal writings. Whatever they may be in terms of their origin, their content or their age, the 'apocrypha' are downgraded as heretical and therefore excluded from any ecclesiastical use. We cannot establish what effect Athanasius' letter had outside of Egypt. We may conjecture that it advanced the recognition of the seven 'catholic' epistles in the East, but it could not remove the opposition to the Apocalypse. This book only achieved its firm place in the canon of the Greek Church in the 10th century.

In the West the completion of the canon came about earlier. After Hebrews and part of the 'catholic' epistles (probably under the influence of the Greek Church) had won canonical status in the course of the 4th century, the number of the twenty-seven books was at the end of the 4th century firmly documented, as the catalogue of the so-called *Decretum Gelasianum* shows (translation below, pp.38ff.). Certainly there were still uncertainties here and there (cf. Kümmel, pp. 351f.), but on the whole the range of the NT stands fast.

It may be briefly noted that in the areas in which the Syriac tongue was dominant the development of the canon took a somewhat different course. On the one hand the Diatessaron of Tatian was here in use down to the 5th century, in place of the 'separated' four Gospels. On the other, judgment as to parts of the 'Apostolos' long remained very vacillating. It is striking that 3 Corinthians, which was originally a part of the apocryphal Acts of Paul (see vol. II, chapter XV 3), was in Syria widely treated as canonical.

From the 5th century on there was a gradual assimilation, but at very varying pace, to the rest of the Church. The East Syrians retained a canon of twenty-two books (without the four minor 'catholic' letters and the Apocalypse), while among the West Syrians an assimilation took place.[47]

These differences as to the extent of the canon, however, do not alter the fact that in all regions of the Church in the 4th century the fundamental decision has been taken: the Church has a holy scripture of Old and New Testaments, which stands as a closed entity (despite variations in compass) over against the apocryphal, i.e. heretical, writings.

7. This brief sketch of the history of the NT canon has probably made it clear that in view of the not very extensive source material it is difficult to present the development without any gaps. Only too often we can guess at connections, but not prove them. Despite this it is probably also clear that a treatment of the apocryphal literature cannot leave aside a consideration of the

history of the canon. The following aspects are of significance:

a) The collection of twenty-seven writings which prevailed in the Church from the 4th century on as a complete and normative holy scripture (alongside the OT) was not created by any decree of Church government, but grew together in a long process. The presupposition for the genesis of such a collection was the living use of the individual writings in the churches. It was readily comprehensible that the need for clarity as to what was 'genuine' and 'true' Jesus tradition and apostolic tradition should lead to a collection recognised by the Church. Since the number of the apocryphal documents increased considerably in the course of the 2nd century, delimitation had to ensue. But this also means that the writings later canonised and the 'apocryphal' stand in some relation to one another - which must be determined for each individual text.

b) The Old Testament had from the beginning a firm place in the Church, but was always subject to interpretation by faith in Jesus Christ. The 'new scripture' is thus superior to the old, but grew together with it into the two-part Bible. Here the differences in compass for a long time evidently did not have the weight which one might assume. The reason is probably to be seen in the fact that the plurality was measured against the *regula fidei*. It was by this norm also that the fate of writings which were later excluded from Church use as 'apocrypha' was decided.

c) Even if the New Testament came into being chiefly for reasons within the Church, the development was still furthered by Marcion and by Gnosticism. The production of apocryphal gospels and acts which began in the course of the 2nd century necessitated a clear separation between 'true' and 'false' tradition. Since these works largely availed themselves of the literary *Gattungen* which were also used in Church literature, their dissemination in the churches was the easier, but on the other hand a testing of their content became necessary (cf. the example of Serapion; above p.26).

The history of the canon is thus on the one side to be understood as the history of the collecting and fixation of traditions. As such it has a certain parallel in the rise and diffusion of the literature which later was called 'apocryphal'. On the other hand it is also determined by the taking-shape of Church doctrine. For the acceptance or rejection of a writing, already at an early date, usually also included an evaluation of its content. It is understandable that in the 4th century, when the doctrine began to become more uniform, the canon also was heading towards its completion.

8. To elucidate what has been said in the survey of the history of the canon, a series of texts will here be presented which have already been mentioned, and which are important for the history of the collection of the NT. These are a) *Canon lists*, i.e. texts from which the content of the canon can be clearly seen - such texts were compiled, for various reasons, from the end of the 2nd century or from the 3rd century - and b) *testimonies of Church Fathers*, which are of significance as evidence for the growth of the canon and the assessment of the apocrypha. The choice of the lists, as of the texts, has been governed by the point of view that the delimitation between 'canonical' and 'apocryphal' in the different stages of the development of the canon should be manifest, and further that texts should be chosen in which the titles of apocryphal writings are named.

Further texts: in Th. Zahn, *Gesch. des ntl. Kanons* II 1, 1890; F.W. Grosheide, *Some Early Lists of the Books of the New Testament*, Textus minores 1, Leiden 1948.
Detailed bibliography: Marek Starowieyski (ed.), *Apokryfy Nowego Testamentu*, vol. I 2, Lublin 1980, 626ff.

a) Canon Catalogues
1. *The Canon Muratori*

In a manuscript of the 8th century in the Ambrosian Library in Milan, probably written in Bobbio, L.A. Muratori (1672-1750) discovered a catalogue of the NT writings with comments. He published this text, called after him the Canon Muratori, in 1740. Four fragments of the Canon were found in 1897 in four manuscripts of the 11th and 12th centuries in Montecassino. The beginning and probably also the end of the catalogue are missing. Presumably the text derives from the West (Rome ?) and was composed about 200. The Latin version goes back to a Greek original. For its interpretation see above, pp. 27ff.

Text: Zahn, *Gesch. d.ntl.Kanons* II 1, 1-143 (with commentary); H. Lietzmann, KlT 1, ²1933; G. Bardy in DBS V, 1957, cols. 1399-1408. From the abundant literature we may mention: H. Lietzmann, *Wie wurden die Bücher des NT hl. Schrift?*, 1907, pp. 52ff.; K. Stendhal, 'The Apocalypse of John and the Epistles of Paul in the Muratorian Fragment', in *FS O.A. Piper*, London 1962, pp. 239-245; H. von Campenhausen, *Formation* pp. 243-261; A.C. Sundberg, 'Canon Muratori', in HTR 66, 1973, 1-41; J. Beumer, 'Das Fragmentum Muratori', in ThPh 48, 1973, 534-550; H. Burckhardt, 'Motive und Maßstäbe der Kanonsbildung nach dem C.M.', in *ThZ* 30, 1974, 207-211.
Further lit.: Erbetta I 29.

The following translation is intended to adhere closely to the line division of the Latin text.

. . . .

at which however he was present and so he has set it down.
The third Gospel book, that according to Luke.
This physician Luke after Christ's ascension (resurrection?),
since Paul had taken him with him as an expert in the way   (of
    the teaching),
composed it in his own name   5.
according to (his) thinking. Yet neither did he himself see
the Lord in the flesh; and therefore, as he was able to ascertain it,
    so he begins
 to tell the story from the birth of John.
The fourth of the Gospels, that of John, (one) of the disciples.
When his fellow-disciples and bishops urged him,   10.
he said: Fast with me from today for three days, and what
will be revealed to each one
let us relate to one another. In the same night it was
revealed to Andrew, one of the apostles,   that,
whilst all were to go over (it), John in his own name   15.

should write everything down. And therefore, though various
rudiments (or: tendencies?) are taught in the several
Gospel books, yet that matters
nothing for the faith of believers,   since by the one and guiding
     (original?) Spirit
everything is declared in all: concerning the birth,   20.
concerning the passion, concerning the resurrection,
concerning the intercourse with his disciples
and concerning his two comings,
the first despised in lowliness, which has   come to pass,
the second glorious in kingly power,   25.
which is yet to come. What
wonder then if John, being thus always true to himself,
adduces particular points in his epistles also,
where he says of himself: What we have seen with our eyes
and have heard with our ears and   30.
our hands have handled, that have we written to you.
For so he confesses (himself) not merely an eye and ear witness,
but also a writer of all the marvels of the Lord in
order. But the acts of all apostles
are written in one book. For the 'most excellent Theophilus'   35.
     Luke
summarises the several things that in his own presence
have come to pass, as also by the omission of the passion of Peter
he makes quite clear, and equally by (the omission) of the journey
     of Paul, who from
the city (of Rome) proceeded to Spain. The epistles, however,
of Paul themselves make clear to those who wish to know it   40.
which there are (i.e. from Paul), from what place and for what
     cause they were written.
First of all to the Corinthians (to whom) he forbids the heresy
of schism, then to the Galatians (to whom he forbids)
     circumcision,
and then to the Romans,(to whom) he explains that Christ
is the rule of the scriptures and moreover their principle,   45.
he has written at considerable length. We must deal with these
severally, since the blessed
apostle Paul himself, following the rule of his predecessor
John, writes by name only to seven
churches in the following order: to the Corinthians   50.
the first (epistle), to the Ephesians the second, to the Philippians
the third, to the Colossians the fourth, to the Galatians the
fifth, to the Thessalonians the sixth, to the Romans
the seventh. Although he wrote to the Corinthians and to the
Thessalonians once more for their reproof,   55.
 it is yet clearly recognisable that over the whole earth one church

is spread. For John also in the
Revelation writes indeed to seven churches,
yet speaks to all. But to Philemon one,
and to Titus one, and to Timothy two, (written) out of goodwill   60.
and love, are yet held sacred to the glory of the catholic Church
for the ordering of ecclesiastical
discipline.There is current also (an epistle) to
the Laodiceans, another to the Alexandrians, forged in Paul's
name for the sect of Marcion, and several others,   65.
which cannot be received in the catholic Church;
for it will not do to mix gall with honey.
Further an epistle of Jude and two with the title (or: two of the
          above mentioned)
John are accepted in the catholic Church, and the Wisdom
written by friends of Solomon in his honour.   70.
Also of the revelations we accept only those of John and
Peter, which (latter) some of our
people do not want to have read in the Church. But Hermas
wrote the Shepherd quite lately in our time in the city
of Rome, when on the throne of   75.
the church of the city of Rome the bishop Pius, his brother,
was seated. And therefore it ought indeed to be read, but
it cannot be read publicly in the Church to the other people either
          among
the prophets, whose number is settled, or among
the apostles to the end of time.   80.
But we accept nothing whatever
from Arsinous or Valentinus and Miltiades(?), who have also
composed a new psalm book for Marcion,
together with Basilides of Asia Minor,
the founder of the Cataphrygians.   85.

2. *The catalogue in the Codex Claromontanus*

In the bilingual manuscript of the Pauline epistles known under the name *Codex Claromontanus* (Cod. D 06; now Paris. gr.107, written in the 6th century), after Philemon and before Hebrews there is a catalogue of the biblical writings of the Old and New Testaments with a statement of the 'lines', i.e. of the extent of the several writings. Its NT portion is given here. According to Jülicher (in opposition to Zahn) the catalogue belongs to the 4th century and is probably of Western origin(cf. p.30 above).

Text: Zahn, *Gesch. d. ntl. Kanons* II 1, 157-172 (with commentary); Preuschen, *Analecta* II², 40-42.

Gospels 4	
Matthew	2600 lines
John	2000 lines
Mark	1600 lines
Luke	2900 lines
Epistles of Paul	
To the Romans	1040 lines
To the Corinthians I	1060 lines
To the Corinthians II	<>70 lines
To the Galatians	350 lines
To the Ephesians	375 lines

(three lines seem to have fallen out here:
Philippians, 1 and 2 Thessalonians are missing)

To Timothy I	208 lines
To Timothy II	289 lines
To Titus	140 lines
To the Colossians	251 lines
To Philemon	50 lines
To Peter I	200 lines
To Peter II	140 lines
(Epistle) of James	220 lines
I Epistle of John	220 lines
Epistle of John II	20 lines
Epistle of John III	20 lines
Epistle of Jude	60 lines
Epistle of Barnabas	
(= Epistle to the Hebrews?)	850 lines
Revelation of John	1200 lines
Acts of the Apostles	2600 lines
Shepherd (of Hermas)	4000 lines
Acts of Paul	3560 lines
Revelation of Peter	270 lines

3. *The so-called Decretum Gelasianum*

In the so-called *Decretum Gelasianum de libris recipiendis et non recipiendis*, which upon the whole is probably of South Gallic origin (6th century) but which in several parts can be traced back to Pope Damasus and reflects Roman tradition, we have in the second part a canon catalogue, in the fourth part an enumeration of recognised synods and ecclesiastical writers, and in the fifth part a catalogue of the 'apocrypha' and other writings which are to be rejected. The canon catalogue gives all twenty-seven books of the NT, the canon being therefore settled definitely in this form. The list, already outwardly and sharply separated from it, of the 'apocrypha', i.e. of the writings to be rejected, is given here in translation (according to the edition of v. Dobschütz, [see below], pp.48-60). An identification of the several writings that are cited is dispensed with (cf. on this Dobschütz in his edition). Some of them are apocrypha which are included in the present work; and when they are discussed, reference will be made to the witness of the Decretum Gelasianum: but others are much later writings to which no further consideration can be given in this work.

Text: E. von Dobschütz, TU 38.4, 1912, with commentary. Cf. also E. Schwartz, ZNW 29, 1930, 161-168. Further literature in Erbetta I 27.

The remaining writings which have been compiled or been recognised by heretics or schismatics the Catholic and Apostolic Roman Church does not in any way receive; of these we have thought it right to cite below some which have been handed down and which are to be avoided by catholics.

Further Enumeration of Apocryphal Books:

In the first place we confess that the Synod at Ariminum which was convened by the emperor Constantius, the son of Constantine, through the prefect Taurus is damned from then and now and for ever.

Itinerary (book of travels) under the name of the apostle Peter, which is called The Nine Books of the holy Clement	apocryphal
Acts under the name of the apostle Andrew	apocryphal
Acts under the name of the apostle Thomas	apocryphal
Acts under the name of the apostle Peter	apocryphal
Acts under the name of the apostle Philip	apocryphal
Gospel under the name of Matthias	apocryphal
Gospel under the name of Barnabas	apocryphal
Gospel under the name of James the younger	apocryphal
Gospel under the name of the apostle Peter	apocryphal
Gospel under the name of Thomas, which the Manichaeans use	apocryphal
Gospels under the name of Bartholomaeus	apocryphal
Gospels under the name of Andrew	apocryphal
Gospels which Lucian has forged	apocryphal
Gospels which Hesychius has forged	apocryphal

Book about the childhood of the Redeemer	apocryphal
Book about the birth of the Redeemer and about Mary or the midwife	apocryphal
Book which is called by the name of the Shepherd	apocryphal
All books which Leucius, the disciple of the devil, has made	apocryphal
Book which is called The Foundation	apocryphal
Book which is called The Treasure	apocryphal
Book about the daughters of Adam: Leptogenesis(?)	apocryphal
Cento about Christ, put together in Virgilian lines	apocryphal
Book which is called The Acts of Thecla and of Paul	apocryphal
Book which is ascribed to Nepos	apocryphal
Book of the Sayings, compiled by heretics and denoted by the name of Sixtus	apocryphal
Revelation which is ascribed to Paul	apocryphal
Revelation which is ascribed to Thomas	apocryphal
Revelation which is ascribed to Stephen	apocryphal
Book which is called The Home-going of the Holy Mary	apocryphal
Book which is called the Penitence of Adam	apocryphal
Book about the giant Ogias, of whom the heretics assert that after the flood he fought with the dragon	apocryphal
Book which is called The Testament of Job	apocryphal
Book which is called The Penitence of Origen	apocryphal
Book which is called The Penitence of the Holy Cyprian	apocryphal
Book which is called The Penitence of Jamnes and Mambres	apocryphal
Book which is called The Portion of the Apostles	apocryphal
Book which is called The Grave-plate(?) of the Apostles	apocryphal
Book which is called the Canones of the Apostles	apocryphal
The book Physiologus, compiled by heretics and called by the name of the blessed Ambrose	apocryphal
The History of Eusebius Pamphili	apocryphal
Works of Tertullian	apocryphal
Works of Lactantius	apocryphal
(*later addition*: or of Firmianus or of the African)	

Works of Postumianus and of Gallus	apocryphal
Works of Montanus, of Priscilla and of Maximilla	apocryphal
Works of Faustus the Manichaean	apocryphal
Works of Commodianus	apocryphal
Works of the other Clement, of Alexandria	apocryphal
Works of Thascius Cyprian	apocryphal
Works of Arnobius	apocryphal
Works of Tichonius	apocryphal
Works of Cassian, a presbyter in Gaul	apocryphal
Works of Victorinus of Pettau	apocryphal
Works of Faustus of Riez in Gaul	apocryphal
Works of Frumentius Caecus	apocryphal
Epistle of Jesus to Abgar	apocryphal
Epistle of Abgar to Jesus	apocryphal
Passion (Martyr Acts) of Cyricus and of Iulitta	apocryphal
Passion of Georgius	apocryphal
Writing which is called Interdiction (Exorcism?) of Solomon	apocryphal
All amulets which have been compiled not, as those persons feign, in the name of the angels, but rather in that of the demons	apocryphal

These and the like, what Simon Magus, Nicolaus, Cerinthus, Marcion, Basilides, Ebion, Paul of Samosata, Photinus and Bonosus, who suffered from similar error, also Montanus with his detestable followers, Apollinaris, Valentinus the Manichaean, Faustus the African, Sabellius, Arius, Macedonius, Eunomius, Novatus, Sabbatius, Calistus, Donatus, Eustatius, Iovianus, Pelagius, Iulianus of Eclanum, Caelestius, Maximian, Priscillian from Spain, Nestorius of Constantinople, Maximus the Cynic, Lampetius, Dioscorus, Eutyches, Peter and the other Peter, of whom the one besmirched Alexandria and the other Antioch, Acacius of Constantinople with his associates, and what also all disciples of heresy and of the heretics or schismatics, whose names we have scarcely preserved, have taught or compiled, we acknowledge is to be not merely rejected but excluded from the whole Roman Catholic and Apostolic Church and with its authors and the adherents of its authors to be damned in the inextricable shackles of anathema for ever.

4. *The Stichometry of Nicephorus*

In the detailed version of the *Chronography* of Nicephorus (Patriarch of Constantinople 806-815) there is a canon catalogue, the origin of which has not indeed been clearly settled, but which may perhaps be located in Jerusalem. Whether it is older than c.850 (so Jülicher) remains open to question. It is striking that in the enumeration of the NT books the Revelation of John is wanting. Here, then, a canon of twenty-six books still presents itself. The catalogue of the books of the Old and New Testaments is followed by that of the 'antilegomena' and of the 'apocrypha'.

Text: C. de Boor, *Nicephori archiep. Const. opuscula historica*, 1880, p. 132; Zahn, *Gesch. d.ntl. Kanons* II 1, 297-301; Preuschen, *Analecta* II², 62-64. On Nicephorus cf. Krumbacher, *Gesch. d. Byz. Literatur*, ²1897, pp. 349ff.; H.G. Beck, *Kirche und theol. Lit. im byzantin. Reich*, 1959, pp. 489ff. and index s.v. Nicephorus I.

And the (writings) of the Old Testament which are gainsaid and are not recognised in the Church (ἐκκλησιάζονται = canonised) are the following:

1. 3 Books of the Maccabees	7300 lines
2. The Wisdom of Solomon	1100 lines
3. The Wisdom of Jesus Sirach	2800 lines
4. The Psalms and Odes of Solomon	2100 lines
5. Esther	350 lines
6. Judith	1700 lines
7. Susanna	500 lines
8. Tobith, also (called) Tobias	700 lines

And of the New Testament (writings) the following are gainsaid:

1. The Revelation of John	1400 lines
2. The Revelation of Peter	300 lines
3. The Epistle of Barnabas	1360 lines
4. The Gospel of the Hebrews	2200 lines

Apocrypha of the Old Testament are the following:

1. Enoch	4800 lines
2. (Testaments of the) Patriarchs	5100 lines
3. The Prayer of Joseph	300 lines
4. The Testament of Moses	1100 lines
5. The Assumption of Moses	1400 lines
6. Abraham	300 lines
7. Eldad and Modad	400 lines
8. (Book of the) prophet Elias	316 lines
9. (Book of the) prophet Zephaniah	600 lines
10. (Book of) Zacharias, the father of John	500 lines
11. Pseudepigrapha of Baruch, Habakkuk, Ezekiel and Daniel	

Apocrypha of the New Testament are the following:

1. The Circuit of Paul	3600 lines
2. The Circuit of Peter	2750 lines
3. The Circuit of John	2500 lines
4. The Circuit of Thomas	1600 lines
5. The Gospel of Thomas	1300 lines
6. The Teaching (Didache) of the Apostles	200 lines
7. The 32 (books) of Clement	2600 lines
8. (Writings) of Ignatius, of Polycarp and of Hermas . . .	

5. *Catalogue of the Sixty canonical books*

This list, which probably originated in the 7th century and is transmitted in several manuscripts (for information about these see Zahn, *Gesch. d. ntl. Kanons* II 1, 289f.), reflects the view, widely held in the Greek Church at a later time, of the canon of sixty books (thirty-four OT and twenty-six NT, therefore without the Revelation of John). After the enumeration of the canonical books, in which the complete silence observed regarding the Apocalypse of John is the most serious matter, there follows that of the writings 'outside the sixty' and the 'apocrypha'. **Text:** Zahn, *op. cit.* pp. 290-292; Preuschen, *Analecta* II², 68f

And the following (writings) outside the sixty

1. The Wisdom of Solomon
2. The Wisdom of Sirach
3. Maccabees (I)
4. Maccabees (II)
5. Maccabees (III)
6. Maccabees (IV
7. Esther
8. Judith
9. Tobit

And the following apocryphal (writings)

1. Adam
2. Enoch
3. Lamech
4. The Patriarchs
5. The Prayer of Joseph
6. Eldad and Modad
7. The Testament of Moses
8. The Assumption of Moses
9. The Psalms of Solomon
10. The Revelation of Elias
11. The Vision of Isaiah
12. The Revelation of Zephaniah
13. The Revelation of Zechariah

b) Testimonies of Church Fathers from the 3rd and 4th centuries
1. *Origen*

Eusebius in his Church History (H.E. VI, 25, pp. 572. 10 - 580. 8 Schwartz) has assembled a series of observations by Origen on the canon (cf. above, pp. 30f.):

In expounding the first Psalm he (Origen) gives a catalogue of the sacred scriptures of the Old Testament. Word for word he writes: . . . (there follows an enumeration of the Old Testament books).

These writings he gives in the work mentioned.

In the first book of his Commentary on Matthew, true to the canon of the Church, he testifies that he knows only four Gospels; he writes: 'Concerning the four Gospels, the only ones that meet with no opposition in the Church of God (spread out) under heaven, I have learned by tradition as follows: First was written the Gospel according to Matthew, formerly a publican and later an apostle of Jesus Christ, who published it for believers from Judaism, composed in Hebrew letters; the second is the Gospel according to Mark, who followed the instructions of Peter, who in his catholic epistle has acknowledged him as his son in the words: The (Church) that is at Babylon, elected together with you, saluteth you; and so also doth Marcus my son [1 Pet. 5:13]; the third is that according to Luke who composed the Gospel commended by Paul [2 Cor. 8:18; cf. Orig. *Hom. I on Lk.*, Rauer 10. 8-14] for believers from the Gentiles; the last of all is the Gospel according to John.'

And in the fifth book of his *Commentary on the Gospel of John* the same author (= Origen) speaks as follows about the epistles of the apostles: 'Paul, who was enabled to be a minister *of the new testament not of the letter, but of the Spirit* [2 Cor. 3:6] and fully preached the gospel *from Jerusalem and round about unto Illyricum* [Rom. 15:19], did not write to all the churches which he had instructed; and even to those to which he wrote, he sent only a few lines. Peter, on whom the Church of Christ is built, against which the gates of hell shall not prevail [Mt. 16:18], has left one acknowledged epistle, possibly also a second, but that is disputed. What need be said of him who lay on Jesus' breast [Jn. 13:25; 21:20], of John who has left one Gospel and has confessed that he could write so many that the world could not contain them [Jn. 21:25], and who also has written the Revelation, but was commanded to keep silence and not record the words of the seven thunders [Rev. 10:4]? He has also left an epistle of only a few lines: he has possibly also left a second and third epistle, but not all consider these to be genuine. The two of them indeed do not contain a hundred lines.'

Further in regard to the Epistle to the Hebrews he (= Origen) observes as follows in his Homilies upon it: 'In its style the epistle written to the Hebrews has a character which does not exhibit the rhetorical clumsiness of the apostle, who confesses that he is rude in speech, i.e. in expression [2 Cor. 11:6]. Rather the diction of the epistle is purer Greek, as everyone who is able to estimate differences in modes of expression must acknowledge. That on the other hand the thoughts of the epistle are wonderful and not inferior to those of the writings that are recognised as apostolic, everyone must admit to be true who gives the apostolic text his careful consideration.'

After other comments he (= Origen) adds: 'Expressing my own opinion, I would say that the thoughts proceed from the apostle, but that the expression and composition are those of someone who remembered the apostle's discourses and as it were paraphrased the words of his teacher. If then a church regards this epistle as Paul's, it may in this command our assent: for not without good reason have the ancients handed it down as Paul's. But who actually wrote the epistle, God knows. According to the information that has reached us, some say that Clement, the bishop of Rome, wrote the epistle, and others that Luke, the author of the Gospel and of the Acts of the Apostles, did so.'

From the first *Homily on Luke* (on Lk. 1:1):

According to the Latin translation of Jerome (pp. 3.8-5.20 Rauer)	According to the Greek fragments in *Catenae* (pp. 3,4-6,5 Rauer)
	As the attempt on the part of a man to record the teaching and discourse of God may be presumptuous, he (= Luke) with good reason justifies himself in the preface.
As once upon a time among the Jewish people	As among the ancient people

many engaged in prophetic discourse,
but some were lying prophets

(one of them was Ananias, the son of Azor)

whereas others were truthful prophets

and as among the people there was the gift of grace to distinguish spirits, whereby a section of the prophets was received, but some were rejected as it were by 'expert bankers' [cf. Resch, *Agrapha*, ²1906, pp. 112-128; see below, p. 91], so now also in the new testament (*instrumentum*) have 'many taken in hand' to write gospels, but not all have been accepted.

That there have been written not only the four Gospels, but a whole series from which those that we possess have been chosen and handed down to the churches, is, let it be noted, what we may learn from Luke's preface, which runs thus: 'For as much as many have taken in hand to compose a narrative'.

and as to the people there was granted as a gift of grace power to distinguish spirits by virtue which they discriminated between the true and the false prophets, so also now in the new covenant many have wished to write gospels; the efficient bankers [cf.Resch pp.112-128] have, however, not accepted everything, but have chosen only a few things.

The expression 'they have taken in hand' [the Greek adds: forsooth] involves a covert accusation of those who precipitately and without the gift of grace [the Latin adds: of the Holy Ghost] have set about the writing of gospels.

Matthew to be sure and Mark and John as well as Luke did not 'take in hand' to write, but filled with the Holy Ghost have written the Gospels. 'Many have taken in hand to compose a narrative of the events which are quite definitely familiar among us.' The Church possesses four Gospels, heresy a great many, of which one is entitled 'The Gospel according to the Egyptians', and another 'The Gospel according to the Twelve Apostles'. Basilides also has presumed to write a gospel and to call it by his own name. 'Many have taken in hand' to write, but only four Gospels are recognised.

Matthew to be sure did not 'take in hand' to write, but rather has written from the Holy Ghost; so also have Mark and John and equally also Luke.

Those to be sure who have composed the gospel superscribed 'The Gospel according to the Egyptians' and the one entitled 'The Gospel of the Twelve' have 'taken it in hand'. Moreover, Basilides also has presumed to write a 'Gospel according to Basilides'. Thus 'many have taken it in hand'.

From these the doctrines concerning the person of our Lord and Saviour are to be derived. I know a certain gospel which is called 'The Gospel according to Thomas' and a 'Gospel according to Matthias', and many others have we read - lest we should in any way be considered ignorant because of those who imagine that they possess some knowledge if they are acquainted with these. Nevertheless, among all these we have approved solely what the Church has recognised, which is that only the four Gospels should be accepted.

That is to say there are also in circulation the 'Gospel according to Thomas' and the 'Gospel according to Matthias' and some others. These belong to those who 'have taken it in hand'. But the Church of God has preferred only the four. There is a report noted down in writing that John collected the written gospels in his own lifetime in the reign of Nero, and approved of and recognised those of which the deceit of the devil had not taken possession; but refused and rejected those which he perceived were not truthful.

2. *Eusebius of Caesarea*

Church History III 25 (pp. 250.19-252.24 Schwartz); cf. above, p.31

Here it may be in place to assemble once more the writings of the New Testament which have been mentioned. In the first place is to be set the holy quaternion of the Gospels, on which there follows the Acts of the Apostles. After this there are to be filed the epistles of the holy Paul, and then place must be given to the so-called first epistle of John and likewise to that of Peter. To these writings, provided it is considered proper, the Revelation of John may be added; the opinions with regard to it will be set out at the proper time. These belong to the recognised writings. To the disputed writings, which are nevertheless esteemed by most people, there belong the so-called epistle of James, that of Jude, the second epistle of Peter as also the so-called second and third epistles of John, whether they belong to the Evangelist or to another person of the same name. To the writings that are spurious there must be counted the Acts of Paul, the so-called Shepherd, the Revelation of Peter, also the so-called epistle of Barnabas and the so-called Teachings (διδαχαί) of the Apostles and also, as has been said, the Revelation of John, provided that is considered proper; which some, as has been mentioned, reject but which others reckon among the recognised writings. Moreover, many have also reckoned among these writings the Gospel according to the Hebrews, in which those especially from among the Hebrews who have accepted Christ find delight.

While all these may be reckoned among the disputed writings, we have nevertheless felt ourselves called upon to draw up a catalogue of them, in which we have distinguished between the writings which according to ecclesiastical tradition are true, genuine and unanimously recognised and those which ordinarily exist side by side with them, which, although they do not indeed belong to the canon (ἐνδιάθηκος) but are disputed, yet have attention paid them by most ecclesiastics. We have felt ourselves called upon to draw up this catalogue in order that we may be in a position to know these writings as also those which have been adduced under apostolic names by the heretics, including e.g. the Gospels of Peter and Thomas and Matthias or of any others besides, or the Acts of Andrew and of John as also of other apostles. No ecclesiastical writer standing in the tradition has ever in any of his works considered any of these writings worth mentioning. Moreover their linguistic features are at variance with apostolic usage, and the thought and purpose of what is expressed in them, being in the highest degree contrary to true orthodoxy, show clearly that in them we handle the concoctions of heretics. Wherefore they are not even to be classed with the writings that are spurious, but ought to be rejected as wholly absurd and impious.

Church History II 23.24f. (p.174.12-17 Schwartz):

This [i.e. the report given earlier by Eusebius in II 23] is the history of James, by whom the first of the so-called catholic epistles is said to have been written. It needs, however, to be borne in mind that it is regarded as spurious. Certainly not many of the ancients have mentioned it, and the same is true of the so-called epistle of Jude, which likewise is one of the seven so-called catholic epistles. All the same we know that these also are read publicly with the remaining epistles in most churches.

Church History III 3 (pp. 188.17-190.27 Schwartz):

There is an epistle, the so-called first, by Peter which is generally recognised. The ancients have already used it in their writings as a work that is beyond question. As regards the so-called second epistle of Peter, it has come down to us that it does not belong to the canon (ἐνδιάϑηκος); to many, however, it has appeared helpful and has been highly esteemed with the remaining writings. Certainly the Acts described as his and the Gospel bearing his name as also the Preaching ascribed to him and the so-called Revelation have, we know, by no means been handed down among the catholic writings, for no ecclesiastical writer, whether ancient or modern, has made use of testimonies drawn from them. . . . These are writings bearing the name of Peter, of which, as I have ascertained, only one epistle is genuine and recognised by the ancients. But it is manifest and certain that the fourteen epistles of Paul come from him. It would, however, not be right to overlook the fact that some have rejected the Epistle to the Hebrews, maintaining that it is spoken against as non-Pauline in the Roman church . . . .

The so-called Acts of Paul have certainly not come down to us among the undisputed writings. Since the apostle in the closing salutations of the Epistle to the Romans has made mention among others of Hermas [Rom. 16:14] to whom the book called The Shepherd is ascribed, it is worth noting that this book also has been spoken against by some; on their account it should not be reckoned to the generally recognised writings; by others again it has been rated as extremely necessary, especially for such as need introductory, elementary instruction. For that reason, as we know, it has already been read publicly in [some] churches, and, as I have ascertained, has been used by some of the very ancient writers. This may suffice as information about the divine writings, those which are not spoken against as also those which are not recognised by all.

3. *Athanasius*

From the 39th Festal Letter for the year 367. The text found its way into the Greek canon collections and hence has a widespread tradition. In addition there are translations into Syriac, Armenian and Coptic. Cf. *Clavis Patrum graec.* II, 1974, No. 2102. The translation offered here follows the Greek text of S. Sakkos, ʿΗ λϑʾ ἑορταστικὴ ἐπιστολὴ τοῦ Μ.,ʾΑθανασίου, in Τόμος ἑόρτιος ed. G. Mantzarides, Thessalonica 1974, pp. 131-233(text pp.177-182). German translation of the Coptic text: *Osterfestbriefe des Apa Athanasius*, trans. Pius Merendino, 1965, pp. 94ff. On the interpretation, cf. above, pp.31f. See further M.Tetz, 'Athanasius und die Einheit der Kirche', in ZThK 81, 1984, 196-219.

Since, however, we have spoken of the heretics as dead but of ourselves as possessors of the divine writings unto salvation, and since I am afraid that - as Paul has written to the Corinthians [2 Cor. 11:3] - some guileless persons may be led astray from their purity and holiness by the craftiness of certain men and begin thereafter to pay attention to other books, the so-called apocryphal writings, being deceived by their possession of the same names as the genuine books, I therefore exhort you to patience when, out of regard to the Church's need and benefit, I mention in my letter matters with which you are acquainted. It being my intention to mention these matters, I shall, for the commendation of my venture, follow the example of the evangelist Luke and say [cf. Lk. 1:1-4]: *Since* some *have taken in hand to set in order* for themselves the so-called apocrypha and to mingle them with the God-inspired scripture, concerning which we have attained to a sure persuasion, according to what *the original eye-witnesses and ministers of the word have delivered* unto our fathers, *I also*, having been urged by true brethren and having investigated the matter from the beginning, *have decided* to set forth in order the writings that have been put in the canon, that have been handed down and confirmed as divine, in order that every one who has been led astray may condemn his seducers and that every one who has remained stainless may rejoice, being again reminded of that.

Athanasius now in the first place enumerates the scriptures of the Old Testament. He then proceeds:

Continuing, I must without hesitation mention the scriptures of the New Testament; they are the following: the four Gospels according to Matthew, Mark, Luke and John, after them the Acts of the Apostles and the seven so-called catholic epistles of the apostles - namely, one of James, two of Peter, then three of John and after these one of Jude. In addition there are fourteen epistles of the apostle Paul written in the following order: the first to the Romans, then two to the Corinthians and then after these the one to the Galatians, following it the one to the

Ephesians, thereafter the one to the Philippians and the one to the Colossians and two to the Thessalonians and the epistle to the Hebrews and then immediately two to Timothy, one to Titus and lastly the one to Philemon. Yet further the Revelation of John.

These are the springs of salvation, in order that he who is thirsty may fully refresh himself with the words contained in them. In them alone is the doctrine of piety proclaimed. Let no one add anything to them or take anything away from them . . .

But for the sake of greater accuracy I add, being constrained to write, that there are also other books besides these, which have not indeed been put in the canon, but have been appointed by the Fathers as reading-matter for those who have just come forward and wish to be instructed in the doctrine of piety: the Wisdom of Solomon, the Wisdom of Sirach, Esther, Judith, Tobias, the so-called Teaching (διδαχή) of the Apostles [Coptic adds: I do not mean the Teaching of which it is said that it censures Deuteronomy] and the Shepherd. And although, beloved, the former are in the canon and the latter serve as reading-matter, yet mention is nowhere made of the apocrypha; rather they are a fabrication of the heretics, who write them down when it pleases them and generously assign to them an early date of composition in order that they may be able to draw upon them as supposedly ancient writings and have in them occasion to deceive the guileless.

3. New Testament apocrypha

The term 'New Testament apocrypha' is not a self-designation of the writings to which we today give this name (apart from a few exceptions, see above p. 14f.), nor can it be derived from any ancient collection. There never was a corpus of writings which bore this designation. Rather is it a term by which a rich store of very diverse works is comprehensively described. Any attempt to define more precisely what are 'New Testament apocrypha', and what belongs among them, must therefore take various factors into consideration.

1. The survey of the history of the canon has shown that the formation of the NT cannot be regarded as a process in the course of which some Church authority examined the literature available and used in the churches, accepting a part of it but rejecting another part. Rather is it a question, as we have seen, of a process of the fixation of the Jesus tradition and the apostolic tradition. The fact that in this process (at least in the decisive phase, the second half of the 2nd century) the *regula fidei* played a role as a normative standard points to the close connection between the formation of the canon and the development of Church doctrine and proclamation. At any rate, the acceptance of the writings which then grew together into the canon probably did not take place in the churches without some testing of their agreement with the dominant form of Christian doctrine.

According to a widespread understanding of the term, the writings which we call apocrypha are defined simply as those works which were not accepted into the canon. This is certainly not an adequate definition. In particular, the relation of these works to the canon is very much more complex than one might at first think.

This is already clear from the fact that the apocrypha originated partly before the canonising process, partly parallel with it in time, and partly after the completion of the canon. A small group of older apocrypha was composed contemporaneously with the writings which were later canonised, and thus in certain circumstances these were in rivalry with the texts received into the canon with regard to the authority they claimed (e.g. the Gospel of Peter; see below, pp. 216 ff). Another group, the composition of which falls into the period when the canon was in formation although not yet complete, does indeed consciously link up with *Gattungen* of NT writings, but also took over or created other literary forms. Here the relationship to the nascent canon may sporadically be determined by the fact that by such works people wished to set forth something that was of equal value to (i.e. of the same authority as) the writings recognised by the Church. But above all a role was probably played by the intention of setting over against the Church's literature, or beside it, something which in terms of content was of another stamp. The process of canon formation strengthened these intentions.

Finally there is a large number of apocrypha which arose after the provisional closure of the canon (about 200) and presuppose the collection of writings recognised by the Church. These are mostly works which are to be explained by the motive of supplementation (on this see below, p. 55). They are not intended to supplant the Church's writings in respect of their authority, but simply offer more information than the canonical texts.

For the relation of the apocrypha to the canon we may refer also to a further aspect: it is clear from our account of the history of the canon that this collection arose in a lengthy process, often hard to decipher, in which first of all oral traditions were precipitated into written form, and then written texts of this kind grew together with others (such as letters). The formation of the apocryphal literature appears in large part to have proceeded according to similar laws. In many of these works also traditions are worked up which had been handed on in part orally and in part in writing. That in addition new 'traditions' were consciously shaped (with appeal to recognised authorities) is a special characteristic of the apocryphal literature, but has a parallel in some NT writings. We may therefore say that a definition of the term 'New Testament apocrypha' cannot rest content with the statement that it is a question of writings which were not accepted into the canon. These very heterogeneous works rather hang together in very varied fashion with the phenomenon of the canon. Parallels and differences have to be noticed, but the connection with the canon is important for the understanding of this literature.

2. New Testament apocrypha are writings which in some way, be it in terms of their form or of their content, stand in some relationship with the writings of the New Testament. This statement also - though not false - is not an adequate

definition. Rather we must, as in the question of the relation to the canon, differentiate very precisely with regard to *the relationships of the individual writings*. This holds for the problem of the *Gattungen*[1] and also for the motives which led to the rise of the apocrypha. The two cycles of problems hang together, but may not be misunderstood as purely formal questions of literary history; rather they are closely connected with tendencies of content, i.e. in this case with theological tendencies.

A perusal of the whole material brought together in the present work shows that here we can trace a multiplicity of *literary Gattungen*. There are writings which correspond to the New Testament *Gattungen*. This holds, for example, for some early apocryphal gospels, but also for some pseudo-apostolic letters. Other apocrypha in their literary form are governed less by the NT writings and much more by non-Christian *Gattungen* (like the apocryphal Acts for example). The works in another group have indeed taken over the designations of NT writings, but 'without the right to bear these titles in terms of *Gattung*' (Vielhauer, *Lit. gesch.* p. 5). This applies especially to many gnostic works.

These relationships are discussed in the introductions to the individual sections of our collection. Here reference may be made only to a few fundamental aspects:

a) The division of the apocryphal literature into Gospels, Acts, Epistles and Apocalypses is certainly not incorrect, but should not deceive us as to the fact that behind such general designations works of very distinct stamp lie concealed. Proximity to, and distance from, the NT *Gattungen* must therefore at times be determined for each individual writing.

b) In any classification of an apocryphal text in terms of *Gattung*, we may not start out from the title of the work. The Coptic gnostic texts offer many an example in which titles are taken over for works which belong to another *Gattung* than that described by the title.[2]

c) The fact that many apocrypha (especially the later) attest the acceptance of 'secular' *Gattungen* should not blind us to a different state of affairs: such borrowings from the literature of the surrounding world are frequently connected with an association with New Testament *Gattungen*. This holds good not only for the titles, but also for the individual traditions which are worked up.

The outcome of these propositions is that we must test the form-critical relationships between the apocryphal and the NT literature in regard to the particular case at every turn. A global setting in opposition of Christian 'primitive literature' and 'patristic literature' is accordingly somewhat question-able. Franz Overbeck in an essay in 1882 threw this contrast into relief, and thereby provided decisive impulses not only for the later form-critical work in the NT but also for the whole of early Christian literature (including the apocrypha).[3] It will be useful for our purposes also to give some consideration to Overbeck's theses.

According to Overbeck, the NT writings cannot yet be regarded as the beginning of Christian literature. 'Gospel, Acts and Apocalypse are historical forms which from a quite specific point of time disappear in the Christian

Church' (p. 23). In these writings we have to do with the Christian 'primitive literature', which indeed is not a literature in the strict sense of the word - there is such a literature only from the time of the Apologists, in fact strictly only after Clement of Alexandria. Only from then on can we speak of a Graeco-Roman literature of Christian profession and Christian interest, i.e. of a real Christian literature. 'Against this no-one will seriously oppose the so-called apocryphal literature. For the rise of apocryphal gospels, acts and apocalypses, of which there are actually many before the point of time just indicated, there are admittedly no historical limits, and pieces of this kind could still be written at any time even today. But the very description of this literature as apocryphal shows that in history it leads only a so to speak illegitimate existence and that its recognition depends solely on the fiction of an origin which is either primeval or otherwise lies outside the limits of the existing literature. For its part, the apocryphal literature thus serves only to confirm the statement that gospels, acts and apocalypses are forms which, at a time when what has kept itself alive as Christian literature had only just begun to exist, have already ceased to be even possible in it' (pp. 23 f.).

For the understanding of these statements about primitive literature, apocrypha and Christian literature, it has to be observed that for Overbeck literary history is form history: 'A literature has its history in its forms, and any real literary history will thus be a form history' (p. 13). This is naturally not to be misunderstood in a formal and aesthetic sense. Overbeck to be sure here concentrated on the major forms (gospels, etc.). 'He does not yet know the smaller forms which are contained in these, and which were only worked out much later by research into the history of religions and form criticism' (Vielhauer, *Lit. gesch.* p. 3). This already points to certain limits in Overbeck's view.

We need not in this connection enter into the influences and consequences for NT study, and especially for form-criticism, which resulted from Overbeck's statement.[4] Here we are concerned only with his judgment on the apocrypha and their relation to the 'primitive literature'. This cannot be accepted in this form. On the one hand Overbeck evidently starts out from the view that the NT apocrypha so described themselves, or at least were uniformly so labelled, at a very early date. This, as we have seen, is not correct. On the other hand Overbeck probably has not seen that the chief problem of research into the apocrypha is the question why the 'primitive literature' in part continued in them (this holds at any rate from the point of view of the history of *Gattungen*). Finally, the designation 'illegitimate' for the apocrypha is only applicable if we start out from the presupposition that the canon was very early regarded as the collection of the only legitimate writings. This presupposition, however, is also not correct, but rather a part of Overbeck's view of the history of primitive Christianity, against which there are considerable objections to be raised.

Despite much criticism of Overbeck, some things should for our purposes be held fast on the basis of his statements:

a) The term 'primitive literature' is correct, in so far as it is a matter of a part of the NT writings (cf. also below, p. 55). It is also correct that Christian literature in the proper sense of the word first begins with the Apologists, i.e. in the period in which forms of literature were taken over from the surrounding world for the defence of Christianity. At the same time theological work begins[5] (in the sense of a reflective conception of the faith), and this then leads to a manifold literature of Christian profession which stands in the tradition of ancient models. Here, however, we must not overlook the fact that the 'primitive literature' was further developed, as the apocrypha show. It need not be emphasised that the distinction between the apocrypha and the 'Graeco-Roman literature of Christian profession and Christian interest' (Overbeck, p. 37) is important. But the limits are not to be rigidly drawn.

b) The statement that for the origin of apocryphal gospels, acts and apocalypses there were 'no historical limits' (Overbeck, p. 23) is untenable. This would obliterate the distinction between the apocrypha and the hagiographical literature (see below, pp. 57f.) and at the same time leave out of consideration the historical context in which the two categories are to be seen. As is clear from our survey of the history of the canon, it makes a considerable difference whether a work of this kind originated before or after the middle of the 4th century. Naturally we cannot name any fixed date after which there are no longer any apocrypha but only hagiographical literature. Precisely from the point of view of the history of *Gattungen*, which Overbeck rightly stresses, the transition from the one category to the other is to be seen as a lengthy process, as can be shown from the further development from the old apocryphal Acts. Here too a special significance attaches to the total historical frame in which this development took place (cf. for example the rise of veneration of the saints).

c) The distinction between 'primitive literature' and 'patristic literature' is, according to Overbeck, determined above all by the fact that Christianity entered into contacts with the 'world'. Literature first comes into being when specific forms which exist in the 'world' are taken over. The 'primitive literature', however, is a witness to a community which knows itself separated from the 'world' and therefore has produced no literature in the proper sense of the word. Only with the Apologists does the process of the reception of 'secular' literary forms begin. Behind these statements too there stands a particular conception of the nature of primitive Christianity and of the relation of Christianity to culture, with which we cannot agree.[6] But that there were in early Christianity independent literary forms, not taken over from the 'world', which however did not intend at all to be literature, can be demonstrated, for example, from the Gospels. Only it must be added that evidently very early (and thus *before* the Apologists) 'secular' forms streamed in,[7] and the oldest tradition very soon fell under the influence of the forms of Graeco-Roman literature.[8] This is the case in a special way with the apocrypha. They do not belong to the 'patristic literature' with the origin of which Overbeck deals, but represent a separate category alongside, and in continuation of, the 'primitive literature'.

Despite the objections against many of Overbeck's ideas, we may accept some suggestions for the understanding of the phenomenon of the apocrypha, and that not only with regard to the form-critical aspect but also with an eye to the question of the reception of 'secular' content. This indeed is to be firmly held: The 'primitive literature', i.e. the written deposit of early Christian faith, was transformed through the acceptance of forms of Graeco-Roman literature. But this change was also conditioned by the outreach of Christian preaching into the world, and with it the unfolding of Christian faith with the aid of the intellectual and literary resources of the time. The apocrypha are a particularly important source for the understanding of this process.

3. What *motives* were operative in the rise of apocryphal writings? This question too cannot be answered in global terms. Rather we must investigate for each individual writing what motive or what occasion for its composition can be worked out. This will have to be done in each case in the introductions to the texts in the present work. Here only a few summary remarks may be submitted in advance, on the basis of the detailed observations.

a) For a few early texts we must assume similar motives as for the canonical literature. Traditions were collected and fixed in writing, in order to provide an authoritative norm for the proclamation of the Christian message. This happened above all in the shape of the same 'gospel' *Gattung* such as we meet in the canonical books. Of this group only very little has survived.

b) The authority of writings reporting on the life and work of Jesus, as well as on the teaching of the apostles (Paul's letters also belong here), was in the course of the 2nd century limited by the canonisation process to specific works. There were however in addition churches which ascribed authority to the traditions still living among them, and which hence for their part - sometimes linking up with NT *Gattungen*, sometimes taking over only the name of the *Gattung* - created works in which these traditions were brought together in writing. The Coptic gnostic texts from Nag Hammadi show that this could also lead to the shaping of new literary forms (e.g. dialogues).

c) With the provisional closure of the canon (about 200) a motive which had probably also been operative earlier becomes increasingly important: the aim of supplementing the canonical texts. Here it is a question of filling up 'gaps' in the reports about Jesus and the apostles, but also of presenting and propagating teachings which do not appear in the canonical books. We can see the first beginnings of such supplementing activity in many textual variants and additions in NT writings.[9] At a later period texts handed down were further developed, by taking out a part and building something new upon it. The Infancy Gospels (see below, pp. 414 ff.) are an important example of this kind of expansion. Here the meagre statements of the canonical Gospels are drawn out at length, expanded and supplemented by large additions, and here the influence of literary *Gattungen* of the surrounding world was certainly considerable.

d) This motive of supplementation also plays a role in the apocryphal works which no longer have their basis directly in NT writings, but are simply interested in individual persons who are mentioned in the NT. The apocryphal Acts are an example of this. Here we may set other aspects also into the reckoning: local interests, such as the evangelising of some place or region, had to be taken into account; church usages which developed in the course of time had to be legitimated through writings which declared themselves to be old tradition. All this provided the impulse for works which were indeed more or less oriented towards NT *Gattungen*, but yet already very clearly form a transition to another kind of literature.

e) Supplementation with regard to doctrine as a motive for the origin of apocryphal writings is, as already said, perceptible at an early date. This is not surprising, since the diversity in preaching and in doctrine in the first two centuries was considerable, and only gradually gave way to a uniform orthodoxy.[10] This is reflected in the apocryphal literature. With the advance of 'orthodoxy' the character of this literature also changed: it became propaganda literature for particular groups or opinions. The authors of the writings which are to be understood in this way wished to disseminate teachings and ideas of their groups by creating works linked with *Gattungen* of the 'primitive literature', but at the same time borrowing from 'secular' literary forms, and by these works anchoring these teachings in the past (i.e. in the time of the apostles). Such motives can be identified in the apocryphal Acts (cf. for example the emphasis on continence in the Acts of Paul).

f) For a part of the apocrypha (in particular the Acts of apostles) the motive of 'entertainment' has also been assumed, and here links with *Gattungen* of ancient literature (e.g. the romance) have been pointed out. Now there are certainly individual sections in many works which can be regarded as popular legends or anecdotes with a certain entertainment value. But it should not be overlooked that these pieces - probably at first transmitted orally - were intended to serve not so much for 'entertainment' in our sense but rather for 'edification'. That is, they served to throw into relief the life and deeds of the hero concerned, and so to serve for 'edification' or even for propaganda.[11] Traditions of this kind are then built into the total composition and give it an entertaining or edifying aspect, which is, however, closely bound up with the theological intention of the work. This, to be sure, does not mean that we can apply the term 'popular literature' to the whole of the apocryphal literature.[12] Rather it is one of the important problems of research into the apocrypha to determine ever more precisely the relation between popular narrative tradition and theological composition.

To sum up: the question as to the motives which were operative in the origin of the apocrypha cannot be answered in a single sentence. There are very diverse tendencies, which all play their part. Form-critical treatment of this literature can make a certain development parallel to the canonical writings probable for the early period. At a later period we can trace a further development of the NT *Gattungen*. For the question of motives the variety in faith and doctrine in the early period is not unimportant. For this diversity gained expression for itself in the different versions of the 'Gospel', but led also to other works. With the unification of doctrine (and of the canon) the form of Christian preaching that was not accepted became 'heretical', and its literature a non-orthodox 'tendency-literature'. In addition there are also works of this literature which are not 'heretical', but were intended simply to supplement the canonical literature or to serve for entertainment and for edification.

4. From what has been said so far as to the relation of the apocrypha to the canon and to the *Gattungen* of the 'primitive literature' it follows that we have to do with works which are to be assigned to a particular period in Church history. Fixed dates with regard to a chronological arrangement are, however, not at our disposal. The beginnings above all are largely shrouded in obscurity. We can only point, as already said, to a certain parallelism between the formation of some early apocryphal gospels and the origin of the canonical writings, although we can hardly reckon with a 'gospel' composed before Mark. Everything points to the conclusion that the collections of traditions (in the form of a gospel) which did not find a place in the canon are to be set predominantly, if not exclusively, later than Mark.

For the part of the apocrypha connected with the later 'Apostolos' in the canon, we may also in part reckon with early beginnings. It should be recalled that the composition of the deutero-Pauline letters, which are in part regarded, probably rightly, as products of the Pauline school, is strictly no different from the rise of apocryphal works of the same *Gattung*.

The establishing of the chronological end of the production of apocryphal writings is beset by many difficulties. We cannot specify any firm point in time. But at any rate the sources available, very much more abundant than for the beginnings, allow of a few firm statements.

It has already been said that the closing of the canon in the 4th century marks an important caesura for the apocrypha and their production. For thereby the presuppositions for the production of this kind of literature are finally altered. The canon is now regarded as the sole 'spring of salvation', the legitimate collection of the apostolic traditions or the like. Everything that appears in the garb of the NT *Gattungen* is as a matter of course heretical and excluded from Church use. Certainly tendencies of this kind are probably to be observed even earlier, but they were still not yet so unambiguously set forth.

It is for our purpose not of importance that, as explained in the survey of the history of the canon, the extent of the NT differed in the various regions of the Church, and the uniform stock of twenty-seven books was only generally established very late. Whether the canon included twenty-two or twenty-six or twenty-seven books, all that is important here is the fact that a firmly closed collection of recognised texts, invested with the highest authority, now existed everywhere.

The settlement of the canon, as already mentioned, is not to be separated from other phenomena in the sphere of the Church. In the nascent imperial Church of the 4th century efforts towards a unification in the various fields of Church life are to be observed. Dogma, Church order, liturgy, but above all the holy scripture, must be moulded as uniformly as possible throughout the whole Church. This is connected with a change in popular piety, as the rise of the veneration of the saints and the cult of relics shows. Here a special significance attaches to the nascent monasticism, and we may assign to the monks a share in the production of certain later 'apocrypha' also, which however can no longer strictly be described by this term.

At any rate this briefly sketched development brought it about that the old forms of the NT apocrypha changed: out of the apocrypha comes the hagiographical literature. Gospels are scarcely produced any longer. When the designation 'gospel' is used for a work, this title can scarcely conceal the fact that it is a case of legends of the saints. The apocryphal Acts were particularly strongly affected by the change. The recasting of older writings and the production of new works are determined by the veneration of a 'saint', and this in a wholly different way from that in the old Acts of apostles, even though the starting-points for the further development are already present there.

The apocalypses, which in the older apocryphal literature are in any case not so important, become in later times books of instruction about the last judgment, hell etc. (cf. the Apocalypse of Paul). Even if by their titles they profess to be apocalypses, in terms of *Gattung*-history they are yet something else. This is naturally connected with the fact that in the Church apocalyptic was more and more pushed to one side.

Here we may not overlook the fact that older traditions live on in later texts. Many of the works are indeed nothing but reworkings of the writings of the first three or four centuries. Old *Gattungen* were also used and imitated. But this is an artificial taking-over of older *Gattungen*. The historical context in which this happens has become a different one.

This has consequences for the literary formation. Thus, for example, an influence from Church homiletic on the speeches in the later apocryphal Acts is not to be denied. Since the hagiographical presentation of the lives of the apostles was intended for reading on special occasions, the style of the sermons had to be adapted to Church usage.

These general remarks about the change must suffice here. In regard to many details something will be said in the introductions to the texts presented in this work, while other points probably still require further research.

We cannot locate this change in terms of time by any fixed date. Yet it may probably be maintained that the transition from the NT apocrypha to the hagiographical literature took place in the 4th and 5th centuries. It was a lengthy process, just as the way from the pre-Constantinian Church to the Theodosian Imperial Church was both long and manifold. We can only understand this process when we see it in the whole context of the development of Church history.

For the investigation of the NT apocrypha the later literature is without doubt of inestimable value. For in it many older traditions are preserved, the original context of which has been lost. This is also the reason why in the present collection a temporal limit could not be rigidly adhered to. But here it must always be kept in mind that a hagiographical text does not become a New Testament apocryphon simply because it re-casts and hands on older tradition.

5. In NTApo[3], pp. 27f. I attempted to give a definition of the term 'New Testament Apocrypha'. Since a discussion of this attempt has recently been sparked off, the wording may be repeated here:

'The New Testament Apocrypha are writings which have not been received into the canon, but which by title and other statements lay claim to be in the same class with the writings of the canon, and which from the point of view of Form Criticism further develop and mould the kinds of style created and received in the NT, whilst foreign elements certainly intrude' (p. 27). In amplification it was added: 'When we speak of 'Apocrypha of the NT', we mean by that Gospels which are distinguished by the fact not merely that they did not come into the NT, but also that they were intended to take the place of the four Gospels of the canon (this holds good for the older texts) or to stand as enlargement of them side by side with them. . . . It is further a matter of particular pseudepigraphical Epistles and of elaborately fabricated Acts of Apostles, the writers of which have worked up in novelistic fashion the stories and legends about the apostles and so aimed at supplementing the deficient information which the NT communicates about the destinies of these men. Finally, there also belong here the Apocalypses in so far as they have further evolved the 'revelation' form taken over from Judaism' (p. 28).

These statements, in which an attempt is made to define the heterogeneous apocryphal literature, are not to be separated from what was said at NTApo³, pp. 60ff. on the origin of the apocrypha, and has been taken up afresh above, pp. 50ff.

It was already remarked in NTApo³ (p. 28) that the definition was a working hypothesis, with the aid of which the material can be sifted and arranged. It is thus not a question of a 'canonical' principle which could be rigidly enforced, but of a definition with the help of which the material which may rightly be reckoned to the NT apocrypha can be selected from the heterogeneous mass of the texts. If in the process texts which properly belong to hagiography are accepted into the collection, this can be justified on the ground that older traditions live on in them.

The definition given in NTApo³ has frequently been accepted. Erbetta and Moraldi (cf. below, p. 68) have taken it over, although they have considerably increased the number of texts included. R. McLachlan Wilson has used it in his comprehensive article 'Apokryphen II' (TRE III, 1978, 316ff.) as a useful working basis. He has in addition evaluated the gnostic library of Nag Hammadi, published in the interval, with regard to this problem.

Against this definition Eric Junod has voiced considerable doubts, and has attempted a definition of his own of this literature.[13] There are three points in particular on which he raises objections:

a) The chronological delimitation in NTApo³ is very problematic. The restriction to writings of the first three centuries, which in any case is not strictly adhered to and was further modified by Erbetta and Moraldi, is governed too much by the presupposition that a writing belongs to the apocrypha simply because it was not accepted into the canon.

b) A definition of the term which starts from the position that the apocrypha claimed an equal rank with the canonical writings can only be applied to a small group of the works presented in NTApo³. In most other texts no such claim can be identified.

c) The form-critical aspect, which for NTApo³ plays a major role, cannot be decisive. The literary forms of most apocrypha have nothing to do with the NT

Gattungen. In particular we should not allow ourselves to be led on a false track by the (often secondary) titles.

On the whole, Junod considers the definition given in NTApo³ too narrow, and he pleads for a wider conception. In particular he would replace the term 'New Testament apocrypha' by a different one: 'Ancient Christian apocrypha'.[14] The connection with the NT would then no longer be the exclusive point of reference, and Old Testament apocrypha accepted or worked over by the Church would also be included. Finally Junod gives a definition of his own:

Christian Apocrypha are: 'anonymous or pseudepigraphical texts of Christian origin, which stand in some relation to the books of the NT or the OT, because they are devoted to events which are narrated or mentioned in these books, or because they are devoted to events which can be understood as a continuation of events presented or mentioned in these books, because they concentrate upon persons who appear in these books, or because their literary *Gattung* is related to those of the biblical writings'.[15] We cannot here enter into a detailed discussion of Junod's theses. Only a few important points may be briefly addressed:

a) The inclusion of the OT apocrypha in the circle of the 'Christian apocrypha' is not very meaningful. The reception and also the reworking of these texts in the Church is indeed a different process from the production of works which - in whatever fashion - are rooted in NT traditions.

b) Behind Junod's definition stands the opinion expressed at another point, that there is no temporal limit for the rise of apocrypha, indeed the production is uninterrupted even down to today (p. 412). This is to be contested, because here the distinction between the apocrypha proper and the hagiographical literature is overlooked. Certainly the transition from the one category to the other is fluid, but the boundaries may not be completely obliterated. Above all we have to think of the fact that the *Sitz im Leben* is different (cf. above, pp. 54f.).

c) Junod's objection against too strong an emphasis on the form-critical and *gattungsgeschichtlich* points of view is only partly justified. Naturally it is perfectly clear that we may not assess a work on the basis of its title (often a secondary accretion). For example, the Gospel of Truth is not a gospel, and in form critical terms stands in no kind of relation to the NT Gospels. On the other hand, the question of the form critical connection between apocrypha and canonical literature is probably more complex than appears at first sight. Here it is not only a matter of comparing an apocryphal gospel, for example, with the canonical texts, but we must also ask to what extent the separate traditions which are worked up in apocryphal texts are comparable with separate pieces in the NT writings. The work is certainly rendered more difficult by the fact that it is not a case of technical theological literature, but of texts in which popular narrative traditions are worked up under particular theological aspects into works which represent an independent entity.

Even if we thus adhere to a narrow conception of 'New Testament apocrypha', this is not to reject the intention of the projected 'Corpus of the Christian apocrypha' (see below, p.69) as misguided. An undertaking which collects and sets forth the whole of the material connected with the mass of early Church documents which we call NT apocrypha can only be welcomed. But the boundaries which exist between the literature of the first centuries, which came into being as a sidestream alongside the canonical writings, and the hagiographical works of the Byzantine and early mediaeval Church are not to be overlooked. Here it is a question not only of differences in the literary forms, but above all of a fundamental disparity in the historical standpoint.

Finally we may attempt a definition of the term 'New Testament apocrypha' on the basis of the considerations set out above.

New Testament apocrypha are writings which originated in the first centuries of Church history, and which through title, *Gattung* or content stand in a definite connection with the NT writings. The relation to the canonical works is very different in individual apocrypha, and must be determined in each separate case. The motives which led to the rise of apocrypha are also by no means uniform. Above all, in any decision as to what are NT apocrypha the historical conditions in which they are set must be taken into account. This not only holds for the boundaries with the hagiographical literature but is especially important for the connections with the NT canon, whether nascent or closed.

In this literature we have to do with :

Gospels, which are not only characterised by the fact that they did not come into the NT, which rather in part sought to claim the same rank as the canonical Gospels (this holds for the oldest texts), or which in some way sought to supplement the canonical texts;

pseudepigraphical Letters, which were probably for the most part intended to disseminate didactic supplements or corrections;

Acts of apostles, which developed the reports and legends about the apostles in novelistic fashion (and often in very great detail), and so sought to supplement the defective knowledge which might be derived from the NT about these men; here motives of propaganda for particular theological teachings often played a role;

Apocalypses, which in part reworked Jewish texts, but in part also further developed the form of the 'revelations' taken over from Judaism.

This attempt at a comprehensive definition takes into consideration the aspects set out above, but it too is not a definition which craves 'canonical' validity. It is, however, a practical working hypothesis, with which this literature in all its complexity may be correctly comprehended and evaluated.

4. The continuance and influence of the New Testament apocrypha

There is still no comprehensive study of the continuation and the influence of the apocryphal literature. It is probably also something to be achieved only with great difficulty, for here we are dealing with quite distinct problems on many levels. The abundance of the material in many languages makes a comprehensive view well-nigh impossible.

It would be an important task to work out the continuation of the apocrypha in the hagiographical literature of the Middle Ages, of which we have already spoken. This requires above all a taking stock of the Byzantine and mediaeval literature of this kind in the different languages. To this end a series of works are already available, which have to be fully utilised (see below).

In addition to the question of the literary continuation (and reworking) of the apocrypha, there is the other question of the influences exercised upon movements and opinions in Church history, especially upon some phenomena outside the official Church. The identification of an influence upon such things as poetry in the Middle Ages could also provide information about the continuing operative force of this literature.

The influence of NT apocrypha on art is quite immense. Many motifs of mediaeval painting (including the eastern icons) are taken from these works, even though frequently not directly from the ancient texts but from their later remodellings.

This enumeration of the problems is certainly not complete, and can easily be expanded. However, it cannot be the task of this introduction to discuss in detail all the questions mentioned. It must suffice to give a few indications, together with some references to resources and literature to which the reader may turn for further orientation.

1. In the discussion up to this point it has already been frequently indicated that the NT apocrypha lived on in various ways. However, probably only a small part of the texts was known in their original wording in the Middle Ages (e.g. the Protevangelium Jacobi; Apocalypse of Paul). These are in particular relatively late apocrypha, which already herald the transition to the hagiographical literature. What is more important is that in many mediaeval texts in East and West traditions are worked over and handed on, which go back to the old apocrypha.

In the Greek area it is in particular the Menologies, the collections of lives of saints, which contain much old material.[1] We can form some impression of the significance attaching to the Menologies from the example of the Acts of John, of which we now have the Junod-Kaestli edition[2] in which the whole of the material is worked over: the greater part of the text is handed down in menology manuscripts.

Like the later Greek writings of this kind, the versions in the different languages may also be helpful for the reconstruction of the content and structure of the ancient texts. At the same time these translations are a valuable source for the influence of the apocrypha in the different regions of the Church. The abundance of the extant manuscripts and the number of the languages involved ought not to deter us from pressing ahead with the investigation of this late tradition. In the present collection reference is made from time to time to the versions, in so far as they are of significance for the ancient texts.

Many apocrypha were evidently early translated into *Latin* (e.g. the Protevangelium Jacobi, Acts of Peter, Acts of Paul and Thecla). Albert Siegmund has assembled some examples in his work 'Die Uberlieferung der griechischen christlichen Literatur in der lateinischen Kirche bis zum 12.Jh' (1949). This work, however, needs completion, and a comprehensive stock-taking is urgently necessary. The *Bibliotheca hagiographica Latina* and the *Repertorium biblicum medii aevi* published by F. Stegmüller are important resources.[3] The work by McNamara referred to below (p. 63) also contains valuable references.

For the *oriental versions* we are largely reduced to gathering together the rich extant material from the many (and widely scattered) separate editions or from works of reference. The multiplicity of the texts handed down, however, also shows how widely apocryphal traditions were diffused in the different areas and how they were received in different ways. For the apocryphal gospels there are many bibliographical references in A. de Santos Otero.[4] The *Bibliographia hagiographica orientalis*[5] is an important resource for the oriental tradition of the Acts of apostles.

Syriac texts are available in many editions.[6] There is a survey of *Coptic versions*, which in part are specially important, in W. Grossouw, 'De Apocriefen van het Oude en Nieuwe Testament in de koptische Letterkunde' (*Studia Catholica* 10, 1933-34, 434-446, and 11, 1934-35, 19-36). This work too, however, must today be supplemented, since in the interval new finds have been added.[7] G. Graf's *Literaturgeschichte*[8] offers important information for the *Arabic tradition*. For the *Ethiopic apocrypha* cf. the references in de Santos (4th ed.), p. 12 and Erbetta I 1, 44. S.J. Voicu, 'Gli Apocrifi armeni' (in *Augustinianum* 23, 1983, 161-180, with many references to the literature) deals with the *Armenian apocrypha*. On the *Georgian texts* cf. M.van Esbroeck, 'Gli Apocrifi georgiani' (in *Augustinianum* 23, 1983, 143-159; he too gives copious references to the literature).

Two areas should be dealt with in somewhat greater detail, since for these pioneering and comprehensive works are now available: the apocrypha in Irish and Slavonic tradition.

Irish traditions of apocryphal works and traditions were already known before, but have played hardly any role in research in this field. Ireland however, as is clear from McNamara's work,[9] is a country with a particularly abundant literature which is connected with the apocrypha. 'We have in Irish probably the richest crop of apocrypha in any of the European vernaculars, possibly in any vernacular language. And together with this some early Latin texts of the apocrypha come from Ireland.' This may be a slight exaggeration, especially in view of the Slavonic tradition, but it cannot be denied that the Irish branch of the apocryphal traditions was of great significance in the Middle Ages.

Certainly it is only in very few cases that we have to do with texts containing verbatim passages from apocrypha collected in the present work. But from the comprehensive survey which McNamara offers, in which the whole material is presented with information about manuscripts, editions and literature, the process of transmission from the ancient apocrypha through the Latin translations down to the Irish versions can be clearly recognised. Here it is of some importance that for the period from the 7th to the 9th century knowledge of Latin versions of apocryphal works in Ireland can be demonstrated through manuscript discoveries. Here B. Bischoff has made important contributions.[10] From the 10th century on there followed the transition to the Irish language, which creates a certain barrier for modern research in this field.

In the future we shall have to devote more attention to the Irish area, both with regard to full utilisation for the tradition of the contents of the ancient apocrypha[11] and also in respect of the history of the continuing life and influence of this literature.

Here the associations of the early Irish Church with the Latin Church of the West have to be considered, just as much as the influences of the Irish Church upon the continent. The relations of Ireland with the East, elsewhere attested (cf. the tradition of the Psalms commentary of Theodore of Mopsuestia), could also be important here.

The Irish apocrypha literature is largely dependent on the Latin tradition, and has independently developed it further. The *Slavonic texts* which are to be reckoned to this literature have their models almost exclusively in the Greek and Byzantine area. We must look for the beginnings of activity in translation to the Bulgarian Church in the 10th or 11th century.[12]

For this branch of the transmission of apocryphal traditions we now have the great work of Aurelio de Santos,[13] which marks a first and important step towards the opening-up of the extensive material. De Santos has collected the information about all the accessible manuscripts, arranged it according to the several works, and briefly commented on it. In the process he had to examine an immense number of manuscripts for their content. One comes 'readily to the conviction that we have to reckon with tens of thousands of Old Slavonic manuscripts' (de Santos I, 30), and this mass has now to be evaluated for research into the apocrypha.

The apocryphal traditions in Slavonic speech are for the most part handed down as an element in other books. 'The apocrypha are . . . in general nothing other than a fixed element in the 'Church books'' (de Santos I, 20). Only for a few works can an independent branch of the tradition be demonstrated. De Santos speaks in this connection of the 'parasitic existence' of the apocrypha (I, 20f.). The manner of their incorporation into liturgical books, Menaia, Menologies, collections of homilies, etc., had as its consequence that the revisions of the 'Church books' about which de Santos reports (I, 4ff.) extended to the apocryphal texts contained in them also. These revisions were naturally connected with particular events in Church history (e.g. Hesychasm, the schism of the Old Believers), which then had an effect on the apocryphal texts also. Very early there was an 'index of apocrypha', but all efforts to suppress this literature met with no success, simply because they were transmitted under cover of other texts.

What value does the Slavonic tradition have for the opening-up of the ancient apocrypha? This question is not to be answered in global terms, but has to be investigated for each text separately. For the Infancy Gospel of Thomas (see below, pp. 439ff) de Santos has presented an investigation of this kind, in which he shows 'how the Slavonic texts contribute to the filling up of gaps in the Greek 'textus receptus' and the removal of misunderstandings'.[14] Whether this applies to other apocrypha also has still to be examined.

We can certainly refer to the 'Slavonic borrowing from the Greek sources, which characterises most of the translations' (I, 29). It must, however, be added that the Greek models for the Slavonic versions were mostly already hagiographical recastings of older texts.

This makes no difference to the fact that for various reasons a considerable significance attaches to the Slavonic tradition, and that research in this field still has large tasks in front of it.

2. The influence of the NT apocrypha upon the *Christian art* of the Middle Ages was - as already remarked - very great. Both in the mosaics and icons of the Greek and Slavonic Eastern Church and also in the carved work and paintings of the West we keep on meeting motifs which derive from the apocryphal traditions. 'Without apocryphal motifs the painting of icons . . . would be inconceivable.'[15] This holds for western painting also.

One example - certainly chosen somewhat arbitrarily - may make this general statement plain.

The representations of the birth of Christ[16] in Byzantine art from the 10th century on follow a definite pattern, which one may call a 'canon'. In it specific elements are fixed constituents of the representation: the birth of Christ takes place in a cave; Mary lies at the central point of the picture; the child Jesus rests in or on a stone-built trough (or in a kind of basket); an ox and an ass are looking into the trough.

This 'canon' of representation governed the painting of icons in the Greek area down to the 17th century, and is still employed even today. In the West also we meet with many of these elements, although there the birth of Christ is usually transferred to a stable. But ox and ass appear here also, and that very early (sarcophagi of the 4th and 5th centuries; ivory carvings of the 5th and 6th centuries).

These representations cannot be derived from the canonical Gospels. Rather they are based on apocryphal texts: in the East it is the Protevangelium Jacobi (esp. chapter 18) which is influential, while in the West the Infancy Gospel of Pseudo-Matthew, a combination of the Protevangelium and the Infancy Gospel of Thomas, is drawn upon (esp. chapter 14).

It may be added that the adoration of the newborn Jesus by an ox and an ass goes back to a very old prophetic proof-text[17] (Isa. 1:3 and Hab. 3:2; the two passages are quoted in Ps.-Matthew 14). This was taken up in old apocryphal narratives, and then found its pictorial representation in art.[18] This example of the portrayals of the birth is intended only to indicate how important the NT apocrypha are for the understanding of Church art in both East and West.[19] A comprehensive discussion of their influence in art would go far beyond the limits here appointed, but a few references to the literature may be given.

K. Künstle, *Ikonographie der christlichen Kunst* I-II, 1926-28. - U. Fabricius, *Die Legende im Bild des ersten Jahrtausends der Kirche*, 1956. - G. Schiller, *Ikonographie der christlichen Kunst* I-IV, 1966-80. - E. Kirschbaum (ed.), *Lexikon der christlichen Ikonographie*, 1968ff. - K. Wessel, art. 'Apocrypha', in *Reallexikon zur byzantinischen Kunst* I, 1972, 209-219. There is a detailed bibliography in M. Starowieyski (ed.), *Apokryfy Nowego Testamentu* II 1, 1980, 609-612.

5. On the history of research into the apocryphal literature

Hennecke (NTApo[1], pp. 22-28 and NTApo[2], pp. 31*f.) gave a brief survey of the history of the opening-up of the apocryphal literature. In NTApoHdb, pp. 5-9 there is a collection of editions, commentaries and investigations; this collection of titles is not repeated here. For some partial aspects of the history of research cf. Gérard Poupon, 'Les Actes apocryphes des Apôtres de Lefèvre à Fabricius', in *Les Actes apocryphes des Apôtres*, ed. F. Bovon, Geneva 1981, pp. 25-47; Jean-Daniel Kaestli, 'Les principales orientations de la recherche sur les Actes apocryphes des Apôtres', ibid. pp. 49-67.

Even though apocryphal traditions were known and handed on or reworked in the Middle Ages (see above, pp. 61ff.), scholarly concern with these texts came into operation only gradually, with the work of the Humanists and with the printing of books.

In 1531 Friedrich Nausea published a collection of Latin lives of apostles, which may be regarded as the first attempt at a collection of apocryphal literature. Like most editions in patristics and Church history in that period, this work too was casual in character: people printed just what was in the manuscripts which lay to hand, and this was to the advantage of all kinds of apocrypha. There were also many separate editions in these years, such as for example that of the Protevangelium Jacobi by Bibliander (Basel 1552). Important beyond doubt is the edition of the apocrypha by the Ilfeld rector Michael Neander: *Apocrypha, hoc est, narrationes de Christo, Maria, Josepho, cognatione et familia Christi, extra biblia etc.* (Basel 1564). Neander appended this edition to a collective volume containing in particular a Graeco-Latin adaptation of Luther's Smaller Catechism, intended for school purposes. From this association it is clear that Neander concerned himself with the apocrypha above all out of historical and philological interests; the book was intended to provide material for the humanistic training of his pupils. In addition to the Protevangelium of James, the collection of the apocrypha contained: the Abgar legend, Letters of Pilate, a series of Sibylline books, illustrative quotations on New Testament history from profane and ecclesiastical writers, and later testimonies concerning Christ.

The advance in the investigation of Christian antiquity which took place towards the end of the 17th century (Cotelier, Ittig, Cave, the Bollandists) was also to the advantage of the apocrypha (on this period cf. above all Poupon's essay mentioned above). In 1703 the great Hamburg collector Johann Albert Fabricius published his *Codex Apocryphus Novi Testamenti*, which has retained its value down to modern times. In volume I Fabricius brought together Infancy Gospels, the Gospel of Nicodemus and Letters of Pilate, the Letter of Lentulus, fragments of apocryphal gospels. Volume II contains: *Acta, Epistolae, Apocalypses aliaque scripta Apostolis falso inscripta*. Finally volume III brought liturgies under apostolic names and supplements, as well as the Shepherd of Hermas. At the same time in England Jeremiah Jones translated into English the pieces of apocryphal literature which had become known to him, in order with his work to counter the Deistic attacks on the sole authority of the NT writings. His work thus stands largely under the banner of polemic. He is concerned to demonstrate the spuriousness and the heretical character of this literature.

As in every field of historical theology, so in that of research into the apocrypha the 19th century brought an abundance of new editions and numerous investigations. At the beginning stands the edition of the apocryphal gospels by Thilo, a Halle theologian who planned a complete edition of all apocrypha but only got as far as volume I (*Codex apocryphus Novi Testamenti*, Leipzig 1832). This publication stimulated a series of further investigations, but also brought it about that the apocryphal gospels came strongly into the foreground, over against the other texts. The editions of apocryphal texts by Constantine Tischendorf led far beyond Thilo; he was concerned for good manuscripts, and applied to these texts the fundamental principles of philology (*Acta apostolorum apocrypha*, 1851; *Evangelia apocrypha*, 1852; *Apocalypses apocryphae*, 1866; the gospels appeared in a second edition in 1876, the Acts were published in a second edition by Lipsius-Bonnet 1891-1903, with a reprint in 1959).

Since Tischendorf (or Lipsius-Bonnet), work in the field of the NT apocrypha has advanced further. But there has not been a scientifically based complete edition of this literature (on the new plans for one, see below, p. 69). Even the excellent bilingual collection of the apocryphal gospels by Aurelio de Santos Otero cannot be, and is not intended to be, a substitute for such an edition (*Los Evangelios Apócrifos. Colección de textos griegos y latinos, versión crítica, estudios introductorios, comentarios e ilustraciones*: Biblioteca de Autores Cristianos 148, Madrid 1956, 6th ed., 1988). Yet this work, the scholarly level of which is generally recognised, marks a great advance for the elucidation of this part of the apocrypha. Up to that point there was no comparable collection which so comprehensively brought together the texts from different languages, translated them and provided the necessary introductions. The extensive bibliography is of particular value. De Santos, who has also rendered pioneer service in the field of the Slavonic tradition of the apocrypha (cf. above, p. 64.), has succeeded in creating an instrument which is of the greatest utility for further work on the apocryphal gospels.

The historico-critical approach, which F.C. Baur made the inalienable possession of theology, had a markedly fertilising effect upon work on the apocrypha. Especially in the second half of the 19th century and at the beginning of our own, a wealth of studies was devoted to our texts. In addition there was an unexpected swarm of new discoveries: manuscripts and papyri brought ever new texts to light, which were then edited and investigated. As the Nag Hammadi discovery shows, this period of new finds is still by no means over. That in the work on the new discoveries, and also on the texts long known, the historico-critical method and in addition the religio-historical approach have been, and must be, decisive is generally recognised.

In 1904 Edgar Hennecke published the first edition of his *Neutestamentliche Apokryphen in deutscher Übersetzung*, followed in the same year by his *Handbuch zu den Neutestamentlichen Apokryphen*. In this collection, which soon carried the day because of its scholarly importance, the texts especially of the 2nd and 3rd centuries were brought together. In the 2nd edition, which appeared in 1924, the term apocrypha was no longer so strictly adhered to (consideration of the 'Voices of the Church'!), while Montague Rhodes James in his English *Apocryphal New Testament* (Oxford 1924) held much more strongly to the forms and *Gattungen* of the NT, and also took later texts into consideration.

In the 3rd edition of Hennecke's collection (NTApo [3] I, 1959; II, 1964; the 4th edition of 1968/71 was only a revised reprint. English trans. I, 1963; II, 1965; 2nd impression I, 1973; II, 1974) an attempt was made on the one hand to give the *gattungsgeschichtlich* aspect once again a stronger validity, and on the other to give the appropriate space to the many new discoveries made since 1924. That here the texts from the Coptic gnostic library of Nag Hammadi could still not be presented in detail was due to the legal situation of the time. Nevertheless the imposing survey of the gnostic gospels and related literature by H-C. Puech (NTApo[3] I, 231-362) showed that with these texts many new problems have ensued for research into the apocrypha. In the present revision an attempt has been made to do justice to the new requirements.

It should be observed here, without detracting from the great significance of the Nag Hammadi library, that work on the NT apocrypha ought not to be focussed too one-sidedly upon these texts. They document an important part of the religious and spiritual development of the early centuries and contribute much to an understanding of a part of the apocrypha - but only a part. Many other texts which we may reckon to the NT apocrypha have nothing at all to do with Gnosticism, or only very little.

The third edition of 'Hennecke' evidently had a stimulating effect upon research. Since then not only have many separate studies appeared, to which reference is made as required in the present work, but also some collections have been published in various languages, which take their orientation largely from NTApo[3]. However, as a result of an imprecise definition of 'New Testament apocrypha', texts have frequently been included to which no consideration is given in our collection. This holds for the two Italian works of Erbetta[1] and Moraldi,[2] but also for the Polish translation published by Starowieyski.[3] The Dutch version by Klijn[4] presents only a selection.

The volumes mentioned on the one hand show - not least through their sometimes very good bibliographies - the present state of the continually growing research in this field, but on the other are also a sign of an increasing interest in the apocrypha.

More important than these publications are the works which have as their aim the taking stock of the material in different languages. In addition to the Syriac, Coptic and Arabic traditions, which have already frequently been worked over earlier (cf. NTApo[3]) and also still attract considerable attention (cf. the references in Starowieyski II, 614ff.), the works in the Slavonic sphere (A. de Santos Otero) and the Irish (M. McNamara) particularly call for mention (they have already been referred to above, pp. 63f.). Here in laborious effort the wealth of texts in manuscripts (and in print) is brought together and sifted, and this is important for research into the apocrypha from two points of view. For one thing, it is now possible to investigate more accurately the continuing existence of apocryphal traditions in the different areas, as well as their influence on piety and on art (cf. above, p. 65). For another, these texts can now also be examined to see whether remains of early Church writings, i.e. genuine apocrypha, can be identified in their wording. This will be possible only in a few cases, since the hagiographical literature (and it is largely with this that we are concerned) presents recasting of the apocrypha and not precise textual transmission. At any rate this state of affairs must not be overlooked.[5] This, however, makes no difference to the fact that through these new resources new possibilities are opened up both for research into the apocrypha and for mediaeval hagiography, and it is well to make use of them.

The work of the group of scholars in France and Switzerland active under the leadership of F. Bovon shows what advances have been made in this field in the interval, and how the many new aspects can be made effective. The aim is a complete critical edition of the texts transmitted in the different languages. The apocryphal Acts are being worked on by the Swiss group, the gospels in Paris. The edition is to appear as a separate series in the *Corpus Christianorum* (Steenbrugge). An agreement has been reached for collaboration with the *Sources Chrétiennes*. M. Geerard is preparing a *Clavis Apocryphorum*, which will without doubt be an important tool for research.

The publications which have so far appeared - in addition to some companion works[6] special mention should be made of the edition of the Acts of John by Junod and Kaestli[7] - make it clear that here a new epoch in the history of research is beginning. In this undertaking the whole of the material necessary to the establishing of the text and for the understanding of the 'Christian apocrypha' (as they are called by this group, see above p. 60) will be comprehensively collected, presented and commented on.

We shall not enter yet again into the question of the expansion of the term 'New Testament apocrypha', to my mind problematic, and the lack of precision bound up with it (see above, p. 60ff.). Even if there are considerable reservations against it, a wide-ranging stock-taking is on the other hand certainly necessary for the edition and the interpretation of the literature. One can only hope that the enterprise may proceed successfully.

The present revision of NTApo[3] has adhered to a narrower definition of the term 'New Testament apocrypha', for the reasons set out above (p. 58ff.). An attempt has been made to present in translation the texts which in my opinion belong to this literature. That some later texts are also given consideration is no inconsistency, but results from the facts of the tradition. The aim of these volumes is to offer to the reader the texts which in the proper sense may be called New Testament apocrypha, but without, through sticking to principles, being too narrow-minded about many a problematic case.

Notes

General Introduction

1. On the problems of the OT canon and the Apocrypha, see *Le canon de l'Ancien Testament. Sa formation et son histoire*, ed. Jean-Daniel Kaestli and Otto Wermelinger, Geneva 1984 (with detailed bibliography).

1. The concepts: canon, testament, apocrypha

1. Text in E. Preuschen, *Analecta II*, [2]1910, 70f. Whether Canon LX is secondary cannot be discussed here.

2. Eusebius' statements about Origen (H.E. VI 25.3) cannot be claimed as evidence for a use of the word 'canon' as equivalent to the Bible. G. Wanke (Art. 'Bibel I', in TRE VI, 1980, 1) points to the fact that the term canon is used so much as a matter of course in Athanasius and Amphilochius that 'an older usage must be assumed (Credner: beginning of fourth century)'.

3. Evidence for this section in Zahn, *Grundriß* and Beyer, TDNT.

4. R. Pfeiffer, *History of Classical Scholarship*, Oxford 1968, p. 207.

5. Cf. the commentaries on the passages. At Phil. 3:16 there are readings in which κανων occurs, but these are secondary glosses.

6. Cf. Zahn, *Grundriß* 5, note 20; R.P.C. Hanson, *Tradition in the Early Church*, London 1962, pp. 75ff.

7. H. Frhr. von Campenhausen, 'Das Bekenntnis Eusebs von Caesarea (Nicaea 325)', in ZNW 67, 1976, 123-139; quotation from p. 131 (there also further literature).

8. Thus in the Greek as in the Latin Church the concept took on numerous meanings: decree of a council, list of the clergy, part of the mass, etc.; cf. Beyer *op. cit.*, pp. 601f.; Lampe, *Patristic Greek Lexicon* pp. 701ff.

9. Zahn, *Grundriß* 8ff.; Vielhauer, *Lit. gesch.*, p. 776.

10. Beyer, *op. cit.* p. 601; Jülicher, *Einleitung* 555; NTApo[3], pp. 23f.

11. Jülicher, p. 555.

12. J. Behm, TDNT II 134. Cf. also E. Kutsch, Art. 'Bund', in TRE VII, 1981, 397-410.

13. Cf. Zahn, *Geschichte* I 1, 103; von Campenhausen, *Formation*, p. 267.

14. Von Campenhausen, *Ib.* p. 267.

15. Ib. p. 267.

16. Ib. p. 268.

17. Ib. p. 268.

18. Cf. the collection in E. Preuschen, *Analecta II*, [2]1910. Some specimens are printed below, pp. 34ff. Cf. also Erbetta I 1, 24 ff. (Lit.).

19. C. A.Credner offers a reprint of this document (*Zur Geschichte des Canons*, Halle 1847, pp. 316-412.

20. Here we are concerned only with the history of the term as a *terminus technicus* within the Church. Cf. above all Oepke's article in TDNT.

21. Cf. Zahn, *Geschichte* I, 123ff.

22. Cf. also Robert McLachlan Wilson, Art. 'Apokryphen II', in TRE III, 1978, 316ff.

23. Iren. *adv. Haer.* I 20.1; Tert. *De pud.* 10.12

24. On Origen cf. Oepke, *op. cit.*, pp. 994f.

2. On the history of the New Testament canon

1. A certain exception is formed by the Manichean collection of apocryphal Acts of Apostles, on which see Schäferdiek in vol. II, chapter XV.

2. The following discussion is not an exhaustive history of the canon. It is intended simply to delineate the most important aspects in outline. It should be observed that this sketch belongs to an introduction to the NT apocrypha, and thus must give special prominence to what seems important for the understanding of this literature. No attempt has been made to provide a detailed apparatus with evidence, for which reference may be made to the literature cited.

3. It remains questionable whether the spectacular new arrangements attempted by Sundberg are really helpful. Cf. A.C. Sundberg, 'Towards a Revised History of the New Testament Canon', in *Studia Evangelica IV*, (TU 102), 1968, 452-461; id. 'Canon Muratori: a Fourth Century List', in HTR 66, 1973, 1-41. The interesting and informative essays of Farmer and Farkasfalvy are also not convincing in their appraisal.

4. Cf. the volume quoted above, p. 9, note 1.

5. A.Harnack, *Lehrbuch der Dogmengeschichte* I, [4]1909, 379f.

6. Reference ought to be made here to many works on the history of the 2nd century. By way of example I mention only the problem of the *regula fidei*, on which Hanson especially has made decisively new contributions (*Tradition in the Early Church*, London 1962).

7. Cf. my article in TRE, where also the literature is listed.

8. On this section cf. Lietzmann, pp. 24ff.; Helmut Köster, *Synoptische Uberlieferung bei den Apostolischen Vätern*, (TU 65), 1957; Donald A. Hagner, *The Use of the Old and NT in Clement of Rome* 1973.

9. The fragments are collected in Funk-Bihlmeyer, *Die Apostolischen Väter*, [2]1956, pp. 133-140. There are also editions of the text in two recent studies: Josef Kürzinger, *Papias von Hierapolis und die Evangelien des Neuen Testaments* (= Eichstätter Materialien Bd. 4), 1983. Ulrich H.J. Körtner, *Papias von Hierapolis. Ein Beitrag zur Geschichte des frühen Christentums*, (FRLANT 133), 1983.

10. Cf. also von Campenhausen, *Formation*, pp. 129ff.

11. On the literary *Gattung* cf. Vielhauer, *Lit. gesch.* pp. 767f., who above all works out the difference from ὑπομνήματα (Hegesippus).

12. Cf. Arthur J. Bellinzoni, *The Sayings of Jesus in the Writings of Justin Martyr*, 1967.

13. On this problem cf. Vielhauer, pp. 252ff. and below pp. 77ff.

14. Cf. E. Haenchen, *Acts* (ET Oxford 1971), pp. 8f.

15. Günter Klein, *Die zwölf Apostel* 192ff., (FRLANT 77), 1961, p. 200.

16. Cf. W. Bauer, *Orthodoxy and Heresy in Earliest Christianity* (ET Philadelphia 1971, pp. 213ff.; German, pp. 215ff.).

17. On this cf. Kümmel, *Introduction*, pp. 338f.

18. On this see Bauer's book mentioned in note 16 above. His theses merit further attention, even though there is much to correct in detail.

19. Cf. above all von Campenhausen's discussion (*Formation*, pp. 82ff.) of the Letter of Ptolemy to Flora (Epiph. *Haer.* 33), a particularly important document for this problem.

20. So M. Krause in Foerster, *Gnosis* II (ET Oxford 1974), 8.

21. Many of these texts are treated in the present work. Cf. also Robert McLachlan Wilson, Art. 'Apokryphen II', in TRE III, 1978, 319f.

22. In the present context only brief reference can be made to Marcion's significance for the history of the canon. The problems have been often and abundantly discussed, the literature is immense, but new points of view are rare. From the literature we may mention:

A. von Harnack, *Marcion. Das Evangelium vom fremden Gott* [2]1924 (= Darmstadt 1960); E.C. Blackman, *Marcion and his Influence*, London 1948; von Campenhausen, *Formation*, pp. 148ff.; Kümmel, *Introduction*, pp. 342f.

23. Harnack, p. 151; von Campenhausen, p. 148; Kümmel, p. 343.

24. Von Campenhausen, p. 155.

25. On this see vol. II, chapter XIV, section 2.

26. Cf. Zahn, *Geschichte* I 1, 4ff.; Harnack, *Entstehung*, pp. 26ff. (*Origins of the NT* 1925).

27. Cf. von Campenhausen, *Formation*, pp. 221ff.; H. Paulsen, 'Die Bedeutung des Montanismus für die Herausbildung des Kanons', *Vig. Chr.* 32, 1978, 19-52. On Montanism generally, cf. also vol. II, chapter XIX, introduction.

28. Cf. the volume cited at p. 9, note 1 above, particularly the contribution of E.Junod, 'La formation et la composition de l'Ancien Testament dans l'Eglise grecque des quatre premiers siècles' (pp. 105-134).

29. On Tatian, cf. M. Elze, *Tatian und seine Theologie*, 1960.

30. Cf. Robert M. Grant, 'The Bible of Theophilus of Antioch', JBL 66, 1947, 173-196.

31. 'The formation of the Canon is not simply a process of Church tradition or proclamation, but at least also the deposit of the formation of Church doctrine': E. Käsemann in *Das Neue Testament als Kanon*, ed. E. Käsemann, 1970, p. 399.

32. For the details cf. W.O. Dulière, 'Le canon néotestamentaire et les écrits chrétiens approuvés par Irénée', *Nouv. Clio* 6, 1954, 199-224.

33. Cf. among others von Campenhausen, *Formation*, pp. 197ff.

34. Cf. Helmut Merkel, *Widersprüche zwischen den Evangelien*, 1971, pp. 51ff.

35. Texts in Preuschen, *Analecta* II[2], 24ff.

36. Cf. von Campenhausen, *Formation*, pp. 243ff., where many references to the extensive literature will also be found.

37. Albert C. Sundberg (see above, note 3). We cannot here enter into detailed debate with Sundberg. It would however be too simplistic to dismiss Sundberg's hypothesis as 'arbitrary', as Kümmel does (*Einleitung*, p. 434), for Sundberg has presented many arguments and proofs worthy of consideration. But to my mind he starts out from false presuppositions. For one thing he sees the history of the canon too much from the point of view of the closed canon of the 4th century, and thereby fails to see how tortuous and entangled from the beginning were the ways that led to this collection of NT writings. He does not observe that in the process contingencies of many kinds, which we can no longer recognise, played their part in individual communities or regions. He also does not take account of the fact that the canon was not the result of decisions by Church government, but grew up in the churches. Official decisions are first found in the 4th century. The Canon Muratori is not to be compared with these. All this, however, cannot be further developed here. Serious discussion of Sundberg's theses has still to be undertaken.

38. Sundberg's statements on this passage (*op. cit.* pp. 4ff.) are not convincing.

39. Whether we can enrol the author of the Canon Muratori in the 'anti-Montanist front', as von Campenhausen does (*Formation*, p. 259), is questionable.

40. On this see von Campenhausen, *Formation*, pp. 343ff.

41. Cf. the compilation in Zahn, RE[3], pp. 787f.

42. Cf. N.B. Stonehouse, *The Apocalypse in the Early Church. A Study in the History of the NT Canon*, Goes n.d. (1929).

43. Cf. W.A. Bienert, *Dionysius von Alexandrien. Zur Frage des Origenismus im 3 Jh.*, PTS 21, 1978.

44. Cf. Lietzmann, *op. cit.* pp. 99ff.

45. So Kümmel, p. 348. Cf. also Sundberg, *op. cit.* p. 33.

46. Cf. on this the works of M. Tetz, especially 'Athanasius und die Einheit der Kirche', ZThK 81, 1984, 196-219.

47. Cf. Walter Bauer, *Der Apostolos der Syrer*, 1903.

3. New Testament apocrypha

1. 'There is no linguistic rule for the use of 'form' and '*Gattung*'. The two terms are to a large extent promiscuously used in the fundamental form-critical works, and hence in scientific usage. Attempts to introduce a terminological differentiation go in completely different directions, and contribute nothing to a meaningful linguistic ruling. The term 'form' is more general than '*Gattung*' and the expression Form Criticism therefore commends itself, and also on the basis of its origin in the history of research, as the principal term for the method and its subordinate aspects' (Vielhauer, *Lit. gesch.* p. 3, note 5).

2. On the special problems of the title 'Gospel' cf. Vielhauer, *op. cit.* pp. 257f.

3. Franz Overbeck, 'Über die Anfänge der patristischen Literatur', in *Hist. Zeitschr.* 48, 1882, 412-472; reprinted Basel 1954 (quoted from this). On Overbeck, cf. M. Tetz, 'Über Formengeschichte in der Kirchengeschichte', in ThZ 17, 1961, 413ff.; id. 'Altchristliche Literaturgeschichte - Patrologie', in ThR NF 32, 1967, 1ff.

4. On this cf. Ph. Vielhauer, 'Franz Overbeck und die neutestamentliche Wissenschaft', in *Ev. Theol.* 10, 1950/51, 193ff. (reprinted in Vielhauer, *Aufsätze zum Neuen Testament* 1965, pp. 235ff.).

5. Cf. W. Schneemelcher, 'Lehre und Offenbarung bei dem Apologeten Justin', in *Theologie - Grund und Grenzen* (FS H. Dolch), ed. H. Waldenfels, 1982, pp. 521-532.

6. Cf. W. Schneemelcher, *Das Urchristentum*, 1981.

7. This holds already for Luke's Acts. Cf. the works of M. Dibelius and E. Haenchen, as well as the recent commentaries on Acts.

8. Cf. for the *Gattung* of the Gospels: A. Dihle, 'Die Evangelien und die griechische Biographie', in *Das Evangelium und die Evangelien*, ed. P. Stuhlmacher, (WUNT 28), 1983, pp. 383-411.

9. Cf. for example the variants to Mt. 8:13 and 23:14, as well as the additions in Mk. 16:9ff. and Jn. 7:53ff. The many variants in Codex D of Acts could also be mentioned, but probably represent a special problem.

10. Cf. still W. Bauer, *Orthodoxy and Heresy in Earliest Christianity* (ET Philadelphia 1971). Also important is: Helmut Koester and James M. Robinson, *Trajectories through Early Christianity*, 1971.

11. H. Koester has rightly stressed the connection between 'entertainment' and theological tendencies: 'these books do not simply seek to edify and to minister to the popular desire to be entertained. However desirous of pious edification the mass of Christian people might have been, the basic theological and christological conviction which made it possible to fulfil these desires was the same religious 'divine man' motif that had already contributed to the success of Paul's opponents in 2 Corinthians' (*op. cit.* [see note 10], p. 192).

12. The term 'popular literature' plays a role in form-critical work on the Gospels. Cf. Ferdinand Hahn (ed.), *Zur Formgeschichte des Evangeliums*, Wege der Forschung 81), 1985, pp. 427ff.

13. Eric Junod, 'Apocryphes du NT ou Apocryphes chrétiens anciens? Remarques sur la désignation d'un Corpus et indications bibliographiques sur les instruments de travail recents', in *Etudes théol. et rel.* 58, 1983, 408-421. This essay is connected with the work on a new edition of the apocrypha within the frame of the Corpus Christianorum, on which see below, p.69.

14. This is evidently accepted in the undertaking mentioned in note 13.

15. Junod, *op. cit.* p. 412. The French text runs: 'textes anonymes ou pseudépigraphes d'origine chrétienne qui entretiennent un rapport avec les livres du NT et aussi de l'AT parce qu'ils sont consacrés à des événements racontés ou évoqués dans ces livres ou parce qu'ils sont consacrés à des événements qui se situent dans le prolongement d'événements racontés ou évoqués dans ces livres, parce qu'ils sont centrés sur des personnages apparaissant dans ces livres, parce que leur genre littéraire s'apparente à ceux d'écrits bibliques'.

4. The continuance and influence of the New Testament apocrypha

1. The basic work is: Albert Ehrhard, *Überlieferung und Bestand der hagiographischen und homiletischen Literatur der griechischen Kirche von den Anfängen bis zum Ende des 16.Jhs.* I-III, 1937-1952, TU 50-52. Cf. also *Bibliotheca hagiographica graeca*, [3]ed. F. Halkin, 1957 (= BHG); Auctarium 1969.

2. *Acta Johannis. Praefatio, textus; textus alii, commentarius, indices, cura Eric Junod et Jean-Daniel Kaestli,* CChr SA 1-2, Turnhout 1983. See my review in *Rivista di Storia e Letteratura Religiosa* 22, 1986, 358-371.

3. *Bibliotheca hagiographica latina,* ed. Socii Bollandiani, I-II (Subs. hagiographica 6) [2]1949 (= BHL); Supplementum [2]1911. *Repertorium biblicum medii aevi,* ed. F. Stegmüller, I-IV, Madrid 1940-1961. Martin McNamara, *The Apocrypha in the Irish Church,* Dublin 1975.

4. Aurelio de Santos Otero, *Los Evangelios Apócrifos,* (Biblioteca de Autores Cristianos 148), [6]1988, xiiif and 11f.

5. *Bibliotheca hagiographica orientalis,* ed. Socii Bollandiani (Subs. hagiographica 10) 1910.

6. Cf. A.Baumstark,*Geschichte der syrischen Literatur*, 1922. A. de Santos, *op. cit.* pp.11f.

7. Cf. also the interesting and important contribution of T. Orlandi, 'Gli Apocrifi copti' (in *Augustinianum* 23, 1983, 57-71). Nothing need here be said about the Coptic texts from Nag Hammadi. So far as they are to be counted among the apocrypha, they are presented in this work, and the necessary references given.

8. Georg Graf, *Geschichte der christlichen arabischen Literatur* I-V, Studi e testi 118; 133; 146; 147; 172, Rome 1944-53; an English translation - in 6 vols is intimated by Editions Briel of Cambridge, Mass. The question of the influence of NT apocrypha on Islam cannot be further pursued here. It must be divided into three subordinate questions:

a) Can the use of any apocryphal texts or traditions be established in Christian Arab communities before Mohammed? There certainly were Christian communities in Arab localities from the 3rd century. But: 'Even if the beginnings of Christian Arabic literature in pre-Islamic times are to be presumed, still texts and firm reports only begin from about the eighth century' (J.Aßfalg, in *Kleines Wörterbuch des christlichen Orients,* 1975, p. 20).

b) What apocryphal traditions or texts can be traced in the Koran, and did they have any significance for the teaching of Mohammed? It is not to be doubted that for example the Protevangelium Jacobi is used in Sura 19, and that in other Suras also Mary-traditions from apocryphal sources appear to be known. It is however very questionable whether these apocryphal reports had any very great influence on Mohammed's ideas.

c) What role did apocryphal works play in the Christian Arabic literature originating from the 8th century on? There is an abundance of texts, mostly translations from Syriac or Coptic originals, which shows the popularity of the apocrypha. Many works travelled from the Arabic area to the Ethiopic; cf. the survey of the corpus of the Acts of apostles which I. Guidi published in R.A. Lipsius, *Die apokr. Apostelgesch.*, Erg. heft 1890, pp. 89ff. On the whole subject cf. Graf, *op. cit.* I, 224ff.

9. M. McNamara (see above, note 3).

10. Cf. B.Bischoff, 'Wendepunkt in der Geschichte der lateinischen Exegese im Frühmittelaltertum', in *Sacris Erudiri* 6, 1954, 189-281 (= Mittelalt. Studien I, 1966, 205-273).

11. This holds, for example, for the Protevangelium and the Infancy Gospel of Thomas; on the Irish witnesses for the Acts of John cf. vol. II, chapter XV 2.

12. Cf. A. de Santos Otero, *Das kirchenslavische Evangelium des Thomas*, PTS 6, 1967, esp. pp. 34f.

13. A. de Santos Otero, *Die handschriftliche Überlieferung der altslavischen Apokryphen* I, (PTS 20), 1978; II, (PTS 23), 1981.

14. *Überlieferung* I, 29. For the work on the Gospel of Thomas see above, note 12.

15. A. de Santos Otero, *Überlieferung* I, 22.

16. Cf. Christa Schaffer, *Gott der Herr - Er ist uns erschienen. Mit Bildteil von K. Gamber*, (Studia Patristica et Liturgica, Beih. 7), 1982.

17. Cf. Joseph Ziegler, 'Ochs und Esel an der Krippe', in MThZ 3, 1952, 385-402.

18. By way of supplement we may mention also a particularly instructive example of the use of an apocryphal text as the basis for pictorial representations: the mosaics in a former monastery in Constantinople (today Kahriye Camii in Istanbul). The mosaics, commissioned by Theodore Metochites (c. 1260-1332), are among the most beautiful witnesses to Byzantine art in the 14th century. In the inner narthex the life of Mary is presented in a cycle (of originally twenty pictures) closely connected with the Protevangelium Jacobi. Cf. P.A. Underwood, The *Kariye Djami* I-IV, Princeton 1966-75 (vol. IV deals with the artistic endowment of the church).

19. In recent times Selma Lagerlöf and Felix Timmermanns, for example, have also gone back to apocryphal material. On the use of parts of the Acts of John in modern times, cf. Schäferdiek, vol. II, chapter XV 2.

5. On the history of research into the apocryphal literature

1. Mario Erbetta, *Gli Apocrifi del Nuovo Testamento*. Vol. I 1-2: 'Vangeli', 1975-1981. Vol. II: 'Atti e Leggende', 1966. Vol. III: 'Lettere e Apocalissi', 1969.

2. Luigi Moraldi, *Apocrifi del Nuovo Testamento*, 2 vols., 1971. Cf. my review in *Rivista di Storia e Letteratura Religiosa* 11, 1975, 113-119.

3. *Apokryphy Nowego Testamentu. Pod redakcja ks. Marka Starowieyskiego*. Tom. I (in 2 vols.): 'Evangelie Apokryfiezne', Lublin 1980.

4. A.F.J. Klijn, *Apokriefen van het Nieuwe Testament*, vol. I, Kampen 1984.

5. As an example we may mention the episode from the ancient Acts of John, which appears in revised form in an Irish translation from the Latin: McNamara, *The Apocrypha in the Irish Church*, Dublin 1975, pp. 95-98; *Acta Johannis*, ed. Junod-Kaestli, I 109ff.; Schäferdiek in vol. II, chapter XV.

6. Cf. the reports of F. Bovon, 'Vers une nouvelle édition de la littérature apocryphe chrétienne', *Augustinianum* 23, 1983, 373-378, and J-.D. Dubois, 'The New Series Apocryphorum of the Corpus Christianorum', *The Second Century* 4, 1984, 29-36.

7. See above, p. 62, note 2.

A. GOSPELS
Non-Biblical Material about Jesus

Introduction

Wilhelm Schneemelcher

Literature (Selection): a) J. Schniewind, *Euangelion. Ursprung und erste Gestalt des Begriffes Evangelium*, (BFChrTh, 2R., 13 and 25), 1927-31. G. Friedrich, Art εὐαγγελίζομαι etc., TDNT II, 1964, 707-737; bibliographical supplement in ThWNT X, 1979, 1087f. P. Stuhlmacher, *Das paulinische Evangelium. I. Vorgeschichte*, (FRLANT 95), 1968. Id. (ed.), *Das Evangelium und die Evangelien. Vorträge vom Tübinger Symposium 1982*, (WUNT 28), 1983. G. Strecker, 'Das Evangelium Jesu Christi', in *Jesus Christus in Historie und Theologie* (FS Conzelmann), 1975, pp. 503-548. Id. Art. εὐαγγέλιον in ExWtbNT II, 1981, cols. 176-186.

b) M. Dibelius, *Die Formgeschichte des Evangeliums* ([1]1919) [3]1959 (ET *From Tradition to Gospel*, 1934). K.L. Schmidt, *Der Rahmen der Geschichte Jesu* ([1]1919), [2]1964. R. Bultmann, *Die Geschichte der Synoptischen Tradition*, (FRLANT 29, [1]1921) [3]1957 (with supplement; ET *The History of the Synoptic Tradition*, [2]1968). Vielhauer, *Lit. gesch.* 1978, pp. 255ff. H. Koester, 'One Jesus and Four Primitive Gospels', in Koester/ Robinson, *Trajectories through Early Christianity*, 1971, pp. 158-204. Id. 'Apocryphal and Canonical Gospels', HTR 73, 1980, 105-130. Id. Art. 'Formgeschichte/Formenkritik II', TRE XI, 1983, 286-299. P. Stuhlmacher (ed.), *Das Evangelium . . .* (see above). M. Hengel, *Die Evangelienüberschriften*, (SHAW, Phil.-hist. 1984, 3), 1984. Willem S. Vorster, 'Der Ort der Gattung Evangelium in der Literaturgeschichte', *Verkündigung und Forschung* 29/1, 1984, 2-25 (Lit.).

1. The texts and reports brought together in this section under the heading 'Gospels. Non-Biblical Material about Jesus' appear at first sight to be a motley and manifold collection, the unity of which is at least questionable.

a) There are in the first place texts (in part only fragments of lost works) which belong to the oldest stratum of the Church tradition, but whose relation to the canonical Gospels must in each case be separately determined. Their classification in the history of the Jesus tradition in the 1st and 2nd centuries must also be investigated in each particular case (Agrapha, fragments of unknown gospels).

b) A second group is formed by the texts which do indeed show connections with the canonical Gospel tradition, but which have further developed the tradition in a particular theological direction (e.g. Coptic Gospel of Thomas, Jewish-Christian Gospels, Gospel of Peter, Gospel of the Egyptians).

c) Some texts seem to admit of being reckoned to the 'Gospel' *Gattung* only with qualifications. They are indeed so called in their titles, and in other cases the title has come to be accepted. But the differences from the canonical texts and those listed under a) and b) are so considerable that it is questionable whether we may reckon them to this *Gattung*. These works, however, may nevertheless be considered here, since in them too the connection with the Person of Jesus is the decisive theme and their message is generally also intended to be 'Gospel', i.e. the message of salvation (e.g. Gospel of Philip; some texts from chapter IX also belong here).

d) A special kind of text is represented by the 'Dialogues' (see below, pp. 228ff). Linking up with resurrection narratives, taking over older sayings traditions and drawing upon Greek models, this independent *Gattung* was created above all by gnostics, and for various reasons must be drawn into the circle of the apocryphal gospel literature.

e) A further group of works is characterised by the motive of supplementation. The production of such texts begins from the 2nd century on (Protevangelium Jacobi), and in them the intention is to fill the gaps in the life of Jesus which exist in the canonical Gospels. The childhood of Jesus in particular, but also his passion and resurrection, stands at the centre of interest (the Pilate literature, the Gospel of Nicodemus and the Gospel of Bartholomew must also be added here).[1]

This brief survey is intended simply to convey a first impression of the variety of the material dealt with here. The division into groups can only be a first indication of the problems which arise with the complexity of the texts. The bringing together in this volume of works so distinct is justified by the fact that all the texts in some way relate to the person, life and work of Jesus, and that not in the style of theological reflection but in association with the 'Gospel' *Gattung*. Certainly, the differences in form and content, theological tendency and motivation are so considerable that we cannot affirm that all these texts belong to a homogeneous 'Gospel' *Gattung* (this is what the addition 'non-Biblical material about Jesus' is meant to indicate). But on the other hand they do represent a special category within the early Christian literature.

For the better understanding of these relationships, it will be useful first to say something about the term 'Gospel' and its transformation into the description of a *Gattung*, and then to discuss briefly the problem of the nature of a 'Gospel' text[2].

2. a) When in the present collection reference is made to a 'gospel' or 'gospels', it is always texts transmitted in writing that are meant, hence a gospel *book* or gospel *books*. This is not the original *meaning* of the Greek word εὐαγγέλιον. The word is rather an expression for something non-literary: (glad) tidings brought by word of mouth, but also the reward given to the bearer of the tidings.

The taking-over of this Greek term by early Christianity as a comprehensive description for the glad tidings of salvation in Jesus Christ is now as ever variously explained. 'While in regard to the verb εὐαγγελίζεσθαι there is a certain consensus that its roots go back to Semitic-speaking early Judaism and the Old Testament, the origin and declarative function of the word 'Evangelium' are still variously explained.'[3]. So P. Stuhlmacher described the state of the discussion. He himself inclines 'to understand εὐαγγέλιον as a translation term for a (prophetic) message . . . and thus to explain it from the linguistic usage of

Semitic-speaking Judaism and the Old Testament'.[4]. On the other hand G. Strecker has established 'that an unambiguous O.T.-Jewish or hellenistic-Greek genealogy for εὐ. cannot be provided. The NT proclamation of the εὐ. can take to itself both O.T.-Jewish and also hellenistic-Greek elements of tradition. Here the primary attachment of the substantive εὐ. to Graeco-hellenistic tradition is evident. It is just through this that the new thing which Christian proclamation has to declare is articulated in a way that could be understood in its environment.'[5]. This cautious statement is probably more convincing than the effort (often with an apologetic ring) to derive this term too from the Old Testament and Jewish tradition.

This problem however need not be further discussed here. For our purposes it is enough to hold fast the fact that the designation of the orally proclaimed message of salvation by the word εὐαγγέλιον (hence a Greek word, which should probably be noted) was evidently already current in hellenistic (Jewish-Christian?) Christianity before Paul, who found it already in use.

b) How did it come about that the term 'Gospel' became *the designation for a written presentation* of the life and work of Jesus, 'that the pregnant theological term became a literary designation'[6]? An unambiguous answer to this question cannot be given, since the sources say nothing about the process of making it a literary term[7]. The impulse for this development probably came from Mk. 1:1. There the written presentation of the story of Jesus is described as 'Gospel'. It is however to be observed that with the words 'Beginning of the Gospel of Jesus Christ' (Mk. 1:1) the author of Mark understood the account which he put together as part of the proclamation of salvation, i.e. he thus gave the proper sense of the term 'Gospel' its full validity.

Only in the middle of the 2nd century can we unambiguously demonstrate the use of the word 'Gospel' as a literary term. The author of the so-called 2 Clement refers with a quotation formula ('for the Lord says in the Gospel', 8.5) to a book. Justin shows through the plural εὐαγγέλια that he is using this word as the description of a literary *Gattung* (I *Apol.* 66.3: 'the apostles in the memoirs, which are called 'Gospels').

Alongside this use as a literary term, the original significance (Gospel = message of salvation) was evidently still influential. The κατά–superscriptions (εὐαγγέλιον κατὰ Μᾶρκον etc.) point to this. For they have the sense: 'the one Gospel according to (the presentation of) Mark' (Vielhauer, p. 225). The statement of the Canon Muratori about Luke (see above, p. 34) is to be understood in similar fashion: 'the third book of the Gospel, according to Luke'. The age of these κατά– titles is probably scarcely to be determined exactly[8].

The use of the word 'Gospel' as a literary term brought it about that similar works which were rejected by the Church could also be described as 'gospel'. The κατά– titles too were applied to them (Gospel of Peter, etc.). We cannot, however, tell when and where these ascriptions to a fictitious author or to a group took place. To some extent these may be the original designations of the texts concerned. We may further note the fact that the Coptic gnostic library of Nag Hammadi contains works which carry the designation 'gospel' (Thomas, Philip, Gospel of Truth, Gospel of the Egyptians). Now here we have very varied kinds of text, and it is also not certain when and where the title 'gospel' was associated with them (cf. the introductions to the relevant sections in this volume). However this phenomenon is to be explained in detail, it could be that here the original significance of 'Gospel' = 'message of salvation' is still operative (cf. Vielhauer, *Lit. gesch.* p. 258). It is no accident that it is precisely in gnostic works that we find the adoption in its older significance of a term which in the interval has become a literary concept. These works are indeed intended to impart knowledge as a liberating message, to some extent hark back to older traditions (sayings collections) in the process and can therefore from their point of view describe such texts as 'gospel' with a certain justice.

3. The word 'gospel' was thus transformed from a pregnant theological term into a literary designation, although the original theological content was probably never completely lost. How then is the *literary Gattung 'Gospel'* to be defined?

In recent years there has been a profusion of attempts to answer this question by adducing many ancient or modern literary *Gattungen*[9]. In highly imaginative fashion, hellenistic memoirs, biographies, aretalogies[10], tragedies, tragicomedies, apocalypses, OT historical narratives, Passover haggada, Midrashim, the Mishnah and other texts have all been mooted as analogies to the 'Gospel' *Gattung*. This confusing and often sterile discussion need not be presented here. Only one complex which is important for our investigation will be dealt with. Many of the newer works on this problem of the 'Gospel' *Gattung* are marked by an aversion to the form-critical method which has long been dominant[11]. This is, however - despite all objections - still a well-tried aid in the investigation of early Christianity and its literary and historical associations[12]. For the understanding of the apocryphal gospels also (as for example the works of H. Koester show) important insights are to be obtained along this road. Here only a few points may be addressed:

a) Building on the so-called two-document theory, which explains the relationship of the three Synoptic Gospels to one another, form-critical research has investigated the traditional material incorporated in the canonical Gospels. Scholars concentrated in particular on the small units of the traditional material, and sought to bring out not only their literary form (parable, apophthegm, etc.) but also their *Sitz im Leben*. This led to the recognition that in the Gospels we are dealing with 'popular literature', i.e. that these texts are rooted in the life of the early Christian communities (preaching, catechesis, mission, public worship) and are not to be regarded as literary works by individual authors. It may already be noted here that the same holds for many apocryphal texts.

b) It is no contradiction of this that we must regard the author of Mark as the man who first created through his work the new *Gattung* 'Gospel', for which there are no parallels before, or outside of, Christianity. For he did not as an author invent and shape his material, but collected traditional material and presented it under specific theological leading ideas. A similar judgment is to be passed on the work of the authors of Matthew and Luke, who in addition to Mark's Gospel incorporated the Sayings Source Q and their own special material. They too were not men of letters who wanted to create a literary work, but collected and arranged what was in their communities living tradition, and was now for the future also to be held fast as the message of salvation.

c) It has been said that this unique genre of text the 'Gospel' is a creation of the kerygma[13]. This formulation is not very happy (what does *kerygma* mean?), but points to the fact that this *Gattung* developed out of the needs of the community. This does not mean that the whole Jesus tradition is an 'invention' of the community. A part of the tradition certainly goes back to the earthly Jesus. But the much-discussed question of the 'authenticity' of the words of Jesus and the reports about him is set free from its apologetic straitjacket precisely through form-critical research, because here we are working with adequate standards and not with modern preconceived opinions.

d) The association of this *Gattung* which originated in early Christianity with the term 'Gospel' is already present in Mark, but as we have seen only prevailed in the 2nd century. We may not, however, overlook the fact that it was not the compilations of Mark, Matthew or Luke which were first understood as part of the proclamation of salvation; rather the tradition which existed before them already had this intention. This holds for example for the sayings source (Q), the purpose of which was to preserve the preaching of Jesus as the inalienable basis of the Church's witness[14].

e) The sayings source Q which was used by Matthew and Luke was probably not the only collection of the kind in the early period. Mark appears to have gone back to collected sayings material (cf. Mk. 4:1; 12:38) which cannot be identified with Q. We may not therefore confine the history of the Synoptic tradition of the words of Jesus to the origin and development of Q, but must also take note of other strands of tradition. This is important for the apocryphal texts, because such traditions (in addition to Q) may possibly have lived on in them. For the narrative material we shall have to assess the development somewhat differently. This branch of the tradition was more open to development under the influence of extra-Christian forms, as can be recognised from the apocryphal texts[15].

f) Building on the work of form-criticism, New Testament scholarship in recent decades has turned with greater concentration to the question of the redaction of the individual Gospels. In particular the theological intentions which determined the shaping of the Gospels were worked out: on the basis of the results of this 'redaction-critical' analysis attempts were then made, and are being made, to determine more accurately the place of the individual Gospels in the history of primitive Christianity (which, however, in view of our meagre source-material, can only yield hypothetical results). This certainly meaningful and necessary work has, however, not shaken the thesis that the authors of the canonical Gospels were not men of letters who wanted to create a literary work. Even if the framework into which they built the traditions that came down to them (sometimes indeed altering these traditions) was stamped by their own theological intentions, the decisive act was still the collection and with it the fixation of the Jesus tradition. This is probably the most important criterion for an explanation of the 'Gospel' genre of text.

These remarks are intended only to highlight a few aspects which result from form-critical work for the question of the *Gattung* 'Gospel', and which at the same time are important for the further consideration as to what the apocryphal gospels are. To sum up, it may be said that 'Gospel', despite objections often raised, is a *Gattung* which arose in primitive Christianity out of the particular needs of the communities of the time. This genre of text has no analogies in ancient literature, and in particular is not biography[16]. A major feature is their collective character. The authors of the Gospels have brought together traditions (sayings and narrative material) and built them into a framework which in each case is of a theologically different stamp. This work of compilation is rooted in the faith and life of the community, but at the same time aims at the strengthening and propagation of faith in Christ.

4) The work of form-criticism developed out of synoptic research, and has mainly centred in this field. The form-critical method has, however, also been successfully applied to the Gospel of John, even if this Gospel poses a host of other problems. With regard to genre of text, John cannot simply be set on a completely equal footing with the Synoptics. We need not discuss here the relationship of John to the Synoptics, but in our context it must be emphasised 'that John in terms of literary history does not represent a further development of the Synoptic type'[17]. The same holds also for a part of the apocryphal gospels.

This is not, however, to say that John and the early apocryphal texts (e.g. the Jewish Christian Gospels) belong to another *Gattung*. Like the Synoptics, they are 'gospels'. For the description of this *Gattung* attempted above applies to them also: the collection and working-up of traditions, whether in the form of individual pericopes or of complexes already formed (e.g. the 'signs source' in John), are also characteristic of these works. They too are rooted in the faith and life of the communities in which they came into being, and are meant to be a message of salvation. Despite the differences from the Synoptics they belong to the same *Gattung*.

It is beyond doubt an important task to examine the apocryphal texts to see whether traditions which reach back into the period before the composition of the canonical writings are worked into them. Here the form-critical method can be helpful[18]. Even if the connections can often be explained only hypothetically, it still appears to be certain that for a part of the apocryphal texts the same laws were operative in their origin as for the canonical works.

This statement, however, probably holds good only for a part of the texts brought together in this volume. With regard to genre of text we must also pay attention to the differentiation outlined on pp. 50ff. above. Thus some texts are to be regarded as works 'which consist of Jesus traditions, whether sayings or narrative material, irrespective of whether they show the title 'Gospel' *expressis verbis* or not'[19], i.e. they correspond to the 'Gospel' *Gattung*, even on a very narrow definition.

Other texts are evidently connected with the canonical Gospels, perhaps also employ similar traditions, but their *Gattung* cannot be unambiguously determined. This holds especially for the works in which theological purposes conceal or even shatter the form of a 'gospel', but specific elements of the *Gattung* are still preserved.

In addition we have the phenomenon that old traditions and new purposes can be incorporated into another *Gattung*, in which however the 'gospel' tradition stands out so clearly that we may reckon these texts also to the apocryphal gospels in the wider sense (e.g. a part of the 'Dialogues of the Redeemer', in which sayings traditions are still operative; see below, pp. 228ff.). On the whole we may say that there is no independent and uniform *Gattung* of 'apocryphal gospels'. But the texts assembled here under this title belong together not only by the fact that they have the person and work of Jesus Christ for their content, but also because it is characteristic of them that in various ways they are modified or influenced by the 'Gospel' *Gattung*.

Here it is to be noted that in the course of the historical development the connection with the 'Gospel' genre declines and other elements gain an influence over the shaping. Thus we can observe in the so-called Infancy Gospels (see below, pp. 414ff.) how personal legends alter the 'Gospel' *Gattung*, and the way to the hagiographical literature thus opens up. It is clear that this development is connected with the final closing of the canon. For with this the presuppositions for the production of apocryphal texts had decisively altered.

For most of the texts presented here we must, however, adhere to the position that - despite all the demonstrable deviations and the use of independent traditions - a connection with the content and the *Gattung* of the canonical Gospels is decisive.

5) Finally, something may be briefly said about modern attempts to fill the 'gaps' in the life of Jesus. Works of this kind are mostly concerned to demonstrate, through ostensibly ancient texts, the connections of Jesus with Egyptian or oriental wisdom and so to supplement the defective picture of the canonical Gospels. Sensationalism and commercial interest are here often combined with anti-Church feeling: the 'official' Church has hitherto allegedly suppressed all the 'authentic' sources for the life and work of Jesus, in order to maintain its own dogmatic position unassailed; now through the new documents the truth has finally come to light. These clumsy efforts accordingly stand in the tradition of the 18th-century Enlightenment. For some of this literature it can also be established that it is intended to serve as propaganda for new groups, e.g. the Ahmadiyya sect.

a) In 1910 appeared the so-called *Letter of Benan*, allegedly a report by an Egyptian doctor, originally written in Greek in 83 A.D., then rendered into Coptic and finally translated into German and published by Ernst Edler von der Planitz[20]. Benan the writer came to know Jesus during his youth in Egypt. Jesus had been brought there by his mother immediately after his birth, to be educated under an Egyptian astrologer. After an interlude in Jerusalem, Jesus from the age of twelve once again lived in Egypt, and in this period mastered Egyptian and Jewish wisdom (the *Therapeutae*), before he returned to Palestine. When Benan sets out after three years to learn what has become of his friend Jesus, he arrives in the very nick of time for the crucifixion, and also experiences the first appearances of the risen Jesus. In the further course of his life, Benan frequently encounters the spreading Christian communities, without himself becoming a Christian. 'The letter . . . is a forgery, as shameless as it is senseless, the sources of which Carl Schmidt demonstrated in a serious work[21] when the credulity even of pastors had dangerously surrendered to this clumsy fabrication, which does not even disdain the stimulus of eroticism in the story of Jesus' life.'[22]

b) If the Letter of Benan was intended to demonstrate that Jesus was rooted in Egyptian and Jewish wisdom, and so to close the 'gaps' in the Gospels, other such works which have met with great response in very recent times are interested in the *Indian influences* upon Jesus. Here we must distinguish two different starting-points. On the one hand it is a case of Jesus dwelling in India during his early years, and of the influence which Buddhism and other Indian wisdom gained over him during this period. On the other the theory is advanced that Jesus did not die on the cross, but was only seemingly dead. He was healed so quickly by Essenes that he was able to travel to India, where he died at the age of over a hundred years and was buried in Srinagar in Kashmir.

For the first theory it is in particular the book by *Nicolas Notovitch*, a Russian adventurer and journalist[23], that is repeatedly copied, even today: *La vie inconnue de Jésus Christ*, Paris [8]1984 (German: *Die Lücke im Leben Jesu*, 1894). In this work the author describes how during a 'voyage of discovery' he was tended for some days, after an accident, in the Hemis monastery in Ladakh. During these days a senior lama read to him texts about the life of Issa (= Jesus) from two Tibetan manuscripts. He noted down what the interpreter translated (Notovitch did not possess a knowledge of the relevant language). These notes he then worked up some years later into the book mentioned.

The content of this fantastic report need not be reproduced here. Yarns are spun about the history of Israel, just as about Jesus' sojourn in India and the influence of Buddhism upon him. Shortly after the appearance of the book the reports of travel experiences were already unmasked as lies. The fantasies about Jesus in India were also soon recognised as pure invention. It may be added that down to today nobody has had a glimpse of the manuscripts with the alleged narratives about Jesus[24].

Notovitch's book has been dug up again in recent times. Here its content has been combined with the theories of Ghulam Ahmad, founder of the Ahmadiyya sect, a syncretistic community emanating from Islam. These fanciful ideas (Jesus' grave in Srinagar, etc.) were taken up by H. Kersten, S. Obermeier and others, and with the help of the sensationalist press these fables were given a wide publicity[25].

Kersten for example attempted to work up Notovitch and Ahmadiyya legends with many other alleged witnesses into a complete picture[26]. Thus Levi's *Aquarian Gospel* (1908)[27] is pressed into service, along with the Turin shroud and the Qumran texts. The main thesis is - as already said - that after his Crucifixion Jesus returned to India and died there. We need not enter into details. Such works, in which fantasy, untruth and ignorance (above all in the linguistic area) are combined, and which are in addition marked by anti-Church feeling, have nothing to do with historical research.

In our context we must only raise the further question, whether these modern fictions are in any way to be compared with the apocryphal texts which are presented in this volume. Can we eventually show analogous motives for the origin of apocryphal gospels (e.g. the Infancy Gospels) and the modern Life of

Jesus forgeries? This question must clearly be answered in the negative.

For one thing, the apocryphal gospels (including the later ones), even when they have taken up all kinds of legendary motifs from their environment, are always related to the Jesus who is spoken of in the canonical Gospels. Certainly the intention is to 'supplement' what is narrated there. But the connection is always present. Absurd attempts to demonstrate a dependence of Jesus on Egyptian or Indian wisdom, with the help of alleged new discoveries, do not appear in this form in the texts.

This is connected, on the other hand, with the fact that the apocryphal texts generally, like the canonical Gospels, have their origin in the traditions of the communities in which they arose. Most of them, despite their often very clear theological tendencies, which are considerably different from those of the 'orthodox' literature, are based on older traditions of the communities. In contrast the modern fictions were cobbled together by individual authors from various motives (sensationalism, the quest for gain, hostility to the Church). This literature thus arose under quite different conditions, and is therefore not to be compared with the apocryphal gospels of the early centuries.

Notes
A. Gospels
Non-Biblical Material about Jesus

Introduction

1. Two texts are not considered here, although they are described as apocryphal gospels:
a) The *Arabic Gospel of John*, discovered in 1931 in a manuscript in the Ambrosian Library in Milan. This is a text of the 14th century, which goes back to an Ethiopic work. Whether older material is incorporated in it remains questionable.
Edition: I. Galbiati (ed.), *Johannis Evangelium apocryphum arabice*, Liber I-II, Milan 1957.
Literature: de Santos, pp. 23f. and xivf.

b) The *Gospel of Barnabas*, handed down in Italian and Spanish. It was already known in the 18th century (Tolland), but has received more detailed attention only in recent times. This gospel is a work of the 16th century, and evidently belongs in the area of the history of the Moriscoes. It is very doubtful that older material (of Jewish Christian origin) is included in it.
Edition: *Évangile de Barnabé*. Recherches sur la composition par L. Cirillo. Texte et traduction par L. Cirillo et M. Frémaux, Paris 1977.
Literature: de Santos, pp. 24f. and xv. J. Slomp, *Het Pseudo-Evangelie van Barnabas*, Hertogenbosch 1981 (German, without bibliography: *Das 'Barnabas-evangelium'*, 1982). R. Stichel, "Bemerkungen zum Barnabasevangelium", in *Byzantinoslavica* 43, 1982, 189-201. M. de Epalza, "Le milieu Hispano- moresque de l'Évangile islamisant de Barnabé (XVIe-XVIIe siècle)", in *Islamochristiana* 8, 1982, 159-183.
These two texts are examples of the production of works which are indeed described as gospels and which are also interesting sources for the period of their origin, but do not belong in a collection of early Church apocrypha.

2. The detailed discussion of the history of the term and of the formation of the Gospels presented in NTApo³, pp. 71-80 is not repeated here. It would today have to be much more detailed, and would then strain the limits of this book.

3. P. Stuhlmacher, 'Zum Thema: Das Evangelium und die Evangelien', in the volume edited by him (see Lit. above), p. 20. This volume is an impressive witness for one school of research, marked in particular by its antithesis to form-criticism with all its implications.

4. *Ib.* 20. In greater detail: P. Stuhlmacher, *Das paulinische Evangelium, I. Vorgeschichte*, 1968.

5. G. Strecker, Art. εὐαγγέλιον, ExWtbNT II, 1981, col. 180. Cf. also Strecker in *FS Conzelmann*, 1975, pp. 505ff.

6. Vielhauer, *Lit. gesch.* p. 253.

7. On this problem cf. Vielhauer, *Lit. gesch.* pp. 252-258. M. Hengel (*Die Evangelienüberschriften*, p. 8) thinks that Vielhauer's treatment of the problem 'despite many correct insights is on the whole not very satisfactory'. In view of their different basic positions, this is understandable. If, however, we approach the problem from different presuppositions, we shall regard Hengel's arguments as 'not very satisfactory'. It should be observed that neither the question of the transformation of 'Gospel' into a literary term nor the problem of the κατά–superscriptions can be seen in isolation. The question of the origin of the Gospels and the problem of determining the *Gattung* are closely associated with this complex of themes.

8. Hengel in the discussion mentioned above conjectures a very early time of origin (*c.* 69-100). This, unfortunately, is not capable of proof.

9. Cf. the comprehensive critical report by W.S. Vorster (see Lit. above). Vorster thinks 'that the narrative model best explains the problem of the Gospel *Gattung*' (p. 24). 'Gospels are narratives about the words and deeds of Jesus, and are intended to be read in their entirety. The authors of these writings have related the story of Jesus with an eye to their hearers, each in his own fashion, with the aid of traditional material' (p. 25). This charitably sober conclusion which Vorster draws from his report shows indeed that the numerous attempts to determine the *Gattung* afresh, undertaken with great acumen and stupendous erudition, have not yielded much result.

10. This term is especially popular in American research. Koester and Robinson for example use it quite nonchalantly. On this Vorster writes: 'The major problem in this hypothesis lies in the fact that there probably never was such a genre of text as the 'aretalogy'. It is therefore a highly dubious proceeding to explain other genres of text from a genre which never existed' (p. 15). D. Esser already pointed out the problems posed by this term as the description of a literary *Gattung* ('Formgeschichtliche Studien zur hellenistischen und frühchristlichen Literatur' [Evang. Theol. Diss. Bonn 1969], pp. 98ff.). 'What is described as aretalogy in classical philology includes quite diverse literary *Gattungen*: hymns, votive inscriptions, letters, satires, romances. 'Aretalogy' describes not the form but the content and purpose of very diverse literary *Gattungen*' (Vielhauer, *Lit. gesch.* p. 310). We must therefore be very cautious in the use of this term for the definition of the 'Gospel' *Gattung*. This is not to deny that aretalogical elements are to be found in the traditional material.

11. This is very clear in the contributions to the 1982 Tübingen symposium, edited by P. Stuhlmacher (see Lit. above).

12. The basic works by M. Dibelius, K.L. Schmidt and R. Bultmann are noted in the literature above. There is a brilliant description in Vielhauer, *Lit. gesch.* pp. 255ff.

13. Cf. Koester, *Trajectories*, p. 161.

14. Cf. the essays of Robinson, *Trajectories*, pp. 71ff.; Koester, *ib.* pp. 158ff.

15. We may refer here to Koester's essay 'One Jesus and Four Primitive Gospels' (*Trajectories*, pp. 158-204), which stresses the connections of the Gospel sources with the *Gattungen* of the apocryphal gospels. Even if we cannot follow Koester in every respect, this essay is very important for the question of the *Gattung*.

16. On the problem of the relation of the Gospels to ancient biography, cf. A. Dihle, 'Die Evangelien und die griechische Biographie', in *Das Evangelium und die Evangelien* (see Lit. above), pp. 383-411.

17. Vielhauer, *Lit. gesch.* p. 420.

18. Cf. the works by H. Koester listed in the literature above.

19. Vielhauer, *Lit. gesch.* p. 614.

20. *Ein Jugendfreund Jesu. Brief des ägyptischen Artzes Benan aus der Zeit Domitians*, ed. Ernst Edler von der Planitz, 1910. In total 5 volumes: text, commentary and comprehensive presentation.

21. Carl Schmidt, *Der Benanbrief*, (TU 44.1), 1921.

22. Jülicher-Fascher, Art. 'Benanbrief', RGG[2] I, col. 887. There also a reference to Spiridion Gopčevič, *Die Wahrheit über Jesus nach den ausgegrabenen Aufzeichnungen seines Jugendfreundes*, 1925. Jülicher-Fascher describe Gopčevič as a 'disciple' of von der Planitz. Since the work was not accessible to me, I have not been able to check the relation of the two writings to one another.

23. On the personality of Notovitch, cf. N. Klatt, 'Jesus in Indien', in *Orientierungen und Berichte* 13, 1986 (Evgl. Zentralstelle für Weltanschauungsfragen).

24. Günter Grönbold's book *Jesus in Indien. Das Ende einer Legende* (1985) is a devastating assessment of these fantasies. The author has comprehensively worked over the whole complex of 'Jesus in India', and as an expert in Indian and Tibetan studies has exposed the fraud. An extensive bibliography is given in the book.

25. Details of the literature in Grönbold (note 24 above).

26. H. Kersten, *Jesus lebte in Indien* (Knaur Sachbuch), 1983.

27. *The Aquarian Gospel of Jesus the Christ*, 1908 (German translation: Levi H. Dowling, *Das Wassermann-Evangelium von Jesus dem Christus* 1980 [!]).

I. Isolated Sayings of the Lord
Otfried Hofius

Introduction

1. Literature: *Collections of Material*: E. Klostermann, *Apocrypha* II. 'Evangelien'(KlT 8), ³1929. Id. *Apocrypha* III. 'Agrapha usw.', (KlT 11), ²1911. A. Resch, *Agrapha. Außerkanonische Evangelienfragmente* (TU 5.4), 1889; ² rev. ed.: *Agrapha. Außerkanonische Schriftfragmente*, (TU NF 15. 3, 4,) 1906 (= Darmstadt 1967). De Santos⁴, pp. 108-122.

Studies (sometimes with further collections of material): M. Asin y Palacios, *Logia et agrapha Domini Jesu apud Moslemicos scriptores, asceticos praesertim, usitata*, PO 13.3, 1916, 327-431; 19.4, 1926, 529-624. A. Baker, 'Justin's Agraphon in the Dialogue with Trypho', JBL 87, 1968, pp. 277-287. J.B. Bauer, 'Echte Jesusworte?' in W.C. van Unnik, *Evangelien aus dem Nilsand*, 1960, 108-150. W. Bauer, *Das Leben Jesu im Zeitalter der neutestamentlichen Apokryphen*, 1909 (= Darmstadt 1967) pp. 351-360, 377-415. F. Cabrol, Art. 'Agrapha', DACL 1, 1907, 979-984. R. Haardt, 'Das koptische Thomasevangelium und die außerbiblischen Herrenworte', in K. Schubert (ed.), *Der historische Jesus und der Christus unseres Glaubens*, 1962, pp. 257-287. A. Harnack, 'Über einige Worte Jesu, die nicht in den kanonischen Evangelien stehen', SPAW 169, 1904, 170-208. E. Hennecke, Art. 'Agrapha', RE³ 23, 1913, 16-25. Id. in NTApo¹, pp. 7-11; NTApoHdb, pp. 13-21; NTApo², pp. 32-38. O. Hofius, Art. 'Agrapha', TRE II, 1978, 103-110. Id. 'Unbekannte Jesusworte', in P. Stuhlmacher (ed.), *Das Evangelium und die Evangelien*, (WUNT 28), 1983, pp. 355-382. U. Holzmeister, 'Unbeachtete patristische Agrapha', ZKTh 38, 1914, 113-143; 39, 1915, 98-118, 801-803. E. Jacquier, 'Les sentences du Seigneur extracanoniques (Les Agrapha)', RB 15, 1918, 93-135. J. Jeremias, *Unbekannte Jesusworte*, 1948, (AThANT 16); ²1951, BFChrTh 45.2; 3rd completely rev. ed. in collaboration with O. Hofius 1963 = ⁴1965 (ET *Unknown Sayings of Jesus* ², 1964). Id. 'Zur überlieferungsgeschichte des Agraphon 'Die Welt ist eine Brücke'', NAWG, Phil.-hist. Kl., 1953 (vol. 4), 95-103. Id. in NTApo³, pp. 85-90. J. Karawidopoulos, 'Ein Agraphon in einem liturgischen Text der griechischen Kirche', ZNW 62, 1971, 299f. H. Koester, 'Die außerkanonischen Herrenworte als Produkte der christlichen Gemeinde', ZNW 48, 1957, 220-237. S. Leanza, *I detti extracanonici di Gesù*, Messina 1977. A. Resch (see above). J.H. Ropes, *Die Sprüche Jesu, die in den kanonischen Evangelien nicht überliefert sind. Eine kritische Bearbeitung des von D. Alfred Resch gesammelten Materials* (TU 14.2,) 1896. Id. Art. 'Agrapha', DB extra vol., 1904, pp. 343-352. J. Ruwet, 'Les 'Agrapha' dans les oeuvres de Clément d'Alexandrie', *Bib.* 30, 1949, 133-160. L. Vaganay, Art. 'Agrapha', DBS 1, 1928, cols. 159-198. P. Vielhauer, *Geschichte der urchristlichen Literatur*, 1975, pp. 615-618. R.McL. Wilson, TRE III, 1978, 322f.

Further literature is listed in the following *Bibliographies:* Resch², pp. 14-17; Ropes, DB extra vol., p. 352; Vaganay, cols. 193-198; Jeremias, NTApo³, pp. 85f.; de Santos⁴, pp. 110f. and xxiii; Leanza, pp. 11-13; Hofius, TRE II, 109f.

2. Definition: By an 'isolated saying of Jesus' - an 'agraphon' - we must understand a saying ascribed to the *earthly* Jesus which is *not* handed down in the oldest version of the four canonical Gospels. According to this definition the following do not count as agrapha: a) all texts outside the Gospels which are presented as words of the pre-existent Christ or of the risen or exalted Lord; b) OT prophetic sayings and NT words of apostles, which some early Christian writer adduces as 'words of the Lord' only because according to his conviction the pre-existent Christ spoke through the mouth of the prophets, the exalted Lord through the mouth of the apostles; c) the numerous cases in which a saying of Jesus contained in the canonical Gospels is simply freely quoted, or reproduced in a form which deviates only externally.

3. The Sources: a) the New Testament (Acts 20:35)[1]; b) variant readings in some Gospel manuscripts (see especially Lk. 6:5 D, also for example the secondary additions to Mt. 20:28; Lk. 9:55; 10:16); c) the fragments of apocryphal gospels (POx 840, PEgerton 2, POx 1224, Jewish-Christian Gospels)[2] and the legendary reports about the childhood, activity and passion of Jesus; d) pseudepigraphical Acts and letters of apostles; e) the Christian authors from the 2nd century on,[3] as well as some liturgies and Church orders from the early Church; f) the Christian gnostic literature (especially the Coptic Gospel of Thomas,[4] the logia of which are intended to be understood as words of revelation uttered by Jesus before Easter); g) Manichean and Mandean writings;[5] h) the rabbinic literature (only *one* example: b.'A.Z. 17a par. Qoh.R. 1 §24 on V.8) and the Toledoth Jeshu;[6] i) the Koran (e.g. 3.49[43]ff.; 43.63f.; 61.6) as well as the writings of Islamic ascetics and mystics.[7] There is no complete edition of the extensive material representing the present state of research. The older collections of Resch [2], Klostermann and (for the Islamic agrapha) Asin y Palacios are still indispensable. De Santos[4] (pp. 112-122) offers an instructive selection, but not all the texts included by him belong to the agrapha in the sense defined above.

4. Critical Evaluation of the Material: Fundamental works in this field were published especially by Ropes, Klostermann, W. Bauer, Hennecke, Vaganay and Jeremias. From a methodical point of view, it proved to make sense to undertake a process of elimination which attempted to discover those agrapha which might in terms of content and the history of tradition be set alongside the sayings of Jesus in the Synoptic Gospels.

a) If we apply this criterion of selection, a considerable number of agrapha must immediately be excluded on grounds of *content*. Among these are: 1. the sayings firmly anchored in the framework of legendary narratives about Jesus, and therefore freely invented along with their context (e.g. the words of the child Jesus in the Infancy Gospels); 2. all those sayings, whether newly formed or obtained through the remodelling of canonical sayings, which make Jesus represent heretical opinions (e.g. the gnostic logia of the Coptic Gospel of Thomas); 3. the sayings formulated with polemical intent, which are meant to discredit Jesus or the Church's Christology (e.g. the Talmudic agraphon (see above §3) and the Mandean agrapha); 4. the wisdom sayings of varied provenance which were ascribed to Jesus by Islamic authors because of the respect accorded to him (e.g. the agraphon quoted in note 7).

b) The remaining material consists predominantly of sayings which in terms of content are unassailable, but against which suspicions may be raised on grounds of the *history of tradition*: 1. Not infrequently biblical or extra-biblical quotations are erroneously (occasionally also deliberately) transferred to Jesus, in which case the linguistic formulation may show certain variations. Thus for example the agraphon 'It is more blessed to give than to receive' (Acts 20:35) has behind it a maxim current in the Graeco-Roman world. The two well-known agrapha 'There will be divisions and factions' (Justin, *Dial.* 35.3) and 'No one can attain the kingdom of heaven who has not passed through temptation' (Tertullian, *De Bapt.* 20.2) are also erroneous transferences: the first originated from 1 Cor. 11:18f., the second from Acts 14:22b. — 2. Some agrapha are indebted to the language and theology of the Gospel of John. Thus we may for example conjecture in the background of the saying 'Those who are with me have not known me' (Acts of Peter: Actus Vercellenses 10) the question of Jesus in John 14: 9. — 3. The group of sayings which clearly betray their dependence on the synoptic tradition is relatively large. Three from the Coptic Gospel of Thomas may serve as representative examples:[8] Gos. Thom. 25 is a development from Mt. 19:19b or Mk. 12:31a par. (= Lev. 19:18b); Gos. Thom. 48 owes its origin to the combination of Mt. 18:19 and Mt. 17:20; Gos. Thom. 102 is a new formation analogous to Mt. 23:13 (cf. Gos. Thom. 39a), taking up a Greek proverb. — 4. Occasionally a narrative note in the canonical Gospels has provided the stimulus for the formation of a saying of the Lord. Thus the agraphon 'Pray and do not grow weary' (Aphraates, *Dem.* IV 16) grew out of Lk. 18:1.

c) The critical process of elimination leads to a very small *residue* of agrapha 'whose attestation and subject-matter do not give rise to objections of weight, which are perfectly compatible with the synoptic tradition, and whose authenticity admits of serious consideration'.[9] Jeremias (*Unknown Sayings of Jesus²*) noted eighteen agrapha; this figure however, must still be reduced by about a half.[10] There then remain the seven agrapha adduced below, as well as the word of Jesus to the chief priest Levi in POx 840 (see below, pp. 94f.) and the parable of the Great Fish (Gos.Thom. 8; see below, p. 118). If we set a very critical standard, then even here in five cases doubts on grounds of the history of tradition are not entirely to be excluded: No. 1 could be a meagre summary of Mt. 24:27f., 40f. par.; no. 2 a secondary application of Mt. 6:33 par. to prayer; no. 3 an 'epexegesis of 1 Thess. 5:21' (W. Bauer); the woe in POx 840 a new formation dependent on Mt. 23:27f.; and the parable in Gos. Thom. 8 simply a formation analogous to Mt.13:45f. par., Gos. Thom.76.

d) Only the four agrapha listed under numbers 4-7 are certainly *not derivative in terms of tradition history*. No. 5 does indeed border on Lk. 12:49 and Mk. 9:49, but this does not in any way allow us to assume dependence; and no. 7 can scarcely be conceived as a secondary modification of the love commandment of Lev. 19:18b (quoted in Mt. 19:19b; Mk. 12:31a par.).

5. The question of authenticity: The question of authenticity is not settled by the identification of agrapha which are not derivative in terms of tradition history, but only posed. At most one might consider whether authentic sayings of Jesus are present in the agrapha 5, 6 and 7. *BAC 148:*

1. As you are found,
   so will you be led away [sc. to judgment]

   (Syriac Liber Graduum, Serm. III 3; XV 4)

2. Ask for the great things,
   And God will add to you what is small

   (Clem. Alex. *Strom.* I 24.158)

109
(§ 17)

3. Be competent money-changers!

   (Ps. Clem. Hom. II 51.1; III 50.2; XVIII 20.4)

4. On the same day he [Jesus] saw a man working on the sabbath. He said to him: 'Man, if you know what you are doing, you are blessed; but if you do not know, you are accursed and a transgressor of the law!'

   (Luke 6: 5 D)

107-8
(§ 8)

5. He who is near me
   is near the fire;
   he who is far from me
   is far from the kingdom

   (Gos.Thom. 82; Origen, *In Jer.hom.* lat.III 3;
   Didymus, *In Psalm.* 88.8)

6. (He who today) stands far off will tomorrow be (near to you)

   (POx 1224)

7. And only then shall you be glad,
   when you look on your brother with love

   (Gospel of the Hebrews, according to Jerome, *In Ephes.* 5.4)

37
(§ 15)

Notes

I. Isolated Sayings of the Lord

1. There is *no* agraphon in 1 Thess. 4:15-17; see O. Hofius, 'Unbekannte Jesusworte', *op. cit.* 357ff. Jeremias (*Unknown Sayings of Jesus*[2] 14, 80ff.) takes a different view, seeing in 1 Thess. 4:16-17a 'the oldest of the sayings outside the Gospels'(p. 80).
2. Cf. the material presented below, pp. 94f.; 96ff.; 100f.; 134ff.
3. Cf. the survey in Jeremias, *op. cit.* pp. 20ff.
4. See the translation below, pp. 117ff.
5. For Manichean agrapha see below, pp. 402ff.; Mandean evidence in M. Lidzbarski, *Ginza* (QRG 13.4), 1925, pp. 29 and 47ff.
6. G. Schlichting, *Ein jüdisches Leben Jesu*, (WUNT 24), 1982, pp. 78ff. passim.
7. The saying to be read on an Arabic inscription in the ruined city of Fathpur-Sikri in North India also belongs to this group of Islamic agrapha: 'The world is a bridge. Pass over it, but build not your dwelling there!'
8. For the text of the logia see below, pp. 120; 124 and 129.
9. Jeremias, *op. cit.* pp. 42f.
10. On this see Hofius, TRE II 107f.; id. 'Unbekannte Jesusworte', *op. cit.* pp. 363ff.

II. Fragments of Unknown Gospels

Joachim Jeremias † and Wilhelm Schneemelcher

Introduction

W. Schneemelcher

It is clear from all kinds of quotations and references in early Christian writers that there was a considerable number of apocryphal gospels. Sometimes quotations are given from these works, but elsewhere only the title is mentioned. We may also suspect in some statements in the Church literature that the gospel named by the author concerned never actually existed (e.g. the gospels of Cerinthus, Apelles, Bardesanes).

Some gospels which were formerly known only by name have come to light in recent decades through papyrus and manuscript discoveries (e.g. the Gospel of Peter, the Coptic Gospel of Thomas), and are included in the present collection. In addition texts have turned up (especially on papyrus) which have been regarded as fragments of unknown gospels or extracts from such works. Since the Fayyum fragment (see below) became known in 1885, and then the Oxyrhynchus Papyrus 1 (see below, p. 121) in 1897, soon followed by many other texts, these fragments - often enough mere shreds - have time and again exercised a great attraction: an almost boundless number of studies has been devoted to them, and a vast number of hypotheses has been attached to them, which often enough quickly crumbled into dust. In this connection the lack of method, manifest over and over again and above all in the 'age of discovery', is astonishing. Every fragment was immediately assigned to some one gospel, although not even the slightest clues for so doing were available. We have now become very much more cautious, particularly since new finds are continually making clearer the gaps in our knowledge of this 'minor literature' in Egypt.

Several papyri which hitherto have always been mentioned in this connection may be eliminated straight away, since it has been proved that they do not contain gospel fragments or extracts from gospels. Thus POx 1081 (Greek text in Wessely, PO XVIII, 269ff.; Klostermann, KIT 8³ 25) was identified by Puech as part of the *Sophia Jesu Christi* (H.-C. Puech, 'Les nouveaux écrits gnostiques', in *Coptic Studies in Honor of W.E. Crum*, 1950, p. 98; cf. W. Till, *Die gnostischen Schriften des kopt. Pap. Berol. 8502*, (TU 60), 1955, 216ff.). As regards POx 210 (text edited by B.P. Grenfell and A.S. Hunt, OP II, 1899, 9f.) the editors advanced the conjecture that in it we have before us remains or excerpts from an apocryphal gospel, possibly the Gospel of the Egyptians. But A. Deissmann (ThLZ 26, 1901, col. 72) pointed out that because of the fragmentary character of the scanty remains a near guess as to the provenance of this text is out of the question. That judgment still holds good. Finally, in the case of POx 1384 also (text: OP XI, 1915, 238-241), the editors have indulged in guesses as to whether the texts, which here turn up among medical prescriptions, do not come from an apocryphal gospel. But the text is so short and the situation so difficult to understand that we must abstain from any assignment. Even if it should be the case that its source is some apocryphal writing, it could only be one of the later legendary formations (the papyrus was written in the 5th or 6th century).

The fragment POx 2949 (text: OP XLI, 1972, 15f.: 'late second or early third century') need not be dealt with in detail, since all that emerges from its few lines is that it is a fragment of a text in which Joseph of Arimathea asks Pilate for the body of Jesus. The editors conjecture some proximity to the Gospel of Peter, but it remains questionable whether it is a case of the remains of a gospel at all.

Equally uncertain is the identification of PBerol. 11 710, which Lietzmann explained as the remains of an apocryphal gospel (text: H. Lietzmann, ZNW 22, 1923, 153f.). The two small leaves from the 6th century, which probably served as an amulet, contain a confession of Jesus as Son of God and Lamb of God by Nathaniel, as well as Jesus' answer: 'Walk in the sun.' We cannot say whether the text belongs to a later legend or to an apocryphal gospel.

In the following survey a few important fragments are selected. An approximate completeness in bibliographical statements is just as little striven after as an exhaustive enumeration and refutation of all the conjectures that have been thrown out regarding the reconstruction or derivation of the texts. There is a compilation of the Greek texts (a selection) in Klostermann, *Apocrypha II* (KlT 8)[3], 1929, 19ff. and above all in Ch. Wessely, *Les plus anciens monuments du Christianisme écrits sur Papyrus*, PO IV 2, Paris 1908, 57ff. and XVIII 3, Paris 1924, 264ff. (with the older literature); cf. also Giuseppe Bonaccorsi, *Vangeli Apocrifi I*, Florence 1948; de Santos[6], pp. 76-101; Erbetta I 1, 102-110. On the papyrological questions cf. J. van Haelst, *Catalogue des papyrus littéraires, juifs et chrétiens*, Paris 1976; K. Aland, *Repertorium der griechischen christlichen Papyri* I, 1976, (PTS 18).

1. Oxyrhynchus Papyrus 840

Joachim Jeremias † and Wilhelm Schneemelcher

In December 1905 Grenfell and Hunt found in Oxyrhynchus (now Behnesa in the Middle Egypt) a leaf of a parchment book of the smallest size (8.5 x 7 cm.) written on both sides in microscopically small letters, which had probably served as an amulet (4th or 5th century). The first seven lines contain the conclusion of a discourse of Jesus delivered in Jerusalem, in which he warns his disciples against a deceptive confidence. There follows a visit to the Temple court where a sharp discussion takes place between Jesus and a Pharisaic chief priest named Levi, who takes Jesus and his disciples to task for neglecting the purification rules laid down for the treading of the court of the Israelites (called 'the place of purification'). This neglect of theirs answers to what is recorded in Mk. 7:1ff. and Mt. 15:1ff. regarding Jesus' attitude to rabbinical precept; and the severity and vigour with which in his rejoinder Jesus castigates the Pharisaic hypocrisy which sought through scrupulously careful observance of the ritual of cleanliness to delude men as to the abominable nature of what was within them, has in substance an exact parallel in Mt. 23:27f.

The text in form and content represents without doubt a variant of synoptic narratives. We may therefore speak of 'an unknown gospel of Synoptic type'. It must however be added that we cannot make any statements about the content and structure of the whole work. The age of this gospel also cannot be precisely determined.

Text: B.P. Grenfell and A.S. Hunt, OP V, London 1908, no. 840; id. *Fragment of an Uncanonical Gospel from Oxyrhynchus*, Oxford 1908; H.B. Swete, *Zwei neue Evangelienfragmente*, (KlT 31), Bonn-Berlin[1]1908 = [2]1924, pp. 3-9; Aland, *Synopsis* p. 584 (index). **Literature:** A Büchler in *The Jewish Quart. Review* 20, 1907-8, 330-346; E.J. Goodspeed in *Biblical World* NS 31, 1908, 142-146; A. Harnack in *Preuss. Jb.* 131, 1908, 201-210 = *Aus Wissenschaft und Leben* II, Giessen 1911, 237-250; E. Preuschen in ZNW 9, 1908, 1-11; E. Schürer in ThLZ 33, 1908, cols. 170-172; A. Sulzbach in ZNW 9, 1908, 175f.; L. Blau, *ib.* pp. 204-215; A. Marmorstein, *ib.* 15, 1914, 336-338; E. Riggenbach, *ib.* 25, 1926, 140-144; J. Jeremias in *Coni. Neotest.* XI in honorem A. Fridrichsen, 1947, pp. 97-108: id. *Unknown Sayings of Jesus*, [2]1964, pp. 47ff.; de Santos[6], pp. 74-78; Vielhauer, *Lit. gesch.* pp. 639-641.

First before he does wrong (?) he thinks out everything that is crafty. But be ye on your guard that the same thing may not happen to you as does to them.[1] For not only among the living do evil doers among men receive retribution, but they must also suffer punishment and great torment.

And he took them [the disciples] with him into the place of purification itself and walked about in the Temple court.[2] And a Pharisaic chief priest, Levi (?) by name, fell in with them and s<aid> to the Saviour: Who gave thee leave to <trea>d this place of purification and to look upon <the>se holy utensils without having bathed thyself and even without thy disciples having <wa>shed their f<eet>?[3] On the contrary, being defi<led>,

94

thou hast trodden the Temple court, this clean p<lace>, although no<one who> has <not> first bathed <himself> or <chang>ed his clot<hes> may tread it and <venture> to vi<ew> <these> holy utensils! Forthwith <the Saviour> s<tood> still with h<is> disciples and <answered>: How stands it (then) with thee, thou art forsooth (also) here in the Temple court. Art thou then clean? He said to him: I am clean. For I have bathed myself in the pool of David and have gone down by the one stair and come up by the other and have put on white and clean clothes, and (only) then have I come hither and have viewed these holy utensils. Then said the Saviour to him: Woe unto you blind that see not![4] Thou hast bathed thyself in water that is poured out, in which dogs and swine[5] lie night and day and thou hast washed thyself and hast chafed thine outer skin, which prostitutes also and flute-girls[6] anoint, bathe, chafe and rouge, in order to arouse desire in men, but within they are full of scorpions and of <bad>ness <of every kind>.[7] But I and <my disciples>, of whom thou sayest that we have not im<mersed> ourselves, <have been im>mersed in the liv<ing . . . > water[8] which comes down from < . . . B>ut woe unto them that . . . .

Notes

II. Fragments of Unknown Gospels

1. Oxyrhynchus Papyrus 840

1. Cf. Lk. 13:5.
2. Cf. Mk. 11:27.
3. Cf. Jn. 13:10.
4. Cf. Mt. 15:14; 23:16f., 19, 24, 26.
5. Cf. Mt. 7:6; Rev. 22:15.
6. Cf. Gospel of the Nazarenes No. 18 (p. 162 below).
7. Cf. Mt. 23:27f.
8. Cf. Jn. 4:14.

2. Papyrus Egerton 2

Joachim Jeremias † and Wilhelm Schneemelcher

P. Egerton 2 (= P. London Christ. 1) was first published by H.I. Bell and T.C. Skeat in 1935. It consists of two leaves and the remains of a third, which in the first edition and also in later studies were dated to the period around or before A.D. 150 (so also van Haelst, *Catalogue* No. 586 and Aland, *Repertorium* No. Ap 14). This dating is called in question by the discovery of a fragment identified by its editor M. Gronewald as part of P.Egerton 2, which supplements it by some five lines: P.Köln no. 255.[1] In Gronewald's opinion the writing of the papyrus shows characteristics which allow us to assume a date close to P.Bodmer II (P[66] of John). This however according to E.G.Turner[2] is to be placed about 200 rather than about 150. Even when we take into account the difficulties of an exact dating, we must with regard to PEgerton 2 be much more cautious with an early date than hitherto. In particular many hypotheses bound up with this text become very questionable. The new discovery is taken into consideration in the translation below.

'The text consists of the fragments of four pericopes, of which the first (*ll*. 1-31) bears Johannine marks, the second (*ll*. 32-41) and third (*ll*. 43-59) exhibit parallels to Synoptic stories, whilst the fourth (*ll*. 60-75), the text of which has been handed down in a particularly fragmentary condition, describes an apocryphal miracle wrought by Jesus on the bank of the Jordan. The 'Johannine' fragment presents first the conclusion of a trial (*ll*. 1-5), the occasion of which was a transgression of the law on the part of Jesus; since two sayings follow from Jn. 5, the matter dealt with may be a violation by Jesus of the Sabbath. There follows a controversial discourse, made up of Johannine logia, with the rulers of the people (*ll*. 5-20), which reaches its climax in an agraphon of violent threatening. If, as is likely, the narrative continued in *ll*. 22-31, a self-assertion of Jesus will have followed which was felt to be blasphemous and so provoked an attempt to stone him, blasphemy being one of the offences for which the punishment was stoning (cf. Jn. 8:59; 10:31). Only very loosely connected to this, there follows the healing of the leper.

The two Synoptic pericopes, the healing of a leper and a discourse about tribute-money (*ll*. 32-59), are distinguished by the fact that they show contacts with all the three Synoptics; the material is simultaneously reduced and enlarged. In five places (see Jeremias in *Theol. Blätter* 15, 1936, cols. 40-42) there are transitions to other Gospel passages occasioned by verbal reminiscences, and this leads to the conclusion that both stories have been reproduced from memory. The scene at the Jordan (*ll*. 60-75) begins with a question (by Jesus) which clearly has as its subject the mystery of the resurrection typified in a grain of seed: Jesus himself answers the question by a miracle on the bank of the Jordan, causing, as it seems, the sowing and the ripening of the grain to follow immediately upon one another, as an index doubtless to the omnipotence of God which brings forth life out of death.

The value which we assign to the text is determined by our judgment as to its relation to the canonical Gospels, especially to the Fourth. There are contacts with all four Gospels. The juxtaposition of Johannine (I) and Synoptic material (II and III) and the fact that the Johannine material is shot through with Synoptic phrases and the Synoptic with Johannine usage, permits the conjecture that the author knew all and every one of the canonical Gospels. Only he had no one of them before him as a written text. On the contrary the above-mentioned digressions in II and III, which were occasioned by verbal reminiscences and which also occur in I, show that the material has been reproduced from memory. Consequently we may have before us an instance of the overlapping of written and oral tradition: although the tradition was already fixed in writing, it was still widely reproduced from memory and in this way, enriched with extra-canonical material (IV), found new expression in writing. The text shows no historical knowledge that carries us beyond the canonical Gospels. The reproduction of the story of the healing of the leper shows in its beginning (wandering with lepers) and at its end ('the priests', in the plural) that Palestinian circumstances were not well known to the author; also the question about tribute-money is robbed of its typically Jewish tone through being worded in general terms' (Jeremias).

This assessment of PEgerton 2 by Jeremias was largely taken over by Vielhauer (*Lit. gesch.* pp. 636ff.). In addition he drew attention to the fact that the two 'synoptic' sections show an advanced stage in terms of tradition history. This, if the early dating has to be corrected, is only to be expected. Furthermore Vielhauer emphasises that PEgerton 2 is evidence for the way in which 'the tradition already fixed in writing, but reproduced from memory, was altered in its oral reproduction' (*op. cit.* p. 638). The papyrus shows 'how little the putting into writing of the Life of Jesus material by Mark, his successors and John brought the oral Jesus tradition to a standstill' (*ibid.*).

H. Koester has presented a different interpretation of the text.[3] Starting from an extremely early dating (beginning of 2nd century A.D.) he thinks it is a case of a text which is older than the Fourth Gospel. 'With its language that contains Johannine elements but reveals a greater affinity to the Synoptic tradition, it belongs to a stage of a tradition that preceded the canonical Gospels' (*History* 2, 182). Here he takes up the thesis of Mayeda, who affirmed the independence of PEgerton from the Gospels. But he goes even further when he evaluates this gospel fragment for his view of the history of the debate between the early community and Judaism. For Koester this text is a witness for the 'formation of the controversial material later taken up in the Johannine discourses'.

Apart from the probably untenable early dating, we cannot follow Koester in other respects either. Neirynck has convincingly shown for the section in which the healing of the leper is reported that the text is 'post-synoptic', and that the author probably knew the three Synoptics, but especially Luke.[4] The generalisation of the question of the tribute-money, mentioned by Jeremias, also speaks against the thesis that this papyrus documents an early stage in the history of the tradition.

Text: H.I. Bell and T.C. Skeat, *Fragments of an Unknown Gospel*, London 1935; id., *The New Gospel Fragments*, London 1935 (with corrections). Aland, *Synopsis* p. 584 (index). **Literature** (with suggestions for restoration of the text): M.J. Lagrange, *Critique textuelle* II, Paris 1935, 633-649 (= *Rev. Bibl.* 44, 1935, 47ff.); M. Dibelius in *Dt. Lit. Ztg.* 57, 1936, cols. 3-11; C.H. Dodd, *A New Gospel*, Manchester 1936 (= BJRL 20, 1936 56ff.; reprinted in *New Testament Studies*, Manchester 1953, pp. 12ff.); K.F.W. Schmidt - J. Jeremias in *Theol. Blätter* 15, 1936, cols, 34-45 (cf. H. I Bell, cols. 72-74); further older literature in G. Mayeda, *Das Leben-Jesu-Fragment Papyrus Egerton* 2, Bern 1946 (cf. H.I. Bell in HTR 42, 1949, 53-63); J. Jeremias, *Unknown Sayings of Jesus*, [5]1964 (index); Ugo Gallizia, 'Il P. Egerton 2', in *Aegyptus. Riv. ital. di egittologia e di papirologia* 36, 1956, 29-72 and 178-234; Vielhauer, *Gesch. d. urchr. Lit.* pp. 636-639; H. Koester and F. Neirynck, see notes 3 and 4.

BAC
148:
93-96

f.1[v] (*ll.* 1-20)

(I) . . . <to> the lawyer<s: 'Punish e>very one who act<s contrary to the l>aw, but not me! . . . (5) . . . what he does, as he does it.' <And> having turn<ed> to <the> rulers of the people he <sp>oke the following saying; *'(Ye) search the scriptures* in which *ye think that ye have life; these are they* (10) *which bear witness of me.*[5] *Do not think that I came to accuse* <you> *to* my *Father! There is one<that ac>cuses <you>, even Moses, on whom ye have set your hope.'*[6] And when they sa(15)<id>: *'We know that God* <hath> *spok<en> to Moses, but* as for thee, *we know not <whence thou art>'*[7] Jesus answered and said unto them: 'Now (already) accusation is raised[8] against <your> (20) unbelief in regard to the things testified by him. For if <you> had <believed Moses>, you would have believed <me>; *for <concerning> me he <wrote> to your fathers'.*[9]

f.1[r] (*ll.* 22-41)

. . . <to gather> *stones* together *to stone him.*[10] And the <rul>ers laid (25) their hands on him that they might arrest him and <deliver> him to the multitude. But they w<ere not able> *to arrest* him *because the hour* of his betrayal <was> *not yet c*<ome>.[11] (30) But *he* himself, the Lord, *escaped out of their han>ds*[12] and turned away from them. (II) *And behold a leper drew near* <to him> *and said*: 'Master Jesus, wandering with lepers and eating with them (35) in the inn, I also <became> a <leper>. If <thou> therefore <wilt>, I am made *clean.*' Immediately the Lord <said to him>: *'I will, be thou made clean.'* <And thereupon> *the leprosy* departed *from him.* But Jesus (40) <said> to him: 'Go and show thyself to <the priests> and *offer <for thy > purification* as <Moses commanded>, and *sin no more* . . . '[13]

f. 2[r] (*ll.* 43-59)

(III) . . . <ca>me to him to put him to the pro<of> and to tempt him, whilst <they said>: (45) *'Master* Jesus, *we know that thou art come* <*from God>,*[14] for *what* thou *doest bears a test<imony>*[15] (to thee) (which) (goes) beyond (that) of al(l) the prophets. <Wherefore *tell*> *us*: is it *admissible <to p>ay* to the kings the (charges) appertaining to their rule? *<Should we> pay <th-> (50) em or not? But Jesus saw through* their <in>tention,[16] *became <angry>*[17] and said to them: '*Why call ye me* with yo<ur mou>th Master and *yet <do> not what I say?[18] Well has Is<aiah> prophesied <concerning y>(55)ou* saying: *This <people* honours> *me with* the <*ir li>ps but their heart is far from me; <their worship is> vain. <They teach> precepts <of men>.*'[19]

f. 2ᵛ (lines 60-75)[20]

(IV) <The grain of wheat> . . . (60) . . . in the place shut in . . . it was laid beneath and invisible . . . its wealth imponderable?[21] And as they were in perplexity at his strange question, (65) Jesus as he walked stood <on the> bank of the <riv>er Jordan, stretched out <hi>s right hand, <fill>ed it with . . . and sowed . . . on the (70) . . . And then . . . water . . . And . . . before <their eyes>, brought fruit . . . much . . . to the jo(75)<y?> . . .

Notes
2. Papyrus Egerton 2

1. Text and commentary have appeared in *Kölner Papyri (PKöln)* vol. VI = Abh. RWA, Sonderreihe Papyrologica Coloniensia 7, 1987. I thank Herr R. Merkelbach and Herr M. Gronewald, who made it possible for me to use the manuscript of the relevant section (the translator would also thank Prof. D. Lührmann for facilitating access to the published text).
2. *Greek Manuscripts of the Ancient World*, Oxford 1971, pp. 13.
3. Helmut Koester, *History and Literature of Early Christianity*, 1982, II, 181f.; id. 'Apocryphal and Canonical Gospels', in HTR 73, 1980, 105-130, esp. pp. 119ff.
4. F. Neirynck, 'Papyrus Egerton 2 and the Healing of the Leper', ETL 61, 1985, 153-160.
5. Jn. 5:39.
6. Jn. 5:45.
7. Jn. 9:29.
8. Cf.Jn. 12:31.
9. Jn. 5:46.
10. Jn. 10:31.
11. Jn. 7:30.
12. Jn. 10:39.
13. Mk. 1:40-44; Mt. 8:2-4; Lk. 5:12-14.
14. Jn. 3:2.
15. Jn. 10:25.
16. Mk. 12:13-15; Mt. 22:15-18; Lk. 22:20-23; Jn.5:14
17. Cf. Mk. 1:43.
18. Lk. 6:46.
19. Isa. 29:13 LXX; Mk. 7.6f.; Mt. 15:7f.
20. No completely satisfying reconstruction of the text has yet been found for fol.2ᵛ.
21. Cf. Jn. 12:24?.

3. Oxyrhynchus Papyrus 1224

Wilhelm Schneemelcher

The remains of a papyrus book, the writing of which points to the beginning of the 4th century, were also published by Grenfell and Hunt (POx 1224 = OP X, 1914, 1-10). The pages were numbered (there can still be recognised the numbers 139, 174 and 176; with these there belong 138 or 140, 173 and 175). The condition of the pages permits only a partially trustworthy reading of them. In the present state of our knowledge the identification of the fragments with a gospel is not possible.

Text: Wessely, PO XVIII, 266ff.; Klostermann, *op. cit.*, p. 26; Bonaccorsi, *op. cit.*, p. 40 (where, however, only one fragment is given); Aland, *Synopsis*, p. 584 (index).

p. 175
And the scribes and <Pharisees
and priests, when they sa<w
him, were angry <that with sinners in the midst he <reclined
at table. But Jesus heard <it and said:
The he<althy need not the physician.

p. 176
And pray for
your enemies. For he who is not
against you> is for you.
He who today> is far off - tomorrow will be
near to you> . . . .

The remaining fragments are not translated here, since they are handed down in too poor a state. With p. 175 cf. Mk. 2:16-17 and par. With p. 176 cf. Mt. 5:44 (Lk. 6:27f.) and Mk. 9:40 (Lk. 9:50). Cf. also Jeremias, *Unknown Sayings of Jesus*, [2]1964, p. 130 (index).

4. Papyrus Cairensis 10 735

Wilhelm Schneemelcher

Grenfell and Hunt also claimed as a survival from a non-canonical gospel the content of a page of papyrus of the 6th or 7th century (*Catalogue général des antiquités égyptiennes du Musée du Caire*, X, Oxford 1903, No. 10 735). But A. Deissmann brought forward objections to this assumption and was of opinion that here it is a matter rather of a text from a commentary or from a homily (A. Deissmann, 'Das angebliche Evangelienfragment von Kairo' in AR 7, 1904, 387-392; reprinted in *Licht vom Osten*⁴, 1923, pp. 368-371, (ET 1927, pp. 430-434). The objections expressed by Deissmann still stand, although his completions and explanations are not accepted. But an identification of the text has not so far been possible. Only this is settled, that it has to do with the proclamation of the birth of Jesus and the flight to Egypt, i.e. that here material from a gospel is presented - but whether as excerpt or homily remains open.

Text: In addition to Deissmann, *op. cit.*, also in Klostermann *op. cit*, p. 24; Bonaccorsi, *op. cit.* pp. 32ff. Aland, *Synopsis*, p. 584 (index).

Recto
The angel of the Lord spake: Jo<seph, arise,
take Mary, thy w<ife and
flee to Egypt < . . . .

. . . .

. . . .
every gift and if < . . . .
his friends . . . < . . . .
of the king . . < . . . .

. . . .
Verso
(*According to Deissmann's reconstruction*)
   . . . > should interpret to thee. The
archistrategus however> said to the virgin: Behold,
Elisabeth, thy relat>ive has also conceived, and it is the s>ixth month for her who
was called barren. In> the sixth, that is <in the month Thoth,
did his mother> conceive John.
But it behoved> the archistra-
tegus to an>nounce <beforehand John, the> servant who goes before his Lord's> coming . . .

With the recto cf. Mt. 2:13; with the verso Lk. 1:36.

5. The so-called Fayyum Fragment
Wilhelm Schneemelcher

In the papyrus collection of the Archduke Rainer in Vienna G. Bickell found in 1885 a fragment of the 3rd century (PVindob. G 2325) which caused considerable sensation, the opinion being that it provided a first step to the formation of the Synoptic Gospels (cf. Mk. 14:27, 29f.). The publication of the papyrus (*Mittheilungen aus der Sammlung der Papyrus Erzh. Rainer* I, 1887, 54-61) was followed by a wealth of hypotheses (cf. literature in NTApo Hdb, p. 21 and NTApo[2], p. 38). But here also a secondary, indeed an abridged, rendering of the synoptic material has to be assumed, and the text must be considered an excerpt or fragment of a gospel hitherto unknown to us. The brevity of the fragment forbids sure statements of any kind: the completions also remain questionable.
Text: It is also in Wessely, PO IV2.79ff.; Klostermann, *op. cit.* p. 23; Bonaccorsi, *op. cit.* pp. 30ff.; Aland, *Synopsis*, p. 444; de Santos[6], pp. 80f. (Lit.).

After> the meal according to custom (?) (he said:) <All ye
in this> night will be offend-
ed, as> it is written: I will smite the <shepherd,
and the> sheep will be scattered.
When> Peter <said>: Even if all, <not I,
Jesus said:> Before the cock crows twice, <thrice
wilt thou> de<ny me today.

6. The Strasbourg Coptic Papyrus

Wilhelm Schneemelcher

On shreds of papyrus from the 5th or 6th century, which in 1899 came into the possession of the Strasbourg Landes- und Universitätsbibliothek, were found, as Carl Schmidt recognised, the remains of an apocryphal gospel. The first attempt to set the small pieces in order and restore a coherent text was undertaken by Adolf Jacoby, W. Spiegelberg being responsible for the Coptic part (Adolf Jacoby, *Ein neues Evangelienfragment*, Strasbourg 1900). This effort met with a justly severe criticism from C. Schmidt (GGA 1900, pp. 481-506), who for his part advanced a reconstruction of his own for almost all the lines, and thereby made it possible to read with comprehension. The shreds indeed are preserved in such a sorry condition that any reconstruction must remain subject to considerable uncertainty (cf. the illustrations in Jacoby).

The two leaves, remains of an extensive manuscript, are designated Copt. 5 and Copt. 6. The recto of Copt. 5 contains a prayer of Jesus, in which there may be distant echoes of John 17. Certainly the text of the verso, which is separated from the recto only by two or three broken-off lines (which must have contained the end of the prayer), shows that the situation in which this prayer of Jesus is supposed to have been uttered is that of his farewell to the disciples (before the Passion or after the Resurrection?). The prayer is cast in the form of brief sentences, rounded off from time to time by an Amen (cf. the hymn in the Acts of John c. 94-95). On the verso the quotations from Matthew are remarkable, while on the recto there is evidently a reference to I Cor. 15. Unfortunately it cannot be said how Copt. 6 is to be related to Copt. 5, since only 6 and not 5 shows any pagination. From the few lines it is, however, clear that in Copt. 6 we have the end of this apocryphon. This ending might suggest that the fragment derives from a work which belongs to the *Gattung* of the 'Dialogues' (see below pp.234ff.). On the other hand the content of Copt 5 - so far as we can recognise it - certainly speaks against this. We cannot pass beyond conjectures.

All attempts to assign these fragments to a particular gospel have proved abortive. Jacoby maintained that it was a question of a fragment from the Gospel of the Egyptians; Schmidt conjectured (very cautiously!) that the text belonged to the (Jewish-Christian!) 'Gospel of the Twelve', since the apostles here speak in the plural. But F. Haase rightly rejected all speculations of the kind (*Literarkritische Untersuchungen zur orientalisch-apokryphen Evangelienliteratur*, 1913, pp. 1-11; further literature there). Equally unanswerable is the question of the original language: the number of Greek loan-words is in this text rather smaller than greater than in the other Coptic texts. The age of the apocryphon can scarcely be established, but in view of the use of the NT we can hardly go back beyond the beginning of the 3rd century.

The translation is given according to the text revised by C. Schmidt (NTApo², p. 66), with a few variations resulting from a fresh examination of the Coptic text.

103

I. Copt. 5 (Recto):

<that> he may be recognised by
<his hospitality? . . . >
   and be praised
through his fruits, for (since?)

. . . . . many of . . . .
. . . . Amen. Give me now thy
<power>, O Father, that
<they> with me may endure
<the world>. Amen. <I have>
received the diadem (sceptre?)
of the kingdom <. . . the> diadem of him who is
. . . <while men despise them
<in their> lowliness, since they
have not <recognized them>. I
   am become king
<through thee>, Father. Thou
   wilt
make <all> subject to me.
<Amen>. Through whom will

<the last> enemy be destroyed?
Through <Christ>. Amen.
Through whom is
the sting of death <destroyed>?[7]
<Through the> Only-begotten.
Amen. To whom belongs <the>
   dominion?
<It belongs to the Son>. Amen.
   <Through

whom has all come into being?
Through>
. . . .

(Verso):

<When> now <Jesus had> com-
pleted all <the praise? of his
   Father>[1]
then he turned to us and spake
<to us>:

The hour is nigh,[2]
when I shall be taken from you.[3]
The Spirit <is> willing,
but the flesh <is> weak.[4] <Wait>
now and watch <with me>.[5]
But we, the apost<les, we>
wept, <and> said <to him>:

. . . .<son>
of God . . . <will>
himself . . . .

He answered and said <to us>:

Fear ye not the
destruction (of the body) but ,
<fear ye>
rather . . . [6]
the power <of darkness?>

Be mindful of all that <I>
have said unto you: *<if>*
they have persecuted <me>,
<they will>
also persecute you . . . .[8] <Ye(?)>

now rejoice, that I have
<over come> the world,[9] and I

(2-3 lines missing)

2. Copt 6 (Recto): p. 157
(that I) may reveal to you all
my glory and show you
all your power and the secret
of your apostolate . . . . .

(Verso): p. 158
Our eyes penetrated all places,
we beheld the glory[10] of his
godhead and all the glory of
< his> dominion. He clothed
    <us>
<with> the power <of our>
    apostle<ship>

Notes

The Strasbourg Coptic Papyrus

1. <cf. Mt. 26:30?>
2. Mt. 26:45.
3. Mt. 9:15 and par.
4. Mt. 26:41.
5. Mt. 26:38.
6. Cf. Mt. 10:28.
7. Cf. 1 Cor. 15:25f., 55.
8. Jn. 15:20.
9. Cf. Jn. 16:33.
10. Jn.1:14.

Appendix: the 'secret Gospel' of Mark

H. Merkel

Literature: M. Smith, *Clement of Alexandria and a Secret Gospel of Mark*, Cambridge, Mass. 1973; id. *The Secret Gospel. The Discovery and Interpretation of the Secret Gospel according to Mark*, New York 1973.

Reviews of Smith: P. Achtemeier, JBL 93, 1974, 625-628; R.P.C. Hanson, JTS 25, 1974, 513-521; H.C. Kee, JAAR 43, 1975, 326-329; H. Koester, AHR 80, 1975, 620-622; C.C. Richardson, TS 35, 1974, 571-577; E. Trocmé, RHPhR 55, 1975, 291f.

Studies: R.E. Brown, 'The Relation of 'The Secret Gospel of Mark' to the Fourth Gospel', CBQ 36, 1974, 466-485; F.F. Bruce, 'The 'Secret' Gospel of Mark' (E.M. Wood Lecture 1974), London 1974; R.H. Fuller, 'Longer Mark: Forgery, Interpolation or Old Tradition?' in: *The Center for Hermeneutical Studies in Hellenistic and Modern Culture, Protocol of the 18th Colloquy*, ed. W. Wuellner, 1975, pp. 1-11; R.M. Grant, 'Morton Smith's Two Books', ATR 56, 1974, 58-65; P.W. van der Horst, 'Het 'Geheime Markusevangelie'. Over een nieuwe vondst', NedThT 33, 1979, 27-51; H. Merkel, 'Auf den Spuren des Urmarkus? Ein neuer Fund und seine Beurteilung', ZThK 71, 1974, 123-144; C.E. Murgia, 'Secret Mark: Real or Fake?' in R.H. Fuller (see above), pp. 35-40; H. Musurillo, 'Morton Smith's Secret Gospel', *Thought* 48, 1974, 327-331; P. Parker, 'On Professor Morton Smith's Find at Mar-Saba', ATR 56, 1974, 53-57; Q. Quesnell, 'The Mar Saba Clementine: A Question of Evidence', CBQ 37, 1975, 48-67; W. Wink, 'Jesus as Magician', USQR 30, 1974, 3-14; E.M. Yamauchi, 'A Secret Gospel of Jesus as 'Magus'?' CScR 4, 1975, 238-251.

Replies by Smith: 'Merkel on the Longer Text of Mark', ZThK 72, 1975, 133-150; 'On the Authenticity of the Mar Saba Letter of Clement', CBQ 36, 1976, 196-199 (with an answer by Q. Quesnell, *ibid.* pp. 200-203); 'Response by Dr Morton Smith', in R.H. Fuller (see above), pp. 12-15; 'Clement of Alexandria and Secret Mark: The Score at the End of the First Decade', HTR 75, 1982, 449-461.

Introduction

1. The Discovery of the Text: During a stay in the Greek Orthodox monastery of Mar Saba, south-east of Jerusalem, Morton Smith in the summer of 1958 found a handwritten entry on the last (unprinted) pages of an edition of the works of Ignatius of Antioch dating from 1646. It presents an extract from a letter of Clement of Alexandria to one Theodore, whom he seeks to warn against a Gospel of Mark falsified by the gnostic sect of the Carpocratians; in the process, Clement concedes that it gives a 'more spiritual' version of Mark, and quotes from it.

M. Smith photographed this text, which breaks off in mid-sentence on the third page, but did nothing about safeguarding the original, which to this day has not been accessible to anyone else. Only in 1973 did he publish the text with an extensive commentary; at the same time he published a popular presentation of the story of the discovery and his work upon it. Several palaeographers to whom Smith had made photographs of the text available dated the manuscript from the late 17th down to the early 19th century.[1]

Through detailed linguistic investigations, M. Smith makes it probable that it could be a question of a genuine letter of Clement of Alexandria.[2]

Smith further wished to prove that the two quotations go back to the Aramaic original version of Mark, which served as a source for the canonical Mark and also for the Gospel of John; an admirer of Mark's Gospel expanded it by passages from the Aramaic source, which he translated in conscious imitation of Mark's style.[3]

The passage inserted between Mk. 10:34 and 35 deals with the resurrection from the dead of a young man, whom Jesus later baptises in a possibly homosexual act. Here Smith sees the historical Jesus accurately portrayed, since he considers him a magus possessed by the Spirit. The libertinism of Jesus was suppressed only later, by James the Lord's brother and by Paul.[4]

2. On the Discussion of the Problems: It has still to be settled whether the letter derives from Clement of Alexandria or not. Over against the linguistic indications which speak for authenticity, differences of substance as compared with the rest of Clement's writing have been noted.[5] One might also have expected that a learned copyist of the 18th century would give the source from which he made his copy.[6] Finally, it is striking that the text contains none of the errors typical in manuscript tradition.[7]

Even if the letter is authentic, however, we can deduce no more than that an expanded version of Mark was in existence in Alexandria about A.D. 170. When Smith seeks to go back to the last years of the 1st century for the composition of the expanded Mark, that rests on pure speculation.[8]

In the quotations from the 'secret Gospel', is it really a question of translation from the Aramaic? Smith refers to three 'semitisms', which, however, often occur in the Synoptics;[9] as Smith himself admits,[10] such semitisms are easily imitated. Anyone who reads the text impartially will rather gain the impression that here the raising of Lazarus in Jn. 11 is adapted in an abridged form, with the admixture of numerous echoes of Synoptic pericopes. PEgerton 2 and some gnostic texts, for example, offer analogies for this kind of development and reminting of the Gospels.[11] Smith rejects such parallels without argument,[12] since he would see in the secret Gospel a variant of Mark. Thus he denies any connections with the language of Matthew[13] as with that of John,[14] and the verbatim quotation from Lk. 18:23 in III 6 is charged to the account of a glossator or a later copyist, as is the allusion to Lk. 9:53 in III 16. Reference has frequently been made to the methodologically questionable character of such a procedure.[15] Finally, even the Marcan character of the fragment is not without its problems. 'The style is certainly Mark's, but it is too Marcan to be Mark'; such was already C.C. Richardson's verdict in 1974, and E. Best in 1979 confirmed this judgment in detail.[16] In Mark itself the Marcan peculiarities of style are nowhere so piled up as in the 'secret Gospel'!

Accordingly, everything points to the view that the 'secret Gospel' is an apocryphon resting on the foundation of the canonical Gospels.[17] On this ground alone any conclusions relating to the historical Jesus are not possible.[18]

The time of origin of the 'secret Gospel' probably lies not before the middle of the 2nd century.

Fragments of the 'Secret Gospel of Mark'

Frag. 1   (*II 23*) And they came to Bethany.[19] And there was a woman there, whose brother was dead.[20] (24) And she came and fell down before Jesus and said to him:[21] Son of David, (25) have mercy on me.[22] But the disciples rebuked her.[23] And in anger[24] (26) Jesus went away with her[25] into the garden where the tomb was;[26] and (*III 1*) immediately a loud voice was heard from the tomb;[27] and Jesus went forward and (2) rolled away the stone from the door of the tomb.[28] And immediately he went in where (3) the young man was,[29] stretched out his hand and raised him up, (4) grasping him by the hand.[30] But the young man looked upon him and loved him,[31] and (5) began to entreat him that he might remain with him.[32] And when they had gone out (6) from the tomb, they went into the young man's house; for he was rich.[33] And after (7) six days[34] Jesus commissioned him; and in the evening the young man (8) came to him,[35] clothed only in a linen cloth upon his naked body.[36] And (9) he remained with him that night;[37] for Jesus (10) was teaching him the mysteries of the Kingdom of God.[38] And from there he went away (11) and returned to the other bank of the Jordan.[39]

Frag. 2   (*III 14*) He came to Jericho.[40] And there were (15) there the sisters of the young man whom Jesus loved,[41] and (16) his mother and Salome;[42] and Jesus did not receive them.[43]

Notes

Appendix: the 'secret Gospel' of Mark

1. M. Smith, *Clement of Alexandria* . . . pp. 1-4. Q. Quesnell rightly censures the very summary reproduction of the expert opinions.
2. M. Smith, *op. cit*. pp. 5-85.
3. *Ibid*. pp. 86-194.
4. *Ibid*. pp. 195-265.
5. Smith, p. 31, quotes W. Völker's observation that Clement does indeed know a gnostic tradition in the Church, but this is said to be unwritten; moreover the letter presupposes a conception of the Church which is more strongly institutionalised than it appears elsewhere in Clement. Smith, p. 37, quotes the objection of J. Munck, that the description of the Carpocratians in the third book of the *Stromateis* is very different from the one given here. W.G. Kümmel (ThR 40, 1975, 302) mentions reservations expressed by H. von Campenhausen against authenticity: 'Not only the manner of the transmission speaks against it, but also the description of a church archive containing secret writings, the recommendation of a falsehood to be fortified by a false oath on polemical grounds, the idea of two stages of secret teaching of Jesus, and the report of Mark's migration to Alexandria contradict everything that we know from Clement.'
6. H. Musurillo, p. 330.
7. C.E. Murgia, p. 40.
8. H. Merkel, pp. 129f.
9. M. Smith, *op. cit*. pp. 133f. On the two cases of the pleonastic addition of the personal

pronoun after relatives (in II 23 and III 15) it is for that matter to be noted that this is 'an error not unknown to classical and later Greek' (Blaß-Debrunner-Funk, *A Greek Grammar of the NT*, 1961, § 297).

10. M. Smith, *op. cit.* p. 134.

11. Cf. R.E. Brown, pp. 476f.; R.M. Grant, pp. 60f.; P.W. van der Horst, pp. 46f.; H. Merkel, pp. 137f.

12. M. Smith, *op. cit.* 95: 'Fortunately ... there is no need to rely on this material of which the interpretation is so uncertain. The Gospel described by Clement's letter was unquestionably (!) a variant form of Mark.'

13. Cf. the tabular survey in R.E. Brown, pp. 471-474; Merkel, pp. 132f.

14. R.E. Brown, pp. 474ff.; E.C. Hobbs, 'Response to R.H .Fuller', pp. 19-25; Merkel, pp.131ff.

15. R.E. Brown, p. 469, note 11; P.W. van der Horst, p. 45; Merkel, p. 132. The libertine interpretation of Jesus rests strongly on a similar act of violence in III 9, where Smith replaces the transmitted verbal form 'he taught' by 'he handed over' (*op. cit.* p. 183). ' . . . as there is only one copy, guessing is free' (R.P.C. Hanson, p. 516).

16. C.C. Richardson, p. 573; E. Best, JSNT 4, 1979, 71-76.

17. This rules out R.H. Fuller's attempt to discover an older form of the resurrection story in the first fragment with the help of considerations of tradition and redaction criticism. The features in the 'secret Gospel' which seem to him more original as compared with Jn. 11 are merely borrowings from the Synoptics.

18. M. Smith's conclusions have been rejected by practically all critics; nevertheless he has set them out afresh in his book *Jesus the Magician*, London 1978 (German: *Jesus der Magier*, Munich 1981; on this cf. J.A. Bühner, 'Jesus und die antike Magie', EvTh 43, 1983, 156-175).

19. Mk. 8:22 D; Jn. 12: 1.

20. Cf. Jn. 11: 2, 32.

21. Cf. Mt.15:25; Jn. 11:32.

22. Mk. 10:48; Mt. 15:22.

23. Cf. Mk. 10:13; Mt. 19:13.

24. Cf. Mk. 10:14; 1:41 D; Jn. 11:33.

25. Cf. Mk. 5:24.

26. Cf. Jn. 19:41.

27. Cf. Mk. 5:7; Jn. 11:43.

28. Cf. Mt. 28:2.

29. Cf. Mk. 5:40.

30. Cf. Mk. 1:31; 5:41; 9:27; Lk. 7:14.

31. Cf. Mk. 10:21.

32. Cf. Mk. 5:18.

33. Lk. 18:23.

34. Cf. Mk. 9:1; Jn. 12:1.

35. Cf. Mt. 27:57; Jn. 3:2.

36. Mk. 14:51.

37. Cf. Jn. 1:39.

38. Cf. Mk. 4:11.

39. Cf. Mk. 3:8; 10: 1; Jn. 3:22, 26; 10:40.

40. Mk. 10:46.

41. Cf. Jn. 11:5; 13:23; 19:26; 21:7, 20.

42. Cf. Mk. 15:41; 16:1.

43. Cf. Lk. 9:53.

III. The Coptic Gospel of Thomas

Beate Blatz

Introduction

1. Literature: *Facsimile: The Facsimile Edition of the Nag Hammadi Codices*, published under the Auspices of the Department of Antiquities of the Arab Republic of Egypt in Conjunction with the UNESCO, Codex II, Leiden 1974, p. 32-51.

Editions: A. Guillaumont, H.-Ch. Puech, G. Quispel, W. Till and Yassah 'Abd Al Masih, *The Gospel according to Thomas*. Text edited and translated, Leiden 1959. Jean Doresse, *Les livres secrets des Gnostiques d'Égypte*, vol. II: 'L'Évangile selon Thomas ou les paroles secrètes de Jésus', Paris 1959 (ET in *The Secret Books of the Egyptian Gnostics*, London 1960, pp. 333-383). J. Leipoldt, *Das Evangelium nach Thomas, koptisch und deutsch*, TU 101, 1967. B. Layton (ed.), *Nag Hammadi Codex II 2-7, together with XIII 2*, Brit. Lib. Or. 4926 (1) and P. Oxy. 1, 654, 655*, vol. I, (NHS 20), Leiden 1989.

Translations: Guillaumont et al. (see above); Leipoldt (see above); H. Quecke in: W.C. van Unnik, *Evangelien aus dem Nilsand*, 1960, pp. 161-173. J.E. Ménard, *L'Évangile selon Thomas*, Leiden 1975. H. Koester and T. Lambdin, in: *The Nag Hammadi Library in English*, ed. James M. Robinson, Leiden 1977, pp. 117-130 (revised ed. 1988, pp. 124-138). Cf. also de Santos[6] 1988, pp. 678-705 (Lit.).

Studies: the literature devoted to this important text is immense, and cannot be adduced here. Some references are given in the notes. A survey is provided by D.M. Scholer, *Nag Hammadi Bibliography 1948-1969*, Leiden 1971. This bibliography is continued in the 'Supplements' in *Novum Testamentum* (since 1971).

2. Attestation: According to the Pistis Sophia (chapters 42 and 43)[1] Jesus after his resurrection commissioned Philip, Matthew and also Thomas to set down his words in writing. We may conclude from this that Thomas was to be regarded as the guarantor for, or author of, a gospel. In fact a work with the title 'Gospel of Thomas' is known in the tradition from the 3rd century on.

In his report on the Naassenes Hippolytus († 235) mentions a 'Gospel of Thomas' and also quotes from this work.[2] About A.D. 233 Origen in his first homily on Luke mentions the Gospel of Thomas in addition to the Gospel of Matthias among the heterodox gospels.[3] His testimony was taken over in a Latin translation or paraphrase by Jerome,[4] Ambrose[5] and the Venerable Bede.[6] In the Greek area Eusebius of Caesarea, probably following Origen, includes a Gospel of Thomas in the group of apocrypha of purely heterodox character; he inserts it between the Gospel of Peter and that of Matthias.[7] Philip of Side about 430, referring to Eusebius in a fragment of his *Church History*, says that 'most of the elders' had 'completely rejected' the so-called Gospel of Thomas (τὸ λεγόμενον Θῶμα εὐαγγέλιον) as well as the Gospel of the Hebrews and that of Peter, 'saying that these writings were the work of heretics'.[8] In addition he counts the Gospel of the Egyptians, the Gospel of the Twelve and the Gospel of Basilides among the 'false gospels'.

A series of Greek witnesses[9] reckon a 'Gospel according to Thomas' among the writings which were used by the Manicheans or even, as is occasionally asserted, composed by them. Cyril and those who copied him naturally do not describe the author as an apostle, but as a disciple of Mani who was also called Thomas. The testimonies of pseudo-Leontius and Timothy of Constantinople are worthy of note: they both link the Gospel of Thomas closely with the Gospel of Philip, which they mention immediately after it. Timothy in addition expressly distinguishes the Gospel of Thomas from another apocryphon, the infancy stories of the Lord, by setting the two works at different places in his list of Manichean writings (under no. 9 and no. 13).

The pseudo-Gelasian decree also includes an 'Evangelium nomine Thomae, quibus Manichaei utuntur, apocryphum' in its catalogue of the *libri non recipiendi*.[10] Here it is not clear whether it is a question of the (heretical) Gospel of Thomas or of the Infancy Gospel ascribed to Thomas. The same holds also for two other references to a Gospel of Thomas, one in the Stichometry of Nicephorus[11], the other in the 'Synopsis' of ps.-Athanasius.[12]

3. Extant Remains: down to the discovery of the Nag Hammadi documents, nothing was known of the text of the Gospel of Thomas apart from the 'quotation' in Hippolytus.[13] With the discovery of the Coptic gnostic library we now have a collection of 114 logia, written in Sahidic,[14] which is described in the colophon as 'Gospel according to Thomas'. The introduction confirms this title.

Codex II from Nag Hammadi, which contains the Gospel of Thomas, is dated to about 400. It can, however, be demonstrated that the manuscript had a significantly older Coptic *Vorlage*.

As early as 1952 H.-Ch. Puech established that parts of this gospel had already long been known in Greek,[15] namely in the Oxyrhynchus Papyri 1, 654 and 655.[16] Independently of Puech, G. Garitte also recognised that they belonged together,[17] but drew very far-reaching conclusions with regard to the relations between the Greek and the Coptic texts, which however have proved untenable. For this question it is to be noted that the sequence of the sayings in the Coptic text deviates from that in POx (in POx 1 logia 30 and 77 stand together), and that there are also occasional differences in text (cf. log. 5 with POx 654). In addition a stronger gnosticising tendency is to be assumed for the Coptic text. It has to be affirmed that the extant Greek text, which derives from three different copies of the gospel, was not the direct *Vorlage* for the Coptic text contained in Codex II from Nag Hammadi (and naturally not the converse). 'Between the Greek and the Coptic version the Gospel of Thomas has undergone a development.'[18]

The fragments from the Oxyrhynchus papyri are set alongside the translation offered below, in order to make plain the relationship as well as the differences between the two versions.

4. Position within the early Christian literature: the second tractate in Codex II of Nag Hammadi is not identical with the Infancy Gospel of Thomas (on which see below, pp.439ff.). Rather the work may be identified as the 'Gospel of Thomas' which the ancient witnesses reckoned among the Manichean scriptures.[19] This is already suggested, first, by the fact that in the manuscript the Gospel of Thomas from Nag Hammadi has its place before the Gospel of Philip (see below, pp. 179ff.), as in the catalogues of ps.-Leontius and Timothy. In addition, there is a series of parallels between individual logia and Manichean texts.[20] It is certain that the Gospel of Thomas was known and used in Manicheism.

There is much to be said for the view that this knowledge of the Gospel of Thomas in Manicheism was transmitted through Syria. It is also widely assumed today that this work originated in Syria, even though the extant witnesses to the text derive from Egypt, and moreover it is possible to demonstrate some parallels with the Gospel of the Egyptians.[21] These parallels should not, however, be over-rated, since to some extent it is probably a question of 'wandering sayings' (e.g. log. 22 and 37).

The origin of the Gospel of Thomas in Syria can be deduced from many pointers. We may refer first to the statements of the prologue, according to which 'Didymus Judas Thomas' is alleged to be the author or redactor of this gospel. This striking form of the name occurs in the Acts of Thomas and in other works which had their home in Syria.[22] The Syrian background of this text is clear not only from this form of the name but also from the rank which is assigned to Thomas (cf. log. 13; cf. also Puech, NTApo³, pp. 286f.). This is confirmed by other parallels, identified especially by A. Baker and G. Quispel. The Syrian 'native soil' is just as clear in imagery and parables, in which reference is made to a return to a primordial condition and to the removal of separation and division, as in the role assigned to the 'little ones' (log. 46). Mention may also be made of parallels to the Liber Graduum.[23] The question of the relation between the Gospel of Thomas and the Diatessaron, which arises in this connection, is to be answered - according to Ménard and Quispel[24] - in the terms that the two texts originated in the same Syrian milieu and go back to the same Syrian *Vorlage*. To what extent we may assume a common Jewish-Christian tradition as the basis[25] remains in dispute.

Reference has been made to the proximity of this text to the Naassene use of Scripture.[26] According to Hippolytus, these gnostics harmonised texts from the canonical Gospels, as can be shown from the example of the Parable of the Sower.[27] Something similar is said to be true of the Gospel of Thomas (cf. log. 19, 39 and 45). It is, however, very questionable whether any analogy can actually be demonstrated.

5. Literary *Gattung*, sources and relation to the canonical Gospels: the *Gattung* of the Gospel of Thomas can be unambiguously defined: it is a collection of sayings. The book is thus evidence for the existence of such collections (as a literary *Gattung*). The introduction and log. 1 make it clear that this collection of sayings of Jesus is intended to be a message of salvation, and this genre of text may therefore be described as a 'sayings gospel'.[28] Here we should not overlook the difference from the gnostic revelation documents (e.g. the 'dialogues', see below, pp. 228ff.). For the Gospel of Thomas it is not a question of secret instruction, nor is it intended to supplement the Jesus tradition. This work 'is severed from the story of Jesus and represents the 'Gospel' in autarchic fashion, in that it hands on the 'hidden words' of the 'living', ever-present Jesus'.[29] There is no reference to the activity of Jesus, or to his death and resurrection. The individual words here gathered together are the 'Gospel'.

It is scarcely possible to identify any principle of arrangement in this collection. 'Only catch-word linkings combine several sayings into fairly small groups.'[30] It is precisely in this stringing-together of individual sayings that the Gospel of Thomas gives an impression of great antiquity.

The redactor, however, possibly found some small groups of sayings already together, and took them into his collection. This cannot be proved for certain, but may be suspected. Connected with this question is the problem of the sources of Thomas, which even today is still disputed. The work beyond doubt contains material of very diverse origin. Roughly half of the sayings have parallels in the Synoptic Gospels. The other logia are partly completely unknown words of Jesus, partly 'agrapha' which were already known. These logia can also be distinguished according to whether they have a Synoptic character in form and content, or are 'gnostic' sayings. This complex situation makes it very difficult to answer the question how Thomas and the canonical Gospels are related to one another. In research up to the present, efforts have been made to demonstrate both the dependence and the independence of the sayings.[31]

This problem cannot be discussed in detail here. It can only be said in summary fashion that we must regard the Gospel of Thomas as a collection of sayings which goes back to one or more earlier stages and is not directly dependent on the canonical Gospels or the sayings source Q. This collection is to be regarded as a phenomenon parallel to Q, and belongs to the early history of the formation of the Gospels.[32]

6. Place and time of origin: The grounds for the assumption of a Syrian provenance for the Gospel of Thomas have already been reported.[33] It is not possible to determine the place of origin more precisely. In the same way the time of composition cannot be stated exactly. We can only say that there is much in favour of the view that Thomas originated about the middle of the 2nd century in eastern Syria, although admittedly the collected sayings material may in part go back even into the 1st century.

7. Theological themes: 'The Gospel of Thomas in literary terms has several strata, hence resists any theological characterisation and poses difficult methodological problems for any such undertaking.'[34] We can, therefore, point out only some important aspects here.

Jesus appears as the living one, i.e. the risen one, the Son of the living Father, who has laid aside all earthly form. Jesus is the revealer, who imparts to the disciples the secret of his - and their - origin. He is the one who explains this secret to the disciples. His heavenly form is recognisable only to the elect. Jesus is one with the Father, one with the kingdom of light, from him all has proceeded, and he is contained in all. Apocalyptic descriptions are lacking in the Gospel of Thomas, as are Son of Man sayings. Jesus is also not the Messiah expected by the prophets (log.52).

The world is negatively assessed (log. 55, 56 and 80). The human body is a corpse. The opposition of world, body and death on the one hand and the kingdom of the Father, knowledge and life on the other governs the language of Thomas (cf. also log. 3, 35 and 103). Man, even though 'drunk', i.e. without knowledge, is still of divine origin (log. 3, 85 and 87), created after the divine image (log. 50; cf. also log. 83 and 84). Those who 'have ears to hear' (log. 24 and often[35]), who understand the message of Jesus and recognise his true form, these also learn that they themselves belong to the world of light, the One.

The 'kingdom' (the 'kingdom of the Father' or 'kingdom of heaven') is a central concept in the Gospel of Thomas.[36] Here the difference from Jesus' preaching of the kingdom in the Synoptic Gospels becomes especially clear: the eschatological outlook towards the future is almost completely lacking. Certainly there is reference to 'entering' or 'finding', and that in a future sense. But these statements are closely connected with the statement that the disciple derives from the kingdom (log. 49). Only the present character of the kingdom seems to be important, and this is strongly spiritualised (log. 113[37]). 'Frequently it appears that return to the 'kingdom' not only presupposes the gnostic idea of the pre-existence of the soul, but that the 'kingdom' is a concept interchangeable with the divine self of the disciple (= the gnostic).'[38]

With this is connected a further peculiarity of the Gospel of Thomas: there are scarcely any signs of the formation of a community, and ecclesiological ideas are completely lacking. Access to the 'kingdom' is promised to individuals, reached by the call of Jesus. It is the 'little ones', the 'single ones', the 'solitary', who attain the 'kingdom' and with it 'rest'.[39] 'In terms of the history of theology many lines run together in the Gospel of Thomas, and from it to other writings, although it cannot be assigned to any particular group. The roots reach far back into the proclamation of Jesus, in Jewish-Christian gnostic circles (perhaps in Transjordan); it belongs in the strongly gnosticising reverence for Thomas in east Syria, in which also the ascetic (encratite) tendencies of the Gospel of Thomas probably have their home. There are also some connections with Valentinian ideas (e.g. that of the 'bridal chamber', log. 75). But in the Nag Hammadi library the Gospel of Thomas appears to be a foreign body; for the present we do not yet know its 'true kinsman'.'[40]

Notes
III. The Coptic Gospel of Thomas

Introduction

1. Carl Schmidt and Violet MacDermot, *Pistis Sophia*, (NHS 9), Leiden 1978, pp. 71f.
2. *Ref.* V 7.20, Marcovich p. 147.103ff. Cf. J.E. Ménard, *L'Évangile selon Thomas*, (NHS 5), Leiden 1975, p. 6.
3. *Luc. hom.* I, Rauer 5.13f.; cf. above p. 46.
4. *Luc. hom. lat.*, Rauer 5.11-13.
5. *Expositio evangelii Lucae* I 2, Schenkl 10.20-11.1.
6. *In Lucae evangelium expositio* I, prol. PL XCII, 307 C.
7. Eusebius, H.E. III 25.6; cf. above, p. 47.
8. Philip of Side (in: Codex Baroccianus 142): C. de Boor, TU V 2, 1888, 169, No. 4
9. Cyril of Jerusalem, *Cat.* IV 36 and VI 31; PG XXXIII 500 B and 593 A.—ps.-Leontius of Byzantium, *de Sectis* III 2; PG LXXXVI 1, 1213 C.—Timothy of Constantinople, *de Recept. Haeret.* PG LXXXVI 1, 21 C.— Acts of the second Council of Nicaea 787, VI 5, Mansi XIII 292B.
10. E. von Dobschutz, *Das Decretum Gelasianum*, (TU 38.4), 1912, pp. 11 and 295f.; cf. above p. 38.
11. PG C 1060 B; cf. above, p. 42.
12. PG XXVIII 432 B.
13. The 'quotation' probably has some connection with log. 4; see below, p. 117.
14. The text shows Achmimic and sub-Achmimic elements.
15. H-C.Puech, 'Une collection de Paroles de Jésus récemment retrouvée: L'Évangile selon Thomas', in *Comptes rendus de l'Academie des Inscriptions et Belles Lettres*, 1957, pp. 59ff.
16. On the papyri cf. NTApo[3] I 97ff. and 278ff.; J.A. Fitzmyer, 'The Oxyrhynchus Logoi of Jesus and the Coptic Gospel According to Thomas', in ThSt 20, 1959, 505-560; R.A. Kraft, 'Oxyrhynchus Papyrus 655 Reconsidered', in HTR 54, 1961, 252-262.
17. Cf. 'Les Logoi d'Oxyrhynque et l'Apocryphe copte dit 'Évangile de Thomas'', in *Le Muséon* 73, 1960, 151-172. See Guillaumont's response, *ib.* pp. 325-333, with Garitte's rejoinder, *ib.* pp. 335-349.
18. Vielhauer, *Lit. gesch.* p. 620.
19. Cyril of Jerusalem, see note 9 above; Peter of Sicily, *Hist. Man.* 16, PG CIV 1265C.
20. Turfan fragment T II D II 134, in SPAW 1934, 856. Kephalaia X 42.24-43.21
21. E.g. log. 22, 37 and 61; on these see below, pp. 120ff. Cf. G. Quispel, 'The Gospel of Thomas revisited', in B. Barc (ed.), *Colloque international sur les Textes de Nag Hammadi*, Louvain 1981, pp. 218-266.
22. Cf. W. Bauer, NTApo[3] II 59; U. Monneret de Villard, *'Le leggende orientali sui Magi evangelici'* (Studi e Testi 163), Rome 1952, p. 46, note 1. Act. Thom. c. 1, Aa 100.4f.; cf. also c. 39, Aa 156.12-15.
23. Cf. A. Baker, 'Pseudo-Macarius and the Gospel of Thomas', in *Vig.Chr.* 18, 1964, 215-225; id. 'The Gospel of Thomas and the Syriac Liber Graduum', in NTS 12, 1965, 291-294; id. 'Fasting to the World', in JBL 84, 1965, 291-294; G. Quispel (note 21 above); Werner Jäger, *Two Rediscovered Works of Ancient Christian Literature*, Leiden 1954, pp. 275.6 and 83.11.
24. Ménard, *op. cit.* (see Lit.), pp. 18ff.; Quispel, *op. cit.* (note 21), p. 252; A. Baker, 'The Gospel of Thomas and the Diatessaron', in JTS 16, 1965, 449-454.
25. Quispel, *op. cit.* (note 21), p. 252.

26. Ménard, *op. cit.*; R.M. Grant and D.N. Freedman, *The Secret Sayings of Jesus*, 1960, pp. 92ff.

27. Hippol. *Ref.* V 8.29; cf. log. 9.

28. So especially H. Koester in his contributions to the problem of the Gospels, see above, pp. 77ff.

29. Vielhauer, *Lit. gesch.* p. 623.

30. *Ibid.*

31. Cf. the report in Vielhauer, *op. cit.* pp. 624ff.; H. Koester in ANRW 25/2, 1492ff.

32. Cf. the various contributions of Koester (see above, pp. 77ff. and below, pp. 228ff.), who is, however, not at all points convincing. In particular he often seems to incline to a too early dating.

33. See above, pp. 112f. Contrast B. Aland, 'Kann das Thomasevangelium aus Edessa stammen?', *Nov. Test.* 12, 1970, 284ff.

34. Vielhauer, *Lit. gesch.* p. 633.

35. On the 'awakening formula', which occurs relatively frequently (log. 8, 21, 24, 63, 65, 96), cf. Vielhauer *op. cit.* p. 623.

36. Cf. log. 3, 20, 22, 27, 46, 49, 54, 76, 82, 96, 98, 107, 109, 113, 114.

37. With log. 113 cf. also Manichean Psalm-Book 160.20f.

38. Vielhauer, *Lit. gesch.* p. 634, with reference to log. 27, 49 and 11.

39. Cf. log. 4, 16, 22, 50, 51, etc.

40. Vielhauer, *Lit. gesch.* p. 635.

Translation

NHC II 2, 32.10-51.28

POx 654

Lines 1-5

These are the secret words which the living Jesus spoke, and which Didymus Judas Thomas wrote down[1] (1) And he said: He who shall find the interpretation of these words shall not taste of death[3].

These are the words which < . . . Jesus spoke, the living, a<nd . . and Thomas, and he said < . . . these words < . . . will he not taste.[2]

Lines 5-9

(2) Jesus said: He who seeks, let him not cease seeking until he finds; and when he finds he will be troubled, and when he is troubled he will be amazed, and he will reign over the All.[4]

<Jesus says: Let not him cease who is se<eking... has found, and when he has found < . . . . has been amazed (?) he will reign an<d find rest

Lines 9-21

(3) Jesus said: If those who lead you say to you: See, the kingdom is in heaven, then the birds of the heaven will go before you; if they say to you: It is in the sea, then the fish will go before you. But the kingdom is within you, and it is outside of you. When you know yourselves, then you will be known, (p. 33) and you will know that you are the sons of the living Father. But if you do not know yourselves, then you are in poverty, and you are poverty.[5]

J<esus> says . . . who draw us (you?) < . . . the kingdom in hea<ven . . . the birds of the hea<ven . . . it is under the earth < . . . the fish of the se<a . . . . . . > you. And the kingdom < . . . is within you < . . . he who (?) knows, will fi<nd this . . . if you shall know yourselves < . . . you are of the Father, of the <living know yourselves in < . . .

And you are po<verty (?)[6]

Lines 21-27

4) Jesus said: The man aged in days will not hesitate to ask a little child of seven days about the place of life, and he shall live; for there are many first who shall be last, and they will become a single one.[7]

<Jesus says: A m<an> will not hesitate . . . . . > to ask a <child . . . . . > about the place of the < . . . . . > that many (first) shall <be the last (and) the last the first and < . . .[8]

117

(5) Jesus said: Recognise what is before you, and what is hidden from you will be revealed to you; for there is nothing hidden that will not be made manifest[9].

Jesus says:< . . .
lies (before) your sight and < . . .
from you, will be revealed < . . .
Nothing (?)
is hidden that <will> not <be made
mani<fest,
and buried that <will> not <be raised
up (?)[10]

6) His disciples asked him (and) said to him: Do you want us to fast? And how shall we pray (and) give alms? What diet should we observe? Jesus said: Do not lie, and what you abhor, do not do; for all things are manifest in the sight of heaven; for there is nothing hidden which will not be revealed, and there is nothing covered which will remain without being uncovered.[12]

<His disciples> ask him <and
s>ay: How should we fas<t and how
should we pr>ay and how < . . . . . .
. >and what should we observe<. . .
. . > Jesus says < . . . .
. . . . > do not do < . . . .
. . . . > truth < . . .
. . . . > hidden < . . . [11]

(7) Jesus said: Blessed is the lion which the man eats, and the lion will become man; and cursed is the man whom the lion eats, and the lion will become man.[13]

. . . . . blessed is . . .
. . . .
. . . .[14]

(8) And he said: Man is like a wise fisherman who cast his net into the sea; he drew it up from the sea full of small fish; among them he found a large good fish, the wise fisherman; he threw all the small fish (p. 34) into the sea, he chose the large fish without difficulty. He who has ears to hear, let him hear![15]

(9) Jesus said: Look, the sower went out, he filled his hand (and) cast (the seed). Some fell upon the road; the birds came, they gathered them. Others fell upon the rock, and struck no root in the ground, nor did they produce any ears. And others fell on the thorns; they choked the seed and the worm ate them. And others fell on the good earth, and it produced good fruit; it yielded sixty per measure and a hundred and twenty per measure.[16]

(10) Jesus said: I have cast a fire upon the world, and see, I watch over it until it is ablaze.[17]

(11) Jesus said: This heaven will pass away, and the one above it will pass away; and those who are dead are not alive, and those who are living will not die. In the days when you ate of what is dead, you made of it what is living. When you come to be light, what will you do? On the day when you were one, you became two. But when you have become two, what will you do?[18]

(12) The disciples said to Jesus: We know that you will depart from us; who is it who will be great over us? Jesus said to them: Wherever you have come, you will go to James the Just, for whose sake heaven and earth came into being.[19]

(13) Jesus said to his disciples: Compare me, tell me whom I am like. Simon Peter said to him: You are like a righteous angel. Matthew said to him: (p. 35) You are like a wise philosopher. Thomas said to him: Master, my mouth is wholly incapable of saying whom you are like. Jesus said: I am not your master, for you have drunk, you have become drunk from the bubbling spring which I have caused to gush forth (?). And he took him, withdrew, (and) spoke to him three words. Now when Thomas came (back) to his companions, they asked him: What did Jesus say to you? Thomas said to them: If I tell you one of the words which he said to me, you will take up stones (and) throw them at me; and a fire will come out of the stones (and) burn you up.[20]

(14) Jesus said to them: If you fast, you will put a sin to your charge; and if you pray, you will be condemned; and if you give alms, you will do harm to your spirits. And if you go into any land and walk about in the regions, if they receive you, eat what is set before you; heal the sick among them. For what goes into your mouth will not defile you; but what comes out of your mouth, that is what will defile you.[21]

(15) Jesus said: When you see him who was not born of woman, fall down upon your faces and worship him; that one is your Father.[22]

(16) Jesus said: Perhaps men think that I am come to cast peace upon the world; and they do not know that I am come to cast dissensions upon the earth, fire, sword, war. For there will be five who (p. 36) are in a house: three shall be against two and two against three, the father against the son and the son against the father, and they shall stand as solitaries.[23]

(17) Jesus said: I will give you what no eye has seen and what no ear has heard and what no hand has touched and what has not entered into the heart of man.[24]

(18) The disciples said to Jesus: Tell us how our end will be. Jesus said: Since you have discovered the beginning, why do you seek the end? For where the beginning is, there will the end be. Blessed is he who shall stand at the beginning (in the beginning), and he shall know the end, and shall not taste death.[25]

(19) Jesus said: Blessed is he who was before he came into being. If you become disciples to me (and) listen to my words, these stones will minister to you. For you have five trees in Paradise which do not change, either in summer or in winter, and their leaves do not fall. He who knows them shall not taste of death.[26]

(20) The disciples said to Jesus: Tell us what the kingdom of heaven is like. He said to them: It is like a grain of mustard-seed, the smallest of all seeds; but when it falls on tilled ground, it puts forth a great branch and becomes shelter for the birds of heaven.[27]

(21) Mariham said to Jesus: Whom are your disciples like? He said: They are like (p. 37) little children who have settled in a field which does not belong to them. When the owners of the field come, they will say: Leave us our field. They are naked before them, in order to leave it to them and give them (back) their field. Therefore I say: If the master of the house knows that the thief is coming, he will keep watch before he comes, and will not let him dig through into his house of his kingdom to carry off his things. You, then, be watchful over against the world; gird your loins with great strength, that the robbers may find no way to come at you. For the advantage for which you look, they will find. May there be among you a man of understanding! When the fruit ripened, he came quickly, his sickle in his hand, and reaped it. He who has ears to hear, let him hear.[28]

(22) Jesus saw some infants who were being suckled. He said to his disciples: These infants being suckled are like those who enter the kingdom. They said to him: If we then become children, shall we enter the kingdom? Jesus said to them: When you make the two one, and when you make the inside as the outside, and the outside as the inside, and the upper as the lower, and when you make the male and the female into a single one, so that the male is not male and the female not female, and when you make eyes in place of an eye, and a hand in place of a hand, and a foot in place of a foot, an image in place of an image, then shall you enter [the kingdom].[29]

(p. 38)(23) Jesus said: I shall choose you, one out of a thousand and two out of ten thousand, and they shall stand as a single one.[30]

(24) His disciples said: Teach us about the place where you are, for it is necessary for us to seek it. He said to them: He who has ears, let him hear! There is light within a man of light, and he lights the whole world. If he does not shine, there is darkness.[31]

(25) Jesus said: Love your brother as your soul; watch over him like the apple of your eye.[32]

POx 1

(Verso) 11   *(Page number)*
                 (Lines 1-4)

(26) Jesus said: You see the mote
which is in your brother's eye; but
you do not see the beam which is in
your own eye.
When you cast out the beam from
your own eye, then you will see   and then you may see clearly
(clearly) to cast out the mote from   to pull out the mote
your brother's eye.[33]   that (is) in the eye
                                          of your brother

                                              (Lines 4-11)

(27) <Jesus> said: If you do not fast   Jesus says:
to the world, you will not find the   If you do not fast
kingdom; if you do not keep the   (as to) the world, you will not
Sabbath as Sabbath, you will not   find the kingdom
see the Father.[34]   of God, and if you do not
                                          keep the Sabbath as Sab-
                                          bath, you will not see the
                                          Father.
                                              (Lines 11-22)

(28) Jesus said: I stood in the midst   Jesus says: I stood (up)
of the world, and I appeared to them   in the midst of the world,
in the flesh. I found them all drunk;   and in the flesh I appeared
I found none among them thirsting,   to them and found them all
and my soul was afflicted for the   drunk, and
sons of men; for they are blind in   none found I a-
their heart, and they do not see that   thirst among them, and my
they came empty into the world,   soul is troubled (or: feels pain)
(and)empty they seek to leave the   for the sons of men,
world again. But now they are drunk.   because they are blind in their
When they have thrown off their   heart and do <not> see
wine, they will repent.[35]   . . . .[36]

(29) Jesus said: If the flesh came
into existence because of the spirit,
it is a marvel. But if the spirit (came
into existence) because of the body,
it is a marvel of marvels. But as for
me, I wonder at this, (p. 39) how

this great wealth made its home in this poverty.[37]

. . . . th>e poverty [38].

(Lines 23-36)

(30) Jesus said: Where there are three gods, they are gods; where there are two or one, I am with him.[39]

<Jesus sa>ys: <Wh>erever there are three gods, there> they are gods. And wh>ere o<ne> is alone with himself?>, I am with hi<m>. Li<f>t up the stone, and there you will find me; cleave the wood, and I am there.[40]

(31) Jesus said: No prophet is accepted in his own village, no doctor heals those who know him.[41]

Jesus says: A prophet is not acceptable in his own country, neither does a doctor work cures on those who know him.

(Lines 36-41)

(32) Jesus said: A city that is built on a high mountain and fortified cannot fall, nor can it be hidden.[42]

Jesus says: A city which is built on the top of a high <m>ountain and firmly stablished can neither fal-l> nor remain hid-d>en.

(Lines 41-43)

(33) Jesus said: What you hear with your ear (and) with the other ear, proclaim it on your roof-tops. For no one lights a lamp to set it under a bushel, or to put it in a hidden place; but he sets it on the lamp-stand, that all who go in and come out may see its light.[43]

Jesus says: <What> you hear i>n your o<ne e>ar, that

(34) Jesus said: If a blind man leads a blind man, they both fall into a pit.[44]

(35) Jesus said: It is not possible for anyone to go into the strong man's house (and) take it by force, unless he binds his hands; then will he plunder his house.[45]

POx 655

Fragment Ia

(36) Jesus said: Be not anxious from morning to evening and from evening to morning about what you shall put on.[46]

From early until <late nor> from eveni<ng> until> early neither <about food> for you, what you should eat nor> about c<lothing for you>, what you should pu>t on. Much bet>ter <are> you than <the li>lies which card not neither do they spin. And have no <garment> . . . . . . also.

Fragment Ib

you? Who can add to your age? He himself will give to you your garment.[47]

(37) His disciples said: On what day will you be revealed to us, and on what day shall we see you? Jesus said: When you unclothe yourselves and are not ashamed, and take your garments and lay them beneath your feet like the little children (and) trample on them, then [you will (p. 40) see] the Son of the Living One, and you will not be afraid.[48]

His disciples say to him: When will you be manifest to us and when shall we see you? He says: When you undress and are not ashamed . . . . [49]

(38) Jesus said: Many times have you desired to hear these words which I speak to you, and you have no other from whom to hear them. Days will come when you will seek me (and) you will not find me.[50]

(39) Jesus said: The Pharisees and the scribes have taken the keys of knowledge (and) have hidden them. They did not go in, and those who wished to go in they did not allow. But you, be wise as serpents and innocent as doves.[51]

they have <received the keys of <knowledge and have hid<den them, they themselves do <not> go in <and those who <wish to go> in <they have not al<lowed. But you, be wise as <serpents and without guile <as do- ves . . . . [52]

(40) Jesus said: A vine has been planted outside of the Father; and since it is not established, it will be plucked out with its roots (and) will perish.[53]

(41) Jesus said: He who has in his hand, to him shall be given; and he who has not, from him shall be taken even the little that he has.[54]

(42) Jesus said: Become passers-by![55]

(43) His disciples said to him: Who are you, that you say these things to us? <Jesus said to them:> From what I say to you, do you not know who I am? But you have become like the Jews; for they love the tree (and) hate its fruit, and they love the fruit (and) hate the tree.[56]

(44) Jesus said: He who blasphemes against the Father will be forgiven, and he who blasphemes against the Son will be forgiven; but he who blasphemes against the Holy Spirit will not be forgiven, either on earth or in heaven.[57]

(45) Jesus said: Grapes are not harvested from thorn-bushes, nor are figs gathered from hawthorns, [f]or they yield no fruit. (p. 41) [A go]od man brings forth good from his treasure; a bad man brings forth evil things from his evil treasure, which is in his heart, and he says evil things, for out of the abundance of his heart he brings forth evil things.[58]

(46) Jesus said: From Adam to John the Baptist there is among the children of women none higher than John the Baptist, for his eyes were not destroyed (?). But I have said: Whoever among you becomes small will know the kingdom and will be higher than John.[59]

(47) Jesus said: It is not possible for a man to ride two horses or stretch two bows; and it is not possible for a servant to serve two masters, unless he honours the one and insults the other. No one drinks old wine and immediately desires to drink new wine. And new wine is not poured into old wineskins, lest they burst; nor is old wine poured into a new wineskin, lest it spoil. An old patch is not sewn on a new garment, for a rent would result.[60]

(48) Jesus said: If two make peace with one another in this one house, they will say to the mountain: Be removed, and it will be removed.[61]

(49) Jesus said: Blessed are the solitary and the elect, for you will find the kingdom, for you came forth from it, (and) you will return to it again.[62]

(50) Jesus said: If they say to you: Whence have you come?, say to them: We have come from the light, the place where the light came into being of itself. It [established itself] (p. 42), and it revealed itself in their image. If they say to you: Who are you?, say: We are his sons, and we are the elect of the living Father. If they ask you: What is the sign of your Father in you?, say to them: It is movement and rest.[63]

(51) His disciples said to him: On what day will the rest of the dead come into being, and on what day will the new world come? He said to them: What you await has come, but you do not know it.[64]

(52) His disciples said to him: Twenty-four prophets spoke in Israel, and they all spoke of you. He said to them: You have abandoned the living one before your eyes, and spoken about the dead.[65]

(53) His disciples said to him: Is circumcision useful or not? He said to them: If it were useful, their father would beget them from their mother (already) circumcised. But the true circumcision in the Spirit has proved useful in every way.[66]

(54) Jesus said: Blessed are the poor, for yours is the kingdom of heaven.[67]

(55) Jesus said: He who does not hate his father and his mother cannot be a disciple to me. And (he who does not) hate his brothers and sisters and take up his cross like me, will not be worthy of me.[68]

(56) Jesus said: He who has known the world has found a corpse; and he who has found a corpse, the world is not worthy of him.[69]

(57) Jesus said: The kingdom of the Father is like a man who had [good] seed. His enemy came by night (p. 43) and sowed weeds among the good seed. The man did not allow them to pull up the weeds. He said to them: Lest you go to pull up the weeds, (and) pull up the wheat with it. For on the day of the harvest the weeds will be manifest; they will be pulled up and burned.[70]

(58) Jesus said: Blessed is the man who has suffered; he has found life.[71]

(59) Jesus said: Look upon the Living One so long as you live, that you may not die and seek to see him, and be unable to see him.[72]

(60) <They saw> a Samaritan carrying a lamb, who was going to Judaea. He said to his disciples: (What will) this man (do) with the lamb? They said to him: Kill it and eat it. He said to them: While it is alive he will not eat it, but (only) when he kills it (and) it becomes a corpse. They said to him: Otherwise he cannot do it. He said to them: You also, seek a place for yourselves in rest, that you may not become a corpse and be eaten.[73]

(61) Jesus said: Two will rest upon a bed; one will die, the other live. Salome said: Who are you, man, whose son? You have mounted my bed and eaten from my table. Jesus said to her: I am he who comes forth from the one who is equal; I was given of the things of my Father. <Salome said:> I am your disciple. <Jesus said to her:> Therefore I say: If he is equal, he is full of light; but if he is divided, he will be full of darkness.[74]

(62) Jesus said: I speak my mysteries to those [who are worthy (p. 44) of my] mysteries. What your right hand does, let not your left hand know what it does.[75]

(63) Jesus said: There was a rich man who had many possessions. He said: I will use my possessions to sow and reap and plant, to fill my barns with fruit, that I may have need of nothing. These were his thoughts in his heart; and in that night he died. He who has ears, let him hear.[76]

(64) Jesus said: A man had guests; and when he had prepared the dinner, he sent his servant to invite the guests. He went to the first, and said to him:

My master invites you. He said: I have money with some merchants; they are coming to me this evening. I will go and give them my orders. I ask to be excused from the dinner. He went to another (and) said to him: My master has invited you. He said to him: I have bought a house, and I am asked for a day. I shall not have time. He went to another (and) said to him: My master invites you. He said to him: My friend is about to be married, and I am to arrange the dinner. I shall not be able to come. I ask to be excused from the dinner. He went to another, he said to him: My master invites you. He said to him: I have bought a farm; I am going to collect the rent. I shall not be able to come. I ask to be excused. The servant came back (and) said to his master: Those whom you invited to the dinner have asked to be excused. The master said to his servant: Go out to the roads, bring those whom you find, that they may dine. Traders and merchants [shall] not [enter] the places of my Father.[77]

(p. 45)(65) He said: A good man had a vineyard; he leased it to tenants, that they might work in it (and) he receive the fruits from them. He sent his servant, that the tenants might give him the fruits of the vineyard. They seized his servant, beat him, (and) all but killed him. The servant went away (and) told his master. His master said: Perhaps <they> did not know <him>. He sent another servant; the tenants beat the other also. Then the master sent his son. He said: Perhaps they will have respect for my son. Those tenants, since they knew that he was the heir of the vineyard, they seized him and killed him. He who has ears, let him hear.[78]

(66) Jesus said: Show me the stone which the builders rejected; it is the cornerstone.[79]

(67) Jesus said: He who knows the all, (but) fails (to know) himself, misses everything.[80]

(68) Jesus said: Blessed are you when you are hated and persecuted, and they will find no place where you have been persecuted.[81]

(69) Jesus said: Blessed are those who have been persecuted in their heart; these are they who have known the Father in truth. Blessed are the hungry, for the belly of him who desires will be filled.[82]

(70) Jesus said: If you have gained this within you, what you have will save you. If you do not have this in [you], what you do not have in you [will] kill you.

(71) Jesus said: I will des[troy this] house, and none shall be able to build it [again].[83]

(p. 46) (72) [A man said] to him: Speak to my brothers, that they may divide my father's possessions with me. He said to him: O man, who made me a divider? He turned to his disciples. He said to them: I am not a divider, am I?[84]

(73) Jesus said: The harvest is indeed great, but the labourers are few. But pray the Lord, that he send forth labourers into the harvest.[85]

(74) He said: Lord, there are many about the well, but no one in the well.[86]

(75) Jesus said: There are many standing at the door, but it is the solitary who will enter the bridal chamber.

(76) Jesus said: The kingdom of the Father is like a merchant who had a load (of goods) and found a pearl. That merchant was wise. He sold the load and bought for himself the pearl alone. You also, seek after his treasure which does not fail (but) endures, where moth does not come near to devour nor worm to destroy.[87]

(77) Jesus said: I am the light that is above them all. I am the all; the all came forth from me, and the all attained to me. Cleave a (piece of) wood, I am there. Raise up a stone, and you will find me there.[88]

(78) Jesus said: Why did you come out into the field? To see a reed shaken by the wind? And to see a man clothed in soft raiment? [Look, your] kings and your great men, (p. 47) these are the ones who wear soft clothing, and they [will] not be able to know the truth.[89]

(79) A woman in the crowd said to him: Blessed is the womb which bore you, and the breasts which nourished you. He said to [her]: Blessed are those who have heard the word of the Father (and) have kept it in truth. For there will be days when you will say: Blessed is the womb which has not conceived, and the breasts which have not given suck.[90]

(80) Jesus said: He who has known the world has found the body; and he who has found the body, the world is not worthy of him.

(81) Jesus said: He who has become rich, let him become king, and he who has power, let him renounce (it).[91]

(82) Jesus said: He who is near to me is near the fire, and he who is far from me is far from the kingdom.[92]

(83) Jesus said: The images are revealed to man, and the light which is in them is hidden in the image of the light of the Father. He will reveal himself, and his image is hidden by his light.[93]

(84) Jesus said: When you see your likeness, you rejoice. But when you see your images which came into existence before you, which neither die nor are made manifest, how much will you bear?

(85) Adam came into being out of a great power and a great wealth, and he was not worthy of you; for if he had been worthy, [he would] not [have tasted] of death.[94]

(86) Jesus said: [The foxes] (p. 48) [have] the[ir holes] and the birds have [their] nest, but the Son of Man has no place to lay his head and rest.[95]

(87) Jesus said: Wretched is the body which depends on a body, and wretched is the soul which depends on these two.[96]

(88) Jesus said: The angels and the prophets will come to you, and they will give you what is yours. You also, give them what is in your hands, and say to yourselves: On what day will they come to take what is theirs?[97]

(89) Jesus said: Why do you wash the outside of the cup? Do you not understand that he who made the inside is also he who made the outside?[98]

(90) Jesus said: Come to me, for my yoke is easy and my lordship is gentle, and you will find rest for yourselves.[99]

(91) They said to him: Tell us who you are, that we may believe in you. He said to them: You test the face of the sky and of the earth, and him who is before you you have not known, and you do not know (how) to test this moment[100]

(92) Jesus said: Seek, and you will find; but the things you asked me in those days and I did not tell you then, now I desire to tell them, but you do not ask about them.[101]

(93) <Jesus said:> Do not give what is holy to the dogs, lest they cast it on the dung-heap. Do not cast the pearls to the swine, lest they make it [. . .].[102]

(94) Jesus [said:] He who seeks will find, [and he who knocks], to him will be opened.[103]

(95) [Jesus said:] If you have money, (p. 49) do not lend at interest, but give [. . .] to him from whom you will not receive it back.[104]

(96) Jesus [said:] The kingdom of the Father is like a woman. She took a little leaven, [hid] it in dough, (and) made large loaves of it. He who has ears, let him hear.[105]

(97) Jesus said: The kingdom of the [Father] is like a woman carrying a jar full of meal. While she was walking [on a] distant road, the handle of the jar broke (and) the meal poured out behind her on the road. She was unaware, she had not noticed the misfortune. When she came to her house, she put the jar down (and) found it empty.

(98) Jesus said: The kingdom of the Father is like a man who wanted to kill a powerful man. He drew the sword in his house and drove it into the wall, that he might know that his hand would be strong (enough). Then he slew the powerful man.

(99) The disciples said to him: Your brothers and your mother are standing outside. He said to them: Those here who do the will of my Father, these are my brothers and my mother; they are the ones who will enter into the kingdom of my Father.[106]

(100) They showed Jesus a gold piece and said to him: Caesar's men demand tribute from us. He said to them: What belongs to Caesar, give to Caesar; what belongs to God, give to God; and what is mine, give it to me.[107]

(101) <Jesus said:> He who does not hate his father and his mother like me cannot be a [disciple] to me. And he who does [not] love [his father] and his mother like me cannot be a [disciple] to me. For my mother [. . .] (p. 50), but [my] true [mother] gave me life.[108]

(102) Jesus said: Woe to the Pharisees, for they are like a dog lying in the manger of the cattle; for he neither eats not does he let the cattle eat.[109]

(103) Jesus said: Blessed is the man who knows [in which] part (of the night) the robbers are coming, that he may rise and gather his [...] and gird up his loins before they come in.[110]

(104) They said [to him]: Come, let us pray today and fast. Jesus said: What then is the sin that I have done, or in what have I been overcome? But when the bridegroom comes out from the bridal chamber, then let them fast and pray.[111]

(105) Jesus said: He who knows father and mother will be called the son of a harlot.[112]

(106) Jesus said: When you make the two one, you will become sons of man, and when you say: Mountain, move away, it will move away.[113]

(107) Jesus said: The kingdom is like a shepherd who had a hundred sheep; one of them, the biggest, went astray; he left (the) ninety-nine (and) sought after the one until he found it. After he had laboured, he said to the sheep: I love you more than the ninety-nine.[114]

(108) Jesus said: He who drinks from my mouth will become like me, and I will become like him, and the hidden things will be revealed to him.[115]

(109) Jesus said: The kingdom is like a man who had in his field a [hidden] treasure, of which he knew nothing. And [after] he died he left it to his [son. The] son also did not know; he took (p.51) the field and sold it. The man who bought it came (and) as he was ploughing [found] the treasure. He began to lend money at interest to whomever he wished.[116]

(110) Jesus said: He who has found the world (and) become rich, let him renounce the world.

(111) Jesus said: The heavens will be rolled up and likewise the earth in your presence, and the living one, (come forth) from the Living One, will not see death or <fear>, because Jesus says: He who finds himself, of him the world is not worthy.[117]

(112) Jesus said: Woe to the flesh that depends on the soul; woe to the soul that depends on the flesh.[118]

(113) His disciples said to him: On what day will the kingdom come? <Jesus said:> It will not come while people watch for it; they will not say: Look, here it is, or: Look, there it is; but the kingdom of the father is spread out over the earth, and men do not see it.[119]

(114) Simon Peter said to them: Let Mariham go out from among us, for women are not worthy of the life. Jesus said: Look, I will lead her that I may make her male, in order that she too may become a living spirit resembling you males. For every woman who makes herself male will enter into the kingdom of heaven.[120]

The Gospel according to Thomas

Notes

III. The Coptic Gospel of Thomas

Translation

1. Cf. H.-Ch. Puech in NTApo³ I, 285-286.

2. POx 654, 1 and 655 are presented here in translation, without noting all the possible restorations of the lacunae. On the papyri, cf. J.A. Fitzmyer, 'The Oxyrhynchus Logoi of Jesus and the Coptic Gospel according to Thomas', in TS 20, 1959, 505-560; R.A. Kraft, 'Oxyrhynchus Papyrus 655 Reconsidered', in HTR 54, 1961, 253-262. In line 3 the extant text has 'and Thomas'; but it is probably to be restored: '(who) also [sc. is called] Thomas'; in Greek: ὁ καὶ Θωμᾶς).

3. Cf. Jn. 8:51; log. 18; log. 19. J.E. Ménard, op. cit. pp. 77ff. For the knowledge of this logion in Manicheism, cf. Augustine, c. Epist. Fundament. 11; c. Felicem I 1; Turfan fragment T II D II 134, SPAW 1934, 856.

4. Cf. Clem. Alex. Strom. II 9.45.5; V 14.96.3. Clement in the first passage assigns the saying to the Gospel of the Hebrews (cf. below, p. 136). Cf. also Pistis Sophia c. 100, p. 161.24ff. and c. 102, p. 164.23ff. (Schmidt-Till; chapter-numbers are the same in Schmidt-MacDermot, but the page-numbers there are those of Schmidt's Coptic text, and therefore differ); Act. Thom. c. 136 (Aa II 2, 243.8-10). Cf. Mt. 7:7-8 (Lk. 11:9-10).

5. Cf. Lk. 17:21b. - Mt. 5:45.

6. The Greek text is very fragmentary. However with the aid of the Coptic text the lacunae can to some extent be restored. Cf. Fitzmyer, op. cit. pp. 519ff.

7. Cf. Mt. 11:25 par. - Mk. 10:31 par. - Manich. Psalm-Book 192.2-3 Allberry, Hippolytus (Ref. V 7.20, Marcovich 147.103ff.) probably had this logion before him as a text from the Gospel of Thomas, although in a somewhat different version.

8. Restoration of lines 26f. does not necessarily have to follow the Gospel of Thomas. Also possible is: 'and they will attain to life' (cf. Mk. 10:30f.).

9. Cf. Mk.. 4:22 par. (see Huck-Greeven, Synopsis of the First Three Gospels, ¹³1981, p. 92. Reference is made to the Synopsis in the following notes when the abundant material in Greeven yields information for the connection of the Gospel of Thomas with the Gospel tradition). Manich. Kephalaia LXV, vol. I, 163.28f. Schmidt-Böhlig.

10. The restoration of line 31 is uncertain, but very natural. In the Coptic the last element of the saying is missing. Cf. Fitzmyer, op. cit. pp. 525f.

11. In the papyrus the logion is too badly preserved to be restored with any certainty. However,it is clear from the little that remains that we have here a tradition parallel to logion 6. Cf. Fitzmyer, op. cit. pp. 527ff.

12.-Cf.Mt.6:1 18(Huck-Greeven,pp.35ff.);Eph.4:25(Col.3:9);Mk.4:22par.(Huck-Greeven, p.92).

13. Cf. J.E. Ménard, L'Évangile selon Philippe, 1967, pp. 179, 211. B. Gaertner, The Theology of the Gospel of Thomas, pp. 163ff. R.M. Grant, 'Two Notes on the Gospel of Thomas', in Vig.Chr. 13, 1959, 170-180.

14. Only a few letters survive from this part of the papyrus, and only in line 40 can they be restored as two words. Whether the Greek version of log. 7 stood here cannot be proved, but merely conjectured. Fitzmyer (p. 528) restores: 'Ha]ppy is [he who does not do these things. For all] will be mani[fest before the Father who] is [in heaven].' He thus assumes a version different from the Coptic text.

15. Cf. Mt. 13:47-50. C.H. Hunzinger, 'Außersynoptisches Traditionsgut im Thomas-Evangelium', ThLZ 85,1960, cols. 843-846. On the 'awakening formula' at the end of the logion cf. Mk. 4:9 par.; Rev. 2:7; 13:1; Hippol. Ref. V 8.29; VIII 9.1; above, p. 116, note 35.

16. Cf. Mk. 4:3-9 par; Hippol., Ref. V 8.29; VIII 9.1. Ménard, NHS V, 91ff.

17. Cf. Lk. 12:49. Manich. Kephalaia I, p. 5.3; XXXVIII, p. 102.32ff. Polotsky-Böhlig.

18. Cf. Mk. 13:31 par; Hippol. *Ref.* V 8.32 (on which see E.-M. Cornelis, 'Quelques éléments pour une comparaison entre l'Évangile selon Thomas et la Notice d'Hippolyte sur les Naassènes', *Vig.Chr.* 15, 1961, 83-104). Manich. Kephalaia I, XVI, p. 54.23f. Polotsky-Böhlig. Turfan fragment M 2: Henning-Andreas, 'Mitteliranische Manichaica aus Chinesisch-Turkestan III', SPAW 1934, 850.

19. Cf. Mk. 9:33-37 par. (Huck-Greeven, pp. 141f.). On James the Just see below,pp.473ff.

20. Cf. Mk. 8:27-30 par. Mt. 23:8; Jn. 13:13; Jn. 4:10ff; Acta Thomae c. 37; 39; 147.

21. Cf. Mt. 6:1-6, 16-18; Lk. 10:8; Mk. 7:18f. par; Pistis Sophia c. 111, 182.5ff. Schmidt-Till.

22. Cf. Clem. Alex. *Exc. ex Theod.* 68; R.M. Grant, 'The Mystery of Marriage in the Gospel of Philip', *Vig.Chr.* 15, 1961, 134ff.

23. Cf. Mt. 10:34-36; Lk. 12:49-53.

24. Cf. 1 Cor. 2:9 (Testament of Jacob?; see H. Koester in HTR 73, 1980, 115). Turfan fragment M 789, in APAW 1904, II; 68.

25. Cf. Clem. Alex. *Exc. ex Theod.* 78.2. Plotinus, *Enn.* II 2.3; V 1.3, 7; 3.5, 7, 17; 5.47,8.

26. Cf. Iren. *Epideixis* c. 43; Resch, *Agrapha*², pp. 285f. 2 Book of Jeu c. 50, p.316.22f. Schmidt-Till. H.Ch. Puech, *Le manichéisme. Son fondateur. Sa doctrine*, Paris 1949, pp. 159, note 285. Mk. 9:1 par.

27. Cf. Mk. 4:30-32 par.

28. Cf. Lk. 12:39f. par. (Huck-Greeven, p. 160); Mk. 13:33ff. par; Pistis Sophia c. 120, 200.32ff. Schmidt-Till. Mk. 4:29.

29. Cf. Mk. 10:13-16 par. (Huck-Greeven, p. 178). Mt. 18:3 (Huck-Greeven, p. 143). On the parallels in the tradition of the Gospel of the Egyptians (2 Clement, Acts of Philip, etc.) see below, pp. 212f.

30. Cf. Pistis Sophia c. 134, p.229.21 Schmidt-Till. Irenaeus, *adv.Haer.* I 24.6; Epiphanius, *Pan.* 24.5.4.

31. Cf. Mt. 6:22f. par. (Huck-Greeven, p. 38); Jn. 7:34ff. Cf. also log. 2; log. 77.

32. Cf. Mk. 12:31 par.

33. Cf. Mt. 7:3-5 par.

34. Cf. Clem. Alex. *Strom.* III 15.99.4; Justin, *Dial.* 12.3; Baker, JBL 84, 1965, 291ff. Jn.14:9.

35. Cf. Ménard, *op. cit.* pp. 121ff.

36. Fitzmyer (*op. cit.* pp. 536ff.) assumes a lacuna of sixteen lines between the two fragments verso 11-22 and recto 23.

37. Cf. log. 87; log. 112.

38. A restoration of the Greek text, of which only one word survives, is not possible, even though it is to be assumed that here a version parallel to logion 29 was handed down.

39. Cf. Mt. 18:20; Clem. Alex. *Strom.* III 68.1ff; Ménard, *op. cit.* p. 126.

40. The second part of this saying is transmitted as logion 77 in the Coptic Gospel of Thomas. This - and also the deviations of the two versions from one another in the first part - proves that the Coptic version cannot be a direct translation of a Greek version such as is handed down in POx 1 (see above, p. 111 and Fitzmyer, *op. cit.* pp. 538ff.).

41. Cf. Mk. 6:4 par. (Huck-Greeven, p. 105); Jn. 4:44.

42. Cf. Mt. 5:14.

43. Cf. Mt. 10:27 par. Mk. 4:21 par. (Huck-Greeven, pp. 91f.).

44. Cf. Lk. 6:39 par. (Huck-Greeven, p. 74). Ménard, *op. cit.* pp. 133f.

45. Cf. Mk. 3:27 par.

46. Cf. Mt, 6:25ff. par.

47. In this logion too the differences between the Greek and the Coptic text show that we have to do with different versions. The reading long accepted in line 9 (αὐξάνει) has been put right by several scholars: οὐ ξαίνει (ξαίνειν = to card, a technical term in wool manufacture). Cf. T.F. Glasson, JTS 13, 1962, 331f.; R. Merkelbach, ZPE 54, 1984, 64.

48. Cf. Jn. 14:22; 1 Jn. 3:2. Log. 22. Clem. Alex. *Strom.* III 91ff.; 2 Clem. 12.1-2; on this passage, belonging to the Gospel of the Egyptians, see below, pp. 210f. Mt. 16:16.

49. In POx 655 there follow eleven or twelve lines, of which however only one or two letters survive in each case. Fitzmyer (*op. cit.* pp. 548ff.) has attempted to fill the gaps on the basis of the Coptic text.

50. Cf. Mt. 13:16f. par.; Mk. 2:20 par.; Lk. 17:22; Jn. 7:33ff.; 13:33. On the first part of the logion cf. Puech in NTApo³ I, 301, who refers to Iren. *adv. Haer.* I 20.2 and other parallels.

51. Cf. Lk. 11:52; Mt. 23:13 (Huck-Greeven, pp. 214; 157). Mt. 10:16.

52. This section too is badly preserved, but can to some extent be restored on the basis of the Coptic text. Cf. Fitzmyer, *op. cit.* pp. 550f.

53. Cf. Mt. 15:13. Ménard, *op. cit.* p. 142.

54. Cf. Mk. 4:25 par. (Huck-Greeven, pp. 92f.).

55. Cf. J. Jeremias, *Unknown Sayings of Jesus,* ²1964, pp. 111ff.

56. Cf. Jn. 8:25. Lk. 6:43f. par. (Huck-Greeven, pp. 75f.).

57. Cf. Mk. 3:28 par.

58. Cf. Lk. 6:44ff. par. (Huck-Greeven, p. 75f.).

59. Cf. Mt. 11:11; Lk. 7:28. Macarius, *Hom.* 29, p.234.67ff. Dörries-Kröger (PTS 4).

60. Cf. Mt. 6:24; Lk. 16:13. Mk. 2:21f. par. G. Quispel, *Vig.Chr.* 13, 1959, 91; E. Haenchen, *Die Botschaft des Thomasevangeliums,* 1961, p. 51, note 53. Manich. Psalm-book 223.2ff. Allberry.

61. Cf. Mk. 11:23 par. (Huck-Greeven, p. 198). H. Achelis-J. Flemming, *Die syrische Didascalia* (TU XXV 2), 1904, p. 345.

62. Cf. log. 4; log. 16; log. 23; log. 50; log. 75. M. Harl in REG 73, 1960, 464-474.

63. Cf. Irenaeus, *adv. Haer.* I 21.5; Epiphanius, *Pan.* 36.3.2-6.

64. Cf. Mk. 9:13 par.; Lk. 21:7; Mt. 17:11f. P. Vielhauer, 'ΑΝΑΠΑΥΣΙΣ. Zum gnostischen Hintergrund des Thomasevangeliums' (1964), in id. *Aufsätze zum NT,* 1965, pp. 215-234.

65. Cf. Lk. 24: 5; Jn. 5:39f.; 8:53. Puech in NTApo³ I, 302.

66. Cf. Rom. 2:25, 29; 3:1.

67. Cf. Lk. 6:20 par.

68. Cf. Mt. 10:37f. par.

69. Cf. Manich. Psalm-book 63.22ff. Allberry.

70. Cf. Mt. 13:24-30. Epiphanius, *Pan.* 66.65. Waldschmidt-Lentz, 'Die Stellung Jesu im Manichäismus', APAW, hist.-phil. Klasse 4, 1926, 27f.; Clem. Alex. *Exc. ex Theod.* 53.

71. Cf. Barn. 7.11 (on which see H. Windisch in HdbNT Ergbd., 1920, p. 347); K. Wengst in *Schriften des Urchristentums* 1984, p. 199 note 128.

72. Cf. Jn. 8:21.

73. Cf. Manich. Psalm-book 172.15ff. Allberry.

74. Cf. Lk. 17:34. For the role of Salome, cf. Gospel of the Egyptians (below, pp.209ff.); Pistis Sophia c. 54,p. 65.30ff.; c. 58, p.73.27ff. Schmidt-Till, and other passages. Mt.11:27par.

75. Cf. Mt. 6:3. Second Book of Jeu c. 43, p. 305.1ff. Schmidt-Till.

76. Cf. Lk. 12:16-21.

77. Cf. Lk. 14:16-24 par.

78. Cf. Mk. 12:1-12 par. (Huck-Greeven, pp. 202f.).

79. Cf. Ps. 118:22; Mk. 12:10 par.

80. Cf. Mk. 8:36 par. Log. 2.

81. Cf. Mt. 5:11 par (Huck-Greeven, p. 30). Log. 69.

82. Cf. Mt. 5:8, 10 par.; Mt. 5:6 par. (Huck-Greeven, p. 30).

83. Cf. Mk. 14:58 par.; Mk. 15:29 par.; Jn. 2:19.

84. Cf. Lk. 12:13f.

85. Cf. Mt. 9:37 par. (Huck-Greeven, p. 107).

86. Cf. Origen, *c. Cels.* VIII 15f.

87. Cf. Mt. 13:45f.; Mt. 6:20 par.; J.-E. Ménard, *op. cit.* pp. 176f.

88. Cf. Jn. 8:12. Clem. Alex. *Exc. ex Theod.* 35.1. In POx 1 the second part of logion 77 is attached to logion 30; see above, p. 122.

89. Cf. Mt. 11:7f. par.

90. Cf. Lk. 11:27f.; Lk. 23:29. Mt. 24:19 par.

91. Cf. log. 110; log. 111.

92. Cf. Mk. 12:34; Lk. 12:49; Mt. 3:11. J. Jeremias, *Unwritten Sayings of Jesus*, [2]1964, pp. 66ff.

93. Cf. Paraphrase of Shem, NHC VII 1, p. 1ff. Three Steles of Seth, NHC VII 5, p.118ff. Irenaeus, *adv. Haer.* I 5. Acts of John 26-29, pp. 117.1-118.19 Junod-Kaestli.

94. Cf. J.-E. Ménard, *op. cit.* pp. 186f.

95. Cf. Mt. 8:20 par.

96. Cf. log. 29; log. 112.

97. Cf. Mt. 16:27 par. (Huck-Greeven, p. 134). Origen, *In Joh.* XIII 49, §324. S. Giet, *L'énigme de la Didaché*, Paris 1970, p. 227.

98. Cf. Mt. 23:25f. par.; Acta Archelai 24.2, p. 35.38ff. Beeson. A. Baker, JTS 16, 1965, 449-454.

99. Cf. Mt. 11:28-30. Vielhauer, ΑΝΑΠΑΥΣΙΣ, pp. 225ff.

100. Cf. Mt. 16:1-3 par. (Huck-Greeven, p. 126). Log. 5.

101. Cf. Mt. 7:7 par. Irenaeus, *adv. Haer.* II 13.10; II 30.2.

102. Cf. Mt. 7:6. Hippol. *Ref.* V 8.33; IX 17.1. Clem. Alex. *Strom.* I 12.55.3.

103. Cf. Mt. 7:7 par. Log. 2; log. 92. Pistis Sophia c. 83, p. 119.5ff.; c. 133, p. 227.25ff. Schmidt-Till.

104. Cf. Mt. 5:42 par. Liber Graduum, cols. 305.5-7; 325. 21-22.

105. Cf. Mt. 13:13 par. Iren. *adv. Haer.* I 8.3. Hippol. *Ref.* V 8.8.

106. Cf. Mk. 3:31-35 par. (Huck-Greeven, p. 85).

107. Cf. Mk. 12:13-17 par. (Huck-Greeven, pp. 205ff.). J.E. Ménard, *op. cit.* p. 200.

108. Cf. Mt. 10:37-39 par.; Mt. 16:24 par. (Huck-Greeven, pp. 130ff.). Log. 55.

109. Cf. Mt. 23:13ff. par. (Huck-Greeven, pp. 214f.). G. Moravcsik, 'Hunde in der Krippe. Zur Geschichte eines griechischen Sprichwortes', *Act. Ant.* 12, 1964, 77-86.

110. Cf. Lk. 12:35ff. par. (Huck-Greeven, p. 160).

111. Cf. Mt. 9:14f. par. Log. 6; log. 14.

112. Cf. Origen, *c. Cels.* I 28. Liber Graduum, col. 660.10

113. Cf. log. 22; log. 48. Mt. 21:20ff. par. (Huck-Greeven, pp. 197ff.).

114. Cf. Mt. 18:12-14 par. Iren. *adv. Haer.* I 8.4.

115. Cf. Jn. 7:37. Log. 13.

116. Cf. Mt. 13:44.

117. Cf. Isa. 34:4. Log. 2; log. 56.

118. Cf. log. 87.

119. Cf. Lk. 17:20-21; Lk. 17:23 par. Log. 3; log. 51.

120. Cf. log. 22. Clem. Alex. *Exc. ex Theod.* 21.2f.; H.-Ch. Puech in NTApo[3] I, 303; 343.

IV. Jewish-Christian Gospels

Philipp Vielhauer † and Georg Strecker

Literature: E. Amman, *Dictionnaire de la Bible*, Suppl. 1, 1926, pp. 470-475. F. Amiot, *La Bible apocryphe, Evangiles apocryphes*, 1975. G. Bardy, 'Saint Jérôme et l'évangile selon les Hébreux', *Mélanges de science religieuse* 3, 1946, 5ff. (= Bardy, 'Jérôme'). J.B. Bauer, 'Die Entstehung apokrypher Evangelien', BiLit 38, 1964, 268-271; id. *Die neutestamentlichen Apokryphen*, 1968. W. Bauer, *Das Leben Jesu im Zeitalter der neutestamentlichen Apokryphen*, 1909; id. Art. 'Ebionitenevangelium', RGG ²II, 6; id. Art. 'Hebräerevangelium', RGG ²II, 1674; id. Art. 'Nazaräerevangelium', RGG ²IV, 473; id. *Rechtgläubigkeit und Ketzerei im ältesten Christentum*, BHTh 10, ²1964 (ET *Orthodoxy and Heresy in Earliest Christianity*, 1971; = Bauer, *Orthodoxy*). D.A. Bertrand, 'L'Évangile des Ébionites. Une harmonie évangélique antérieure au Diatessaron', NTS 26, 1980, 548-563 (= Bertrand, 'Ebionites'). B. Bischoff, 'Wendepunkt in der Geschichte der lateinischen Exegese im Frühmittelalter', *Sacris erudiri* 6, 1954, 189-281 (= Bischoff, 'Wendepunkte'). S.G.F. Brandon, *The Fall of Jerusalem and the Christian Church*, 1951. S.P. Brock, 'A New Testimonium to the 'Gospel according to the Hebrews'', NTS 18, 1971, 220-222 (= Brock, 'Testimonium'). E.A.W. Budge, *Miscellaneous Coptic Texts in the Dialect of Upper Egypt*, 1915 (= Budge, *Texts*). J.B. Colon, *Dictionnaire de la Bible*, Suppl. 4, 1949, 1298-1315. O. Cullmann, 'The Significance of the Qumran Texts for Research into the Beginnings of Christianity', JBL 74, 1955, 213-225; id. Art. 'Ebionitenevangelium', RGG ³III, 298; id. 'Die neuentdeckten Qumrantexte und das Judenchristentum der Pseudoklementinen', BZNW 21, 1954, 35-51. M. Dibelius, *Geschichte der urchristlichen Literatur*, TB 58, ²1975 (= Dibelius, *Geschichte; ET A Fresh Approach to the NT and Early Christian Literature*, London 1937). J.A. Fitzmyer, 'The Qumran Scrolls, the Ebionites and Their Literature', in *The Scrolls and the New Testament*, ed. K. Stendahl, 1957, pp. 208-231. L. Goppelt, *Christentum und Judentum im ersten und zweiten Jahrhundert*, 1954. J. Jeremias/O. Hofius, *Unbekannte Jesusworte*, ³1963 (ET *Unknown Sayings of Jesus*, ²1964; = Jeremias, *Sayings*). E. Klostermann, *Apocrypha II: Evangelien*, KlT 8, ²1910 (= Klostermann, *Apocrypha*). E. Lohse, Art. 'Nazaräerevangelium', RGG ³IV, 1385f. W. Michaelis, *Die apokryphen Schriften zum NT*, 1956 (= Michaelis, *Schriften*). E. Preuschen, *Antilegomena*, ²1905. A. de Santos Otero, *Los Evangelios Apocrifos*, BAC 148, ⁶1988 (= de Santos, *Evangelios*). A. Schmidtke, *Neue Fragmente und Untersuchungen zu den judenchristlichen Evangelien*, TU 37.1, 1911 (= Schmidtke, *Fragmente*); id. 'Zum Hebräerevangelium', ZNW 35, 1936, 24-44 (= Schmidtke, 'Hebräerevangelium'). W. Schneemelcher, 'Bemerkungen zum Kirchenbegriff der apokryphen Evangelien', *Ges.Aufs.* 1974, 139-153. H.J. Schoeps, *Theologie und Geschichte des Judenchristentums*, 1949 (= Schoeps, *Judenchristentum*); id. *Aus frühchristlicher Zeit*, 1950; id. *Urgemeinde, Judenchristentum, Gnosis*, 1956; id. 'Die ebionitische Wahrheit des Christentums', in *The Background of the NT and its Eschatology* (FS C.H. Dodd), 1956, pp. 115-123. G. Strecker, Art. 'Ebioniten', RAC IV,

487-500 (= Strecker, 'Ebioniten'); id. 'Zum Problem des Judenchristentums' Appendix I to W. Bauer, *Rechtgläubigkeit und Ketzerei [BHTh 10]*, ²1964, pp. 245-287 (ET *Orthodoxy and Heresy*, 1971, pp. 241-285); id. *Das Judenchristentum in den Pseudoklementinen*, TU 70, ²1981 (= Strecker, *Judenchristentum*). H.W. Surkau, Art. 'Hebräerevangelium', RGG ³II, 109. P. Vielhauer, 'Judenchristliche Evangelien', NTApo⁴ I, 1968, 75-108 (ET 117-165); id. *Geschichte der urchristlichen Literatur* 1975 = reprint 1978 (= Vielhauer, *Geschichte*). H. Waitz, 'Das Evangelium der zwölf Apostel (Ebionitenevangelium)' I, ZNW 13, 1912, 338-348; II, ZNW 14, 1913, 38-64; III, ZNW 14, 1913, 117-132 (= Waitz, Evangelium); id./E. Hennecke *et al.*, 'Evangelien. Außerbiblisches über Jesus', NTApo², 1924, pp. 1-110 (= Waitz, 'Evangelien'); id. 'Neue Untersuchungen uber die sogenannten judenchristlichen Evangelien', ZNW 36, 1937, 60-81 (= Waitz, 'Untersuchungen'). R.McL. Wilson, Art. 'Apokryphen II 6.4: Judenchristliche Evangelien', TRE III, 327-330 (= Wilson, 'Evangelien').

Abbreviations: JG = Jewish-Christian gospels; GE = Gospel of the Ebionites; GH = Gospel of the Hebrews; GN = Gospel of the Nazaraeans.

Introduction: The Testimonies of the Early Church regarding Jewish-Christian Gospels

In the second edition of this work H. Waitz rightly described the problem of the Jewish-Christian Gospels (JG) as one of the most difficult which the apocryphal literature presents, 'difficult because of the scantiness and indefiniteness of the patristic testimonies, difficult also because the results of scientific investigation are often self-contradictory' (p. 10). There are preserved, mostly as citations in the Church Fathers, only small fragments from which conclusions as to the character of the whole book are difficult to draw, and also accounts which are in themselves often very vague and in their entirety make possible a whole kaleidoscope of interpretations. The Church Fathers hand down the title of only one JG, that of the Gospel of the Hebrews (GH). On the basis of their accounts it is possible to see in this GH either with Jerome the Gospel of the Nazaraeans (GN) or with Epiphanius that of the Ebionites (GE) or with Eusebius an independent entity and so to distinguish it from each of these. A problem in itself is the relationship of a 'Gospel of the Twelve (Apostles)' - it is mentioned by Origen and identified by Jerome with the GH - to these or to one of these JG (on this see below, p. 166). Thus the number of the JG - whether there be one, two or three such gospels - is uncertain, the identification of the several fragments is also uncertain and, finally, the character and the relationship to one another of the several JG is uncertain.

Reflecting these uncertainties, investigation has led to numerous hypotheses but to no generally recognised result. Information about its position, which until now has not changed, is given in an article by Waitz 'Untersuchungen'. The older view that there was only one JG or two adaptations of this JG has been abandoned, and now two theories are in competition, of which the one distinguishes two and the other three JG. The first of these, which depends upon some degree of confidence in the accounts of Jerome, distinguishes the Gospel of the Hebrews (= the Gospel of the Nazaraeans) and the Gospel of the Ebionites (= the Gospel of the Twelve Apostles)[1] - so, e.g., Klostermann; the other considers that the Gospel of the Nazaraeans,[2] the Gospel of the Hebrews and the Gospel of the Ebionites are different entities - so, with differences in detail, Waitz, Dibelius and Bauer. Schmidtke's identification of the Gospel of the Ebionites with the Gospel of the Hebrews has met with violent rejection.

It seems to me that the assumption of three JG most easily does justice to the texts and accounts and their uncertainties. But as regards the state of the sources the statement of Dibelius cannot be firmly enough underlined: 'Enlightenment is to be expected not from new hypotheses but only from new discoveries' (*Geschichte der urchristlichen Literatur* I, 1926, 55). How right he was the discovery at Nag Hammadi has shown (see below on Clement of Alexandria). The following investigation concentrates on critical analysis and does not purpose to cover over the gaps in our knowledge of the JG with hypothetical constructions. It starts from the position that three JG are to be distinguished, and divides the fragments among the different books. In the process its hypothetical character, which comes to light not only in the assignment of the individual fragments but also with regard to the relation of the GE and the Gospel of the Twelve Apostles and the use of sometimes questionable sources, is always made clear.

1. Irenaeus gives the earliest testimony - it is admittedly indirect - to the existence of a JG. He reports that the Jewish-Christian sect of the Ebionites used only one gospel, that of Matthew (*Adv. Haer.* I 26.2; III 11.7). But when in other places he says that they had eliminated the virgin birth (III 21.1; V 1. 3), it is clear that the gospel used by them cannot have been the canonical Mt., and that Irenaeus had not himself seen this book; otherwise he would not have been able to identify it with Mt. This JG had apparently no special title.

2. Clement of Alexandria on the other hand mentions a 'Gospel according to the Hebrews' and quotes from it an apocryphal saying of Jesus (*Strom.* II 9. 45). He adduces this saying once again in *Strom.* V 14. 96 in a longer version, but without stating where he found it. That this version gives the full text is clear from POx. 654, in which the logion in question in its longer version occurs as the second of six sayings of the Lord. Waitz ('Evangelien', pp. 49-52) has assigned the complete text of the papyrus to the GH. But he has done so wrongly, for this text is found in its entirety in the same sequence in the Coptic Gospel of Thomas discovered at Nag Hammadi (see pp. 117ff. above). This discovery makes it doubtful if the saying quoted by Clement should be assigned to the GH. It is, however, quite possible that it stood in both gospels. If in this state of affairs conclusions as to the character of the GH in respect of its form and content must be reserved, Clement testifies nevertheless to the existence of a 'Gospel according to the Hebrews' that was well known in Egypt.

3. Origen: he also quotes the 'Gospel according to the Hebrews' (*in Joh.* vol. II, 12) and indeed a saying of Jesus about his being carried away: his mother, the Holy Spirit, took him by one of his hairs and carried him to the high mountain Tabor. This account is adduced once again by Origen but without any statement as to where he found it (*in Jer*. vol. XV, 4). In this quotation we have to do with a variant of the story not of the transfiguration but of the temptation (Mt. 4:1-11 and pars.; cf. Walter Bauer, *Das Leben Jesu*, pp. 143ff.; Waitz, 'Evangelien' 13). The deviations from the canonical account are very considerable; out of the report given by the Evangelist has come an account given by Jesus himself of his experience, the devil is replaced by the Holy Spirit, and the Holy Spirit is identified with the mother of Jesus. This last trait presupposes the semitic conception of the Spirit, since in the semitic tongues the Spirit is *femini generis*, but it does not imply that the GH was originally written in Hebrew or in Aramaic (Waitz, p. 52; for further particulars see Bauer, *loc. cit*). The mythological conception of the Holy Spirit as the mother of Jesus separates the GH from the canonical nativity narratives and also from the conception of Joseph as the father of Jesus that obtained among the Ebionites of whose gospel Irenaeus speaks; the GH cannot have been identical with that gospel.

A further quotation from the GH occurs in the Latin revision of Origen's commentary on Matthew (*in Mt.*, vol. XV, p. 389 Benz-Klostermann), a fictional development of Mt. 19:16-24. Schmidtke (*Fragmente*, pp. 90-94) has with reason made it probable that this quotation was inserted in the commentary not by Origen himself but by the later reviser and also that it does not come from the GH used by Origen (otherwise Bardy, 'Jérôme', p. 29). Certain indications, such as the singling out of Simon (*dixit Simoni discipulo suo*) connect this pericope with the gospel fragment in Jerome, *adv. Pelag.* (*dixit illi Simon discipulus eius*), whilst the address *Simon, fili Jonae* (not: Simon, son of John; so Waitz, 'Evangelien', p. 13) points rather to Mt. 16:17 than to the scholium of the Judaikon, which in this place gives 'son of John' (Cod. Ev. 566).

4. Eusebius: The accounts of the JG given by Eusebius are in his *Church History* (*Historia Ecclesiastica*, H.E.), partly in his comments on the history of the canon and partly in the information he gives about Papias and Hegesippus; he adduces direct quotations from JG only in his *Theophania*.

In his statements about the compass of the canon Eusebius mentions the GH and its constituency.

> To these [i.e. to the spurious writings] some reckon the Gospel according to the Hebrews, in which especially those Hebrews who have become converted to Christ find delight (H.E. III. 25.5).

The readers of the GH were above all Jewish Christians; the designation 'Hebrews' indicates where they belonged as a people, but not their tongue; according to the context these Jewish Christians in the time of Eusebius used the GH side by side with the four canonical Gospels. It was otherwise with a special school of thought among the Ebionites: the members of this school, in contrast to the ordinary Ebionites, recognised the virgin birth of Jesus although they called his pre-existence in question (H.E. III 27. 1-3).[3]

> . . . as they use only the so-called Gospel according to the Hebrews, they attach little value to the rest (H.E. III 27.4).

Since two fragments of the GH assume the pre-existence of Jesus, this Ebionite group either did not dispute it or did not read the GH. But apart from this question, this note shows that for Eusebius the GH was not identical with the gospel which according to Irenaeus was used by the ordinary Ebionites.

The note of Papias of Hierapolis (c. 150) quoted by Eusebius, that Mt. collected the sayings of the Lord in 'the Hebrew tongue' and that every one interpreted them as he was able (H.E. III 39.16), was meant to defend the Gospel of Matthew from being used improperly, as in the opinion of this churchman of Asia Minor heretics were using it (W. Bauer, *Orthodoxy*, pp. 184ff., 204f.); but it is at most an indirect witness for a specifically Jewish-Christian gospel, if Schmidtke's conjecture should be right (*Fragmente*, pp. 46f.), that the statements of Papias were occasioned by accounts of an Aramaic revision of the Gospel of Matthew.

> After observing that Papias also used 1 Jn. and 1 Pet., Eusebius says:And he has adduced another story of a woman who was accused of many sins before the Lord, which is contained in the Gospel accordng to the Hebrews (H.E. III 39.17).

The statement of the place where this story was found clearly comes not from Papias but from Eusebius (Schmidtke, *Fragmente*, pp. 149ff.; Waitz, 'Evangelien', p. 11; id. 'Untersuchungen', p. 68). What story is meant is uncertain. As it cannot be identical with Lk. 7:36-50 - otherwise Eusebius would not have assigned it to the apocryphal GH - it has since Rufinus been readily equated with the *pericope adulterae* (Jn. 7:53-8:11), which originally did not belong to Jn. and is found there for the first time in codex D; but it is already attested earlier by the Syriac *Didascalia* (Achelis-Flemming, TU 25. 2, 1904, 38f.), and here the woman is not called an adulteress but a sinner, as in Jn. 8:3 D (cf. W. Bauer, *Das Johannesevangelium*, [3]1933, pp. 115ff.; U. Becker, *Jesus und die Ehebrecherin. Untersuchungen zur Text- und Überlieferungsgeschichte von Joh 7, 53-8, 11*, BZNW 28, 1963). But this evidence does not suffice either for the identification of the story adduced by Papias with the pseudo-Johannine pericope in the version of cod. D or for conclusions as to the literary character of the apocryphal gospel. That the story adduced by Papias lies before us in Jn. 7:53ff. is merely a possible hypothesis; if Eusebius localises it in the GH, he must have found it there; and nothing justifies our assigning it to the GN and fixing its original position between Mt. 22:22 and 23 (against Waitz, 'Evangelien', pp. 11f., 18).

> Regarding Hegesippus (c.180) and his 'Memoirs' Eusebius reports: He quotes both from the Gospel according to the Hebrews and from the Syriac (Gospel) and in particular some words in the Hebrew tongue, showing that he was a convert from the Hebrews (H.E. IV 22.8).

The attempts frequently undertaken to equate the GH and the 'Syriac Gospel' with one another are abortive; because of the Greek syntax Eusebius' sentence can only be understood as meaning that Hegesippus quoted two different gospels, the GH and a Syriac one, i.e. one written in Aramaic, and that Eusebius also distinguishes these. The 'Hebrew tongue' is, as elsewhere in Eusebius, the Aramaic, the 'mother-tongue' of the 'Hebrews'; the quotations 'in the Hebrew tongue' come therefore not from the GH but from the 'Syriac Gospel'. That Eusebius designated this as 'Syriac', contrary to his usage elsewhere, may be put down to Hegesippus' account (Schmidtke, *Fragmente*, pp. 51ff.). Although Eusebius speaks frequently elsewhere of the 'Hebrew' proto-Matthew (III 24.6; 39.16; V 8.2; VI 25.4), he nowhere identifies it with the 'Syriac' Gospel known to Hegesippus; this identification therefore ought not to be ascribed to him (against Schmidtke, *loc. cit.*); the early Church historian was more sparing of such hypotheses than the moderns. From the fact that in the H.E. he gives no quotations from either of the two JG it ought not to be concluded that at the time he wrote the H.E. he did not know them (against Schmidtke and Waitz): he at least knew the GH if he identified the Papias story of the woman that was a sinner, and of the Syriac Gospel he knew at any rate the quotations in the Memoirs of Hegesippus.

In the *Theophania* (c. 333) Eusebius adduces two quotations from JG and introduces them in a peculiar way:

> ... as we have found somewhere or other in the Gospel which is (in circulation) among the Jews in the Hebrew tongue ... (*Theoph.* IV 12). Since the Gospel that has come down to us in the Hebrew script turns the threat not against him who ... , I put myself the question whether according to Matthew ... (Mai, *Nova Patr. Bibl.* IV, 1, 155).

In this JG it is clearly not a matter of the GH, for this is regularly given the fixed designation 'Gospel according to the Hebrews', but of a gospel of no fixed name; Eusebius characterises it by its tongue, script and constituency as an Aramaic gospel. He clearly puts a space between it and the Greek Mt., to which on both occasions he adduces it as a parallel; but nothing indicates that he considered it as its Aramaic original (against Schmidtke, *Fragmente* 55ff.). If in the H.E. he treats the 'Hebrew' Mt. as a bygone entity and as a curious fact records that an exemplar of it had survived among the Indians down to the time of Pantaemus (V 10.3), then in the *Theophania* he would assuredly have underlined the new appearance of the original Matthew otherwise than by the phrase 'the Gospel that has come down to us in the Hebrew script', had he seen the former in the latter. Again, he does not connect it with the Syriac Gospel known to Hegesippus; it is uncertain whether he regarded the two as identical, but likely that they were identical; for of the existence of two JG in the Aramaic tongue nothing is otherwise known.

Eusebius thus knew two JG: first the GH also mentioned by Hegesippus, Clement and Origen, which was already known to Papias and which was supposed to have been used as their only gospel by a particular group of the heretical Ebionites; and second an Aramaic gospel from which Hegesippus and he himself quote.

5. Epiphanius in his *Panarion* enlarges at great length regarding the Jewish-Christian sects of the Nazoreans and Ebionites. *Haer.* 29 is devoted to the history and teaching of the Nazoreans, the Syrian Jewish-Christians; Schmidtke (*Fragmente*, pp. 95-126) has analysed this conglomerate of tradition and phantasy and with regard to the home of this sect has come to the conclusion (pp. 98ff.) that the only substantiated piece of information is 'this sect dwells in Beroea in Coelesyria' (29. 7. 7). Their canon comprised not merely the New but also the whole of the Old Testament, and the latter the Nazoreans read in Hebrew (29.7.2.4). In conclusion Epiphanius speaks of the Gospels:

> They have the Gospel according to Matthew complete and in Hebrew. For this is evidently still preserved among them, as it was originally written, in Hebrew script. But I do not know whether they have removed the genealogy from Abraham to Christ (*Haer.* 29.9.4).

Two points are here worthy of note: (1) the Gospel of the Nazoreans is the complete 'Hebrew' original Matthew; (2) as his last observation shows, Epiphanius had not himself seen the book, but also he had not heard of anything (such as misrepresentation or abridgement) against it.

How is this note to be judged against the background of what has already been said? Eusebius had sharply distinguished between the 'Hebrew' original of Matthew, which he knew merely as a forgotten entity of the past, and the 'Gospel (written) in Hebrew letters which has come down to us', the 'Gospel which is (in circulation) among the Jews in the Hebrew tongue'. If we are unwilling to assume that there were different 'Hebrew' gospels among the Jewish-Christian sects, then nothing stands in the way of the assumption that the 'Jews' of Eusebius are the Nazoreans of Epiphanius and that the gospel composed in 'Hebrew' of these latter is the gospel composed in the Hebrew script and tongue of the former. The identification, which Eusebius has avoided, of the JG with the Hebrew original Matthew occurs for the first time in Epiphanius, but is probably to be accredited to his tradition. Since he can impute to it nothing heretical or non-Matthaean, the Gospel of the Nazoreans must have been an Aramaic version of Mt. (and was possibly identical with the Syriac Gospel known to Hegesippus). It is to be underlined that Epiphanius as little as Eusebius designates this 'Hebrew', i.e. Aramaic JG as GH.

Epiphanius gives more numerous accounts of the Gospel of the Ebionites (*Haer.* 30), and he also communicates a few fragments from it. After relating a little about Ebion, the alleged founder of the sect, and his Christology, he says with regard to the Ebionites:

> And they too receive the Gospel according to Matthew. For this they too use, as do the followers of Cerinthus and Merinthus, to the exclusion of all others. But they call it (the Gospel) according to the Hebrews, for, to speak truthfully, Matthew alone of New Testament writers presents and proclaims the gospel in Hebrew and in the Hebrew script (*Haer.* 30.3.7).

In the opinion of this Church Father the only gospel which the Ebionites use is the Gospel of Matthew; but evidently they call it not the Gospel of Matthew but the Gospel according to the Hebrews and do so, as he adds in an aetiological comment, because Matthew wrote his Gospel 'in Hebrew'. It is striking that in giving this description he does not identify the Gospel of the Nazoreans with that of the Ebionites; he neither states that the latter was still read in Hebrew, as he has said of the former, nor does he call the former GH, as he names the latter. That the two cannot be identical and are not so for Epiphanius, is shown by another note on the Gospel of the Ebionites:

> In the Gospel used by them, that called 'according to Matthew', which however is not wholly complete but falsified and mutilated - they call it

the 'Hebrew (Gospel)' - it is recorded . . . (*Haer*. 30.13.2).

As title Epiphanius no longer gives GH but the Hebrew Gospel. But both mean the same thing: the book composed originally in Hebrew in accordance with *Haer*. 30. 3. 7. All the same, as regards the Gospel of the Ebionites it is not a question of the Hebrew original Matthew: whilst the Gospel of the Nazoreans is the Hebrew and complete Mt., that of the Ebionites is merely a 'so-called Matthew' and as compared with the real Mt. is falsified and abridged. Over these abridgements and falsifications the Church Father very much loses his temper in the following:

> They have cut away the genealogy in Matthew and, as has already been said, have let the Gospel begin in this way: It came to pass, it is said, in the days of Herod, the king of Judaea, when Caiaphas was high priest, that there came a certain man John by name and baptised with the baptism of repentance in the river Jordan (*Haer*. 30.14.3).

Since the gospel begins with the appearance of the Baptist, it lacks the whole nativity narrative Mt. 1 and 2. The fragments adduced below may convey an impression of the distortions.

The statements of Epiphanius regarding the Gospel of the Ebionites agree with those of Irenaeus in this, that the Ebionites use only a single gospel and that this is a Gospel of Matthew; further in this, that this sect denies the virgin birth. That the gospel in question cannot then have been the canonical Mt., Irenaeus does not indeed say, but Epiphanius does so all the more clearly. New in Epiphanius as compared with Irenaeus is the communication of the title, the Gospel of the Hebrews or the Hebrew Gospel, and the aetiology of the Church Father for this title. That the Ebionites themselves gave it that name is, however, more than doubtful. For on the one hand the earlier ecclesiastical writers never associate the GH with Mt. On the other hand Epiphanius bestows this title (GH) even on Tatian's Gospel Harmony which was rejected by the great Church:

> It is said that from him [Tatian] there comes the Diatessaron, which is also called the Gospel according to the Hebrews (*Haer*. 46.1).

On the motive of this identification see Schmidtke, *Fragmente*, pp. 172f. This assuredly false statement casts suspicion on the entitling also of the Gospel of the Ebionites; it certainly does not rest on trustworthy tradition, but is a combination made by Epiphanius. He may have been inspired to associate the two documents by the comment of Eusebius (H.E. III 27. 4) that a special school of thought among the Ebionites used only the GH; a further link in the equation is his own aetiological explanation of the title.

Whence Epiphanius obtained his knowledge of the Gospel of the Ebionites is disputed. The assumption that he had it in his hands and made excerpts from it (Waitz, 'Evangelien', pp. 14f.) is the one nearest at hand and least cumbered with hypotheses. Whilst he knows the Gospel of the Nazoreans only from hearsay and with regard to the GH is aware of little more than the title, the Gospel of the Ebionites is familiar to him, as his citations show. This last must be differentiated in accordance with his own statements from the Gospel of the Nazoreans and also, for the reasons already mentioned, from the GH. We are concerned here with three different entities.

6. Jerome: the most numerous citations and the most numerous but also the most perplexing accounts of JG have been handed down by Jerome. Critical investigations have not yet led to any generally recognised result. It is above all uncertain how far the statements of this Church Father ought to be trusted and how far conclusions ought to be drawn from them as to the tongue, compass and literary character of the JG. The identification of the several fragments is a further problem; in the present state of research no complete certainty can be obtained in regard to either of these two questions. Only this is certain, that Jerome has always only one JG in mind. The styling varies: he calls it on seven occasions the Gospel according to the Hebrews, on two occasions the Gospel of the Hebrews, on three occasions the Hebrew Gospel, on two occasions the Hebrew Gospel according to Matthew, and on two occasions he tells us that this designation is an hypothesis of others; also on one occasion he calls it the Gospel according to the Apostles. Thus he means always the GH and regards it as the Hebrew original Matthew.

Jerome cites his JG for the first time in his *Commentary on Ephesians* (on 5:4), which appeared in 386-387, and does so with the introductory formula: 'As we also read in the Hebrew Gospel', without describing it more closely as later he always does; that seems to indicate that he took the citation not from the gospel itself, but from one of his exegetical texts, which however cannot now be identified. The next citation - the report by Jesus, adduced also by Origen, of his being carried away by his mother, the Holy Spirit - is found in the *Commentary on Micah* (on 7:6), written between 390 and 392, and is introduced:

> He who ... believes in the Gospel according to the Hebrews which I have recently translated.

This translation must therefore have appeared shortly before 390. In spite of the certainty with which Jerome speaks of it, doubt cannot be suppressed; for Origen cites this passage of the GH twice without giving any hint that the GH was not composed originally in Greek, and it cannot be understood why Jerome should have translated a book that already for a long time had been available in Greek.

In the *de viris inlustribus* (392-393) he speaks repeatedly of the GH.

> Also the Gospel which is called 'according to the Hebrews' and which was recently translated by me into Greek and Latin speech, which Origen also used frequently ... (*vir. inl.* 2)

According to that, the original of the GH was composed in a semitic tongue. The reference to Origen probably indicates that Jerome took the citation from him and not from the GH itself (Schmidtke, *Fragmente*, p. 135; Bardy, 'Jérôme', pp. 9f.). The semitic original is for him the 'Hebrew' proto-Matthew:

> Matthew in Judaea was the first to compose the gospel of Christ in the Hebrew character and speech for the sake of those who came over to the faith from Judaism; who he was who later translated it into Greek is no longer known with certainty. Further the Hebrew text itself is still preserved in the library at Caesarea which the martyr Pamphilus collected with great care. The Nazaraeans in Beroea, a city of Syria, who use this

book, also permitted me to copy it. In it it is to be noted that wherever the evangelist adduces testimonies from the OT - be this done by himself or by our Lord and Saviour - he follows not the Septuagint translation but the Hebrew original text.(*vir. inl.* 3)

Jerome can hardly have seen the Hebrew original of Mt. in the library at Caesarea, for Eusebius never says anything about such a treasure in his library and never identifies an unknown JG with the Hebrew original of Matthew. What we are concerned with here must be an Aramaic gospel - the one from which come the citations in the *Theophania* - and this Jerome equates with the original Matthew. Whether he knew the Caesarean exemplar from having himself seen it, is open to question. At all events he does not imply that he derives his information from it. For he notes - in order of course to show his familiarity with this work - that this gospel was used by the Nazareans in Beroea and that he had copied it with their permission. Since in his citations from JG he again and again refers to the Nazaraeans (or Nazarenes), he obviously implies that he obtained his information amongst them. The Coelesyrian Beroea near Aleppo was in fact a centre of the Nazoraeans, i.e. of the Syrian Jewish-Christians (Epiphanius, *Haer.* 29.7.7; 30.2.7; Bardy, 'Jérôme', p. 11). Jerome can have had contact with them only during his stay in the desert of Chalcis, i.e. between 373 and 376 (Bardy, p. 11); but then it is altogether inconceivable that he kept the Gospel of the Nazaraeans so long to himself and was silent about it, and cited it for the first time in 386. It is equally inconceivable that the differences between the Gospel of the Nazaraeans and the canonical Matthew can have struck him so little that he could consider the latter to be the translation of the former. The conclusion is inevitable that it was not the Nazaraeans who communicated to him his knowledge of this gospel.

In critical examination of the JG the paragraph *de viris inlustribus* 16 has played a decisive role. In it Jerome asserts that Ignatius quotes the GH in his *Epistle to Polycarp*:

> Ignatius . . . writes in particular (an epistle) to Polycarp . . . , in which he also adduces a testimony about the person of Christ from the Gospel which was recently translated by me; he says: 'And I have also seen him in the flesh after the resurrection and believe that he is. And when he came to Peter and to those who were with Peter, he said to them: Behold, handle me and see that I am no bodiless demon. And forthwith they touched him and believed.'

Years later (in 408-409) in his *Commentary on Isaiah* (XVIII, preface) he cites the saying about the bodiless demon, but without reference to Ignatius:

> Since that is to say the disciples took him for a spirit or according to the Gospel of the Hebrews, which the Nazaraeans read, for a bodiless demon...

The statement of *de viris inlustribus* 16 is much disputed; whilst it serves Waitz as basis for far-reaching constructions, Bardy categorically calls its accuracy in question. The fact cannot be denied that in this passage Jerome makes two solid mistakes. In the first place the passage cited from Ignatius stands not in his epistle to Polycarp but in that to the Smyrnaeans; and then Jerome understands the first sentence ('and I have also seen him in the flesh after the resurrection', etc.) as part of the fragment said to be quoted by Ignatius, whereas it is actually an avowal on the part of Ignatius. Ignatius writes:

> And I know and believe that even after his resurrection he was in the flesh. And when he came to those about Peter, he said to them: Lay hold, handle me and see that I am no bodiless demon. And forthwith they touched him and believed, being closely joined to his flesh and spirit (*Smyrn*. 3.1f.).

The statement of the Church Father that the passage stood in the Gospel of the Nazaraeans which he had translated is wrecked on the fact that the decisive notion 'bodiless demon' cannot be the translation of a semitic original.[4] That eliminates an Aramaic gospel as source; a Greek text, perhaps the GH as such, is at most what can be considered. Moreover it has long been recognised and acknowledged that when writing the *de viris inlustribus* Jerome had before him neither the text of the apocryphal gospel nor that of the epistles of Ignatius, but the *Ecclesiastical History* of Eusebius who (III 36.11) adduces Ign. *Smyrn*. 3.1f.; Jerome cites the text only as far as Eusebius gives it; his assigning of it to the epistle to Polycarp finds its explanation in cursory reading, and his misunderstanding of the first sentence in the fact that he did not take in the context of the Ignatian expositions. Two points tell against the derivation of *Smyrn*. 3.2 from a JG:

(i) Eusebius says expressly that he does not know the source of the Ignatian sentence (H.E. III 36.11); since he knew the GH and an Aramaic JG and the latter according to Jerome was at hand in the library at Caesarea, Eusebius could have identified the passage in question without more ado, had it stood in a JG; that he came to know the Aramaic JG only after he had written the H.E. is a way out of the difficulty with which Schmidtke and Waitz would vindicate Jerome's statement about the source and make Ignatius a witness of the Gospel of the Nazaraeans. (ii) Origen (*de princ*. I prooem. 8) says that the word of the risen Jesus 'I am no bodiless demon' stood in an apocryphal 'Teaching of Peter'. That speaks decisively against Jerome's statement about the source and eliminates also the GH known to Origen and cited by him. We may leave aside the question whether the expression *Petri doctrina* is Rufinus' rendering of κήρυγμα Πέτρου (so above all Bardy, 'Jérôme', pp. 13f.); the attribution of the sentence to this *Kerygma* or to a lost Teaching of Peter remains an assumption.

What makes the identification of the Ignatian sentence uncertain is simply the expression 'bodiless demon'; otherwise Eusebius would not have hesitated to see in *Smyrn*. 3.2 a free rendering of Lk. 24:36-41, where the risen Jesus says: 'Handle me and see, for a spirit hath not flesh and bones as ye see me have' (vs. 39). It is true that Walter Bauer also is of opinion that Ignatius does not formulate *Smyrn* 3. 2 independently but follows here a strange context, since he connects vs. 2 to what goes before it with 'and when' instead of, as the logical procedure would have been, with 'then when' (W. Bauer, *Die apostolischen Väter II. Die Briefe des Ignatius v. Antiochia und der Polykarpbrief*, HNT [Ergänzungsband], 1920, p. 266 [²1985 ed. H. Paulsen]). Nevertheless, as argument for the derivation of the tradition cited by Ignatius this not quite correct linkage seems to me to have less weight than the similarity of the passage with Lk. 24:36ff.: the situation is the same, and the emphasis on Peter answers to the estimate of him in the 2nd century and is besides justified by Lk. 24:33f. The word of the risen Jesus in vs. 39b: 'Handle me and see, for a spirit has not flesh and bones as ye see me have', is given a Greek formulation in *Smyrn*. 3. 2 and above all, as the context shows, is pointed against Docetism. Immediately before (in *Smyrn*. 2) Ignatius calls the docetic heretics 'bodiless and demonic'. The latter term is a polemical distortion of the term 'pneumatic' which the Gnostics applied to themselves, and the former refers to the gnostic understanding of redemption as the liberation of the spirit from the matter of corporeality. The characterisation of the Docetics in *Smyrn*. 2 and the logion in *Smyrn*. 3. 2 harmonise terminologically the one with the other, and this they do in using and distorting the gnostic terminology.

In my opinion the anti-docetic tendency of Ignatius and the actual front-line in which he stood sufficiently explain the formulation of the saying of the Lord and make the assumption of any source other than Lk. 24:36ff. unnecessary. In the Ignatian rendering, which was easier to remember and of greater striking power than the Lucan, the logion passed into the Teaching of Peter. The dominating position of Peter and the absence of any reference to doubt on the part of the disciples do not in any way show that the Ignatian text is original, but that from the point of view of tradition-history it is secondary as compared with Luke (against Waitz, 'Evangelien', pp. 10f. and 'Untersuchungen', p. 67). Jerome was led to make his false identification simply through the uncanonical formulation of the saying and through the comment of Eusebius that he did not know Ignatius' source. Ignatius, *Smyrn*. 3. 2 drops out as a fragment of an apocryphal JG and therefore as an index to its dating.

Jerome adduces the majority of his quotations from his JG in the *Commentary on Matthew* written shortly before 398. Of the formulae of introduction only the one to the story of the healing of the man with the withered hand is noteworthy:

> In the Gospel which the Nazarenes and the Ebionites use, which we
> recently translated out of the Hebrew tongue into the Greek and which is
> called by most people the authentic (Gospel) of Matthew . . .

In contrast to *de vir. inl*. 2 and 3 there is no more mention of a translation into Latin, and that this JG is to be equated with the 'Hebrew' proto-Matthew is no longer described as an individual opinion but as that of 'most people', who these are being left open; and this change in emphasis occurs later still (*In Ps. cxxxv tract*.: in the Hebrew Gospel according to Matthew; *adv. Pelag*. III, 2: . . . as most assume, according to Matthew; see below). The mentioning of the Ebionites as readers of this gospel is singular in Jerome and probably a literary reminiscence from his reading of Epiphanius.

In his writings composed after the *Commentary on Matthew* Jerome no longer states that he had translated the JG. The introductory formulae characterise it as 'written in Hebrew letters' (*Epist*. 120, 8 *ad Hedib*.) or as composed 'in the Hebrew speech' (*Com. in Is*. on 11:2) and usually also as read among the Nazaraeans. The most detailed citation formula is found in the *Dial. adv. Pelag*. III 2, which appeared towards the end of 415; it introduces two citations:

> In the Gospel according to the Hebrews, which is in the Chaldaean and
> Syriac tongue, but written in Hebrew letters, and which the Nazarenes use

to this day as (the Gospel) according to the Apostles or, as most people suppose, according to Matthew, which is also in stock in the library of Caesarea, the story tells . . .

after the citation:

And in the same volume: . . .

What in these statements goes beyond what Jerome has already said about his JG is first the precise statement regarding the tongue and secondly the identification of it with a 'Gospel according to the Apostles'. As the original tongue he no longer gives Hebrew but the 'Chaldaean and Syriac dialect', by which he clearly means Aramaic; in these different statements we are concerned not with a fundamental antithesis or with an indication that Jerome was informed only in 415 about the actual tongue of the JG, but with a terminological difference which finds its explanation in the fact that where Jerome speaks of a 'Hebrew Gospel' he makes use of the inexact, popular designation (Bardy 'Jérôme'. p. 19) - by the 'Gospel according to the Apostles' he certainly understands the Gospel according to the Twelve Apostles which he also mentions in the prologue to his *Commentary on Matthew* side by side with other apocryphal gospels, which Origen in his *Homily on Lk. i* calls the 'Gospel of the Twelve' (in Jerome's translation: *Juxta duodecim apostolos*), which is also mentioned elsewhere (by Ambrose and Theophylact) but never cited. The statement that the Aramaic Gospel of the Nazaraeans was identical with this is supported, however, by no other evidence and is for that reason unreliable.[5]

This detailed review made in chronological order of the learned framework within which Jerome sets his citations has been necessary in order to find out what measure of confidence ought to be put in the Church Father's statements. It is a very small measure. But the recognition of this should give no occasion to daring hypotheses; these can only increase the confusion which Jerome has brought about. In the following summary it is a question merely as to what can in a measure be counted as certain.

It is clear that Jerome has always only one gospel in mind, that he designates this as the GH and that he equates it with the Aramaic Gospel of the Nazaraeans. But this equation is false and does not make head against the clear distinction between the GH (drafted in Greek) and an Aramaic JG, particularly since Clement and Origen say nothing of a semitic original form of the GH. Jerome thus reluctantly confirms the existence of two JG, the GH and an Aramaic gospel.

That the latter was at hand in the library in Caesareas is not to be disputed; it is at any rate likely on the ground of the citations of Eusebius in his *Theophany*. It will likewise be correct that the Nazaraeans used such an Aramaic gospel, since Epiphanius also testifies to this. That the Aramaic gospel, evidence of which is given by Hegesippus and Eusebius, is identical with the GN, is not indeed absolutely certain, but perfectly possible, even very probable, and is assumed in what follows.

The following statements of Jerome are, however, open to question: first that he got to know the Gospel of the Nazaraeans among the Nazaraeans of the Syrian Beroea, secondly that he copied it there and thirdly that he translated it 'recently', i.e. between 386 and 390. As has already been said, the chronology tells against the first two of these assertions. He must have got to know the book at another time and in another way; Bardy even thinks that he did not actually know the Nazaraeans, for he speaks of them almost in stereotyped phrases and what he records about them he could have read in Epiphanius (so Schmidtke also). Several arguments tell against the third assertion. No one has seen or mentioned the translation, and Jerome himself mentions it only between 390 and 397 and thereafter no more. It is true that the different statements regarding the original tongue (Hebrew, Chaldaean, Syriac) do not prove that he was not quite certain about that; the fact, however, that in 392-393 he speaks of a translation into Greek and Latin but in 397 only of a translation into Greek, is puzzling. The fact that in texts which he demonstrably came upon in Greek and assuredly did not translate out of Aramaic he speaks of a translation, must intensify to scepticism our doubt as to his statements. It is therefore widely recognised that Jerome did not translate the Gospel of the Nazaraeans. He had obviously only purposed to translate it; and although unable to carry out this purpose, he spoke of it as an accomplished fact (Bardy, 'Jérôme', pp. 32f.).

The erroneous equation of the Greek GH and the Aramaic GN shows at all events that Jerome knew accurately neither of these two Gospels, for otherwise the differences in their content and character must have struck him. Apparently he worked only with fragments, a fact which also explains how he could ascribe them all to one and the same book. Whence he had the fragments cannot be said with certainty. It is disputed whether he himself had looked into the Aramaic GN and had made a note of some things that he found in it (so Waitz, 'Evangelien', p. 15) or had not done so (so Schmidtke, *Fragmente*, pp. 66f., 246ff.); this question cannot by any means be settled. On his visit to Caesarea the opportunity was at all events afforded him of examining the exemplar in the library there. He certainly drew citations from literature of second rank, especially from commentaries. Origen can be identified as the source of some of his citations; as regards the others no certain or probable statement of their source can be made; all conjectures which would assert more about it are futile. That holds good in particular of the hypothesis, brought forward with as much drive as constructive power by Schmidtke, that Jerome borrowed the fragments of the GH from the commentaries of Origen and those of the GN from the commentaries of Apollinaris of Laodicea; for in the first place in the literary remains of Apollinaris nothing is found which justifies such a conjecture (Bardy, 'Jérôme', p.6 note 2 ; 30), and besides in no citation does Jerome appeal to him as his authority, as anyhow he appeals once to Origen. The fact that he had heard and read Apollinaris is no cogent reason for the assertion that he had from him the citations in question. At all events the thesis of Schmidtke, which many have accepted, is not indisputable because the opposite cannot be proved; even as a working hypothesis it is not suitable.

Such being the state of affairs, no complete certainty can be arrived at in the matter of the identification of the several fragments. The canon drawn up confidently by Waitz, 'Evangelien', p. 15): 'The question merely is in what cases Jerome has followed either Origen or Apollinaris or has obtained them on his own', does not suffice, after what has just been adduced, for a decision as to whether a fragment belongs to the GH or to the GN. It has already been said that the citation twice repeated about the 'bodiless demon' is to be eliminated since it did not originate in any JG. As this instance shows, the possibility must be reckoned with that Jerome has also elsewhere attested certain texts which appealed to him and handed them down as coming from a JG; this element of uncertainty cannot be eliminated.

The trustworthy testimony of Origen must pass as evidence of membership in the GH. According to it the story of the carrying-away of Jesus by his mother, the Holy Spirit (*in Mich.* 7. 7; *in Is.* 40. 19; *in Ezech.* 16. 13), belongs assuredly to the GH, and also in all likelihood the appearance of Christ to James (*vir. inl.* 2), for which Jerome refers to the authority of the Alexandrian.

Criteria for derivation from the Aramaic GN must be: (*a*) indications that the text has a semitic basis and (*b*) the Synoptic character of the text or its affinity in particular with Mt., since the GH, according to all that we know of it, diverged very much from the synoptic type. According to (*a*) we shall be inclined to refer to the GN the Aramaic readings and the corrections of evangelic OT-citations made to bring them into accord with the original text of the OT. But here also a warning must be given against a too great certainty: the explanation of the name Barabbas as 'son of their teacher' is in a semitic text extremely questionable (Waitz, 'Evangelien', pp. 19f.). The derivation of the two quotations in Mt. 2:15, 23 from the Hebrew Bible may be conjectured with equal justice or injustice for the text of the canonical Matthew also, and the assertion that instead of ἐπιούσιος in the petition for bread in the Lord's Prayer there stood 'mahar' *crastinus* may be a conjecture on the part of Jerome; and that at the time of Jesus' death according to the GN it was not the veil of the Temple that was rent but the lintel that collapsed is according to Schmidtke 'Jerome's own invention' (*Fragmente*, p. 80), according to Bardy a gleaning by Jerome from Eusebius' *Chronicon* ('Jérôme', pp. 19-22). If, however, the tradition in question comes from a JG, it may be ascribed to the GN rather than to the GH, for the collapse of the lintel can be understood as a coarsening of the synoptic motif of the rending of the veil of the Temple.

In view of its synoptic character (*b*) one will ascribe the story of the man with the withered hand (*in Matt.* on 12:13) to the GN. So also in the case of the two citations in *adv. Pelag.* III 2 we do well to handle them as variants of synoptic and indeed Matthaean texts. The first, the conversation of Jesus with his mother and brethren before his baptism, is connected in theme (the baptism of Jesus in spite of his sinlessness) with the conversation with the Baptist in Mt. 3:14f. The second, the conversation about forgivingness, is, as the dialogue form shows, a colouring of the dialogue in Mt. 18:21f. (and not of the single saying Lk. 17:4); moreover the last sentence has been handed down in Greek as the version of the Judaikon (see No. 15b below). Since there are neither formal nor material reasons for a different derivation of the two fragments, they are to be referred to the GN.

Ordinarily the other baptism story (*in Is.* 11. 2) is also reckoned to the GN. For that Jerome's statement that the story came from the gospel composed 'in the Hebrew speech' is not a sufficient reason, particularly as it is wanting in his

Commentary on Matthew, in which he cites the GN five times; but *one* characteristic trait - the sounding forth of the voice *after* Jesus has left the water - which is found only here and in Mt. 3:16, goes to prove the derivation of the passage from the GN. But there are also considerable differences: the 'resting' of the Spirit on Jesus has no parallel in the Synoptics, although it has one in the 'abiding' of the Spirit upon him in Jn. 1:32f.; further it is not a voice from heaven that speaks but the Spirit resting on Jesus, and it speaks not in the third person as in Mt., but in the second person as in Mk. and Lk. And above all the content of the saying is a great deal more mythological than it is in the Synoptics; it assumes the notions of the pre-existence and the transfiguration of the Redeemer and in its motif of the eschatological 'rest' ('that I may rest in thee': 'thou art my rest') it points to the GH (cf. Clem. Alex. *Strom.* II 9. 45; V 14. 96). These peculiarities make it questionable whether this passage belongs to the same baptism story as does the conversation of Jesus with his mother and his brethren (*adv. Pelag.* III 2); accordingly I would - with reserve - assign it to the GH.

The derivation of the citations *in Eph.* on 5:4 and *in Ezech.* on 18:7 is altogether uncertain. Jerome has probably taken the first - it is also the earliest which he adduces - from one of his exegetical sources, but from which cannot be made out, and for that reason it cannot be concluded to which JG the fragment belongs (Schmidtke, *Fragmente*, pp. 75-79: Apollinaris and the GN; Bardy, 'Jérôme', p. 5f.: Origen and the GH); since on the one hand the association of Apollinaris with the GN rests solely upon conjectures on the part of Schmidtke which admit of no proof (J. Reuss, *Matthäuskommentare aus der griechischen Kirche*, TU 61, 1957, 26 is to the point), and since on the other hand Jerome can have obtained his knowledge of an Aramaic GN only after the writing of his *Commentary on Ephesians* (Bardy, 'Jérôme', p. 7ff.), the assignation proposed by Bardy has a little more likelihood. Since moreover the saying exhibits no semitisms and shows no close relationship to a synoptic saying of the Lord, it may be entered among the fragments of the GH. For the identification of the second citation no evidence that is at all likely can be adduced. Only because actual synoptic parallels are wanting, because Jerome in his *Commentary on Ezekiel* (on 16:13) gives a genuine GH-citation, and because of the material relationship of this saying to the one just discussed, it may be assigned with it to the GH.

7. The so-called 'Zion Gospel Edition': in the *subscriptiones* of thirty-six Gospel manuscripts dating from the 9th to the 13th centuries there is a reference to a gospel described as τὸ Ἰουδαϊκόν , and two of these manuscripts (codices 566 and 899) adduce readings of the Judaikon as marginal notes to Matthew. Codex 1424, which does not have the subscriptions, presents the largest number, namely ten of the thirteen Judaikon readings on Mt., and for eight of them it is the sole witness. The subscriptions refer to the standard exemplar on the 'holy mount', Zion, in Jerusalem.

Schmidtke (*Fragmente*, pp. 1-32) has investigated this group and shown that it goes back to a Gospel edition that was preserved in a basilica on Zion in Jerusalem and which he has accordingly called the 'Zion Gospel Edition'. He puts its origin in 370-500 (this is disputed by Ernst von Dobschütz in Nestle's *Einführung in das griechische NT*, [4]1923, p. 51). His statement that the Judaikon readings given in this Gospel edition go back to the lost *Commentary on Matthew* by Apollinaris of Laodicea, cannot be proved. The designation τὸ 'Ιουδαϊκόν characterises the book as a JG which cannot be one of the four canonical Gospels. But neither can it be identified with the GH, for otherwise the latter common title would certainly have been given. Since it is nowhere characterised as heretical, we cannot here be concerned with the Gospel of the Ebionites. Moreover it is nearly related to Mt. and is clearly a variant of the Gospel of Matthew. The title Judaikon may also point to the 'Jewish' speech, the Aramaic. The Greek citations from the Judaikon are certainly *ad hoc* renderings. The relationship to Mt. and to many JG-citations in Jerome (especially the identity of the reading for Mt. 18:22 with the concluding sentence of the second fragment in *adv. Pelag.* III 2) suggests the conclusion that the Judaikon and the GN were closely related to one another, if not identical.

8. Cyril of Jerusalem: in the Coptic translation of a discourse of Cyril of Jerusalem he (Cyril) puts a citation from the GH into the mouth of a heretical monk from 'the neighbourhood of Maiôma near Gaza' (ed. by Budge, *Texts*, Coptic, p. 60, English, p. 637). We are concerned here with a fragment of the story of the birth of Jesus: When Jesus wished to come into the world, God the Father entrusted Him to a mighty power which was called Michael; this came into the world and was named Mary. In the Greek writings of Cyril this discourse is not preserved; V. Burch ('The Gospel according to the Hebrews: Some new matter chiefly from Coptic sources', JTS 21, 1920, 310-315) regards it as a sort of excursus on the twelfth Catechesis. But it is questionable whether it actually goes back to Cyril, and above all whether the citation really comes from the GH. This question forces itself upon us in view of the different conceptions of the mother of Jesus in the GH fragment on the carrying away of Jesus (Origen and Jerome) and in the present passage. Whilst there the mother is designated the Holy Spirit, here she passes as the incarnation of a 'mighty power' which in its pre-existence is called Michael; our hesitations are strengthened if Burch's thesis is correct, that the 'mighty power' denotes a star and that Michael is to be understood as a star angel. But we know the GH too little to be able to deny this fragment to it; we are possibly concerned here with a corrupted fragment of the GH or with a fragment of a corrupted GH.[6]

9. Nicephorus: in the Stichometry of Nicephorus (*Nicephori opusc. hist.* ed. de Boor 1880, p. 134; see pp. 41f. above) it is recorded under the rubric New Testament Antilegomena: '4. The Gospel according to the Hebrews: 2200 lines'. For the Gospel of Matthew there are reckoned 2500 lines.

10. Testimonies from the Middle Ages: references are also found in writers of the Middle Ages to the GH or the GN. Haimo of Auxerre (*c.* 850) in his *Commentary on Isaiah* (on 53:12) cites the word of Jesus: 'Father, forgive them' (Lk. 23:34) and adds: 'For as it is said in the Gospel of the Nazaraeans', many thousands of the Jews who were standing round the cross became believers. Here it is deserving of notice that what is spoken of is a Gospel of the Nazaraeans, therefore one with a title which Jerome never uses. It is questionable whether this citation actually comes from the GN; the GN is clearly a working-up of Mt., but Haimo's citation is based on Lk. 23:48 and GosPet 7.25. It is certain that another apocryphal dictum, which according to Haimo's *Commentary on Hebrews* (on 13:4) 'the blessed apostle Matthew' gives 'somewhere' (Klostermann, *Apocrypha*, p. 12, No. 28), does not belong to a JG.

In a 13th-century English MS of the *Aurora* of Peter of Riga, a Bible put in verse (12th cent.), a marginal note on the cleansing of the Temple gives a citation which may 'be read in the books of the Gospels which the Nazarenes use'.[7]

In the 'Celtic Catechesis' of the Breton Vaticanus Regin. lat. 49 of the 9th century a statement is made according to the 'Gospel of the Hebrews' about the day of the last judgment (Dom A. Wilmart, 'Analecta Reginensia' in *Studi e Testi* 59, 1933, 58). More recently Bischoff has published two unknown fragments of the GH from Irish commentaries (Wendepunkte): (i) a 'Historical Commentary on Luke' mentions that the 'Gospel according to the Hebrews' gave the miracles that Jesus had wrought in Bethsaida and Chorazin; (ii) in his *Commentary on Matthew* Sedulius Scotus adduces from the 'Gospel which is entitled according to the Hebrews' a fictional expansion of the episode of the Magi. Fictional development of Mt. is generally characteristic of the GN; we have before us a case such as we have many a time in Jerome, a text being ascribed to the GH which according to its literary character should be assigned rather to the GN. Moreover Bischoff conjectures that the statements regarding names in an Irish commentary on Matthew (Wendepunkte, p. 252) and in the 'Historical Commentary on Luke' (*ibid.* p. 262) go back to the same apocryphal passage.[8]

Finally in a theological miscellany manuscript (14th-15th cent.) of German origin Bischoff has discovered a *historia passionis domini* (14th cent., first half), in which the latest authority adduced is Nicolas de Lyra and which contains several citations from the 'Gospel of the Nazaraeans'. In a letter Bischoff has in an extremely friendly and kindly way put the relative passages at our disposal.

As far, then, as into the 14th century we come across citations from the JG; the designation alternates between GH and GN. Whether this alternation should be appraised as evidence for our distinction between the two JG seems to me to be open to question. For it is quite possible that we have to do not with direct citations from such a gospel book but rather with borrowings from *catenae* or commentaries. But the influence of Jerome on this exegetical tradition is unmistakable. This tradition was evidently carried on in particular by the Irish, and Bischoff thinks, probably rightly, that the citation in Haimo of Auxerre and the scholion in the Aurora go back to Irish intervention. How far these citations and references are trustworthy testimonies for the content of the GN and the GH must remain open.

11. Conclusion: the foregoing investigation has come to the conclusion that three JG are to be distinguished:

(1) *The Gospel of the Nazaraeans*, a gospel read in a semitic speech (Aramaic or Syriac), which is attested by Hegesippus and Eusebius, Epiphanius and Jerome, which according to the latter was in use among the Nazaraeans, the Syrian Jewish Christians, and which showed a close relationship to the canonical Matthew.

(2) *The Gospel of the Ebionites*, the gospel of heretical Jewish Christians, composed in Greek, of which Irenaeus knew and from which Epiphanius quotes, which was related more to Mt. than to any other of the canonical Gospels, but differed from it in essential respects.

(3) *The Gospel of the Hebrews*, the JG that is mentioned most often, was perhaps already used by Papias and in the time of Eusebius still belonged to the Antilegomena; its most important witnesses are Clement of Alexandria and Origen. The few fragments that have been preserved indicate no special relationship to one of the canonical Gospels, but contain syncretistic elements and show the heretical character of the Jewish Christian users of the GH.

In the present state of research it is not yet possible to fit these JG into place in the history of Jewish Christianity or in the history of its theology. Analysis of the pseudo-Clementines has shown how complex an entity Jewish Christianity was (Strecker, *Judenchristentum*); the relevant accounts of the early Church heresiologists have not yet been sufficiently investigated; the clarification of the connection between the Qumran sect and the primitive Church and Jewish Christianity is still in full swing; it would then be premature to attempt to fix the JG historically. Here our only or main concern must be the clearing up of the literary question which these books occasion.

Notes

IV. Jewish-Christian Gospels

Introduction: the testimonies of the Early Church regarding Jewish-Christian gospels

1. On the Gospel of the Twelve Apostles, see below, pp. 374ff.

2. The designation of this JG varies in the sources. Where it is not a question of a quotation, the designation Gospel of the Nazaraeans has been used, although the group from which the work comes was probably called the Nazoreans.

3. This information comes from Origen (c. Celsum V 65, p. 68 Koetschau). There is dispute as to what sort of a group we are here concerned with (cf. Schoeps, Theologie, p. 16; Strecker, 'Ebioniten', pp. 496f.).

4. Neither in Hebrew nor in Aramaic is there an equivalent for the Greek ἀσώματος. On the other hand this Greek vocable, as a loan word (asomata = 'incorporalia' and asomataja = 'incorporalis') taken over into the Syriac, is attested for the first time in Ephraem and in the Breviarium Chaldaicum (Brockelmann, Lexicon Syriacum, ²1928, 35b). Cf. also on this logion H. Köster, Synoptische Überlieferung bei den Apostolischen Vätern (TU 65), 1957, pp. 50ff.

5. On the Gospel of the Twelve, see below, pp. 374ff.

6. On GH 1 cf. D.A.Bertrand, 'Le baptême de Jésus. Histoire de l'exégèse aux deux premiers siècles', BGBE 14, 1973 (further literature there on pp. 144ff.).

7. Cf. GN No. 25 below. This observation is hardly a citation from the GN, but a literary reminiscence on the part of the scholiast from Jerome, Com. on Mt. on 21:12: 'A certain fiery and starry light radiated from his eyes and the majesty of Godhead gleamed in his face' (cf. James p. 8).

8. Cf. also M. McNamara, The Apocrypha in the Irish Church, 1975, pp. 7f. and 40ff.

1. The Gospel of the Nazaraeans

Introduction.

1. Content and compass: in content and compass the GN was closely related to Mt. That is shown first and foremost by the readings of the Judaikon, but also by the other fragments that have been preserved. If the observation of Jerome, *de vir. inl.* 3 (GN 1) refers not merely to Mt. 2:15, 23 but also to the GN, then the latter contained the Matthaean nativity narrative, with the lack of which even Epiphanius could not charge it. Also its story of the baptism had as its basis the Matthaean report. Moreover the GN contained the story of the temptation, the sermon on the mount, the mission discourse, the discourse about the Baptist together with the cry of jubilation, the healing of the withered hand, the sayings against a mania for marvels, about the washing of hands, and about the demand for signs, the confession of Peter, the discourse to the disciples, the story of the rich man, the discourse to the Pharisees, the parable of the entrusted pounds, the denial of Peter, the release of Barabbas, the miracles at the time of the crucifixion, the watchmen at the grave. Since in the fragments only peculiarities that are more or less striking are handed down, it may be concluded that the content of the GN was roughly identical with that of Mt. and consequently that the GN was merely a secondary form of Mt., the character of which has still to be discussed. The Easter stories must have been similar to those in Mt., for the Christophany in Ign. *Smyrn.* 3. 2 does not belong to the GN (see above, pp. 143f.). That the *pericope adulterae* (Jn. 7:53-8:11) does not belong to it, has already been said. So also the encounter of Jesus with the high priest (POx 840; see above, pp. 94f.) belongs to another context.

Waitz finds traces of, and citations from, the GN in the Epistle of Barnabas, in Justin and in the Didascalia; but he has failed to give either a compelling or a likely proof of his thesis. It is a question of fictional developments of stories or of new formations or recastings of sayings of the Lord, of documents of 'rampant' tradition, which may have been transmitted in writing, but also orally, and to identify which with certainty is meanwhile a hopeless undertaking.

2. Language: according to the testimony of Hegesippus and Eusebius, of Epiphanius and Jerome, the GN was written in Syriac or Aramaic. Among scholars, however, it is disputed whether the GN was originally drafted in Aramaic or was a translation from the Greek. Closely bound up with this is the question whether the GN represents or discloses an earlier tradition than the canonical Gospel of Matthew, but this question cannot be decided on philological grounds alone. The Aramaic or Hebrew expressions which are handed down in the fragments are adduced both for Aramaic (Hebrew) and for Greek as the original tongue of the GN, but the scantiness and uncertainty of the material permit of no conclusion that is absolutely sure.

The fragments in question are Nos. 5, 12 and 20; in addition two observations of Jerome must also be taken into account, and these we will consider first.

> (On Bethlehem of Judaea) . . . that is an error on the part of the copyist. We believe i.e. that, as we read in the Hebrew, 'Judah' and not 'Judaea' was originally written by the Evangelist. (Jerome, *Com. on Mt.*, on 1:5)

The question is whether in this conjecture regarding the original text of Mt. 2:5 the Church Father meant by the expression *in ipso Hebraico* the Hebrew text of the citation (Micah 5:1) or the 'Hebrew Gospel' (= GN). In favour of the first there is the immediate impression and then Jerome's statement that Mt. in his Old Testament citations follows the Hebrew text. Since however 'Judah' stands in the Hebrew and in the Septuagint, but in both cases not in immediate connection with Bethlehem - 'And thou Bethlehem-Ephrath, thou least among the districts of Judah' (Massoretic text, and so also the LXX) - it is often supposed that the note refers not to the Hebrew text of Micah 5:1 but to the 'Hebrew Gospel'. In that case, however, Jerome would certainly have expressed himself more clearly (cf. the formulae of citation in his *Commentary on Matthew* Nos. 5, 10, 17, 20), especially as this would then be his first reference to the JG in his *Commentary on Matthew*. But since in his opinion this JG represents the original Mt. and therefore all the more in the matter of its Old Testament citations must follow its original text, the same perplexity confronts us. It is best solved by the assumption that Jerome referred to the original text of the OT, but did not accurately remember it.

The other observation is found in the *Epistle to Damasus*, in which he answers a question of his as to the meaning of 'Hosanna to the son of David':

> Finally Matthew, who composed the Gospel in the Hebrew speech, has written: 'Osanna barrama', i.e. Hosanna in the highest.
> (Jerome, *Epist.* XX, 5; Klostermann, *Apocrypha* 9 No. 12)

The old question whether by the Hebrew Mt. Jerome means the JG that he usually values so much is settled by a reference to the chronology; Damasus addressed his question to Jerome in 383, the latter mentions a JG for the first time in 386-387 and speaks of a 'Hebrew' JG first in 390-393; thereby another question, whether 'Hosanna in the highest' stood in the place of or side by side with 'Hosanna to the son of David', is decided in the latter sense. And finally yet another question, whether Jerome read the expression *Osanna barrama* in a 'Hebrew' gospel text or merely conjectured it, falls to the ground; moreover the retranslation is wrong: for 'height of heaven' is *rama* neither in Hebrew nor in Aramaic, but in Hebrew *marom* or *meromim* and in Aramaic *marom* or *meroma*.[1] This therefore like the foregoing observation of Jerome drops out so far as concerns the question as to the original tongue of the GN.

No. 12 provides no decision on the matter. If the Judaikon in Mt. 15:5 read 'Corban' instead of 'offering', as does the parallel Mk. 7:11, it here used a Hebrew-Aramaic *terminus technicus* which must of necessity have stood in a Hebrew or Aramaic rendering of this saying, whether we have here the original text or the Aramaic translation of the Greek word.

The situation is different in No. 5, the rendering of the petition for bread in the Lord's prayer: 'Give us today our bread of tomorrow.' The *maḥar* given by Jerome as the text of the GN cannot be the original Aramaic or Hebrew text of this petition; otherwise this vocable would not have been rendered in like manner in Mt. and Lk. by ἐπιούσιος, a rare expression and one hard to interpret. Jerome himself understands ἐπιούσιος as *supersubstantialis*, and so not as equivalent to *mahar*; accordingly he has not himself translated back into Aramaic and given out his retroversion as the original text. If the GN actually contained the vocable *mahar* in the petition for bread - and that there is no reason to doubt - then the conclusion is inevitable that this reading is 'merely an erroneous translation, resting on a misunderstanding, of the original *epiûsios*' (Waitz, 'Evangelien', p. 19). The rendering of the petition for bread in the GN is the earliest attempt to explain it. The Aramaic GN thus assumes, at least here, the Greek text of Matthew.

Jerome's statement in No. 20 that in the GN the name Barabbas was 'interpreted' as 'son of their teacher' is difficult to grasp. For *bar-abba* is a frequent personal name (cf. H.L.Strack/ P. Billerbeck, *Das Evangelium nach Matthäus erläutert aus Talmud und Midrasch I*, [8]1982, p. 1031) and means 'son of the abba' or 'son of the father'; if 'father' is understood as 'teacher', it then means 'son of the teacher'; for the latter meaning there may also be assumed *bar-rabba* or *bar-rabban* (the name being written then with two r's). But in either case the translation 'son of *their* teacher' is wrong. It is obscure why a name that was so well-known and the meaning of which was so obvious should have had to be 'interpreted' in an Aramaic gospel, and what this interpretation can have looked like ('*bar-abba*, i.e. *bar-rabba*'? But what sense would this explanation have had?); and it is altogether incredible that a person who spoke Aramaic translated his name as 'son of *their* teacher' and so wrongly. Accordingly Waitz postulates a Greek original for the Aramaic GN, in which there stood (similarly as in Acts 4:36) this wrong explanation of the name, and from that he concludes that the original tongue of the GN was Greek and therefore that the Aramaic GN was a translation; 'in an original Greek GN such an addition had a meaning: in an original Aramaic GN it would have been meaningless' ('Evangelien', p. 20).

This thesis assumes, however, (i) that the writer of the Greek GN read the name only in the accusative (Βαραββᾶν) and did not understand it as such; (ii) that in consequence of an imperfect acquaintance with Aramaic he misunderstood the termination of the word, and (iii) that the Aramaic translator accepted this wrong translation of the Aramaic name and retranslated it into Aramaic. This hypothesis is burdened by so many improbabilities that it collapses under them. Now Jerome also brings forward the interpretation of the name in his *Onomasticon* (Lagarde, *Onomastica sacra*, 2nd ed., p. 93):*barraban*, the son of their teacher. That is Syriac, not Hebrew.

There is here no reference to the Aramaic JG as the place where this translation was found. In the *Onomasticon* it is a question simply of the traditional interpretation of semitic names. In a Greek Origen-scholion of unknown date (in Gallandi, *Bibliotheca*, vol. XIV app. p. 81, cited in Klostermann, *Apocrypha*, p. 10, note on lines 9ff.) it is said:

> For clearly the brigand bore a patronymic, Barabbas, which being interpreted is 'son of the teacher'. Conformably the name Barabban means 'son of our teacher'.

In the second interpretation the termination 'an' is understood as a personal suffix of the first person. A similar scholion is found in the Codex S (028) and in other manuscripts at Mt. 27:17:

> Barabbas, which being interpreted is 'son of the teacher' (cf. Tischendorf, NTG octava *ad loc.*).

These scholia testify to a tolerably extensive onomastic tradition which manifestly does not go back to Jerome, since it is nowhere carried back to him and since it nowhere contains the objectionable personal pronoun 'their' given by him. In his remark about the name Barabbas it may be a question of such a tradition and not of a citation from the GN. Since it is questionable whether Jerome had had the GN actually in his hands, since it is established that his commentaries are compilations, and since it is certain that he attributed to the esteemed JG much that he had found elsewhere, no absolute certainty is to be attributed to his statement of the place where he found this meaning of the name. Rather we must reckon with the possibility of an error. He probably found the interpretation 'son of the teacher' or 'son of our teacher' in one of the commentaries which he used, of his own accord inserted the personal pronoun 'their' in order to distinguish this 'teacher' from the 'teacher' of Christians, and localised the whole in his JG. At all events the interpretation of the name given by Jerome is linguistically so impossible that it can have stood neither in an Aramaic original nor in an Aramaic translation; this note does not suffice as a basis capable of bearing the postulate of a Greek GN as the original of the Aramaic.

After what has been said in the introduction to the JG under Nos. 4 and 6 the further arguments of Waitz for the existence of a Greek GN anterior to the Aramaic (Ign. *Smyrn.* 3. 2; Jn. 7:53-8:11; Waitz, 'Evangelien', p. 19) are futile.

The fragments Nos. 5 and 7 certainly assume a Greek text, but no other than that of the canonical Mt. The GN was clearly an Aramaic version of the Greek Mt., but, as the fictional enlargements of canonical scenes, many corrections and deletions and the insertion of new sayings of the Lord show, it was no accurate translation, but a targumistic rendering of the canonical Gospel of Mt.

3. Literary Character: So far as can be discovered from the fragments the GN was a gospel of the synoptic type (Wilson, 'Evangelien', pp. 327-330 thinks otherwise). Alike in its narratives and in its discourse material it proves itself for the most part secondary in comparison with Mt.

In the narratives a fictional development of the tradition can often be detected. Especially significant is the Nazaraean variant in No. 16 of the story of the rich young man (Mt. 19:16-30). The one rich man has become two; such doublings, which can also be observed e.g. in Mt. (cf. Mt. 20:29ff. with Mk. 10:46ff.), are signs of a later stage of the tradition. The situation is fictionally delineated (Jesus and Peter are seated; the rich man who has been spoken to scratches his head); J. Jeremias (*Unknown Sayings*, pp. 46f.) points out 'Palestinian colouring': the phrase 'sons of Abraham'; 'brother' in the sense of fellow-countryman; the animation of what is inanimate (nothing 'comes forth' from the goods that are in the house); such traits show the semitic character of this JG. The saying of Jesus is more detailed; with a graphic description of the prevailing misery it comments upon the requirement to fulfil the law and the prophets. Here there is a suggestion of a social motive which is not yet present in Mt. 19:16ff. Whilst in Mt. vs. 21 the giving away of one's goods to the poor expresses how extremely serious a thing it is to follow Christ, in the GN it is motivated by charity; the transformation of eschatological into ethical ideas, so characteristic of the development of the tradition, is evident. The investigation of this pericope, ascribed to the GH, by A.F.J. Klijn confirms its dependence on Matthew and in addition identifies agreements with Luke and with variant synoptic readings. The witnesses claimed for Tatian's Diatessaron (Ephraem, Aphraates) also offer parallels and make the question of relationship appear meaningful. The conclusion here is that the Diatessaron was influenced by the 'GH' text, and evidently presupposes an Aramaic or Syriac stage of the tradition ('The Question of the Rich Young Man in a Jewish-Christian Gospel', NT 8, 1966, 149-155).

No. 10 shows a similar secondary character. The story of the healing of the withered hand is fictionally enlarged by a request from the sick man, and further it is given a different point through a social motive.

The conversation of Jesus with his mother and his brethren (No. 2) is a variant of the conversation with the Baptist and is determined by the dogmatic idea of the sinlessness of Jesus.

If the passion story told in the GN (No. 21) actually reported the collapse of the lintel instead of the rending of the veil of the temple - a trait which recurs in the mediaeval *Historia passionis domini* (No. 36) - then here also we have to do with a fictional development, which has perhaps been influenced by the account in Josephus of calamitous omens of the destruction of the Temple (*Bell. Jud.* VI 293-300) or by Eusebius (*Chronicon*, ad annum 32, ed. Helm, [2]1956, p. 175; cf. Bardy, 'Jérôme', pp. 19ff.).

The mediaeval fragments of the JG show the growth of fictional and legendary interests. These determine the working-up of the Magi episode, No. 28 (the introduction of Joseph, who is wanting in the Matthaean Magi legend; the colourful description of the circumstances; on a cave as the place of Jesus' birth cf. Justin, *Dial.* 78 and *Protev. Jacobi*, 18, 19, 21. 3 and W. Bauer, *Leben Jesu*, pp. 61ff.; the dress described characterises the Magi as Persians, more accurately as servants of Mithras, as they are also characterised in representations of this scene in Christian art; cf. A. Dieterich, 'Die Weisen aus dem Morgenlande', ZNW 3, 1902, 4f.). A legendary interest in secondary characters is also found in Nos. 29, 30, 33; edifying traits in the martyrdom style in Nos. 24 and 35.

As regards the discourse material of the GN there are occasions when a late stage of the tradition history can clearly be recognised. No. 18 can claim no originality in comparison with Mt. 25:14ff. In the saying on forgivingness (No. 15) the sin of the brother is, as compared with Mt. 18:21f., limited to sins of the tongue, to insulting language; Jeremias however pleads for the authenticity of the Nazarene version (*Unknown Sayings*, pp. 94ff.). J.B. Bauer has convincingly shown that Jerome is not the author of the Latin recension of the text, which may stand very close to its Greek *Vorlage*. According to him *etenim* (*in prophetis*) and the expression *sermo peccati* are alien to the Vulgate language of Jerome (BZ NF 4, 1960, 122-128). The semitic stamp of the latter expression makes it worthy of consideration that the text originally affirmed of the prophets not 'sinful speech' but 'sin' (cf. also M.J. Lagrange, 'L'Évangile selon les Hébreux', RB 31, 1922, 334-339; A. de Santos Otero, *Evangelios*, p. 42 with note 32, p. 46; Michaelis, *Schriften*, pp. 124, 127 - with reference to Mt. 5:37, where because of the semitic stamp the translation should likewise not be literal). There has often been discussion as to whether the combination of Lk. 17:4 with Mt. 18:21f. makes it legitimate to draw any conclusion about Tatian's Diatessaron, but the question of relationship is at best left open (J.B. Bauer, *op. cit.* p. 125) and may here be set aside. The saying in No. 23 has no synoptic parallel, but on the other hand it contains two 'Johannine' expressions: 'I choose' (cf. Jn. 6:70; 13:18; 15:16, 19) and 'whom my Father giveth me' (cf. Jn. 6:37, 39; 17:2, 6, 24); these expressions Jeremias (*op. cit.* p. 5, note 2) considers post-Johannine. At all events we can see here, as already in Q (Mt. 11:25ff. and par.) an infiltration of 'Johannine' motifs. The Judaikon reading at Mt. 7:5 (No. 6), which is actually a variant of Mt. 7:21f., has an apocryphal parallel in 2 Clem. 4. 5:

> Though ye be gathered together in my bosom and do not my commandments, I will cast you away and will say to you: Depart from me, I know you not whence ye are, ye workers of iniquity.

On the tradition-history of this saying cf. Bultmann, *Die Geschichte der synoptischen Tradition*, 1979, pp. 98, 122f. (ET 1968, pp. 94, 116f.). It is a point of importance that in place of the original 'Lord, Lord' saying there appears 'to be in my bosom', that the 'symbol of the cultic-legal piety' (Dibelius) is replaced by a formula of mystical communion (on this term cf. W. Bauer, *Das Johannesevangelium*, [3]1933, on 1:18); Dibelius rightly sees here 'the intrusion of exotic expressions' (*Geschichte*, p. 53).

Its literary character shows the GN secondary as compared with the canonical Mt; again, from the point of view of form-criticism and the history of tradition, as well as from that of language, it presents no proto-Matthew but a development of the Greek Gospel of Matthew (against Waitz). 'It is scarcely to be assumed that in it we are dealing with an independent development of older Aramaic traditions; this assumption is already prohibited by the close relationship with Mt. On the other hand the Aramaic (Syriac) GN cannot be explained as a retroversion of the Greek Mt; the novelistic expansions, new formations, abbreviations and corrections forbid that. In literary terms the GN may best be characterised as a targum-like rendering of the canonical Mt' (Vielhauer, *Geschichte*, p. 652).

4. Time and place of origin: the *terminus a quo* is accordingly the writing of Mt., the *terminus ad quem* is Hegesippus (180), who is the first to testify to the existence of the GN. It will have appeared in the first half of the second century.

The place of its origin is uncertain. We must think of regions in which Aramaic-speaking Jewish Christian churches continued down to the time of Jerome. It is quite possible that the GN originated where according to the testimony of Epiphanius and Jerome it was in use as *the* Gospel, in Beroea (Aleppo) in Coelesyria.

The circles in which it arose, those of Syrian Jewish Christians (Nazaraeans), were clearly not 'heretical' but belonged, so far as the GN permits us to make out, to the great Church; 'in content and character it was not more Jewish Christian than Mt.' (Waitz, 'Evangelien', p. 28).

Fragments

1. To these [*namely the citations in which Mt. follows not the Septuagint but the Hebrew original text*] belong the two: 'Out of Egypt have I called my son'[2] and 'For he shall be called a Nazaraean.'[3]

(Jerome, vir. inl. 3)

2. Behold, the mother of the Lord and his brethren[4] said to him: John the Baptist baptises unto the remission of sins,[5] let us go and be baptised by him.[6] But he said to them: Wherein have I sinned that I should go and be baptised by him?[7] Unless what I have said is ignorance (a sin of ignorance).[8]

(Jerome, adv. Pelag. III 2)

3. The Jewish Gospel has not 'into the holy city'[9] but 'to Jerusalem'.[10]

(Variant to Mt. 4:5 in the Zion Gospel Edition)

4. The phrase 'without a cause'[11] is lacking in some witnesses and in the Jewish Gospel.

(Variant to Mt. 5:22, ibid.)

5. In the so-called Gospel according to the Hebrews instead of 'essential to existence' I found '*maḥar* ', which means 'of tomorrow', so that the sense is:

Our bread of tomorrow - that is, of the future - give us this day.[12]

(Jerome, Com. on Mt. on 6:11 and Tract. on Ps. cxxxv)

6. The Jewish Gospel reads here as follows:

If ye be in my bosom and do not the will of my Father in heaven, I will cast you out of my bosom.[13]

(Variant to Mt. 7:5, or better to Mt. 7:21ff., in the Zion Gospel Edition)

7. The Jewish Gospel: (wise) more than serpents.

(Variant to Mt. 10:16, ibid.)

8. The Jewish Gospel has: (the kingdom of heaven) is plundered.

(Variant to Mt. 11:12, ibid.)

9. The Jewish Gospel: I thank thee.

(Variant to Mt. 11:25, ibid.)

10. In the Gospel which the Nazarenes and the Ebionites use, which we have recently translated out of Hebrew into Greek, and which is called by most people the authentic (Gospel) of Matthew, the man who had the withered hand[14] is described as a mason who pleaded for help in the following words:

I was a mason and earned (my) living with (my) hands; I beseech thee, Jesus, to restore to me my health that I may not with ignominy have to beg for my bread.

(Jerome, Com. on Mt., on 12:13)

11. The Jewish Gospel does not have: three d(ays and nights).

(Variant to Mt. 12:40 in the Zion Gospel Edition)

12. The Jewish Gospel: what you should obtain from us is corban.

(Variant to Mt. 15:5, *ibid.*)

13. What is marked with an asterisk[15] is not found in other manuscripts, also it is not found in the Jewish Gospel.

(Variant to Mt. 16:2f., *ibid.*)

14. The Jewish Gospel: son of John.[16]

(Variant to Mt. 16:17, *ibid.*)

15a. He [*namely Jesus*] said: If thy brother has sinned with a word and has made thee reparation, receive him seven times in a day.[17] Simon his disciple said to him: Seven times in a day? The Lord answered and said to him: Yea, I say unto thee, until seventy times seven times.[18] For in the prophets also, after they were anointed with the Holy Spirit, the word of sin [*sinful discourse?*][19] was found.

(Jerome, *adv. Pelag.* III 2)

15b. The Jewish Gospel has after 'seventy times seven times': For in the prophets also, after they were anointed with the Holy Spirit, the word of sin [*sinful discourse?*] was found.

(Variant to Mt. 18:22 in the Zion Gospel Edition)

16. The other of the two rich men said to him:[20] Master, what good thing must I do that I may live? He said to him: Man, fulfil the law and the prophets. He answered him: That have I done. He said to him: Go and sell all that thou possessest and distribute it among the poor, and then come and follow me. But the rich man then began to scratch his head and it [*the saying*] pleased him not. And the Lord said to him: How canst thou say, I have fulfilled the law and the prophets? For it stands written in the law: Love thy neighbour as thyself;[21] and behold, many of thy brethren, sons of Abraham, are begrimed with dirt and die of hunger - and thy house is full of many good things and nothing at all comes forth from it to them! And he turned and said to Simon, his disciple, who was sitting by him: Simon, son of Jona, it is easier for a camel to go through the eye of a needle than for a rich man to enter into the kingdom of heaven.

(Origen, *Com. on Mt.* XV 14 on 19:16ff. in the Latin rendering)

17. In the Gospel which the Nazarenes use, instead of 'son of Barachias'[22] we have found written 'son of Joiada'.[23]

(Jerome, *Com. on Mt.* on 23:35)

18. But since the Gospel [*written*] in Hebrew characters which has come into our hands enters the threat not against the man who had hid [*the talent*], but against him who had lived dissolutely[24] - for he [*the master*] had three servants: one who squandered his master's substance with harlots and flute-girls,[25] one who multiplied the gain, and one who hid the talent; and accordingly one was accepted (with joy), another

merely rebuked, but the other cast into prison - I wonder whether in Matthew the threat which is uttered after the word against the man who did nothing may refer not to him, but by epanalepsis to the first who had feasted and drunk with the drunken.

(Eusebius, *Theophania* IV 22 on Mt. 25:14f.; Klostermann, *Apocrypha*, p. 9, No. 15).

19. The Jewish Gospel: And he denied and swore and damned himself.

(Variant to Mt. 26:74 in the Zion Gospel Edition)

20. Barabbas . . . is interpreted in the so-called Gospel according to the Hebrews as 'son of their teacher'.

(Jerome, *Com. on Mt.* on 27:16)

21. But in the Gospel which is written in Hebrew characters we read not that the veil of the temple was rent, but that the lintel of the temple of wondrous size collapsed.

(Jerome, *Epist.* 120 *to Hedibia* and *Com. on Mt.* on 27:51)

22. The Jewish Gospel: And he delivered to them armed men that they might sit over against the cave and guard it day and night.

(Variant to Mt. 27:65 in the Zion Gospel Edition)

23. He [Christ] himself taught the reason for the separations of souls[26] that take place in houses, as we have found somewhere in the Gospel that is spread abroad among the Jews in the Hebrew tongue, in which it is said: I chose[27] for myself the most worthy:[28] the most worthy are those whom my Father in heaven has given me.[29]

(Eusebius, *Theophania* - In Syriac - IV 12 on Mt. 10:34-36)

Examples from the Middle Ages:

24. As it is said in the Gospel of the Nazaraeans:
At this word of the Lord[30] many thousands of the Jews who were standing round the cross became believers.[31]

(Haimo of Auxerre, *Com. on Is.* on 53:12)

25. In the Gospel books which the Nazarenes use we read:
Rays went forth from his eyes, by which they were affrighted and fled.[32]

(Marginal note in a manuscript of the *Aurora* of Peter of Riga)

26. These eight days of the Passover at which Christ, the Son of God, rose again[33] signify eight days after the recurrence[?] of the Passover[34] at which all the seed of Adam will be judged,[35] as is proclaimed in the Gospel of the Hebrews; and for this reason the learned believe that the day of judgment will be at Easter time, because on that day Christ rose again, that on that day also the saints should rise again.

(From the *Catéchèse celtique* of the Breton Vaticanus Regin. lat. 49; *Studi e Testi*, 59, 1933, 58)

27. In these cities (namely Chorazin and Bethsaida) many wonders have been wrought,[36] as their number the Gospel according to the Hebrews gives 53.

('Historical Commentary on Luke' on Lk. 10:13; MS: Clm 6235, fol. 56[r]: cited in Bischoff, 'Wendepunkte', p. 262)

28. For thus the Gospel which is entitled 'According to the Hebrews' reports:

When[37] Joseph looked out with his eyes, he saw a crowd of pilgrims who were coming in company to the cave,[38] and he said: I will arise and go out to meet them. And when Joseph went out, he said to Simon:[39] It seems to me as if those coming were soothsayers, for lo, every moment they look up to heaven and confer one with another. But they seem also to be strangers, for their appearance differs from ours; for their dress is very rich and their complexion quite dark; they have caps on their heads and their garments seem to me to be silky, and they have breeches on their legs. And lo, they have halted and are looking at me, and lo, they have again set themselves in motion and are coming here.

From these words it is clear that not merely three men, but a crowd of pilgrims came to the Lord, even if according to some the foremost leaders of this crowd were named with the definite names Melchus, Caspar and Phadizarda.

(Sedulius Scotus, *Com. on Mt.*; MSS: Berlin, Phil. 1660, 9th cent. fol. 17[v]; Vienna 740, 9th cent. fol. 15[r.v.]; cited Bischoff, 'Wendepunkte', pp. 203f.)

29. On Mt. 9:20 (a woman with an issue of blood) named Mariosa

on Mt. 12:10 'a man' by name Malchus and he was a mason.

on Mt. 12:42 'the queen', namely Meroe, 'of the south', that is Aethiopia.

(*Com. on Mt.*; MS: Würzburg, M. p. th. fol. 61, 8th-9th cent., cited in Bischoff, *op. cit.* p. 252)

30. on Lk. 8:42 'the daughter', that is the synagogue, whose name is Mariossa.

on Lk. 11:31 'the queen of the south' whose name is Meruae.

('Historical Com. on Lk.'; MS: Clm. 6235 fol. 55[v] and 57[v], cited in Bischoff, *op. cit.* p. 262)

From the *Historia passionis Domini*, MS: Theolog. Sammelhandschrift, 14th-15th cent., foll. 8-71 (14th cent.)

31. (And he wiped their feet.)[40] And as it is said in the Gospel of the Nazaraeans: He kissed the feet of each one of them.[41]

(fol. 25[v])

32. And how the angel strengthened Christ in his struggle in prayer,[42] is told in the Gospel of the Nazaraeans. And the same is also adduced by Anselm in his lamentation: Be constant, Lord, for now comes the time in which through thy passion mankind sold in Adam will be ransomed.[43]

(fol. 32[r])

33. In the Gospel of the Nazaraeans the reason is given why John was known to the high priest.[44] As he was the son of the poor fisherman Zebedee,[45] he had often brought fish to the palace of the high priests Annas and Caiaphas. And John went out to the damsel that kept the door and secured from her permission for his companion Peter, who stood weeping loudly before the door, to come in.

(fol. 35ʳ)

34. We read in the Gospel of the Nazaraeans that the Jews bribed four soldiers to scourge the Lord[46] so severely that the blood might flow from every part of his body. They had also bribed the same soldiers to the end that they crucified him, as it is said in Jn. 19...

(fol. 44ʳ)

35. (Father, forgive them, for they know not what they do.[47]) Note that in the Gospel of the Nazaraeans we have to read that at this virtuous discourse of Christ eight thousand were later converted to the faith; namely three thousand on the day of Pentecost as stated in the Acts of the Apostles 2,[48] and subsequently five thousand about whom we are informed in the Acts of the Apostles 10 (?)[49]

(fol. 55ʳ)

36. Also in the Gospel of the Nazaraeans we read that at the time of Christ's death the lintel of the Temple, of immense size, had split[50] (Josephus says the same and adds that overhead awful voices were heard which said: Let us depart from this abode).[51].

(fol. 65ʳ)

Notes

1. The Gospel of the Nazaraeans

1. Cf. L. Köhler-W. Baumgartner, *Lexikon in Veteris Testamenti Libros*, 1953, 893b; id. *Hebräisches und aramäisches Lexikon zum Alten Testament*, ³1974, pp. 598f.; G.H. Dalman, *Aramäisches-neuhebräisches Handwörterbuch zu Targum, Talmud und Midrasch*, ³1938, 252b. In the Syriac the word is *merauma*, and that precisely in our passage; *rama* in the sense of 'heaven' is first documented in Ephraem; cf. C. Brockelmann, *Lexicon Syriacum*, ²1928, 720b.
2. Cf. Mt. 2:15; Hos. 11:1.
3. Cf. Mt. 2:23 (Lev. 21:12; Jud. 13:5; Isa. 11:1; 53:2).
4. Cf. Mt. 12:46 par.
5. Cf. Mk. 1:4; Lk. 3:3.
6. Cf. Mt. 3:13; Mk. 1:9.
7. Cf. Mt. 3:14.
8. Cf. Lev. 4:2; 5:18b.
9. Cf. Mt. 4:5.
10. Cf. Lk. 4:9.
11. Cf. Mt. 5:22 ℵ² DW Θ 0233 f¹·¹³ M it sy co: Jrˡᵃᵗ.

12. Cf. Mt. 6:11 (Lk. 11:3).
13. Cf. Mt. 7:21, 23; 2 Clem. 4. 5.
14. Cf. Mt. 12:9ff. par.
15. Cf. Mt. 16:2f. (onwards from 'When it was evening'); the saying is also lacking in ℵBXΓf¹³ al sy ˢ·ᶜ sa boᵖᵗ ; Or
16. Cf. Mt. 16:17; Jn. 1:42; 21:15ff.
17. Cf. Lk. 17:4.
18. Cf. Mt. 18:21f.
19. Cf. Jas. 3:2.
20. Cf. Mt. 19:16-24.
21. Cf. Lev. 19:18.
22. Cf. Mt. 23:35; Zech. 1:1.
23. Cf. 2 Chron. 24:20ff.
24. Cf. Mt. 25:14-30.
25. Cf. P. Ox. 840.
26. Cf. Mt. 10:34ff.
27. Cf. Jn. 13:18; 15:16, 19.
28. Cf. Mt. 10:13.
29. Cf. Jn. 6:37, 39; 17:2, 6, 9; Mt. 11:27.
30. Cf. Lk. 23:34.
31. Cf. Lk. 23:48; Gospel of Peter 7, 25; GN 35.
32. Cf. Mt. 21:12ff.
33. Cf. Mk. 16:1-8 par.
34. Cf. Rom. 4:25.
35. Cf. Rev. 20:11ff.
36. Cf. Lk. 10:13; Mt. 11:20f.
37. Cf. Mt. 2:9ff.
38. Justin, *Dial.* 78; Protev. Jacobi 18, 19, 21.
39. Cf. Mk. 6:3?
40. Cf. Jn. 13:5.
41. Cf. Lk. 7:38-45.
42. Cf. Lk. 22:43ff.
43. Cf. Gal. 3:13.
44. Cf. Jn. 18:15ff.
45. Cf. Mk. 1:19f.
46. Cf. Mk. 15:15-20; Mt. 27:27-31; Jn. 19:1-3.
47. Cf. Lk. 23:34; GN 24.
48. Cf. Acts 2:41.
49. Cf. Acts 4:4.
50. Cf. GN 21.
51. Cf. Josephus, *Bell. Jud.* VI 293-300.

2. The Gospel of the Ebionites

Introduction

1. Testimony: Epiphanius testifies to a JG which was used by the Jewish Christian sect of the Ebionites, which must have been an abridged and falsified Gospel of Matthew, and which he incorrectly entitles the 'Gospel of Hebrews' and the 'Hebrew Gospel' (see pp. 140f. above). What title it actually bore is unknown. In the rest of the heresiological literature it is neither attested nor quoted. For our knowledge of it we are dependent on the accounts and quotations in Epiphanius.

Origen (*Hom. on Lk.* 1:1) and Jerome (Introduction to his *Com. on Mt.* and *adv. Pelag.* III 2) mention a 'Gospel according to the Twelve' or 'according to the Apostles', which the latter identifies with the Aramaic GH read among the Nazaraeans (see pp.145f. above). This identification is not to be trusted; for against Jerome, who in other respects also is unreliable, Origen clearly distinguishes between the GH and the Gospel of the Twelve (O. Bardenhewer, *Geschichte der altkirchlichen Literatur*, I, 1902, 384, is much to the point). The fact that Jerome wrongly identifies the gospel *secundum apostolos* with the GH and describes it as *juxta Matthaeum* recalls the introduction which Epiphanius prefaces to his presentation of the fragments of the Gospel of the Ebionites, according to which the GE 'is called after Matthew' and is identical with the 'Hebrew gospel' (*Haer.* 30.13.2f.). The fragment which Epiphanius quotes at this point has for its content the call of the 'twelve apostles for a testimony to Israel'.

Since according to Origen the Gospel of the Twelve is said to be a gospel of synoptic type, but on the other hand did not rank for him as a document of the Church, both of which are also true for the GE, and in addition the twelve apostles are said to appear as informants in both cases, Waitz identified the Gospel of the Twelve with the GE ('Evangelium', pp. 345ff.). The Syriac sources named by Schmidtke (*Fragmente*, pp. 170ff.), with the help of which he seeks to show the gnostic character of the Gospel of the Twelve (on the character of the Quqājē cf. H.J.W. Drijvers, 'Quq and the Quqites. An Unknown Sect in Edessa in the Second Century A.D.', in id. *East of Antioch*, 1984, XIV, 104-129), and in consequence denies an identification with the GE, are too uncertain, since it cannot be made clear whether the Syrian sect of the Quqājē had a Gospel of the Twelve (to the point: Waitz *op. cit.* pp. 46f.; cf. Drijvers, *op. cit.* pp. 123ff.).

Despite the arguments advanced by Waitz, it remains questionable whether the fragment cited by Epiphanius is to be reckoned to the GE, since the narrative style (first person plural: 'who chose *us*') deviates from the GE fragments handed down. In addition there are difficulties about the positioning of the fragment. Its inclusion here as fragment No. 4 is a makeshift expedient, which does indeed correspond to the chronological place in the gospel narrative, but cannot remove the formal impediment. Possibly Epiphanius shows by bringing it forward that he has come upon a fragment of a tradition independent of the GE, which suggests the conjecture that an independent Gospel of the Twelve was in existence in the time of Epiphanius.

2. Content and compass: Waitz has sought to reconstruct the content and compass of the GE by assigning to it Gospel citations from the *Kerygmata Petrou* and another source-document of the pseudo-Clementines ('Evangelium', pp. 48ff.; 'Evangelien', pp. 39f.). But G. Strecker has in my opinion shown convincingly that no JG is cited in the pseudo-Clementines (*Judenchristentum*, Section D, pp. 117-136; cf. id. 'Die Makarismen der Bergpredigt', in id., *Eschaton und Historie*, 1979, pp. 108-131, 112). Also the two citations from Origen, *de Princ*. IV 22 and Clement Alex. *Strom.* V 10, 63, which Waitz adduces ('Evangelien', pp. 47f., Nos. 37 and 59b) cannot with certainty be carried back to the GE. There remain only the fragments that have been handed down by Epiphanius.

These have to do with John the Baptist and his work, the call of the disciples and the baptism of Jesus, and contain a parallel to Mt. 12:46-50, one to Mt. 5:17 and one to Mt. 26:17ff.; Lk. 22:15. The GE began, as Epiphanius states emphatically, not with the nativity narrative but with the appearance of the Baptist; it contained an account of the last supper and then also probably a history of the passion and Easter, about which, however, we know nothing in detail. It may be that No. 6 comes from a kind of Sermon on the mount from which Epiphanius cites this one saying merely because of its peculiarity.

The structure of the GE is not entirely clear. No. 1 (appearance of the Baptist) forms the beginning. Then follow presumably the characterisation of the Baptist (No. 2) and the baptism of Jesus (No. 3). Epiphanius' introductory remark 'and after it has narrated many things' relates to the preceding passages, and does not necessarily presuppose the election pericope; this is therefore, in accordance with the canonical design, to be inserted as No. 4, even if in the process questions remain open; so does the problem whether two fragments were secondarily combined or whether we have a coherent text.

3. The Language: the GE was originally composed in Greek. Proof of that is furnished by the account of the food of the Baptist (No. 2) in which the locusts (ἀκρίς Mk. 1:6; Mt. 3:4) are missing and only 'wild honey, the taste of which was as manna, as a cake (ἐγκρίς) dipped in oil' is mentioned. This characterisation of the honey is borrowed from Num. 11:8, where the taste of the manna is so described; 'but without the similarity of the Greek words the author would hardly have lighted here on the manna' (Dibelius, *Geschichte*, p. 58). Dibelius also points out that the GE adheres considerably to the text of the Synoptic Gospels, and that goes to prove a composition in Greek.

4. Character: in literary character the GE is a Gospel of the synoptic type. It may be especially related to Mt. (No. 6 has a parallel in Mt. alone), but it also assumes the two other Synoptics. The chronological and biographical statements in the account of the Baptist, the statement about the age of Jesus and the saying No. 7 come from Lk. (cf. the notes to the fragments). In the story of the baptism of Jesus all the three synoptic accounts are utilised: it gives the voice from heaven three times, according to Mk. 1:11, Lk. 3:22 D it and Mt. 3:17. The original version alleged by R. Merkelbach, according to which the core of the Baptist narrative was the report of the shining of a light and this narrative was then secondarily assimilated to the synoptic tradition through the motif of the descent of the Holy Spirit in the form of a dove ('Kritische Beiträge 4. Ein Fragment des Ebionitenevangeliums', in *Studien zur Textgeschichte und Textkritik*, ed. K. Dahlmann and R. Merkelbach, 1959, pp. 164f.), is not very probable, especially since the motif of the shining of a light recurs in late manuscripts (cf. D.A. Bertrand, *Le baptême de Jésus. Histoire de l' exégèse aux premiers siècles*, BGBE 14, 1973, 44-46, 129). The dependence of the GE on the GN asserted by Waitz ('Evangelien', pp. 42f.), and after him by Schoeps, does not exist, since the evidences for this thesis have not been proven to belong to the GE. Rather is the GE to be described, with Bertrand, as a 'gospel harmony' ('L'Évangile des Ébionites', NTS 26, 1980, 548-563, 551), since in it the Synoptic Gospels find an additive application. In contrast to the Diatessaron of Tatian there is admittedly no use in it of John; nor is there any indication that the differences between the Gospels are consciously suppressed. So far as a harmonising tendency is present, it serves rather a novelistic interest, which takes up the concrete features of the synoptic gospel tradition or amplifies them independently. Thus the food of the Baptist ('wild honey' according to Mk. 1:6 par. Mt. 3:4) is elucidated by the addition mentioned above (p. 167) from Num. 11:8, 'whose taste was that of manna'; or, linking up with Lk. 1:5, Herod becomes 'king of Judaea'.

The deletion of the nativity story (Mt. 1 and 2) goes back to a dogmatic tendency. The Ebionites denied the virgin birth of Jesus; according to their Christology the divine sonship of Jesus rests not upon his divine begetting and wonderful birth, but on the union of the Holy Spirit with him at the time of his baptism (No. 3). That this 'entry' of the Holy Spirit is something other than his descent upon Jesus (Mk. 1:10; Mt. 3:16; Lk. 3:22), and thus no adoption or inspiration but the union of a heavenly being with the man Jesus, resulting in the Christ, the Son of God, so that in this trait there is to be discerned a gnostic characteristic of Ebionite Christology (so Dibelius, *Geschichte*, p. 56; Vielhauer, *Geschichte*, p. 655), is improbable. The strong dependence on the synoptic tradition leads one rather to think of the Marcan or Lucan conception of the baptism of Jesus. By setting the different synoptic passages about the baptism of Jesus side by side, it is brought about that Jesus is 'presented' before the Baptist as Son of God, and through his homage is 'acclaimed' as such. The ordaining of the twelve apostles for Israel underlines the Jewish character of this gospel (No. 4). Jesus' task is to do away with the 'sacrifices' (No. 6); in this saying the hostility of the Ebionites against the Temple cult is documented. No. 7 and probably also the account of the food of the Baptist (deletion of the locusts) point to vegetarianism.

A specific Christology, hostility to the cult, and vegetarianism - these dogmatic elements distinguish the Jewish Christianity of the Ebionites from that of the Nazaraeans and characterise it as deviating from the Christianity of the Great Church, as 'heretical'. A closer description of this Jewish Christianity is not possible on the basis of the GE fragments.

5. Time and place of origin: since the GE presupposes the Synoptics, it can have originated at the earliest in the beginning of the 2nd century. Irenaeus (*c.* 175) knew of its existence, although only from hearsay. Accordingly the origin of the GE is to be dated in the first half of the 2nd century.

The place of origin is uncertain. It was possibly composed in the region east of Jordan, where according to the accounts of the Church Fathers the Ebionites had their headquarters and where Epiphanius will have seen the book and made excerpts from it.

Fragments:

1. And the beginning of their Gospel runs:

It came to pass in the days of Herod the king of Judaea,[1] <when Caiaphas was high priest,[2]> that there came <one>, John <by name,> and baptised with the baptism of repentance in the river Jordan.[3] It was said of him that he was of the lineage of Aaron the priest, a son of Zacharias and Elisabeth;[4] and all went out to him.[5]

(Epiphanius, *Haer*. 30.13.6)

2. And

It came to pass that John was baptising;[6] and there went out to him Pharisees and were baptised,[7] and all Jerusalem.[8] And John had a garment of camel's hair and a leathern girdle about his loins, and his food, as it saith, was wild honey,[9] the taste of which was that of manna, as a cake dipped in oil.[10]

Thus they were resolved to pervert the word of truth into a lie and to put a cake in the place of locusts.

(*ibid.* 30.13.4f.)

3. And after much has been recorded it proceeds:

When the people were baptised,[11] Jesus also came and was baptised by John.[12] And as he came up from the water, the heavens were opened and he saw the Holy Spirit in the form of a dove that descended[13] and entered into him. And a voice (sounded) from heaven that said: Thou art my beloved Son, in thee I am well pleased.[14] And again: I have this day begotten thee.[15] And immediately a great light shone round about the place.[16] When John saw this, it saith, he saith unto him:

Who art thou, Lord? And again a voice from heaven (rang out) to him: This is my beloved Son in whom I am well pleased.[17] And then, it saith, John fell down before him and said: I beseech thee, Lord baptise thou me. But he prevented him and said: Suffer it; for thus it is fitting that everything should be fulfilled.[18]

(*ibid.* 30.13.7f.)

BAC
148; 50
(§ 2)

4. In the Gospel that is in general use amongst them, which is called according to Matthew, which however is not whole (and) complete but forged and mutilated - they call it the Hebrew Gospel - it is reported:

There appeared a certain man named Jesus of about thirty years of age,[19] who chose us.[20] And when he came to Capernaum,[21] he entered into the house of Simon[22] whose surname was Peter,[23] and opened his mouth and said: As I passed along the Lake of Tiberias,[24] I chose John and James the sons of Zebedee, and Simon and Andrew and Thaddaeus and Simon the Zealot and Judas the Iscariot,[25] and thee, Matthew, I called as thou didst sit at the receipt of custom, and thou didst follow me.[26] You therefore I will to be twelve apostles for a testimony unto Israel.[27]

(*ibid.* 30.13.2f.)

5. Moreover they deny that he was a man, evidently on the ground of the word which the Saviour spoke when it was reported to him: 'Behold, thy mother and thy brethren stand without', namely:

Who is my mother and who are my brethren? And he stretched forth his hand towards his disciples and said: These are my brethren and mother and sisters, who do the will of my Father.[28]

(*ibid.* 30.14.5)

BAC
148: 52
(§ 6)

6. They say that he [Christ] was not begotten of God the Father, but created as one of the archangels . . . that he rules over the angels and all the creatures of the Almighty, and that he came and declared, as their Gospel, which is called [*according to Matthew? according to the Hebrews?*], reports:

I am come to do away with sacrifices,[29] and if ye cease not from sacrificing, the wrath of God will not cease from you.[30]

(*ibid.* 30.16.4f.)

BAC
148: 52
(§ 7)

7. But they abandon the proper sequence of the words and pervert the saying,[31] as is plain to all from the readings attached, and have let the disciples say:

Where wilt thou that we prepare for thee the passover? and him to answer to that:

Do I desire with desire at this Passover to eat flesh with you?

(*ibid.* 30.22.4)

Notes

2. The Gospel of the Ebionites

1. Cf. Lk. 1:5; Justin, *Dial.* 103.3.
2. Cf. Lk. 3:2.
3. Cf. Mk. 1:4f.; Lk. 3:3.
4. Cf. Lk. 1:5-18; 3:2.
5. Cf. Mt. 3:5; Mk. 1:5.
6. Cf. Mk. 1:4 (Mt. 3:1).
7. Cf. Mt. 3:7.
8. Cf. Mt. 3:5; Mk. 1:5.
9. Cf. Mt. 3:4; Mk. 1:6.
10. Cf. Exod. 16:31; Num. 11:8.
11. Cf. Lk. 3:21.
12. Cf. Lk. 3:21; Mt. 3:13; Mk. 1:9.
13. Cf. Mt. 3:16 par.
14. Cf. Mk. 1:11.
15. Cf. Lk. 3:23 D; Ps. 2:7.
16. On the shining of a light at the baptism of Jesus cf. Walter Bauer, *Leben Jesu*, pp. 134-139.
17. Cf. Mt. 3:17.
18. Cf. Mt. 3:14f.
19. Cf. Lk. 3:23.
20. Cf. Lk. 6:13.
21. Cf. Mk. 1:21; Lk. 4:31.
22. Cf. Mk. 1:29; Lk. 4:38.
23. Cf. Mt. 4:18.
24. Cf. Mk. 1:16; Mt. 4:18.
25. Cf. Mt. 10:2-4 par.
26. Cf. Mt. 9:9.
27. Cf. Mt. 10:2, 6; Mk. 3:14; Lk. 6:13; Barn. 8:3.
28. Cf. Mt. 12:47-50.
29. Cf. Mt. 5:17f.
30. Cf. Jn. 3:36b.
31. Cf. Mt. 26:17ff. par.; Lk. 22:15.

3. The Gospel of the Hebrews

Introduction.

1. Contents and compass: it is not known how the GH began; but if the Cyril fragment (No. 1) belonged to it, then in its introduction the pre-existence and birth of Jesus must have been recorded, and indeed largely otherwise than they are in the prologue to Jn. and in the nativity narratives of Mt. and Lk.; No. 1, the account of the descent of Jesus, seems to be a fragment which belongs essentially between the two accounts. No. 3 belongs obviously to a story of the temptation. It is not clear into what context the sayings (4, 5, 6) should be fitted, since synoptic parallels are wanting.

At its end, or somewhere near its end, the GH told the story of an appearance of Christ to James; in it two lost accounts are assumed, which however we can still trace by inference: the one was an account of the last supper according to which James the brother of the Lord had been present and had vowed to abstain from food until he had seen Jesus risen from the dead - a pledge which assumes that at the last supper Jesus had spoken of His death and resurrection; the other was an account of the resurrection according to which it must have taken place in the sight of those who guarded the sepulchre, for Jesus gives the linen cloth to the priest's servant; and this trait presupposes an account of the burial. It is clear that the account of Easter given in the GH departed considerably from those of the canonical Gospels (cf. Waitz, "Evangelien", pp. 58f.).

The fragments of the GH that have been preserved give us no idea of its compass. According to the Stichometry of Nicephorus it comprised 2200 lines, therefore only 300 fewer than the canonical Mt.

2. Character: as literature and in substance the GH differs considerably from the canonical Gospels and also from the GN and the GE. Its stories and sayings scarcely permit of their being understood as developments of synoptic or Johannine texts.

The appearance of the risen Christ to James is an independent legend, which has formed round an historical kernel of which the oldest witness is 1 Cor. 15:7. But that the first appearance of the risen Christ was to James, and that he was present at the last supper, contradicts the New Testament tradition; the target of the account is the setting free of the Lord's brother from his vow of abstinence; here a special interest in the person of James is evident. This interest gives the Christophany of the GH the character of a personal legend. The handing-over of the linen cloth to the priest's servant points to a legendary working-up of the resurrection story; if, as is probable, the linen cloth was intended to prove to the "priest" (the high priest) the reality of Jesus' resurrection, then an anti-docetic motive here makes its appearance. The account of the baptism (No. 2) is hardly a fictional or legendary development of the synoptic parallels, but a mythical variant (see below).

It is interesting that Jesus himself tells the story of the temptation (No. 3), as in the GE he tells of the choice of the apostles; possibly this was intended to explain how the disciples came to know about Jesus' temptation (Dibelius, *Geschichte*, p. 57); but as the example from the GE shows, in the I-form of the narrative we may have to do with a popular expedient in composition.

Among the sayings No. 4 is cast in a form that is worthy of note, the form of a rhetorical "chain" which in the New Testament occurs above all in Paul and in the epistle of James and to which Dibelius has devoted an instructive study (*Der Brief des Jakobus*, KEK 15, [11]1964, 126-129). The chain in No. 4 is a *climax* and portrays the way of salvation (seek - find - marvel - reign - rest). The saying has been handed down in four versions; it has already been said (p. 136) that the version which Clement first presents (No. 4a) is, as P.Ox. 654 shows, abbreviated compared with the later version (4b); the version of P. Ox. may be the more original since it is less polished, while on the other hand that of the Coptic Gospel of Thomas (see above, p. 117) presents a different chain: seek - find - be bewildered - marvel - reign. To the question which this difference occasions no answer can yet be given in the present state of investigation (on the relation of the Gospel of Thomas to the Gospel of the Hebrews, cf. Puech in NTApo[3] pp. 297f., 310).

The Jewish-Christian character of the GH is indicated not merely by the title (as to that see below) but above all by the emphasis on James the brother of the Lord, who according to the reports of the NT (Gal. 2; Acts 15; 21:18f.) and of Hegesippus (Eusebius, H.E. II 23.4-18) was the champion of a strict Jewish Christianity and leader of the early Jerusalem Church. Since contrary to the historical facts he is distinguished as a participant of Jesus' last supper and as the first witness and consequently the most important guarantor of the resurrection, it is clear that for the GH he is the highest authority in the circle of Jesus' acquaintances. This trait also has a striking parallel in the Coptic Gospel of Thomas (cf. logion 12, p. 119 above; on the James tradition: D. Kirchner, "Epistula Jacobi Apocrypha: die erste Schrift aus Nag-Hammadi-Codex I", Diss. theol., Berlin 1977; cf. also below, pp. 285ff.; W.P. Funk, *Die zweite Apokalypse des Jakobus Nag-Hammadi-Codex V*, 1976; cf. also below, pp.313ff.; A. Böhlig, "Der jüdische und judenchristliche Hintergrund in den gnostischen Schriften von Nag Hammadi", in id., *Mysterion und Wahrheit*, AGJU 6, 1968, 102-111). The understanding of the Holy Spirit as a female is also Jewish or semitic.

This Jewish Christianity however contains syncretistic-gnostic elements. The account of the carrying away of Jesus (No. 3) shows a strong mythological trait, the Holy Ghost being designated the mother of Jesus; what form was taken by the speculation here presupposed with regard to Jesus' birth is uncertain. But if, in spite of the objections urged in the introduction par. 8 (see above, p. 150), the Coptic Cyril fragment belongs to the GH, then the Holy Spirit is to be identified with the "mighty power in heaven" and Mary to be understood as the incarnation of the heavenly power. Not merely for Jesus but also for his mother the pre-existence and incarnation myth may have been assumed. That the mighty power in heaven was called Michael is not surprising, in view of his importance in Egyptian magical texts and in the *Pistis Sophia* (cf. W. Bauer, *Rechtgläubigkeit*, p. 57; ET *Orthodoxy*, p. 53) and in the last analysis is no decisive objection to the identification of the "mighty power" with the Holy Spirit. In the Coptic Epistle of James of the Cod. Jung, Jesus describes himself as "son of the Holy Spirit" (H.-Ch. Puech and G. Quispel, "Les écrits gnostiques du Codex Jung", *Vig.Chr.* 8, 1954, 12; see below, p. 293).

The story of the baptism (No. 2) also bears upon it mythical imprints. In the first place what happens is presented as inspiration and adoption. But the fact that it is not the voice (of God) which speaks out of the opened heaven as in the synoptic story of the baptism, but the Holy Spirit that has come down, and also the content of the words tell against the view that not until his baptism was Jesus inaugurated as Son of God. It is true that the last sentence has the ring of an adoption formula, but that ring is as faint as it is in Lk. 3:22 (contrasted with Mk. 1:11); for the two foregoing sentences assume Jesus' sonship, as the address "my Son" shows, and they characterise it otherwise than as messianic dignity ("thou art my rest"). The Holy Spirit waits for the coming of his Son, clearly for his coming forth from pre-existence; he has waited for him in all the prophets, but till now in vain; he waits for him that he may "rest" upon him. This "resting" of the Spirit upon his Son is clearly something other than the resting of the Spirit of the Lord upon the Messiah (Isa. 11:2), and is not inspiration but complete and final union of the Spirit with his Son ("the whole fount of the Spirit" comes down upon him: "thou art my rest"). The Holy Spirit speaks here as does the hypostatised divine Wisdom in the Jewish Wisdom Literature. As the Spirit waited in vain to find "his rest" in all the prophets until the Son came, so Wisdom "seeks" her "rest" in vain in all peoples until she finds it in Israel.

> With all these I sought rest (ἀνάπαυσις);
> And in whose inheritance shall I lodge?

> (Ecclus. 24:7)

And as the Spirit knows rest in no prophet, so from primaeval times Wisdom passes into ever new souls:

> From generation to generation passing into holy souls:
> She maketh (men) friends of God and prophets.

> (Wisd. 7:27)

The "rest" that the Holy Spirit waits for and finally finds in his Son is the eschatological rest. This is also the objective of the pre-existent Redeemer who, according to the Jewish-Christian-gnostic *Kerygmata Petrou*, after endless change in form becomes incarnate in Jesus:

> From the beginning of the world he runs through the ages, changing his form at the same time as his name, until in his time, anointed of God's mercy for his toil, he shall find his rest for ever.

> (ps. Clem.*Hom.* III 20.2;cf.*Rec.*II 22.4)

To the circle of such gnostic speculations belongs the Christology of the baptism pericope of the GH.

The chain-saying No. 4 with its *climax* "seek - find - marvel - reign - rest" points to the same religious milieu. It is not in the least an equivalent of Mt. 7:7, but with its notion of "rest"[1] has a New Testament parallel only in Mt. 11:28f. But even this passage is a foreign body in the synoptic tradition (cf. Dibelius, *Die Formgeschichte des Evangeliums* [5]1966, pp. 279-287; ET 1934, pp. 279ff.). Our saying describes the steps of the revelation of salvation and of the way of salvation. This description is characteristic of the Hermetic gnosis, as Dibelius has pointed out (*op. cit.* p. 285, note 2; ET p. 284, note 2); here also "to marvel" is found as a step (*Corp. Hermet.* IV 2; XIV 4) and the "rest" as eschatological salvation (*Corp. Hermet.* IX 10; XIII 20). The Jewish-Christian pseudo-Clementines speak in different ways of the "rest" as eschatological salvation: according to the *Kerygmata Petrou* the true prophet makes known "the word of rest" (*Hom.* III 26.5), and instruction as to who the true prophet is and as to how he is found is said "to bring to rest" (*Hom.* I 20.1); according to the basic writing one reaches "the haven of rest" (*Ep. Clem.* 13.3; 16.3), and in a prayer which goes back to the homilist "rest" is the last and highest of many affirmations about God ("Lord and Master of all, Father and God . . . thou art rest": *Hom.* III 72.1f.). In Clement of Alexandria there occurs the sentence: "For I shall take you up into rest (and into the enjoyment) of inexpressible and ineffable good things . . . " (*Quis dives salvetur* 23.3, cited by Dibelius, *op. cit.* p. 281, note 2). These examples of gentile, Jewish-Christian and churchly gnosis may make plain the atmosphere out of which there arose the "mystic" piety that reveals itself in our saying.

Because of the scantiness of the material we cannot say how strongly this mystic-gnostic religiosity has influenced the GH, whether it is an essential or merely an infused element. The two other sayings (5 and 6) with their demand for brotherly love stand much closer to the preaching of Jesus and could - as is not seldom the case - also be assigned to the GN (cf. Wilson, "Evangelien", p. 328). A fragment to which S.P. Brock has drawn attention corresponds to the same type as Nos. 5 and 6: in a Psalm-commentary preserved in the Tura papyri, traced back to Didymus the Blind (to be distinguished from the Psalm commentary of Didymus handed down in *catenae*), there is the following Greek text, in which the author comes to speak about the problem of the double names in the biblical tradition:

> (Scripture) seems to call Matthew "Levi" in the Gospel of Luke. Yet it is not a question of one and the same person. Rather Matthias, who was installed (as apostle) in place of Judas, and Levi are the same person with a double name. This is clear from the Gospel of the Hebrews.
>
> (Didymus the Blind, Psalm commentary (Tura papyrus) III, ed. and trans. M. Gronewald, *Papyrologische Texte und Abhandlungen* 8, 1968, p. 198:, p. 184. 9-10)[2]

While in Matthew Levi the tax-collector (Lk. 5:27, 29) is identified with Matthew (Mt. 9:9), the identification of the disciple Levi and the subsequently elected twelfth apostle Matthias is not attested elsewhere. Somewhere close to our text are the report of Clement of Alexandria that the chief collector Zacchaeus

(Lk. 19:2ff.) bore the name of Matthias (*Strom* IV 6.35.2), or the designation of the apostle Matthias as a "rich man" who left everything in order to follow Jesus (cf. Lk. 19:8) in the "Book of the Resurrection of Christ" ascribed to the apostle Bartholomew (E.A.W. Budge, *Coptic Apocrypha in the Dialect of Upper Egypt*, London 1913, Coptic p. 30, English p. 204). It may be left open here whether only this identification of Matthias with the tax-collector appeared in the "GH", and it was Didymus who first linked him with the name of Levi (Brock, "Testimonium", p. 222), or whether this identification originally belonged to the text of the "GH". At any rate a confusion of the name Matthias with Matthew was not only possible in the reading of a Greek text.

3. Title, country and time of origin: the GH is the only JG the title of which ("the Gospel according to the Hebrews") has been handed down. "When it is a matter of marking their nationality Greek-speaking Jews also are called Hebrews" (W. Bauer, *Rechtgläubigkeit*, p. 56 (ET *Orthodoxy*, p. 52); Bauer's position is contested by H.E.W. Turner, *The Pattern of Christian Truth: A Study in the Relations between Orthodoxy and Heresy in the Early Church*, 1954). The title characterises the book as the Gospel of Greek-speaking Jewish-Christian circles, and that in distinction from, and in contrast with, the Gospel of other and Gentile-Christian circles - for a distinction from the Gospels according to Matthew or Luke can hardly be implied in such a title. An analogous instance presents itself in the "Gospel according to the Egyptians". Bauer has made it probable that these two designations were provided to distinguish the Gospels of two churches existing in the same area, and that the Gospel of the Egyptians was the Gospel of the Egyptian Gentile-Christians, the GH the Gospel of the Egyptian Jewish-Christians (*op. cit.* pp. 54-57 [ET, pp. 50-53]; but cf. below, p. 214). If the GH was used in Egypt and given that name there, then it may also have originated there. Egypt is indicated as its place of origin also by the fact that its principal witnesses are the Alexandrians Clement and Origen, by the religio-historical character of the fragments Nos. 1 and 4, and also by the conception of Jesus as the Son of the Holy Spirit, which is documented for Egypt by the Coptic Epistle of James (Puech-Quispel, *op. cit.* pp. 7-22; see below, p. 293). The GH was known to Hegesippus and must therefore have originated, as did the two other JG, in the first half of the 2nd century. Since a literary dependence upon one of the other JG cannot be made out, the time of origin of the GH cannot be determined more closely.

Fragments:

1. It is written in the Gospel of the Hebrews:

When Christ wished to come upon the earth to men, the good Father summoned a mighty power in heaven, which was called Michael, and entrusted Christ to the care thereof. And the power came into the world and it was called Mary, and Christ was in her womb seven months.

(From the Coptic translation of a discourse ascribed to Cyril of Jerusalem ed. E.A.W. Budge, *Texts*, Coptic p. 60, English p. 637)

2. According to the Gospel written in the Hebrew speech, which the Nazaraeans read, the whole fount of the Holy Spirit shall descend upon him . . . Further in the Gospel which we have just mentioned we find the following written:

And it came to pass when the Lord was come up out of the water,[3] the whole fount of the Holy Spirit descended upon him and rested on him[4] and said to him: My Son,[5] in all the prophets was I waiting for thee that thou shouldest come and I might rest in thee.[6] For thou art my rest;[7] thou art my first-begotten Son[8] that reignest for ever.[9]

(Jerome, *Comm. on Is.* IV on Is. 11:2)

3. And if any accept the Gospel of the Hebrews - here the Saviour says:

Even so did my mother, the Holy Spirit,[10] take me by one of my hairs and carry me away[11] on to the great mountain[12] Tabor.

(Origen, *Com. on Jn.* II 12; *Hom. on Jer.* XV 4; Jerome, *Com. on Micah* 7:6; *Com. on Is.* 40:9; *Com. on Ezek.* 16:13)

4a. As also it stands written in the Gospel of the Hebrews:

He that marvels shall reign, and he that has reigned shall rest.

(Clem. Alex. *Strom.* II 9.45)

4b. To those words[13] this is equivalent:[14]

He that seeks will not rest until he finds; and he that has found shall marvel; and he that has marvelled shall reign; and he that has reigned shall rest.[15]

(Clem. Alex. *Strom.* V 14.96; cf. POx 654 and the Coptic Gospel of Thomas, p. 117 above)

5. As we have read in the Hebrew Gospel, the Lord says to his disciples:

And never be ye joyful, save when ye behold your brother with love.[16]

(Jerome, *Com. on Eph.* 5:4)

6. In the Gospel according to the Hebrews, which the Nazaraeans are wont to read, there is counted among the most grievous offences:

He that has grieved the spirit of his brother.[17]

(Jerome, *Com. on Ezek.* 18:7)

177

3AC
48:38
(§17)

7. The Gospel called according to the Hebrews which was recently translated by me into Greek and Latin, which Origen frequently uses, records after the resurrection of the Saviour:

And when the Lord had given the linen cloth to the servant of the priest, he went to James and appeared to him.[18] For James had sworn that he would not eat bread from that hour in which he had drunk the cup of the Lord until[19] he should see him risen from among them that sleep. And shortly thereafter the Lord said: Bring a table and bread! And immediately it is added: he took the bread, blessed it and brake it and gave it[20] to James the Just and said to him: My brother, eat thy bread, for the Son of man is risen from among them that sleep.[21]

(Jerome, *Vir.inl.* 2)

Notes

3. The Gospel of the Hebrews

1. On "rest" cf. P. Vielhauer, "ΑΝΑΠΑΥΣΙΣ. Zum gnostischen Hintergrund des Thomasevangeliums", TB 31, 1965, 215-234.
2. Cf. D. Lührmann, "Das Bruchstuck aus dem Hebräer-Evangelium bei Didymus von Alexandrien", *Nov.Test.* 29, 1987, 265-279.
3. Cf. Mt. 3:16.
4. Cf. Isa. 11:2; 61:1.
5. In the Coptic Epistle of James of the cod. Jung the risen Christ says to James and the disciples: "Soyez Élus, ressemblez au Fils de l'Esprit Saint" (Puech-Quispel, *Vig.Chr.* 8, 1954, 12).
6. Cf. Ecclus. 24:7.
7. Cf. Ps. 132:14.
8. Cf. Ps. 2:7; Lk. 3:22 D; Mk. 1:11; Exod. 4:22; Jer. 31:9; Col. 1:15; Hebr. 1:6.
9. Cf. Ps. 89:29f.; Lk. 1:33.
10. Cf. Mk. 1:12; Mt. 4:1.
11. Cf. Ezek. 8:3; Bel and the Dragon 36.
12. Cf. Mt. 4:8.
13. Plato, *Timaeus* 90.
14. Cf. Mt. 7:7; Lk. 11:9.
15. Cf. Mt. 11:28f.; Clem. Alex. *Quis dives salvetur* 23.3; *Corp. Hermet.* 13.20.
16. Cf. Lk. 15:31f.
17. Cf. Mt. 18:6.
18. Cf. 1 Cor. 15:7.
19. Cf. Mk. 14:25 par.
20. Cf. Mk. 14:22 par; 1 Cor. 11:23f.
21. Cf. Mk. 8:31 par.

V. The Gospel of Philip

Hans-Martin Schenke

1. Literature: *Facsimile: The Facsimile Edition of the Nag Hammadi Codices*, published under the Auspices of the Department of Antiquities of the Arab Republic of Egypt in Conjunction with the United Nations Educational, Scientific and Cultural Organization, Codex II, Leiden 1974, pl. (4-5), 63-98.

Editions of the Text: B. Layton (ed.), *Nag Hammadi Codex II 2-7, Together with XIII 2* ,Brit. Lib. Or. 4926 (1) and P. Oxy. 1, 654, 655*, vol. I (= Nag Hammadi Studies 20), Leiden 1989. J.-E. Ménard, *L'Évangile selon Philippe*, Strasbourg 1967. W.C. Till, *Das Evangelium nach Philippos* (= PTS 2), 1963.

Translations: C.J. de Catanzaro, 'The Gospel According to Philip', JTS NS 13, 1962, 35-71. B. Frid, 'Filippusevangeliet' (= SyBU 17), Lund 1966. W.W. Isenberg, 'The Gospel of Philip', in *The Nag Hammadi Library in English*, ed. J.M. Robinson, San Francisco 1977, pp. 131-151; rev. ed. 1988, 139-60.id. [The Gospel According to Philip, Translation] in *Nag Hammadi Codex II 2-7*, ed. B. Layton, I, 131-215 (with Coptic text) R. Kasser, 'Bibliothèque Gnostique VIII/IX: L'Évangile selon Philippe', *Revue de théologie et de philosophie* 20, 1970, 12-35, 82-106. M. Krause, 'Coptic Sources', in *Gnosis* II, ed. W. Foerster (ET by K.H. Kuhn), Oxford 1974, 76-101. B. Layton, 'The Gospel According to Philip, A Valentinian Anthology', in Layton, *The Gnostic Scriptures* 1987, pp. 325-353. H.-M. Schenke, 'Das Evangelium nach Philippus', ThLZ 84, 1959, cols. 1-26; id. 'Das Evangelium nach Philippus', in J. Leipoldt/H.-M. Schenke, *Koptisch-gnostische Schriften aus den Papyrus-Codices von Nag- Hamadi* (= Theologische Forschung 20), 1960, pp. 31-65, 81f.

Select further literature (for complete coverage cf. D.M. Scholer, *Nag Hammadi Bibliography 1948-1969* [= Nag Hammadi Studies 1], Leiden 1971, pp. 165-171, and the annual supplement under 'Bibliographia Gnostica' in *Novum Testamentum* since vol. 13, 1971): G.L. Borchert, 'An Analysis of the Literary Arrangement and Theological Views in the Gnostic Gospel of Philip' (Dissertation, Princeton Theological Seminary 1966). A.H.C. van Eijk, 'The Gospel of Philip and Clement of Alexandria: Gnostic and Ecclesiastical Theology on the Resurrection and the Eucharist', *Vig.Chr.* 25, 1971, 94-120. H.-G. Gaffron, 'Studien zum koptischen Philippusevangelium unter besonderer Berucksichtigung der Sakramente' (Ev. theol. Diss. Bonn, 1969). R.M. Grant, 'The Mystery of Marriage in the Gospel of Philip', *Vig.Chr.* 15, 1961, 129-140. A. Helmbold, 'Translation Problems in the Gospel of Philip', *New Testament Studies* 11, 1964, 90-93. W.W. Isenberg, 'The Coptic Gospel According to Philip' (Ph.D. Dissertation, University of Chicago, 1968); id. [The Gospel according to Philip] 'Introduction', in B. Layton [ed.], *Nag Hammadi Codex II 2-7*, I, 131-139. Y. Janssens, 'L'Évangile selon Philippe', *Le Muséon* 81, 1968, 79-133. R. Kasser, 'L'Évangile selon Philippe: Propositions pour quelques reconstitutions nouvelles', *Le Muséon* 81, 1968, 407-414. K. Koschorke, 'Die 'Namen' im Philippusevangelium', ZNW 64, 1973, 307-322. M. Krause, [review of Till's edition], ZKG 75, 1964, 168-182. K. Niederwimmer, 'Die Freiheit des Gnostikers nach dem Philippusevangelium', in O. Böcher/K. Haacker [eds.], *Verborum Veritas*: Festschrift für G. Stählin, 1970, pp. 361-374. H.-Ch. Puech, 'The Gospel of Philip', NTApo[3] I, 271-278. H.-M. Schenke, 'Die Arbeit am Philippus-Evangelium', ThLZ 90, 1965, cols. 321-332; id. 'Aus dem Evangelium Philippi', in J. Leipoldt/W. Grundmann, *Umwelt des Urchristentums*, Bd. II: Texte, 1967, 375-388. E. Segelberg, 'The Coptic-Gnostic Gospel according to Philip and its Sacrificial System', *Numen* 7, 1960, 189-200; id. 'The Antiochene Background of the Gospel of Philip', *Bull. Soc. Archéol. Copte* 18, 1965/66, 205-223; id. 'The Gospel of Philip and the New Testament', *The New Testament and Gnosis*: Essays in honour of R.McL. Wilson [ed. A.H.B. Logan/ A.J.M. Wedderburn], Edinburgh 1983, pp. 204-212. J.-M. Sevrin, 'Les noces spirituelles dans l'Évangile de Philippe', *Le Muséon* 77, 1974, 143-193. W.J. Stroud, 'The Problem of Dating the Chenoboskion Gospel of Philip' (Th.D. Dissertation, The Iliff School of Theology 1971); id. 'Ritual in the Chenoboskion Gospel of Philip', *Iliff Review* 28:2, 1971, 29-35. C. Trautmann, 'Le Parenté dans l'Évangile selon Philippe', *Colloque international sur les textes de Nag Hammadi [Québec, 22-25 Août 1978]*, ed. B. Barc [= Bibliothèque copte de Nag Hammadi, Section 'Études' 1], Quebec 1981, pp. 267-278. M.A. Williams, 'Realized Eschatology in the Gospel of Philip', *Restoration Quarterly* 14, 1971, 1-17. R.McL. Wilson, *The Gospel of Philip*, London and New York 1962; id. 'The New Testament in the Nag Hammadi Gospel of Philip', *New Testament Studies* 9, 1962/63, 291-294.

2. Attestation: the existence of the Gospel of Philip, or of a Gospel of Philip (Gos. Phil.), is directly attested on the one hand by Epiphanius (*Haer.* 26.13.2-3; Holl I 292.13-293.1), on the other hand and later by Timotheus of Constantinople (*de Receptione Haereticorum*; PG 86.1.21 C) and ps.-Leontius of Byzantium (*de Sectis* III 2; PG 86.1.1213 C). According to Epiphanius it was in use in the 4th century among libertine gnostics in Egypt; he also gives a verbatim quotation from it. According to Timotheus and ps.-Leontius, the Manicheans also use it, in addition to the Gospel of Thomas mentioned immediately before it. We may (or perhaps must) understand as an indirect witness for the existence of the/ a Gos. Phil. a passage in the Pistis Sophia (C. Schmidt, *Koptisch-gnostische Schriften I*, [4]1981, 44.14-47.8), in so far as there Philip appears along with Thomas and Matthew as a writer of the teachings and deeds of Jesus, with special emphasis on the teachings (see chapters 42-43 of Book I in MacDermot's translation [NHS 9] at pp. 143, 145 and 147).

The identity of the Gos. Phil. thus attested with the one that has survived and is presented here is of course problematic. The passage quoted by Epiphanius is not to be found in the text that has come down to us. Epiphanius says: 'They produce a spurious gospel composed in the name of the holy disciple Philip, saying that 'The Lord revealed to me what the soul must say as it ascends into heaven, and how it must answer each of the higher powers: 'I have known myself, and I have collected myself from every side; I have sowed no children for the Archon, but I have uprooted his roots and I have collected the members that were scattered, and I know who thou art. For I am one of those from on high.' And so it is allowed to go. But if it is found to have begotten a son, it is held fast here below until it can recover its own children and restore them to itself' (tr. after G.C. Stead, in Foerster, *Gnosis* I (ET 1972), 324-325; cf. Puech, NTApo[3] I, 273f.).

While the Gos. Phil. of Epiphanius' 'gnostics' thus clearly resists any identification with our Gos. Phil., there are no such difficulties with the Gos. Phil. of the Manicheans and that presupposed by the Pistis Sophia - because references to the content are there completely lacking. Indeed, in this case the connection with the Gospel of Thomas, attested or presupposed, might absolutely commend an identification with our Gos. Phil., which in the manuscript stands immediately after the Gospel of Thomas. Must we then see in the Gos. Phil. of Epiphanius' 'gnostics' a second Gos. Phil., quite different from ours? Should we after all, however we co-ordinate the other witnesses, reckon with two Gos. Phil.?

Against my own earlier view in this matter, and against a clear tendency among scholars, I would no longer answer this question in the affirmative without more ado, but would rather hold it perfectly possible that there was always only *one* Gos. Phil., and that all the testimonies refer to the one known to us. Our Gos. Phil. has such a well-marked character of its own, and is of such a fascination, that it is difficult to imagine how another document with the same title could have asserted itself alongside it. In addition the very theme with which the quotation in Epiphanius deals, the ascent of the soul after death through the archontic spheres, actually occurs in our Gos. Phil., and with striking frequency (cf.§§ 49, 59, 61c, 61d, 63a, 67d, 77, 97, 106, 107a, 107b, 127). It would thus be entirely comprehensible if the 'gnostics' expanded the Gos. Phil. before them by inserting a passage which directly dealt with this theme according to their views. And it would again be by no means accidental that in the refutation of their heresy just this specific passage should have been singled out as a revealing quotation. Such 'supplements' after all are well known from the textual history of other writings, and in no way affect the identity of a document.

The introductory phrase 'The Lord revealed to me', which does not harmonise with the textual *Gattung* of our present Gos. Phil., may be connected with a certain history through which the quotation itself has passed. The quotation in fact probably stands in a double framework: Epiphanius is quoting some authority, and it is his text which contains the quotation from the Gos. Phil. Again, the demarcation at the end of the quotation is problematic, and has been variously placed by scholars. But since for direct or indirect users of the Gos. Phil. this text contains the teachings of Jesus written down by Philip, it would not be too surprising if an original 'In the Gospel of Philip stands written the revelation of the Lord', and so on, had become our present '(Philip says in his gospel): The Lord revealed to me', etc. This suggestion is, however, valid only on the presupposition that the 'me' of the introductory phrase is to be related to Philip, which for a constituent element (even perhaps a secondary one) in the actual Gos. Phil. is anything but a matter of course.

3. Tradition: the Gos. Phil. has come down to us only in a Coptic version, and only in a single copy. This stands immediately after the Gospel of Thomas in the codex now counted as number II in the Cairo collection of the Nag Hammadi papyri (Coptic Museum, Department of Manuscripts, inv. 10544). This is a single-quire papyrus codex (28.4 x 15.8 cm.), complete with its sheepskin cover, and has no original pagination. According to the page numbering which has become usual among scholars, taking account only of the inscribed pages, the Gos. Phil. stands on pp. 51 (line 29) to 86 (line 19). As in the codex as a whole, the pages of our text are written in one column, which shows no kind of text-division, marginal aids or decoration. The time of the manufacture of the codex, which is important as the *terminus post quem non* for the composition of the Gos. Phil., cannot be directly determined (with the aid of dated documents transmitted by chance along with it); for the cover of Codex II is one of the three in which no scrap papyrus (used for stiffening the cover) was any longer found. However, from the dates found in documents from the remaining eight covers of codices in the Nag Hammadi collection - the three most important come from the cover of Codex VII - we may probably deduce for our codex also (and accordingly for our Coptic copy of the Gos. Phil.) an origin in the first half of the 4th century, especially since the palaeographical assessment of Codex II agrees with this.

The copy preserved in Codex II is not in a state to present the Gos. Phil. in an undamaged form. Even if the copy has been ever so carefully executed, more or less typical errors still occur, which neither the copyist nor a corrector has noticed and which thus have remained uncorrected. In the following translation the corrections of such passages are taken for granted, duly marked, and as a rule explained in the notes. Where no explanation is given, a { } appearing in the text signifies the deletion of a simple dittography (§§ 39, 48, 55b), a word in angled brackets < > the supplying of a missing grammatical element (§§ 94a, 97, 103), points within angled brackets < . . . > an anacoluthon; where a longer passage in angled brackets < > stands in immediate proximity to { } (namely in §§ 61b, 72a), this means that in the context of an attempt at a critical restoration of the damaged original text one and the same piece of text has been *moved* from the one place to the other. The real defect of this our only witness consists, however, in the very apparent fact that the papyrus leaves which contain the text show damage at the upper and especially the lower margin, increasing in extent towards the middle of the document and decreasing again towards the end. The resultant lacunae have indeed been restored - on the basis of the efforts of a whole generation of scholars - so far as is possible with some certainty or probability (such restora-tions are as usual placed in square brackets []). But there remain lacunae which defy restoration.

4. Original language, time and place of origin: the Coptic version of the Gos. Phil. which has come down to us in one copy must - as is the rule for Coptic literature - represent a translation from the Greek. Greek is probably also to be regarded as the original language in which the Gos. Phil. was composed. We can only estimate how much time lies between the composition of this Greek original and the emergence of our witness. The only fixed point at the other side, the *terminus ante quem non*, is the activity of the gnostic leader Valentinus (in Rome about 138-158), since the Gos. Phil. contains clearly Valentinian teachings, as will be shown in detail later. Since their character and the manner in which they appear seem to presuppose a certain development in the Valentinian school, we may not remain too close to the time of Valentinus himself for the presumptive time of composition. But Isenberg's dating to the second half of the 3rd century may still lie about half a century too late. The older view, often expressed, which would have the Gos. Phil. composed even in the 2nd century may still be considerably more probable.

Determining the place of composition is even more difficult. The only indications there are point to Syria. These are in particular the interest in Syriac words or Syriac etymologies (§§ 19, 47, 53); Isenberg mentions in addition both the familiarity with eastern sacramental practice and sacramental catechism and also the plea for encratite ethics. It is however problematic whether in a document of this kind we may really draw conclusions for the origin of the *whole* from indications which occur in separate *parts*. If however we do - especially when we add the connection on several levels with the Gospel of Thomas, certainly native to Syria - then it is at any rate east Syria, i.e. a genuinely bilingual milieu such as Edessa (Layton), that we should think of, rather than simply the region around Antioch in west Syria (so e.g. Krause).

Nothing can be discovered about the actual author of the Gos. Phil. - over against the fictitious authorship of Philip - or about the original purpose of the composition of his book. If there was an individual author at all, then from the character of his work he was in reality a collector or compiler.

5. The genre of the text and its title: what kind of a text the Gos. Phil. in essence really represents (apart, that is, from its title) is, or was for a long time, very much a matter of debate. It is, however, essentially a question of a simple alternative. The view advanced in connection with the first translation, that the text has the character of a collection and thus is something like a *florilegium*, was immediately opposed by the contention that there is a continuous and coherent text in Gos. Phil.; thus according to Krause it is 'a treatise, which uses different materials, including material derived from a source containing sayings' (*Gnosis* II, 76), according to Gaffron 'a didactic and monitory document, which presents the gnostic message in the most varied forms of speech, in loose sequence and without any strict thematic linking in its execution' (*Studien* p. 220). It now however looks as if in the course of the further work on the elucidation of the Gos. Phil. (especially Isenberg, Layton) the theory of the *florilegium* or anthology character of the text has been confirmed, and as if this is already on the point of becoming generally accepted. Here Isenberg and Layton - like Wilson already before them - point to the *Excerpta ex Theodoto* of Clement of Alexandria as the closest formal parallel.

The discovery, or the assertion, that the Gos. Phil. is a *florilegium* or collection of excerpts was from the beginning bound up with the introduction of a numbering of the 127 text-units recognised as independent of one another, which however should for preference no longer be described (on the analogy of the Gospel of Thomas) as 'sayings', but in neutral terms as 'paragraphs', if not directly as 'excerpts' (so now Layton). This old paragraph division (from §1 to 127), which has been widely adopted, even by scholars who did not share the anthology theory behind it, is in principle retained here also. The problem is that in the course of the work on the Gos. Phil. considerable advances have been achieved (over against the first sketch) in the recognition of the caesurae between the individual excerpts. And it is nothing less than the objective understanding of the Gos. Phil. as a whole that depends upon the recognition of which sentences and how many here form a larger textual unit, and where exactly the next one begins; that is, at what point a sentence-break coincides with a caesura in the text, and indeed also perhaps when there is further discussion of the same subject as before - but now from an abruptly altered point of view. If the advance in our knowledge here relates only to the more exact determination of the beginning or end of an excerpt, this presents no problems for the numbering itself. There is however a whole host of cases where more searching exegesis has shown that a piece of text originally regarded as a unit in reality consists of several (cf. for example the liberating division of §26). The only logical course would have been a completely new paragraph division (Layton introduces one, but counts only 107 excerpts, whereas to my mind there are no fewer than 175). However, to avoid the confusion which this would entail, we have resorted to the expedient of retaining and expanding the original numbering, but subdividing the affected paragraphs into a, b, c, etc. At the points concerned, therefore, the numbering is not to be understood as if for example §§9a and 9b stood in a closer objective relationship to one another than 7 and 8 or 10 and 11.

What has been gathered into this *florilegium* is a number of theological statements, some shorter, some longer, on questions of the sacraments and of ethics. They stand side by side without connecting links, or linked only by association of ideas or by catchwords, occasionally indeed without any explicit point of reference, and represent quite diverse kinds of text with their differing styles: aphorism, logion, comparison, metaphor, parable, paraenesis, polemic, exegesis, discourse. Not infrequently what originally and objectively belongs together appears - for whatever reason (Isenberg thinks it the intention of the compiler) - to have been rent asunder. How wide the literary field was on which these flowers were plucked, we naturally do not know. But what Isenberg suggests on this question deserves to be retained as a borderline hypothesis, namely that it is perfectly possible that almost all these excerpts derive from a single work, which must then have been a comprehensive Christian-gnostic sacramental catechesis. For the rest, neither the anthology or excerpt character of our text nor the 'disorder' of its components should deceive us as to the fact that the whole is governed and dominated by a quite specific and irreplaceable spirit living on the boldness of the images and metaphors, and a touch of greatness in the mysterious and enigmatic character of its statements. Otherwise it would probably scarcely have come about that this text was very soon regarded as a gospel.

This understanding of the anthology before us as a gospel, as the saving teaching of Jesus Christ, and that according to Philip, finds expression only in the colophon - thus neither in the *incipit* nor anywhere else in the framework, and certainly not in the body of the work. And this colophon is not so clearly set apart from the text as are the other titles of the documents which appear in this codex; it rather looks as if it had been inserted here only subsequently by the scribe of this codex. But there are many possible explanations for this, and that it was the scribe of this Coptic copy who first made the text into the Gospel of Philip is probably the most unlikely. Standing immediately after the Gospel of Thomas, with which according to our witnesses the Gospel of Philip must have shared a common history of transmission, our text must from the outset have been written out by the copyist of Codex II as the 'Gospel according to Philip'. How long or how soon after its conception our *florilegium* became the Gospel of Philip in the understanding of its users is unknown. Here we presume as a matter of course that the creator of our text himself, the excerptor or compiler, did not so understand his work, but rather as what it actually is, namely an excerpt - perhaps simply for private use. The most likely assumption might be that the new understanding of the text is directly connected with its 'publication' and general diffusion, so that we might say: whatever it was previously, it was disseminated as 'the Gospel according to Philip'. The interpretation of this text as a gospel was facilitated by the fact that a quite imposing number of the excerpts (§§ 5, 9a, 9b, 17c, 18, 19, 20, 21, 23b, 26a, 32, 34, 46, 47, 53, 54, 55b, 57, 68, 69a, 69c, 69d, 70, 72a, 72b, 72c, 81a, 81b, 82a, 83, 89, 93, 97) deal with Jesus or Christ or the Lord or 'him' as the bringer of salvation, whether it is that words of the Lord (known or unknown) are quoted or that there is some narrative or reflection concerning him. In the realm of apocryphal literature the description 'gospel' is by no means restricted to the type of text so called in the New Testament. In addition one cannot avoid the suspicion that the analogy with the Gospel of Thomas, however relative and restricted we may assess it to have been, has also played a part.

That this text, now understood as a gospel, was *at the same time* - as we may probably assume - attributed to Philip is certainly connected with the fact that he is the only apostle mentioned in it by name, even if only once (§91). That, however, is quite enough for the attribution; in the canonical Gospel of Matthew, for example, Matthew does not appear much more often. Again, this Philip to whom the teaching in the text is accordingly traced back is no mere name or shadow from the New Testament, but the complex and attractive figure from early Christian tradition who bore this name, whether it be that here the two NT figures, the disciple and apostle Philip on the one hand and the evangelist Philip on the other, have been secondarily fused, or that the tradition has so to speak bypassed the NT and the cleavage in the one historically important and legendary figure which we find in the NT has simply been left out of the reckoning. In addition to the long known witnesses to this Philip tradition (the Philip stories in Acts, Philip as interlocutor in the Gospel of John, the Acts of Philip), a new and important witness which confirms and underlines the significance of this figure and the relative independence of this tradition from the NT has now appeared in the so-called 'Letter of Peter to Philip' (Nag Hammadi Codex VIII 2; see below, pp. 342ff.). When we see the ascription of our text to Philip in this wider perspective of the Philip tradition, the question finally imposes itself upon us whether there may not be here and there in the text, without any occurrence of the name of Philip, material from the Philip tradition which was readily recognisable to the users of the time and contributed to this ascription.

6. Internal character: our Gos. Phil. represents a quite special kind of Christianity. It is a gnostic and indeed a Valentinian text: compiled by a Valentinian for Valentinians, drawn from works many of which (if not all, as Layton assumes) were Valentinian, used as a gospel first by Valentinian communities. At the same time it is Valentinian only to the extent and in the degree that is possible in a text of this kind, that is, an anthology. This characterisation results from the fact that clearly Valentinian *theologoumena* are found in the Gos. Phil., and that the most characteristic feature of the teachings and ideas found in it, which so to speak determines its profile, is Valentinian. In addition to an abundance of allusions in the Gos. Phil. as a whole, paragraphs 26b, 61a, 61b, 67b and 67c clearly contain the specifically Valentinian doctrine of the Saviour as the Bridegroom of the lower Sophia, and the angels of the Saviour as the bridegrooms of the seed of the lower Sophia. A further proof-text for Valentinian origin is § 39, where it is a question of the Valentinian name for the lower Sophia, 'Achamoth', whether it is that this is applied to both Sophias, to the higher in the form Echamoth, to the lower in the form Echmoth, or whether the intention is only to distinguish the Valentinian technical term from the normal word for Wisdom. In § 125a the Valentinian view of the relative redemption of the psychic Demiurge is presented. Frequently there is reference - more or less clearly - to the mystery of the bridal chamber (§§66, 68, 74, 76, 98). Such a mystery is indeed attested only for the Valentinian school of the Marcosians (cf. Irenaeus, *adv. Haer.* I 21 3, and on this W. Bousset, *Hauptprobleme der Gnosis*, 1907, pp. 315-318), although it is probably to be assumed for other Valentinians also. In addition to these cardinal passages for a Valentinian origin there are many other sections which only take on colour on a Valentinian interpretation. However, although thus of a Valentinian character, the Gos. Phil. (in keeping with its nature) cannot be traced back to, or identified with, a particular Valentinian school. Its Valentinian excerpts may have been brought together from works of different schools. Again, all the gnostic elements which are found in it need not be Valentinian. We must rather from the outset reckon with the possibility that material from other gnostic movements has also flowed into the Gos. Phil., since indeed it could very early be used by non-Valentinian gnostics too.

This gnostic and specifically Valentinian character of the Gos. Phil. is, however, irrelevant in the context of NT apocrypha, although it ought not to be left without mention or explanation. What is interesting within the present frame is rather everything that is not specifically gnostic or specifically Valentinian, and this relates to by far the greater quantity of the material contained in the Gos. Phil. This is, on the one hand, non-Valentinian material, whether it was collected from common Christian tradition or literature or (though essentially unaffected) flowed already through Valentinian channels, and, on the other, views and practices in which the Valentinians were no different from the developing Great Church. The Gos. Phil. is of particular importance in this perspective for the transmission and use of the sayings of the Lord, for discourse in similes and parables, and generally as a witness for the catechetical tradition and practice of early Christianity.

7. Content: because of the literary genre represented by the Gos. Phil., it is not possible - at least without more ado - to give a summary of its content. It is entirely out of the question to extract anything like a theology of the Gos. Phil. from the text. Its content rather invites us to take each excerpt methodically in itself and endeavour to ascertain its meaning in comparison with similar statements within and outside the Gos. Phil. Moreover, partial formal or thematic relationships then emerge within the gospel. Thus for example, according to Isenberg, §§ 77, 106, 107a, 107b, 63a, 63b, 63c, 64 originally belong together, and that in this sequence; likewise §§ 99c, 45 and §§ 51, 80.

In a very general sense we can naturally grasp and describe the content of the Gos. Phil. with the help of particular constantly recurring major themes. First of all, discussions about Adam and paradise are frequent (§§ 13, 14, 15, 28, 41, 42, 71, 78, 79, 80, 83, 84, 92, 94a, 94b). Speculations about the (difference of the) acts of creating and begetting also constantly recur (§§ 1, 29, 41, 84, 86, 99a, 99b, 99c, 102a, 102b, 120, 121a, 121b). Especially interesting are the many excerpts which on different levels of significance deal with bride, bridegroom and bridal chamber (above all §§ 31, 61a, 61b, 67b, 67c, 74, 82a, 122a, 122b, 122c, 122d; but also §§ 60, 66, 68, 73, 76, 77, 79, 80, 87, 95, 98, 102a, 102c, 103, 125a, 126c, 127) and those in which it is a question of the sacraments, namely baptism, chrism, the eucharist, redemption and the mystery of the bridal chamber (§§ 24, 25, 43, 59, 66, 67b, 67c, 67d, 68, 74, 75, 76, 90a, 90b, 92, 95, 97, 98, 100, 101, 108, 109, 111a, 111b, 122c, 125b). The relation of the sacraments to one another is, however, not clear. Thus Gaffron takes baptism and chrism together, and understands only these as initiation rites, while he interprets the sacrament of the bridal chamber, the beginning of which again is the rite of the redemption, as a sacrament for the dying. Isenberg, on the contrary, considers it more probable that all the sacraments mentioned are only five different stages of a complex initiation ritual.

The elucidation of the content of the Gos. Phil. on the basis of its major themes can still be substantially refined. Thus Layton prefaces to his translation of the Gos. Phil. an index of no fewer than 45 key concepts and themes. In such an approach it is then even possible to gather the essential ideas of the Gos. Phil. systematically together, as Isenberg convincingly demonstrates in his 'Introduction', where he selects as section headings: Animals, free men and virgins, bridal chamber, sacraments, analogies and parables, biblical allusions.

The Gospel of Philip*

1. A Hebrew man produces Hebrews; and such [peo]ple are called 'proselytes'. But a p[rosel]yte does not produce proselytes. [Some peop]le are as they [come into being], and produce still othe[rs]; [for the others] (p. 52) [it] must suffice that they come into being (at all).

2. The [slave] seeks only to become free, but he does not seek after the possessions of his master. But for the son (it is) not (enough) only that he is a son, but he lays claim to the inheritance of the father.

3. Those who are heirs to the dead are themselves dead; and it is (only) to the dead that they are heirs. Those who are heirs to him who lives are alive; and they are heirs to him who lives - *and* to the dead. - Dead ones inherit nothing. For how could one who is dead inherit? - If he who is dead is heir to him who lives, he (who lives) will not die (thereby), but rather he who is dead will come to life.

4. A Gentile man does not die, for he has never lived that he should die. He who has come to believe in the truth has found life, and this man is in danger of dying. For he is alive since the day Christ came.

5. The world is created. The cities are adorned. The dead are carried out.

6. When we were Hebrews, we were orphans and had (only) our mother, but when we became Christians we obtained father and mother.[1]

7. Those who sow in the winter reap in the summer. The winter is the world.[2] The summer is the other aeon. Let us sow in the world, that we may reap in the summer! Because of this it is fitting for us not to pray (for anything [*sc.* reward]) in the winter.[3] What follows on the winter is the summer. But if anyone reaps in the winter, he will not (really) reap, but (only) pluck out.

8. Since such a (man or field) will produce fruit [for the Na]me, it (the fruit) will not only come forth [daily], but [not] even on the Sabbath is [his power] without fruit.

9a. Christ came (p. 53) to ransom some, to save others, to redeem others. It is those who were strangers that he ransomed < . . . >. He made them his own. - And he took back his own, which he had laid down as a pledge[4] of his own free will.

9b. It applies not only when he appeared that 'he laid down the soul, when he wished'. But since the world has come into being he has laid down the soul. At the time when he wished, then he came for the first time to take it (again). Since it had been laid down as a pledge,[4] it was under the robbers and had been taken captive. But he rescued it. - And that which is good in the world he saved as well as that which is evil.

10. Light and darkness, life and death, the right and the left, are brothers one to another. It is not possible for them to separate from one another.

Because of this, neither is the good good, nor the evil evil, nor is life life, nor death death. - Because of this each one will be resolved into its original nature. But those who are exalted above the world are indissoluble and eternal.

11. The names which are given to worldly (things) are the cause of a great deception. For they turn their (i.e. men's) heart away from what is established to what is not established. So he who hears (the name) 'God' does not think of him who is established, but has thought of him who is not established. So is it also with (the names) 'Father', 'Son, 'Holy Spirit', 'Life', 'Light', 'Resurrection', 'Church' [and] all the other (names). People do not think of what is established, but they think of what is not established. [Nevertheless] they could point to what is established. - The nam[es which are heard] belong to this world. [Let no-one] (p. 54) deceive [himself]! [If they belonged] to the (other) aeon, they would never be named in the world, nor would they have been assigned to worldly things. They have an end in the (other) aeon.[5]

12a. One single name is not uttered in the world, the name which the Father gave to the Son, which is above all things; this is the name of the Father. For the Son would not become Father if he had not put on the name of the Father. - So far as such a name is concerned, - those who have it do indeed think of it, but they do not utter it. Those who do not have it cannot (even) think of it.

12b. But the truth brought forth names in the world for our sakes, (the truth) to which one cannot refer without names. The truth is one single thing. And it is manifold, and (that) for our sakes, to teach us about this alone in love through many.[6]

13. The archons wanted to deceive man, since they saw that he had a kinship with the truly good. They took the name of the good and gave it to what is not good, in order (first) to deceive him through the names and bind them to what is not good, and then, as if they were doing them a favour, to cause them to remove from the 'not good' and transfer them to the 'good' which they think is so. For they wished to take the free man and make him their slave for ever.

14. There are powers which bring [benefit] to man, (only) because they did not wish him to [be saved], that their existence might be enduring. For if man [is saved], sacrifices will [no longer] take place. - [   ] and (indeed) animals were offered up (p. 55) to the powers; for animals (also) were those to whom (the sacrifice) was offered. They were offered up alive, but when they were offered they died. Man (on the other hand) was offered up to (the true) God dead, and he came (thereby) to life.[7]

15. Before Christ came, there was no bread in the world, just as paradise, the place where Adam was, had many trees for food for the beasts, but no

wheat as food for man. Man fed like the beasts[8]. But when Christ came, the perfect man, he brought bread from heaven, that man might feed on the food of man.

16a. The archons thought that it was by their own power and will that they were doing what they did. But the Holy Spirit secretly contrived everything through them, as he wished.

16b. Truth is sown everywhere, the truth which exists from the beginning. And many see it as it is sown. But few are they who see it as it is reaped.

17a. Some said: 'Mary conceived by the Holy Spirit.' They are in error! They do not know what they are saying! When did a woman ever conceive by a woman?[9]

17b. Mary is the virgin whom no power defiled. This is a great curse for the Hebrews, namely the apostles and the apostolic men. This virgin whom no power defiled [wishes that] the powers might defile themselves.

17c. And the Lord [would] not [have] said: 'My F[ather who art] in heaven' if [he] had not (also) had [ano]ther father; but he would have said simply: ['My Father'].

18. The Lord said to the dis[ciples: 'Take (something)] (p. 56) from every [ho]use and bring it into the house of the Father! But do not steal in the house of the Father and do not take anything away!'

19. 'Jesus' is a hidden name. 'Christ' is a revealed name. Because of this, (the word) 'Jesus' does not exist in any other tongue, but (in every language) his name is 'Jesus', just as he is called. As for 'Christ', on the other hand, his name in Syriac is 'Messiah', but in Greek it is 'Christ'. In general, all other (peoples) have it according to the language of each one of them. 'The Nazarene' is the revealed (name) of the hidden (name contained in it).[10]

20. Christ has everything in himself, whether man or angel or mystery, and the Father.

21. Those who say that the Lord first died and then rose up are in error. For he rose up first and then died. If anyone does not first attain the resurrection, he will not (be able to) die. As God lives, that one would d[ie].[11]

22. No one will hide a costly and precious object in a costly vessel. But many times some-one has cast countless myriads into a vessel worth a farthing. So it is with the soul. It is a precious thing, and came to be in a despised body.

23a. Some are afraid lest they rise naked.[12] Because of this they wish to rise in the flesh. And they do not know that those who bear the f[lesh] are [precisely] the naked. Those who are [able] to lay (it) aside [are precisely those who] are not naked.

23b. 'Flesh [and blood cannot] inherit the kingdom [of God].'[13] What is this (flesh) which cannot (p. 57) inherit? This which we bear. But what is this which can inherit? It is the (flesh) of Jesus and his blood! Because of this he said: 'He who shall not eat my flesh and drink my blood has no life in him.'[14] Of what kind is this (flesh)? His flesh is the Word, and his blood is the Holy Spirit![15] He who has received these has food and drink and clothing.

23c. I blame the others, who say that it (the flesh) will not rise. Then both are at fault. You say that the flesh will not rise. But tell me what will rise, that we may honour you (as a teacher). You say: The spirit in the flesh, and it is also this (spark of) light in the flesh. But this too (which you have mentioned) is something which exists (only) *in* the flesh. For whatever you name, you (yet) name nothing that exists outside the flesh. It is (therefore) necessary to rise in this flesh, since everything is in it.[16]

24. In this world those who put on garments are more precious than the garments. In the kingdom of heaven the garments are more precious than those who have put them on.[17]

25. Through water and fire the whole place is purified - the visible through the visible, the hidden through the hidden. There are some things which are hidden through what is visible. There is water in water; there is fire in a chrism.

26a. Jesus deceived everyone. For he did not show himself as he was; but he showed himself as [they would] be able to see him. [But] he showed himself [to them all]: He [showed] himself to the great as great. He sho[wed himself to] the small as small. He [showed himself] (p. 58) [to the] angels as an angel and to men as a man. Because of this his *logos* hid itself from everyone. Some indeed saw him, thinking that they had seen themselves. But when he appeared to his disciples in glory on the mountain, he was not small - he became great - but he made the disciples great, that they might be able to see him in his greatness.

26b. He[18] said on that day in the thanksgiving: 'You who have united the perfect light with the Holy Spirit, unite the angels also with us, the images!'

27a. Do not despise the lamb! For without it it is not possible to see the king.

27b. No one will be able to enter in before the king if he is naked.

28. The heavenly man has more children than the earthly. If the children of Adam are numerous, although they die, how much more the children of the perfect man, who do not die but are continually begotten.

29. The father produces a child. The child (for his part) has not the ability to produce a child. For he who has (just) been begotten has not (yet) the ability (himself) to beget. Rather the child gets brothers for himself, not children.

30. All who are begotten in the world are begotten of nature. And the others are in [this one] from [whom] they are begotten, [and] are nourished there. - Man rec[eives nour]ishment from the promise, (to enter in) to [the place] above. [   ] it (the promise?) from the mouth. [And if] the Logos came forth there, (p. 59) he would be nourished from the mouth and become perfect.

31. The perfect conceive through a kiss and give birth. Because of this we also kiss one another. We receive conception from the grace which we have among us.[19]

32. There were three (women) who kept company with the Lord at all times: Mary his mother, <his>[20] sister and Magdalene, who is called his companion. His sister, his mother and his companion were all called Mary.

33. 'The Father' and 'the Son' are simple names; 'the Holy Spirit' is a double name. For they (Father and Son) are everywhere: they are above, they are below; they are in the hidden, they are in the visible. The Holy Spirit is (on the one hand) in the visible: (then) he is below; (on the other hand) he is in the hidden: (then) he is above.

34. The saints are (also) ministered to by the evil powers. For they have become blind through the Holy Spirit, that they may think they are serving the men who belong to them when they act for (the benefit of) the saints. - Because of this (it is said): A disciple asked the Lord one day for a worldly thing, and he said to him: 'Ask your mother (for it), and she will give you (it) from what is alien to us.'

35. The apostles said to the disciples: 'May our whole offering obtain 'salt'!' They called [Sophia] 'salt'. Without it no offering is acceptable.[21]

36. But Sophia is barren [(and) without] children. Because of this she is called '[the pillar](?) of salt'.[22] Wherever they shall [   ] in their way, [there] the Holy Spirit [   ]. (p. 60) [An]d (so) her children are (none the less) many.

37. What the father possesses belongs to the son. And the son himself, so long as he is small, is not entrusted with what is his own. When he becomes a man, his father gives him all that he possesses.[23]

38. You who have gone astray! What the Spirit brings forth, that also goes astray through him. Because of this (it is said): through one and the same breath the fire blazes and is quenched.

39. Echamoth is one thing, and Echmoth is another. Echamoth is simply Wisdom, but Echmoth is the Wisdom of death, that is: the wisdom [   ] who *knows* death, who is called 'the little Wisdom'.

40. There are animals which are obedient to man, like the bull, the ass and (many) others of this kind. (And) there are other (animals) which are not obedient and live apart in the deserts. Man ploughs the field with the

animals which are obedient. And thereby he feeds himself and the animals, whether those that are obedient or those that are not obedient. So it is with the perfect man. Through powers which are obedient he ploughs, preparing for everything to come into being. - It is because of this that the whole place has stability, whether the good or the evil, the right and the left. The Holy Spirit tends everything and rules over all the powers, [those which] are obedient and those which are not obedient and separated. For he remains [firmly resolved] to cage them in, so that [even if] they wish they may not get out.

41. [He who] was moulded (Adam) was [noble. And you would] expect that his children are (likewise) noble (p. 61) *figures*. (Only) if he was not moulded but begotten would you expect that his *seed* is noble. But now he was (simply) moulded, and (yet) he begot (noble *seed*). What kind of nobility is this!

42. First adultery came into being, afterwards the murderer (Cain). And he was begotten in adultery. For he was the son of the serpent. Because of this he became a murderer, as his father also (was).[24] And he slew his brother (Abel). - But any intercourse which has taken place between those unlike one another is adultery.

43. God is a dyer. As the good dyes, which are called 'genuine', 'die' (only) *with* the (materials) which were dyed with them, so it is with those whom God has dyed: since his dyes are immortal, they (also) become immortal through his medicines. - But God baptises those whom he baptises in water.[25]

44. It is impossible for anyone to see anything of what is established, unless he becomes like them. It is not as with a man when he is in the world, who sees the sun without being a sun, and sees heaven and earth and all other things, without being these - it is not so in (the realm of) the truth. But: you saw something of that place, and you became these. You saw the Spirit and became spirit. You saw Christ and became Christ. You saw the [Father] and will become Father. - Because of this, [here] you see everything and [do not see] yourself. But [there] you see yourself; for what you see (there), that you will [become].

45. Faith receives, love gives. N[obody can] (p. 62) receive without faith; nobody can give without love. Because of this (it holds good): in order to receive, we believe; and in order to love, we give. - For if anyone gives, (but) not with love, he has no benefit from what he has given.

46. He who has received (anything, but) not the Lord, is still a Hebrew.

47. The apostles who were before us called <him>[26] thus: 'Jesus the Nazorean, Messiah', that is, 'Jesus the Nazorean, the Christ'. The last name is 'Christ'. The first is 'Jesus'. That in the middle is 'the Nazarene'. Messiah has two meanings: 'Christ' and 'the measured'.[27] Jesus in Hebrew means 'the redemption'.[28] Nazara is 'the truth'. The Nazarene ac-

cordingly means '<the man of> the truth'.[29] Christ is the one who was measured. 'The Nazarene' and 'Jesus' are those who have measured <him>.[30]

48. When a pearl is cast down in the mud, {} it does not become less valuable, nor does it (only) become valuable when it is anointed with balsam oil. But it has always the (same) worth in the eyes of its owner. So with the children of God, wherever they may be. They have still the (same) value in the eyes of their Father.

49. If you say 'I am a Jew', no one will be moved. If you say 'I am a Roman', no one will be disturbed. If you say 'I [am a] Greek', 'a barbarian', 'a slave', 'a [free] man', no one will be troubled. [If] you [say] 'I am a Christian', the [world] will tremble. May I [even] so re[ceive him] whose name the [world] cannot endure [to hear].

50. God is a man-eater. (p. 63) Because of this man [is sacrificed] for him. Before man was sacrificed, animals were sacrificed. For these were no gods, for whom they sacrificed.

51. Vessels of glass and vessels of earthenware are made with the aid of fire. But if vessels of glass break, they are made again; for they came into being through a breath. But if earthenware vessels break they are destroyed; for they came into being without breath.

52. An ass turning a millstone covered a hundred miles walking. When it was loosed, it found that it was still at the same place. There are also human beings of this sort: they travel great distances, without drawing near to any goal. When evening came upon them, they saw neither city nor village, neither anything man-made nor anything natural. There is no power there (to help), no angel. In vain did these wretches labour.

53. The eucharist is Jesus. For <it>[31] is called in Syriac 'Pharisatha', which means 'the spread out'. For it happened that Jesus was crucified to the world.[32]

54. The Lord went into the dye-works of Levi. He took seventy-two (cloths of different) colours and threw them into the vat. He took them out (again) all white. And he said: 'Even so is the Son of Man come as a dyer.'[33]

55a. The Sophia who is called barren is the mother of the [angels] and [the] companion of the S[aviour].

55b. The S[aviour lov]ed [Ma]ry Mag[da]lene more than [all] the disciples,[34] and kissed on her [mouth] often. The other [disciples] (p. 64) [   ]. They said to him: 'Why do you love her more than all of us?' The Saviour answered and said to them {}: 'Why do I not love you like her?'

56. If a blind man and one who sees are both together in the darkness, they are no different from one another. When the light comes, then he who sees will see the light, and the blind will remain in darkness.

57. The Lord said: 'Blessed is he who is before he came into being.[35] For

he who is, both came into being and shall be.'

58. The pre-eminence of man is not visible, but lies in secret. Because of this he is lord over the beasts which are stronger and greater than he by the standard of the visible and the hidden. And this gives them their continuance. But if man separates from them, they kill one another and bite one another. - And they devoured one another, because they did not find any food. But now they have found food, since man began to till the ground.

59. If anyone goes down into the water and comes up again without having received anything, and says 'I am a Christian', he has borrowed the name at interest. But if he receives the Holy Spirit, he possesses the name as a gift. - He who has received a gift does not have it taken away. But he who has received something at interest, it will be demanded back from him. So it happens with us, when anyone submits to a mystery.[36]

60. The mystery of marriage is great.[37] For [with]out it the wor[ld] would [not] exi[st]. For [the ex]istence of the [wor]ld [depends on] men. But the existence [of men depends on] marriage. - Understand [what great] power [undef]iled intercourse possesses! Its image (p. 65) consists in defile[ment].

61a. Among the forms of the unclean spirit there are male and female. It is the males which unite with the souls which dwell in a female form; but the female are those which unite with those which are in a male form, in an illicit way. And none can escape these, because they lay hold of him, unless he receives a male power and a female, namely the Bridegroom and the Bride. But one receives (them) from the mirrored bridal chamber.

61b. When the foolish women see a man sitting alone, they come to him, sport with him, and defile him. So also when foolish men see a beautiful woman sitting alone, they prevail upon her, do violence to her, wishing to defile her. But when they see the man and his wife sitting together, the women cannot go in to the man, nor can the men go in to the woman, <nor can anyone else venture to go in to the man or his wife>. So it is when the image and the angel are united with one another { }.

61c. He who leaves the world, and (thus) cannot be held fast any longer because he *was* in the world, is manifestly exalted above the desire of the [and] above fear. He is master over the [   ]. He is superior to envy. If [he   ] comes, he is seized and throttled. And how will [he] be able to escape the g[reat clutch]ing powers? How will he be able to con[ceal himself from them]?

61d. There are [of]ten people who [say:] 'We are faithful', in order that they [may not see] (p. 66) [any unclean spirit] or demon. For if they had the Holy Spirit, no unclean spirit would molest them.

62. You should not be afraid of the flesh, nor should you love it! If you are afraid of it, it will dominate you. If you love it, it will swallow you

up and strangle you.

63a. (Man) is either in this world or in the resurrection or in the places of the midst - far be it from me that I be found in them. - In this world there is good and evil. Its (the world's) good is not good; and its evil is not evil. But there is something evil after this world, which is truly evil, namely what is called 'the Midst'. That is death. - So long as we are in this world, it is fitting for us to acquire for ourselves the resurrection, that when we strip off the flesh we may be found in (the place of) rest and not roam about in the Midst.[38]

63b. Truly, many go astray on the way.

63c. Truly, it is good to come forth from the world before one has sinned.

64. There are some who neither wish nor are able (to do something); but the others, even if they wish, have no profit, since they have not done it. Does the wish then make them sinners? But if they do not wish, (it is so). Righteousness will hide itself from both groups. And [it is not] the wish, not the fulfilment.

65. An apostolic man saw [i]n [a] vision some (people) who were [im]prisoned in a house of fire, bound with fiery [chains] and cast [into a] fiery [, because   ] them in [their false f]ait[h]. And it was said to <him>[39] [: 'These might have] saved [their souls], [but] they did not wish. (So) they have received [this place of] punishment' - which is called (p. 67) out[er] darkness, because it [   ].[40]

66. Out of water and fire the soul and the spirit came into being. Out of water, fire and light the son of the bridechamber <came into being>.[41] The fire signifies the chrism, the light signifies the fire. I do not mean this (earthly) fire, which has no form, but that other (heavenly) fire, whose form is white, which is radiant, beautiful and bestows beauty.

67a. Truth did not come into the world naked, but it came in types and images. It (the world) cannot receive it otherwise.

67b. There is a rebirth and an image of rebirth. It is truly necessary to be reborn through the image.

67c. Of what a nature is the resurrection! And the image must rise again through the image. The bridegroom and the image must enter through the image into the truth, which is the *apocatastasis*.

67d. (So) it is fitting for those who have not only obtained the *names* of the Father, the Son and the Holy Spirit, but have obtained *these very things* <for themselves>.[42] If anyone does not obtain *them* for himself, the *name* also will be taken from him. - But one receives them in the chrism with the bals[am] of the power of the cr[oss]. Th[is] (power) the apostles called '[the r]ight and the left'. Such a one is no longer a [Christ]ian, but a Christ.

68. The Lord [did] everything in a mystery: baptism, chrism, eucharist, redemption and bridal chamber.

69a. [Because of this] he said: 'I am come to make [the lo]wer like the up[per and the ou]ter like the in[ner][43] [and to] unite them at th[at] place.' [But he spoke in these] places through sym[bols and images].

69b. Those who say: '[There is a heavenly one, and] there is one above [her]' are in error. - F[or] so far as the visible is concerned, that (p. 68) heav[enly] one is the one who [is] called 'the lower'; and the one to whom the hidden realm belongs, he is the one who is above him.

69c. For it is rightly said: 'The inner, the outer, and what is outside the outer'. Because of this the Lord called perdition 'the outer darkness';[44] there is no other outside of it.

69d. He said: 'My Father who is in secret'. He said: 'Go into your chamber, shut your door behind you, and pray to your Father who is in secret',[45] which means: he who is within all. But that which is within all is the Pleroma. Beyond that there is nothing other within it. This is the one of whom it is said: 'He who is above them'.

70. Before Christ some came out whence they could no longer go in; and they went in where they could no longer come out. But Christ came. Those who had gone in he brought out; and those who had come out he brought in.

71. When Eve was [i]n A[d]am, there was no death. But when she separated [from] him, death came into being. Again, if <she>[46] en[ter]s (into him) and he takes <her>[46] to himself, death will no longer exist.[47]

72a. 'My God, my God, why { } [have] you forsaken me?'[48] <The Lord> spoke these (words) on the cross. For there he w[as] separated.

72b. [   ] who was begotten from the one who [   ] through God.

72c. The [Lord] is [risen] from the dead. [He did not come as he w]as, but [his body] was [wholly] perfect. [It consists of] flesh. But this [flesh] is true [fle]sh. [Our flesh how]ever is not true flesh, but an image of the true.(p. 69)

73. The bridal chamber is not for the animals, nor is it for the slaves or for the defiled women; but it is (only) for free men and virgins.

74. Through the Holy Spirit we are born again. But we are born through Christ - (in baptism) with the two. We are anointed with the Spirit. When we were born, we were united.

75. No one can see himself, either in water or in a mirror, without light; nor can you on the other hand see in the light without water or mirror. Because of this it is necessary to baptise with the two, with the light and the water. But the light is the chrism.

76. There were three buildings as places of offering in Jerusalem: the one which opens to the west was called 'the holy'; another which opens to the south was called 'the holy of the holy'; the third which opens to the east was called 'the holy of the holies', where only the high priest might enter. Baptism is the 'holy' house. [The] redem[ption] is 'the holy of the holy'.

'The [hol]y of the holies' is the bridal chamber. - [Bap]tism has after it the resurrec[tion and the] redemption. The redemption is in the bridal chamber. But [the] bridal chamber is in what is superior to [them], to [which we] belong. You cannot find anything that is [like it. - Those who] are those who worship [in spirit and in truth].⁴⁹ [They do not worship] in Jerusalem. There are people in Jerusalem who [do indeed worship in Jerus]alem, [but] wait [for the mysteries] which are call[ed 'the hol]y of the holies', [the veil of which] was rent. [Our] bridal chamber is [nothing other] than the image [of the bridal chamber which] (p. 70) [is] above. That is why its veil was rent from top to bottom. - For it would have been necessary for some from below to go upward.

77. As for those who have put on the perfect light, the powers cannot see them, and (thus) are not able to hold them back. But one will put on this light in the mystery of the union.

78. If the woman had not separated from the man, she would not have died with the man. The separation from him became the origin of death. Because of this Christ came, to remove the separation which existed from the beginning and again unite the two, in order to give life to those who have died in (the time of) the separation and to unite them.

79. But the woman is united to her husband in the bridal chamber. But those who have united in the bridal chamber can no longer be separated. That is why Eve separated from Adam, because she had not united with him in the bridal chamber.

80. The soul of Adam came into being from a breath.⁵⁰ Its consort is the [spirit. The spirit] which was given to him is his mother. The soul was [taken] from him and replaced by [spirit]. Since when he had united (with the spirit) he [spo]ke words which are too high for the powers, they were envious of him. They [separated] the spiri[tual un]ion themselves [ ], which is hidden [oc]casion [ ] themselves alone [b]ridal chamber, in order that [ ].

81a. Jesus revealed [himself in the Jo]rdan⁵¹ (as) the ful[ness of the] kingdom of heaven.

81b. He [who came into being] before the All (p. 71) was born again. He [who had] previously [been] anointed, was anointed again. He [who] had been redeemed, again redeemed (others).⁵²

82a. Truly, it is necessary to utter a mystery. The Father of the All united with the virgin who had fallen. And a fiery (star) shone forth for him that day and revealed the great bridal chamber.⁵³ Because of this (it holds true): on that day his body came into being. He left the bridal chamber. - As the one who came into being from the bridegroom and the bride, so Jesus established everything in it through these.

82b. And it is necessary that each one of the disciples enter into his rest.

83. Adam came into being from two virgins: from the Spirit and from the

virgin earth. - For this reason Christ was born of a virgin, that he might set right the fall which occurred at the beginning.

84. There are two trees in paradise. The one produces [animals], the other produces men. Adam [ate] of the tree which produces anim[als]. [He be]came an animal and begat an[imals]. Because of this the children of Adam worship the (gods in the form of) an[imals]. The tree the fruit [of which he ate] is the [(tree) of knowledge]. [Because] of this, [sins] became many. [If he had] eaten the [fruit of the other tree], the fruit of [the tree of life which] produces men, [the gods would wor]ship men.

85. A[s in] God created men [that men] (p. 72) might create[54] God, so in the world men make gods and they worship their creations. It would be fitting for the gods to worship men.[55]

86. As the truth is, the works of man come into being from his power. Because of this they are called 'the powers'; they are his works. As for his children, they came into being from rest. Because of this (it holds good): his power dwells in his works; but rest is visible in the children. And you will find that this extends even to the image. Indeed, this is the man after the image. He does his works by his power, but out of rest he begets his children.

87. In this world the slaves serve the free men. In the kingdom of heaven the free will minister to the slaves: the children of the bride-[chamber] will minister to the children of the marriage.

88. [The] children of the bridal chamber have one [and the same] name: rest. When [they are with one] another, they do not need to take on any form. [They possess] the vision [per]ception. They are more [ ] among those who are in the [ ] the glories of the gl[ories] are not.

89. [ ] went down to the wat[er in order to ful]fil it (and) purify it.[56] [those were fulfil]led who have [received baptism] in his name. For he said[: 'In this manner] shall we fulfil (p. 73) all righteousness'.[57]

90a. Those who say that they will die first and (only then) rise again are in error. If they do not first receive the resurrection while they are still alive, when they die they will receive nothing.

90b. So also they speak about baptism, saying: 'Baptism is a great thing; for if (people) receive it, they will live.'

91. Philip the apostle said: 'Joseph the carpenter planted a garden, because he needed wood for his trade. It was he who made the cross from the trees which he planted. And (so) his seed hung on that which he planted. His seed was Jesus, but the planting was the cross.'

92. But the tree of life stands in the midst of paradise. And indeed (it is) the olive-tree. From it came the chrism. Through it <came>[58] the resurrection.[59]

93. This world is an eater of carrion. Whatever is eaten in it is itself already mor[tal]. The truth is an eater of what is still living. Because of

this none of those who are nourished from the [truth] will die.[60] - Jesus came from [that] place and brought food from there. And to those who wished he gave [life, that they might] not (any longer) die.

94a. G[od pl]anted a [para]dise. Man [lived in the para]dise. There are so[me who exi]st together with some [ ] of God. In [the] those who are in [it as] I will. This parad[ise is the place where] they will say to me: '[Eat of] this or do not eat, [as you] (p. 74) will!' This (is) the place where I shall eat all things.

94b. There is the tree of knowledge. That one slew Adam. But this passage (says): the tree of knowledge awakened man to life. The tree was the Law. It is able (only) to impart the knowledge of good and evil. It neither freed him from evil nor did it set him in the good, but it brought death upon those who ate of it. For when it said: 'Eat this, do not eat this', it became the beginning of death.

95. The chrism is superior to baptism. For from the chrism we were called 'Christians', not from the baptism. Christ also was (so) called because of the anointing. For the Father anointed the Son. But the Son anointed the apostles. And the apostles anointed us. - He who is anointed possesses all things. He has the resurrection, the light, the cross.

96a. So far as the Holy Spirit is concerned, the Father gave him this in the bridal chamber, and he received (it).

96b. The Father was in the Son and the Son in the Father. That is [the] king[dom] of heaven.

97. Well did the Lord say: 'Some went into the kingdom of heaven laughing and came out [lau]gh[ing].' A[nd an]other (said): '[It is] a Christian.' [He] sa[id aga]in: 'And immediately, [after this man had gone] down to the water, he came [up as lord] over all things. Because [of this the redemption is not a] trifle; but [since he] des[pised] these rags [he went laughing into] the kingdom of [heaven]. If he despises [the body] and scorns it as a trifle, [he will come out] laughing.'

98. So it is also (p. 75) with the bread and the cup and the oil, even if there is another (mystery) that is (still) higher than these.

99a. The world came into being through a mistake. For he who created it wished to create it imperishable and immortal. He fell away, and did not attain to (his) hope. For incorruptibility does not belong to the world, as incorruptibility also does not belong to him who created the world.

99b. For incorruptibility does not belong to things, but to children. And nothing will be able to achieve incorruptibility unless it becomes a child.

99c. But he who does not have the ability to receive, how much more will he be unable to give?

100. The cup of prayer <for which thanks is given>[61] contains wine as well as water. It represents the blood { } and fills with the Holy Spirit. And this is all that constitutes the perfect man. When we drink this (cup), we

shall receive for ourselves the perfect man.

101. The living water is corporal. It is fitting that (in it) we should put on the living man. Because of this (it holds good): when he goes down to the water, he unclothes himself, that he may put this one on.[62]

102a. A horse begets a horse; a man begets a man; a god begets a god.[63] So it is with [the] bride[groom] and [the br]ide: they come from the [   ].

102b. There was no Jew [   ] from the Greeks [   ] was. And [   ] from the Jews [   ] to Christians. An[other race came into being, and] these bl[essed ones] were called: 'the chosen spir[itual] race', (p. 76) 'the true man', 'the Son of Man' and 'the seed of the Son of Man'. This true race is well known in the world.

102c. These are the place where the children of the bride-chamber are.

103. While in this world the union consists <of> man and wife - representing power and weakness - in the (other) aeon the form of the union is (entirely) different.

104a. But we call them by these names. But there are others. They are exalted above every name that is named.

104b. And they are higher than the strong. For where strength is, there also are those who are superior to the strength.

104c. Those are not: the one and the other. But these two are one and the same. This is what cannot enter into any heart of flesh.[64]

105. Must not anyone who possesses all things also know all this? Some if they do not know it will also not enjoy what they possess. But those who have come to know it will also enjoy it.

106. The perfect man not only cannot be restrained, but also cannot be seen. For if he is seen he will be put under restraint. No one will be able to receive for himself this grace in any other way, un[less] he puts on the perfect light [and] himself becomes perfect li[ght]. He [who has put] it on will enter [   ]. This is the perfect [   ].

107a. [It is necessary] that we become [who]lly [   ] before we come [out of the world].

107b. He who shall receive all things [but does not   himself] from these places [   ] will not be able to [   ] that place, but will [go to the M]idst as imperfect.[65] (p. 77) Only Jesus knows the end of this one.

108. The holy man is altogether holy, including his body. For if he has received the bread, he will make it holy, or the cup, or anything else that he receives, purifying them. And how will he not purify the body also?

109a. As Jesus filled the water of baptism (with Spirit),[66] so he emptied out death. Because of this (it holds good): we do indeed go down into the water, but we do not go down into death.

109b. (This came about) that we might not be emptied by the spirit of the world. When it blows, it causes the winter to come. When the Holy Spirit blows, the summer comes.

110a. He who has the knowledge of the truth is free.[67] But the free man does not sin. For (it is said): 'he who commits sin is the slave of sin'.[68] The truth is the mother (of the free), but knowledge is the <father>.[69] Those to whom it is not permitted to sin the world calls 'free'. These are they to whom it is not permitted to sin. 'The knowledge' of the truth 'lifts up',[70] that is, it makes them free and causes them to be lifted up above the whole place. 'But love builds up.'[71] He who has become free through knowledge is a servant for love's sake to those who have not yet been able to receive the freedom of knowledge. But knowledge makes them capable (of this) by [causing them] to become free.

110b. Love [says of] nothing that it [belongs] to it, [al]though [yet everything] belongs to it. It does not [say: 'That is mine'] or 'this is mine', but ['all'] that belongs [to me] is yours'.[72]

111a. [Spiritual] love is wine and fragrance. They all enjoy (p. 78) it, those who anoint themselves with it. They also enjoy (it) who stand nearby, so long as the anointed are standing there. If those anointed with ointment withdraw from them and go away, those who are not anointed and only stand near them remain in their (own) evil odour.[73]

111b. The Samaritan gave nothing to the wounded man except wine and oil.[74] This is nothing other than the ointment. And it healed the wounds. For (it is said): 'Love covers a multitude of sins.'[75]

112. He whom a woman loves, the (children) she will bear are like him: if her husband, they are like her husband; if it is an adulterer, they are like the adulterer. Often if a woman sleeps with her husband of necessity, but her heart is with the adulterer with whom she is wont to consort, the (child) she bears is born in the likeness of the adulterer. But you who are united with the Son of God, do not love the world, but love the Lord, that those whom you shall bring forth may not be like the world but like the Lord!

113. Man mingles with man, horse mingles with horse, ass mingles with ass. The kinds associate with those of like kind.[76] So also the spirit mingles with spirit and the lo[gos unites] with the logos and [the l]i[ght] associates [with the light]. If [you] become man, it is [the man] who [will] love you. If you become [spirit], it is the spirit that will unite with you. If [you] become logos, it is the logos which (p. 79) will associate with you. If [you] become light, it is the light which will unite with you. If you become (one of) those above, those above will rest upon you. If you become horse or ass or bull or dog or sheep or any other of the animals which are outside and those which are below, neither man nor spirit nor logos nor light can love you, nor can those above or those within find rest in you, and you have no part in them.

114. He who is a slave against his will can become free. He who has

become free through the favour of his master and has sold himself into slavery can no longer become free.

115. The husbandry of the world is through four kinds: they gather into the barn through water, earth, wind and light. And the husbandry of God is likewise through four: faith and hope and love and knowledge. Our earth is faith: it is this in which we take root. The water is hope: it is this through which we are [nour]ished. The wind is love: it is <this>[77] through <which> we grow. But the light [is] knowledge: it is this through which we [ripen].

116a. Grace is [fourfold: it is] earthly; it is [heavenly;   ] highest heaven [   ] in [   ].

116b. [Bles]sed is he because he has not grieved (p. 80) any souls! This is Jesus Christ. He encountered the whole place and (yet) did not burden anyone. Because of this (it holds good): blessed is one of this kind! For he is a perfect man.

117. So far as this is concerned, the word tells us about it, how difficult it is to bring it about. How can we accomplish this great (undertaking)? How will it give rest to everyone?

118. First of all, it is not fitting to grieve anyone - whether great or small, unbeliever or believer - then to give rest to those who are at rest in the things that are good. There are some to whom it is an advantage to give rest to one who is faring well. He who does good may not give rest to these. For he does not attain what he wishes. But (also) he cannot grieve (them), unless he causes them to bring themselves into tribulation. But he who fares well often causes them grief. It is not his fault, but it is their wickedness which causes them grief. - He who has the nature (for it) gives joy to the good. But some through this are sorely grieved.

119. A householder acquired all kinds of things: children, slaves, cattle, dogs, pigs, wheat, barley, chaff, grass, [castor] oil, meat and acorns. [But] he was a wise man, and knew the food for each. Before the children he set [pre]pa[red] bread [and meat]. To the slaves he gave cas[tor oil and m]eal. To the cattle he threw barley, chaff and grass. [To the] dogs he cast bones. [And to the pigs] he threw acorns (p. 81) and scraps of bread (?). So it is with the disciple of God. If he is wise and understands discipleship, the bodily forms will not deceive him, but he will look to the state of the soul of each one and speak with him (accordingly). There are many animals in the world which bear a human form. If he recognises them, to the pigs he will throw acorns, to the cattle barley, chaff and grass, to the dogs bones. To the slaves he will give what is preliminary, but to the children what is perfect.

120. There is the Son of Man, and there is the son of the Son of Man. As to the Son of Man, that is the Lord; and the son of the Son of Man is the one who creates in the power of the Son of Man. - The Son of Man

received from God the ability to create. He (also) has the ability to beget. 121a. He who has received the ability to create is (himself) a creature. He who has received the ability to beget is an offspring. He who creates cannot beget. He who begets is able (also) to create. It is admittedly (also) said of one who creates that he 'begets'. But his 'offspring' is a creation, because these 'offspring' are not his children but [his works]. 121b. He who creates works [openly] and is himself visible. He who begets begets in [secret] and is himself hidden, [because] he sur[passes] the image. [Again] (it is said): He who cre[ates] cr[eates (works)] openly. But he who begets [begets] children in secret.

122a. [No one can] know when [the man] (p. 82) and his wife unite with one another, except them alone. For the marriage of this world is a mystery for those who have taken a wife. If the marriage of defilement is so secret, how much more is the undefiled marriage a true mystery! It is not fleshly, but pure. It has nothing to do with desire, but with the will. It does not belong to the darkness or the night, but to the day and the light.

122b. If a marriage has become (openly) exposed, it has become harlotry. And the bride has played the harlot not only if she has received the seed of another man, but even if she has left her bedchamber and been seen. She ought to show herself only to her father, her mother, the friend of the bridegroom[78] and the children of the bridegroom.[79]

122c. To these it is permitted to enter every day into the wedding hall. But as for the others, let them desire at least to hear her (the bride's) voice and enjoy (the fragrance of) her ointment.[80] And let them feed on the crumbs that fall from the table, like the dogs[81].

122d. Bridegrooms and brides belong to the bridal chamber. No one can see the bridegroom and the bride, unless [he] become such a one.

123a. When Abraham [attained] to seeing what he was to see,[82] he circumcised the flesh of the foreskin, by which he [shows us] that it is necessary to destroy the flesh.

123b. [Most] (things) of the world have continuance and life only so long as their [inward parts] are hidden. [If they] become visible, they are dead. Corresponding to the ex[ample] of the visible man: [so long] as the entrails of the man are hidden, the man is (p. 83) alive. When his entrails are exposed and come out of his abdomen, the man will die. So it is also with the tree: so long as its root is hidden, it sprouts and grows (?). If its root is exposed, the tree dries up. So it is with all kinds of things in the world, not only the visible but also the hidden. For so long as the root of wickedness is hidden, it is strong. But when it is recognised, it has dissolved. And if it becomes visible, it has perished. That is why the Word says: 'Already the axe is laid at the root of the trees',[83] not to cut it away - what is cut away sprouts again. Rather the axe delves deep down until it brings out the root. Jesus tore out the root of the whole place, but others (only) partially. As for us, let each one of us dig down after the root of evil which is in him, and pluck it out from his heart even to the root. But it will be plucked out if we recognise it. But if we are ignorant of it, it strikes root in us and brings forth its fruit in our hearts. It is master over us, and we are its slaves. It takes us captive, so that we do what we do [not] want. What we want, we do [not] do.[84] [It] is powerful, because we have not recognised it. So long as [it] exists, it is active.

123c. Ign[orance] is the mother of [all] evil. Ignorance will end in [death]. [For] those who derive from ign[or]ance neither existed nor exist nor will exist. [But those who belong to the truth] (p. 84) will become perfect when the whole truth is revealed. For the truth is like ignorance: so long as it is hidden, it rests in itself; but when it comes to the light and is recognised, it is praised, inasmuch as it is stronger than ignorance and error. It gives freedom. The Logos said: 'If you know the truth, the truth will make you free.'[85] Ignorance is a slave, knowledge is freedom. If we recognise the truth, we shall find the fruits of the truth in us. If we unite with it, it will receive our fulfilment.

124. Now we hold on to the visible things of the creation, and say that *they* are strong and honoured, but the hidden things are weak and despised. It is <not>[86] so with the visible things of the truth: they are weak and despised, but the hidden things are strong and honoured. But the mysteries of the truth are visible only as types and images.

125a. But the bedchamber is hidden. It is the holy of the holy one. The veil at first concealed how God controlled the creation. But when the veil is rent and the things within become visible, this house will be left deserted, or rather will be dest[royed]. Then (also) all piety will flee [from] here, not (however) into the most holy place - for it cannot mix with the unmixed l[ight] and the [flawless] Pleroma - but it will remain under the wings of the cross [and under its] arms. This ark will be [their] deliverance when the flood (p. 85) of water prevails over them. If any belong to the tribe of the priesthood, they will be able to enter within the veil with the high priest. - That is why the veil was not only rent above - otherwise only the upper part would have been opened; nor is it only below that it was rent - otherwise it would have revealed only the lower part; but it was rent from top to bottom. The upper part opened itself to us <together with> the lower, that we might enter into the secret of the truth. This is truly the honoured which is strong. But we shall go in there through despised symbols and things that are weak. They are indeed despised compared with the perfect glory. There is glory that excels glory; there is power that excels power. That is why (it is said): the perfect and the hidden things of the truth have been opened for us, and the holy of the holies has been revealed, and the bedchamber has invited us in.

125b. So long as it is hidden, wickedness is indeed of no account, but it has not (yet) been removed from the midst of the seed of the Holy Spirit; (and so) they are (still) slaves of wickedness. But when it is revealed, then will the perfect light pour out upon every one, and all those who are in it will receive [the chrism]. Then the slaves will be free, [and] the captives delivered.

126a. E[very] plant [which] my heavenly Father has [not] planted [will be] rooted out.[87]

126b. What is separated will be united; [what is empty] will be filled.

126c. All who shall [enter] into the bedchamber will kindle the li[ght]. For [   ] as in the marriages which take place [and] in the night, the fire [shines] (p. 86) the night through and goes out. But the mysteries of this marriage are completed in the day and in the light. That day or its light does not set.

127. If anyone becomes a son of the bridal chamber, he will receive the light. If anyone does not receive it while he is in this world, he will not receive it in the other place. He who shall receive that light will not be seen, nor can he be detained. And none shall be able to molest such a one, whether he (still) dwells in the world or departs from the world. He has already received the truth in the images. The world has become the aeon; for the aeon has become a Pleroma for him. And as such it is visible to him alone, not hidden in the darkess and the night, but hidden in a perfect day and a holy light.

Notes

V. The Gospel of Philip

* In the manuscript the title appears only in the colophon. This translation has been prepared in close collaboration with Prof. Schenke, who has introduced some further revisions of the published German version.

1. Cf. Philo in Reitzenstein, *Die hellenistischen Mysterienreligionen*, Darmstadt ³1956, p. 270 (ET Pittsburgh 1978, p. 343); Gospel of Thomas, logion 105.

2. Cf. Hermas, *Sim.* III 2; IV 2.

3. On the prohibition of prayer, cf. Gospel of Thomas, logion 14; Clem. Alex. *Strom* VII 41; Origen, *de Orat.* V 1.

4. Cf. Pistis Sophia (C. Schmidt, *Koptisch-gnostische Schriften* I, ⁴1981, 76, 2-5); Apocalypse of Esdras 6.3, 17, 21 (Rießler, p. 135); Apocalypse of Sedrach 9.2 (Rießler, p. 161); Ps.-Phokylides 106 (Rießler, p. 866).

5. On the name-speculations here and elsewhere in the Gospel of Philip cf. e.g. Justin, *Apol.* I 61.14f.

6. On §§ 11 and 12 cf. Clem. Alex. *Exc. ex Theod.* 31.4: 'the name - the names'.

7. Cf. for the general background for example Porphyry, *de Abst.* 2.40, 42; Athenagoras, *Apol.* 26f.

8. Cf. Life of Adam and Eve (Rießler, p. 668).

9. It is the semitic background of the word which is responsible for the fact that here and elsewhere the Spirit is regarded as feminine.

10. Etymology on the basis of the Hebrew *nasar* 'to hide' may also be included.

11. In the manuscript only the initial letter of the Coptic verb is written, and thereafter the space for the two remaining letters is inexplicably left empty.

12. Cf. 2 Cor. 5:3.

13. 1 Cor. 15:20.

14. Jn. 6:53f.

15. Cf. Ignatius, *Trall.* 8; *Rom.* 7.3.

16. Cf. Hermas, *Sim.* V 7.

17. On the motif of the heavenly garments cf. W. Bousset, *Hauptprobleme der Gnosis*, 1907, p.303, note 2.

18. 'He' perhaps refers to the apostle Philip.

19. Cf. Plutarch, *Is. et Os.* 74; Barn. 10.8; Physiologus 21; Philo, *Rer. Div. Her.* 51; Paraphrase of Shem (NHC VII 1) 23.16ff.; Hippol. *Ref.* VI 10.2.

20. The manuscript wrongly has 'her'.

21. Cf. on the one hand Lev. 2:13 and Mk. 9:49 (with *varia lectio*), and on the other Col. 4:5f. Perhaps in the background there is also the eucharist with bread and salt; on this cf. Ps.-Clem. *Hom.* 14.1.4; 13.4.3; Acts of Thomas 29; and Lietzmann, *Messe und Herrenmahl*, 1926, pp. 239-241.

22. Cf. 1 Clem. 11.2; ZP XXXVI 301; but above all Iren. *adv. Haer.* IV 31.3, where Lot's wife who became a pillar of salt (*statua salis*) is interpreted positively as an image of the Church.

23. Cf. Gal. 4:1f.

24. Cf. Jn. 8:44.

25. Cf. Plutarch, *On the E at Delphi* 20.

26. This word is missing in the manuscript.

27. *mšḥ* also with the meaning 'to measure': cf. Brockelmann, *Lex. syr.* 406b.

28. Interpreting Ješûᶜă as jᵉšûᶜā.

29. The manuscript has 'the truth'. The same etymology in Iren. *adv. Haer.* I 21.3.

30. The manuscript has 'them'.

31. The manuscript has 'he'. The salient point, however, is that Pharisatha is in reality a description not of Jesus but of the eucharist; cf. Brockelmann, *Lex. syr.* 600a middle. For the rest, etymological speculation on the basis of the two like-sounding words *prs* 'to divide, break bread' and *prś* 'to spread out', which in Syriac are also written alike.

32. Cf. the *Church Order* of Hippolytus 31.8: '(Jesus Christ) who ... spread out his hands, since he suffered' (NTApo² p. 575); Clem. Alex. *Protr.* XI 111.2.

33. Cf. the Infancy Gospel of Thomas (below, p. 453).

34. I.e. Mary Magdalene corresponds to the type of the Beloved Disciple.

35. Cf. Gospel of Thomas, logion 19a.

36. Cf. for image and subject for example the Gospel of Truth (NHC 1 3) 40.9; Irenaeus, *adv. Haer.* I 6.4; Hermas, *Sim.* IX 13.

37. Eph. 5:32.

38. For 'the Midst' as hell, cf. C. Elsas, *Neuplatonische und gnostische Weltablehnung in der Schule Plotins*, 1975, p. 235.

39. The manuscript has 'them'.

40. Part of a 'vision of hell' after the manner of the (vulgar Christian) Apocalypses of Peter and Paul. There is comparable material also in the Book of Thomas (NHCII 7; cf. below, pp. 232ff.).

41. In the manuscript the verb has been inadvertently omitted.

42. The manuscript mistakenly has 'for yourself'.

43. Cf. Gospel of Thomas, logion 22; 2 Clem. 12.2; Acts of Philip 34 (cf. also above, p. 120, and below, pp. 212f.).

44. Cf. Mt. 8:12; 22:13; 25:30.

45. Cf. Mt. 6:6.

46. The manuscript has 'he' and 'him'.

47. Cf. Gospel of Thomas, logion 22; 106; 114; 2 Clem. 12.2.

48. Cf. Mk. 15:34 par.

49. Cf. Jn. 4:23.

50. Cf. Gen. 2:7.

51. *Sc.* at his baptism.

52. Cf. Acts of John 95.

53. Cf. Ignatius, *Eph.* 19.2.

54. Perhaps to be corrected to 'worship'.

55. Cf. Apoc. Adam 33.3 (Rießler, p. 15); 4.3 (Rießler, pp. 15f.).

56. Cf. Ignatius, *Eph.* 18.2.

57. Mt. 3:15.

58. In the manuscript the verb is mistakenly omitted.

59. Cf. Ps.-Clem. *Recog.* I 45; the Ophites (according to Origen, *c. Cels.* VI 27), where the newly initiated must say: 'I have been anointed with white ointment from the tree of life'; and Bousset, *Hauptprobleme*, pp. 304f.

60. Cf. Gospel of Thomas, logion 11b; Hippol. *Ref.* V 8.32.

61. Cf. 1 Cor. 10:16.

62. Cf. Bousset, *Hauptprobleme*, p. 296, note 1.

63. Cf. Philostr. *Vit. Ap.* VI 40.

64. Cf. 1 Cor. 2:9.

65. On 'the Midst' as hell, cf. Elsas, *Weltablehnung*, p. 235.

66. Cf. Ignatius, *Eph.* 18.2; and thereon H. Schlier, *Religionsgeschichtliche Untersuchungen zu den Ignatiusbriefen*, BZNW 8, 1929, 43-48.

67. Cf. Jn. 8:32.

68. Jn. 8:34.

69. As the result of a wrongly written letter, the manuscript has a meaningless 'agreement'.

70. 1 Cor. 8:1. Cf. Clem. Alex. *Strom.* VII 104.5-105.2.

71. 1 Cor. 8:1.

72. On §§ 109 and 110 cf. J.B. Bauer, ThLZ 86, 1961, cols. 551-554.

73. Cf. Philo, *Somn.* I 178.

74. Cf. Lk. 10:34.

75. 1 Peter 4:8.

76. Cf. Philostr. *Vit. Ap.* VI 40.

77. The manuscript has 'he' and 'whom'.

78. Cf. Jn. 3:29.

79. Cf. Mk. 2:19 par.

80. Cf. Mt. 25:1-12.

81. Cf. Mk. 7:24-30 par.

82. Cf. Jn. 8:56.

83. Mt. 3:10 par.

84. Cf. Rom. 7:19.

85. Jn. 8:32.

86. A negative has presumably been omitted in the manuscript.

87. Mt. 15:13.

VI. The Gospel of the Egyptians

Wilhelm Schneemelcher

Literature: Texts in Klostermann, *Apocrypha II* (KlT)³ 8, 15f.; Aland, *Synopsis*, p. 585 (index). Harnack, *Lit. gesch. I*, 12-14; *II* 1, 612-622; W. Bauer, *Rechtgläubigkeit und Ketzerei im ältesten Christentum*, ²1963, pp. 54ff. (ET *Orthodoxy and Heresy*, 1971, pp. 50ff.); H. Köster, *Synoptische Überlieferung bei den Apostolischen Vätern*, TU 65, 1957; M. Hornschuh, 'Erwägungen zum 'Evangelium der Ägypter', insbesondere zur Bedeutung seines Titels', *Vig.Chr.* 18, 1964, 6-13; Vielhauer, *Lit. gesch.* pp. 662-665; de Santos, pp. 53-57.

In his first Homily on Lk., along with other apocryphal gospels, Origen also mentions a Gospel of the Egyptians (for the text see p. 46 above). From the text nothing emerges regarding the content and character of this gospel, only it is clear that in Origen's time it was already no longer recognised by the Church. Almost nothing of it has been preserved, and the few lines that have been handed down scarcely permit of any far-reaching conclusions, although learned phantasy has time and again attempted to close these gaps in our knowledge. The Greek Gospel of the Egyptians is not identical with the 'Gospel of the Egyptians' recently found at Nag Hammadi (see p. 413 below).

1. Fragments and reports: the chief source of the little knowledge that we have is Clement of Alexandria, who evidently knew the Gospel of the Egyptians and cites it. In *Stromateis* III, which is devoted to the discussion of marriage questions and of sexuality in general, Clement has to join issues with Encratites and others. In doing so he states that these groups (he mentions in addition the name of Julius Cassianus) use the Gospel of the Egyptians, but nothing is said as to the sort of use they made of it.

To refute those who object to marriage and the begetting of children Clement adduces what follows:

(*a*) When Salome asked, 'How long will death have power?' the Lord answered, 'So long as ye women bear children' - not as if life was something bad and creation evil, but as teaching the sequence of nature.

(Strom. III 45; Stählin II 217.6-10)

There is a reference to this saying in a later passage in which Clement again turns against the Encratites and gives the source of the saying:

(*b*) Those who are opposed to God's creation because of continence, which has a fair-sounding name, also quote the words addressed to Salome which I mentioned earlier. They are handed down, as I believe, in the Gospel of the Egyptians. For, they say: the Saviour himself said, 'I am come to undo the works of the female', by the female meaning lust, and by the works birth and decay.

(Strom. III 63: Stählin II 225.1-6)

The Lord - so Clement proceeds - has indeed actually made an end to the works of lust, but birth and decay, i.e. the system of the world, persist.

BAC
148:56
(§3)

(c) Since then the Word has alluded to the consummation, Salome saith rightly, 'Until when shall men die?' Now Scripture uses the term 'man' in the two senses, of the visible outward form and of the soul, and again of the redeemed man and of him who is not redeemed. And sin is called the death of the soul. Wherefore the Lord answers advisedly, 'So long as women bear children', i.e. so long as lusts are powerful.

(*Strom.* III 64; Stählin II 225.15-21)

After further counter-arguments (with quotations from scripture) it is said:

BAC
148:56
(§4)

(d) Why do they not also adduce what follows the words spoken to Salome, these people who do anything but walk by the gospel rule according to truth? For when she said, 'I have then done well in not bearing children', as if it were improper to engage in procreation, then the Lord answered and said, 'Eat every plant, but that which has bitterness eat not'.

(*Strom.* III 66; Stählin II 226.11-16)

Clement's concern is to make it clear that marriage and childbearing are just as little sinful as is continence. In this connection he combats a false interpretation of Mt. 18:20:

(e) For they declare that the Lord meant to say: with the greater number there is the Creator, God, the primal cause of existence, but with the one, the elect one, there is the Redeemer, the Son of another, to wit the good God.

(*Strom.* III 68; Stählin II 227.2-5)

Although the context suggests that this last saying, which may of course have been taken from any writing of the opponents, should be associated with the previously used Gospel of the Egyptians, yet that cannot be done, since Clement gives no indication that that is where it belongs. For the whole polemic he has used, it is clear, only the dialogue of Salome with Christ on death and on the problem of sexuality (on Salome see below). To this dialogue, however, there must also be reckoned a passage which appears in Clement in another context: in his polemic against Julius Cassianus (on him see Hilgenfeld, *Ketzergesch. d. Urchr.* pp. 546ff.), whom he looks upon as the founder of the doctrine of Docetism, he quotes from his writing 'On Continence or on Castration':

(f) If such an arrangement [*namely, the institution of different sexes*] were of God, to whom we aspire, then he would not have praised eunuchs (cf. Mt. 19:12) and the prophet would not have said that they are no unfruitful tree (Isa. 56:3).

Contending further for the impious doctrine he adds:'And how could a charge not be rightly brought against the Saviour, if he has transformed us and freed us from error, and delivered us from sexual intercourse?' In this matter his teaching is similar to that of Tatian. But he emerged from the school of Valentinus. Therefore Cassianus now says, When Salome asked when what she had inquired about would be known, the Lord said, 'When you have trampled on the garment of shame and when the two become one and the male with the female (is) neither male nor female'.

Now in the first place we have not this word in the four Gospels that have been handed down to us, but in the Gospel of the Egyptians. Further he seems to me to fail to recognise that by the male impulse is meant wrath and by the female lust.

(Strom. III 91ff.; Stählin II 238.14-30)

It has been conjectured (O. Stählin, ed. in loc.) that the Gospel of the Egyptians has been used in yet another passage:

(g) Again the Lord says: He who has married should not repudiate his wife, and he who has not married should not marry.

(Strom. III 97; Stählin II 241.3f.)

But Clement does not indicate that here he uses some apocryphon. One easily assumes a free use of 1 Cor. 7:27, 32-36.

It is clear then from the texts given thus far that Clement knew the Gospel of the Egyptians and that he did not regard it as being on a par with the four canonical Gospels, yet did not wholly disapprove of it; cf. (a), (c) and (d). He is aware of the use of this Gospel by the Encratites and Julius Cassianus. From yet another text it is clear that Theodotus, from whom Clement made excerpts, also used this Gospel:

(h) And when the Saviour says to Salome that death will reign as long as women bear children, he does not thereby slander procreation, for that indeed is necessary for the redemption of believers.

(Exc. ex Theod. 67; Stählin III 129.3-6)

Here use is made of the same discourse which we came across in the passages given above, but we are told nothing more about it.

The Gospel of the Egyptians must also have been used by the Naassenes, a Gnostic group whom Hippolytus attacks in his Refutatio (after 222):

(i) They inquire yet further what the soul is, whence it originates and of what nature it is . . . This, however, they search for not in the scriptures but in esoteric doctrines [or teachers of esoteric doctrine?]. Now they say

211

that the soul is very hard to find and to perceive. For it does not always remain in the same fashion or form or in one condition . . . And these various changes (*of the soul*) they find recorded in the so-called Gospel of the Egyptians.

(Hippol. *Ref.* V 7.8f.; Marcovich 145.36-43)

Since Hippolytus does not quote literally but contents himself with this general reference to the use and interpretation of the Gospel of the Egyptians by the Naassenes, there is not much that one can do with his statements. In particular they provide no basis for a reconstruction of this lost Gospel or for assigning other fragments to it. Some (e.g. Zahn, *Gesch. d. ntl. Kanons* II 2, p. 630, note 1) have been minded to derive yet other sayings in Hippolytus from this Gospel, but scarcely with reason (cf. the compilation of the passages in Preuschen, *Antilegomena*[2], pp. 12f.). Certainly we have no means of proving that any such assigning of these sayings is correct.

Finally Epiphanius of Salamis (4th century) refers to the fact that the Sabellians used the Gospel of the Egyptians:

BAC
148:57
(§ 8)

(j) Their whole error, however, and the strength of it they derive from some apocrypha, above all from the so-called Gospel of the Egyptians, as some name it. For in it many such mysterious things are handed down as having come secretly from the Saviour, as that he had revealed to the disciples that the Father, the Son and the Holy Spirit are one and the same person.

(Epiph. *Haer.* 62.2; Holl II 391.4ff.)

Let alone that Epiphanius gives no literal quotation, his statement is in other respects also not very illuminating. For it is quite possible that here he merely brings together his description of the heterodox teaching of the Sabellians and the Gospel of the Egyptians, which for him was of course also heretical. The Sabellians may as a matter of fact have used this gospel. But any drawing of conclusions as to its character from the notice in Epiphanius is forbidden.

2. The Gospel of the Egyptians in other writings: a part of Jesus' answer to Salome (*f* above) also appears in the so-called *Second Epistle of Clement*. But only a fragment of the answer is preserved there, and the wording is new:
(k) Let us now every hour expect the kingdom of God in love and righteousness, since we know not the day of God's appearing. For the Lord himself, on being asked by someone when his kingdom should come, said: When the two shall be one and that which is without as that which is within, and the male with the female neither male nor female.

(2 Clem. 12. 1-2)

It is probably not to be disputed that this saying of Jesus is very closely connected with the quotation (*f*). The possibility that here the Gospel of the Egyptians is quoted therefore does indeed exist. Now there are logia of a similar tenor in other apocryphal writings:

Jesus said to them: When you make the two one, and when you make the inside as the outside and the outside as the inside, and the upper as the lower; and when you make the male and the female into a single one, so that the male is not male and the female female, and when you make eyes in place of an eye and a hand instead of a hand and a foot instead of a foot, an image in place of an image, then will you enter the kingdom.

(Coptic Gospel of Thomas, logion 22)

Jesus said: When you unclothe yourselves and are not ashamed, and take your clothes and lay them under your feet like little children and trample on them, then you will see the Son of the living One, and you will not be afraid.

(Coptic Gospel of Thomas, logion 37)

Concerning this the Lord says in a mystery: Unless you make what is on the right hand as what is on the left and what is on the left hand as what is on the right, and what is above as what is below, and what is behind as what is before, you will not know the kingdom of God.

(Acts of Peter, Act. Vercell. c. 38)

For the Lord said to me: If you do not make your lower part into the higher, and the left into the right, you will not enter into my kingdom.

(Acts of Philip c. 140)

The relation of these passages to the Gospel of the Egyptians (we might also refer to Gos. Phil. 69a, see above, p. 197) can scarcely be determined beyond cavil. We cannot exclude the possibility that there is some connection. However, the differences show that the Gospel of the Egyptians was probably not the written *Vorlage*. Rather we might assume that the saying is 'as its variants show, a wandering saying', or became one (Vielhauer, *Lit. gesch.* p. 663).

Whether the conversation with Salome (and particularly this logion) was originally transmitted in the Gospel of the Egyptians, or stood in a sayings collection, or was disseminated in oral tradition, cannot be said in the present state of our sources.

The logion in 2 Clem 12.2, which possibly derives directly from the Gospel of the Egyptians or at least is connected with the traditions handed down in it, has led many scholars to assign all the sayings of Jesus in 2 Clem to this apocryphon. M. Schneckenburger in 1834 already used this passage for his untenable hypothesis of a close relationship between the Gospel of the Egyptians and that of the Ebionites or that of the Hebrews[1]. After Köster's penetrating investigation of all the relevant passages in 2 Clem,[2] an assignment to the Gospel of the Egyptians (apart from 12.2) can no longer be maintained.

Many other attempts to improve the meagre knowledge imparted by Clement of Alexandria by drawing in other texts have also proved abortive. Thus Th. Zahn thought that there was a connection between the Gospel of the Egyptians and the Gospel of Peter (*Gesch. des ntl. Kanons* II 2, 635f.). He thought that Cassian did not use the Gospel of the Egyptians, but another, and that the Gospel of Peter, although the material of the two gospels was closely related. D. Völter then changed into an identity the relationship which Zahn had conjectured but had not proved.[3] This attempt however met with no approval. The extant fragments of the two apocrypha do not allow of any such hypothesis. The attribution of the logia in POx 1 and 655 to the Gospel of the Egyptians[4] has become untenable through the discovery of the Coptic Gospel of Thomas (see above, pp. 110ff.). We may advance many conjectures about the relation between the Gospel of Thomas and that of the Egyptians, but unfortunately we can prove nothing. The statement that the Gospel of the Egyptians 'used the Gospel of the Hebrews and worked it up' (so Quispel, *Vig.Chr.* 11, 1957, 143) is pure conjecture.

For the apocryphal sayings of the Lord in the so-called Epistle of Titus[5] E. Hennecke assumed derivation from the Gospel of the Egyptians.[6] This too is a hypothesis which cannot be proven.

It may also be mentioned that A. Jacoby wished to ascribe the Strasbourg Coptic fragment edited by him (for the text see above, pp. 103ff.) to the Gospel of the Egyptians, which was already shown by C. Schmidt (GGA 1900, 481-506) to be nonsense. The baptism account published by Jacoby (*Ein bisher unbeachteter apokrypher Bericht über die Taufe Jesu nebst Beiträgen zur Geschichte der Didascalia der 12 Apostel*, Strasbourg 1902) was claimed for the Gospel of the Egyptians by A. Baumstark (*Oriens Christianus* 2, 1902, 466). This hypothesis, however, could only be maintained if we actually knew as much about the Gospel of the Egyptians as Baumstark thinks - which is not the case. At any rate we shall not follow these highly fantastic expositions.

The outcome of this review is then that apart from the fragments in Clement which are expressly declared to be parts of the Gospel of the Egyptians nothing can be claimed with certainty for this apocryphal gospel.

3. Name, tendencies, localisation and date: because of the few extant fragments, precise statements can scarcely be made about the content, structure, theology and composition of this gospel. The following firm data must suffice:

In the 2nd century there was in Egypt a gospel which bore the name Εὐαγγέλιον κατὰ Αἰγυπτίους. W. Bauer thought that the construction of the title with κατά as with the canonical Gospels was a substitute for the *genitivus auctoris*, and drew important consequences from this.[7] The gospel in his view goes back to a period 'in which the Christians of Egypt used this gospel, and only this gospel, as their 'life of Jesus'' (*Orthodoxy*, p. 50). In contrast to the Alexandrian and Jewish-Christian Gospel of the Hebrews, it was the gospel of the gentile Christians of Egypt.

Two objections in particular must be raised against these theses of Bauer. For one thing, after the illuminating expositions of M. Hengel the interpretation of the κατα as a substitute for the genitive probably cannot be maintained. Rather it is intended by this form of title to express the idea 'that the Gospel is here narrated in the special form of the evangelist concerned'. This holds in the first place for the canonical Gospels. Other 'gospels' then by analogy took over this form of title.[8] Here Hengel presupposes a great antiquity for the gospel superscriptions, which is not so certain as he thinks.

On the other hand Hornschuh has contested with instructive reasons Bauer's view that the Gospel of the Egyptians was *the* gospel of the gentile Christians in Egypt (in contrast to the Jewish-Christian Gospel of the Hebrews). The Gospel of the Egyptians 'owes its origin to an older circle of Egyptian Encratites, which we cannot associate with any of the traditional sect names. For later gnostics the apocryphon, which we cannot claim as a document of consistent Gnosis, ranked as an authority. The title 'Gospel of the Egyptians' cannot have originated in Egypt.'[9] This summary characterisation, which rests above all on an investigation of the term 'Egyptians', is probably correct. It remains only to ask whether the Gospel of the Egyptians, of which we have only the paltry remains in Clement of Alexandria, was a gospel in the style of the canonical Gospels, or belonged to the *Gattung* of the 'Dialogues of the Redeemer'. The extant fragments all clearly derive from the dialogue of Jesus with Salome, and thus correspond to the 'Dialogue' *Gattung*, such as we know elsewhere as gnostic 'gospels' (see below, pp. 228ff.). But this question cannot be answered. However, the fact that at least the 'Dialogue' *Gattung* is also used is an important pointer to a proximity to Gnosis, which is also to be recognised in the encratite tendencies. The time of composition cannot be determined exactly. The Gospel of the Egyptians belongs in the second century, presumably in the first half.

Notes

VI. The Gospel of the Egyptians

1. M. Schneckenburger, *Über das Evangelium der Ägypter*, Bern 1834.
2. *Synoptische Überlieferung*, pp. 62-111. It is a question of the following passages: 2 Clem 2.4; 3.2; 4.2; 4.5; 5.2-4; 6.1; 6.2; 8.5; 9.11; 11.2-4; 11.7; 12.1-2; 13.4. Most of the citations belong in the context of the synoptic tradition and its influence. We cannot here enter into the question to what extent Köster's assessments require to be modified.
3. D. Völter, *Petrusevangelium oder Ägyptierevangelium?* 1893; id. 'Petrusevangelium oder Ägyptierevangelium', ZNW 6, 1905, 368-372.
4. Cf. A. Harnack, *Über die jüngst entdeckten Sprüche Jesu*, 1897; E. Hennecke in NTApo[2], pp. 56ff.
5. Edition by de Bruyne, *Revue Bénédictine* 37, 1925, 47-52. Translation by A. de Santos Otero, NTApo[3] II, 141-166 = [5]vol. II, chapter XIV 4.
6. E. Hennecke, 'Zur christlichen Apokryphenliteratur', ZKG 45, 1927, 317, note 3. Zahn had already referred to the possible relationships between Priscillian and the Gospel of the Egyptians (*Gesch.* II 2, 629, note 2; older literature on this question there). H. Chadwick (*Priscillian of Avila*, 1976, pp. 109f.) expresses himself with greater reserve.
7. W. Bauer, *Wörterbuch z. NT*, s.v. κατά 7c (Bauer-Arndt-Gingrich, *Lexicon*[2] 408a); id. *Orthodoxy*, pp. 50ff.
8. M. Hengel, 'Die Evangelienüberschriften' (SAHW 1984, 3), 9f. and 18f.
9. M. Hornschuh, *Vig.Chr.* 18, 1964, 13.

VII. The Gospel of Peter

Christian Maurer and Wilhelm Schneemelcher

Introduction

Wilhelm Schneemelcher

1. Literature: *Facsimile*: O. von Gebhardt, *Das Evangelium und die Apokalypse des Petrus. Die neuentdeckten Bruchstücke nach einer Photographie der Handschrift zu Gizeh in Lichtdruck herausgegeben*, 1893.

Editions: U. Bouriant, 'Fragments du texte grec du livre d'Énoch et de quelques écrits attribués à saint Pierre', *Mémoires publiés par les membres de la mission archéologique française au Caire*, IX 1, Paris 1892. H.B. Swete, *The Apocryphal Gospel of Peter. The Greek Text of the newly discovered Fragment,*[2] London 1893. E. Klostermann, *Apocrypha I* (KlT 3),[3] 1933. A. de Santos Otero, *Los Evangelios Apócrifos* BAC 148, Madrid [4]1984, pp. 375-393;[6]1988, pp. 369-387. M.G. Mara, *Évangile de Pierre. Introduction, texte critique, traduction commentaire et index*, (SC 201), Paris 1973 (Lit.). A. Fuchs, *Das Petrusevangelium. Mit 2 Beiträgen von F.Weißengruber und unter Mitarb. von Chr. Eckmair*, Studien zum NT und seiner Umwelt, B 12), Linz 1978 (Wortkonkordanz und grammatischen Untersuchungen).

Studies: A. Harnack, *Bruchstücke des Evangeliums und der Apokalypse des Petrus* (TU 9.2),[2]1893. H. von Schubert, *Die Composition des pseudo-petrinischen Evangelien-Fragments*, 1893. Th. Zahn, *Das Evangelium des Petrus*, 1893. L. Vaganay, *L'Évangile de Pierre*, (Études Bibliques), Paris 1930 (with detailed bibliography). M. Dibelius, 'Die alttestamentlichen Motive in der Leidensgeschichte des Petrus-und des Johannes-Evangeliums', in FS von Baudissin, BeihZAW 33, 1918, 125ff. (= *Botschaft und Geschichte*. Ges. Aufs. von M. Dibelius, ed. G. Bornkamm I, 1953, 221-247). A.F.J. Klijn, 'Het Evangelie van Petrus en de Westerse Text', *Nederlandse Theol. Tijdschrift* 16, 1961, 264-270. O. Perler, 'L'Évangile de Pierre et Méliton de Sardes', *Rev.Bibl.* 71, 1964, 584-590. J. Denker, 'Die theologiegeschichtliche Stellung des Petrusevangeliums. Ein Beitrag zur Frühgeschichte des Doketismus', (Europ. Hochschulschr. XXIII, 36), 1975. N. Brox, ''Doketismus' - eine Problemanzeige', ZKG 95, 1984, 301-314. J.W. McCant, 'The Gospel of Peter: Docetism reconsidered', NTS 30, 1984, 258-273. B.A. Johnson, 'The Gospel of Peter: Between Apocalypse and Romance', *Studia Patristica* XVI, ed. E.A. Livingstone, (TU 129), 1985, 170-174. Vielhauer, *Lit. gesch.* pp. 641-648. Erbetta I 1, 135-145. Starowieyski I 2, 409-419.

2. Attestation: a Gospel of Peter (= Gos.Pet.) is frequently mentioned in the Church literature of the early centuries. With one exception, however, exact statements about its compass, content and origin are not combined with these reports, and no quotation from this apocryphon has been handed down.

Origen in his *Commentary on Matthew* (vol. X 17, ed. Klostermann, GCS 40.1, 1935, p. 21.26ff.) reports that some people affirm that the brothers of Jesus sprang from a first marriage of Joseph (cf. for this Protev. Jac. 9.2). In this they rely on the tradition of the so-called Gospel of Peter. Origen however adds: 'or the book of James'. It is therefore at least questionable, if not indeed excluded, that Origen knew the Gos.Pet. itself.

Eusebius mentions the Gos.Pet. twice among the writings not recognised in the Church (H.E. III 3.2; III 25.6; see above, p. 46), without however saying anything about its content. Jerome (*Vir. Ill.* 1) and the Decretum Gelasianum (see above, p. 37) go back to Eusebius.

More important than these references is the quotation handed on by Eusebius (H.E. VI 12.3-6) from a work (a letter?) by Serapion of Antioch (end of 2nd century) 'On the so-called Gospel of Peter'. Serapion came across the Gospel of Peter in the community at Rhossos, and at first sanctioned its reading. Later, on more careful examination, he recognised that alongside much orthodox material there are in it also heretical opinions, which he brings into connection with 'Docetists'.

3. The fragment of the text: these few reports about the Gos.Pet. were supplemented and superseded in surprising fashion by a parchment manuscript of the 8th/9th century found in the grave of a monk at Akhmim in Upper Egypt in the winter of 1886/1887. This manuscript contains fragments of a gospel, the Greek Apocalypse of Peter and the Greek Enoch. The identification of the first text as part of the Gos.Pet., above all on the basis of vss. 26f. and vs. 30, is today generally recognised. Also there seems in the 1st century to have been only one gospel under the name of Peter. At any rate we know of no other work under this name. The Akhmim text begins with Pilate's washing of his hands, which is not indeed recorded in the extant lines but can probably be deduced to have preceded. Then follow the sections about the condemnation, death and resurrection of Jesus. The fragment breaks off with the departure of Peter, Andrew and Levi 'to the sea'. This was probably the introduction to the report of the appearance of the risen Jesus at the lake of Tiberias, which has not survived.

As the ornaments at the beginning and end show, the copyist of this Akhmim manuscript had only this part of the Gos.Pet. before him. Any speculation about the structure or the rest of the content of the Gos.Pet. as a whole is in the present state of our knowledge meaningless.

The text of the fragment was divided by Robinson into fourteen chapters and by Harnack into sixty verses. Both numberings are noted in the translation offered below.

R.A. Coles in 1972 published two small papyrus fragments (POx 2949), which Dieter Lührmann identified as remains of the Gos.Pet.[1]. It is a matter of one piece with thirteen fragmentary lines and another with five. However, the amount of readable text is so scrappy that while we may indeed consider Lührmann's identification to be correct, we do not gain much help for the text of the Gos. Pet. But the discovery is important because it proves that the Gos. Pet. was used in Egypt at the end of the second century or the beginning of the 3rd (such is the dating by the editors).

4. Utilisation: after the discovery of the Akhmim fragment, numerous efforts were made to demonstrate quotations from the Gos. Pet. or traces of its use in writings of the early centuries. The search for such evidence ranged from Justin in the middle of the 2nd century to Aphraates in the 4th. A comprehensive critical examination of the material in question, such as Denker (pp. 9-30) has undertaken, leads however to the conclusion that in most cases use of the Gos. Pet. cannot be proved. The similarities, already often worked out, between individual works of early Church literature and the Gos. Pet. can usually be adequately explained on the view that the Gos. Pet. stands 'in a broad stream of West Syrian gospel tradition' (Denker, p. 30).

This is also suggested by the probable use of the Gos. Pet. in Manichean texts. In the Turfan fragment M 18 quoted below (p. 402) the influence of the Gos. Pet. is not to be overlooked.[2] Since the Turfan material has not been completely made accessible (see below, p. 411), we cannot yet determine more precisely the extent of the use of the Gos. Pet. in Manichean texts. But if such use can actually be shown, we may probably assume a passage across Syria (or starting from Syria).[3]

5. Relation to the canonical Gospels: the debate about the relation of this text to the NT Gospels began immediately after the Gos. Pet. fragment became known. At first the literary-critical method was paramount, i.e. the effort to show that individual sentences in the Gos. Pet. were citations from the canonical Gospels (cf. above all Th. Zahn). This led easily to the picture of a 'forger' who - as it were at a writing-table - put together a mosaic from the texts of the three or four NT Gospels. Martin Dibelius in particular pointed out[4] that we should probably have a different picture of the origin of the Gos. Pet.: the author used the traditional material of the Gospels from memory, and supplemented it by oral preaching traditions (above all traditions of Old Testament exegesis).

Vielhauer in his *Literaturgeschichte* took up this interpretation. The Gos. Pet. already shows itself to be a late work through the 'I' of the author, ostensibly Peter. It presupposes the four NT Gospels, but not yet the canon of the four Gospels. In terms of source-criticism, however, the presentation cannot be parcelled out without remainder. In terms of the history of tradition also the Gos. Pet. proves to be secondary. 'It shows not only an enhanced delight in the fantastic and the miraculous, but above all a shifting of the theological interest from the Cross to the Resurrection' (p. 646). On the other side certain archaic elements are not to be overlooked, particularly in the references to the OT. The 'way of presenting the suffering of Jesus with the help of OT sayings without quotation formulae is in terms of tradition history older than the explicit scriptural proof, it represents the oldest form in which the Passion was portrayed, but is likewise intended to substantiate the fulfilment of OT prophecies in the Passion and its details' (p. 646). These archaic features probably reached the author through homiletic traditions.

Mara also assumes a knowledge of the canonical Gospels. In its narrative, he thinks, the Gos.Pet. follows the Synoptics, but in its theology the Gospel of John. What is more important is that in this gospel the passion and glorification of Jesus are set in the light of the OT. This is also, according to Mara, the basis for the many connections of the Gos.Pet. with other early Christian writings, to which reference is repeatedly made in his commentary. The Gos.Pet. does not stand in isolation in the history of early Christianity. Mara appears to attach great significance to the oral tradition which could be worked up in the Gos.Pet.

Denker represents another view. He rejects the literary-critical method, with reason, and comes to the conclusion: 'The Gos.Pet. does not allow any recognition that it presupposes the redactional work of the four canonical Gospels. Dependence upon them therefore cannot be proved. The author of the Gos.Pet. will not have known them, or at least he takes no notice of them. He rather attaches himself to his (catechetical) community tradition' (pp. 56f.). Denker sees in the Gos.Pet. an independent creation on the basis of the oral tradition known to the author, above all the OT exegetical tradition (77). The OT was for the author an important source. But he used it selectively: Isaiah, the Psalms and some other passages are particularly important for him.[5] Now these statements are probably connected with the total understanding of the Gos.Pet. which Denker advocates. For him the Gos.Pet. is a Jewish-Christian Gospel which must be placed chronologically very early (c. 100-130). This problem has still to be discussed below. Here it may merely be remarked that the verbal agreements between the Gos.Pet. and the canonical Gospels are too numerous to allow us to uphold so sharp a rejection of their knowledge and use.

Yet another view of the problem is that of H. Köster, who appraises Denker's work positively.[6] He sets the Gos.Pet. in the total context of early Christian gospel formation, and thinks that the kinship between the Gos.Pet. and the canonical Gospels is to be explained on the basis that an old tradition (an epiphany story) is in each case worked into a different context. Here the Gos. Pet. is even given a pre-eminence, since in it the old tradition is preserved complete. Köster is inclined to agree with the view 'that in this document we have older versions of the Passion and resurrection stories, in which traditions and sources used by the canonical Gospels are further developed independently of them'.[7] According to this, the question of the agreements between the four NT Gospels and the Gos.Pet. is to be answered on the basis that all the texts go back to a common old tradition, which has however been differently developed.

Now such a development would indeed be possible, but can scarcely be proved. Above all, this conception seems to be contradicted by the fact that the author betrays no knowledge of the situation in Palestine in the time of Jesus, which one would expect to find at least in some way in an old tradition. In particular the Jewish institutions are evidently unknown to him (Mara has laid special stress on this). But this does not exactly speak for old tradition in the Gos.Pet.

In view of these very divergent opinions it is difficult to form any precise judgment on the relations between the Gos.Pet. and the canonical Gospels. Many questions remain open. The verbal echoes and the deviations are just as clear as the secondary character of many features and the archaic elements. 'The fragment contains both old and new, in literary and in theological terms it is complex' (Vielhauer, p. 646).

Since an exact dating of the Gos.Pet. is scarcely possible (see below), we cannot attain to any certainty on this question from this side either. It may finally be recalled yet again that we possess only the Akhmim fragment, hence probably only a small portion of the complete Gos.Pet.

6. The Gos.Pet. in the history of theology: in the Serapion quotation in Eusebius (H.E. VI 12.3-6), the Gos.Pet. is put in relation, not very precisely defined, with the 'Docetists'. Even if 'most of it corresponds to the correct doctrine of the Redeemer', Serapion has discovered other things which he describes as the false teaching of the successors of those "whom we call Docetae'. Unfortunately Eusebius has quoted nothing of the exposition which Serapion promises of this docetic error. After the appearance of the Akhmim fragment, search was understandably made for docetic statements in this text. In particular verses 10 ('but he was silent, as if he felt no pain') and 19 (the dying cry: 'My power, O power, thou hast forsaken me'; also 'and having said this, he was taken up') were interpreted as evidence for the docetism of the Gos.Pet.

Apart from the fact that we have only this one fragment of the Gos.Pet.and therefore can say nothing about the tendency of the whole work, we may not regard the passages mentioned as unambiguously docetic statements.[8] The emphasis on the reality of the resurrection and also the inclination towards a pre-existence Christology (vs. 56) tell against the docetic character of the Gos.Pet.

In addition, we ought in any case to be somewhat cautious in our use of the term 'docetic'. N. Brox has expressed himself emphatically against a widespread nebulous use of the term, and has sought an exact definition which links up with the original usage (e.g. in Clement of Alexandria).[9] Docetism is 'the doctrine according to which the phenomenon of Christ, his historical and bodily existence, and thus above all the human form of Jesus, was altogether mere semblance without any true reality. The human existence and suffering of Christ as pure semblance: this idea served to eliminate the incarnation and Passion of the heavenly Redeemer where they gave offence. Polemic was directed especially against the (bodily) birth and Passion ... Jesus Christ as divine Redeemer, who had no contact with matter, however fleeting, because by his very nature and his mission he could not and must not have it' (p. 306). An equation of Docetism so defined with gnostic Christology is false, as can also be shown in the texts from Nag Hammadi. If we apply these briefly summarised reflections of Brox to the Gos. Pet., then the question of the docetic or gnostic character of the work is to be answered with an unambiguous negative.

The combination of docetic tendencies with an alleged origin in 'Jewish Christianity' is also not very plausible. It may be that 'the early Christological Docetism was of value for the Jewish Christian concern for the inviolability of (Jewish) monotheism' (Brox, p. 314). But Brox himself admits the uncertainty of the assumption of a connection of Docetism and Jewish Christianity.

Denker's attempt to prove the Gos.Pet. a Jewish-Christian gospel does not rest so much on the alleged Docetism of the fragment, which is regarded rather as a consequence of its Jewish-Christian conception. For Denker other factors are more important (apologetic, angelomorphic Christology, etc.). He works with a very vaguely conceived idea of 'Jewish Christianity': 'I would define the Jewish Christianity of the Gos.Pet. as a Christian thought especially of the period between the two Jewish Wars, which expresses itself in ideas and forms borrowed from Judaism' (p. 86). Jewish Christianity is not only 'Ebionitism', but includes more movements than only this one.

It is very questionable whether justice is really done to the very complex phenomenon of Jewish Christianity with this definition of terms. For the Gos.Pet. one can probably only then make a beginning if on the one hand we can prove the complete independence of this text from the canonical Gospels and their traditions, and if on the other hand we disregard the fact that the reception of the OT in primitive Christianity also led to an influence of individual concepts, ideas and forms which ran parallel in Church and Synagogue.

The anti-Jewish polemic in the Gos.Pet., which cannot be overlooked, also speaks against a Jewish-Christian origin. With this polemic the Gos.Pet. stands in a long tradition (cf. e.g. 1 Thess. 2:15), which is also visible in the passover homily of Melito of Sardis, the proximity of which to the Gos.Pet. Perler has shown. This apologetic, however, seems scarcely compatible with a Jewish-Christian origin.

In the present state of our knowledge it cannot be said in what group in early Christianity the Gos.Pet. originated. Serapion of Antioch established, probably correctly, the presence side by side of 'correct doctrine' and views which deviated from it. We may further understand from his words that this gospel was used in a community which did not adhere to any sect or heresy, but rather was in fellowship with the community of Antioch. This juxtaposition of 'correct' and 'false' teaching is matched by the remarkable combination of different traditions which we have sketched above. Here the tradition of OT exegesis in an anti-Jewish sense was evidently an important constituent (at least in the fragment known to us). This shows that the Gos.Pet. may not be seen in isolation, but belongs with many another writing. Everything speaks for the view that the Gos.Pet. originated in a community which cannot be characterised by any description of heretics, whether old or new. Eventual later use by groups outside the Great Church (e.g. by gnostics) says nothing about its origin.

7. Place and time: an exact dating is not possible. We can only establish that according to the testimony of Serapion the Gos. Pet. must have originated some time before c. 190. If we assume knowledge of the four canonical Gospels, we shall not place the Gos.Pet. too early in the 2nd century. On the other hand the older traditions which can be shown are an indication that it cannot be dated too late. We can scarcely get beyond conjectures. The middle of the 2nd century is a natural hypothesis. Nor can we name the place of origin. The Gos.Pet. is attested by Serapion for Syria, by POx 2949 in Egypt. Asia Minor has also been proposed as the land of origin (cf. Melito of Sardis). But Syria appears to be more natural.

Notes

The Gospel of Peter

Introduction

1. POx 2949, in *The Oxyrhynchus Papyri*, XLI, ed. G.M. Browne *et al.*, London 1972, 15f. Dieter Lührmann, 'POx 2949: EvPet 3-5 in einer Handschrift des 2/3 Jahrhunderts', ZNW 72, 1981, 217-226.

2. Cf. W. Sundermann, 'Christliche Evangelientexte in der Überlieferung der iranisch-manichäischen Literatur', *Mitt. des Inst. für Orientforschung*, (Berlin), 14, 1968, 386-405 (esp. p. 389).

3. On the diffusion of Syrian literature, especially apocryphal works, as far as central Asia, cf. J.P. Asmussen, 'The Sogdian and Uighur-Turkish Christian Literature in Central Asia before the Real Rise of Islam. A Survey', in *Indological and Buddhist Studies* (FS J.W. de Jong), Canberra 1982, pp. 11-29. On the question of the relation of the Pilate literature to the Gos.Pet. cf. Denker, pp. 24ff., who assumes use only for recension B. But this problem probably requires a closer investigation.

4. Dibelius' essay 'Die alttestamentlichen Motive...' marks a decisive new beginning in the study of the Gos.Pet., and is still influential.

5. The problem of the testimonia collections, to which Mara frequently refers, is not given any special treatment by Denker.

6. Cf. H. Köster, 'Apocryphal and Canonical Gospels', HThR 73, 1980, 105-130; id. 'Überlieferung und Geschichte der frühchristlichen Evangelienliteratur', ANRW 2512, 1984, 1463-1542.

7. ANRW 1488, appealing to Denker and B.A. Johnson, 'The Empty Tomb Tradition in the Gospel of Peter', Harvard Univ. Diss. (unfortunately not accessible to me; cf. however the essay by Johnson in *Studia Patristica* XVI, mentioned above).

8. Cf. Mara and Vielhauer.

9. N. Brox, 'Doketismus' - eine Problemanzeige', ZKG 95, 1984, 301-314. The essay is important not only for the Gos. Pet., but can be helpful for other apocrypha also.

Translation of the Akhmim Fragment*

Christian Maurer

1. 1. But of the Jews none washed their hands,[1] neither Herod nor any one of his judges. And as they would not wash, Pilate arose. 2. And then Herod the king commanded that the Lord should be marched off, saying to them, 'What I have commanded you to do to him, do ye.'

2. 3. Now there stood there Joseph, the friend of Pilate and of the Lord, and knowing that they were about to crucify him he came to Pilate and begged the body[2] of the Lord for burial. 4. And Pilate sent to Herod and begged his body. 5. And Herod said, 'Brother Pilate, even if no one had begged him, we should bury him, since the Sabbath is drawing on.[3] For it stands written in the law: The sun should not set on one that has been put to death.'[4]

And he delivered[5] him to the people on the day before the unleavened bread,[6] their feast.

3. 6. So they took the Lord and pushed him in great haste and said, 'Let us hale the Son of God now that we have gotten power over him.' 7. And they put upon him a purple robe and set him on the judgment seat and said, 'Judge righteously, O King of Israel!'[7] 8. And one of them brought a crown of thorns and put it on the Lord's head. 9. And others who stood by spat on his face, and others buffeted him on the cheeks, others nudged him with a reed,[8] and some scourged him, saying, 'With such honour let us honour the Son of God.'

4. 10. And they brought two malefactors and crucified the Lord in the midst between them.[9] But he held his peace,[10] as if he felt no pain. 11. And when they had set up the cross, they wrote upon it: This is the King of Israel.[9] 12. And they laid down his garments before him and divided them among themselves and cast the lot upon them.[9] 13. But one of the malefactors rebuked them, saying, 'We have landed in suffering for the deeds of wickedness which we have committed, but this man, who has become the saviour of men, what wrong has he done you?'[11] 14. And they were wroth with him and commanded that his legs should not be broken,[12] so that he might die in torments.

5. 15. Now it was midday and a darkness covered all Judaea. And they became anxious and uneasy lest the sun had already set, since he was still alive. <For> it stands written for them: the sun should not set on one that has been put to death.[13] 16. And one of them said, 'Give him to drink gall with vinegar.' And they mixed it and gave him to drink.[14] 17. And they fulfilled all things and completed the measure of their sins on their head.[15] 18. And many went about with lamps, since they

supposed that it was night, <and> they stumbled.[16] 19. And the Lord called out and cried, 'My power, O power, thou hast forsaken me!'[17] And having said this he was taken up. 20. And at the same hour the veil of the temple in Jerusalem was rent in two.[18]

6. 21. And then the Jews drew the nails[19] from the hands of the Lord and laid him on the earth. And the whole earth shook and there came a great fear.[20] 22. Then the sun shone (again), and it was found to be the ninth hour.[21] 23. And the Jews rejoiced and gave his body to Joseph that he might bury it, since he had seen all the good that he (= Jesus) had done. 24. And he took the Lord, washed him, wrapped him in linen[22] and brought him into his own sepulchre, called Joseph's Garden.[23]

7. 25. Then the Jews and the elders and the priests, perceiving what great evil they had done to themselves, began to lament and to say, 'Woe on our sins, the judgment and the end of Jerusalem is drawn nigh.'[24] 26. But I mourned with my fellows, and being wounded in heart we hid ourselves, for we were sought after by them as evildoers and as persons who wanted to set fire to the Temple. 27. Because of all these things we were fasting and sat mourning and weeping night and day until the sabbath.[25]

8. 28. But the scribes and pharisees and elders, being assembled together and hearing that all the people were murmuring and beating their breasts, saying, 'If at his death these exceeding great signs have come to pass, behold how righteous he was!',[26] - 29. were afraid and came to Pilate,[27] entreating him and saying, 30. 'Give us soldiers that we may watch his sepulchre for three days, lest his disciples come and steal him away and the people suppose that he is risen from the dead, and do us harm.' 31. And Pilate gave them Petronius the centurion with soldiers to watch the sepulchre. And with them there came elders and scribes to the sepulchre. 32. And all who were there, together with the centurion and the soldiers, rolled thither a great stone and laid it against the entrance to the sepulchre 33. and put on it seven seals, pitched a tent and kept watch.[28]

9. 34. Early in the morning, when the sabbath dawned, there came a crowd from Jerusalem and the country round about to see the sepulchre that had been sealed.

35. Now in the night in which the Lord's day dawned, when the soldiers, two by two in every watch, were keeping guard, there rang out a loud voice in heaven, 36. and they saw the heavens opened[29] and two men come down from there in a great brightness and draw nigh to the sepulchre. 37. That stone which had been laid against the entrance to the sepulchre started of itself to roll and gave way to the side, and the sepulchre was opened, and both the young men entered in.[30]

10. 38. When now those soldiers saw this, they awakened the centurion and the elders - for they also were there to assist at the watch. 39. And whilst they were relating what they had seen, they saw again three men come out from the sepulchre, and two of them sustaining the other, and a cross following them,[31] 40. and the heads of the two reaching to heaven, but that of him who was led of them by the hand overpassing the heavens. 41. And they heard a voice out of the heavens crying, 'Hast thou preached to them that sleep?',[32] 42. and from the cross there was heard the answer, 'Yea'.

11. 43. Those men therefore took counsel with one another to go and report this to Pilate. 44. And whilst they were still deliberating, the heavens were again seen to open, and a man descended and entered into the sepulchre. 45. When those who were of the centurion's company saw this, they hastened by night to Pilate, abandoning the sepulchre which they were guarding, and reported everything that they had seen, being full of disquietude and saying, 'In truth he was the Son of God.'[33] 46. Pilate answered and said, 'I am clean from the blood of the Son of God, upon such a thing have you decided.'[34] 47. Then all came to him, beseeching him and urgently calling upon him to command the centurion and the soldiers to tell no one what they had seen. 48. 'For it is better for us', they said, 'to make ourselves guilty of the greatest sin before God than to fall into the hands of the people of the Jews and be stoned.'[35] 49. Pilate therefore commanded the centurion and the soldiers to say nothing.[36]

12. 50. Early in the morning of the Lord's day Mary Magdalene,[37] a woman disciple of the Lord - for fear of the Jews,[38] since (they) were inflamed with wrath, she had not done at the sepulchre of the Lord what women are wont to do for those beloved of them who die - took 51. with her her women friends and came to the sepulchre where he was laid. 52. And they feared lest the Jews should see them, and said, 'Although we could not weep and lament on that day when he was crucified, yet let us now do so at his sepulchre. 53. But who will roll away for us the stone also that is set on the entrance to the sepulchre, that we may go in and sit beside him and do what is due? - 54. For the stone was great,[39] - and we fear lest any one see us. And if we cannot do so, let us at least put down at the entrance what we bring for a memorial of him and let us weep and lament until we have again gone home.'

13. 55. So they went and found the sepulchre opened. And they came near, stooped down and saw there a young man sitting in the midst of the sepulchre, comely and clothed with a brightly shining robe, who said to them, 56. 'Wherefore are ye come? Whom seek ye? Not him that was crucified? He is risen and gone. But if ye believe not, stoop this way and

see the place where he lay, for he is not here. For he is risen and is gone thither whence he was sent.' 57. Then the woman fled affrighted.[40]

14. 58. Now it was the last day of unleavened bread and many went away and repaired to their homes, since the feast was at an end. 59. But we, the twelve disciples of the Lord, wept and mourned, and each one, very grieved for what had come to pass, went to his own home. 60. But I, Simon Peter, and my brother Andrew took our nets and went to the sea.[41] And there was with us Levi, the son of Alphaeus, whom the Lord - (had called away from the custom-house (?), cf. Mk. 2:14).

Notes

Translation of the Akhmim Fragment

* We have dispensed with the italicising of words and phrases which also appear in the NT reports, in order not to arouse the impression that in the Gos.Pet. we have a gospel harmony artificially put together.

1. Cf. Mt. 27:24.
2. Mk. 15:43 par.
3. Cf. Lk. 23:54.
4. Cf. Jn. 19:31; Deut. 21:22ff.; Josh. 8:29; 10:27.
5. Cf. Mk. 15:15 par.
6. Cf. Mk. 14:12 par.
7. Cf. Justin, *Apol.* 1. 35; Jn. 19:13.
8. To vss. 6-9 cf. Mk. 14:65; 15:16-20 par.
9. Cf. Mk. 15:24ff. par.
10. Cf. Mk. 14:61 and par.; 15:5 par.
11. Cf. Lk. 23:39ff.
12. Cf. Jn. 19:31ff.
13. Mk. 15:33 par.; Am. 8:9; cf. note 4 above.
14. Cf. Mt. 27:34, 48 par.; Ps. 68:22.
15. Cf. Jn. 19:28, 30.
16. Cf. Jn. 11:10.
17. Cf. Mk. 15:34 par.; Ps. 21:2.
18. Mk. 15:38 par.
19. Jn. 20:25, 27.
20. Mt. 27:51, 54.
21. Cf. Mk. 15:33 par.
22. Cf. Mk. 15:46 par.
23. Jn. 19:41.
24. Cf. Lk. 23:48 *var. lect.*
25. Cf. Mk. 2:20 par.; 16:10.
26. Cf. Lk. 23:47f.
27. With vss. 29-33 cf. Mt. 27:62-66.
28. Cf. Mk. 15:46 par.; Mt. 27:66.
29. Cf. Mt. 3:16f. par.

30. With vss. 35-37 cf. Mt. 28:1f.
31. Cf. Mk. 16:3 cod. k; Asc. Is. III 17; Epist. Apost. 16 (27).
32. Cf. 1 Pet. 3:19.
33. Mk. 15:39 par.
34. Cf. Mt. 27:24.
35. Cf. Jn. 11:50.
36. With vss. 47-49 cf. Mt. 28:11-15.
37. Cf. Mt. 28:1 par.
38. Cf. Jn. 20:19.
39. Cf. Mk. 16:3f.
40. With vss. 55-57 cf. Mk. 16:1-8.
41. Cf. Jn. 21:1ff.

VIII. Dialogues of the Redeemer

Introduction

Wilhelm Schneemelcher

In 1919 Carl Schmidt, in collaboration with I. Wajnberg, published the Epistula Apostolorum under the title 'Gespräche Jesu mit seinen Jüngern nach der Auferstehung. Ein Katholisch-Apostolisches Sendschreiben des 2. Jahrhunderts' (see below, pp. 249ff.). The two-part title, which is not handed down in the manuscripts but deduced by the editors, indicates the problem of the *Gattung* of this text: it begins as a letter, but is in its main body a dialogue of Jesus with the apostles. We can describe this work as a revelation discourse in the form of a dialogue with a 'gospel' framework[1].

In NT Apo[3] this 'Epistula Apostolorum' was placed together with the Freer Logion (see below, pp. 248f.) and the Strasbourg Coptic fragment (see above, pp. 103ff.) under the heading 'Conversations between Jesus and his disciples after the Resurrection' (I, 188-230), without any detailed discussion of the literary *Gattung* (the genre, as it is often called today).

In his comprehensive survey 'Gnostic gospels and related documents' (NT Apo[3], I, 231-362) H.-Ch. Puech drew attention to many texts which present similar dialogues of the risen Jesus with his disciples, and which are described by him as 'typically gnostic gospels'. Here it is mostly a question of works which first became known through the discovery of the Coptic gnostic library of Nag Hammadi. Now when Puech wrote his contribution the texts from this library were for the most part still not published. His report could therefore be only a first survey, which however in many respects still has value even today (cf. below, pp. 354ff.). The problem of the *Gattung* 'dialogues of the Redeemer', i.e. in Puech's view the 'typically gnostic gospels', could at this point still not be comprehensively dealt with.[2]

In the interval the texts from Nag Hammadi have become accessible.[3] A vast number of studies has been devoted to them, and many hypotheses have been linked with these texts. The question of their genre, their literary genus, is one of the problems which have resulted from this work.

Among the Nag Hammadi texts there is a number of works which could be described as 'dialogues'. Closer examination however shows a considerable variety, so that the question arises whether there is a uniform 'dialogue' *Gattung*, in the sense of a 'gnostic gospel' genre.

Kurt Rudolph has devoted an important essay to this question.[4] He demonstrates that the gnostic texts link up with the ancient literary form of the 'dialogue', and at the same time take up elements of the erotapocrisis (question and answer) literature.[5] Rudolph rightly stresses the intention of the gnostic works: they serve to convey salvation and for the formation of doctrine. 'Through this literature Gnosis seeks to explain itself' (p. 103). That this clarification of doctrine ministers to salvation, which consists in 'knowledge', is an essential presupposition of this *Gattung*, which is an independent literary form belonging to Gnosis which originated through the development of older stylistic forms.

P. Vielhauer, who concurs with Rudolph's arguments,[6] rightly draws attention to the fact that the Easter stories in the gospel tradition are the point of departure for this literary *Gattung*. In fact these dialogues (except for the Ap. Jas.; see below, pp. 285ff.) are set out as instruction for the disciples by the risen Lord in the period after Easter. The stage-setting is not uniform (e.g. the place of the conversation is given in various ways). What is more important is that these conversations are indeed conceived in questions and answers, but strictly are not genuine dialogues. 'Jesus is throughout the leading figure, his partners in the conversation only those instructed' (Vielhauer, p. 683). This, however, corresponds with the aim of this gnostic literary form developed out of various *Gattungen*.

The Epistula Apostolorum shows that there were also non-gnostic works of this kind.[7] 'This in church circles is singular, and is evidently a conscious taking over of one of the most typical gnostic forms for substantiating authoritative teaching; it is thus a case of an attempt to combat the gnostic opponents with their own weapons' (Vielhauer, p. 687).

In several contributions H. Koester has applied himself intensively to the problem of the 'dialogue gospels', although from other points of view.[8] At first he had interpreted the gnostic 'revelations' on the basis of the theophany narratives, and placed them in association with the *Gattung* of the apocalypses.[9] In this interpretation the tradition of apocalyptic sayings of Jesus which is to be assumed before the Gospels already plays for Koester an important role. 'The gnostic gospel, even in its developed form, remains the representative of a *Gattung* which goes back to very early pre-canonical developments of the gospel tradition'.[10]

Koester then further developed these ideas (above all in his major contribution in ANRW 25.2), and sought to build them up into a total picture of the origin of the gospels as a *Gattung*. For the history of the gospel literature the source documents which can be deduced from canonical as from apocryphal writings are in his view of fundamental importance for the understanding of this *Gattung*. Koester seeks in this way to carry the form-critical work on the canonical Gospels further with the help of the Nag Hammadi texts. This need not be further discussed here. Only the conclusions for the *Gattung* of the 'dialogue' as a gnostic gospel type which result from this conception require brief consideration.

These dialogues according to Koester are to be inserted in the context of the sayings tradition. Even before Paul's letters and before the canonical Gospels there were collections of the logia of Jesus. Alongside wisdom sayings, to which a special significance attaches, prophetic and apocalyptic sayings were also collected and handed on. The sayings source Q was according to Koester an apocalyptic book of sayings, in which the wisdom tradition receded into the background. On the other hand the Coptic Gospel of Thomas presents several wisdom sayings, although with a gnostic adjustment. In other texts from the Nag Hammadi discovery (e.g. the Dialogue of the Saviour; see below, pp. 300ff.) Koester sees a development of, and in part also a conscious commenting on, the Gospel tradition.

We may formulate it, in somewhat cursory and epigrammatic fashion: the 'dialogues', which Rudolph regards as an independent gnostic development of Greek literary *Gattungen*, are understood by Koester as a continuation of older sayings collections, which is at the same time interpretation. It is worthy of note that Koester sets the 'sayings sources' which he deduces very early (e.g. for one *Vorlage* of the Dialogue of the Saviour he even assumes the 1st century as the period of origin). He can thus bring the sources deduced from canonical and apocryphal sources into association with one another and attempt to reconstruct the history of the oldest logia tradition. However, it remains questionable whether these hypotheses can actually be confirmed. We cannot however overlook the fact that the task of a form-critical investigation of the gnostic 'dialogue gospels' and their source material has been recognised by Koester, and taken in hand.

It has already been said that Koester regards the extant texts of this *Gattung* (to which he also reckons the Gospel of the Egyptians; see above, pp. 209ff.) as a development of the sayings tradition into longer conversations and discourses of Jesus. Here in his view the logia tradition which has been worked over is still perfectly recognisable. In other texts we may observe that the original dialogue form fades away, and so a longer connected discourse of Jesus comes into being, which however also rests upon an interpretation of sayings of Jesus (Koester here refers to the discourses of Jesus in John's Gospel). A further development of the *Gattung* can according to Koester be identified in the gnostic revelation documents, which indeed no longer have any connection with the wisdom sayings tradition but yet are probably modelled on the example of older dialogues. This brief sketch of Koester's conception must here suffice. Further work on the texts will show how much of his theories can be retained. At some points considerable reservations are certainly appropriate, particularly when it is a question of texts the tradition of which is not so certain as many a reconstruction would seem to suggest.

One point has still to be dealt with in conclusion: is Koester's conception thus depicted a substitute for the (indeed well grounded) explanation of the 'dialogues' by Rudolph? This one cannot say. For the two attempts to clarify the problem of the literary *Gattung* of the 'gnostic dialogue gospel' start out from different presuppositions. Rudolph is concerned to explain the special stamp of this *Gattung*, as it appears in the gnostic texts, from the Greek and Hellenistic pre-history of this genre of text. Koester, in the interests of a total view of the 'gospel' *Gattung* and its history, is more interested in the traditions lying before the texts which have come down to us, and their relation to the tradition worked up in the canonical Gospels. We may not harmonise the two approaches over-hastily. But they are also not mutually exclusive. For even if the gnostic 'dialogues' are to be regarded as a *Gattung* which rests upon Greek models (including the *erotapokriseis*), this does not exclude the possibility that in these texts older traditions, such as sayings collections, are incorporated. However, one must probably be somewhat more reserved with hypotheses about such collections - both in regard to their number and their age - than is the case with Koester.

This sketch, which makes no claim to be a complete discussion of the problems, is intended only to indicate the discussion about the genre of some texts which has been started off by the Nag Hammadi discovery. It will be clear that works of this *Gattung* belong in a collection of NT apocrypha. They are not gospels in the sense familiar to us, but are intended to be 'Gospel', that is, a saving message, and they proclaim this message in the form of a conversation of Jesus with his disciples. In the following section eight texts are selected, which are to be reckoned to this *Gattung*. They are not uniform in form and content, but rather show sundry differences. But thereby the problems of this kind of 'gnostic gospel' will also become apparent.

Notes

VIII. Dialogues of the Redeemer

Introduction

1. Cf. Vielhauer, *Lit. gesch.* pp. 683-687.
2. Koester's critical remarks (*Trajectories*, p. 194, note 122 and ANRW, p. 1492, note 156) are therefore inappropriate polemic, and overlook the fact that in 1956 people were not so 'clever' as in 1971 or 1984.
3. Facsimile: *The Facsimile Edition of the Nag Hammadi Codices*, 12 vols., Leiden 1972ff. English trans. *The Nag Hammadi Library in English*, ed. J.M. Robinson, New York etc. 1977, rev. ed. 1988.
4. K. Rudolph, 'Der gnostische 'Dialog' als literarisches Genus', in *Probleme der koptischen Literatur*, ed. P. Nagel, Wiss. Beitr. Univ. Halle-Wittenberg 1968, pp. 85-107.
5. Rudolph here carries further the work of G. Bardy, M. Hoffmann, H. Dörrie and H. Dörries. Cf. the references to the literature in his essay.
6. *Lit. gesch.* pp. 680ff.
7. No far-reaching conclusions can be drawn from the Freer Logion.
8. H. Koester, 'One Jesus and Four Primitive Gospels', in H. Koester and J.M. Robinson, *Trajectories through Early Christianity*, 1971, pp. 158-204; id. 'Dialog und Spruchüber-lieferung in den gnostischen Texten von Nag Hammadi', *Ev.Theol.* 39, 1979, 532-556; id. 'Apocryphal and Canonical Gospels', HTR 73, 1980, 105-130; id. 'Überlieferung und Geschichte der frühchristlichen Evangelienliteratur', ANRW 25/2, 1984, 1463-1542.
9. *Trajectories*, pp. 193ff. Against this, Vielhauer, *Lit. gesch.* pp. 690f.
10. *Entwicklungslinien*, p. 184 (this sentence does not seem to appear in so many words in the English version).

1. The Book of Thomas

Hans-Martin Schenke
(translated by Einar Thomassen)

Introduction

1. Bibliography: *Facsimile: The Fascimile Edition of the Nag Hammadi Codices* published under the Auspices of the Department of Antiquities of the Arab Republic of Egypt in Conjunction with the United Nations Educational, Scientific and Cultural Organization. Codex II, Leiden 1974, pl. (6.), 150-157.

Editions: M. Krause, *Gnostische und hermetische Schriften aus Codex II und Codex VI*,(Abhandlungen des Deutschen Archäologischen Instituts Kairo, Koptische Reihe 2), Glückstadt 1971, pp. (22-24, 31-36,) 88-106. B. Layton (ed.), *Nag Hammadi Codex II, 2-7, together with XIII, 2*, Brit. Lib. Or. 4926(1) and P. Oxy. 1, 654, 655*, II,(NHS 21), Leiden 1988, 171-205 (265-281). H.-M. Schenke, *Das Thomas-Buch (Nag Hammadi Codex II, 7) neu herausgegeben, übersetzt und erklärt*, (TU 138), Berlin 1989. J.D. Turner, *The Book of Thomas the Contender from Codex II of the Cairo Gnostic Library from Nag Hammadi (CG II, 7): The Coptic Text with Translation, Introduction and Commentary*, (Society of Biblical Literature, Dissertation Series 23), Missoula (Montana) 1975. R. Kuntzmann, *Le Livre de Thomas (NH II, 7): Texte établi et présenté*, (BCNH, Section 'Textes' 16), Québec 1986.

Translations: D. Kirchner, ''Das Buch des Thomas' - Die siebte Schrift aus Nag-Hammadi-Codex II', ThLZ 102, 1977, 793-804. M. Krause, 'Coptic Sources', in W. Foerster (ed.), *Gnosis, II*, Oxford 1974, 110-118. J.D. Turner, 'The Book of Thomas the Contender', in J.M. Robinson (ed.), *The Nag Hammadi Library in English*, San Francisco, pp. 188-194 (3rd rev. ed. 1988, pp. 199-207). J.D. Turner, ['The Book of Thomas the Contender Writing to the Perfect. Translation'], in B. Layton (ed.), *Nag Hammadi Codex II, 2-7*, II, 181-205.

Further select bibliography (for a complete bibliography cf. D.M. Scholer, *Nag Hammadi Bibliography 1948-1969*, (NHS I), Leiden 1971, p. 174, and the annual supplement 'Bibliographia Gnostica' in *Novum Testamentum* from vol. 13, 1971): G.M. Browne, 'Ad CG II 7, 139:20', *The Bulletin of the American Society of Papyrologists* 15, 1978, 191-193. S. Emmel, 'Unique Photographic Evidence for Nag Hammadi Texts: CG II 2-7, III 5 and XIII 2*', *The Bulletin of the American Society of Papyrologists* 14, 1977, 109-121. H. Koester, *Introduction to the New Testament*, vol. II: 'History and Literature of Early Christianity', Philadelphia 1982, p. 208. R. Kuntzmann, 'L'identification dans le Livre de Thomas l'Athlète', in B. Barc (ed.), *Colloque international sur les textes de Nag Hammadi (Québec, 22-25 août 1978)*. (BCNH, Section 'Études' 1), Québec 1981, pp. 279-87. P. Nagel, 'Thomas der Mitstreiter (zu NHC II, 7: p. 138, 8)', in *Mélanges offerts à M. Werner Vycichl*, Société d'Égyptologie Genève,Bulletin No. 4, 1980, pp. 65-71. P. Perkins, *The Gnostic Dialogue: The Early Church and the Crisis of Gnosticism* Theological Inquiries), New York 1980, pp. 56, 67, 71-73, 99-107, 183, 189. H.-Ch. Puech, 'The Book of Thomas the Athlete', in NTApo³ I, 307-308. H. Quecke, [review of Krause's edition], *Orientalia* 42, 1973, 530-34; *id.* [review of Turner's edition], *Biblica*, 57,1976, 429-32. H.-M. Schenke, 'Sprachliche und exegetische Probleme in den beiden letzten Schriften des Codex II von Nag Hammadi', OLZ 70, 1975, 5-13; *id.* 'The Book of Thomas (NHC II.7): A Revision of a Pseudepigraphical Epistle of Jacob the Contender', in A.H.B. Logan/A.J.M. Wedderburn (eds.), *The New Testament and Gnosis:*

Essays in honour of R. McL. Wilson, Edinburgh 1983, pp. 213-228; *id.* 'Radikale sexuelle Enthaltsamkeit als hellenistisch-jüdische Vollkommenheitsideal im Thomas-Buch (NHC II, 7)', in U. Bianchi (ed.), *La Tradizione dell'Enkrateia: Motivazioni ontologiche e protologiche. Atti del Colloquio Internazionale Milano, 20-23 aprile 1982*, Rome 1985, pp. 263-291. J.D. Turner, 'A New Link in the Syrian Judas Thomas Tradition', in M. Krause (ed.), *Essays on the Nag Hammadi Texts in Honour of A. Böhlig*, (Nag Hammadi Studies 3), Leiden 1972, pp. 109-119; *id.* ['The Book of Thomas the Contender Writing to the Perfect.'] Introduction, in B. Layton (ed.), *Nag Hammadi Codex II, 2-7*, II, 173-178.

2. Transmission: the existence of the writing which we name The Book of Thomas after the first half of its subscript title (abbreviated in this section Book Thom.), is not attested at all in early Christian literature. It has become known to us exclusively through the accidental rediscovery of the text itself. Moreover, the text discovered is only a Coptic translation and is preserved in a single copy only. It is the seventh and last tractate in what is now counted as Codex II of the Cairo collection of Nag Hammadi papyri (Coptic Museum, Department of Manuscripts, inv. 10544). This is a single quire papyrus codex (size 28.4 x 15.8 cm) without original pagination. According to the numeration of the pages generally adopted by scholars, Book Thom. is written on p. 138 (line 1) to p. 145 (line 19). As regards the date of manufacture of the codex, which has importance as a *terminus post quem non* for the composition of Book Thom., the available evidence points to the first half of the 4th cent.

The extant copy of Book Thom. is carefully executed. But it is not perfect, as is always the case with a single textual witness, which can never provide a perfect text. A number of more or less typical errors occur. Where they were noticed by the copyist, or a corrector, they were corrected. Some minor or more significant mistakes have nevertheless escaped the critical attention of those who produced the text. The following translation presupposes the necessary emendation of such passages. To the extent that it is at all possible to represent such emendations in a translation they have been marked and provided with explanatory notes. For this purpose angular brackets < > have been used to indicate emendatory additions, and braces { } for emendatory deletions. Angular brackets with three dots <...> indicate an anacoluthon. In addition to these errors the text is also affected by physical damage, in some places extensive, especially at the bottom edge of the pages. The lacunae which thus occur - as usual indicated by square brackets [ ] - cannot always be restored with sufficient certainty or probability. Round brackets ( ) on the other hand have nothing to do with the imperfections of our text witness, they merely enclose paraphrasing components of the translation.

3. Original language, provenance, date: although the sole, accidentally preserved and imperfect witness to the textual history of Book Thom. has come down to us in Coptic, in NHC II, 7, it was, as indicated above, not originally composed in that language. As in the case of most specimens of Coptic literature we have to assume Greek as the original language. Although no obvious evidence for this can be found in Book Thom., a trained eye is nevertheless able to recognise here and there the Greek substratum underneath the Coptic surface.

And in interpreting the text it is sometimes very helpful to refer to a hypothetical reconstruction of a Greek original.

The question of the provenance of this literary piece is more difficult to answer. In its present shape, i.e. as a 'Book of Thomas', it points in the direction of the homeland of the Judas Thomas tradition which characterises the literary framework of the document, in other words East Syria, where the Gospel of Thomas as well belongs and originated. As far as the tradition contained in Book Thom. is concerned, however, it is best explained by an Alexandrian environment. If the available evidence can be trusted, this tradition must already have had a certain history behind it before it reached East Syria and became the contents of Book Thom.

For an answer to the question of the date of composition of the original Book of Thomas, i.e. how long it was written before the *terminus post quem non* of the extant copy of a translation of the text (first half of the 4th cent.), we hardly possess any indications. The only thing that can be said is that its *incipit* presupposes the Gospel of Thomas and that Book Thom. therefore must have originated *after* the Gospel of Thomas. The date of the Gospel of Thomas, however, is itself much disputed. It is thus pure guesswork which leads Turner to assume the first half of the 3rd cent. as the date of origin of Book Thom. Koester is equally justified in situating it already in the 2nd cent. At all events the problem of the date of Book Thom. loses much of its importance in view of the necessity of applying a literary-critical perspective, in which Book Thom. emerges as merely a thin and superficial framing of a basic document which is neither gnostic nor Christian; thereby we find ourselves in what to a certain extent is a 'timeless' sphere.

4. Literary genre and title: in its external form Book Thom. presents itself as a Gnostic revelation dialogue between the resurrection Jesus and Judas Thomas about ethical and eschatological questions. In this respect it belongs to the genre of dialogues of the Saviour. As a dialogue, however, it is very peculiar and extremely difficult to understand. The dialogue ends in the middle of the text (p. 142) and turns into a monologue by Jesus, or, differently put, what begins as a dialogue ends as a collection of sayings. Concluding title and *incipit* contradict one another. Moreover, in the tradition Thomas never carries the title 'the Contender', the meaning of which in any case is enigmatic. The responses of Thomas exceed by far any tolerable degree of discipular incomprehension; Jesus and Thomas seem to be talking about completely different things. A further problem consists in the fact that in several respects and in many places the contents do not fit the dialogue framework, so that the text becomes simply incomprehensible. As examples of this type of textual problems may above all be mentioned, first, the passage on p. 139 (lines 12-20),[1] where the otherwise uncomprehending Thomas suddenly begins to instruct the Revealer: 'For this reason I say to you, O Lord', etc. (it is not far from as if Thomas had started off with a 'Truly'), and secondly, the way in which the sun is referred to (cf. in particular how it is described as a good servant (of salvation) on p. 139, (lines 28-31). One of the typical, but much more delicate, problems also appears at the very beginning, when Jesus says 'listen to me, while *you* still have time/ opportunity (to do so) in the world', and not 'while *I* still have time left in the world'.

It is probably indisputable that these problems and the phenomenon of the text as such can be solved, or explained, only by means of literary criticism. The only question is: what *kind* of literary criticism? According to the suggestion of J.D. Turner, Book Thom. is redactionally composed from two sources. One work, consisting of pp. 138.4-142.21[26], was a dialogue between Thomas and the Saviour, perhaps entitled 'The Book of Thomas the Contender writing to the Perfect'. The second work, embracing pp. 142.26-145.16, was a collection of the Saviour's sayings gathered into a homily. It is the latter work which may have been entitled 'The secret words which the Saviour spoke, and which I, Matthew wrote down'. A redactor has joined together, Turner claims, these two works, and prefaced the whole with an *incipit* title composed on analogy with the original title of the second work and designating Matthew as the scribe of the whole. The subscript title, however, which names Thomas as the scribe of the whole, is in reality only the title of the first source document, but having been placed at the end of the newly formed whole it has become the overall title (cf., e.g., Turner's diss., p. 215). And with regard to the contents Turner places both source documents as well as the new whole within the *Gattungsgeschichte* of the sayings of Jesus in the sphere of a syncretistic (ascetic, midly gnosticising) Christianity, where the process leads by way of the implicit interpretation of the sayings as parts of sayings collections ultimately to the creation of new sayings in the framework of the revelation dialogue (cf. diss., pp. 224f.).

Turner's literary-critical theory is developed under consideration of practically all the problematic aspects and obstacles of the text referred to above. It is only a matter of a different assessment of the priorities among the commonly recognised problems if I am of the opinion that the same method must lead to a completely different conclusion. Evidently a *horizontal* not a *vertical* division is to be made. It is the whole framework of Book Thom., i.e. precisely the dialogue between Jesus and Thomas, which is alone responsible for all its present peculiarities and which can be shown to have been secondarily forced upon the material. With no great difficulty the framework may be bracketed out, whereby the text emerges as being *in reality* quite comprehensible, attractive and significant, something which cannot be said of it in its present form. The framework must be bracketed out, not merely removed or cut away. In accordance with observations which have previously been made regarding sayings materials transformed into dialogues, one has to take into consideration that parts of the basic material may have been used even in the formulation of the question of the respective dialogue partner.

As a demonstration of what we here claim, and as an illustration of the hypothesis of a basic document, the beginning at least of a reconstruction of it may here be quoted:

Listen to me, while you still have opportunity in the world! Examine yourself, and understand who you are, how you exist and how you will come to be! You should not remain ignorant of yourself! You have begun to understand. For you have already understood what the knowledge of the truth is. You have already, though you are still ignorant, attained knowledge. And you shall be named 'the one who knows himself'. For he who has not known himself has known nothing. But he who has known himself has also already obtained knowledge about the depth of the All.

Behold what is hidden from men, that is, that on which they stumble if they do not recognise it. But it is difficult to perform the truth before men. If the things that are visible to you are hidden before you, how, then, will you be able to hear about the things which are not visible? If the deeds of the truth that are visible in the world are difficult for you to perform, how indeed, then, will you perform those (deeds) of the exalted Majesty and of the Fullness, which are not visible? How, then, will you be named 'doers (of the truth)'? Therefore: You are beginners! And: You have not yet attained the measure of perfection.

[Al]l bodies [have come into being in the same way] that the beasts are begotten (- that is) wi[thout reas]on. T[herefo]re they are in this way v[isi]ble as well, (that is) as [a creature str]etching [out after another creatu]re. [Because] of this, however, those who are above [do not exist in the same way] as the ones who are visible, but [they] live from their own root. And it is their fruits that nourish them. But these visible bodies eat from the creatures which are like themselves. Because of this, then, the bodies change. But that which changes will perish and disappear, and has then no more hope of life. For this body is bestial. So just as the body of the beasts perishes, so also will these modelled forms perish. Does it not derive from intercourse, just as that of the beasts? If it too derives from that, how can it be better than them? Because of this, then, you are minors! <How long will it take> until you become perfect<?>

Those who speak of matters that are invisible and difficult to explain are like those who aim their arrows at a target at night. To be sure, they shoot their arrows just like people <who (do not know what they do [?])>. For it is the target they are aiming at, but that is not visible. But when the light comes forth and hides the darkness, then the performance of each will be visible.

It is the light that enlightens. Through light only is there light. Behold the visible light here; it rises, but sets as well. Only for your sakes does this visible light shine, not in ord[er] that you may stay in this place, but rather that you may come back o[ut] of it. But when all the elect have abandoned bestiality, then this light will (also) withdraw up to its own home. And its own home will receive it (again), because it was a good servant. Oh, inscrutable love of the light! (etc.)

Removed from its framework the text emerges as a platonising, Hellenistic-Jewish wisdom writing. Put briefly, the literary character of Book Thom. is similar to that of The Sophia of Jesus Christ (NHC III 4 and BG 3). Just like Soph. Jes. Chr., Book Thom. is the Christian 'dramatisation' of a non-Christian 'prose' model. But whereas the basic writing of Soph. Jes. Chr. has been preserved in the shape of the Letter of Eugnostos (NHC III 3 and V 1), the basic writing of Book Thom. can only be extracted or reconstructed from that text itself.

It is also within this perspective that the question of the concluding title of Book Thom. belongs. This title has two parts. It reads: 'The Book of Thomas. The Contender writes to the Perfect.'. Any other rendering (and corresponding abbreviation), however firmly established, is erroneous, i.e., the title consists of two syntactically quite independent phrases, of which the second even has the characteristic form of an *epistolary prescript*. The crucial question is now whether this formal peculiarity of the concluding title might be directly connected with the literary character of the tractate itself as a Jewish source secondarily reworked as a Christian dialogue. This seems to be an evident explanation. The first title, 'The Book of Thomas', applies to the tractate as it now is, i.e., it refers specifically to its present framework as a dialogue. Whereas there exists no intrinsically compelling liaison between the first and the second title, the second title, with its concepts of the contender and the perfect, contains precisely such ideas as are entirely central to the material lying underneath the frame. I.e., the second title seems suited to cover the model of Book Thom. And it is only in the light of the material (by bracketing out the dialogue frame) that the designation 'the Contender', at first sight so enigmatic, now unexpectedly becomes transparent. For in that environment where the assumed model may well have originated, i.e. in the environment of platonising Jewish wisdom ideology, whose main witness for us is Philo of Alexandria, there is only *one* Contender, and that is Jacob the patriarch. If in this environment one speaks of '*the* Contender,' for which also the term '*the* Ascetic' serves as a synonym, then everyone knows that the reference is to Jacob. This is so because Jacob is here understood as the ideal and type of the man who does not yet possess wisdom and virtue, but who always strives for them in a coninuous struggle against the passions. To this one must add the fact that even the materials of Book Thom. themselves in certain places reveal paraenetic Jacob motifs. In concrete terms, what all this means is this: It may be assumed that the second concluding title of Book Thom. was in fact the original title of the basic writing of Book Thom. and that accordingly the basic writing referred to presented itself as a (pseudepigraphical) *letter* of the Contender (Jacob) to the perfect, and that means that it was in a sense a document of the kind which A. Meyer envisaged as the basis for the Letter of James in the New Testament.[2]

On the other hand, this means that the 'author' of Book Thom., the man who has given our tractate its present shape, and thus also must be held responsible for the redaction of the full concluding title, has not only reshaped the body of his model, but also its concluding title, by joining it and adapting its meaning to the new title devised for the text in its new shape, 'The Book of Thomas'. Together with the entire doctrine of the model, Thomas thus also 'inherits' the title of Contender. To the 'author' of Book Thom., Thomas and 'the Contender' would have been identical, of course, i.e., when formulating, or composing, this title for the book, he apparently assumed that 'the Contender' of whom the second title speaks would be the same person as the one called Thomas. Since the Thomas of the Syrian Judas Thomas tradition, though the title

'Contender', as said above, is not attested for him, nevertheless bears the essential traits of a spiritual struggler, he is no unsuitable 'heir' to the doctrine and title of 'the Contender' (Jacob).

5. Internal character: although the most essential aspect of the internal character of Book Thom. has already received attention in various ways, this internal character is nevertheless also to be dealt with separately in its own right. The particular problem in this connection is to determine its Christian nature.

The first question which must be asked in this respect is whether Book Thom., viz. the work in its present shape, can be called Christian *gnostic* in a real sense. The fact that it belongs to the Nag Hammadi discovery, i.e. to the so-called Coptic gnostic library of Nag Hammadi, does not automatically make it a gnostic text. In the course of investigation into the writings of Nag Hammadi it has in fact become clear that although the majority of them are genuinely gnostic, this is by no means the case with all. In order to decide this, each tractate must be studied in its own right and allowed to speak for itself. As for Book Thom. it seems definitely to belong to the tractates which contain no unequivocal and specific gnostic ideas. If its Christian gnostic character nevertheless cannot, or should not, simply be ruled out altogether, this is because it presents itself after all in the form of a gnostic revelation dialogue, and because it is embedded in the Syrian Judas Thomas tradition, which seems as a whole to have come under gnostic influence, and in particular also because of its literary dependence on the Gospel of Thomas, which in its present shape has a decided gnostic emphasis.

The second question concerns the amount of Christian material in Book Thom. This question has a special bias. The problem is whether apart from the evidently Christian framework with its dialogue between Jesus and Judas Thomas there is *in fact* no Christian content in the text, or what more there is that might be considered Christian elements. To begin with there is in the middle of the text a passage which is clearly Christian. This is the following words on p. 141 (lines 10-13): 'Because of the love of faith which they had previously they will be brought back into the visible (world). Those, however, who can see are not parts of the visible (world). Without the first love . . . ' But this piece can be shown by means of a more detailed exegesis to be a redactional interpolation which belongs on the same level as the dialogue frame.

More problematic and more interesting is, however, the fact that there are also beyond doubt several phrases and sentences which have such a strong affinity with passages of the New Testament that one at first sight would incline to regard them as echoes of these passages, i.e. as dependent upon the respective New Testament books and traditions. This applies to three parallels to Jn. 3, two on p. 138 (in the section lines 21-36) and one on p. 140 (in the section lines 5-18) [cf. notes 4, 5 and 9]; the introductory formula 'Truly, I tell you' (p. 142 [lines 27,29f]); the second of the (three) beatitudes: 'Blessed are you who are mocked and not esteemed! On account of the love which your Lord has toward you' (p. 145 [lines 3-5]); the third beatitude: 'Blessed are you who weep and are oppressed by those who ha[ve n]o hope. For you will be released from all bonds' (p. 145 [lines 5-8]; and finally the exhortation which introduces the final promise: 'Watch and pray that you will not remain in the flesh, but that you may escape from the bitter chains of this life!' (p. 145 [lines 8-10]).

However, the New Testament phrases and sentences which might be considered as sources belong to such parts of the New Testament which themselves represent, or at least might represent, material that is borrowed and inherited (from Judaism), i.e., they are in themselves not specifically Christian, and it would therefore be quite conceivable that the passages in question in Book Thom. do not owe their familiar-looking appearance to Christianity, but directly to its foundations. But even if such phrases in our material were nevertheless to be regarded as Christian, this would have no real relevance for the determination of the internal character of the material as a whole, since the overwhelming mass of the material clearly represents traditions and ideas that are of a quite different nature and essentially non-Christian, and even alien to Christianity. Moreover, the question of the nature of the material should not be regarded in a static fashion. On the contrary, the material, being paraenetical, is in movement. And before it came to be embedded in a Christian frame it presumably was put to practical use by the Christian groups in question, and during this process Christian material can easily have drifted into the text.

6. Content and significance: the content of Book Thom. is paraenesis. Its purpose is to propagate an ascetical way of life, in particular to propagate sexual abstinence. Moreover, this ideal of perfection is advocated with unusual one-sidedness. The key word and main theme in this respect is the concept of fire. The concept is elaborated in a double fashion: one is warned of the fire of erotic and sexual desire, and one is threatened with the tormenting fire of hell. The two aspects are joined together by the corresponding principle that the means of sin is at the same time the means of its punishment. The path towards avoidance, or mastery, of the dangers, and towards the realisation of the ideal leads by way of self-knowledge. The direction of the duty of self-knowledge may be described in the following way: 'Know your double nature, so that you do not turn into a beast by succumbing to lust, and fall down into hell, but that your soul may come to heaven. Take heed not to deserve the 'woe to you', but the 'blessed are you'!' Important here is moreover the fact that in self-knowledge there is also growth, in other words, that the person who is addressed in this way is understood as someone who still finds himself on the path towards perfection. In the description of what is to be avoided, the concept of bestiality plays an important role throughout. On the other hand it has to do with the necessity of avoiding the dangers, when Book Thom. speaks of the ethical merit of fleeing. The description of the infernal punishments which await the fools who do not follow the prescribed path of wisdom, or who even oppose it, takes up much space and links Book Thom. with the Apocalypse of Peter, and shows that both draw upon the same tradition.

Book Thom. is a rich new source for the form-critical investigation of the literature of early Christianity. This source is particularly relevant for the transmission of the words of Jesus. In various recent works H. Koester has sought to draw attention to the importance of non-canonical early Christian writings for the sayings tradition.[3] Of the Nag Hammadi writings, the Gospel of Thomas, the Dialogue of the Saviour, and recently also the Apocryphon of James, play a central role for him. In this 'Koester-perspective' Book Thom. should also be given a prominent position.

In a wider framework still, one may say that the significance of Book Thom. is that it enriches with an entire dimension our perception of the Jewish sapiential tradition and of its reception within Christianity.

Notes

The Book of Thomas

Introduction

1. Although the lines of the pages in the codex are not indicated in the following translation, for the sake of readability, line-references have nevertheless been supplied in this introduction in order to facilitate control and further study.
2. *Das Rätsel des Jacobusbriefes*, (BZNW 10), 1930.
3. 'Dialog und Spruchüberlieferung in den gnostischen Texten von Nag Hammadi', *Ev.Th.* 39, 1979, 532-556; 'Gnostic Writings as Witnesses for the Development of the Sayings Tradition', in B. Layton (ed.), *The Rediscovery of Gnosticism. Proceedings of the International Conference on Gnosticism at Yale, New Haven, Connecticut, March 28-31, 1978*, vol. I: 'The School of Valentinus', (Studies in the History of Religions 41.1), Leiden 1980, pp. 238-256 (256-261); 'Apocryphal and Canonical Gospels', HTR 73, 1980, 105-130.

240

The Book of Thomas

The Contender Writes to the Perfect¹

The secret words that the Saviour spoke to Judas Thomas² and which I, Matthew, wrote down. I was passing by and heard them speak with one another.

The Saviour said: 'Brother Thomas, listen to me, while you still have opportunity in the world, that I may reveal to you what you have pondered in your heart.

'Now since it has been said that you are my twin and my sole true friend,³ examine yourself and understand who you are, how you exist and how you will come to be! Since you are called my brother, you should not remain ignorant of yourself. And I know that you have begun to understand. For you have already understood that I am the knowledge of the truth. Now while you have been walking with me, you have already, though you are still ignorant, attained knowledge. And you shall be named 'the one who knows himself'. For he who has not known himself has known nothing. But he who has known himself has also already obtained knowledge about the depth of the All. So, therefore, you (alone) my brother Thomas have beheld what is hidden from men, that is, that on which they stumble if they do not recognise it.'

But Thomas said to the Lord: 'Therefore I beg you to tell me what I ask you before your ascension. [An]d only when I hear from you (the truth) about that which is hidden, will I be able to speak about it. And I am aware that it is difficult to perform the truth before men.'⁴

The Saviour answered, saying: 'If the things that are visible to you are hidden before you, how, then, will you be able to hear about the things that are not visible? If the deeds of the truth that are visible in the world are difficult for you to perform, how indeed, then, will you perform those (deeds) of the exalted Majesty and of the Fullness, which are not visible?⁵ How, then, will you be named 'doers (of the truth)'?⁴ Therefore: You are beginners! And: You have not yet attained the measure of perfection.'

But Thomas answered and said to the Saviour: 'Tell us about [t]he things which you say are not visible, b[ut are] hidden from us!'

The Saviour said: '[Al]l bodies [have come into being in the same way] that the beasts are begotten (- that is) wi[thout reas]on. T[herefo]re they are in this way v[isi]ble as well, (that is) as [a creature str]etching [out after another creatu]re. [Because] of this, however, those who are above [do not exist in the same way] as the ones who are visible, but [they] (p. 139) live from their own root. And it is their fruits that nourish

241

them. But these visible bodies eat from the creatures which are like themselves. Because of this, then, the bodies change. But that which changes will perish and disappear,and has then no more hope of life. For this body is bestial. So just as the body of the beasts perishes, so also will these modelled forms perish. Does it not derive from inter-course, just as that of the beasts? If it too derives from that, how can it be better than them? Because of this, then, you are minors! <How long will it take>[6] until you become perfect<?>'

But Thomas answered: 'For this reason I say to you, O Lord: Those who speak of matters that are invisible and difficult to explain are like those who aim their arrows at a target at night. To be sure, they shoot their arrows just like people <who (do not know what they do [?])>.[7] For it is the target they are aiming at, but that is not visible. But when the light comes forth and hides the darkness, then the performance of each will be visible. But it is you, our light, that enlightens, O Lord.'

Jesus said: 'Through light only is there light.'

Thomas spoke, saying: 'O Lo[rd], the visible light here, which shines for the sake of men, why does it not only rise, but set as well?'

The Saviour said: 'O blessed Thomas, only for your sakes does this visible light shine, not in ord[er] that you may stay in this place, but rather that you may come back o[ut] of it. But when all the elect have abandoned bestiality, then this light will (also) withdraw up to its own home. And its own home will receive it (again) because it was a good servant.'

Then the Saviour continued and said: 'Oh, inscrutable love of the light! Oh, bitter fire! You burn in the bodies of men and in their marrow, burning in them night and d[ay]. You consume the limbs of men, [make t]heir hearts drunk and their souls deranged. Y[ou dominate] t[h]em, males and females, [by] da[y and n]ight. You agitate them [with] an [agitat]ion which [agitates] secretly and openly. For [when] the males are [agita]ted, [it draws them to the fema]les, and the females to [the males. Therefore it is] (p. 140) said: 'Anyone who seeks the truth from her who is truly wise will make himself wings so as to fly when he has to flee the desire which burns the spirits of men.' And: 'He will make himself wings when he has to flee every visible spirit.''

Thomas answered, saying: 'O Lord, this is precisely why I am asking you as <(a teacher[?])>,[8] (that is) because I have understood that it is (only) you we can profit from, just as you say.'

Again the Saviour answered and said: 'Therefore we[9] have to speak to you. For this is the doctrine for the perfect. If, then, you wish to be perfect, you must observe these (words). If (you do) not (observe them), your name is 'Ignorant', since it is not possible that a wise man dwell together with a fool. For the wise man is filled with every wisdom. To the fool, however, the good and the bad are the same. For the wise man will be nourished by the truth, and he will become 'like the tree growing by the torrent stream'.[10]

'There are in fact those who have wings as they are chasing after what is visible, that which is far removed from the truth. For that which guides them, which is the fire, will give them an illusion of truth [an]d will shine on them with peri[shable] beauty. And it will imprison them by dark delight and captivate them through stinking pleasure. And it will make them blind through insatiable lust. And it will burn their souls and b[e] for them like a stake stuck in their heart which they never will be able to pull out, and like a bit in a (horse's) mouth which drags them according to the desire proper to it.

'Indeed, it has fettered them with its chains; and all their limbs it has bound with the bitter bond of desire for these visible things which perish, change and are transformed. In accordance with the attraction they were pulled down from above. They are constantly being killed, as they are drawn to all the beasts of uncleanness.'

Thomas answered and sa[id:] 'It is obvious. And [it] has also been said: '[. . .] those who do not know [. . . of the] soul'.'

[The Saviour] answered, say[ing: 'Blessed is] the wise man who [sought after the truth. For wh]en he found it, he came to rest (p. 141) upon it forever and was no longer afraid of those who wanted to confuse him.'[11]

Thomas answered and said: '(Thus) it is profitable for us, O Lord, to come and rest in that which is our own?'

The Saviour said: 'Yes, that is gainful. And it is good for you because the visible (parts) of men will dissolve. For 'the vessel of their flesh will dissolve'. And even when it disintegrates it will be part of the visible (world), of that which can be seen. And then the visible fire will give them pain. Because of the love of faith which they had previously they will be brought back into the visible (world). Those, whoever, who can see are not parts of the visible (world). Without the first love they will perish. < . . . >[12] with concern for this life and the ardour of the fire for a short time, until that which is visible will dissolve. Then shapeless phantoms will come into existence and linger in the tombs forever upon the corpses with pain and corruption of the soul.'

But Thomas answered and said: 'What do we have to say in the face of these (people)? What are we to say to blind men? What teaching are we to present to these m[ise]rable mortals who say, 'We wanted to [attain] good, not curse.' Moreover, they will rep[eat] that 'Had we not been begotten in the flesh we would not have known [ini]quity.''

The Saviour said: 'Truly, with regard to th[ose] do not consider them as men, but regard them a[s be]asts! For just as the beasts devour [one a]nother, so also men of this sort 'devour' one another. But they have forfeited (their) [king]ship; for they love the delight of the fire and are slaves to death, they chase after the deeds of uncleanness and fulfil the lust of their fathers. They will be thrown into the abyss and be chastised through the necessity (which arises) from the bitterness of their evil nature. For, 'they will be whipped so that they rush headlong to the place they do not know'.

'And it is not with endurance that they will [abstain] from their limbs, but [you will] become weak! And they rejoice in [the] f[ire, loving] madness and derangement, because they are [fools]. [They] are pursuing derangement without realising [their mad]ness, [belie]ving that they a[re] wise. [They . . . the l]ove of their body [. . .], (p. 142) their mind being turned towards themselves, while their thought dwells on their affairs. But it is the fire that will consume them.'

But Thomas answered and said: 'O Lord, what will happen to that which has been thrown into them? Indeed, I am very concerned about them. For many are those who oppose them.'

The Saviour answered and said: 'What is it that is clear to yourself?'

Judas, who is called Thomas, said: 'It is you, O Lord, whom it befits to speak, and I to listen to you.'

The Saviour answered: 'Listen to what I am going to tell you and believe in the truth! The one who sows and that which is sown will dissolve by their fire - within the fire and the water - [a]nd they will hide in the tombs of darkness. And after a long time the fruits of the evil trees will be made manifest, as they are punished and as they are killed, by the mouth of beasts and men (and) as a result of the rains, the winds, the air and the light that shines above.'

But Thomas answered: 'You have indeed persuaded us, O Lord. We have reasoned in our heart and it is clear (to us) that this [is s]o, and (that) your word is free of envy. But these wor[ds wh]ich you speak to us are laughing-stocks to the wo[rl]d and something one turns up his nose at because they are not understood. How, then, can we go out to [p]reach them, considering that we are reckoned [as naught i]n the world?'

The Saviour answered and said: '[Tru]ly, I tell you: He who will listen to [your w]ord and turn away his face or tu[rn] up his nose at it, or smirk in this way - truly I tell you that he will be handed over to the Ruler above, he who rules over all the powers as their king, and he will turn that one away and have him thrown from on high down into the abyss and he will be locked up in a narrow and dark place; and so he will not be able to turn around or to move because of the great depth of Tartaros and the [burd]ensome bi[tter]ness of Hades. Whoever relies o[n that] which [i]s [brought] to him [wh]en [they . . .], wi[ll] not be forgiven [his ma]dness ; he [will receive his judgment. Whoever has] pursued you [will be de]livered [to the an]gel Tartarouchos [with whom is flaming f]ire which pursues them, (p. 143) [while] fiery scourges cast spark upon spark into the face of the one who is pursued. If he flees to the west he will fi[nd] the fire. If he turns to the south he will also find it there. If he turns to the north the horror of boiling fire meets him again. But he does not find the way to the east so that he may flee there and be saved. For he did not find it at the time when he was in the bo[dy], so that he might find it (again) on the day of judgment.'

Then the Saviour continued, saying: 'Woe to you, godless ones who have no hope, who rely on that which will not endure!

'Woe to you who put your hope in the flesh and in the prison which will perish - how long will you remain oblivious? - and in the 'imperish-ables' of whom you think that they will not perish! If you[r] hope is founded upon the world and your god is this life, then you will wreck your souls.

'Woe to you for the fire that burns in you! For it is insatiable.

'Woe to you because of the wheel that turns around - in your thoughts!

'Woe to you on account of the burning within you! For it will devour your flesh visibly and tear apart your souls invisibly, and make you ready <to . . . >¹³ among one another.

'Wo[e t]o you, captives! For you are fettered in ca[v]es. You laugh and rejoice over senseless ina[ni]ties. You do not conceive your perdition, nor do y[o]u conceive that in which you are, nor hav[e y]ou understood that you dwell in darkness and dea[th]. Instead you are drunk with the fire and [filled] with bitterness. Your mind is deranged on account of the [bu]rning wi[th]in you. And sweet to you are the poison and the stab of your enemies. And the darkness has risen for you as the light. For you have given up your freedom for enslavement; you have darkened your minds. And you have given up your thoughts to folly; and you have filled your thou[ght]s with the smoke of the fire within you. And your light [has hi]dden in the [dark] cloud. [A]nd the garment which you wear you have l[oved, though it is de]filed. and yo[u] have been taken in possession [by] the ho[pe which does] not exist. And w[ho] it is that [you ha]ve beli[eved] in you [do not] kn[ow. And you a]re all in yo[ur fetters. And you pr]ide yourselves as if y[ou were in freedom. And] (p. 144) you have submerged your souls in the water of dark[ness]. You have run off according to your own desires.

'Woe to you who have got into perdition and do not see the light of the sun, who judges everything, who looks upon everything, for it will turn against all (your) 'heroic' deeds aimed at subduing your enemies! Nor do you consider the moon, how by night and day it looks down and sees the corpses of you[r] massacres.

'Woe to you who love the company of women and the adulterated intercourse with them!

'And woe to you for the masters of your body! For they will grieve you.

'Woe to you for the workings of the evil demons!

'Woe to you who drag your limbs into the fire! Who is it that will rain a refreshing dew[14] upon you that may quench such a mighty fire in you along with your burning? Who is it that will grant you the sun to rise on you so as to disperse the darkness within you and hide the darkness and the polluted water?

'The sun and the moon will give you fragrance - together with the air, the wind, the earth and the water. For if the sun does not shine upon these bodies they will rot and [pe]rish, [in] the way that happens with weeds or grass. When the sun shines on it it becomes strong and chokes the grapevine. But if the grapevine is strong and shades the weeds [an]d all the other grass growing up together with it, and [spre]ad[s] out and becomes wide, then it alone in[her]its the land on which it grows and becomes master of every place it has shaded. So then as it grows, it becomes master of all the land and flourishes for its owner and pleases him greatly. For he would have had to suffer great labours because of the weeds before he could have uprooted them. But now the grapevine itself has done away with them. And it has choked them and they have died and become earth.'

Then Jesus c[on]tinued, and said to them: 'Wo[e t]o [you]! For you have not received the doctrine. And those who w[ish to receive it], will suffer when they preach. [For you will chase them] and (thereby) run into y[our own ne]ts. Y[ou] will send th[em do]wn be[fore lions[15] and y]ou will kill them daily, (p. 145) so that they may rise from death.

'Blessed are you who know the stumbling blocks in advance and who flee that which is alien!

'Blessed are you who are mocked and not esteemed! On account of the love which your Lord has toward you.

'Blessed are you who weep and are oppressed by those who ha[ve n]o hope! For you will be released from all bonds.

'Watch and pray that you will not remain in the flesh, but that you may escape from the bitter chains of this life! And as you pray you will find rest, < . . . >[16] that you have left behind the suffering and the disgrace.[17] For when you escape from the sufferings and the passions of the body, you will receive a place of rest from the Good One. And you will reign with the Sovereign, you joined with him and he joined with you, from now on forever and ever.'

Amen.

Notes

The Book of Thomas

The Contender Writes to the Perfect

1. In the manuscript this (double) title appears only as a subscript title at the end.
2. Cf. the *incipit* of the Gospel of Thomas.
3. Thomas is thus designated as the Beloved Disciple. P. Nagel, however, wishes to see behind the Coptic expression which is translated above as 'my sole true friend' a misinterpreted 'my fellow contender'.
4. For 'performing the truth' cf. Jn. 3:21; 1 Jn. 1:6.
5. For the structure of this phrase cf. Jn. 3:12.
6. The text, though grammatically sound, is here probably out of order. There has probably been an omission. Cf. the end of paragraph 5.
7. The text of the manuscript is corrupt.
8. The text of the manuscript is corrupt.
9. Cf. the equally sudden 'we' in Jn. 3:11.
10. Cf. Ps. 1:3.
11. Cf. the Gospel of Thomas, logion 2 par.
12. Corruption or anacoluthon; some words like 'They live their lives' must be supplied; cf. Lk. 8:14; 21:34.
13. The text of the manuscript is corrupt.
14. The dew which puts out fire is a motif from the tradition of the three young men in the furnace; cf. Dan. 3:50 LXX.
15. A motif from the tradition of Daniel in the den of lions; cf. Dan. 6:6, 8, 13, 18 LXX; Bel and the Dragon 31-32 LXX.
16. The text of the manuscript is corrupt. An expression such as 'and you will be amazed' must be supplied.
17. Cf. the Gospel of Thomas, logion 2 par.

2. The Freer Logion
Joachim Jeremias †

The Gospel MS W. (4th or 5th century) has, like most manuscripts, the longer spurious ending after Mk. 16:8 (i.e. vss. 9-20), but inserts into it a dialogue between the disciples and the risen Lord, the beginning of which is also transmitted by Jerome (*c. Pelag* II. 15). In the longer ending of Mark it is described how the risen Lord, early on the first day of the week, appeared first to Mary Magdalene and then in another form 'to two of them' as they walked; then follows the appearance to the eleven as a third occasion. While the corresponding passage in Lk. (24:41f.) records that their unbelief is overcome when the risen Lord eats before them. Mk. 16:14 simply mentions a reproach and immediately goes on to the mission charge. In the Freer Logion this gap is eliminated by the insertion of a dialogue between the risen Lord and the disciples. There the disciples charge Satan and the unclean spirits with responsibility for their unbelief and ask about the immediate *parousia*. To this request the risen Lord replies that the power of Satan has truly reached its end, but that certain signs must yet be fulfilled; then follows the mission charge.

Although an apocryphal amplification, the piece shows itself ancient by the highly eschatological tone (which comes out in the request of the disciples) and by its Jewish-apocalyptic terminology. The striking designation of the *parousia* as a revealing of the 'righteousness' of Christ is related to Old Testament usage, for there the righteousness of God and triumph of God are connected (Jud. 5:11; Isa. 5:16; cf. Mt. 6:33; Jn. 16:8; 1 Tim. 3:16).

Text: H.A. Sanders in *Biblical World* NS 31, 1908, 140-142, and in *American Journal of Archaeology*, ser II, 12, 1908, 52-54; H.B. Swete, *Zwei neue Evangelienfragmente* (KlT 31), [1]1908 =[2]1924; Nestle-Aland, NTgr[26], p. 148.
Literature: E.J. Goodspeed in *Biblical World* NS 31, 1908, 220-226; C.R. Gregory, *Das Freer-Logion*, Leipzig 1908; A. Harnack in ThLZ 33, 1908, cols.168-170; C. Schmidt in ThLZ 33, 1908, cols.359f.; H. von Soden in ChW 22, 1908, 482-486; E. Helzle, *Der Schluss des Markusevangeliums (Mk. 16:9-20) und das Freer-Logion (Mk. 16:14 W), ihre Tendenzen und ihr gegenseitiges Verhältnis*. Phil. Diss. Tübingen 1959 (cf. ThLZ 85, 1960, cols. 470-472); Vielhauer, *Lit. gesch.* pp. 680ff.

[*Mark 16:14:* Afterward he appeared to the eleven as they reclined at table and reproached them for their unbelief and hardness of heart, for they had not believed those who had seen him after he arose.] And they excused themselves with the words, 'This aeon (age) of lawlessness and unbelief[1] is under Satan,[2] who through the unclean spirits[3] does not allow the true power of God[4] to be comprehended. Therefore,' they said to Christ, 'reveal your righteousness[5] now.' And Christ replied to them, 'The measure of the years of Satan's power[6] is filled up.[7] But other fearful things draw near, also (for those) for whom I, because they have sinned, was delivered to death, that they might turn back to the truth and sin no more[8] in order to inherit the spiritual and imperishable glory of righteousness (preserved) in heaven.[9]

[*Verse 15:* Now then, go into all the world,' *etc.*]

[The whole is contained in the Gospel MS W. (4th-5th cent.) from Egypt, now in the Freer Museum in Washington; the words of the apostles are also in Jerome, *c. Pelag.* II 15.]

Notes

2. The Freer Logion

1. Cf. 2 Cor. 4:4; Gal. 1:4.
2. Cf. Jn. 14:30; Eph. 2:2.
3. Cf. Mk. 1:23, 26 etc.
4. Cf. Mk. 12:24; 1 Cor. 6:14; Eph. 1:19f.
5. Cf. Mt. 6:33; Jn. 16:8; 1 Tim. 3:16.
6. Cf. Lk. 10:18; Jn. 12:31; 16:11.
7. Cf. Mk. 1:15.
8. Cf. Jn. 5:14; 8:11.
9. Cf. 1 Pet. 1:4; 2 Tim. 4:8.

3. Epistula Apostolorum

C. Detlef G. Muller

1. Editions of the text: Louis Guerrier (avec le concours de Sylvain Grébaut), *Le Testament en Galilée de Notre Seigneur Jésus Christ*, (PO IX 3), Paris 1913 (1982). Carl Schmidt, *Gespräche Jesu mit seinen Jüngern nach der Auferstehung. Ein katholisch-apostolisches Sendschreiben des 2.Jh.* (Trans. of Ethiopic text by Isaak Wajnberg), TU 43, 1919 (reprint 1967). German translation: Hugo Duensing, *Epistula Apostolorum*, (KlT 152), 1925.

Literature: H. Lietzmann, 'Notizen' (on Schmidt's edition), ZNW 20, 1921, 173-176. H. Duensing, review of Schmidt in GGA 184, 1922, 241-252. C. Schmidt, review of Duensing in OLZ 28, 1925, cols. 855-859. L. Gry, 'La date de la Parousie d'après l'Epistula Apostolorum', *Rev.Bibl.* 49, 1940, 86-97. A.A.T. Ehrhardt, 'Judaeo-Christians in Egypt, the Epistula Apostolorum and the Gospel to the Hebrews', *Studia Evangelica III*, (ed. F.L. Cross), TU 88, 1964, 360-382. M. Hornschuh, *Studien zur Epistula Apostolorum*, (PTS 5), 1965. J. Aßfalg in Kindlers Lit. Lex. I, 1965, col. 794. R. Staats, 'Die törichten Jungfrauen von Mt 25 in gnostischer und antignostischer Literatur', *Christentum und Gnosis*, (ed. W. Eltester, BZNW 37), 1969, pp. 98-115; id. 'Ogdoas als ein Symbol für die Auferstehung', *Vig.Chr.* 26, 1972, 29-52. Erbetta III 37-62. Moraldi II 1669-1702.

2. Transmission and attestation: as early as 1895 Carl Schmidt discovered the first Coptic fragments at the Institut de la Mission archéologique française in Cairo, and was able to fill up the gaps with the aid of Pierre Lacau. In addition J. Bick was fortunate enough to find a Latin leaf, which he examined along with E. Hauler, in a palimpsest manuscript, the Cod. Palat. Vindobonensis 16, formerly Bobbiensis. In the interval Louis Guerrier was able to identify the complete Ethiopic text, extant in several manuscripts, and publish it in collaboration with Sylvain Grébaut in 1913. The Ethiopic version is alone complete, and with its five manuscripts shows the importance of this text for the Ethiopians. This tradition is not uniform, and must be divided into at least two main groups. We have to reckon with the probability that the Coptic tradition came to Ethiopia by the usual way through Arabic. An early translation direct from the Greek into Ethiopic is not, however, completely to be excluded, although any such 'Urtext' cannot be isolated from the extant - frequently altered - Ethiopic tradition. The extra-Ethiopic tradition, which is much too meagre, does not allow us to trace even in a preliminary way the course of the transmission. In 1919 Carl Schmidt, assisted by Isaak Wajnberg, brought out the standard complete edition, and in 1925 Hugo Duensing published a German translation of the whole tradition, which works the various strands together or sets them side by side.

3. Content: the text purports to be a letter from the college of the apostles, enumerated by name, to the churches in the four regions of the world. As in all the apocryphal tradition, appeal is made to a special revelation of the risen Lord after the resurrection. The Epistula Apostolorum emphasises the position of the Saviour as God and Son of God, enters into the incarnation and his works of power even as a child and again in the biblical miracles, beginning from the wedding at Cana. Against Cerinthus and Simon the human suffering (crucifixion) of the Son of God is stressed, and also the reality of the resurrection. In addition the Saviour reveals to his disciples how in heaven he had at his disposal the wisdom and power of the Father, and in his descent was made like the angels and archangels of the various heavenly spheres and thus remained unrecognised. This is also why he appeared to the Virgin Mary in the form of the archangel Gabriel, and entered into her. On the occasion of passover (the commemoration of the Saviour's death), a disciple not identified by name is to be cast into prison. On the evidence of the list of names at the beginning, probably only Peter (cf. Acts 12) can be intended here. It is interesting that in the revelation of the time of the return of Christ there is reference to 'the coming of my Father', which is given a basis through the complete unity of Father and Son. The command to the apostles to proclaim the Gospel is in general bound up with detailed eschatological revelations. An important point is the express reference to the resurrection of the flesh together with soul and spirit before the judgment. Over and above this, the Saviour descended to the heroes of the old covenant, in order to enable them also to participate in the baptism of life and the forgiveness of sins. Within the frame of Jesus' dispositions regarding the authority and the preaching of the apostles, Saul/Paul also is mentioned, and his status confirmed. The further revelations regarding the terrors of the end-time and the deliverance of the apostles and the faithful won by them conform with the usual apocalyptic framework. After this conversation the Saviour ascends into heaven, to the accompaniment of natural phenomena.

4. Place and time of composition; significance: the content and the manuscript tradition do not allow any exact identification of the place of composition. The original is lost. It seems to have been composed in the Greek language. The content and the form of the tradition point to Lower Egypt. Alexandria, that great spiritual centre of exchange, must come into the reckoning at least for its dissemination, if not absolutely for its composition. The free handling of the holy scriptures is typical for Egypt. Here the biblical canon was established as obligatory only in 367 in the 39th Festal Letter of Athanasius (see above, pp. 49f.). The Gospel of Mark, of which our text knows only the spurious ending, was at that time still unknown in parts of Upper Egypt. In contrast, the Epistula Apostolorum makes all the more use of the Gospel of John and its Logos Christology. It is worthy of note that the Saviour 'came into being' (*sc.* rose again) on the eighth day, the day of the Lord. The ogdoad played a role in Gnosticism - particularly among the Valentinians - but also in more orthodox movements, and offered itself as a theme for cosmological and astrological speculation. Hellenistic-Jewish Christianity above all seems to have stressed the eighth day.

We must conjecture that the document originated in these circles, which were also surely Egyptianised. It is not free from gnostic motifs, but as a whole its homeland is in hellenised Egyptian Jewish Christianity. Its tendency is rather anti-gnostic. It certainly combats movements which match that description, yet is rooted in the syncretistic milieu of Lower Egypt; this fits in with the Hermetic and Essene knowledge which can be identified in the author. The bluntly anti-docetic tendency and the emphasis on the resurrection of the flesh are Egyptian. So too in general is the Christology of the document, and also the close association of Father and Son at the return for judgment. As in Egypt 'the godhead works not directly but through the ruler, who is its embodiment and instrument' (S. Morenz, *Gott und Mensch im alten Ägypten*, 1965, p. 74), so here the Father works through the Son as his incarnation and instrument. Other connections between the Epistula Apostolorum and the Near East (e.g. with Symeon of Mesopotamia, according to Staats) and Asia Minor, in addition to the Egyptian basic features, are easily explained if we see in the author a school head from the hellenistic-Jewish Christianity of Alexandria or its neighbourhood, the point of irruption into Egypt for all oriental ideas and teachers. This also fits with the special mention of the additional apostle Paul, who played no role in Egyptian-Jewish Christianity and must here be commended for the first time. But possibly the author is in this way answering the regard in which this apostle was held among gentile gnostics.

An origin about the middle of the 2nd century may be postulated for the document, in agreement with the date of the *parousia* mentioned in it. The Epistula Jacobi Apocrypha was probably known to the author (A.A.T. Ehrhardt).

Epistula Apostolorum[1]
(The title is inferred from the text)

1. (*Chaps. 1-6 in Eth. only.*) What Jesus Christ revealed to his disciples as a letter, and how Jesus Christ revealed the letter of the council of the apostles, the disciples of Jesus Christ, to the Catholics; which was written because of the false apostles Simon and Cerinthus, that no one should follow them - for in them is deceit with which they kill men - that you may be established and not waver, not be shaken and not turn away from *the word of the Gospel*[2] that you have heard. As we have heard (it),[3] kept (it), and have written (it) for the whole world, so we entrust (it) to you, our sons and daughters, in joy and in the name of God the Father, the ruler of the world, and in Jesus Christ. May Grace increase upon you.

2. (We,) John and Thomas and Peter and Andrew and James and Philip and Bartholomew and Matthew and Nathanael and Judas Zelotes and Cephas,[4] we have written (*or*, write) to the churches of the East and West, towards North and South, recounting and proclaiming to you concerning our Lord Jesus Christ, as we have written; and we have *heard* and *felt* him after he had risen from the dead;[5] and how he has revealed to us things great, astonishing, real.

3. We know this: our Lord and Saviour Jesus Christ (is) God and Son of God, who was sent from God, the ruler of the entire world, the maker and creator of what *is named with every name*,[6] who is over all authority (as) *Lord of lords and King of kings*,[7] the ruler of the rulers, the heavenly one who is over the Cherubim[8] and Seraphim and sits *at the right hand of the throne* of the Father,[9] who by his word commanded the heavens and built the earth and all that is in it and bounded the sea that it should not go beyond its boundaries,[10] and (caused) deeps and springs to bubble up and flow over the earth day and night; who established the sun, moon, and stars in heaven, who separated light from darkness;[11] who commanded hell, and in the twinkling of an eye summons the rain for the wintertime, and fog, frost, and hail, and the days in their time; who shakes and makes firm; who has created man according to his image and likeness;[12] who spoke in parables through the patriarchs and prophets and in truth through him whom the apostles declared and the disciples touched.[13] And God, the Lord (= the Father), and the Son of God, we believe: *the word* which *became flesh*[14] through the holy virgin Mary, was hidden in her birth-pangs by the Holy Spirit, and was born not by the lust of the flesh but by the will of God,[15] and was wrapped (in swaddling clothes)[16] and made known at Bethlehem; and that he was reared and grew up as we saw.

252

4. This is what our Lord Jesus Christ did, who was delivered by Joseph and Mary his mother to where he might learn letters. And he who taught him said to him as he taught him, 'Say Alpha.' He answered and said to him, 'First you tell me what Beta is.'[17] And truly (it was) a real thing which was done.

5. Then *there was a marriage in Cana of Galilee*.[18] And he was invited with his mother and his brothers.[19] And he made water into wine and awakened the dead and made the lame to walk;[20] for him whose hand was withered, he stretched it out again,[21] and the *woman who suffered twelve years from a haemorrhage touched the edge of his garment* and was immediately whole; and while we reflected and wondered concerning the miracle he performed, he said to us, '*Who touched me?*' And we said to him, 'O Lord, the crowd of people touched you.' And he answered and said to us, '*I noticed that a power went out from me*.' Immediately that woman came before him, answered and said to him, 'Lord, I touched you.' And he answered and said to her, 'Go, *your faith has made you whole.*'[22] Then he made the deaf to hear and the blind to see, and he exorcised those who were possessed,[23] and he cleansed the lepers.[24] And the demon Legion, that a man had, met with Jesus, cried and said, 'Before the day of our destruction has come you have come to turn us out.' But the Lord Jesus rebuked him and said to him, 'Go out of this man without doing anything to him.' And he went into the swine and drowned them in the sea, and they were choked.[25] Then he walked on the sea, and the winds blew, and he rebuked them, and the waves of the sea became calm.[26] And when we, his disciples, had no denarii, we said to him, 'Master, what should we do about the tax-collector?' And he answered and said to us, 'One of you *cast the hook*, the net, into the deep and draw out a fish, and he will find a denarius in it. Give that to the tax-collector for me and for you.'[27] Then when we had no bread *except five loaves and two fish, he commanded* the people *to lie down*, and their number amounted to *5000 besides children and women*, whom we served with pieces of bread; *and they were filled*, and there was (some) left over, and we carried away *twelve baskets full* of pieces,[28] asking and saying, 'What meaning is there in these five loaves?' They are a picture of our faith concerning the great Christianity and that is in the Father, the ruler of the entire world, and in Jesus Christ our Saviour, and in the Holy Spirit, the Paraclete, and in the holy Church and in the forgiveness of sins.

6. And these things our Lord and Saviour revealed and showed to us, and likewise we to you, that you, reflecting upon eternal life, may be associates in the grace of the Lord and in our service and in our glory. Be firm, without wavering, in the knowledge and investigation of our Lord Jesus Christ, and he will prove gracious and will save always in all never-ending eternity.

7. (*Here begins the Coptic.*) Cerinthus and Simon have come to go through the world. But they are enemies of our Lord Jesus Christ,

Ethiopic

who in reality alienate those who believe in the true word and deed, namely Jesus Christ. Therefore take care and beware of them,[29] for in them is affliction and contamination and death, the end of which will be destruction and judgment.

Coptic

for they pervert the words and the object, which is Jesus Christ. Now keep yourselves away from them,[29] for death is in them and a great stain of corruption - these to whom shall be judgment and the end and eternal perdition.

8. Because of that we have not hesitated

with the true testimony of our Lord and Saviour Jesus Christ, how he acted while we saw him, and how he constantly both explained and caused our thoughts within us.

to write to you concerning the testimony of our Saviour Christ, what he did when we were behind him watching and yet again in thoughts and deeds.

9.He of whom we are witnesses we know as the one crucified in the days of Pontius Pilate and of the prince Archelaus, who was crucified between two thieves;[30] and was taken down from the wood of the cross together with them; and he was buried in a place which is called the place of the skull (κρανίου τόπος),[31] to which three women came, Sarah, Martha and Mary Magdalene. They carried ointment to pour out

He concerning whom we bear witness that this is the Lord who was crucified by Pontius Pilate and Archelaus between the two thieves[30]

and who was buried in a place called the place of the skull.[31] There went to that place three women: Mary, the daughter of Martha and Mary Magdalene. They took ointment to pour

upon his body,[32] weeping and mourning[33] over what had happened.

And they approached the tomb and found the stone where it had been rolled away from the tomb,[35] and they opened the door

But when they had approached the tomb they looked inside[34]

and did not find his (*Coptic*: the) body.[36]

10. And (*Copt.*: But) as they were mourning and weeping, the Lord appeared to them and said to them, '(*Copt.*: For whom are you weeping? Now) do not weep;[37] I am he whom you seek.[38] But let one of you go to your brothers and say (*Eth.*: to them),[39] 'Come, our (*Copt.*: the) Master has risen from the dead.''[40]

And Mary came to us and told us. And we said to her, 'What have we to do with you, O woman? He that is dead and buried, can he then live?' And we did not believe her,[41] that our Saviour had risen from the dead.	Martha came and told it to us. We said to her, 'What do you want with us, O woman? He who has died is buried, and could it be possible for him to live?' We did not believe her,[41] that the Saviour had risen from the dead.

Then she went back to our (*Copt.*: the) Lord and said to him,
'None of them believed me

concerning your resurrection'. And he said to her,	that you are alive.' He said,

Let another one of you go (*Copt.*: to them) saying this again to them.'

And Sarah came and gave us the same news, and we accused her of lying. And she returned to our Lord and spoke to him as Mary had.	Mary came and told us again, and we did not believe her. She returned to the Lord and she also told it to him.

11. Then (*Eth.*: And then) the Lord said to Mary and (*Copt.*: and also) to her sisters, 'Let us go to them.' And he came[42] and found us inside, veiled.

And we doubted and did not believe. He came before us like a ghost[43] and we did not believe that it was he. But it was he. And thus he said to us, 'Come, and	He called us out. But we thought it was a ghost,[43] and we did not believe it was the Lord. Then he said to us, 'Come,

do not be afraid.[44] I am your teacher (*Copt.*: <master>) whom you, Peter, denied three times (*Eth.*: before the cock crowed);[45] and now do you deny again?'

And we went to him, thinking and doubting[46] whether it was he. And he said to us,	But we went to him, doubting[46] in our hearts whether it was possibly he. Then he said to us,

'Why do you (*Copt.*: still) doubt and (*Eth.*: why) are you not believing?[47] (*Eth.*: believing that) I am he who spoke to you concerning my flesh, my death, and my resurrection.

And that you may know that it is I, lay your hand, Peter, (and your finger) in the nailprint of my hands; and you, Thomas, in my side;[48] and also you, Andrew, see whether my foot steps on the ground and leaves a footprint.

That you may know that it is I, put your finger, Peter, in the nailprints of my hands; and you, Thomas, put your finger in the spear-wounds of my side;[48] but you, Andrew, look at my feet and see if they do not touch the ground.

For it is written in the prophet,

'But a ghost, a demon, leaves no print on the ground.''[49]

'The foot of a ghost or a demon does not join to the ground.''[49]

12. But now we felt him,[50] that he had truly risen in the flesh. And then we fell on our faces before him, asked him for pardon and entreated him because we had not believed him. Then our Lord and Saviour said to us, 'Stand up and I will reveal to you what is on earth, and what is above heaven, and your resurrection that is in the kingdom of heaven, concerning which my Father has sent me, that I may take up[52] you and those who believe in me.'

But we touched him[50] that we might truly know whether he had risen in the flesh, and we fell on our faces confessing our sin, that we had been unbelieving. Then the Lord our redeemer said, 'Rise up, and I will reveal to you what is above heaven and what is in heaven, and your rest that is in the kingdom of heaven.[51] For my Father has given me the power to take up[52] you and those who believe in me.'

13. And what he revealed is this, as he said to us,[53] 'While I was coming from the Father of all, passing by the heavens, wherein I put on the wisdom of the Father and by his power clothed myself in his power, I was like the heavens. And passing by the angels and archangels in their form and as one of them, I passed by the orders, dominions, and princes, possessing the measure of the wisdom of the Father who sent me. And the archangels Michael and Gabriel, Raphael and Uriel followed me (*Lat. adds*: secretly) until the fifth firmament of heaven, while I appeared as one of them. This kind of power was given

But what he revealed is this that he said,[53] 'But it happened, as I was about to come down from the Father of all, I passed by the heavens; I put on the wisdom of the Father and the power of his might.

I was in the heavens, and I passed by the angels and archangels in their form, as if I were one of them among the dominions and powers. I passed through them, possessing the wisdom of him who sent me. But the chief leader of the angels is Michael, and Gabriel and Uriel and Raphael, but they followed me to the fifth firmament, thinking in their hearts that I was one of them. But the me by the Father. Then I made the archangels to become distracted with the voice and go up to the altar[54] of the Father and serve the Father in their work until I should return to him. I did this thus in the likeness[55] of his wisdom. For I became all in all with them, that I, fulfilling the will of the mercy of the Father and the glory of him who sent me, might return to him.[57]

14. Do you know that the angel Gabriel came and brought the message to Mary?'[58] And we said to him, 'Yes, O Lord.' And he answered and said to us, 'Do you not remember that I previously said to you that I became like an angel to the angels?' And we said to him, 'Yes, O Lord.' And he said to us, 'At that time I appeared in the form of the archangel Gabriel to (the virgin: *not in all MSS*) Mary[59] and spoke with her, and her heart received (me); she believed and laughed;[60] and I, the Word, went into her and became flesh;[61] and I myself was servant[62] for myself; and in the likeness of an angel, like him will I do, and after it I will go to my Father.

15. And you therefore celebrate the remembrance of my death,[63] which is the Passover;

Father gave me powerof this nature

And in that day I adorned the archangels with a wondrous voice that they might go up to the altar[54] of the Father and serve and complete the service until I should go to him. Thus I did it through the wisdom of the likeness. For I became all things in everything that I might fulfil the plan[56] of the Father of glory who sent me, and might return to him.[57] For you know that the angel Gabriel brought the message to Mary.'[58] We answered, 'Yes, O Lord.' Then he answered and said to us, 'Do you not then remember that a little while ago I told you: I became an angel among the angels. I became all things in everything?' We said to him, 'Yes, O Lord.' Then he answered and said to us, 'On that day, when I took the form of the angel Gabriel, I appeared to Mary[59] and spoke with her. Her heart received me and she believed; I formed myself and entered into her womb; I became flesh,[61] for I alone was servant[62] to myself with respect to Mary in an appearance of the form of an angel. So will I do, after I have gone to the Father.

And you remember my death.[63] If now the passover takes place,then will one of you (*Eth.*: .

who stands beside me) be thrown into prison for my name's sake,[64] and he will

be very grieved and sorrowful, for while you celebrate the passover he who is in custody did not celebrate it with you. And I will send my power in the form of (my) angel, and the door of the prison will open, and he will come out and

be in sorrow and care that you celebrate the passover while he is in prison and far from you; for he will sorrow that he does not celebrate the passover with you. I will send my power in the form of the angel Gabriel, and the doors of the prison come to you to watch with you and to rest. And when you complete my Agape and my remembrance[65] at the crowing of the cock,[66] he will again be taken and thrown in prison for a testimony,[67] until he comes out to preach, as I have commanded you.' And we said to him, 'O Lord, have *you* then not completed the drinking of the passover?[68] Must we, then, do it again?' And he said to us, 'Yes, until I come from the Father with my wounds.'

16. And we said to him, 'O Lord, great is this that you say and reveal to us. In what kind of power and form are you about to come?' And he said to us, 'Truly I say to you, I will come as the sun which bursts forth; thus will I, shining seven times brighter than it in glory,[70] while I am carried on the wings of the clouds in splendour with my cross going on before me,[71] come to the earth to judge *the living and the dead.*'[72]

17. And we said to him, 'O Lord, how many years yet?' And he said to us, 'When the hundred and fiftieth year is completed, between pentecost and passover will the coming of my Father take place.' And we said to him, 'O Lord, now you said to us, '*I* will come', and then you said, 'he who sent me will come'.' And he said to us, '*I am*

will be opened. He will go out and come to you; he will spend a night of the watch with you and stay with you until the cock crows.[66] But when you complete the remembrance[65] that is for me, and the Agape, he will again be thrown into prison for a testimony,[67] until he comes out from there and preaches what I have delivered to you.' And we said to him, 'O Lord, is it perhaps necessary again that we take the cup and drink?' He said to us, 'Yes, it is necessary until the day when I come with those who were killed for my sake.'[69]

We said to him, 'O Lord, what you have revealed to us beforehand is great. In a power of what sort or in an appearance of what order will you come?' But he answered, saying, 'Truly I say to you, I will come as does the sun that shines, and shining seven times brighter than it[70] in my brightness; with the wings of the clouds carrying me in splendour and the sign of the cross before me,[71] I will come down to the earth to judge *the living and the dead.*'[72]

But we said to him, 'O Lord, after how many years yet will this happen?' He said to us, 'When the hundredth part and the twentieth part is completed, between pentecost and the feast of unleavened bread, will the coming of the Father take place.' But we said to him, 'Here now, what have you said to us, '*I* will come', and how do you say, 'It is he who sent me who will come'?' Then he said to us, '*I am* wholly *in the Father and the Father in me.*[73] Then we said to him, 'Will you really leave us until your coming? Where will we find a teacher?' And he answered and said to us, 'Do you not know that until now I am both here and there with him who sent me?' And *we* said to him, 'O Lord, is it possible that you should be both here and there?' And he said to us, 'I am wholly in the Father and the Father in me after his image and after his likeness[74] and after his power and after his perfection and after his light, and I am his perfect word.'[75]

18. This is, when he was crucified, had died and risen again, as he said this, and the work that was thus accomplished in the flesh, that he was crucified, and his ascension - this is the fulfilling of the number. 'And the wonders and his image and everything perfect you will see in me with respect to redemption which takes place through me, and while I go to the Father and into heaven.[77] But look, *a new commandment I give you, that you love one another*[78]

wholly *in my Father and my Father is in me*[73]

with regard to the resemblance[74] of form and of power and of perfection and of light and (with regard to) the full measure and the voice. I am the word.[75]

I have become to him a thing, which is this. I am the perfect thought in the type. I came into being on the eighth day which is the day of the Lord.[76] But the whole completion of the completion you will see through the redemption that has happened to me, and you will see me, while I go to heaven to my Father who is in heaven.[77] But look now, *I give you a new commandment; love one another*[78] and [*One leaf missing in the Coptic.*]

and obey each other and (that) continual peace reign among you. *Love your enemies, and what you do not want done to you, that do to no one else.*[79]

19. And both preach and teach this to those who believe in me, and preach concerning the (heavenly[80]) kingdom of my Father,[81] and as my Father has given me the power (*addition in Paris No. 199:* so I give it to you) that you may bring near the children of the heavenly Father. Preach, and they will believe. You (it is) whose duty is to lead his children into heaven.' And we said to him, 'O Lord, it is possible for you to do what you have told us; but how will we be able to do (it)?' And he said to us, 'Truly I say to you, preach and teach, as I will be with you.[82] For I am well pleased to be with you, that you may become *joint heirs* with me[83] of the kingdom

259

of heaven of him who sent me. Truly I say to you, you will be my brothers and companions, for my Father has delighted in you and in those who will believe in me through you. Truly I say to you, such and so great a joy has my Father prepared (for you) that angels and powers desired and will desire to view and to see it, but they will not be allowed to see the greatness of my Father.'[84] And we said to him, 'O Lord, what kind (of thing) is this that you tell us?'

And he said to us, 'You will see a light brighter than light and more perfect than perfection. And the Son will be perfected through the Father, the light - for the Father is perfect - (the Son) whom death and resurrection make perfect, and the one accomplishment surpasses the other. And I am fully the right hand of the Father; I am in him who accomplishes.' And we twelve said to him, 'O Lord, in all things you have become to us salvation and life. Do you speak (*or,* while you speak) to us of such a hope?' And he said to us, 'Have confidence and be of good courage. Truly I say to you,[85] such a rest will be yours where there is no eating and drinking and no mourning and singing (*or* care) and neither earthly garment nor perishing. And you will not have part in the creation of below, but will belong to the incorruptibility of my Father, you who will not perish. As I am continually in the Father, so also you (are) in me.'[86] And we said again to him, 'In what form?[87] Of an angel or that of flesh?' And for this he answered and said to us, 'I have put on your flesh, in which I was born and died and was buried and rose again through my heavenly Father, that it might be fulfilled that was said by the prophet David[88] concerning my

He said to us, 'You will see a light . . . , in that it is more exalted than that which shines . . . [*restored after the Ethiopic text*] the perfection that is perfected in . . . I am fully the right hand of the Father . . . me, which is the fullness.' But we said to him, 'O Lord, in all things you have become to us salvation and life. You have proclaimed to us these words of this kind.' He said to us, 'Have confidence and be of a peaceful heart. Truly I say to you,[85] your rest will be in heaven (?) in the place where there is neither eating nor drinking, neither rejoicing nor mourning nor perishing of those who are in it. You have no part in . . . , but you (*restored*) will receive of the incorruptibility of my Father. As I (*restored from first 'of'*) am in him, so you will rest yourselves (?) in me.'[86]

Again we said to him, 'In what form?[87] In the manner of angels, or in flesh?' [*restored after the Ethiopic text*] He answered and said to us, 'Look. I have put on (your) flesh, in which I was born and crucified and rose again through my Father who is (in heaven), that the prophecy of the prophet David death and resurrection: '*O Lord, how numerous have they become that oppress me; many have risen up against me. Many say to my soul, 'He has no salvation by his God.' But you, O Lord, are my refuge, my glory, and he who lifts up my head. With my voice I cried to God, and he heard me from the mount of his sanctuary. I lay down and fell asleep; and I rose up, for God* raised me up. *I was not afraid of thousands* of people *who surrounded me and rose up against me. Arise, O Lord my God, and save me. For you have smitten (and trodden down*: only in Stuttgart Cod. Orient. fol. no. 49*) all who show me enmity without cause; and you have shattered the teeth of sinners. Deliverance is of God, and your blessing* (be) *upon your people.*'[89]

All that was said by the prophets was thus performed and has taken place and is completed in me, for I spoke in (or, by) them;[90] how much more will what I myself have made known to you really happen, that he who sent me may be glorified[91] by you and by those who believe in me.'

might be fulfilled[88] concerning what he foretold about me and my death and my resurrection, saying, '*O Lord, numerous have they become that strive with me, and many have risen up against me. Many say to my soul, There is no deliverance for you with God. But you, O Lord, are my protector; you are my glory and he who lifts up my head. With my voice I cried out to the Lord, and he heard me. I lay down and fell asleep; I rose up, for you, O Lord, are my protector. I will not be afraid of tens of thousands of people who set themselves against me round about. Rise up, O Lord; save me, my God. For you have cast down all who are my enemies without cause; the teeth of sinners you have broken. To the Lord is salvation and his delight in his people.*'[89]

But if all the words that were spoken by the prophets are fulfilled in me - for I was in them[90] - how much more will what I say to you truly [what I say to you (*dittography*)] happen, that he who sent me may be glorified[91] by you and by those who believe in me.'

20. (*Copt.*: But) After he had said this to us, we said to him, 'O Lord, in all things you have shown yourself merciful to us and have saved us; you have revealed all (*Eth.*: all this) to us. Yet (*Eth.*: Yet one thing) might we ask you, if you permit us.' (*Eth.*: And) He answered and said to us, 'I know

that you are listening and long to listen; concerning what you wish, ask me. Look; ask me and keep in mind what you hear, and it will be agreeable with me to speak with you.

that you will endure and that your heart is pleased when you hear me. But ask me concerning what you wish, and I will speak well with you.

21. (*Copt.*: For) Truly I say to you, as the (*Copt.*: my) Father awakened me from the dead, in the same manner you also will arise[92]

in the flesh, and he will cause you to rise up above the heavens to the place of which I have spoken to you from the beginning (*or*, already), which he who sent me has prepared for you. And for this cause have I perfected all mercy: without being begotten I was born (*or*, begotten) of man, and without having flesh I put on flesh and grew up, that (I might regenerate) you who were begotten in the flesh, and	and be taken up above the heavens to the place of which I have spoken to you from the beginning (before), to the place which he who sent me has prepared for you. And thus will I complete all arrangements (for salvation): being unbegotten and (yet) begotten of man, being without flesh (and yet) I have worn flesh,[93] for on that account have I come, that you . . . (*from here the Coptic is defective and fragmentary*)

in regeneration you obtain the resurrection in your flesh,[94] a garment that will not pass away, with all who hope and believe in him *who sent me*;[95] for my Father has found pleasure in you; and to whoever I will I give the hope of the kingdom.' Then we said to him, 'It is great, how you cause to hope, and how you speak.' He answered and said to us, 'Believe (*must mean*, Do you believe) that everything I say to you will happen.' And we answered him and said to him, 'Yes, O Lord.' And he said to us, 'Truly I say to you that I have received all power[96] from my Father that I may bring back those in darkness into light[97] and those in corruptibility into incorruptibility and those in error into righteousness and those in death into life, and that those in captivity may be loosed, as what is impossible on the part of men is possible on the part of the Father.[98] I am the hope of the hopeless, the helper of those who have no helper, the treasure of those in need, the physician of the sick, the resurrection of the dead.'[99]

22. After he had said this to us, we said to him, 'O Lord, is it really in store for the flesh to be judged (together) with the soul and spirit,[100] and will (one of these) (*Copt.*: really) rest in heaven and the other (*Copt.*: however) be punished eternally while it is (still) alive?[101]' And (*Copt.*: But) he said to us, 'How long do you still ask and inquire?'

23. And (*not in Copt.*) we said again to him, 'O Lord,

but it is necessary, since you have commanded us to preach, prophesy, and teach, that we, having heard accurately from you, may be good preachers and may teach them, that they may believe in you. Therefore	there is a necessity upon us to inquire through you, for you command us to preach, that we ourselves may learn with certainty through you and be profitable preachers, and (that) those who will

we question you.'

be instructed by us may believe in you. Therefore we question you frequently.

24. He answered and said to us, 'Truly I say to you, the flesh of every man will rise with his soul alive (*Paris No. 51 omits 'alive'*) and his spirit.'

He answered us, saying, 'Truly I say to you, the resurrection of the flesh will happen while the soul and the spirit are in it.'

And we said to him, 'O Lord,

then can what is departed and scattered become alive? Not as if we deny it do we ask; rather we believe that what you say has happened and will happen.' And he said to us, being angry, 'You of little faith,[102] how long yet do you ask me? And inquire (only) without anguish after what you wish to hear.

is it then possible that what is dissolved and destroyed should be whole? Not as unbelieving do we ask you - nor is it impossible for you - rather we really believe that what you say will happen.' And he was angry with us, saying to us, 'O you of little faith,[103] until what day do you ask? But what you wish, say to me, and I will tell it to you without grudging. Only

Keep my commandments,[104] and do what I tell you,

without delay and without reserve and without respect of persons;[105] serve in the strait, direct and narrow way.[106] And thereby will the Father in every respect rejoice concerning you.'

and do not turn away your face from anyone, that I also may not turn my face away from you; rather without delay and without reserve . . . (and) without respect of persons[105] serve in the way that is direct and strait and oppressed (narrow).[106] So it is also with my Father. He will rejoice concerning you.'

25. And we said again to him, 'O Lord, look; we have you to derision with the many questions.' And he said to us,

Again we said to him, 'O Lord, already we are ashamed that we repeatedly question and trouble you.' Then he answered and said to us,

'I know that in faith and with (*Copt.*: from) your whole heart you question me. Therefore (*Eth.*: And) I am glad because of you. (*Copt.*: For) Truly I say to you

I am pleased, and my Father in me[107] rejoices, that you thus inquire and ask. Your boldness makes me

I am glad, and my Father who is in me,[107] that you question me. For your boldness affords me rejoicing

263

rejoice, and it affords yourselves life.' And when he had said this to us, we were glad, for he had spoken to us in gentleness. And we said again to him, 'Our Lord, in all things you have shown yourself gracious toward us and grant us life; for all we have asked you you have told us.' Then he said to us, 'Does the flesh or the spirit fall away?' And we said to him, 'The flesh'. And he said to us, 'Now what has fallen will arise, and what is ill will be sound, that my Father may be praised therein; as he has done to me, so I (will do) to you and to all who believe in me.

and gives yourselves (life).' But when he had said this to us we were glad that we asked him. And we said to him, 'O Lord, in all things you make us alive and pity us. Only now will you make known to us what we will ask you?' Then he said to us, 'What is it then that passes away? Is it the flesh (or) the spirit?' We said to him, 'The flesh is perishable.' Then he said to us, 'What has fallen will arise, and what is lost will be found and what is weak will recover, that in what is thus done may be revealed the glory of my Father. As he has done to me, so will I do to all of you who believe.

26. (*Copt.*: But) Truly I say to you, the flesh will rise alive with the soul, that

they may confess and be judged with the work

their accounting may take place on that day, concerning what

which they have done, *whether it is good or bad*,[108] in order that

there may be a selection[109] and exhibition for those who have believed and have done the commandment of my Father who sent me. Then will the righteous judgment take place; for thus my Father wills, and he said to me, 'My son, on *the day of judgment*[110] you will not fear the rich and not spare (*Paris Nos. 90 and 199:* pity) the poor; rather deliver each one to eternal punishment[111] according to his sins.' But to those who have loved me and do love me and who have done my commandment I will grant rest in life in the kingdom of my heavenly Father.[112] Look, see what kind of power he has granted me, and he has given me, that . . . what I want and as I have wanted . . . and in whom I have awakened hope.[113]

a selection[109] may take place of believers who have done the commandments of my Father who sent me. And thus will the judgment take place in severity. For my Father said to me, 'My son, on *the day of judgment*[110] you will neither fear the rich nor will you have pity on the poor; rather according to the sin of each one will you deliver him to eternal punishment.'[111] But to my beloved ones who have done the commandments of my Father who sent me I will grant rest of life in the kingdom of my Father who is in heaven,[112] and they will see what he has granted me; and he has given me power that I may do what I wish, and that I may give to . . . and to those whom I have determined to give and to grant.[113]

27. And on that account I have descended and have spoken with Abraham and Isaac and Jacob, to your fathers the prophets, and have brought to them news[115] that they may come from the rest which is below into heaven, and have given them the right hand of the baptism of life and forgiveness[116] and pardon for all wickedness as to you, so from now on also to those who believe in me. But whoever believes in me and does not do my commandment[117] receives, although he believes in my name, no benefit from it. He has run a course in vain.[118] His end is determined for ruin and for punishment of great pain, for he has sinned against my commandment.

28. But to you I have given that you should be children of the light in God and should be pure from all wickedness and from all power of the judgment (*probably should be*: rulers, *or* archons); and to those who believe in me through you I will do the same, and as I have said and promised to you, that he should go out of prison and should be rescued from the chains and the spears (*probably should be*: archons) and the terrible fire.'[120] And we said to him, 'O Lord, in every respect you have made us rejoice and have given us rest; for in faithfulness and truthfulness you have preached to our fathers and to the prophets, and even so to us and to every man.' And he said to us, 'Truly I say to you, you and all who believe and also they who yet will believe in him *who sent me*[121] I will cause

On that account I have descended to the place of Lazarus,[114] and have preached to the righteous and to the prophets,[115] that they may come forth from the rest which is below and go up to what is (above) . . . (;in that I stretch out) my right hand over them . . . of life and forgiveness and deliverance from all evil, as I have done to you and to those who believe in me. But if someone believes in me and does not do my commandments,[117] although he has acknowledged my name he receives no benefit from it. He has run a futile course.[118] For such will be in error and in (ruin), since they have disregarded my commandments.

(But so much more) you, the children of life, I have redeemed from all evil and from (the power of) the archons,[119] and all who through you will believe in me. For what I have promised you I will also give to them, that they may come out of the prison and the chains of the archons and the powerful fire.'[120] We answered and said to him, 'O Lord, you have given rest of (life to us?) and have given . . . in wonders (for the strengthening?) of faith; will you now yourself preach this (to us)? You have preached to the (fathers) and to the prophets.' Then he said to us, 'Truly I say to you, all who have believed in me and who I will (lead) up to heaven, to the place which my Father has give will believe in him *who sent me*[121] you the chosen kingdom (prepared) for the elect,[122] and I will

265

to rise up into heaven, to the place which the Father has prepared for the elect[122] and most elect, (the Father) who will give the rest[123] that he has promised, and eternal life.[124]

29. But those who have sinned against my commandment, who teach something else, subtract from and add to and work for their own glory, alienating those who rightly believe in me (I will deliver them to ruin: *only Stuttgart Cod. Orient. fol. No. 49*).'[125] And we said to him, 'O Lord, will there exist another teaching and grievance (?)?' And he said to us, 'As those who fulfil what is good and beautiful, so (also) the wicked shall be manifest.[126] And then a righteous judgment will take place according to their work, how they have acted;[127] and they will be delivered to ruin.' And we said to him, 'Blessed are we, for we see and hear you as you speak to us, and our eyes have seen such mighty deeds that you have done.'[128] And he answered and said to us, 'But much more *blessed* will they be *who do not see* me *and (yet) believe* in me,[129] for they will be called children of the kingdom[130] and (will be) perfect in the perfect one;[131] to these I will become eternal life in the kingdom of my Father.'[132] And we said again to him, 'O Lord, how will it be possible to believe that you will leave us, as you said: There is coming a time and an hour[133] when it is in store for you to go to your Father?'[135]

(lead) up to heaven, to the place which my Father has (prepared) for the elect,[122] and I will give you the chosen kingdom in rest,[123] and eternal life.[124]

But those who have transgressed (my) commandments and have taught another teaching, (in that they dissolve) the written (teaching) and add . . . their own, teaching with other words (those who believe) in me rightly, if they are brought to ruin by such things (they will receive) eternal punishment.' But we said to him, 'O Lord, then will there exist teaching from others, besides what you have told us?' He said to us, 'It is necessary that they exist, that what is evil and what is good should be manifest.[126] And thus will the judgment to those who do these works be revealed, and according to their works[127] will they be judged and delivered to death.' We said again to him, 'O Lord, blessed are we, who see you and hear you as you (speak) such (words), for our eyes have seen these great wonders that you have done.'[128] He answered and said to us, 'Much more *blessed* are they *who have not seen and (yet) have believed*,[129] for such will be called children of the kingdom,[130] and they will be perfect (in) the perfect one[131] and I will be life (to them) in the kingdom of my Father.'[132] Again we said to him, 'O Lord, in what way will one be able to believe that you will go and leave us, as you said to us, 'A day will come and an hour[134] when I shall go up to my Father'?'[135]

266

30. He answered and said to us, 'Go and preach[136] to the twelve tribes of Israel[137] and to the gentiles and Israel and to the land of Israel towards East and West, North and South;[138] and many will believe in me, the son of God.'[139] And we said to him, 'O Lord, who will believe us and who will listen to us and how can we do and teach and tell the wonders and signs and mighty deeds,[140] as you have done?' And he answered and said to us, 'Go and preach (and teach: *addition in Paris No. 90*) concerning (the coming and: *addition in Paris No. 90*) the mercy of my Father. As my Father has done through me, I will also do through you in that I am with you, and I will give you my peace and my spirit[141] and my power, (that it may happen to you; *not in all MSS*) that they believe. Also to them will this power be given and transmitted that they may give it to the gentiles.

But he said to us, 'Go you and preach[136] to the twelve tribes[137] and preach also to the gentiles and to the whole land of Israel from sunrise to sunset and from South to North,[138] and many will believe in the son of God.'[139] But we said to him, 'O Lord, who will believe us or who will listen to us (while we do, teach and tell) the powers and the signs that you have done, and the (wonders)?'[140] Then he answered and said to us, 'Go and preach the mercy of my Father; and what he has done through me will I myself do through you in that I am in you, and I will give you my peace, and from my spirit I will give you a power that you may prophesy to them to eternal life. But to the others will I myself also give my power, that they may teach the other nations. (*In the Coptic there follows a gap of four pages*)

31. And look, you will meet a man whose name is Saul, which being interpreted means Paul.[142] He is a Jew,[143] circumcised according to the command of the law,[144] and he will hear my voice from heaven[145] with terror, fear and trembling; and his eyes will be darkened[146] and by your hand be crossed with spittle. And do all to him as I have done to you. Deliver him to others![147] And this man - immediately his eyes will be opened,[148] and he will praise God, my heavenly Father. And he will become strong among the nations and will preach and teach, and many will be delighted when they hear and will be saved. Then will he be hated and delivered into the hand of his enemy, and he will testify before (mortal and perishable: *the bracketed adjectives are not uniformly in all MSS*) kings,[149] and upon him will come the completion of the testimony to me; because he had persecuted[150] and hated me, he will be converted to me and preach and teach, and he will be among my elect, a chosen vessel and a wall that does not fall.[151] The last of the last will become a preacher to the gentiles,[152] perfect in (*or*, through) the will of my Father.

As you have learned from the scriptures that your fathers the prophets spoke concerning me, and it is fulfilled in me' - this certain thing he said - 'so you must become a leader to them. And every word which I have spoken to you and which you have written concerning me, that I am the word of the Father[153] and the Father is in me,[154] so you must become also to that man, as it befits you. Teach and remind (him) what has been said in the scriptures and fulfilled concerning me, and then he will be for the salvation of the gentiles.'[155]

32. And we said to him, 'O master, do we have together with them *one* hope of the inheritance?'[156] He answered and said to us, 'Are the fingers of the hand alike or the ears of corn in the field? Or do the fruit-bearing trees give the same fruit? Do they not bring forth fruit according to their nature?' And we said to him, 'O Lord, are you speaking again in parables to us?' And he said to us, 'Do not be grieved. Truly I say to you, you are my brothers, companions in the kingdom of heaven with my Father, for so has it pleased him. Truly I say to you, also to those whom you shall have taught and who have become believers in me will I give this hope.'

33. And we said again to him, 'When, Lord, will we meet that man, and when will you go to your Father and to our God and Lord?' And he answered and said to us, 'That man will set out from the land of Cilicia[157] to Damascus in Syria[158] to tear asunder the Church[159] which you must create. It is I who will speak (to him) through you, and he will come quickly. He will be (strong: *only Paris No. 199*) in this faith, *that the word of the prophet may be fulfilled*[160] where it says,[161] 'Behold, out of the land of Syria I will begin to call a new Jerusalem, and I will subdue Zion and it will be captured; and the barren one who has no children will be fruitful[162] and will be called the daughter of my Father, but to me, my bride; for so has it pleased him who sent me.' But that man will I turn aside, that he may not go there and complete his evil plan. And glory of my Father will come in through him. For after I have gone away and remain with my Father, I will speak with him from heaven,[163] and it will all happen as I have predicted to you concerning him.'

34. And we said again to him, 'O Lord, such meaningful things you have spoken and preached to us and have revealed to us great things never yet spoken, and in every respect you have comforted us and have shown yourself gracious to us. For after your resurrection you revealed all this to us that we might be really saved. But you told us only that signs and wonders would happen in heaven and upon earth before the end of the world comes.[164] Teach us, that we thus may recognise it.' And he said to us, 'I will teach you, and not only what will happen to you, but (also) to those whom you shall teach and who shall believe,[165] and there are such as will hear this man and will believe in me. In those years and in those days this will happen.' And we said to him again, 'O Lord, what is it then

that will happen?' And he said to us, 'Then will the believers and also they who do not believe see a trumpet in heaven, and the sight of great stars that are visible while it is day, and a dragon (*only Paris No. 51 and Stuttgart Cod. Orient. fol. No. 49; British Museum Or. 793 and Paris No. 90*: stars and wonders; *Paris No. 199 has a scribal error*) reaching from heaven to earth, and stars that are like fire falling down[166] and great hailstones of severe fire,[167] and how sun and moon fight against each other, and constantly the frightening of thunder and lightning, thunderclaps and earthquakes,[168] how cities fall down and in their ruin men die,[169] constant drought from the failing of the rain, a great plague and an extensive and often quick death, so that those who die will lack a grave; and the going out (*or*, carrying out) of children and relatives will be on *one* bed (*or*, bier). And the relative will not turn toward his child, nor the child to his relative; and a man will not turn toward his neighbour. But those forsaken who were left behind will rise up and see those who forsook them, in that they did (not)[170] bring them out because (there was) plague. Everything is hatred and affliction and jealousy, and they will take from the one and give to another; and what comes after this will be worse than this. (Mourn those who have not listened to his commandment.)[171]

35. Then my Father will become angry because of the wickedness of men; for their offences are many and the horror of their impurity is much against them in the corruption of their life.' And we said to him, 'What, Lord, what (is allotted) to those who hope in you?' And he answered and said to us, 'How long are you still slow of heart?[172] Truly I say to you, as the prophet David has spoken concerning me and my people, so will it also be concerning those who shall believe in me. But there will be in the world deceivers and enemies (*Paris Nos. 90 and 199*: blasphemers) of righteousness,[173] and they will meet the prophecy of David who said, '*Their feet are quick to shed blood*[174] and their *tongue weaves deceit.*[175] and *the venom of serpents is under their lips.*[174] And I see you as you *wander* with a *thief and your share is with a fornicator.*[176] *While you sit there* furthermore *you slander your brother, and set a trap for the son of your mother.*[177] What do you think? *Should I be like you?*[178] And now see how the prophet of God has spoken concerning everything, that all may be fulfilled that was said before.'

36. And we said to him again, 'O Lord, *will the Gentiles then not say, 'Where is their God?'*[179] He answered and said to us, 'Thus will the elect be revealed, in that they go out after they have been afflicted by such a distress.' And we said to him, 'Will their exit[180] from the world (take place) through a plague that has tormented them?' And he said to us, 'No, but if they suffer torment, such suffering will be a test for them, whether they have faith[181] and whether they keep in mind these words of mine and obey my commandment.[182] They will rise up, and their waiting will last

(only a) few days, that he who sent me may be glorified, and I with him.[183] For he has sent me to you. I tell you this. But you tell (it) to Israel and to the gentiles, that they may hear; they also are to be saved and believe in me and escape the distress of the plague. And whoever has escaped the distress of death, such a one will be taken and kept in prison, under torture like that of a thief.' And we said to him, 'O Lord, will they be like unto the unbelievers, and will you likewise punish those who have escaped the plague?' And he said to us, 'Believing in my name they have done the work of sinners; they have acted like unbelievers.'[184] And we said again to him, 'O Lord, have they who have escaped in this part no life?' He answered and said to us, 'Whoever has done the glorification of my Father, he is the dwelling-place of my Father.'[185]

37. And we said to him, 'O Lord, teach us what will happen after this.' And he said to us, 'In those years and days there shall be war upon war, and the four corners of the world will be shaken and will make war upon each other. And then a disturbance of the clouds (will cause?) darkness and drought[186] and persecution of those who believe in me, and of the elect. Then dissension, conflict, and evil of action against each other. Among them there are some who believe in my name and (yet) follow evil and teach vain teaching. And men will follow them and will submit themselves to their riches, their depravity, their mania for drinking, and their gifts of bribery; and respect of persons will rule among them.

38. But those who desire to see the face of God and who do not regard the person of the sinful rich and who do not fear the men who lead them astray, but reprove them, they will be crowned in the presence of the Father, as also those who reprove their neighbours will be saved. This is a son of wisdom and of faith. But if he does not become a son of wisdom, then he will hate and persecute and not turn towards

his brother, and will despise (him) and cast him away.

his neighbour, will turn against him and . . . him.

But those who walk in truth and in the knowledge of faith[187]

in me, and have the knowledge of wisdom and perseverance for right-eousness' sake, in that men despise those who strive for poverty and they (nevertheless) endure - great is their reward. Those who are reviled, tormented, persecuted,[188] since they are destitute and men are arrogant against them and they hunger and thirst and

possessing love for me - for they have endured abuse - they will be proud, walking in poverty and tolerating those who hate them and revile them.[188] They have been tormented, being destitute, since men were arrogant against them while they walk in hunger and thirst; but because they have persevered for the blessedness of heaven, they

270

because they have persevered - blessed will they be in heaven, and they will be there with me always.[189] Woe to those who hate and despise them! And *their end is* for *destruction.*'[190]

39. And we said to him, 'O Lord, will all this happen?' And he said to us, 'How will the judgment of righteousness take place for the sinners and the righteous?'[191] And we said to him, 'Will they not in that day say to you, 'You caused to lead toward righteousness and sin and have separated (*British Museum Or. 793*: created) darkness and light, evil and good'?' And he said to us, 'Adam was given the power that he might choose what he wanted from the two;[192] and he chose the light and stretched out his hand and took (it) and left the darkness and withdrew from it (*according to Duensing, perhaps should be*: put it away from himself). Likewise every man is given the ability to believe in the light;[193] this is the life[194] of the Father who sent me. And whoever has believed in me will live,[196] if he has done the work of light. But if he does not acknowledge (*Paris Nos. 51 and 199 without* 'not') that there is the light and does what is (characteristic) of darkness, then he has neither anything that he can say in defence nor will he be able to raise his face and look at the son, which (Son) I am. And I will say to him, 'You have sought and found, have asked and received.[199] What do you blame us for? (*Other MSS*: Why do you not understand us?). Why did

also will be with me eternally.[189] But woe to those who walk in pride and boasting, for *their end is destruction.*'[190]

But we said to him, 'O Lord, what is yours is this, that you do not let us come upon them.' But he answered and said to us, 'How will the judgment come about? Either of the righteous or of the unrighteous?'[191] But we said to him, 'O Lord, in that day they will say to you, 'You did not pursue righteousness and unrighteousness, light and darkness, evil and good.'' Then he said, 'I will answer them saying, 'Adam was given the power to choose one of the two.[192] He chose the light and put his hand upon it; but he forsook the darkness and cast it from him. So have all men the power to believe in the light[193] which is life[194] and which is the Father[195] who sent me.' But everyone who believes (and) does the works of light will live in them.[196] But if there is someone who acknowledges that he is reckoned to the light, while he does the works of darkness[197] - such a one has no defence to make, nor will he be able to lift up his face to (look at the) son of God, which (Son) I am.[198] I will say to him, 'As you sought you have found, and as you asked you have received.[199] In what do you condemn me, O man? Why did you leave me and deny me? Why did you acknowledge me and (yet) deny me?[200] Does not every man have the power to live or to die?'

you withdraw (from me and) from my kingdom? You have acknowledged me and (yet) denied.'[200] Now therefore see that each one is able to live as well as to die (*Other MSS*: to believe). And whoever does my commandment and keeps it[201] will be a son of the light,[202] i.e. of my Father. And for those who keep and do (it), for their sake I came down from heaven; I, the Word, became flesh[204] and died, teaching and guiding, that some shall be saved, but the others eternally ruined, being punished by fire in flesh and spirit.'

Now whoever has kept my commandments[201] will be a son of light,[202] i.e. of the Father who is in me.[203] But on account of those who pervert my words I have come down from heaven. I am the Logos; I became flesh,[204] labouring and teaching that those who are called will be saved,[205] and the lost will be lost eternally. They will be tormented alive and will be scourged in their flesh and in their soul.'

40. And we said to him, 'O Lord, we are truly troubled on their account.' And he said to us, 'You do well, for so are the righteous anxious about the sinners, and they pray and implore God and ask him.' And we said to him, 'O Lord, does no one entreat you?' And he said to us, 'Yes, I will hear the requests of the righteous concerning them.'[206] And we said to him, 'O Lord, all this you have taught us, and have stimulated us and have proved gracious toward us. And we will preach it to those to whom it is fitting. But will there be for us a reward with you?'[207]

But we said to him, 'O Lord, truly we are anxious on their account.' But he said to us, 'You do well, for the righteous are anxious about the sinners, and pray for them, asking my Father.' Again we said to him, 'O Lord, now why is no one afraid of you?' But he said to us, 'Yes, I will hear the prayer of the righteous that they make for them.'[206] But when he had said this to us, we said to him, 'O Lord, in all things you have taught us [. . .]and pitied us and saved us, that we may preach to those who are worthy to be saved, and shall we earn a reward with you?'[207]

41. And he said to us, 'Go and preach and be good ministers and servants.' And we said to him, 'O Lord, you are our father.'[209] And he said to us, 'Are all fathers and all servants, all teachers?' And we said to him, 'O Lord did you not say, 'Do not call (anyone) on earth father and master, for one is your

But he answered and said to us, 'Go, and preach; thus you will become workers[208] . . . and servants.' But we said to him, 'You it is who will preach through us.' Then he answered us saying, 'Do not be all him, 'O Lord, it is you who said, 'Do not call (anyone) father upon earth, for one is your father who is father and teacher, he who is in heaven'?[210] Now you say to us that we should like you become fathers to many children[211] and also teachers and servants.' And he answered and said to us. 'You have rightly said. Truly I say to you, all who have listened to you and have believed in me will receive the light of the seal that is in my hand, and through me you will become fathers and teachers.'

42. And we said to him, 'O Lord, how is it possible for these three to be in one?' And he answered and said to us, 'Truly, truly I say to you, you will be called fathers, for you, full of love and compassion, have revealed to them what (is) in heaven (. . . for) by my hand they will receive the baptism of life and forgiveness of sin.[212] And teachers, for you have delivered to them my word without anguish and have warned them and they have turned back in the things for which you rebuked them. And you were not afraid of their riches and did not respect the face (*or*, the person), but you kept the commandment of the Father and did it. And you have a reward with my heavenly Father;[213] and they shall have forgiveness of sins and eternal life and a share of the kingdom.' And we said to him, 'O Lord, if they had a ten-thousandfold mouth[214] they would not be able to give thanks to you as it is fitting.' And he answered and said to us, 'I say this to you that you may do as I have done to you;[21]

in heaven[210] and your master.' Why do you now say to us, 'You will be fathers of many children[211] and servants and masters'?' But he answered and said to us, 'As you have said. For truly I say to you, whoever will hear you and believe in me, he will receive from you the light of the seal through (me) and baptism through me; you will become fathers and servants and also masters.'

But we said to him, 'O Lord, how now (is it possible) that each one of us should become these three?' But he said to us, 'Truly I say to you, you will first of all be called fathers, for you have revealed to them with seemly hearts and in love the things of the kindom of heaven. And you will be called servants, for they will receive by my hand through you the baptism of life and the forgiveness of their sins.[212] And you will be called masters, for you have given them the word (*logos*) without grudging. You have warned them, and when you warned them they turned back. You were not afraid of their riches and of their face, but you kept the commandments of my Father and performed them. And you will have a great reward with my Father[213] who is in heaven, and they shall have forgiveness of sins and eternal life, and will have a part in the kingdom of heaven.' But we said to him, 'O Lord, even if each one of us had ten thousand tongues[214] to speak with, we would not be able to give thanks to you, for you promise us such things'. Then he answered, saying, 'Only do what I

43. and be as the wise virgins who kindled the light and did not slumber and who went with their lamps to meet the lord, the bridegroom, and have gone in with him into the bridegroom's chamber. But the foolish ones who talked with them were not able to watch, but fell asleep.'[216] And we said to him, 'O Lord, who are the wise and who the foolish?' And he said to us, 'The wise are these five, who are called by the prophet daughters of God,[217] whose names let men hear.' But we were sad and troubled and wept for those who had been shut out. And he said to us, 'The five wise are these: Faith, Love, Joy, Peace, Hope. As soon as they who believe in me have these, they will be leaders[218] to those who believe in me and in him who sent me. I am the Lord and I am the bridegroom; they have received me and have gone with me into the house of the bridegroom, and laid themselves down (at table) with the bridegroom and rejoiced. But the five foolish slept, and when they awoke they came to the house of the bridegroom and knocked at the doors, for they had been shut; and they wept, because they were shut.'[219] And we said to him, 'O Lord, now these their wise sisters who (are) in the house - do they not open to them and are they not sorrowful on their account?' And he said to us, 'Yes they are sorrowful and concerned on their account and entreat the bridegroom and yet are not able to, obtain (anything) on

say to you, as I myself have also done, and you will be like the wise virgins who watched and did not sleep, but (went) out to the lord into the bride-chamber. But the foolish were not able to watch, but fell asleep'.[216] But we said to him, 'O Lord, who are the wise and who are the foolish?' He said to us, 'Five wise and five foolish, these with respect to whom the prophet said, 'They are children of God.'[217] Now hear their names.' But we wept and were sad about those who had fallen asleep. He said to us, 'The five wise are Faith and Love and Grace, Peace and Hope. Among those who believe they who have these will be guides[218] to those who have believed in me and in him who sent me. I am the Lord and I am the bridegroom whom they have received, and they have gone into the house of the bridegroom and have laid themselves down with me in my bridechamber (and rejoiced). But the five foolish slept, they awoke, came to the door of the bridechamber and knocked, for it had been shut.[219] Then they wept and grieved that it was not opened for them.' But we said to him, 'O Lord, and their wise sisters who were within in the house of the bridegroom, did they remain in there without opening to them, and did they not grieve on their account or did they not pray the bridegroom to open to them?' He answered saying, 'They were not

their account.' And we said
to him, 'O Lord, when will they
go in for their sisters' sakes?'
And he said to us, 'Whoever is shut
out is shut out.' And we said
to him, 'O Lord, is this thing
definite? Who now are these
foolish ones?' And he said to
us, 'Listen: Insight, Knowledge,
Obedience, Endurance, Mercy.
These have slept in those who
have believed and acknowledged
me.

44. And since those who slept
did not fulfil my commandment,
they will be outside the kingdom
and the fold of the shepherd;[220] and
whoever remains outside the fold
will the wolf eat.[221] And although
he hears he will be judged (*only in
Paris No. 199*) and will die, and
much suffering and distress and
endurance will come upon him; and
although he is badly pained and
although he is cut into pieces and
lacerated with long and painful
punishment, yet he will not be able
to die quickly.'

45. And we said to him, 'O Lord,
you have revealed everything
to us well.' And he said to us,
'Understand and apprehend these
words.'[223] And we said to him, 'O
Lord, these five it is through which
they (*fem.*) have the expectation of
going into your kingdom; and five
who are shut out, through which
they will be outside your kingdom.
Yet they who have watched and
who have gone in with the Lord,
the bridegroom, will not rejoice

yet able to find grace on their
behalf.' We said to him, 'O Lord,
on what day will they go in for
their sisters' sakes?' Then he said
to us, 'Whoever is shut out is shut
out.' But we said to him, 'O Lord,
(we have understood this word.)
Now who are the foolish?' He said
to us, 'Hear their names. They are
Knowledge (Gnosis) and Wisdom,
Obedience, Forbearance and
Mercy.
These are they which slept in
those who have believed and acknowledged me.
But my commandments were not
fulfilled by those who slept. Consequently they will remain outside
the kingdom and the fold of the
shepherd and his sheep.[220] But
whoever remains outside the fold
of the sheep will the wolves eat,[221]
and he will (be judged?), dying in
much suffering. Rest (?) and perseverance will not be in him, and he
will be (badly?) tormented that he
. . . ; and he will be punished (?) in
great punishment (?), and he will
be under tortures.'[222]

But we said to him, 'O Lord,
you have revealed everything
to us well.' Then he answered
saying to us, 'Do you not
apprehend these words?' We said
to him, 'Yes, O Lord; through
the five will they come into
your kingdom.

Yet they who watched and
were with you, the Lord and
bridegroom, will nevertheless not

because of those who slept'. And he said to us, 'They will rejoice that they have gone in with the Lord, and will be grieved on account of those who slept; for they are their sisters. And these daughters of God are ten.' And we said to him, 'O Lord, it suits your greatness that you show grace to their sisters.' And he said to us, 'This thing is not yours, but his who sent me, and I also agree with him.

46. But you, as you go, preach and teach truly and rightly, respecting and fearing the person of no one, but especially (not) that of the rich, of whom it will be found, that they do not do my commandment,[224] who revel in their riches.'[225] And we said to him, 'O Lord, do you speak to us only of the rich?' And he said to us, 'Also of him who is not rich; as soon as he gives and does not deny to him who has nothing, of such a one (I say this:) he will be called by men a doer.

47. But if someone should fall bearing his burden, i.e. the sin he has committed against the person of his neighbour, then his neighbour should admonish him because of what he has done to his neighbour. And when his neighbour has admonished him and he has returned, then he will be saved,[226] and he who has admonished him will obtain eternal life. But if (he sees) how this one who renders him (something) sins, and encourages him, such a one will be judged in a great judgment. *For a blind man*

rejoice because of those who slept.' He said to us, 'They (will rejoice) that they have gone in with the bridegroom, the Lord; and they are troubled on account of those who slept, for they are their sisters. The ten are the daughters of God the Father.' We then said to him, 'O Lord, it is yours that you ... ' He said to us, ' ... , but his who sent me, and I agree with him.

But you preach and teach in uprightness (and) well, hesitating before no one and fearing no one, but especially (not) the rich, for they do not do my commandments,[224] but flourish in their riches.'[225] But we said to him, 'O Lord, if (it) is the rich (alone)?' He answered saying ('If) anyone who is not rich and possesses a (little) property gives to the needy (and to the poor), then men will call him a benefactor.

But if someone should fall under the load because of the sins he has committed, (then let) his neighbour admonish him for (the good) that he has done to his neighbour. Now if his neighbour has admonished him and he returns he will be saved;[226] (and) he who admonished him will receive a reward and live for ever. For a needy man, if he sees someone sinning who has done him good, and does not admonish him, then he will be judged in an evil judgment. *But a blind man who leads a blind man, who leads a blind man, both will fall into a ditch.*[227] Even so the one who encourages, who respects the person, and also the one whom he encourages and whose person he respects, will both be punished with *one* punishment, as the prophet said, 'Woe to those who encourage, who speak fair to the sinner for the sake of a bribe,[228] *whose God is* their *belly.*'[229] You see how the judgment is? Truly I say to you, in that day I will not fear the rich and will have no pity for the poor.

both are wont to fall into a ditch.[227] And whoever regards the person for (their) sake, (he will be like) the two, as the prophet said, 'Woe to those who regard the person and *(justify the ungodly) for the sake of gifts,*[228] *whose (God is) their belly.*'[229] See now that a judgment (is appointed for them.) For truly I say to you, in that day I will neither fear the rich nor have sympathy with the poor.

48. If you have seen with your eyes how (someone) sins, then correct him, you alone (*or*, under four eyes). *If he listens to you, then you have won* him. *But if he does not listen* to you, then come out with one or at the most two others; correct your brother. But if he (even then) does not listen to you, *so shall he be to you as a gentile and a tax-collector.*[230]

If you see a sinner, then *admonish him between yourself and him. But if he does not listen* to you, *then take with you* another up to three and instruct your brother. If he will not listen to you again, then set him before you as . . . '[230]

(Here the Coptic text breaks off.)

49. If you hear something, then do not give any belief against your brother and do not slander and do not love to listen to slander. For it is written, 'Let your ear listen to nothing against your brother, but (only) if you have seen, censure, correct, and convert him.'' And we said to him, 'Lord, you have taught and exhorted us in everything. But, Lord, among the believers who among them believe in the preaching of your name should there be dissension and dispute and envy and confusion and hatred and distress? For you have nevertheless said, 'They will find fault with one another and have not regarded the person (*or*, without regarding the person).' Do these sin who hate the one who has corrected them?' And he answered and said to us, 'Now why will the judgment take place? That *the wheat may be put in its barn and* its *chaff* thrown into the fire.[231]

50. . . . who thus hate, and he who loves me and finds fault with those who do not do my commandments,[232] these will thus be hated and persecuted, and men will despise and mock (them). They will also deliberately say what is not (true), and there will come a conspiracy against those who love me. But these will rebuke them that they may be

saved. And those who will find fault with them and correct and exhort them will be hated and set apart and despised; and those who wish (to) do good to them will be prevented (from it). But those who have endured this will rank as martyrs with the Father, for they were zealous concerning righteousness and were not zealous with corruptible zeal.' And we said to him, 'Will such, Lord, also happen in our midst?' And he said to us, 'Do not fear what will happen not with many but (only) with few.' And we said to him, 'Tell us in what way.' And he said to us, 'There will come another teaching and a conflict;[233] and in that they seek their own glory[234] and produce worthless teaching an offence of death will come thereby, and they will teach and turn away from my commandment even those who believe in me and bring them out of eternal life. But woe to those who use my word and my commandment for a pretext,[235] and also to those who listen to them and to those who turn away from the life of the teaching, to those who turn away from the commandment of life (*this last clause not in Paris Nos. 51, 90 and 199*), they will be eternally punished with them.'

51. And after he had said this and had ended the discourse with us, he said again to us, 'Look. After three days and three hours he who sent me will come that I may go with him.' And as he spoke there was thunder and lightning and an earthquake, and the heavens divided and a bright *cloud came and took him away.*[236] And (we heard; *only in Paris No. 199*) the voice of many angels as they rejoiced and praised and said, 'Assemble us, O priest,[237] in the light of glory.' And when he (*Paris No. 51, 199 and Stuttgart Cod. Orient. fol. No. 49:* they) had come near to the firmament of heaven, we heard him say, '*Go in peace.*'[238]

Notes

3. Epistula Apostolorum

1. The translation rests on a careful revision of that prepared by Hugo Duensing for the previous edition. So far as they are not specially marked, words in brackets in the Ethiopic part are to facilitate understanding. In the Coptic part, restorations which are not quite certain have been placed in brackets. Where restorations of the lacunae are certain, they are not marked as such. Certain roughnesses in the original text have been retained in the translation.
2. Acts 15:7.
3. Cf. 1 Jn. 1:1.
4. On the list of apostles, cf. the *Apostolic Church Order*, where Peter and Cephas are regarded as different disciples.
5. 1 Jn. 1:1; Jn. 20:27.
6. Eph. 1:21.
7. 1 Tim. 6:15; Rev. 17:14; 19:16.
8. Dan. 3:54 LXX.
9. Cf. Mt. 22:24; 26:64; Mk. 16:19; Acts 2:33; Heb. 1:3; 8:1; 12:2.
10. Job 38:10f.; 1 Clem. 20.6f.
11. Gen. 1:14; 1 Clem. 20.2f.
12. Gen. 1:26f.
13. Cf. Hebr. 1:1.
14. Jn. 1:14.
15. Cf. Jn. 1:13.
16. Lk. 2:7.
17. Infancy Gospel of Thomas 6.3 (see below, p. 445); 14.2 (see below, p. 447); Pseudo-Mt. Infancy Gospel 7, 38. 1.
18. Jn. 2:1ff.
19. Brothers: cf. Jn. 2:12.
20. Lk. 7:14f.; 8:49ff.; Mk. 5:35ff.; Jn. 11:39ff.; Mk. 2:3ff.; Mt. 9:2ff.
21. Mt. 12:10ff.; Mk. 3:3ff.
22. Mt. 9:20ff.; Mk. 5:25ff.; Lk. 8:43ff.
23. Mt. 11:4f.; 15:30; Lk. 7:22; Mt. 9:32f.; Mk. 7:32ff.; 8:22ff.; Jn. 9:1ff.; Mt. 4:24; 8:16; Mk. 1:34.
24. Mt. 8:2f.; Mk. 1:40ff.; Lk. 5:12ff.
25. Mk. 5:1-20; Lk. 8:26-39.
26. Mt. 14:23ff.; Mk. 6:47ff. in connection with Mk. 4:35ff. and par.
27. Mt. 17:24ff.
28. Mt. 14:17ff.; Mk. 6:38ff.; Jn. 6:9ff.
29. Cf. Ignatius, *Trall.* 7.1; *Smyrn.* 7.2; *Trall.* 11.1.
30. Mt. 27:38; Mk. 15:27; Jn. 19:18.
31. Mt. 27:33; Mk. 15:22; Lk. 23:33; Jn. 19:17.
32. Mk. 16:1; Lk. 24:1.
33. Mk. 16:10.
34. Jn. 20:11; Gospel of Peter 55.
35. Lk. 24:2; Mk. 16:4.
36. Lk. 24:3.

37. Jn. 20:14f.; Mk. 16:6.
38. Cf. Jn. 20:15 (18:4).
39. Mt. 28:7.
40. Mt. 28:10; Jn. 20:17.
41. Mk. 16:11ff.; Lk. 24:11-41.
42. Jn. 20:19, 26; Mk. 16:14.
43. Cf. Lk. 24:37, 39.
44. Mt. 28:10.
45. Mt. 26:34, 69ff. and par.
46. Mt. 28:17 (14:31).
47. Jn. 20:27; Mk. 16:14.
48. Cf. Jn. 20:20, 27.
49. Cf. Commodian (probably 3rd cent.): *Carmen apologeticum* V. 564, ed. B. Dombart, CSEL 15, 1887, p. 152: *Vestigium umbra non facit* (a shadow does not make a mark); cf. also Acts of John c. 93.
50. Lk. 24:39; 1 Jn. 1:1; Ignatius, *Smyrn.* 3.2.
51. 2 Clem. 5.5; 6.7.
52. Jn. 12:32.
53. On the following cf. Ascension of Isaiah 10.7ff.
54. Rev. 8:3f.
55. Gen. 1:11, 26/27 is echoed here.
56. Col. 1:25; Eph. 1:10.
57. Jn. 14:12, 28.
58. Lk. 1:26ff.
59. Cf. Reitzenstein, *Zwei religionsgeschichtliche Fragen*, pp. 119ff.
60. Laughed: *Orac. Sibyll.* VIII 466ff.
61. Jn. 1:14.
62. Servant: Pistis Sophia 344. 24 and 403 s.v. (Schmidt-Till, *Koptisch-gnostische Schriften* I, Berlin [3]1962; ET by G. Horner, London 1924 p. 61, 4 lines from bottom).
63. 1 Cor. 11:26.
64. Acts. 12:3ff.; Lk. 21:12; Rev. 2:3; cf. Jn. 15:21.
65. Lk. 22:19; 1 Cor. 11:24f.
66. Mk. 13:35.
67. Testimony: Mk. 13:9.
68. Mt. 26:27f.; Mk. 14:23; 1 Cor. 11:25.
69. Rev. 6:9; 20:4; Didache 16:7; Apoc. Elias 43:10, ed. Steindorff, TU NF 2.3a, 1899, p. 105.
70. Apocalypse of Peter 1.
71. Apoc. Elias 87.32; Apocalypse of Peter 1; cf. Gospel of Peter 10 (39).
72. Acts 10:42; 1 Pet. 4:5; 2 Tim. 4:1.
73. Jn. 10:38; 14:10, 11-20; 17:21, 22, 23; Cf. Acts of John c. 100.
74. Cf. Gen. 1:11, 26/27.
75. Jn. 1:1.
76. Barnabas 15.8; Justin, *Dial.* cc. 24, 41, 138; Clement of Alexandria, *Exc. ex Theod.* 63.1; *Strom.* VII 57.5 and V 106.2-4.
77. Mt. 7:21 *et passim*.
78. Jn. 13:34.
79. Mt. 5:44; Lk. 6:27, 35; Tob. 4:15; Acts 15:20, 29 Cod. D; Didache 1:2; *Apostolic Constitutions* VII 1, ed. Lagarde, p. 193; *Didascaliae Apostolorum Fragmenta Veronensia Latina*, ed. Hauler, p. 3: II, line 12f., note *ad loc.*

80. 'Heavenly' not in all MSS.
81. Lk. 9:2.
82. Mt. 28:18ff.
83. Cf. Rom. 8:17.
84. Cf. 1 Peter 1:12.
85. Synoptic introductory formula.
86. Cf. Jn. 14:20; 15:4f.
87. Cf. Gen. 1:11, 26/27.
88. Cf. Lk. 24:44f.
89. Ps. 3:1-8.
90. Cf. Hebr. 1:1 and 1 Pet. 1:10f.
91. Cf. Jn. 13:31f.
92. Cf. Jn. 5:21; 2 Clem. 9.5.
93. Ignatius, *Eph.* 7.2.
94. 2 Clem. 9.5.
95. Jn. 5:24.
96. Cf. Mt. 28:18.
97. 1 Pet. 2:9; Cf. Odes of Solomon 21.3 and 42.16, ed. Michael Lattke (= Orbis Biblicus et Orientalis 25, 1979/80).
98. Mt. 19:26 and par.
99. Acts of Paul and Thecla c. 37; Liturgy of Mark (in Brightman, *Liturgies*, p. 124, lines 2ff.).
100. Cf. 1 Thess. 5:23.
101. Cf. 2 Clem. 9.1.
102. Cf. Mt. 6:30; 8:26; 14:31; 16:8.
103. *Ibid.*
104. Jn. 14:15; 21; 15:10.
105. Cf. Rom. 2:11; Eph. 6:9; Col. 3:25; Jas. 2:1; Lk. 20:21.
106. Mt. 7:14; Lk. 13:24.
107. Cf. Jn. 14:10.
108. Cf. 2 Cor. 5:10.
109. Cf. 1 Thess. 1:4; 2 Pet. 1:10.
110. Mt. 10:15; 11:22, 24; 2 Pet. 2:9; 3:7; 1 Jn. 4:17; Jude 6.
111. Cf. Mt. 25:46.
112. Cf. 2 Clem. 5.5; 6.7.
113. In this sentence the text has fallen into disorder. Something has evidently dropped out.
114. Cf. Lk. 16:23.
115. Cf. 1 Pet. 3:19.
116. Cf. Barnabas 11.1.
117. Cf. 1 Jn. 2:4.
118. Cf. Gal. 2:2; Phil. 2:16.
119. Archons: cf. 1 Cor. 2:6, 8.
120. Mt. 3:10; Lk. 3:17 and often elsewhere.
121. Cf. Jn. 5:24; 12:44.
122. Mt. 24:22, 24, 31; Mk. 13:20.
123. Cf. 2 Clem. 5.5; 6.7.
124. Jn. 10:28; 17:2.
125. Mt. 25:46.
126. 1 Cor. 11:19; 1 Jn. 2:19; Lk. 17:1.

127. Rom. 2:6.
128. Mt. 13:16f.
129. Cf. Jn. 20:29.
130. Cf. Mt. 13:38.
131. Cf. Mt. 5:48.
132. Mt. 26:29.
133. Cf. Jn. 5:25, 28; 16:25, 32.
134. *Ibid.*.
135. Jn. 16:10, 17 etc.
136. Cf. Mt. 28:19; Mk. 16:15.
137. Mt. 19:28; Lk. 22:30; Acts 26:7; Jas. 1:1; Rev. 21:12.
138. Lk. 13:29; Mk. 16 (second ending).
139. Cf. Jn. 9:35; 12:37.
140. Acts 2:22; 2 Cor. 12:12; 2 Thess. 2:9; Hebr. 2:4.
141. Jn. 14:27; 20:21, 22; Acts 1:8; 2:17f.
142. Acts 13:9.
143. Acts 21:39; 22:3.
144. Phil. 3:5.
145. Acts 9:4; 22:7; 26:14.
146. Acts 9:8f.; 22:11.
147. Here the thought is probably of the blinded Paul's journey to Damascus; Acts 9:6,8.
148. Acts 9:18.
149. Acts 9:15; 1 Clem. 5.7.
150. Acts 9:5; 22:7f.; 26:14f.; Gal. 1:13; 1 Cor. 15:9.
151. Acts 9:15. Cf. Harnack, *Der apokryphe Brief des Paulusschülers Titus*, 'De dispositione sanctimonii', SB Berlin 1925, p. 198; *vas electionis - inexpugnabilis murus.* Cf. Jer. 1:18; 15:20.
152. Gal. 1:16; 2:8f.; Acts 26:17.
153. 1 Jn. 1:1.
154. Jn. 10:38; 14:20.
155. Acts 13:47; 26:18; 28:28.
156. Cf. Eph. 3:6; Acts 26:6.
157. Acts 21:39; 22:3; 23:34.
158. Acts 9:2; 22:5; 26:12 and often elsewhere.
159. Gal. 1:13, 23.
160. Jn. 12:38 and often elsewhere.
161. Source unknown. Cf. Rev. 3:12; 21:2-10; Hebr. 12:22; Gal. 4:26 (probably very free).
162. Cf. Gal. 4:27; Isa. 54:1.
163. Acts 9:4; 22:6f.; 26:14.
164. Cf. Mt. 24; Mk. 13; Lk. 21.
165. Cf. Jn. 17:20.
166. Cf. Rev. 6:13; 8:10; 9:1.
167. Cf. Rev. 8:7; 11:19; 16:21.
168. Cf. Rev. 8:5; 11:19; 16:18.
169. Rev. 11:13; 16:19.
170. *Testament*, ed. Guerrier, PO IX, 40.
171. *Ibid.*
172. Cf. Lk. 24:25.
173. Cf. Acts 13:10.

174. Ps. 13:3 LXX.
175. Ps. 49:19b LXX.
176. Ps. 49:18 LXX.
177. Ps. 49:20 LXX.
178. Ps. 49:21b LXX.
179. Ps. 78:10 LXX.
180. Exit: cf. Wisdom of Solomon 3:2.
181. Cf. Jas. 1:3; 1 Pet. 1:7.
182. Jn. 14:15; 15:10.
183. Cf. Jn. 13:31f.; 14:13.
184. Cf. 1 Jn. 2:4.
185. Cf. Jn. 14:23.
186. Cf. Lk. 21:10f.
187. Cf. Acts 23:1; Phil. 1:27; 2 Jn. 4; 3 Jn. 4; 1 Tim. 2:7.
188. Lk. 6:22-27; Jn. 15:18; 1 Jn. 3:13; Mt. 5:11.
189. Cf. 1 Thess. 4:17.
190. Cf. Phil. 3:19.
191. Cf. Acts 24:15.
192. Cf. Ecclus. 15:16ff.
193. Jn. 12:36.
194. Cf. Jn. 1:4.
195. Cf. 1 Jn. 1:5.
196. Cf. Gal. 3:12; Rom. 10:5.
197. Cf. Rom. 13:12; Eph. 5:11.
198. Cf. Jn. 10:36.
199. Cf. Mt. 7:7; Lk. 11:9f.
200. Cf. Tit. 1:16.
201. Cf. Jn. 14:15 and frequently.
202. Lk. 16:8; Jn. 12:36; Eph. 5:8; 1 Thess. 5:5.
203. Jn. 10:38; 14:10, 11, 20; 17:21, 22, 23; cf. Acts of John 100.
204. Cf. Jn. 1:14.
205. Mt. 22:8; Lk. 14:24; Rev. 17:14.
206. Cf. Jas. 5:16.
207. Cf. Mt. 5:12 and frequently.
208. Mt. 9:37 and frequently.
209. Cf. Jn. 12:26.
210. Mt. 23:8f.
211. Cf. 1 Cor. 4:15.
212. Cf. Barn. 11.1.
213. Cf. Mt. 5:12; Lk. 6:23; Mt. 10:41f.
214. Cf. Theoph. *ad Autol.* 2.12.
215. Cf. Jn. 13:15.
216. Mt. 25:1ff.
217. Cf. Ps. 81:6 LXX.
218. Cf. Mt. 15:14; 23:24.
219. Mt. 25:10.
220. Jn. 10:1f.
221. Cf. Mt. 7:15; 10:16; Jn. 10:12; Acts 20:29.
222. Cf. Rev. 14:10f.
223. Cf. Mk. 8:17.

224. Cf. Mt. 19:23f. and par.; Lk. 6:24; 18:24; 12:15f.; Jas. 1:10f.; 2:1f.; Hermas, *Sim.* 9.20.
225. Cf. Hermas, *Vis.* I 1.8; III 9.6.
226. Cf. Jas. 5:19f.
227. Mt. 15:14; Lk. 6:39.
228. Cf. Isa. 5:23.
229. Phil. 3:19.
230. Mt. 18:15f.
231. Cf. Lk. 3:17; Mt. 3:12; 13:30.
232. Cf. Mt. 5:11; 10:22.
233. Cf. Rom. 16:17.
234. Cf. Jn. 7:18.
235. Mt. 24:5ff.; Rom. 16:18.
236. Acts 1:9.
237. Cf. Hebr. 8:1; 10:11-12; 1 Clem. 36.1.
238. Mk. 5:34; Acts 16:36; Jas. 2:16.

4. The Apocryphon of James

Dankwart Kirchner
(translated by Einar Thomassen)

Introduction

1. Bibliography: *Facsimile: Epistula Iacobi Apocrypha: Codex Jung F.I*^r *- F. VIII*^v *(p. 1-16)*, ed. M. Malinine, H.-Ch. Puech, G. Quispel, W. Till, R. Kasser, R. McL. Wilson and J. Zandee, Zürich-Stuttgart 1968. *The Facsimile Edition of the Nag Hammadi Codices* published under the Auspices of the Department of Antiquities of the Arab Republic of Egypt in Conjunction with the United Nations Educational, Scientific and Cultural Organization, Codex I, Leiden 1977, pl. 5-20.

Editions: Epistula Iacobi Apocrypha: Codex Jung F.I^r *- F. VIII*^v *(p. 1-16)*, ed. M. Malinine *et. al.* (see above, *Facsimile*). D. Kirchner, *Epistula Jacobi Apocrypha: Die erste Schrift aus Nag-Hammadi-Codex I (Codex Jung), neu herausgegeben und kommentiert*, (TU 136), 1989. F.E. Williams, 'The Apocryphon of James: I, 2:1.1-16.30', in *Nag Hammadi Codex I (The Jung Codex): Introductions, Texts, Translations, Indices*, volume ed. H.W. Attridge, (NHS 22), Leiden 1985, 13-53. D. Rouleau, *L'Épître apocryphe de Jacques*, (BCNH, Section 'Textes' 18), Québec 1987.

Translations: Epistula Iacobi Apocrypha: Codex Jung F.I^r *- F. VIII*^v *(p. 1-16)*, ed. M. Malinine *et al.* (see above, *Facsimile*). H.-M. Schenke, 'Der Jakobusbrief aus dem Codex Jung', OLZ 66, 1971, 117-130. D. Kirchner, *Epistula Jacobi Apocrypha* (see above, *Editions*). F.E. Williams, 'The Apocryphon of James', in J.M. Robinson (ed.), *The Nag Hammadi Library in English*, San Francisco 1977, pp. 29-36 (3rd rev. ed. 1988, pp. 29-37). R. Cameron, *The Other Gospels: Non-Canonical Gospel Texts*, Philadelphia 1982, pp. 55-64. M.W. Meyer, *The Secret Teachings of Jesus*, New York 1984, pp. 3-15. F.E. Williams, 'The Apocryphon of James: I,2:1.1-16.30' (see above, *Editions*).

Further select Bibliography (for a complete bibliography cf. D.M. Scholer, *Nag Hammadi Bibliography 1948-1969*, NHS I, Leiden 1971, and the annual supplement 'Bibliographia Gnostica' in *Novum Testamentum* from vol. 13, 1971). S.K. Brown, *James: A Religio-Historical Study of the Relations between Jewish, Gnostic and Catholic Christianity in the Early Period Through an Investigation of the Traditions about James the Lord's Brother*, Ph.D. diss., Brown University, 1972. R. Cameron, *Sayings Traditions in the Apocryphon of James*, (Harvard Theological Studies 34), Philadelphia 1984. C. Colpe, 'Heidnische, jüdische und christliche Überlieferung in den Schriften aus Nag Hammadi VII', JAC 21, 1978, 125-146, esp. pp. 127-131. C. Gianotto, 'La letteratura apocrifa attribuita a Giacomo a Nag Hammadi (NHC I, 2; V,3: V,4)', *Augustinianum* 23, 1983, 111-121. E. Haenchen, 'Literatur zum Codex Jung', ThR, N.F. 30, 1964, 39-82, esp. pp. 45-47. Ch. W. Hedrick, 'Kingdom Sayings and Parables of Jesus in the Apocryphon of James', NTS 29, 1983, 1-24. J. Helderman, 'Anapausis in the Epistula Jacobi Apocrypha', in R. McL. Wilson (ed.), *Nag Hammadi and Gnosis*, (NHS 14), Leiden 1978, pp. 34-43. Y. Janssens, 'Traits de la Passion dans l'Epistula Jacobi Apocrypha', *Le Muséon* 88, 1975, 97-101. K. Kipgen, *Gnosticism in Early Christianity: A Study of the Epistula Iacobi Apocrypha with Particular Reference to Salvation*, D.Phil. diss., Oxford University 1975. D. Kirchner, *Epistula Jacobi Apocrypha* (see above, *Editions*). D. Kirchner, 'Zum Menschenbild in der Epistula Jacobi Apocrypha', in P. Nagel (ed.), *Studien zum Menschenbild in Gnosis und Manichäismus*, Martin-Luther-Universität Halle-Wittenbert, Wissenschaftliche Beiträge 1979/39 (K 5), Halle 1979, pp. 139-145. H. Koester, 'Dialog und Spruchüberlieferung in den gnostischen Texten von Nag Hammadi', *Ev.Th.* 39, 1979, 532-556. H. Koester, 'Apocryphal and Canonical Gospels', HTR 73, 1980, 105-130. H. Koester, 'Formgeschichte/Formenkritik II. Neues Testament', TRE XI, 286-299, esp. pp. 292-296. H. Koester, 'Überlieferung und Geschichte der frühchristlichen Evangelienliteratur', in W. Haase (ed.), ANRW, Principat 25.2, 1984, 1463-1542, esp. pp. 1495-1521. A. Orbe, *Los primeros herejes ante la persecución*, Estudios Valentinianos 5, *Analecta Gregoriana* LXXXIII, Rome 1956, 286-290. P. Perkins, *The Gnostic Dialogue*, New York 1980. P. Perkins, 'Johannine Traditions in *Ap. Jas.* (NHC I,2)', JBL 101, 1982, 403-414. W. Pratscher, *Der Herrenbruder Jakobus und die Jakobustradition*, (FRLANT 139), Göttingen 1987. H.-Ch. Puech/G. Quispel, 'Les écrits gnostiques du Codex Jung', *Vig.Chr.* 8, 1954, 1-51, esp. pp. 7-22. H.-Ch. Puech/G. Quispel/W.C. van Unnik, *The Jung Codex*, London 1955. H.-Ch. Puech, 'The Apocryphon of James (Apocryphon Jacobi)', in NTApo³, I, 333-338. D. Rouleau, 'Les paraboles du Royaume des cieux dans l'Epître apocryphe de Jacques', in B. Barc (ed.), *Colloque international sur les textes de Nag Hammadi*, (BCNH, Section 'Études' 1), Québec 1981, pp. 181-190. K. Rudolph, 'Gnosis und Gnostizismus: Ein Forschungsbericht', ThR, N.F. 34, 1969, 121-175, esp. pp. 169-175. H.-M. Schenke, 'Der Jakobusbrief aus dem Codex Jung', OLZ 66, 1971, 117-130. C. Scholten, *Martyrium und Sophiamythos im Gnostizismus nach den Texten von Nag Hammadi*, (JAC, Erg.-Bd. 14), 1987. J.-M. Sevrin, 'Paroles et paraboles de Jésus dans des écrits gnostiques coptes', in J. Delobel (ed.), *Logia: Les paroles de Jésus - the sayings of Jesus*, (Bibliotheca Ephemeridum Theologicarum Lovaniensium 59), Louvain 1982, pp. 517-528. W.C. van Unnik, 'The Origin of the Recently Discovered 'Apocryphon Jacobi'', *Vig. Chr.* 10, 1956, 149-156. W.C. van Unnik, *Evangelien aus dem Nilsand*, Frankfurt 1960, (*Newly Discovered Gnostic Documents* (SCM Studies in Biblical Theology 30), London 1960). F.E. Williams, 'The Apocryphon of James. I,2:1.1-16.30', in *Nag Hammadi Codex I (The Jung Codex): Notes*, volume ed. H.W. Attridge, (NHS 23), Leiden 1985, pp. 7-37. J. Zandee, 'Gnostische trekken in een apocryphe brief van Jacobus', *NedThT* 17, 1963, 401-422. Also used was a report on D. Kirchner, *Epistula Iacobi Apocrypha* (see above, *Editions*) by A. Böhlig, containing suggestions on the text and its interpretation.

2. Transmission: the Apocryphon of James (Ap. Jas.) from Nag Hammadi Codex I (the Jung Codex) is a document transmitted to us in the Subachmimic Coptic dialect and the existence of which is never alluded to in early Christian literature. It was originally considered to be the first tractate of the codex, since the page-numbers are preserved from p. 7 onwards and thus p. [1] could be ascertained. Later the leaf containing the 'Prayer of the Apostle Paul' was identified as the front flyleaf (pages A/B) of the first quire of this three-quire codex. Pr. Paul is henceforth counted as I,1, and Ap. Jas. as the second tractate of Codex I. The copy is made by the same hand that wrote I,1, I,3 (the Gospel of Truth) and I,5 (the Tripartite Tractate). The pages have from 35 to 41 lines, with considerable variation in the number of letters in each line. This variation is brought about by the unevenness of the handwriting and by the quality of the papyrus. While pages 1-4 are heavily damaged at the top, no single line has been entirely lost. Pages 5-16 show only minor damage. The resulting lacunae in the text may be restored with some confidence. The text is written in one column without subdivisions and is furnished at the end with a small ornament separating Ap. Jas. from Gos. Truth. The copy dates, like the rest of the Nag Hammadi codices, from the first half of the 4th century. The extant text is in good condition, with the normal amount of errors for this kind of copy. In the translation below such errors have been corrected and are indicated by the usual sign { } for deletion of dittographies and by < > for additions in the case of omissions. Square brackets [ ] represent lacunae in the text where the papyrus is damaged. Up to p. 3.1-7 all lacunae have been restored. Additional aids for understanding have been put between round brackets ( ).

3. Original language, date of composition, origin: Ap. Jas. is assumed to have been translated from Greek. This is supported by the dative form *hebraiois* on p. 1. Presumably Greek is also the original language. Genuine indications of any other original language are lacking, since the remark that the text was written down in the Hebrew language is a traditional *topos* known from form-criticism. H.-Ch. Puech assumed a date in the 2nd cent. for Ap. Jas., accepting van Unnik's further delimitation to the period between 125 and 150 and to Egypt (NTApo[3] I, 338). This opinion was generally accepted by scholars. An argument against a later date is the treatment of the sayings tradition in Ap. Jas., which does not yet reveal any dependence on canonised texts. Since Ap. Jas. uses the transmission formula 'recall the words of the Lord', which was still fully valid to Papias (Eusebius, H.E. III 39.2-4), but which in the second half of the 2nd cent. could hardly claim authority any longer, the middle of the 2nd cent. should be regarded as the latest possible date of composition for Ap. Jas. The *terminus post quem* cannot be precisely determined. The fact that Ap. Jas. shares its subject matter with Matthew, John and the First Letter to the Corinthians should, however, allow the assumption that our writing might date from a period as early as the second half of the 1st cent. To regard Egypt as its land of origin has become questionable because of the sayings traditions it contains, and because it shares its subject-matter with other New Testament writings, which suggests a common place of origin. In that case, a Syrian-Palestinian provenance is more plausible than Egypt, and this would also fit in better with James and Peter. The similarities between Ap. Jas. and the Epistula Apostolorum are to be explained by assuming that the latter is reacting to a spiritual situation represented, among others, by Ap. Jas. No literary dependence can be demonstrated. But matters are dealt with and questions answered in Ep. Apost. that are decided in a different way in Ap. Jas. The beginning of Ep. Apost. makes the twelve disciples convene, and presents the writing as having been composed because of Simon and Cerinthus (1[12]). The revelation is summed up in the view that God spoke through patriarchs and prophets in parables and in truth through Jesus, whom the disciples touched (3[14]). Before Easter he performed many miracles witnessed by the disciples (5[16]). Although a special benediction is bestowed upon those who have not seen but believed, the disciples nevertheless accord salvation above all to themselves for having seen, heard and admired his deeds (29[40]).

4. Literary genre, sender and recipient: Ap. Jas. possesses no title, superscript or subscript. In spite of the lacuna on p. 1 there can be no doubt that the opening lines are the prescript of a letter. It is an oriental prescript in two parts. This is followed by the body of the letter, which continues to the first lines of p. 2. Then comes what was asked for, according to the information given in the letter, i.e. a secret teaching. The setting is portrayed in a way typical of such secret teachings. The disciples are gathered together engaged in some activity - in this case with the composition of books. A change of scenery at the end of p. 2 indicates an important change in the setting. The new setting is characterised by a series of revelatory instructions given to the two chosen disciples by the Saviour Jesus in the form of dialogues and discourses. This revelation section concludes with the remark that the Saviour departed (p. 15 top). Next follows an account of a visionary ascent by James and Peter. With a change in setting from the statement that James goes to Jerusalem to pray, to the prayer itself, the revelation framework comes to a close. The prayer, in which the recipient is once more addressed directly, introduces the concluding part of the epistolary framework. In sum, Ap. Jas. may be divided as follows:

Epistolary part pp. 1+2,16: prescript p. 1; contents of letter p. 1+2; conclusion of letter p. 16.
Revelation part pp. 2-16; frame p. 2; revelation dialogue pp. 2-15; vision narrative p. 15; frame p. 16.

The secret teaching seems originally to have existed without the epistolary framework and both of the chosen to have been equally important. It was presumably the author of the epistolary framework who inserted the remark on p. 2 about the second secret teaching written by James as well as the two passages where Jesus speaks to James alone (pp. 8 and 13), in order to give more weight to James. This name, used without any qualifying epithet, undoubtedly refers to James, the Brother of the Lord (Gal. 1:19), or James the Just (Gos. Thom. log. 12; cf. Hegesippus *ap.* Eusebius, H.E. I 23.4-18), and Ap. Jas. is thus with good reason to be ascribed to the 'Jacobean tradition' (M. Hornschuh, in NTApo[3] II, 83). Jesus' answer to James' plea for protection against temptation and persecution (pp. 4-5) clearly alludes to the martyrdom of the Lord's brother (cf. the report of Hegesippus in Eusebius, *loc cit.*). Similarly, the inserted address by Jesus: 'And also to you alone, James, have I said, 'Be saved!' I have commanded you to follow me and I have taught you how to behave before the rulers' (p. 8) could be a reference to his particular martyrdom. The announcement of martyrdom is fully integrated into a theological justification. Genuine 'biographical' aspects are absent (in contrast e.g. to the martyrdom account in the Second Apocalypse of James, NHC V, 4, p. 61). Ap. Jas. joins this apocalypse, as well as the First Apocalypse of James (NHC V, 3), in according a prominent position to James as revealer (1 Apoc. Jas. p. 29, 2 Apoc. Jas. p. 55) and to the locality of Jerusalem. The restoration of the name [Cerin]thus in the prescript is plausible on the following grounds:

(1) According to Irenaeus, *adv. Haer.* I 26, Cerinthus distinguished between Jesus, the son of Joseph and Mary, and his conjunction with the spiritual Christ which took place in baptism. This can be related to the distinction made in Ap. Jas. p. 6: 'Become better than I! Make yourselves like the son of the Holy Spirit!'

This statement distinguishes the pre-Easter Jesus from the risen Redeemer, the Son of the Holy Spirit. The differences between Irenaeus I 26, and Ap Jas. may be explained by the fact that each has in view a different period of the Saviour's work as revealer: Cerinthus the period after baptism and before the crucifixion, Ap. Jas. the period after Easter.

(2) Cerinthus' unbaptised Jesus distinguishes himself in possessing more righteousness, wisdom and knowledge than all other men. What is absent here, the direct soteriological relevance for the believers, is provided in Irenaeus' report on Carpocrates, who is in fact considered to be related to Cerinthus. Whoever behaves in the same way as Jesus will achieve the same as he, or even surpass him. This last implication can also be found in the following admonition in Ap. Jas.: 'Hasten to be saved, without being urged! Rather, be eager on your own accord, and if possible, surpass even me!' (p. 7).

(3) The insistence in Ap. Jas. on being filled by the spirit (p. 2, 3, 4 etc.) has affinity with the notion of metempsychosis, or the reincarnation of the soul, in Irenaeus, *adv. Haer.* I 25.4. The common point consists in the dynamic by which the deficiency of spirit, or the deficient soul, is to be overcome. These thematic affinities nonetheless do not justify the identification of Ap. Jas. with the gospel used by Cerinthus and the Carpocratians (cf. NTApo³ I, 345-346). They do, however, provide a basis for the assumption that Ap. Jas. is not a Valentinian document. The agreements between the Valentinian doctrine transmitted by Irenaeus, *adv. Haer.* I 3.1-2, and Ap. Jas. appear superficial. The *topoi* used by both - veiled speech in the form of parables, the eighteen months spent by Jesus with his disciples after his resurrection - occur in Irenaeus I 3 in the context of speculations about the aeons. These, on their part, are a constituent element of Valentinian doctrine, but are missing in Ap. Jas., as is also the case with the Valentinian trichotomy of choïcs, psychics and spirituals. Ap. Jas. only knows an anthropological tripartition into spirit, soul and body, or flesh (pp. 11-12).

5. Composition and tradition history: the composition of the dialogues and discourses of Ap. Jas. depends on the fact that the questions of the disciples, or their remarks which serve to initiate a dialogue, which Jesus subsequently responds to, make use of in part clearly recognisable sayings traditions. James introduces his plea for protection against temptation by declaring that the disciple is able to obey the Saviour (p. 4 end). This is explained by referring to the disciples' having forsaken their fathers and mothers in order to follow him (cf. Mt. 19:27). From the point of view of tradition history, the statement, 'Lord, we can obey you if you wish', is presumably related to the formula 'Thy will be done on earth as in heaven' of the Lord's Prayer. This, as well as the 6th prayer (Mt. 6:13), is refuted by Jesus by means of a reinterpretation of the tradition, combined with a piece of passion theology. In all sections of the revelation the procedure is comparable. A typical feature here is that the remarks of the disciples are motivated, or provoked, by key words supplied by Jesus in the previous answer discourse. Koester has named this form 'dialogue gospel as sayings interpretation' ('Dialog', *Ev.Th.* 39,534). He points out the difference in arrangement from the Synoptics (TRE XI, 292), but sees on the other hand an affinity with the composition of Johannine dialogues and discourses (ANRW, Principat 25.2, 1521).

6. Contents: one of the key passages for an understanding of the document is found in the revelation framework on p. 2: 'While the twelve disciples were all sitting together, recalling what the Saviour had said to each one of them, whether in secret or openly, . . . ' 'Recalling what the Saviour has said' is a technical term of the early Church, used in Jn. 15:20; Lk. 22:61; Acts 20:35 for the quotation of sayings of the Lord. It was also used with collections of sayings of the Lord, as witnessed by the Papias fragment preserved in Eusebius, H.E. III 39.3-4 (pointed out by Cameron, *Traditions*, pp. 93-100). What is peculiar is that in Ap. Jas. all the exhortations to the disciples to recall (pp. 3, 5, 12) appear with a divergent or even opposite sense from the traditional concept. By taking, for instance, the formula as it occurs on p. 3 in an ironical-paradoxical sense, it becomes possible to appreciate the following woe and benediction with their contrary import. The recollection formula is used in order to interpret sayings traditions through the form of revealed sayings. Sayings which according to Ap. Jas. derive from the earthly Jesus are rejected, since the Jesus of before Easter did not possess the character of revelation. This corresponds to the theory of parables: 'Before I spoke to you in parables and you did not understand. Now I speak to you openly and you still do not understand' (p. 7). The reason given for this view is that the head of prophecy was cut off with John the Baptist, so that Jesus was unable to speak as a prophet and revealer (p. 6). The earthly work of Jesus is seen by Ap. Jas. in this way: he came down in order to be together with the disciples (p. 8) so that they might become the cause of life for others (p. 10). He spoke in parables and was not understood (p. 7). He healed the sick, but a woe is spoken to them in case they found relief in this way (p. 3). Blessed are they who did not need healing (p. 3). He suffered the sufferings of a righteous man to the point of death on the cross and a shameful tomb (p. 5). In his descent Jesus is portrayed as personified Jewish-mythological Wisdom. The statements made by Jesus on suffering which are listed on p. 5 also derive, as a description of the suffering righteous one, from the sphere of wisdom theology (e.g. Wisd. 2:10-20). The picture of Jesus emerging from a fusion of wisdom mythology and the doctrine of the suffering righteous one also serves as a model for the disciple. In this context belongs also the explicit recommendation of temptation (cf. Sir. 2:1). Ap. Jas. does not only reject certain particular prayers, but questions the value of any prayer intended to influence the Father. The argument in Mt. 6:8, directed against the use of many words in prayers, appears on p. 11 in order to make superfluous any prayer of this kind. Ap. Jas. even pronounces a woe to those who think that they need an advocate, and extols those who earn grace through their own efforts. This view as well has its roots in the sapiential tradition which lets Wisdom toil (Sir. 6:19-20 LXX) and then the disciples of Wisdom as well as herself be rewarded with wreath and crown (Prov. 4:9 and Ap. Jas. p. 8). Crucial for a gnostic interpretation of Ap. Jas. is, first, its particular kind of determinism, which emerges e.g. in the 'truly'-formula on p. 14: 'Truly, I tell you: He who receives life and believes in the kingdom will never leave it, not even if the Father wishes him to be persecuted' (cf. pp. 5, 9, 10). This determination is given a dynamic interpretation. Jesus draws James and Peter aside in order to fill them (p. 2). Peter points out to Jesus that they already are full (p. 4). This sounds like something which might have been said by the Corinthian adversaries of Paul in 1 Cor. 4:8. If this is a valid analogy, then Jesus is here made to criticise a static conception of *gnosis* from the position of a dynamic one. That the danger exists of losing the fullness one has acquired is also exemplified by the parable of the city and the foreigners living in front of it (p. 11). A second gnostic feature of Ap. Jas. is its concept of God. A quite typical passage in this respect is found on p. 11: 'Do you perhaps think that the Father is a lover of mankind, or that he is won over by means of prayers, or that he bestows grace on someone because of another, or that he listens to someone who asks (something of him)?' God does not intervene actively in this world. He is remote from the world, which is regarded as the realm of the devil (pp. 4-5). God has loved the chosen one in his providence (p. 5) and will love him even more when he fulfils the will of God.

Translation

(p. 1) [James wr]ites to [his son Cerin]thus. Peace [be with you from] peace, [love from] love, g[race fro]m grace, f[aith f]rom faith, life from holy life. You asked me[1] to send you a secret teaching <which> was revealed to me [an]d Peter by the Lord. I could not turn you away, nor, however, speak with you, so [I have wri]tten it down in Hebrew[2] characters. I send[3] it to you, and to you only, but because you are a servant of the salvation of the saints. Be careful and take heed not to rehearse to many this writing, which the Saviour did not wish to divulge even to all of us, his twelve disciples. But blessed may they be who are saved through faith in this teaching! Ten months ago, however, I sent you another secret teaching[4] revealed to me by the Saviour. (Read and) understand, then, that one (just) as it was revealed to me, James. This one, (p. 2) however, [since] I [have not yet (fully) comprehended it, and since it was] revealed [for you as well, and for] those who belong to you, [exert yourself], and search [after its doctrine!] In this way [you will attain sal]vation. After all [this] you shall re[veal it as well!]

Now, [while] the twelve disciples [were] all sitting together, recalling what the Saviour had said to each one of them, whether in secret or openly, and putting it in books - I m[yself] writ[ing] down what is in th[e] aforesaid (secret teaching) - lo, the Saviour appeared [after] he had been gone from [us] (and) [we had] been wai[ting] for him, 550 days after his resurrection from the dead.[5] We said to him: 'Have you (already) gone away and have you removed yourself from us (forever)?' But Jesus said: 'No. But I shall (soon) go to the place from which I came.[6] If you wish to come with me, come!' They all answered, saying: 'If you bid us, we come.' He said: 'Truly, I tell you, no one will ever enter the kingdom of heaven because I bid him, but only because you are full. Leave James and Peter to me that I may fill them!' And having called these two he drew them aside. The rest he ordered to go on with what they were doing. The Saviour said (to the two): 'Grace has been given to you (p. 3) (*lines 1-6 lacuna*)[7] and [. . .] they have not understood. Do you not, then, desire to be filled? Is your understanding <drunk>?[8] Do you not, then, desire to become sober? So be ashamed, when you are awake and when you sleep! Remember that you have seen the Son of Man, you have spoken with him and you have listened to him. Woe to those who have seen the So[n of M]an![9] Blessed will they be who have not seen the man, who were not together with him, who did not speak with him, who did not listen to anything from him![10] Yours is life. Bear in mind also that he healed you when you were ill, that you might reign. Woe to those who found relief from their illness! For they will relapse into illness. Blessed are <those>[11] who were not ill and knew relief before they became ill! Yours is the kingdom of God. Therefore I tell you, become full and leave no space in you empty. The one who finds this way in will be able to mock you.' Peter then answered: 'Lo, three times you have told us, (p. 4) 'B[ec]ome [full!' But] we are full.'[12] The [Saviour} answered and sa[id: 'Bec[ause of this I tell] you, ['Become full', so] that you do not [decrease.] For [those who decrease] will not [be saved]. For becoming full is goo[d], a[n]d [decr]easing is bad. Just as it is good that you decrease and bad that you instead are filled, so does the fullness decrease and the deficient does not increase,[13] just as the deficient is filled and the fullness is completed to satiety. Therefore you must decrease while you can be filled, and be filled as you can decrease, in order that you may be ab[le] to g[ain] profit [for] yourselves. So be filled through the spirit! But decrease in understanding! For the understanding which <belongs>[14] to the soul is also (of the nature of) soul.'[15] But I answered and said to him: 'O Lord, we can obey you if you wish.[16] For we have left our fathers, our mothers and our villages[17] and have followed you. Provide for us, then, not to be tempted by the evil devil!'[18] The Lord answered and said: 'What is your merit if you do the will of the Father, if being tempted by Satan is not given to you by him as an additional gift?[19] But if you are oppressed and persecuted by Satan and do his (p. 5) will, I [tell] (you) that he will love you, he will make you like me and he will think of you. For you became be[lov]ed already in his providence, in accordance with your election. So will you not cease to love the flesh and to fear suffering? Or do you not know that you have yet to be abused, to be unjustly accused, to be shut up in prison, to be unlawfully condemned, to be crucified <without>[20] reason and to be <shamefully>[21] buried, just like myself, by the evil one? You have the daring to spare the flesh, you whom the spirit encloses like a wall! If you consider the world, how long it existed <before>[22] you and how long it will exist after you, you will find that your life is one single day and your suffering one single hour. Indeed, the good will not enter into the world. So scorn death and concern yourselves with life! Remember my cross and my death, and you shall live!' But I answered and said to him: 'O Lord, do not preach to us of the cross and death, for they are remote (p. 6) from you.' The Lord answered and said: 'Truly, I tell you that none will be saved unless they beli[eve] in my cross. [Fo]r those who ha[ve] believed in my cross, theirs is the kingdom of God. Therefore, seek death, like the dead who seek life! For that which they seek will be revealed to them.[23] And what is there to trouble them? If you turn your attention to death, it will teach you about election. <Tr>uly,[24] I tell you, (. . .) none will be saved of those who fear death. For the kingdom of <God>[25] belongs to those who are killed. Become better than I! Make yourselves like the son of the Holy Spirit!' Then I asked him: 'How can we prophesy to those who request us to prophesy to them? For many are those who ask us and expect to hear a saying from us.' The Lord answered and said: 'Do you not know that the head of prophecy was cut off with John?' But I said: 'O Lord, (. . .)[26] can it be possible to remove the head of prophecy?' The Lord said to me: 'If you know what 'head' means, and that prophecy issues from the head, (then) understand what it means that 'Its head (p. 7) was removed!' Before [I] spoke to you in parables and you did not understand.[27] Now I speak to y[ou] openly and you (still) do not understand.[28] But you served me as a parable among parables and as a visible (model) in open (speech). Hasten to be saved, without being urged! Rather, be eager on your own accord and, if possible, surpass even me! For this is how your Father will love you. Come to hate hypocrisy and evil thinking! For (evil) thinking gives birth to hypocrisy. But hypocrisy is far from truth. Do not allow the kingdom of heaven to wither! For it is like a palm <shoot>[29] whose fruit has dropped down around it. <They>[30] brought forth leaves, and while they were growing they allowed the fountainhead to dry up.[31] In the same way (it is like) the fruit which (also) came forth from that one root. After it had been planted it bore fruit, with many (labours). It would be good, to be sure, if it were possible now to pluck the new plants.[32] (Then) you would find it. Since[33] I was glorified in this way before the present time, why do you hold me back when I hasten to go? (p. 8). For after the su[ffer]ing you forced me to stay with you <yet>[34] another eighteen <months>[35] for the sake of the parables. It was satisfactory for people <who>[36] had listened to <the> teaching, and they understood 'The Sh[ep]herds', 'The Sowing', 'The Building', 'The Lamps of the Virgins', 'The Wage of the Workmen' and 'The Didrachmae and the Woman'. Concern yourselves eagerly with the word! For as to the word, its first part is faith; the second, love; the third, works. For from these issues life. For the word is like a grain of wheat. When someone had sown it, he had faith in it. And when it grew, he loved it, because he saw many grains instead of one. And when he had done his work, he was saved, having prepared it for food. Again, he left some to sow. In this way you can receive the kingdom of heaven. Unless you receive it through *gnosis* you cannot find it. Therefore I tell you, 'Become sober! Do not remain in error!' And many times I have told you all together - and also to you alone, James, have I said, 'Be saved!' I have commanded you to follow me, and I have taught you how to behave before the rulers - 'Behold, I have come down and have spoken and suffered pain,[37] and I have carried off my crown, (p. 9) so as to save you.' For I came down in order to be together with you, so that you in turn may be together with me. And, finding that your houses had no ceiling, I dwelt in the houses that could receive me at the time of my descent.[38] Therefore, trust in me, O my brothers! Understand what the great light is! The Father has no need of me. For a father does not need a son,[39] but it is the son who needs the father. I am on my way to him. For even of you the Father of the Son has no need. Listen to the word! Understand *gnosis*! Love life - and no one will persecute you nor anyone oppress you, save you yourselves! O you wretches, O you miserables, O you pretenders to the truth! O you liars against *gnosis*! O you transgressors against the Spirit! Can you still bear to listen even now, when it was fitting that you should speak from the beginning? Can you bear to sleep even now, when it was fitting that you should be awake from the beginning in order that the kingdom of heaven might receive you?[40] (p. 10) Truly, I tell you, it is easier for a pure one to fall into uncleanness, and a man of light to fall into darkness, than it is for you become rulers - or not to do so. I have remembered your tears, your mourning and your sorrow. They are far away from us. But now, O you who are outside of the Father's inheritance, weep and mourn where it is necessary! And proclaim the good tidings that the Son is ascending as he should. Truly, I tell you, had I been sent to those who listen to me, and had I spoken with them, I would never have come down to earth. So shun these now in the future! Behold, I shall depart from you and go away, and I do not wish to remain with you any longer, just as you yourselves also do not wish it. So hasten now to follow me! Therefore I tell you, it was for your sakes that I came down. You are the beloved. You will become the cause of life among many. Call on the Father! Pray to God often, and he will give to you! Blessed is he who has seen you with himself.[41] He will be proclaimed among the angels, and glorified among the saints. Yours is life! Rejoice and be glad as (p. 11) children of God! Keep the will (of the Father) that you may be saved! Let yourselves be reproached by me and you will save yourselves! I plead for you with the Father, and he will forgive you much.' And when we had heard this, we became glad. For <we>[42] had been distressed at that which <he>[43] had said earlier. But when he saw us rejoicing, he said: 'Woe to you who need an advocate![44] Woe to you, who stand in need of grace! Blessed are they who have spoken out[45] and obtained grace for themselves! Compare yourselves to foreigners: How do they live in front of your city? Why are you troubled, when you expel yourselves and go far from your city? Why do you abandon your dwelling-place of your own accord, making it ready for those who are waiting to settle down in it?[46] O you chosen ones and (yet) fugitives! Woe to you, for you will be captured! Or do you perhaps think that the Father is a lover of mankind,[47] or that he is won over by means of prayers,[48] or that he bestows grace on someone because of another, or that he listens to someone who asks (something of him)?[49] For he knows the will and also that of which the flesh is in need.[50] For does it not yearn for the soul? For without the soul the body cannot sin, just as (p. 12) the soul cannot be saved without [the] spirit. But if the soul is saved from evil, and the spirit is saved as well, then the body becomes free from sin. For the spirit makes the soul <alive>.[51] But the body kills it. That is, it kills itself.[52] Truly, I tell you that he will not forgive any soul its sin, nor the body its guilt.[53] For none of those who have worn the flesh will be saved. For do you think that many have found the kingdom of heaven? Blessed is he who has seen himself as a 'fourth one' in heaven.'[54] When we heard this we became sad. But when he saw that we were sad, he said: 'For this reason I say it to you, that you may know yourselves. For the kingdom of heaven is like an ear of corn which had sprouted in a field. And when it had ripened, it scattered its fruit and again filled the field with ears for another year. As for yourselves, hasten to reap for yourselves an ear of life that you may be filled with the kingdom! And as long as I am still with you, give heed to me and obey me! But when I go away from you, remember me! But remember me because I was with you, (and) you did not know me. Blessed will they be who have known me! Woe to those who have heard and have not believed! Blessed will they be who (p. 13) have not seen, (yet) have be[lieved]![55] But still am I [per]suading you. Fo[r] I reveal myself to you that I may build a house[56] which can be of great avail to you, because you find shelter beneath it, just as it is also able to give support to the house of your neighbours when it threatens to collapse. Truly, I tell you: Woe to those for whose sakes I was sent down to this place! Blessed will they be who ascend to the Father! Still I am reproaching you, you who are. Make yourselves like those who are not, that you may be together with those who are not! Do not allow the kingdom of heaven to become a desert within you! Do not be proud because of the light that illuminates! Rather, be to each other as I myself was to you! For your sakes I have placed myself under the curse, that you may be saved.'[57] But Peter replied to this and said: 'Sometimes you invite us to enter the kingdom of heaven. But then again you turn us away, O Lord. Sometimes you persuade us, draw us to faith and promise life. But then again you push us back from the kingdom of heaven.' But the Lord answered and said to us: 'I have set forth to you the faith many times - moreover I have revealed myself to you, (p. 14) [O Ja]m[e]s - and you have not understood me. Now again I see that you are often glad, and that because you are rejoicing over [the] promise of life. But you are do[wnca]st and sad wh[e]n you are instructed about the kingdom.[58] But through faith [and] *gnosis* you have received life. So disdain the re[jec]tion when you hear it! But when you hear the promise, rejoice the more! Truly, I tell you: He who receives life and believes in the kingdom will never leave it, not even if the Father wishes him to be persecuted. For now this is what I shall tell you. But now I shall go up to the place from which I have come. But you, when I hastened to go, have cast me out, and instead of accompanying me you have pursued me. But give heed to the glory that awaits me! And when you have opened your heart and turned it upwards, listen to the hymns in the heavens! For today I must take (the place) at the right hand of the Father. I have said (my) last word to you. I shall separate from you. For a chariot of spirit has begun to bear me aloft. And now I begin to unclothe myself, that I may clothe myself. Now, give heed: Blessed are they who have proclaimed the Son before he came down, so that, when I have come, I may ascend once more. Thrice blessed[59] (p. 15) are they[60] who we[re] proclaimed by the S[on] before they existed, that you may have a portion among them.' Having said these words, he went away.[61]

But we bent our knees, I and Peter, gave thanks and sent our hearts upwards to heaven. We heard with our ears and saw with our eyes the noise of wars, a trumpet sound and a great turmoil. And when we had passed beyond that place,[62] we sent our mind farther upwards. And we saw with our eyes and heard with our ears hymns and eulogies of angels and rejoicing of angels, and heavenly majesties were singing praises, and we too rejoiced. After this we wished once more to send up our spirit to[63] the majesty. And having ascended we were not allowed to see or hear anything.[64] For the other disciples called us. They asked us, 'What did you hear from the Master?' and, 'What did he say to you?'[65] and, 'Where did he go to?' But we answered them, 'He has ascended', and, 'He has given us a pledge and has promised life to us all and has revealed to us children who will come after us, after commanding (p. 16) [us to] love them since we would be [sa]v[ed] for their sakes.' And when they heard this, they believed indeed in the revelation. But they were vexed because of those who were to be born. Not wishing, however, to give them any grounds for sin, I sent them each to another place. But as for myself I went up to Jerusalem, in order to pray that I might obtain a portion with the beloved, those who are to be made manifest.

Now I pray that the beginning may come from you.[66] For thus may I be saved, as they are enlightened through me, through my faith and through another (faith) which is better than mine. For I wish that mine should be the lesser. So strive to make yourself like them and pray that you may obtain a portion with them! For beyond what I have said the Saviour did not make any revelation to us for their sakes. We do, however, proclaim a portion with those for whom the proclamation was made, those whom the Lord has made his children.

Notes

The Apocryphon of James

Translation

1. ἐπειδή as introduction to the body of a letter should not be translated, cf. Till, *Koptische Grammatik*, p. 347; for the epistolary style, 'You asked me - I send you however'; cf. the letter of Tubias in Deissmann, *Licht vom Osten*[4], pp. 128f. (ET *Light from the Ancient East*, rev. ed. 1927, pp. 162f.); Cameron directs attention to similarly stylised introductions, e.g. Papias (Eusebius, III 39.3-4), *Traditions*, pp. 93-96, 121-122.
2. Cf. Aristeas 3.
3. Coptic uses the perfect of epistolary style.
4. A reference to a previously sent writing is also found in Aristeas 6.
5. Cf. the introductions to the revelations in Soph. Jes. Chr. (BG) 77.9-78.15; Ep. Pet.Phil. 133.12-134.9 (see below, p. 342).
6. Cf. Ap. John (BG) 19.15-16; Jn. 7:33f., etc.
7. A restoration of p. 3.1-7 made by us previously, but which we now regard as questionable, is as follows: '[through the Father, that you may receive my words]. If [the rest of the discip]les [as well] have writ[ten my words in their] books as [if they had understood, bewa]re! [For they have ex]erted [themselves] with[out understanding]. They [have] heard [just] like [fools], and j[ust like the deaf] they have not understood.' For the restorations of the Coptic text and the arguments supporting them cf. Kirchner, TU 136, pp. 85-88; for Schenke's restorations cf. OLZ 66.120, 128.
8. Read *tahe*, for *tahs*.
9. Cf. 1 Cor. 12:3 ΑΝΑΘΕΜΑ ΙΗΣΟΥΣ. The woe is a milder form of the curse. It is only a short step from cursing the one who bears witness to cursing that on which witness is borne, so that for 1 Cor. 12:3, a real background is to be assumed; for this cf. Kirchner, TU136, pp. 91-92.
10. Cf. 1 Jn. 1:1-3.
11. Emend to <*n*>*nete*.
12. Cf. 1 Cor. 4:8.
13. Read *mafmouh*, for *maumouh*.
14. Read *pa*, for *pe*.
15. Read *pe*, for *te*.
16. Cf. Mt. 6:10.
17. Cf. Mt. 19:27.
18. Cf. Mt. 6:13, Lk. 11:4.

19. Cf. Sir. 2:1.
20. Read *mntalogos*.
21. Read *sōs*, for *sou*.
22. Read *hatetenhe*, for *atetenhaeie*.
23. Cameron regards pp. 5.31-6.11 as a parallel to Mk. 8:31-33 par.; *Traditions*, pp. 85-90.
24. Read *se*, for *e*.
25. Read *noute*, for *mou*; Kasser defends 'kingdom of death', *editio princeps*, p. 93.
26. Superfluous *je*.
27. Cf. Mk. 4:33f.; Mt. 13:34f.
28. Cf. Jn. 16:25, 29.
29. Read *slh*, for *ōlh*.
30. Read *au*, for *af*.
31. For the problems presented by this text cf. Kirchner, TU 136, pp. 107-110; Hedrick, *Sayings*, pp. 15f.; Cameron, *Traditions*, pp. 18-27; according to Cameron, the original form of the parable was like this: '(For) it is like a date-palm (shoot) whose fruits dropped down around it so as to cause the productivity (of the date-palm) to dry up': *ib*. p. 25.
32. Cf. νεόφυτος 1 Tim. 3:6
33. Read *epei e*, for *epee*.
34. Read *nhouo*, for *nhoou*.
35. To correspond with the 550 days of p. 2, rather than the 'eighteen days' of the uncorrected text.
36. Read *eausōtm nsa ptsebo*, for *ausōtm nsa tsebo*.
37. Read *ah<i>r skylle*; cf. 1 Enoch 42:1-2; Sir. 24:7-11.
38. Cf. Jn. 1:11.
39. Cf. *Teach. Silv*. 115.10-15.
40. Is this diatribe an allusion to 1 Jn. 1:1-3?
41. Brown translates p. 10.34-38: 'Blessed is he who has seen you with Him when He was preached among the angels and glorified among the saints': *Diss*. p. 62.
42. Read *neahn*, for *neahm*.
43. Read *nentaf*, for *nentan*.
44. Cf. 1 Jn. 2:1; Mt. 7:7.
45. Cf. p. 7.4f.
46. A social illustration of the 'increase and decrease' on pp. 3-4.
47. Besides the NT cf. Ps. Sol. 5:12; Exeg. Soul 135.26-29.
48. Cf. Gos. Thom. log. 14 (above, p. 119).
49. Cf. Jn. 14:13f.; Ign. *Eph*. 10.1.
50. Cf. Mt. 6:8.
51. Read *tnho*, for *taho*.
52. Cf. Gos. Mary 16.13-18.
53. Cf. Mt. 6:12.
54. Presumably an allusion to Mk. 4:3-8, 26-28; Gos. Thom. log. 9, or the parable on 'sowing', p. 8; Kipgen considers that *mahftau* 'fourth one' may be a translation of τέταρτος αὐτός 'with three others': *Diss*. p. 174, note 19.
55. Cf. Jn. 20:29; further Jn. 6:36; Ep. Apost. 29 (40); Ep. Abg. 2 (Lipsius-Bonnet, I, 281:μακάριοι οἱ ἰδόντες με καὶ πιστεύσαντες· τρισμακάριοι δὲ οἱ μὴ ἑωρακότες με καὶ πιστεύσαντες.
56. Cf. Prov. 9.1.
57. Kipgen thinks p. 13.19-25 contains an allusion to Phil. 2:6-9; *Diss*. pp. 156f.

58. The Coptic text may also be divided differently: 'When you should be rejoicing over the promise of life you are downcast, and you are sad when you are instructed about the kingdom'; cf. Schenke, OLZ 6,126; Williams in *Nag Hammadi Codex I*, ed. Attridge, p. 49.

59. A triple benediction; cf. n. 55.

60. In the MS the letters *ei* of the first *neei* have been barred.

61. A typical conclusion of a revelation; cf. Gos. Mary 9.5.

62. Deleting the first *ou* in *ntarnououotb*.

63. Read *arets*, for *aretf*.

64. Cf. Ep. Apost. 19 (30).

65. Cf. Gos. Thom. log. 13 (above, p. 119).

66. Cf. CH I 26; Apoc. Pet. (NHC VII, 3) 71.18.

5. The Dialogue of the Saviour

Beate Blatz
(translation by Einar Thomassen)

Introduction

1. Bibliography: *Editions: The Facsimile Edition of the Nag Hammadi Codices* published under the Auspices of the Arab Republic of Egypt in Conjunction with the UNESCO, Codex III (pp. 120.1-147.23), Leiden 1977. S. Emmel, H. Koester, E. Pagels, *Nag Hammadi Codex III, 5: The Dialogue of the Saviour*, (The Coptic Gnostic Library - NHS 26), Leiden 1984.

Translations: J.M. Robinson (ed.), *The Nag Hammadi Library in English, Translated by the Members of the Coptic Gnostic Project*, Leiden 1977, pp. 230-238 (Koester-Pagels, Attridge); [3]1988 pp. 244-255 (Koester-Pagels, Emmel). Emmel, Koester, Pagels (see above).

Studies: C.H. Dodd, 'The Appearances of the Risen Christ: An Essay in Form Criticism of the Gospels', in D.E. Nineham (ed.), *Studies in the Gospels*, Oxford 1957, pp. 9ff. K. Rudolph, 'Der Gnostische 'Dialog' . . . ' (see above, p. 231). M. Krause and P. Labib, *Gnostische und hermetische Schriften aus Codex II und Codex VI*, 1971. P. Perkins, *Studies in the Form and Development of the Gnostic Revelation Dialogue*, PhD diss. Harvard 1971. F. Wisse, 'Nag Hammadi Codex III: Codicological Introduction', in M. Krause (ed.), *Essays on the Nag Hammadi Texts*, (NHS 6), Leiden 1975, pp. 223-238. M. Krause, 'Der *Dialog des Soter* in Codex III von Nag Hammadi', in M. Krause (ed.), *Gnosis and Gnosticism*, (NHS 8), Leiden 1977, pp. 13-34. S. Emmel, 'Unique Photographic Evidence for Nag Hammadi Texts: CG II, 2-7; III, 5 and XIII, 2', *Bull. of the American Soc. of Papyrologists* 14, 1977, 109-121. E. Pagels, 'Visions, Appearances and Apostolic Authority: Gnostic and Orthodox Traditions', in B. Aland (ed.), *Gnosis: Festschrift für Hans Jonas*, Göttingen 1978, pp. 415-430. S. Emmel, 'A Fragment of Nag Hammadi Codex III in the Beinecke Library: Yale Inv. 1784', *Bull. of the American Soc. of Papyrologists* 17, 1980, 53-60. P. Perkins, *The Gnostic Dialogue: The Early Church and the Crisis of Gnosticism*, New York 1980. H.-M. Schenke, [review of Emmel, Koester, Pagels (see above)], *Enchoria* 14, 1986, 175-187. For the works of H. Koester cf. above, p. 231 n.8.

2. State of preservation of the codex: Nag Hammadi Codex III is unfortunately heavily damaged. At the beginning and end (pp. 5-8, 21-24, 57/58, 117-132, 137/8, 143-147) the damage, and consequently the number of lacunae, is particularly great. The Dialogue of the Saviour (pp. 120.1-147.23) is seriously affected by this. The Coptic codex was written in the 4th cent. Of the seventy leaves which were inventoried at the Coptic Museum in Old Cairo in 1946, sixty-seven are still to be found there today. Some fragments of the final pages have reappeared, however, and are deposited in the Beinecke Library at Yale (cf. Emmel, 'A Fragment . . . '). In his edition Emmel makes use of these fragments.

3. Character: the Dialogue of the Saviour belongs to those writings in which the resurrected Saviour appears to an individual, or to a group of disciples, and reveals to them the true knowledge about his appearance in the world, about his origin and the origin of the Gnostic, the realm of light. The work is thus to be seen in connection with similar texts: the Gospel of Mary (Pap. Ber. 8502), the Sophia of Jesus Christ (Pap. Ber. 8502 and NHC III, 4), the Letter of Peter to Philip (NHC VIII, 2; see below, pp. 342 ff.), the Apocryphon of John (Pap. Ber. 8502 and NHC II, 1), the Apocalypse of Peter (NHC VII, 3), the Pistis Sophia and others (on the question of genre see above, pp. 228 ff.).

NHC III, 5 is, however, the only one among these writings which is entitled 'dialogue'. Kurt Rudolph has pointed out the affinity of the gnostic dialogue with the ancient form of the fictitious or authentic philosophical-didactic discourse.[1] There the dialogue served the purpose of attaining the truth. In contrast to this, the gnostic dialogue wants to convey salvation. The truth is here not in question; the truth is irrevocably declared in the divine revelation. As model for the gnostic dialogue yet another ancient literary genre can be established: the literature of *erotapokriseis*. This literary genre of question and answer served above all the purpose of introduction to specific topics and problems. An amalgamation of *erotapokriseis* literature and revelation literature is found in Hermetic writings. Rudolph sees in the Coptic gnostic writings a cross between the philosophical dialogue and the question-and-answer pattern of the oracles.[2]

4. Composition and structure: the Dialogue of the Saviour possesses no framework narrative. The title is immediately followed by an extensive discourse by the *Soter* (120.2-124.22), in which a prayer is embedded (121.5-122.1). Next follows the dialogue between the Saviour and his disciples (124-147), where Matthew and Judas Thomas, but also Mary Magdalene, are given particular prominence. On several occasions the dialogue is interrupted by actions: in 131.16-18 Judas falls to his knees, offering praise to the *Soter* (cf. Pistis Sophia 8.16; 21.4; 22.2; 29.3 etc.); in 132.23-133.1, after the thirteenth question from the disciples, Jesus picks up a stone in order to make a point; in 135.4-11, following a long discourse by Jesus, Judas has a vision of a high place and of the underworld and turns to Matthew to speak; 136.1-5 appears to signal the end of the dialogue. However, Jesus once more addresses his disciples. In 136.17ff. the conversation is interrupted by the vision of the spirits carrying the soul.

A noteworthy feature is the frequent use of the word τότε 'then'; from the situation in the Letter of Peter to Philip (see below, pp. 342 ff.) it may be inferred that τότε here too marks the breaks between distinct literary units. Elaine Pagels and Helmut Koester recognise in NHC III, 5 five sources which have been woven together:[3]

(1) 120.2-124.22: presumably deriving from the redactor, to judge from the use of the title *Soter*, as distinct from the designation 'Lord' found in other parts of the tractate. This is a gnostic discourse on the passage of the soul through the various heavenly spheres, where it encounters hostile powers. Echoes from the New Testament, especially the Pauline and deutero-Pauline epistles, are notable: 122.4.16 - Col. 1:13; 121.2 - 2 Thess. 2:12; 121.22-23 - Jas. 1:21, 1 Pet. 1:9; 121.20 - Eph. 5:2, Hebr. 10:10-19; 121.10 - 1 Thess. 5:8ff,

Eph. 6:11-17.

(2) 127.23-131.15: a creation myth echoing Gen. 1f., set in the framework of the common gnostic account of the origin of the world and of a dualistic ideology: 129.18 - Gen. 1:14; 129.20ff. - Gen. 2:5. The accent is here not on gnostic re-interpretation of the Biblical myth of creation, but on a reflection upon the concept of 'spirit'.

(3) 133.16-134.24: an explication, based on Western tradition, of the cosmological list, darkness, light, fire, water and wind. The list is interrupted in 134.5-8 by the question concerning the purpose of baptism.

(4) 134.24-137.3: in this section, which contains an apocalyptic vision, the 'original source' and the work of the redactor are clearly distinguishable: in 135.13-15 and 136.17 the 3rd person sing. is used, from which it may be concluded that the original source assumed that the vision was received by one person only. There are, however, three persons, Judas, Matthew and Mary, who receive the vision in NHC III,5.

(5) 124.23ff: the original source, a dialogue between the 'Lord', Judas, Matthew and Mary, where question and answer follow directly upon one another, is interrupted by the redactor in various places. After an introductory dialogue and prayer (124.23-127.22) there follows in 127.23-131.15 a creation myth. Thereafter the original dialogue continues, into which the vision (134.23-137.3) has been incorporated. Koester and Pagels reconstruct the original dialogue as a collection of sayings, similar to Q, or to the Gospel of Thomas, commented upon by the questions of Mary, Judas and Matthew and expounded by the responses of the Lord.[4]

(5) Theology: the first section exhibits a strong tension between present and future eschatology. The purpose of the second section is to make transparent the fact that the cosmos has its origin in the realm of light. The Gnostic must do whatever he can to attain this abode of life. In the third section the *Soter* instructs his disciples about the elements. To understand them and to understand oneself are the preconditions for true baptism. Koester and Pagels see parallels here to Rom 6:3f; Eph. 2:1-6; Col. 3:1-4.[5] In the fourth section the disciples learn more about themselves in visions, after the *Soter* has laid his hands on them, and they attain a deeper understanding of themselves as baptised and chosen disciples. In 137.13-15 the *Soter* makes a distinction between transient vision and eternal vision. The disciples have experienced the transient vision, the eternal one certainly awaits them in the eschatological future. The programme of the Dialogue of the Saviour may be seen in the saying about seeking and finding, marvelling, ruling and resting, as different stages in the attainment of *gnosis*. The disciples have reached the first level of knowledge, i.e. they have sought and found. In 141.3-4, therefore, they ask when they will attain rest. Jesus replies in 141.5-6: You will rest when you lay down this burden i.e. when you have left behind you the body and the world. As for the question concerning the meaning of suffering in the world (140.15ff.) the Dialogue of the Saviour points to the Gnostic's unification with the realm of light (137.22-138.2): the living God is in the Gnostics and they are in him; they do nothing of their own accord, but in order to make manifest the abundance of the revealer (140.18) and to save others (137.16ff.). In the concluding part of the tractate the disciples are given instructions for their future conduct in the world. Their work shall be made perfect, they shall pray and destroy the works of womanhood (141.20ff.; 144.14-16; 144.19ff.).

6. The Dialogue of the Saviour and other writings: the Letter of Peter to Philip, the Sophia of Jesus Christ, the Gospel of Mary, the Gospel of Thomas and the Book of Thomas are comparable to NHC III, 5. All of these are dialogues of the resurrected with his disciples. A comparison leads to the observation, however, that in the case of the Dialogue of the Saviour a framework narrative is absent. On the other hand, events like those taking place in the Dialogue of the Saviour are found only in the Gospel of Mary, the Gospel of Thomas and the Letter of Peter to Philip. The doctrine of the bridal chamber contained in the Dialogue of the Saviour is also found in the Gospel of Thomas, in the Gospel of Philip, in the Exegesis on the Soul, the Authoritative Teaching and the Second Treatise of the Great Seth.[6]

7. Date: in its present shape the Dialogue of the Saviour was probably composed in the 2nd cent. To what extent the assumed sources go back to the 1st cent. (thus Koester) remains doubtful.

Notes

5. The Dialogue of the Saviour

1. K. Rudolph, *op. cit.* p. 86.
2. Rudolph, *ibid.* pp. 89f.; also cf. above, p 228ff.
3. Emmel, Koester, Pagels, *Nag Hammadi Codex III, 5*, pp 2ff.
4. *Ibid.* pp. 3ff.
5. *Ibid.* p. 13.
6. M. Krause, 'Der Dialog des Soter in Codex III von Nag Hammadi', in *Nag Hammadi and Gnosis: Papers read at the First International Congress of Coptology (Cairo, December 1976)*, ed. R. McL. Wilson, (NHS 14), Leiden 1978, pp 66-74.

The Dialogue of the Saviour[1]

1. The Saviour said to his disciples, 'The time has already come, brothers, for us to leave behind our labour and to abide at rest (ἀνάπαυσις). [2] For whoever abides at rest will rest (ἀνάπαυσις) forever. And I say to you, be always above [. . .] time [. . . say] to you [. . .] be afraid [. . .] to you [. . .]. For anger [i]s fearful [. . .] arouse anger [is . . .] but since you have [. . .] come into being from [. . .]. They directed these words against it (*sc.* the anger) with f[e]ar and trembling, and it handed them over to some archons, for nothing could escape from it. But when I came, I opened the path and taught them about the passage which they will pass through, the elect and the solitary,[3] (p. 121) who have [known] the Father, because they have [b]elieved in the truth.[4]

2. And with [a]ll praises which you give, when you offer praise, then do it like this: 'Hear us, Father, just as you heard your only-begotten son and received him [and] gave him rest from many [labours. Y]ou are [the o]ne whose power [. . . yo]ur armour[5] [is . . .] light [. . .] living [. . . whom] they do not touch [. . .] the word of [. . .] repentance [. . .] life [. . .] from you. You are [the] thinking and the [en]tire tranquillity of the solitary ones.' Again: 'He[a]r us, just as you heard your elect. Through your sacrifi[ce][6] will these enter. By means of their [go]od deeds have these saved their souls[7] from these blind li[m]bs so that they may exist (p. 122) eternally. Amen.'

3. I will teach you. When the time of dissolution comes, the first power of darkness[8] will come upon you. Do not be afraid and say, 'Behold, the time has come!' But when you see a single staff [. . .] this [. . .] understand [. . .] the work [. . .] and the archons [. . .] come upon you [. . .]. Truly, fear is the po[wer of darkness]. So if you are afra[id] of what will come upon you, it will engulf you. For there is none among them that will spare you, or show you mercy. But in this way, look at [. . .] in it, since you have mastered every word on earth. It (p. 123) [is what will] take you up to the pl[ace,] there where there is no rule [or ty]rant. When you [. . .] you will see those who [. . .] and also [. . . . I t]ell you that [. . .] the reasoning power [. . .] reasoning power [ex]isting [. . . pla]ce of truth [. . .] but they [. . .]. But you [. . .] truth, this [. . .] living [mind], because of [. . . a]nd your joy [. . .]. So [. . .] in order that [. . .] your souls [. . .] lest the word [. . . which] they have raised [. . . an]d they could not [. . .] what is [in]side [a]nd what [is outsi]de [. . .]. For the crossing-place (p. 124) is fearful [before you]. But you [with a] single mind, pass [it] by! For its depth is great; [its] height [is] enormous [. . .] a single mind [. . .] and the fire [. . .] the waters [. . . a]ll the powers [. . .] you, they will

[. . .] and the po[wer]s [. . .] they [. . .]. I tel[l you that] the soul [. . .] become [. . .] in everyone [. . .] you are the [. . .] and that [. . .] forget [. . .] son [. . .] and which you [. . .] you [. . .].'

4. [Mat]thew said, 'How (p. 125) [. . .]?'

5. The Saviour said, '[. . . kn]ow the things within you [. . .] will remain, you [. . .].'

6. Judas [said], 'Lord, [. . .] the works [. . .] [the]se souls, these [. . .] these little ones, when [. . .] where will they be? [. . .] the spirit [. . .].'

7. The Lord [said], '[. . .] while [. . .] recei[ve th]em. These do not die, [nor] are they destroyed, for they have known [their] consorts and the one who will rec[eive the]m. For the truth seeks [out] the wise and the righteous.'

8. The Saviour sa[id], 'The lamp [of the b]ody is the mind. As long as [the things within] you are kept in order, that is [. . .], your bodies are lu[minous].[9] As long as your hearts are [dar]k, the luminescence you (p. 126) are waiting for [. . .]. I have [. . .] I will go [. . .] my word wit[h . . .] I send to [. . .].'

9. His discip[les said, 'Lord], who is it who seeks and [. . .] reveal?'

10. [The Lord s]aid [to them], 'He who seeks [. . .] reveal [. . .].'[10]

11. Mat[thew said, 'Lord, w]hen I [. . .] and when I speak, who is it who [. . .] who listens?'

12. [The Lord] said, 'It is the one who speaks who also l[istens], and it is the one who can see who also reveals.'

13. [Mar]y said, 'Lord, behold! [As long as I] carry the body whence does it come [that I] weep, and whence that I [laugh]?' 14. The Lord said, '[The body] weeps on account of its works [and all the] rest, and the mind laughs [on] ac[count of] (p. 127) [. . . o]f the spirit. If one does not [stand in the] darkness, he will [not] be able to see [the light]. So I tell you [. . .] light is the darkness. [And if one does not] stand in [the darkness, he will] not [be able to] see the light. [. . .] the lie [. . .] they brought them from [. . .]. You will give [. . . lig]ht and [. . . e]xist forever [. . .]ness [. . .] of one [. . .] ever. Then [al]l the powers which are above as well as those [who are] below will [. . .] you. In that place [there will] be weeping and [gnashing] of teeth[11] over the end of [all] these things.'

15. Judas [s]aid, 'Tell [us, L]ord, what [existed] before [heaven and] earth came into being.' 16. The Lord said, 'There was darkness and water and (p. 128) spirit upon [water].[12] And I say [to you, . . .] that which you seek [and] inquire after, be[hold, it is] within you, an[d . . .] the power and the my[stery . . .] the spirit, for from [. . .] wickedness [. . .] come [. . .] the t[rue] mind [. . .]. Behold [. . .].'

17. [. . .] said, '[Lord,] tell us where [the soul is es]tablished and where [the t]rue [mind] exists.' 18. The Lord s[aid], 'The fire [of the] spirit came

into existence [. . .] both. Because of this, the [. . .] came into existence and the tru[e] mind came into existence with[in] them. If someone se[ts his so]ul up high, then [he will be exalted.'

19. And Matthew as[ked him], (p. 129) '[. . .] who took him [. . .] it is he who is s[trong].' 20. The Lord [sai]d, '[. . . s]tronger than [. . .] you [. . .] to follow you and all the works [. . .] your hearts. For just as your hearts [. . .], so [. . .] you will overcome the powers a[bov]e as well as those below [. . .]. I say to you, let him [who possesses] power renounce [it and re]pent. And [let] him who k[nows] seek and find and rejoice.'[13] 21. Judas [sa]id, 'Behold! [I] see that all things exist [. . .] like signs over [the earth].[14] Therefore they happened in this way.'

22. The Lord [said], 'When the Fa[ther estab]lished the cosmos, he [. . .] water from it. [His] Word came forth from him, (p. 130) and it dwelt in many [. . .]. It was higher than the pat[h . . . encir]cling the whole earth [. . .] the assem[bled] water [. . .] exist[ing] at their outside.[15] [. . .] the water, a great fire [encir]cling them like a wall. [. . .] occasion after many things had become separated [from what] was inside. When the [. . .] had been established, he looked [. . .] and said to it, 'Go and c[ast] forth from yourself so that [the earth may not] be in want from generation to ge[neration an]d from age to age.' T[hen it] cast forth from itself [spr]ings of milk and sp[ring]s [of] honey and oil and w[ine] and go[od] fruits and sweet flavour and good root[s], in [order that] it should not be deficient from generation [to] generation and from age [to] age. 23. But it (sc. the Word) is above [. . .] (p. 131) [. . .] standing [. . .] its beauty [. . .] and outside [there was a gre]at light, [more] powerful [than] the one resembling it, for that [is] the one [which] rules over [all] the aeons [above] and below. [The light was] taken from the fire and it was scattered in the [firma]ment above and [be]low. A[ll] the works [which] depend on them, it is they [which exist] over the heaven above [and ov]er the earth bel[ow]. On them depend all [the wo]rks.'

24. [And] when Ju[das] heard these things, he bowed down and he [worshipped] and he offered praise to the Lord.

25. [Ma]ry addressed <her> brothers, '[These things] which you ask the Son of [Man] about, where will you put them?' 26. [The Lo]rd [said] to her, 'Sister, [no one] will be able to ask about these things ex[cept the one who] has a place (p. 132) to put them in his hea[rt and who is able] to come for[th from this cosmos] and enter [the place of life] so that [he] may not be held back [in] this impoverished cosmos.'

27. [Mat]thew said, 'Lord, I wish [to see] that place of life, [this place] where there is no wickedness, bu[t rather] there is pure light!' 28. The Lord sa[id], 'Brother Matth[ew], you will not be able to see it as [long as you] are wearing flesh.' 29. {Mat}thew said, 'Lord, ev[en if I shall] not

[be able to] see it, let me k[now it]!' 30. The Lord [sa]id, 'E[veryo]ne who has known himself[16] has seen [it in] everything given to him [alone] to do, and has come to [resemble] it in his [g]oodness.'

31. [J]udas answered, saying, 'Tell me, Lord, how [it is that this quak]ing which moves the earth moves.' 32. The Lord picked up a st[one and] held it in his hand, [saying, (p. 133) 'What] do I hold [in] my [hand]?'

33. He said, '[It is] a stone.' 34. He [s]aid to them, 'That which supports [the earth] is that which supports the heaven. When a Word comes forth from the Greatness, it will make its way on that which supports the heaven and the earth. For the earth does not move. If it were to move, it would fall, but (it does not do so) in order that the First Word might not fail. For it was that which established the cosmos. And it (*sc.* the cosmos) came to be in it and it took fragrance from it. For all [things] which do not move I [. . .] them for you, all the sons of me[n. Fo]r you are from [th]at place. [I]n the hearts of those who speak from jo[y] and truth you exist. Even though it issues from [the b]ody of the father among men, without being received by them,[17] still it [does] return up to its place. He who [does not] know [the wo]rk of perfection [kn]ows nothing. Whoever does not stand in the darkness will be unable to see the light.

(p. 134) 35. [W]hoever does not [understand how] fire came into existence will burn in it, because he does not know its root. Whoever does not first understand water knows nothing. For what use is there for him to be baptised in it? Whoever does not understand how the blowing wind came into existence will fly away with it. Whoever does not understand how the body which he carries came into existence will [per]ish with it. And how will he who does n[ot] know [the S]on know the [Father]? And to him who will not know the roo[t] of all things they remain hidden. He who will not know the root of evil is no stranger to it.[18] He who will not understand how he came will not understand how he will go, and he is no str[anger] to this cosmos which w[ill . . .] which will be humiliated.'

36. Then he [. . . J]udas and Matthew and Mar[y] (p. 135) [. . .] the boundary of heaven [and] earth. [An]d when he had placed his [hand] upon them, they hoped that they might [see] it. Judas raised his eyes and saw a very high place, and he saw the place of the abyss below. Judas said to Matthew, 'Brother, who will be able to go up to such a height or down to the abyss?[19] For there is a great fire and a great horror.' At that moment a word came forth from it. As it stood there, he saw how it had come [dow]n. Then he said to it, '[Wh]y have you come down?' 37. And the Son of Man greeted them and said, 'A seed from a power was deficient and it went down to [the] abyss of the earth. And the greatness remembered [it] and sent the Wo[rd t]o it. It brought it up into [his presence] in order that (p. 136) the First Word might not fail.' [Then his di]sciples]

were amazed at all [the things] he had said to them and they accepted them with [fa]ith. And they understood that watching wickedness is futile. 38. Then he said to his disciples, 'Have I not told you that like a visible voice and flash of lightning will the good be taken up to the light?'

39. Then all his disciples offered praise to him and said, 'Lord, before you appeared here, who was it that offered you praise? For all praises exist because of you. Or who is it that blesses you? For all blessing comes fr[om] you.' 40. As they stood there, he saw two spirits carrying with them a single soul in a great flash of lightning. And a word came forth from the Son of Man, saying, 'Give them their clothing!' [And] the small one did as the big one. They were [like] those who received (p. 137) them. [. . .] one another. Then [. . .] disciples whom he had [. . .].

41. Mary [said, ' . . .] see the evi[l . . .] them from the first [. . .] one another.' 42. The Lo[rd] said, '[. . .] when you see them [. . .] become big, they will [. . .]. But when you see that which exists eternally, that is the great vision.' 43. Then they all said to him, 'Tell us about it!' 44. He said to them, 'How do you wish to see it? [In a] transient vision or an eternal vi[sio]n?' Again, he said, 'Str[ive] to save that [which] can follow [you], and to seek after it and to speak from within it, in order that everyt[hing] which you seek after [may] be in harmony with you! For I [say] to you, truly, the living God [dwells] in you [. . .] in him.' 45. Ju[das said, 'Tr]uly I wish [. . .].' 46. The Lo[rd sai]d to him, '[The] living [God] dwells [. . .] entire [. . .] the defi[ciency . . .].'

47. [Ju]das [said,] 'Who [. . .]?' 48. The Lord said, '[. . .] all [the] works which [. . .] the remainder, it is [o]ver them tha[t yo]u [. . .].'

49. Judas said, 'Behold, the archons dwell above us, so it is they who rule over us.' 50. The Lord said, 'It is you who will rule over them! But only when you rid yourselves of envy, will you clothe yourselves in light and enter the bridal chamber.'[20]

51. Judas said, 'How will [our] garments be brought to us?' 52. The Lord said, 'There are some who will bring to you, [and] there are others who will receive [you]. (p. 139) For [it is] they [who will give] you your garments. [For] who [will be] able to pass through that place [which] is [the] retribution? But the garments of life were given to man because he knows the path by which he will travel. And even for me is it difficult to pass through it.' 53. Mary said, 'Thus with regard to 'the trouble of each day',[21] and 'the labourer deserves his keep',[22] and 'the disciple resembles his teacher'.[23] These words she said as a woman who had understood completely.

54. The disciples said to him, 'What is the fullness and what is the deficiency?' 55. He said to them, 'You are from the fullness, and you dwell in the place where the deficiency is. And behold! His light has

poured [d]ow[n] upon me.'

56. Matth[ew] said, 'Tell me, Lord, how the dead die [an]d how the living live!' (p. 140) 57. The [Lord] said, '[You have] asked me about a saying [. . .] which eye has not seen, [no]r have I heard it save from you.[24] But I tell you that when what moves a man is taken away, he is called 'dead'. And when what is alive leaves what is dead, <he> will be called 'alive'.'[25] 58. Judas said, 'Why, for the sake of truth, do they <die> and live?' 59. The Lord said, 'Whatever is born of truth does not die. Whatever is born of woman dies.'[26]

60. Mary said, 'Tell me, Lord, why have I come to this place, to find profit or suffer loss?' 61. The Lord said, 'You make manifest the abundance of the revealer!' 62. Mary said to him, 'Lord, is there then a place which is id[le], or is lacking truth?' 63. The Lord said, 'The place where I am not!' 64. Mary said, 'Lord, you are fearful and won[der]ful, (p. 141) and a [deva]stating [fire] to those who do not know [you].' 65. Matthew said, 'W[h]y do we not rest at [on]ce?' 66. The Lord said, 'When you lay down these burdens.'

67. Matthew said, 'How does the small join itself with the big?' 68. The Lord said, 'When you abandon the works which will not be able to follow you, then you will rest.'

69. Mary said, 'I want to understand all things, [just as] they are.' 70. The Lo[rd] said, 'He who seeks life. For th[is] is their wealth. For the [plea]sure of this cosmos is [false], and its gold and its silver are [a de]lusion.'

71. His [dis]ciples said to him, 'What shall we do, in [ord]er that our work may be perfect?' 72. The Lord [sai]d to them, 'Be [pre]pared in face of everything. [Bl]essed is the man who has found (p. 142) the w[ar and sa]w the battle with his eyes. He did not kill, nor was [he] killed, and nevertheless did he come forth victoriously.

73. J[u]das said, 'Tell me, Lord, what is the beginning of the path?'[27] 74. He said, 'Love and goodness. For if one of these existed among the archons, evil would never have come into being.'

75. Matthew said, 'Lord, you have spoken about the end of everything without distress.' 76. The Lord said, 'You have understood all the things I have said to you and you have accepted them with faith. If you have known them, they are [you]rs. If not, then they are not yours.'

77. They said to him, 'What is the place to which we are going?' 78. The Lor[d] said, 'Stand in the place you can reach!'

79. Mary said, 'Is everything established in this way visible?' 80. The Lord [sa]id, 'I have told you [that] it is the one who can see who reve[als].'

81. His disci[ples], numbering twelve, asked him, 'Teacher [. . .] (p. 143) tran[quillity . . .] teach us [. . .].' 82. The Lord said, '[If you have

understoo]d everything which I have [told you] you will become [immortal,] for you [. . .] everything.'

83. Ma[ry] said, 'There is only one word that I shall [sa]y to the Lord: Because of the mystery of truth that is what we have come to abide in, though for the cosmic (beings) we are manifest.'

84. Judas said to Matthew, 'We [w]ish to understand the sort of garments in which we shall be clothed [when] we leave the corruption of the [fle]sh.' 85. The Lord said, 'The archons [and] the governors possess garments which have been given them for a [ti]me and which do not last. [But] you, as children of truth, are not to clothe yourselves with these transient garments. Rather, I tell you that you will become bles[se]d when you strip your[selv]es!²⁸ For it is not a great thing (p. 144) [. . .] outside.'

86. [. . .] sai[d, ' . . .] I speak, I receive [. . .].' 87. The Lord said, '[. . .] your Father [. . .].'

88. [Ma]ry sai[d, 'Of what] sort is that musta[rd se]ed?²⁹ Is it from heaven or is it from earth?' 89. The Lord said, 'When the Father established for himself the cosmos, he left much over from the Mother of the All. For this reason he speaks and acts.'

90. Judas said, 'From the mind of truth have you told us this. When we pray, how shall we pray?' 91. The Lord said, 'Pray in the place where there is no woman.' 92. Matthew said, 'When he says to us, 'Pray in the place where there is [no wom]an, he means, 'Destroy the works of womanhood', not because there is another [way to give birth], but because they will cease to [give birth].'³⁰ 93. Mary said, 'Will they never be obliterated?' 94. The Lord said, '[They] know that they [also] will dissolve (p. 145) and [the wor]ks of [woman]hood he[re] be de[stroyed as well].' 95. Judas said [to Matth]ew, '[The wo]rks of [woman]hood will dissolve [. . .] the archons will [call] upon [. . .]. In this way will we become prepared [fo]r them.'

96. [The] Lord [sa]id, 'Do they, indeed, see y[ou? Do they se]e those who receive [y]ou? Now, behold a Word. [The one belonging to] heaven is coming forth from the Father [to the] ab[yss], in silence with a flash of li[ghtning], giving birth. Do they see it, or over[power] it? But rather, it is you. Y[ou have] known [the pa]th, the one <which> neither [ang]el nor [au]thority has [known]. Bu[t it bel]ongs to the [Fat]her and the S[on becau]se [the]y are both a single [. . . An]d you wi[ll] travel on [the pat]h which you have [kno]wn. Even [i]f the archons become huge [they will] not be able to pass through it. B[ut liste]n! I [tel]l you [that] it is difficult even [for] me [to pass thro]ugh it!'

(p. 146) 97. [Mary] said [to the Lo]rd, 'When the works [dissolve. . . whi]ch dissolves a [work]?' 98. [The Lord sai]d, '[Indeed, for] you know [. . .] if I dissolve [. . .] will go to his pla[ce].'

99. Judas said, 'How is the spi[rit] apparent?' 100. The Lord said, 'How [is] the sword [apparent]?' 101. Jud[as] said, 'How is the [l]ight apparent?' 102. The Lord said, '[. . .] in it forever.'

103. Jud[as] said, 'Who forgives the works of whom? [The w]orks which [. . .] the cosmos [. . . w]ho forgives the w[o]rks.' 104. The Lord [said], '[W]ho [. . .]? It [is] proper for whoever has understood the [w]or[ks to] do the [wi]ll of the Father.

'And as for y[ou, str]ive to rid yoursel[ves] of an[ger] and [en]vy, and [to st]rip yourselves of your [. . .] and not to [. . .] (p. 147) [. . .] reproach [. . .]. For I say [to you,] you take [. . .] you [. . .] who has sought, having [. . .] this, will r[est . . .] he will live for [ever]. And I say to y[ou . . .] so that you will not lead astray [your] spirits and your souls.'

[The Dialo]gue of the Saviour.

Notes

Translation of the Dialogue of the Saviour

1. The translation has been remade to include restored text, chiefly from Emmel's apparatus, and the suggestions made by Schenke in his review. The notes have been called from the Introduction by Koester and Pagels, from Blatz's notes and from Schenke.
2. Cf. Hebr. 4:10-11.
3. Cf. Gos. Thom. log. 49.
4. Cf. 2 Thess. 2:12.
5. Cf. Eph. 6:11-17.
6. Cf. Eph. 5:2; Hebr. 10:10, 14.
7. Cf. Jas. 1:21; 1 Pet. 1:9.
8. Cf. Col. 1:13.
9. Cf. Mt. 6:22; Gos. Thom. log. 24.
10. Cf. Mt. 7:7; Gos. Thom. log 2, 92, 94.
11. Cf. Mt. 8:12 etc.
12. Cf. Gen. 1:2.
13. Cf. Gos. Thom. log. 2.
14. Cf. Gen. 1:4.
15. Cf. Gen. 2:5.
16. Cf. Gos. Thom. log. 3.
17. Cf. Jn. 1:11,14; Gos. Thom. log. 28.
18. Cf. Gos. Phil. 83.8-28.
19. Cf. Rom. 10:6-7.
20. Cf. Gos. Thom. log 75.
21. Cf. Mt. 6:34b.
22. Cf. Mt. 10:10b.
23. Cf. Jn. 13:16.
24. Cf. Mt. 13:16f. (Lk. 10:23f.); 1 Cor. 2:9; Gos. Thom. log. 17.
25. Cf. Gos. Thom. log. 11.
26. Cf. Gos. Eg. (see above, p 209 ff).
27. Cf. Jn. 14:5.
28. Gos. Thom. log. 37.
29. Cf. Mk. 4:30ff. par.; Gos. Thom. log. 20.
30. Cf. Gos. Eg. (above, p 209 ff).

6. The First Apocalypse of James

Wolf-Peter Funk

1. Literature: *Facsimile: The Facsimile Edition of the Nag Hammadi Codices* published under the Auspices of the Department of Antiquities of the Arab Republic of Egypt in Conjunction with the United Nations Educational, Scientific and Cultural Organization, Codex V, Leiden 1975, pl. 32-52.

Editions of the Text: W.R. Schoedel, 'The (First) Apocalypse of James', in D.M. Parrott (ed.), *Nag Hammadi Codices V, 2-5 and VI with Papyrus Berolinensis 8502, 1 and 4* [= Nag Hammadi Studies 11], Leiden 1979, pp. 65-103. A. Böhlig/P. Labib, *Koptisch-gnostische Apokalypsen aus Codex V von Nag Hammadi im Koptischen Museum zu Alt-Kairo*, Wiss. Zeitschr. der Martin-Luther-Universität Halle-Wittenberg, 1963, Sonderband, pp. 29-55.

Translations: German by A. Böhlig in Böhlig/Labib, *Koptisch-gnostische Apokalypsen*, pp. 34-54. English: W.R. Schoedel/D.M. Parrott, 'The First Apocalypse of James (V, 3)', in J.M. Robinson (ed.), *The Nag Hammadi Library in English*, Leiden 1977, pp. 242-248 (rev. ed. 1988, pp. 260-268). W.R. Schoedel, The (First) Apocalypse of James, in D.M. Parrott (ed.), *Nag Hammadi Codices V, 2-5 and VI*, pp. 69-103. French: R. Kasser, 'Bibliothèque gnostique VI: Les deux Apocalypses de Jacques', RThPh 101, 1968, 163-186. Italian: M. Erbetta, *Gli Apocrifi del Nuovo Testamento*, vol. III: 'Lettere e Apocalissi', Turin 1969, 333-340.

Further literature: A. Böhlig, 'Der jüdische und judenchristliche Hintergrund in gnostischen Texten von Nag Hammadi', in U. Bianchi (ed.), *Le Origini dello Gnosticismo*, Leiden 1967, pp. 109-140 (also in A. Böhlig, *Mysterion und Wahrheit*, Leiden 1968, pp. 80-111). W.-P. Funk, 'Notizen zur Textkonstitution der ersten Apokalypse des Jakobus' (*Enchoria*, in the press). C. Gianotto, 'La letteratura apocrifa attribuita a Giacomo a Nag Hammadi (NHC I, 2; V, 3; V, 4)', *Augustinianum* 23, 1983, 111-121. R. Kasser, 'Textes gnostiques. Remarques à propos des éditions récentes du Livre secret de Jean et des Apocalypses de Paul, Jacques et Adam', *Le Muséon* 78, 1965, 71-98. id. 'Textes gnostiques. Nouvelles remarques à propos des Apocalypses de Paul, Jacques et Adam', *Le Muséon* 78, 1965, 299-312. K. Koschorke, *Die Polemik der Gnostiker gegen das kirchliche Christentum* Nag Hammadi Studies 12, Leiden 1978, pp. 195f. H.-M. Schenke, review of Böhlig/ Labib, *Koptisch-gnostische Apokalypsen*, OLZ 61, 1966, cols. 23-34. W.R. Schoedel, 'Scripture and the seventy-two heavens of the first Apocalypse of James', *Nov.Test.* 12, 1970, 118-129. N. Séd, 'Les douze hebdomades, le char de Sabaoth et les soixante-douze langues', *Nov.Test.* 21, 1979, 156-184. K.W. Tröger, 'Die Passion Jesu Christi in der Gnosis nach den Schriften von Nag Hammadi' (Theol. [Habil.] Dissertation, Humboldt-Universität zu Berlin, 1978), fols. 235-243.

Three works have appeared since this section was completed: a new edition by Armand Veilleux (*La première Apocalypse de Jacques (NH V,3). La seconde Apocalypse de Jacques (NH V,4)*, BCNH Section 'Textes' 17, Quebec 1986) , and two monographs: W. Pratscher, *Der Herrenbruder Jakobus und die Jakobustradition* (FRLANT 139), Göttingen 1987, and C. Scholten, *Martyrium und Sophiamythos im Gnostizismus nach den Texten von Nag Hammadi* (JAC Erg. bd. 14), Münster 1987.

2. Attestation and transmission: nothing is known of a document with the title 'Apocalypse' or 'Revelation of James' from the patristic literature and the other early Christian tradition. Even if there were such a mention, the designation would possibly have to be applied rather to the widely disseminated Protevangelium of James (see below, pp. 421ff.), in the oldest extant manuscript of which (PBodmer V) it occurs as a sub-title (to 'Birth of Mary') or as an identification of the author. In Codex V of the Nag Hammadi discovery (catalogue number 10548 in the Coptic Museum in Old Cairo) there are now two different previously unknown texts with the same title standing directly one after the other.[1] Since their original titles do not in any way distinguish them, it has become customary for scholars to describe these two texts, in accordance with their sequence in the codex, as the 'first' and 'second' Apocalypse of James.

The First Apocalypse of James (1 Apoc. Jas.) stands in the codex, in Coptic (Sahidic dialect), as the third document, on pages 24 (line 10) to 44 (line 10). The codex is a papyrus volume consisting of a single quire, the manufacture of which can be placed about the middle of the 4th century on the basis of the scrap papyrus used for the stiffening of the cover (official documents from the first half of the 4th century). Of inferior quality to begin with, the papyrus has not survived the centuries without considerable damage. Apart from the beginning and the end (the lowest double leaves), such losses are also not uncommonly to be found, to a large extent, in the middle (the topmost double leaves) of the thick papyrus quire of single-quire codices. Since the text of 1 Apoc. Jas. extends exactly to the middle of the codex (= pp.44/45), its last pages (practically the second half of the document, pp. 35-44) are increasingly damaged, and only a torso to some extent survives. Only with great effort - and often not with the certainty one might wish - can we gain from the fragments some impression of what the pages once contained. However, we can today at various points in the text read more than in the time of Böhlig's first edition, since in the interval a whole series of small fragments have been successfully placed. The results of this extremely laborious papyrological detailed work are presented in the facsimile edition and in Schoedel's critical edition. The possibilities for a plausible reconstruction of the text which now sporadically present themselves are, however, far from being completely exhausted in the edition - that is why our translation (especially in the remains of the final pages) occasionally deviates from the text presented in the edition, or goes beyond it. Nevertheless there still remain plenty of small fragments, which for the moment we cannot use for a translation.

The text of the document, possibly in a variant version, is also contained in a papyrus codex, likewise deriving from the 4th century, which first appeared in 1983 (cf. *The Facsimile Edition of the Nag Hammadi Codices. Introduction*, Leiden 1984, p. 21) and according to reports is in a better state of preservation. For the present, however, this codex is not accessible. We may hope from its publication for valuable information to supplement our knowledge of 1 Apoc. Jas. For the present this newly discovered codex - since it contains other gnostic dialogues, but 2 Apoc. Jas. is not among them - is only clear evidence for the independent circulation of 1 Apoc. Jas.

3. Original language, date and place of origin: The Coptic version of 1 Apoc. Jas. preserved in NHC V probably rests ultimately - as is generally assumed - on a translation from the Greek. This assumption may here and there explain certain roughnesses of the text; nevertheless there are no certain indications for it. We have in any case to reckon with the fact that as a copy our present text is the product of a process of transmission within Coptic, and that a large part of its unevennesses is rooted in this process. So long as we have no other witnesses to the text available, it is at many places not possible to decide with certainty whether the text is really in order or, when it does not seem to be in order, how it is to be improved. In our translation we therefore make only extremely rare use of such possibilities.

If we are already reduced to conjectures with regard to the original language, this naturally holds also for the date of the translation into Coptic. It must have taken place at the latest in the first half of the 4th century, yet scarcely earlier than the second half of the 3rd. This still does not say much about the original formation of the document. Here we are reduced to conclusions which result from the content of the text. The Valentinian *theologoumena* utilised in it (cf. especially the doctrines of an upper and a lower Sophia, or of 'Sophia' proper and 'Achamoth', which also occur in the text outside the mystery formulae quoted: p. 36.5, 8) seem to presuppose the fully-developed Valentinian system, and therefore suggest the composition of the document at the earliest towards the end of the 2nd century. The rejection of a bodily fraternal relationship between Jesus and James (p.24.15f.), evidently already presupposed, points in a similar direction. It is however very probable that in the composition of the document older material (especially from the Jewish-Christian or the James tradition) was also used. If this older material however had the dimensions of a major (pre-Valentinian) literary *Vorlage*, then this *Vorlage* would have to be regarded as an independent entity, and not identical with 1 Apoc. Jas.

We must also be prudent in our reflections on the geographical homeland of this document. Reference is made in the text to Addai (here in the Grecised form Addeos = Addaios), the legendary founder of Edessene Christianity, who in general is identified with the Thaddaeus of Mk 3:18 (the most uncertain of the twelve apostles) or as one of the Seventy in Lk 10:1. The role which he plays as bearer of tradition in 1 Apoc. Jas. (p. 36.15-24) seems to point to an East Syrian milieu (Schoedel). In that case we have here an Addai tradition which (in contrast to Euseb. H.E. I 13.11, where Addai is said to be have been sent by the apostle Thomas) appeals to the 'legitimate' successor of Jesus, James the Lord's brother, and thereby possibly establishes a direct connection between East Syrian and Palestinian Jewish Christianity. At any rate the dating of Addai's becoming active which is stated here (p. 36.21f.: ten years after the Jewish War or the exodus of the community) may be more readily regarded as a reflection of actual historical events than that of the Abgar legend[2]. For the present it remains obscure how old the linking of the James tradition with the Addai tradition actually is,[3] and what significance recourse to the Addai tradition had for the composition of the document.

4. Genre and structure of the text: the textual character of 1 Apoc. Jas. is to a decisive extent stamped by the dialogue form. Over wide stretches of the text the lapidary introductions to direct speech ('the Lord said' or 'James said') are the only thing that is 'reported' apart from the speeches. The dialogue form is not merely carried through externally: the speeches themselves, with explicit inquiries and explanations, frequent questions and answers, instruction and confirmation, exhibit pronouncedly interlocutory features. In a certain fashion this holds even for the short hymnic pieces celebrated by James (straining the normal dialogue framework; p. 28.11-20, 22-29), which express in poetic antitheses the quintessence of the Redeemer's mission or the situation of the awakened Gnostic, yet are consistently formulated in the second or first person. Even the revelation speech in the middle of the text is in large part formulated personally. Böhlig in the first edition already aptly characterised the text as a 'pure doctrinal and pastoral discourse'. The 'doctrinal conversation' - as a form of the revelation text - is nothing out of the ordinary (the address 'Rabbi' is worthy of note). The 'pastoral' element on the other hand is striking, for it in fact contributes to the peculiar character of this text and in edifying exhortation goes far beyond the measure usual in comparable texts. It is matched by a literary James figure, whose lamentable spiritual condition derives not only from fear with regard to his own destiny but also from a special sympathy with the suffering Jesus; and this scenery, developed in dialogue form - with a James who is able to compose himself only after repeated insistence - stands clearly at the service of what the document is intended to convey.

The text shows brief narrative sections at three places only. If we leave aside the badly damaged final passage (pp. 43f.), in which presumably the martyrdom of James is reported, the concern in these sections is above all to sketch the background situation in which the conversation is embedded. At the beginning there is no such embedding, and the reader has at first the impression of a pure dialogue text. From the intimations of suffering frequently contained in the words of Jesus, he can gather that this first act of the dialogue is thought of as taking place immediately before the passion. The first brief narrative passage (pp. 30.12-31.5) confirms this by a scant mention of the passion, and thus sets the stage for the second act, which is based upon an appearance of the risen Jesus. This explicit situating of the dialogue parts in the period before *and* after Easter may be a curiosity in a dialogue of the Redeemer which makes no claim to belong to the 'gospel' *Gattung*. In the second even briefer narrative context (p. 32.13-16, 23-28) the background situation for the revelation address proper is explained - both in respect of location (the 'rock' as an enhancement of the mountain of p. 30.19) and also from a psychological point of view (the recipient of the revelation wipes away his tears). The revelation speech itself (pp. 33.2-36.6) is not rent asunder by artificial objections, but carried through with remarkable continuity. Only after the conclusion of a further piece of discourse, which contains the complicated charge regarding transmission (pp. 36.7-38.11), does James again for the first time get a word in. The following final act - introduced by James with the express remark that he would still like to ask something - is from a formal point of view once again similar to the first section.

We shall therefore certainly do no injustice to the text if we regard it - without prejudice to the division into pre-Easter and post-Easter acts, which is conditioned by the situation - as essentially in three parts from the point of view of composition. As Böhlig already pointed out (p. 29), symmetry in the number of the 'acts' before and after Easter cannot be asserted. The speech of Jesus which stands at the centre of the text (pp. 33.1-38.11) is through its length lifted out of the usual dialogue, and essentially forms the core of the whole document. Reference is frequently made to it already in the first 'act', and the last 'act' has a more or less rounding-off character. Accordingly three (or four) major sections may be identified: (1) passion-week dialogue with intimation of suffering (pp. 24.11-30.15); (2) appearance of the risen Jesus (pp. 30.16-38.11): (a) Easter dialogue with interpretation of suffering, and (b) following on it the great revelation discourse; (3) concluding Easter dialogue and martyrdom of James (pp. 38.12-44.8). The ratio of these three sections to one another, measured by codex pages, is approximately 6 : 8 : 6.

5. Title: the title 'apocalypse' cannot here be understood in the sense of the conventional description of a *Gattung*. Since in 1 Apoc. Jas. it is a question of revelation discourses with a quite personal stamp (and secret), we can, if we will, understand the title according to its literal sense as simply 'the revelation (of the Lord) directed to James'. (This conception is however possible only in relation to the title of the presumed Greek original, 'Αποκάλυψις 'Ιακώβου; in Coptic the loan-word *apokalypsis* describes only the genre of the text, not the underlying circumstances). The parallel case of other texts with a more or less dialogue character (especially 2 Apoc. Jas. and the Coptic gnostic Apocalypse of Peter) suggests however that the term 'apocalypse' was also in use as a description of dialogue texts, in so far as they contained important revelations, and that it was not essentially different from 'gospel', 'book', *logos*, 'apocryphon' and similar terms. The mention of names in such titles can scarcely be intended to identify an author (cf. however the striking threefold reference to James in the first person: pp. 24.11; 25.12; 27.18), the more particularly since authorship by James cannot be reconciled with the traditional material developed at p. 36. The intimation of the name is probably always intended to indicate the (principal) partner in the dialogue or the recipient of the revelation. Accordingly the title is to be understood in rather vague terms as 'the apocalypse' or 'revelation' relating to James.

6. Content and purpose: in the course of the dialogue in 1 Apoc. Jas. a whole series of points are touched upon, on which the answers of Jesus are sometimes very general, but sometimes also specific, and occasionally take up a critical position (e.g. 'twelve' instead of 'seven' hebdomads and criticism of the scriptures at p. 26.2-8; on the question of femaleness, pp. 24.26-31; 38.16-23; 41.17-19; and much more). The main theme of 1 Apoc. Jas. is, however, beyond doubt *salvation* in the sense of the liberation of the Gnostic from the torment of earthly existence, his return to his homeland beyond, and his reunion with the primal ground of being: 'Then you will no longer be James, but you are that one who is' (p. 27.8-10). Here redemption is understood in quite practical terms. If one wishes to escape from this present sphere, one is unavoidably confronted by border guards ('toll-collectors' and 'keepers'), who not only bar the way to the ascending soul but wish to lay hold of it for their own purposes. But these powers can be overcome with words - assuming that one knows the right words. The imparting of these 'passwords' stands at the centre of 1 Apoc. Jas., and forms the main content of the great revelation discourse of Jesus. They consist essentially of an appeal by the Gnostic, in frequently varied terms, to his otherworldly origin and his descent from him who was in the beginning. This is enough to confound the border powers, and escape from their dominion.

The formulations of these passwords employed in 1 Apoc. Jas. are in essentials identical with the mystery formulae handed down to us through reports by the Church Fathers on particular groups of the Valentinians (Iren. *Adv. haer.* I 21.5 for the Marcosians; Epiph. *Pan.* 36.3.1-6 for the Heracleonites). They are there in each case presented in two batches in continuous text, and appear as a liturgical element in a sacrament for the dying. In 1 Apoc. Jas., on the other hand, the same formulae are intended in the first place for the personal use of James, and in the first part are imparted not in continuous sequence but individually as answers to prior questions (from the 'toll-collectors'); the distribution is the same, and at the second stage (with the 'keepers') the questions fall away. We have here one of the relatively rare cases of direct literary relationship between an original gnostic document known to us and the patristic literature. One may see in the working out of this interchange of questions and answers a purely literary ('dramatising') trimming; but it is also possible that the dialogue form already stems from the liturgical use. There is, however, no mention of any kind of cultic use in 1 Apoc. Jas. itself. Here the communication of the passwords is rather closely interlocked with the personal equipment of James to meet the things that await him, i.e. his martyrdom. In this connection it is remarkable that in this text practically no distinction is made between earthly and (lower) heavenly powers, and the earthly death-pangs pass over smoothly into the difficulties of the ascent. Just as towards the beginning of the document (in the passion-week dialogue) the earthly Jerusalem has been described as a kind of citadel of the archons (p. 25.18f.), so the powers who impede the ascent make their appearance as it were in the middle of the (anticipated) martyrdom of James (p. 33.2ff.). Accordingly there is basically no suffering unto death with an ascent following, but the suffering leads directly to deliverance.

The christological statements of the document also point in a similar direction. The passion of Jesus is not set out in detail (there is no explicit mention of 'crucifixion' and 'death', only of 'suffering' and 'obligation'), but there can be no doubt that it is taken to be real (Koschorke, *Polemik*, p. 196; Tröger, *Passion*, p. 240). The condition of suffering and the attitude to be adopted to it play a considerable role in the document, with reference both to Jesus and also to James. Since the Redeemer has first to fulfil his obligation in the body of flesh (pp. 29.9f.; 30.12f.) and conceals his true identity as a secret, he is even filled with despondency at the prospect of what lies before him (p. 28.3f.). Only afterwards can he say that the suffering did not affect him himself, for 'I am he who was in me' (p. 31.17f., cf. also the following sentences); only what was appointed for destruction was tortured and destroyed - the flesh, not the Redeemer himself. This may be intended to reject not the reality of the Passion, but a view 'which identified the Redeemer with his bodily nature, capable of suffering, and not rather with that part of him *in* this body which was incapable of suffering' (Koschorke, *Polemik*, p. 196). The proceedings as such do not remain limited to Jesus, but through the mythologising of the martyrdom are in the same way projected on to James, and accordingly - as we may probably infer - to the Gnostic. Thus the way through suffering appears in some degree as the natural way to redemption. The real *leitmotiv* of 1 Apoc. Jas. lies in the encouragement to face suffering - the threat of torment as well as the promise of immediate redemption. The document thus fits very well into any historical situation of persecution. Possibly it was composed in this form with the intention of giving encouragement, in a gnostic fashion, for the facing of martyrdom to adherents of Christianity threatened with persecution.

Note to the translation: there is as yet no recognised chapter division of the text. The numbers inserted with 'p.' indicate the beginning of a new page in the codex (citation usually always by page and line of Codex V). Points within square brackets [. . .] indicate lacunae within a line (usually of one or more words); [. . . . .] means that several lines are missing (presumably more than a sentence). Words in angled brackets < . . . > rest on corrections of defective passages (mostly omissions).

Notes

The First Apocalypse of James

1. On p. 44 of the codex the same title appears twice, once as the closing title of 1 Apoc. Jas. (lines 9-10) and once at the beginning of 2 Apoc. Jas. (lines 11-12). At the beginning of the document (p. 24.10) the title has been added only later.
2. The fragments unfortunately do not convey a very clear picture of the complicated chain of tradition after Addai (pp. 36.24-38.11). For the Abgar legend see below, pp. 492ff.
3. Böhlig (*Kopt.-gnost. Apok.* p. 46) suggests the constructing of a relationship (Thaddaeus as son of James) on the basis of the parallelism of the Thaddaeus of Mk 3:18/Mt 10:3 with the 'Judas of James' of Lk 6:16/Acts 1:13.

6. The First Apocalypse of James

The Lord spoke to me, saying: 'See now the completion of my redemption! I have given you a sign of these things (already before this), James my brother - for not for nothing have I called you 'my brother', although you are not my brother materially, and I know you very well - in order that when I give you a sign <you may take heed. Now I say to you:> Take heed and listen!

'There was once nothing existing outside him who is - he is unnameable and ineffable. I also am an unnameable being from him who is, although (?) I have been [given] many names (?). <We> both[1] <derive> from him who is; but I am before you.

'Since you have enquired about femaleness, (I say to you:) femaleness did exist, but femaleness was not in the first place. And [it] prepared for itself divine powers. But [it] did not yet exist [when (?)] I came forth, (p. 25) for (?) I am an image of him who is. I brought forth [his] image,[2] that the children of him who is might know what is theirs and what is alien. See, I shall reveal to you everything of this mystery. For they will arrest me the day after tomorrow, but my deliverance will be near.'

James said: 'Rabbi! You have said 'They will arrest me' - as for me, what can I do?'

He said to me: 'Do not be afraid, James! You too will be arrested. But (do you) depart from Jerusalem! For this (city) always gives the cup of bitterness to the children of light; it is a dwelling-place for many archons. But your deliverance will deliver (you) from them. That you may know who they are and of what kind they are, you should [flee (?)] Listen! They are not [gods (?)], but [archons]. The twelve [. . . . .] (p. 26) upon his own hebdomad.'

James said: 'Are there then, Rabbi, twelve hebdomads and not seven, as there are in the scriptures?'

The Lord said: 'James! He who spoke through this scripture understood only up to this point. But I will reveal to you what came forth from him who cannot be numbered - I will give a sign concerning their number - (and) as to what came forth from the immeasurable - I will give a sign concerning their measure.'

James said: 'How then, Rabbi? See - I have received their number: they are seventy-two vessels (?)!'[3]

The Lord said: 'These are the seventy-two heavens which are subordinate to them; these are the powers of all their might. They were set up by them. And these are they who were distributed over every place that is under the [authority] of the twelve archons. The insignificant power that is in them [brought forth] for itself angels [and] innumerable hosts. But [he who is] was given [. . .] . . . because of [. . .] he who is [. . .] are innumerable. (p. 27) If you wish to number them now, you will not be able - until you cast away from you the blind thought, this bond of the flesh that surrounds you. Only then will you attain to him who is. Then you will no longer be James, but you are that one who is. And all the innumerable will all have names given to them.'

<James said: 'Then,> Rabbi - in what way shall I attain to him who is, since all these powers and these hosts are armed against me?'

He said to me: 'These powers are not armed against you alone, but also against others: these powers are armed against me. And they are armed with other [powers]. But they are armed against me [with] a judgment. I was not given [. . .] in it . . . [. . .] through them [. . .] . . . here [. . .] suffering. I will . . . [. . .] . . . (p. 28) nor will I reprove them. But there will be in me a silence - and a hidden mystery. But I am faint of heart in the face of their anger.'

James said: 'Rabbi! If they arm themselves against you, yet is there no pretext.
You have come with knowledge,
that you might reprove their forgetfulness.
You have come with recollection,
that you might reprove their ignorance.
But I was concerned because of you.
For you came down into a great ignorance,
but you were not defiled by anything in it.
You came down into thoughtlessness,
but your recollection remained with you.
You walked in mud,
and your garments were not defiled.
Nor were you buried in their filth,
nor did they lay hold of you.
And I was (originally) not like them, but I have clothed myself with everything of theirs.
There is in me forgetfulness,
and yet I remember that which is not theirs.
There is in me [. . .],
and I am in their [. . .].
I found knowledge,
[and . . .] not for their sufferings [. . .].
But I am afraid [of] them, since they have power. (Tell me): What (p. 29) will they do? What will I be able to say? Or what word will I be able to speak, in order to escape them?'

The Lord said: 'James! I praise your understanding and your fear. If you continue to be zealous, do not concern yourself for anything else, but

321

only your redemption. For see, I will complete this destiny here on earth, as (once) I said from the heavens.[4] And I will reveal to you your redemption.'

James said: 'Rabbi - how then? After these things will you appear to us again?[5] After they have arrested you and you complete this destiny, you will go up to him who is!'

The Lord said: 'James! After these things I will make all clear to you - not only for your sake but because of [the] unbelief of men - that [faith] may come into being among them. For many will [attain] to faith [and] they will grow in [. . .] until [they . . .]. (p. 30) And after this I will appear for a reproof to the archons, and will show them that he is invincible. If he is laid hold on, he will lay hold on every one. But now I will go. Be mindful of the things I have told you, and let them enter into your heart.'

James said: 'Lord! I will hasten (to do) as you have said.'

The Lord bade him farewell, and fulfilled the things that were fitting. When James heard of his sufferings, he was greatly distressed.

They were waiting for the sign of his coming; it came after some days. And James was walking on the mountain which is called Gaugela, along with (those of) his disciples who (still) listened to him in (their) distress.[6] He <was ignorant that> there is a comforter, [and] said: 'This is [the] second [. . .].' [Then the] crowd dispersed. But James remained [behind at the place and] prayed [. . .], as (p. 31) was his custom.

And the Lord appeared to him. He abandoned his prayer, embraced him and kissed him. saying: 'Rabbi, I have found you! I heard of your sufferings which you endured, and I was greatly troubled - you know my fellow-feeling. Because of this I had the firm wish[7] not to see this people (any more). They must be judged for the things that they have done. For what they have done is contrary to what is fitting.'

The Lord said: 'James, do not be concerned for me or for this people! I am he who was in me. At no time did I suffer in any way, nor was I distressed. And this people did not do any harm to me. Rather it was imposed upon a figure of the archons, and it was fitting that it should be [destroyed] by them. Also [. . .] the archons [did not] . . . the one who [suffered?] . . . [. . .] angry with [. . .] righteous [. . .] (p. 32) was his servant. Because of this you have this name: 'James the Just'. You see how you will become sober after you have seen me. You have abandoned this prayer because (?) you are a righteous man of God, and have embraced and kissed me[8]. Truly I say to you: You have set in motion a great anger and wrath against yourself. But (this happened) that these other things might come to pass.'

But James was fearful and wept. And he was greatly troubled. They both sat down upon a rock. The Lord said to him: 'James, thus you will be exposed to these sufferings. But do not be sad! For the flesh is weak - it will receive what is appointed for it. But as for you, do not be timid, neither be afraid.' The Lord [paused (?)].

When James heard these things, he wiped away the tears which were in [his eyes] and very bitter (?)[. . .] . . . [. . .].

The Lord [said] to [him: 'James!] See, I will (p. 33) reveal to you your redemption. When you are arrested and exposed to these sufferings, a multitude will arm themselves against you, in order that <they> may lay hold of you. But especially three will lay hold of you, who sit as toll collectors. Not only do they demand tribute, but they also take away souls by theft.

If you fall into their hands, one of them who is their watcher will say to you: 'Who are you, or where are you from?' You are to say to him: 'I am a son, and I am from the Father.' He will say to you: 'What kind of a son are you, and to what father do you belong?' You are to say to him: 'I am from the pre-[existent] Father, and am a son in the pre-existent.' [He will say] to you: 'And [with what charge (?) have you come?]' You are [to say to him: I have come] at the behest (?) of the [pre-existent], that I [may see those who are ours (?), those] who [have become aliens.' He will say to you: 'And of what kind (p. 34) are] these aliens?' You are to say to him: 'They are not altogether aliens, but they are from Achamoth, which is the female. And these she created when[9] she brought this race down from the pre-existent one. Thus they are not aliens, but they are ours. On the one hand they are ours because she who rules over them derives from the pre-existent. On the other hand they are aliens, because the pre-existent did not associate with her at the time when she was about to create them.' When he says to you again: 'Where will you go?', you are to say to him: 'To the place whence I came forth, I will return again.' If you speak these (words), you will escape their attacks.

But if you come into the hands of [the] three controllers - those who carry off souls by theft in that place, [in order to . . . them (?)], you are to [say to them: 'I am] a vessel [which is] more [precious] than [the female who[10] . . .] . . . [. . .] (p. 35) [. . .] of (?) the one who is your [mother. <So long> (?)] as she is [ignorant] concerning her root, you [also] will not become sober [again]. But I will call upon the imperishable Gnosis, who is Sophia, she who is in the Father, who is the mother of Achamoth. Achamoth had no father, nor any male consort, but she is a female from a female. She created you on her own without a male, since she was ignorant of those who live [through] her mother, thinking that she alone existed. But I will cry up to her mother.'

'And then they will be troubled, blaming their root and the race of their mother. But you will go up to [what is] yours, after [you have cast away from you (?)] their fetters (?) [that is, the soul (?) . . . .] (p. 36) the pre-existent one. [They are] prototypes of the twelve disciples and the twelve consorts [. . .] . . . Achamoth, which is translated 'Sophia'.

'But who I am, and (who) the imperishable Sophia (is), through whom you will be redeemed, and (who are) all the children of him who is - these things which they have known and hidden within themselves, you (also) are to hide <them> within you. You are to keep silence! But you are to reveal them to Addai! When you go away, then immediately war will be made with this land - therefore [weep (?)] for him who dwells in Jerusalem! But Addai - let him take these things to his heart. In the tenth year Addai is to sit down and write them out. And when he has written them out [. . .] and they are to give them [to (?) . . .]; he has the [. . .] . . . [. . . . .] (p. 37) [. . . . .] the [first (?) . . .], who is called by the [name] Levi. Then he is to bring forth [. . .] without (?) words. On the basis (?) [of what was (?)] prophesied earlier, (I say:) [he is to take] a wife [outside (?)] Jerusalem in her [. . .]; and he <is to> beget [two] sons from her. [They are] to inherit these things, [and] the understanding of him who [. . .] . . . to exalt (?). And they are to receive [to themselves] from him (something) of his Nous.

'The smaller is greater among them. And let these things be shared with him and hidden within him until [he] comes to the age of seventeen years. [. . . . .] (p. 38) [. . . . .] from [them (?)]. He will be severely persecuted at the hand of his fellow [. . .].[11] He will be proclaimed [through] them; and [he (?) will] proclaim this word. Then [it (?) will become] a seed of [salvation (?)].'

James said: '[I am] encouraged [. . .] and they are [. . . for] my soul. Yet this [other thing] I ask of you: Who are the seven women who have [become] your disciples? And see, all the women bless you! But I wonder how (it is possible that) [power]less vessels have become strong through a perception that is within them.'

The Lord [said]: 'Well do you [. . . . .] (p. 39) [. . . . .] a spirit of [. . .], a spirit of thought, [a spirit] of counsel and [. . .], a spirit of [. . . , a] spirit of knowledge, [a spirit] of fear.[12]

When we had passed through [the] region[13] of [this] archon, who is [called] Adonaios, [then we . . .] him, and [see,] he was ignorant. [And] when I appeared before him, [he] thought that I was [a] son of his. He was gracious [to me] at that time as (to) a son of his. And then, before I appeared in this place, they were cast among [this] people (?). But from that [. . .] the prophets did not [. . . . .] (p. 40) [. . . . .] upon you (?).'

James [said]: 'Rabbi! [. . .] . . . [. . .]. I [. . .] them [all (?)] together - who [are those . . . . . .] among them more [than . . .]?'

The Lord said: '[James], I praise you [because (?) of the] profundity [of your (?) . . .] . . . [. . .] . . . [. . .]. Cast away from [you the] cup, which is the bitterness! For none of [the archons (?) will be able] to stand against you. For you [have begun] to understand [their] roots from beginning to end. Cast away from you all lawlessness, and beware, lest they be envious of you.[14] When you speak the words of this perception, persuade these [four (?)]: Salome, Mary, [Martha (?)] and Arsinoe [. . . . .] (p. 41) [. . . . .] . . . [. . .] . . . [. . .]. To these he [brings] burnt-offerings and offerings. But I [. . .] not in this way, but [I bring (?)] up first-fruits of the im[perishable], that the power [of God] may be manifest. The perishable has gone [up to] the imperishable, and the work of femaleness has attained to the work of this manhood.'

James said: 'Rabbi! Into these three then has their [. . .] been cast. For they have been despised and indeed persecuted by . . . [. . .] . . . .].' (p. 42).

[The Lord said: 'James! . . . .]. See, [I] have [imparted (?)] everything [to you. I] have [. . .] in no respect [. . .]. For you have received [the first-fruits] of knowledge, and [you know] now what is the [place (?)] in [which you will] walk. You will f[ind . . .]. But I will go [hence], and will [reveal (?) . . .], because they have trusted in you, that they may be persuaded - for their blessing and salvation - and that this revelation may come to pass.'

At that time he went immediately and reproved the twelve. He cast [out] from them assurance [concerning] the way of knowledge [. . . . .] (p. 43).

[. . . . .] . . . [. . .] . . . [. . .] The majority of [them . . .] when they saw [that] no charge lay (?) [against him], [departed] from him. [But] the others [. . .] [took him prisoner and] said [. . .]: 'Let us [take] this one [away] from this earth, for he is not worthy of life.' The first, then, were afraid; they rose up, saying: 'We have no part in this blood, for a just man will perish through injustice.' James went away, in order to [. . . . .] (p. 44) [. . . . .] seeing [. . .], for [. . .] . . . him.

The Apocalypse of James

325

The First Apocalypse of James

Notes

The First Apocalypse of James

1. The translations of Böhlig and Schoedel (two names) do not seem grammatically possible to me. The expression must probably be taken adverbially, meaning 'the two' or 'both'. Hence it is to be assumed that something has fallen out.
2. Or: 'the image of his [. . .]'.
3. We know the Coptic noun used here only with the meaning 'clay vessel, jug' (not 'vessel' in general). Probably it is a case of a homonym, the meaning of which is still unknown to us.
4. Possibly there is a corruption here. Read (?): ' . . . as I have said. And from the heavens I will . . . '
5. Or: 'Rabbi! How will you show yourself again to us hereafter?'
6. Or: 'those who listened to him (James), because they had fallen into distress'.
7. Or (?): 'Therefore I wished, as I reflected on it, that I might no (more) see this people.'
8. Or (with Schoedel): 'And you stopped this prayer. Now since you are a just man of God, you have . . . '
9. Or: 'by the fact that . . . '
10. For the bridging of the lacunae cf. the continuous text in Irenaeus, *adv. Haer.* I 21.5: ' . . . more precious than the female who created you'. The present text however varies slightly in what follows from the formula handed down in Irenaeus.
11. Or: 'his [. . .] fellows'.
12. Cf. Isa. 11:2.
13. Or: 'the breadth (of the heaven)'.
14. Or should we understand: '[. . .] take heed that they (*sc.* the wicked) do not vie with you'?

7. The Second Apocalypse of James

Wolf-Peter Funk

1. Literature. *Facsimile: The Facsimile Edition of the Nag Hammadi Codices* published under the Auspices of the Department of Antiquities of the Arab Republic of Egypt in Conjunction with the United Nations Educational, Scientific and Cultural Organization, Codex V, Leiden 1975, pl. 52-73.

Editions of the Text: A. Böhlig/P. Labib, *Koptisch-gnostische Apokalypsen aus Codex V von Nag Hammadi im Koptischen Museum zu Alt-Kairo*, Wiss. Zeitschr. der Martin-Luther-Universitst Halle-Wittenberg, 1963, Sonderband, pp. 56-85. W.-P. Funk, *Die zweite Apokalypse des Jakobus aus Nag-Hammadi-Codex V, neu herausgegeben, übersetzt und erkärt* (TU 119), 1976. C.W.Hedrick, 'The (Second) Apocalypse of James', in D.M. Parrott (ed.), *Nag Hammadi Codices V, 2-5 and VI with Papyrus Berolinensis 8502, 1 and 4* (= Nag Hammadi Studies 11), Leiden 1979, pp. 105-149.

Translations: German by A. Böhlig in Böhlig/Labib, *Koptisch-gnostische Apokalypsen*, pp. 67-85. W.-P. Funk, *Apokalypse*, pp. 11-49, 77-86. English: W.-P. Funk, *Apokalypse*, pp. 221-231. C.W. Hedrick/D.M. Parrott in J.M. Robinson (ed.), *The Nag Hammadi Library in English*, Leiden 1977, pp. 249-255; rev. ed. 1988, pp.270-276. C.W. Hedrick, 'The (Second) Apocalypse of James', in D.M. Parrott (ed.), *Nag Hammadi Codices V, 2-5 and VI*, pp. 111-149. French: R. Kasser, 'Bibliothèque gnostique VI. Les deux Apocalypses de Jacques', RThPh 101, 1968, 163-186. Italian: M. Erbetta, *Gli Apocrifi del Nuovo Testamento*, vol. III: 'Lettere e Apocalissi', Turin 1969, 341-347. Spanish: J. Denker, 'El segundo apocalipsis de Santiago', *Revista Biblica* 45, 1983, 95-107.

Further literature: A. Böhlig, 'Zum Martyrium des Jakobus', *Nov.Test.* 5, 1962, 207-213 (also in Böhlig, *Mysterion und Wahrheit*, Leiden 1968, pp. 112-118). id. 'Der jüdische und judenchristliche Hintergrund in gnostischen Texten von Nag Hammadi', in U. Bianchi (ed.), *Le Origini dello Gnosticismo*, Leiden 1967, pp. 109-140 (also in Böhlig, *Mysterion und Wahrheit*, pp. 80-111). S.K. Brown, 'Jewish and gnostic elements in the second Apocalypse of James (CG V, 4)', *Nov.Test.* 17, 1975, 225-237. W.-P. Funk, 'Notizen zur weiteren Textkonstitution der zweiten Apokalypse des Jakobus', in P.O. Scholz/R. Stempel (eds.), *Nubia et Oriens Christianus* (FS C.D.G. Müller), Cologne 1987, pp. 107-114. R. Kasser, 'Textes gnostiques. Remarques à propos des éditions récentes du Livre secret de Jean et des Apocalypses de Paul, Jacques et Adam', *Le Muséon* 78, 1965, 71-98. id. 'Textes gnostiques. Nouvelles remarques à propos des Apocalypses de Paul, Jacques et Adam', *Le Muséon* 78, 1965, 299-312. K. Koschorke, *Die Polemik der Gnostiker gegen das kirchliche Christentum*, (Nag Hammadi Studies 12), Leiden 1978, pp. 196-198. id. review of Funk, *Apokalypse*, ThLZ 105, 1980, cols. 43-46. W. Myszor, 'Zagadnienie modlitwy gnostików [The question of the Prayer of the Gnostic]', *Tarnowskie Studia Teologiczne* 8, 1981, 35-44. H.-M. Schenke, review of Böhlig/Labib, *Apokalypsen*, OLZ 61, 1966, cols. 23-34. id. 'Exegetische Probleme der zweiten Jakobus-Apokalypse in Nag-Hammadi-Codex V' (Probleme der koptischen Literatur, Wiss. B. Univ. Halle 1968/1, 109-114). K.-W. Tröger, 'Die Passion Jesu Christi in der Gnosis nach den Schriften von Nag Hammadi' (Theol. [Habil.-] Dissertation, Humboldt-Universität zu Berlin, 1978), pp. 194-307.

Three works have appeared since this section was completed: a new edition by Armand Veilleux (*La première Apocalypse de Jacques (NH V,3). La seconde Apocalypse de Jacques (NH V,4)*, BCNH Section 'Textes' 17, Quebec 1986) and two monographs: W. Pratscher, *Der Herrenbruder Jakobus und die Jakobustradition* (FRLANT 139), Göttingen 1987, and C. Scholten, *Martyrium und Sophiamythos im Gnostizismus nach den Texten von Nag Hammadi* (JAC Erg.bd 14), Münster 1987.

2. Attestation and transmission: on the attestation of writings under the title 'Apocalypse of James', see above (pp. 313ff.) on 1 Apoc. Jas. The Second Apocalypse of James (2 Apoc. Jas.) stands, in Coptic (Sahidic dialect), as the fourth document in Codex V from Nag Hammadi (pages 44, line 11, to 64, line 32 = the last line). The original title appears only at the beginning (44.11f.). On the age and character of the papyrus codex, see again what was said on 1 Apoc. Jas.; in regard to the state of preservation the same holds here - with the difference that 2 Apoc. Jas. begins on the badly damaged middle pages of the codex, so that in it the first pages are particularly badly preserved, the last in contrast relatively well. In quite a number of cases important connective sections of the text are affected by the loss of the upper and lower parts of the pages; in the translation an attempt is made to remedy this deficiency so far as possible by indications introduced in brackets. Nothing is known of any parallel transmission of this text.

3. Original language, date and place of origin: although there is no firm evidence for it, it is generally assumed that the extant Coptic copy of 2 Apoc. Jas. goes back to a translation from the Greek. The occasional appearance of a name or a loan-word in a Greek inflected form can be interpreted as an indication of the Coptic translator's lack of attentiveness; here and there the idea of a translation from the Greek is also helpful for our understanding of the Coptic text. The translation into Coptic will have taken place at the latest shortly before the making of the codex (middle of 4th cent.), hence in the first half of the 4th century, but at the earliest in the second half of the 3rd century. We know nothing of the original place and date of origin of the document; for lack of direct connections with literature which can be historically located, no firm indications can be gained from the content itself. We may however raise the question in what period and region the document would best fit according to our conception of it. Along these lines conjectures have been advanced which tend towards the 2nd century (middle, or even first half). In many respects the text stands close to the Fourth Gospel, as well as to the Antitheses of Marcion, although it cannot be recognised to be dependent on either of the two. The prominent role of James the Lord's brother appears to speak for the geographical area of Syria and Palestine rather than for any other.

4. Genre, literary character and literary criticism: 2 Apoc. Jas. is not a dialogue text in the usual sense; it has however in several respects the character of personal discourse. In the first place, the whole text is presented as a transcription by a certain Mareim on the basis of a report given to James's father by a 'priest' who had relations of kinship with the family (pp. 44 and 61). (It is not clear from the text whether instead of these three participants perhaps only two are intended, i.e. whether the 'priest' is to be identified with Mareim.) At any rate the reporter's narrative which forms the frame appears at the beginning of the document (down to just before the end of p. 45) and is taken up again towards the end (p. 60 end [lacuna] - p. 61). The main content of this report - and hence of the document in general - is actually, as announced in the incipit (44.13-15), the 'speech which James the Just delivered in Jerusalem'. The document by no means presupposes that this was the only speech by James in Jerusalem, but seems to regard it as the most important. This speech in turn contains very diverse texts. At the centre stands the appearance of the risen Jesus, with a relatively long speech which is practically never interrupted by questions or objections. In terms of content, this is a very personal speech of revelation addressed by Jesus to his brother, in the course of which however 'ultimate mysteries' are hinted at rather than clearly spoken. Before James relates this occurrence, he appears to quote a still earlier speech of Jesus (pp. 48f.). Only the beginning and end of James's speech are to be understood as addressed to the hearers, and here he concerns himself at the beginning with his own role in particular (as the prototype of the Gnostic), but at the end in a diatribe with the role of the listeners (who have crucified the unrecognised Redeemer) and with the end of the Jerusalem Temple. We cannot however determine the exact structure of James' speech with any certainty, since some crucial passages are lost through lacunae.

If we assume (as some sentences, especially on p. 45, suggest) that the report framing the great speech by James was given to James' father by the priest who was his kinsman during the actual period of distress (i.e. shortly before or during the execution), then the narrative of the course of the execution, or of James' death, given at the end of the document cannot have been a constituent part of this report. We must therefore reckon with the possibility that the final author lost sight of this literary framework - the priest's report to James' father - at the latest somewhere in the text of the present p. 61, or that the last major editorial work consisted in the fusing together of a text of this kind (a speech of James within a framework) and another text (a martyrdom report with James' dying prayer). There has so far been scarcely any opposition to a literary-critical hypothesis along these lines,[1] but owing to the numerous lacunae it cannot be presented with any precision.

In all parts of this literary product, bundled together in a complicated way, there are sections in which we may conjecture, by reason of their stylistic peculiarity or their compactness, that they go back to older traditions - although we cannot identify the author's sources in detail. A special place among these traditional pieces is claimed by the dying prayer of James, inserted into the report of the martyrdom, which is a valuable enrichment of our knowledge of gnostic prayer literature. Along with the so-called 'Prayer of the Apostle Paul' (NHC I 1) it offers a further genuinely Christian example of the *Gattung*, evidently widespread in gnostic circles of the most diverse provenance, of the psalm of ascent (the Sitz im Leben of which may have been a liturgy of ascent variously shaped); for this we previously had almost exclusively Manichean sources (the so-called 'Psalms to Jesus': Man. Ps. Nos. 242-289; cf. also the dying prayer of Thomas in the Acts of Thomas) apart from the penitential laments of the Pistis Sophia.[2]

5. Relation to the James tradition: the text of 2 Apoc. Jas. contains at several points statements which relate to the life of James. Since we are dealing neither with a historiographical work nor with an original document from the Lord's brother, it would be inappropriate to examine these from the point of view of their historical reliability. Nevertheless they may claim a certain interest from the point of view (more one of literary history) of the transmission of data from the life of James, and the formation of a portrait of James, as well as from that of the exegetical understanding of the text itself. These references may be classified in three complexes: (1) the question of relationships; (2) the activity of James; (3) the martyrdom of James.

On the question of relationships we are faced by one (or several) of the major riddles of this document, which is further aggravated by the destruction of some passages but would probably remain even if the text had been handed down complete. The name of James' father and Mary's husband is given not as Joseph but as Theudas (p. 44.18), and the special relationship of Jesus with James consists to all appearances not in the usual (half-)brotherly relationship, but on the one hand in a 'foster-brother' relation through James' mother and on the other in some kind of blood relation through James' father (p. 50). There has been much speculation about the last statement;[3] we probably have to read (despite a small lacuna) with a high degree of certainty 'he (Jesus) is the brother of your (James') father' - whatever is to be understood by 'brother' here.[4] It is, however, to be noted that 2 Apoc. Jas. (in contrast to 1 Apoc. Jas.) contains no express rejection of a bodily brotherhood relationship between Jesus and James, and that here (even more clearly than in 1 Apoc. Jas.) the author works with the latent consciousness of this brotherly relationship (cf. the course of the conversation at p. 50). A certain natural relationship between Jesus and James[5] is in any case of fundamental importance for the development of the main ideas of the document. In addition the family, as already mentioned, is placed in a relation to a Jerusalem Temple priest (pp. 44 and 61; cf. the priest from the Rechabites in Hegesippus, Euseb. H.E. II 23.17).

On the second point it is to be noted that it is above all the rhetorical activity of James that is stressed in 2 Apoc. Jas., and this from two points of view: for one thing he *frequently* delivered speeches (in the court of the Jerusalem Temple)(pp. 45 and 61; cf. Ps. Clem. *Recog.* I 73.3 as well as the Ἀναβαϑμοὶ Ἰακώβου of the Ebionites in Epiphanius, *Haer.* 30.16); for another, it was evidently a particular speech at a great festival (before an international public: p. 45.18-20; cf. Hegesippus in Euseb. H.E. II 23) which finally led to his execution. We are certainly given here examples of James' utterances against the Temple cult (cf. the threat of p. 60.14-23, possibly also the damaged logion p. 45.13-15; cf. Epiphanius, *loc. cit.*). But (in contrast to 1 Apoc. Jas. pp. 30-32) 2 Apoc. Jas. does not appear to refer to James as the great man of prayer (cf. Hegesippus).

As for the report of the execution, it must be said that here a series of traditional details, already known to us from the report of Hegesippus, have been fused with literary cliches and a freely overdrawn portrayal. To the first belong the reproach of 'going astray' (here further below), the formulation of the judgment ('to do away with the Just, for he is of no use to us'), the fall from the pinnacle, and the stoning. The unanimity of the resolve (p. 61.13) appears to be rather a cliche in martyrdoms (cf. already Acts 7:57), and is in any case in conflict with the striking faction-motif in the historiographical James tradition (cf. Josephus, *Ant.* XX 9.1 and also Hegesippus), which clearly recurs in 1 Apoc. Jas. (p. 43). The 'cornerstone' and the fall from a height without fatal consequences pick up again the literary borrowings from Ps. 118, already known from Hegesippus. The rest of the martyr's torments may come from the author's imagination. An arbitrary element - and at the same time the only thing 'gnostic' in this martyrdom report - is the interpolation of the extensive prayer of ascent at the moment of death.[6]

6. Theological accents: the didactic portions of 2 Apoc. Jas. cannot be assigned to any particular group or school, but are none the less to be qualified as 'gnostic'. This is not only because there is no lack of clear reminiscences (elsewhere rooted in a school) of gnostic *mythologoumena* (e.g. pp. 46f.,53f., 58), but above all because it is precisely what is gnostic - the true knowledge in contrast to naive Christianity - that is here the subject. The polemical aspect is, however, by no means in the foreground of the document. Its chief aim is not the denunciation of the ignorant, but the provision of a literary basis for a cultic reverence for James - a James who is appointed for the purpose of opening the gates of heaven to those returning home, and distributing the reward (p. 55), who is envied by the creator (p. 55.25f.), 'the first who will unclothe himself' (p. 56.9f.), indeed the one for whose sake redemption is bestowed on those to be redeemed (p. 56.2-7). Here (after the manner of Peter) the original authority of the earthly representative is carried over into eternity - yet with so much enthusiasm that James is exalted to an extraordinary mythical rank, with aspects of autonomy (cf. Gos. Thom. §12).

Before James can receive the promise of his rank as exclusive mediator of redemption, he must first become a gnostic. This means here that he must first come to know that the salvation intended for him himself is of quite another kind than he hitherto believed. This is what is implicitly done in the speech of Jesus in the centre of the document. Here the theme of relationship provides the author with the decisive metaphors which enable him to comprehend all that is necessary in relatively few sentences. The brotherly relationship in this world is superseded by the brotherhood of the one who derives from above, 'those who are mine - now also thine' (p. 55.19f.; cf. p. 54 and p. 46.20f.). The disparity of the fathers is removed, in that James receives a new father: 'Your father is not my father; but my father has (also) become father to you' (p. 51.19f.). The old promise by the creator-god of all that is visible (the inheritance of the father hitherto) is outbidden by the new promise of the invisible (p. 52.9-16). The pointed contrasting of the known and the unknown father, of the earthly and the heavenly promise (small and great, evil and good), of might and mercy etc. not infrequently leads in this document to antithetic formulations which come very close to some antitheses of Marcion[7] - yet without any polemic against the Jews. This sharpening of the doctrine in the form of theses, its reduction in large measure to the expression of the new self-understanding in personal categories, may be a reflection of actual 'new' belief and 'fresh' knowledge on the part of the circle which produced it (and on the whole probably speaks rather for a relatively high age for the document).

The two-level treatment of the theme of relationship corresponds to a likewise two-level christological conception.[8] James as it were learns to know Jesus as the one who at one and the same time is and is not what others think of him - according to the stage of knowledge at which one is. The risen Jesus who comes to James in his house is doubtless the crucified, 'that one whom you hated and persecuted' (p. 50.8-10), the same person who previously said of himself 'I die in a death' (p. 48.8f.). What James only knows afterwards is that this same Jesus (at the same time and above all) was something completely different, namely 'the invisible, who did not come down upon earth' (p. 58.14-17), 'the stranger' whom 'they could not know in their thoughts' (p. 51.7-9), but 'I saw that he was naked and there was no garment clothing him' (p. 58.20-23). And the main point is this real nature of the Redeemer. 'The crucifixion and the natural relationships of the Saviour are real, yet completely unimportant. The reality of such associations in this world is not denied, but fades away in favour of the reality of the Spirit which alone counts' (Koschorke, *Polemik*, p. 198). This aporia is also symbolically portrayed in the mysterious proceedings which end the epiphany scene (pp. 56f., especially p. 57.10-19). After a fourfold promise of revelation from Jesus, a kiss and a double address as 'my beloved', and the explicit injunction to embrace Jesus, James is at first frustrated: 'I did not find him as I thought.' After a repeated summons James attains to understanding, and experiences a 'mysterium tremendum et fascinosum' (Tröger, *Passion*, p. 204). Even the Redeemer could not impart the real revelation to him in verbal terms. So much the less can the author, who in this way succeeds in confining himself to a few columns, in the well-grounded confidence that he has yet said all that is essential.

Note to the translation: there is no recognised chapter division of the text. The numbers inserted with 'p.' give in each case the beginning of a new page in the codex (citation usually always by page and line of Codex V). Points within square brackets [...] indicate lacunae within a line (usually one or more words); [... ... ...] means that several lines are missing (presumably more than a sentence). Words in angled brackets < ... > rest on corrections of defective passages (occasionally they contain portions of text which were to be deleted { } at another place). An attempt is made to render the frequently confused literal speech more readily comprehensible, as far as the middle of page 61, by the use of various types of quotation mark :> .. <. the priest's report; >> ... << within the priest's report: James' speech and the summons at p. 61.13f.; ' ... ' within James' speech: the scriptural quotation, James' mother and Jesus; ' ... ' within Jesus' speech: words quoted from the Demiurge (also used for some other expressions).

Notes

1. For details on this see Funk, *Apokalypse*, pp. 193-198; cf. also Hedrick, 'The (Second) Apocalypse', p. 107.
2. For the establishing of this *Gattung* cf. the excursus on James' dying prayer in Funk, *Apokalypse*, pp. 211-220.
3. See below, p. 340, note 5.
4. On the possible vagueness of the word 'brother', especially in the phrase 'brother of someone's father', see Funk, 'Notizen', p. 109.
5. On the individual problems see Funk, *Apokalypse*, pp. 90f., 120-122. As a typological parallel for the literary redaction and interpretation of the bodily brother-relationship to Jesus, cf. the introductory chapter in the Book of Thomas (NHC II 6; see above, pp. 241f.)
6. 'Through the death prayer the already existing tradition of the martyrdom of James undergoes a gnostic interpretation in 2 Apoc. Jas. At the same time it also delivers up to this gnostic interpretation the words of the risen Jesus to James: 'My beloved, come to knowledge and understand everything, that you *may come out of this body*, even as I'! (Koschorke, ThLZ 105, col. 44).
7. Cf. the corresponding quotations in Funk, *Apokalypse*, pp. 203f. We may add a reference to antithetical sentences like Jn 4:13f. (in contrast to the 'which I will give him'; cf. 2 Apoc. Jas. p. 52).
8. See on this Koschorke, *Polemik*, pp. 196-198, also ThLZ 105, col. 44f.

The Second Apocalypse of James

This is [the] discourse which James [the] Just delivered in Jerusalem and which Mareim wrote down. One of the priests[1] told it to Theudas, the father of this just man, since he was a relative of his. He said:

>[Hasten] and come with [Mary] your wife and your relatives! . . . [. . . . .] (p. 45) . . . [. . .] . . . [. . . . .] Hasten then! Perhaps, [if] you yourself guide us to him [he will] come to his senses. For see, there are many who are disturbed at his [slander (?)]. They are extremely angry [at him. For he has said (?)]: >>They [do not (?)] pray [. . . . . .]<< For [he has said] these words many times, and others also.

He used to speak these words while the multitude of the peoples was sitting. But (this time) he came in and sat down <not> in the place where it [was] his custom, but he took his seat on the fifth, the 'beautiful', flight of steps. While all our [people . . . . . . (James spoke:)] (p.46) [. . .]

[>>Blessed (?) is the man [who . . .] out of [. . .
    and will come] to [. . .
    of whom it is said] that he is a [. . .]
I am he
    who received a revelation from the Pleroma [of] Imperishability,

who was summoned by him who is great
and obeyed the [Lord] -
(he) who passed through the [worlds] [without being recognised (?)]
who [came down after (?) he] had unclothed [himself],
and walked about naked,
who was found in perishability
although he was to be brought up to imperishability.

This same Lord [came] down as a son who sees and as a brother. He was [rejected (?)] when he was on the way to [him whom] the [Father] begot, in order that (?) [he might . . . him] and induce him to free himself [from the fetters (?) of] death (?) [. . . . .] (p. 47) [. . . . . . who] came to [me in fidel]ity (?) [. . . . .]. Now again am I rich in knowledge. I have a unique [Redeemer]: he who alone was begotten from above and was the first [to] come out of a [. . .]. I am the [. . .]; [. . . . . . to the Father] whom I have come to know. He who[2] was revealed to me was hidden from everyone, and (yet) he will be revealed through him. The two who see - I < . . . >.[3]

It was already prophesied through those (*sc.* the prophets):[4] 'He will be judged with the unrighteous.'

He who lived [without] blasphemy
died through [blasphemy].
He who was cast out
[has been exalted (?)].
He who [was . . .
is . . . .

(p. 48) It is the Lord (?) who so] speaks (?):
'[. . . . .]
I [. . . . . .] flesh,
[and (yet)] I will come out from the flesh in [fulfilment].
I (shall) surely die,
but I will be found in life.
I entered (the world) to be judged,
[and will] come forth [victorious (?)].

I do not judge, [and I do] not [confuse] the servants of his [will], whom I hasten to set free. And if [I] help them, I wish to take them up above him who wishes to rule over them. I am in a secret [way] the brother who scorned (?) this piti[less . . . .] (p. 49) [. . . . .]

I [am the . . .] of imperishability
[and the] first among [those who shall arise (?)].
I [am the] first [son (?)] who was begotten
and who will destroy the dominion of [them] all.
I [am] the beloved.

I am the righteous.
I am the son of the Father.

I speak as [I] have heard.
I command as [I] have [received] the commandment.
I teach you as I have [found].

See, I speak that I may come forth.
    Pay heed to me, that you may see me!
If I have come into being, who then am I?
    For I have come the way I am [not],
    and I will not reveal myself the way I am.
For I existed (on earth only) for a short period of time. [I] did [not] have [. . .] . . . [. . . ..] (p. 50) [... ...].' (*End of Jesus quotation*)
    As I once was sitting and meditating, [he] opened the door and came in to me, that one whom you hated and persecuted. He said to me:
'Hail, my brother!
My brother, hail!'
As I raised my [face] to look at him, (my) mother said to me: 'Do not be afraid, my son, because he said to you 'My brother'. For you were both nourished with the same milk - that is why he calls me 'My mother'. For he is no stranger to us - he is the brother of your father.[5] [I am (?)] not [. . .] . . . [. . . ' After] she [had spoken these words (?) ... ... He said] (p. 51) to me: 'My [brother! . . .] these words [. . .] . . . [. . .]. [Those] whom I shall [find will] come out. [But] I am the stranger, and no [one] knows me in [his] thought, because they know me in [. . .].[6] Rather it would be fitting that others should come to know through you.
    It is to you that I say: Listen and understand!
    For many when they hear will be faint-hearted.
    But you, understand in the way I shall be able to tell you!
Your father is not my father.
    But my father has become a father to you.
(Like) this virgin, about whom you hear, so you also [have chosen (?)] rest [for yourself], [in that you escaped (?)].' When I [did not understand (?), he said]: 'Listen [... ...] virgin [. ...' (I said:) ' ... ...] (p. 52) [. ... .] this virgin. [I] have [understood] how [she returned].' He said to me: '[Take heed! He who] shakes my [promise] does not [act] as I wish. For it is this[7] to which you are to turn [your] face; and this[7] [also] is advantageous for you.
    Your father, whom you consider to be rich,
        will grant that you inherit

all that you see.
But I proclaim to you
   (that I will) give you what I shall say,
   if (only) you listen.
Now then, open your ears!
   And understand!
   And walk (accordingly)!

[When] they come for you - impelled by him who is 'glorious' - wishing to cause confusion and do violence, [pay no heed to them (?),] but [... ...!] And [... ... ...] (p. 53) he [had] set his hand [to something] which [he] did not [understand] - nor did [those] who were sent out by him to make this [creation] which is here. Afterwards, when [he] is put to shame, he will [be troubled] that his labour, which is far removed [from] the aeons, is nothing. And his inheritance will prove to be small - the very one of which he boasted that it was great. His gifts too are not benefits, and his promises are evil counsels. For you do not belong to <the children of> his compassion, but he does violence to you. He wishes to do us injustice. And he will lord it for a time that is appointed for him.

But understand and know the Father who has compassion - he who was not given an inheritance and (whose inheritance) is not limited, nor does it have a (limited) number of days. Rather it is [an] eternal [day] and [light]. It exists [in those places (?) which the ... (sc. the Demiurge)] (p. 54) [himself cannot] perceive and [of which] he (only) made use; for he is not from them. Because of this he [curses (?)] (and) because of this he boasts, that he may not be reproved. For the following reason he is superior to those who are below, (that is,) those whom they looked down upon in order to attain perfection in them: After he had taken captive those from the Father, he seized them and fashioned them to resemble himself; and (in this manner) they are with him.

I saw from the height those who had come into being, and I have (now) indicated how they came into being. They were visited while they were in another form. And while I was watching [I] recognised in those whom I know the way in which I am (myself). In the presence of those who have come to be they will make an [exodus] - since I know that every one who [was brought] down by force (?) to this place (p. 55) will come [to me like] the 'little children'. [I] wish to impart [to him] a revelation through you and the [Spirit of] Power, and he (the Spirit) will give revelation [to those] who are yours; and through you those who wish to enter in will open the good door. And they turn about (on the path they have so far followed?), that they may (henceforth) walk in the way which (leads) before this door, and follow you and enter, [and you] accompany them inside and give to each one the reward that falls to his share. For you are not the redeemer or a helper of strangers. You are an illuminator and redeemer of those who are mine - but now those who are yours. You are to give revelation, and you are to bring good among them all.

You [they shall] admire because of all (your) miracles.
You are the one whom the heavens bless.
You shall he envy,
    [who] gave himself the name 'the [jealous one]'.
You . . . [. . . . . Those who exist in] forgetfulness (?) [these are] (p. 56) those who are instructed about these things with [you].

Because of you [they] will be taught about [these things] and come to rest.

Because of you they will come to reign
    [and] become kings.
Because of [you] pity will be taken
    on those on whom pity is taken.
For just as you are the first who clothed yourself, so also you are the first who will unclothe himself. And you shall become as you were before you unclothed yourself.'

And he kissed me on the mouth (and) embraced me, saying: 'My beloved! See, I will reveal to you what [the] heavens did not know - nor their archons. See, I will reveal to you what he did not know, the one who boasted [saying: 'I am God, and there is no other] (p. 57) apart from me. [But (?)] I am alive, because (?) I am a father.[8] Have I [not power] over all things?' See, I will reveal [to you] all things. My beloved, understand and know them, [that] you may come forth (from this body) even as I am. See, I will reveal to you him who [is hidden]. But now, stretch out your [hand]! Now, embrace me!'

Immediately I stretched out my [hands] - and I did not find him as I thought. But afterwards I heard him saying: 'Understand, and embrace me!' Then I understood, and I was afraid; and (at the same time) I rejoiced with a great joy.

Therefore I say to you: You who judge - you have been judged. You did not spare, but you have been spared. Become sober and [recognise him! For in reality the one whom] you [judged is] another (than you thought)(?). [. . . . .] (p. 58) you did not know.

He was [that one] whom he [could] not [see]
    who created the heaven and the earth and dwelt in it (?).
He was the one [who] is life.
He was the light.
He was the one who will be
    and who again will put [an] end to [what] has begun,

and a beginning to what will come to an end.
He was the Holy Spirit
and the Invisible One, who did not come down upon earth.
He was the virgin
and the one to whom (what) he wishes happens.
I saw that he was naked, and there was no (bodily) garment clothing him.
What he desires happens to him. [. . . . .] (p. 59)

Abandon this difficult way, which has (such) a multitude of forms,
[and] walk according to him who desires [that] you become free men
[with] me, after you have overcome every dominion! For he will not
[judge] you on account of the things which you have done, but he will
have mercy upon you. [For] it was not you who did them, but it was
[your] lord (who did them). He (sc. Jesus) was [not] a wrathful one, but
he was a kind father.

But you have passed judgment on yourselves
and because of this will remain in their fetters.
You have burdened yourselves
and will repent, (and yet) you will in no way profit.
Look upon him who speaks,
and seek after him who is silent!
Know him who came to this place,
and understand him who went away!
I am 'the Just',
and (yet) I do <not> judge.
I am thus not a master,
but I am a helper.

He was rejected before he stretched out his hand. [But] as for me, [he has]
open[ed my ears (?) . . . .] (p. 60) And he makes me hear the
<silencing (?)> of your trumpets, your flutes and your harps [for this]
house. It is the lord who has taken you captive { },[9] closing your ears that
they may not hear the sound of my speech and you in your hearts pay
attention [and be able] to call me 'the Just'.[10] Therefore I say to you <in
the name of the Lord>:[9] 'See, I have given you your house - this of which
you say that God made it, (and) in which he who dwells in it has promised
to give you an inheritance. This I will tear down, to the ruin and derision
of those who are in ignorance.'<< (*End of James' speech?*)

For see, those who (hold the office of) judge are deliberating, in order
to pass [judgment](?) [on all that he has said (?) . . . .] (p. 61) [on]
that day. All the [people] and the crowd were confused, and it was clear
that they were not convinced. And he arose and went away, after speaking
in this [manner].

But he came in (again) the other day (?), and spoke for a few hours.

As for me, I was with the priests. And I revealed nothing of (our) kinship, since they were all saying with one voice: 'Come! Let us stone the Just!'> (*End of priest's report?*)

And they rose up, saying: 'Well then, let us kill this man, that he may be removed from our midst! For he will be of no use to us at all.' And they were there, and they found him standing by the pinnacle of the Temple, beside the mighty cornerstone. And they decided to cast him down from the height, and they cast him down.

But [when] they [looked upon him], they observed [that he was still alive(?). Then] they arose (?) [and went down,] (p. 62) seized him and [abused] him, dragging him on the ground. They stretched him out, rolled a stone on his abdomen, and trampled him with their feet, saying: '(O you) who have gone astray!' Again they raised him up, since he was (still) alive, made him dig a hole, and made him stand in it. When they had covered him up to his abdomen, they stoned him in this manner.

But he stretched out his hands and spoke this prayer - not the one which he was accustomed to say:

'My God and Father,
>who saved me from this hope since it is dead!
>Who made me alive through a mystery of his good pleasure!
Let not these days of this world be prolonged for me,
>but the day of your light
>- in which [no residue (?) of night (?)] remains -
[let it shine (upon me)!]
[Bring me to the place (?) of my] (p. 63) salvation
>and deliver me from this [place of] sojourn!
Do not let your grace be left behind in me,
>but let your grace become pure.
Save me from an evil death!
Bring me from the tomb alive,
>because your grace is alive in me -
>a yearning to be instrumental in a work of fulfilment.[11]
Deliver me from sinful flesh,
>for I have trusted in you with all my strength,
>for you are the life of life![12]
Deliver me from a humiliating enemy,
>and do not give me into the hands of a severe judge!
<Save me> from sin,
>and forgive me all the debts of my days!
For I am alive in you -
>your grace is alive in me.
I have renounced everything,

but you I have openly confessed.
Deliver me from evil affliction!
But now is the [time] and the hour.
Holy [Spirit], send me salvation!
Light [from] light, crown [me] with [imperishable . . .] power!'
After he had spoken, [he] fell silent. His word [was] afterwards [written down. This is (?)] the *logos* [. . .].

Notes

The Second Apocalypse of James

1. Or (with Böhlig and Hedrick): '. . . and which Mareim, one of the priests, wrote. He had told it to Theudas' (division as above: Kasser and Funk). We have to consider whether the text is mutilated, perhaps through a translation error, and originally meant: '. . . and which Mareim wrote. One of the priests, Theudas, reported it to the father of this just man' (Schenke in Funk, *Apokalypse*, p. 90).
2. Or (with Hedrick): 'That which was revealed to me was hidden from everyone and shall (only) be revealed through him'. Or perhaps (?): 'He who was revealed to me and hidden from everyone will reveal himself through his (own) self'.
3. The text at this point appears to be corrupt (Böhlig, Kasser, Hedrick).Either it is a case of an independent sentence, the continuation of which is missing (e.g.: 'the two who see, I <am these> - ' or: 'the two who see - <it is> I <who . . . them>'); or, since the preceding sentence does not have the expected important agent, the whole should be attached there (e.g.: '. . . will be revealed through the <second> who sees - <which is> I').
4. Cf. Is. 53:12 (and Lk. 22:37). Hedrick reads: '. . . proclaimed through these [words]:....'
5. The lacuna is very probably to be filled in this way (with a genitive). Hedrick supplies a different preposition ('on the side of'): 'he is the brother [on the side of] your father', and interprets this as 'your stepbrother' (cf. on this Funk, *Apokalypse*, pp. 121f.). The possibility of this interpretation is however doubtful (one would expect a different Coptic phraseology, e.g. 'your brother-on-the-father's side'. The reconstruction of a genitive relationship underlying the above has given rise to various conjectures (Böhlig: 'the brother of your <milk>', interpreted as 'fosterbrother'; Funk: 'the brother's <son> [= nephew] of your father'). If we take the text literally, then the Theudas mentioned at p. 44.18, the father of James, is apparently a brother of Jesus, and his wife Mary (p. 44.22), the mother of James, is Jesus' fostermother. There would then be no reference at all to the parents of Jesus. But note that 'brother of your father' can mean 'your cousin' (see Gen. 29:12 and cf. Funk, 'Notizen', p. 109).
6. Perhaps: 'for they know me (only) in [this body]'; or (with Hedrick): 'in [this place]'? The solution for an acceptable restoration of lines 5-9 was found by S. Emmel (see H.-M. Schenke's report to the Fourth International Congress of Coptic Studies at Louvain-la-Neuve, 1988: preliminary papers p.67).
7. This relates the two pronouns, by anaphora, to the masculine noun missing in the lacuna in line 5 (here supplied as 'promise'); the pronouns could, however, also be taken as referring to what follows, so that we should have to translate: 'For to this thing shall your face turn, and it is also this that is advantageous to you - (namely:) . . . '
8. There is still no satisfactory solution for the restoration of the lacunae in this passage (Hedrick: 'Am I not alive? Because I am a father, [do] I [not have power] for everything?)'.

9. The phrase 'through the Lord' or '(away) from the Lord' seems out of place in lines 5-7 ('It is the lord . . . '); Schenke thinks it 'presumably a marginal note wrongly inserted'. On the other hand, a corresponding expression (= 'word of the Lord') is required in line 14, to avoid having to relate the 'I' of the attached word of threat to James. Hedrick, however, suggests the possibility of understanding the text as it is handed down: 'The Lord (sc. the Demiurge) has taken you captive from the Lord (sc. Jesus or the Father)' or, with a slight modification of the text, 'from the <height>'.

10. Or (with Hedrick): 'Yet you [will be able to pay] heed in your hearts [and] you will call me 'the Just One'.'

11. Presumably a later insertion.

12. The second 'for' clause, which is here superfluous, fits better a few lines higher up: 'Deliver me from an evil death, for you are the life of life!'

8. The Letter of Peter to Philip

Hans-Gebhard Bethge

1. Literature: *The Facsimile Edition of the Nag Hammadi Codices:* Codex VIII, Leiden 1976; *La Lettre de Pierre à Philippe*. Texte établi et présenté par J. É. Ménard, (BCNH, Section 'Textes' 1), Quebec 1977; 'The Letter of Peter to Philip (VIII 2)' introduced and translated by F. Wisse, in *The Nag Hammadi Library in English*, New York/Hagerstown/ San Francisco/London 1977, pp. 394-398; (rev. ed. 1988, pp. 431-437); 'Der sogenannte 'Brief des Petrus an Philippus' eingeleitet und übersetzt vom Berliner Arbeitskreis für koptisch-gnostische Schriften (federführend: H.-G. Bethge)', ThLZ 103, 1978, 161-170; *The Letter of Peter to Philip*. Text, Translation and Commentary by M.W. Meyer, (SBL Diss. Series 53), Chicago 1981; 'Der Brief des Petrus an Philippus'. Ein neutestamentliches Apokryphon aus dem Fund von Nag Hammadi (NHC VIII, 2)' hg., übers. u. erkl. von H.-G. Bethge, Diss. (B), Berlin 1984. K.-W.Tröger, 'Die Passion Jesu Christi in der Gnosis nach den Schriften von Nag Hammadi', Diss. (B), Berlin 1977, pp. 144-166; K.Koschorke, 'Eine gnostische Pfingstpredigt', ZThK 74, 1977, 323-343; id. 'Eine gnostische Paraphrase des johanneischen Prologs', *Vig. Chr.* 33, 1979, 383-392.

2. Transmission and general character: 'The Letter of Peter to Philip' (Ep.Pet.Phil.[1]) is one of those writings which first became known through the Nag Hammadi discovery. The second and last part of Codex VIII, Ep.Pet. Phil. with its nine on the whole very well preserved pages is of a content, form and character completely different from the preceding - and basically non-Christian - document 'Zostrianos', which is only poorly preserved. Ep. Pet.Phil. however was also handed down outside the Nag Hammadi codices, but the text of the parallel version is so far not yet available for scholarly evaluation.[2]

A document just as important as it is instructive, Ep.Pet.Phil. belongs in the wider context of the New Testament, early Christianity and Gnosis. Like other Nag Hammadi texts, it reveals a part of the history of the influence of portions of the NT. This relates above all to certain passages of Luke's two-volume work and parts of the Fourth Gospel. But at the same time Ep.Pet.Phil. also stands in the tradition of the apocryphal acts of apostles from the 2nd and 3rd centuries.

3. Literary character: in regard to the framework and its treatment, Ep.Pet.Phil. has certain similarities with texts which deal with the meetings and conversations of the risen Jesus with his disciples, for example the end of Luke and the beginning of Acts; the Freer Logion in Mark 16:14; the Epistula Apostolorum and Questions of Bartholomew; the Coptic gnostic texts Soph.Jes.Chr. and Ap.Jas., as well as in its opening framework with the Pistis Sophia. We may however consider as the most remarkable parallel the Petersburg fragments of Acts of Philip, which were already published in 1890 together with fragments of the same work from Borgia manuscripts.[3] They contribute essential material for the understanding of some literary problems of Ep.Pet.Phil.

Jesus there appears to the apostles on the Mount of Olives, gives them the missionary command and calls upon them to divide the field of mission among the Twelve by lot, bids them farewell, and vanishes. The lot appoints Philip for Phrygia. Invoking the name of Jesus, he calls upon Peter to accompany him, and the two set out. On the way Jesus appears to them, promises them suffering but in the end rest, and again returns to heaven. Thereupon Peter and Philip go ahead 'in the power of Christ'. Up to this point, in addition to many differences, there are many common features or parallels with Ep.Pet.Phil. But then follow - without any correspondences - deeds of the apostles. Thus Peter, who is clearly given the pre-eminence, heals a man with a soothsaying spirit and causes a pillar to sink downwards and then rise up again, and the two apostles proceed against the worship of a sparrowhawk and bring people of that town to faith. Thereafter the fragments end.

The present form of Ep.Pet.Phil. is curious. Thus the superscription, clearly thrown into prominence by the writer of the codex (p. 132.10f.), is strictly meaningful in terms of content only for the following 'letter' (pp. 132.12-133.8), but on the other hand ranks as the title for the whole document. Also striking is the torso-character of many passages, e.g. the mythological section pp. 135.8-136.15, where more is presupposed than is actually said. Not only a part of the 'letter' (pp. 132.20-133.5) but also some details (e.g. the content of p. 140.11-13) really lead us to expect a different continuation of the action. This may then hold also, precisely when we consider the whole text of Ep.Pet.Phil., for the conclusion of the document together with the preceding Christophany, even if here, as at the end of the Gospel of Matthew, we come upon a typical closing scene (pp. 140.15-23, 23-27).

The special literary character of Ep.Pet.Phil. rests upon the fact that in this document we have a composition from several elements, sources or traditions, and that within the framework of only partially preserved Acts of apostles, or possibly Acts of Philip, and not so much within the frame of the Lucan Acts. We may imagine the origin of Ep.Pet.Phil. as taking place in a process of several stages:

1. At the beginning stand apocryphal Acts of Philip or of apostles, similar to the fragmentarily preserved Acts of Philip mentioned above. In these, as so often in the acts literature, mission and proclamation, but also opposition and menace, perhaps even martyrdom, play a part.

2. Then come various interpolations:

a) A lengthy passage is inserted with the aim of providing an aetiological explanation for, and at the same time overcoming, an actual threatening situation. This relates to the preponderant part of the didactic dialogue pp.134.18-137.13 + 137.13-138.3, which in its mythological passages is orientated towards a particular but not distinctively Sethian[4] form of the Sophia myth. This insertion, which often recalls corresponding parts, e.g., of Apoc.John, shows initially scarcely any Christian traces in its present sharply abbreviated form in Ep.Pet.Phil., but is later increasingly stamped by Christian tradition.

b) Insertion of a part taken from a Christian gnostic(?) Acts of apostles (pp. 139.9-140.1), which brings the passion of Jesus into connection with the situation of adversity faced by the author/redactor (and the readers). The prominent role of Peter in these passages suggests that the Acts bore his name in the title.

c), d), e) etc . . . Further possible interpolations, which because of the abbreviations (stage 3) are no longer recognisable, at least with any certainty.

Whether these interpolations are the work of one author and lie on the same level in time, or took place in several stages, must remain open.

3. Through abbreviations at the beginning and especially at the end, as well as through redactional revisions, a kind of epitome came into being, which in terms of content concentrated the work essentially upon the theme of suffering. It is readily conceivable that this in principle took place at one stroke.

4. This work, which was given the title of 'Letter of Peter to Philip', was translated from Greek into Coptic and circulated, *inter alia* through its inclusion in NHC VIII.

On the question of the time of origin, we must think for stages 1-3 of the period from the end of the 2nd to the middle of the 3rd century. It is the time on the one hand of the origin of many apocryphal Acts of apostles, and on the other of major persecutions of Christians. On any substantially later dating of the process, the period between the 3rd stage, the translation following it and the diffusion down to NHC VIII would be given too short a measure.

In its present form, Ep.Pet.Phil. is in regard to its framework a piece of an apocryphal Acts of apostles, or possibly of Philip, from which as a result of the history of its origin the original beginning and the continuation of the action are missing, and therefore as a whole a document representing the Acts literature, into which a gnostic dialogue in the form of a didactic discourse has been inserted. In terms of form as well as of content it is not a homogeneous document. By reason of the diverse and sometimes heterogeneous traditions which are worked together in it, and the frame which dominates the content, it cannot be regarded as a genuinely gnostic work.

Gnostic ideas are thus not indeed dominant in Ep.Pet.Phil., but they do none the less have a decisive significance. The manner in which gnostic ideas are reproduced in the fragmentarily summarised myth within the didactic discourse is an indication that not only the creator but also the addressees not only knew but also at least to some extent acknowledged this gnostic content and accent. The allusions were evidently sufficient. The basic questions at the beginning of the discourse (pp. 134.20-135.2) recall the 'classic' questions of *Exc.Theod.* 78.2, but also such passages as Gos. Truth p. 22.14f.; Thom. Cont. p. 138.8-10 and Soph. Jes. Chr. BG p. 117.14-17. It is not possible to recognise in the gnostic passages any specific gnostic school among those known.

The special literary character of Ep.Pet.Phil. and above all the history of its origin serve to explain the role of Philip, which in terms of content is not dominant. His mention at the beginning of the document (pp. 132.10-133.11) may rank as a pointer to the portrayal of his activity in some parts of the work which preceded Ep.Pet.Phil., or lies behind it. The identification of the disciple/apostle Philip[5] with the evangelist,[6] presupposed in Ep.Pet.Phil., also appears occasionally elsewhere in early Church literature.[7] With the prominence given to Peter, Ep.Pet.Phil. not only stands in the line of Luke's Acts but at the same time is in proximity to various witnesses of the primitive or early-Church Peter tradition, which specifically also include persecution and martyrdom.

4. Significant points of content: a) *suffering* and also the threat to the Christians who express themselves in Ep.Pet.Phil. and are addressed by this document, finding themselves in the same situation, are the occasion and at the same time the central theme of the text. This state of affairs already plays a role in parts of the framework not influenced by gnostic ideas. The present intensification of the problem, even to homicidal intentions on the part of opponents not mentioned by name (p. 134.8f.), is to be overcome with the aid of the insertions. The author of Ep.Pet.Phil. seeks with his concentration on this theme to help the addressees to recognise, to explain and to pass through this situation of suffering in a proper manner. As is emphasised on the one hand by appeal to New Testament traditions (pp. 138.23- 139.4), suffering and menace belong of necessity to Christian existence. On the other hand, in the passages by the insertion of which the earlier text which preceded Ep.Pet.Phil. already underwent changes of accent in terms of its content - they now stand out the more strongly because of the epitome character - suffering is regarded for one thing as a consequence of the sin of Eve (p. 139.22f.) and for another - reaching back to elements of a form of the gnostic Sophia myth - as ultimately the work of the archons and as a basic part of the human situation (p. 136.8-15).

In addition to this aetiological explanation, the reference to the passion of Jesus Christ (p. 139.15-28), taken from a Christian-gnostic (?) book of Acts and presented in concentrated form, also serves for the overcoming of suffering in obedience towards Jesus Christ. He really took suffering upon himself, not however out of necessity but for the sake of salvation and figuratively with the Christians in view, hence for their sakes and not his own (p. 138.18), and here not as atoning or vicarious suffering. In contrast to Jesus Christ (p. 139.21f.), the Christians must suffer of necessity (p. 138.19f.).

The text of Ep.Pet.Phil. does not provide any concrete clues as to the immediate circumstances, the place and the moment of the suffering, the persecution and the threat. We have to see this central theme of the document in the context of the situation in which not only the author and addressees of Ep.Pet.Phil. but also other Christians in the 2nd and 3rd centuries found themselves. Ep.Pet.Phil. is therefore not to be regarded as a work in which - as for example in Treat. Seth - the primary concern is with a theoretical discussion, for instance between gnostic and 'Church' Christianity, rather it is the document intended pre-eminently to be helpful in a situation of existential peril brought about by suffering and menace. This central concern allows a reciprocal relationship to become visible, between suffering experienced and anticipated and the self-understanding of those who express themselves and those ad-dressed.

The missionary aspect which frequently appears in Ep.Pet.Phil. is also to be seen from this point of view. It is important for the content, and is not merely a motif employed by the narrator. Missionary activity in preaching is an element in the subjugation and ultimate overcoming of suffering, and at the same time an essential part of the struggle against the archons. Here Ep.Pet.Phil. is not a literary document intended of itself to have a missionary effect, but is meant to serve as missionary equipment.

b) The *soteriology* of Ep.Pet.Phil. is not *a priori* exclusive or particularistic in regard to those to be redeemed, but rather universalistic (p. 132.18f. and often). The salvation of Jesus Christ is for the whole world, but in particular cases requires faith in the name of Jesus (p. 140.17ff.). Missionary work is necessary to bring this about and to further it. In addition to the use of traditional christological titles, not developed in terms of content and orientated towards various traditions, not only from the New Testament, the christological statements placed at the service of Christology in Ep.Pet.Phil. are determined above all by the frequent emphasis on the significance of the activity of the earthly Jesus (pp. 135.4-6; 138.2f., 22-24; 139.11f.), especially his preaching and passion. In the gnostic passages there is in addition visible a redeemer conception such as appears in witnesses which may rank as background to the Johannine prologue.[8] Here as in several gnostic texts (e.g. Ap.John, Soph.Jes.Chr., Gos.Eg.) a Christianisation of an originally non-Christian soteriological conception becomes visible, while elsewhere the soteriology appears to be largely of a genuinely Christian or Christian gnostic colour.

c) The *anthropology* in regard to individual men, in Ep.Pet.Phil. a theme only within the gnostic dialogue in the form of a didactic discourse, is dualistic: the inner man who essentially belongs to the Redeemer (p. 137. 21f.), also called by the Redeemer 'those who are mine' (p. 136.22f.; cf. also p. 137.5f.), is imprisoned in the body created by the archons. The sharply abbreviated anthropogony, in Ep.Pet.Phil. contained only in a passage stamped by an originally non-Christian Gnosis (p. 136.8-15) in connection with the answering of the basic questions (pp. 134.20-135.2), is based on the re-interpretation of Gen. 1-2[9] contained in more detailed form in comparable witnesses of Gnosis, although in Ep.Pet.Phil. it is not given the character of an effective discussion.

In regard to mankind we can recognise in Ep.Pet.Phil. in the context of the missionary activity a factual anthropological dualism, but it is presupposed rather than developed. Jesus is redeemer for all, but not all are redeemed. There are Christians, described like Jesus as φωστηρ (p. 137. 8), and 'dead men' (p. 137.9), which leads to a twofold division.

d) Other topics in Ep.Pet.Phil. stand in direct or indirect connection with the main problems, or play only a minor role or none at all. Thus, perhaps also - as with other themes - as a result of its epitome character, Ep.Pet.Phil. in its concentration on the question of suffering and its overcoming neither develops nor contains any special or indirect *ethic*. The ascetic tendency typical for many Acts of apostles, and also for some Nag Hammadi texts, is missing. Except for the mention of 'rest' as an eschatological blessing (p. 137.11), *eschatology* is not a theme for Ep.Pet. Phil. In *ecclesiology*, which whether deliberately or as a result of the abbreviation is not developed, a rather traditional orientation appears to be presupposed. Here offices as well as structures are lacking, but on the other hand there is a call for public missionary work (p. 137.23ff.). It is

scarcely possible to recognise any Church life within the community represented by Ep.Pet.Phil., except for the prominence given to prayer (pp. 133.19-
134.9; 137.27f. and often) and the indication of some liturgical details (p.
140.13-15).

Notes

8. The Letter of Peter to Philip

1. Abbreviations for the Nag Hammadi documents according to J.M. Robinson, *The Facsimile Edition of the Nag Hammadi Codices: Introduction*, 1984, pp. 96ff.
2. The first information about the existence of this text, which is in a papyrus codex along with a version of 1 Apoc. Jas. and a dialogue of Jesus with his disciples not identical with NHC III 5, was given by J.M. Robinson and S. Emmel at the Third International Congress of Coptic Studies in Warsaw in August 1984.
3. 'Koptische apokryphe Apostelacten', ed. O. von Lemm, *Bulletin de l'Académie Impériale de St Pétersbourg*, Nouvelle Série 1 (33), 1890, 509-581.
4. On Sethianism cf. H.-M.Schenke, 'The Phenomenon and Significance of Gnostic Sethianism', in B.Layton (ed.), *The Rediscovery of Gnosticism. Proceedings of the International Conference on Gnosticism at Yale, New Haven, Connecticut, March 28-31, 1978*, vol. II: 'Sethian Gnosticism', Leiden 1981, pp. 588-616.
5. Cf. Mk. 3:16-19 par.; Jn. 1:43-48; Acts 1:13.
6. Cf. Acts 6:5; 8:1, 5-40.
7. Papias, *ap.* Euseb. H.E. III 39.9; Polycrates, *ap.* Euseb. H.E. III 31.3.
8. Cf. pp.136.16-137.4 and e.g. the third speech of Protennoia in NHC XIII.
9. Cf. the corresponding parts in Ap. John, Hyp. Arch. or Orig. World.

The Letter of Peter, which he sent to Philip

(The 'letter' [pp. 132.12-133.8])

'Peter, the apostle of Jes[us] Christ, to Philip, our beloved brother and fellow-apostle, with the brethren who are with you, greetings! I wish you to know, our brother, [that] we have received commandments from our Lord, the saviour of the whole world, that we should come together, in order to teach and preach concerning the salvation which was promised to us by (p. 133) our Lord Jesus Christ. But you [hel]d yourself apart from us[1] and had no liking for our coming together. And (now) we are to learn how we are to assign ourselves in order to carry the Gospel.[2] Would it therefore be pleasing to you, our brother, to come in accordance with the commands of our God Jesus?'[3]

(Philip's reaction to the letter [p. 133.8-11])

When Philip had received and read this, he went gladly and rejoicing to Peter.

(Gathering of the apostles on the Mount of Olives [p. 133.12-134.9])

Then Peter gathered the other (apostles) together. They went to the mountain which is called 'the Mount of Olives', where they were accustomed to gather with the blessed Christ when he was in the body.[4] Then when the apostles had come together and had fallen on their knees, they prayed thus, saying: 'Father, Father, Father of the light,[5] who possesses the incorruptions,[6] hear us as [thou] hast taken pleasure in thy holy child [Je]sus Christ![7] For he has become for us a light[8] (p. 134) in the darkness. Yea, hear us!' And they prayed again another time, saying: 'Son of Life,[9] Son of Immortality[10] who art in the light, Son, Christ of Immortality, our Redeemer, give to us strength, since they seek after us to slay us.'

(Appearance of Jesus Christ[11] [p.134.9-18])

Then there appeared a great light, so that the mountain shone through the vision of him who appeared. And a voice cried out to them, saying: 'Hear my words, that I may send you! Why do you seek after me? I am Jesus Christ, who is with you for ever.'[12]

(Conversation of the risen Jesus with the apostles
[pp. 134.18-137.13 + 137.13-138.3])

(*Catalogue of basic questions* [pp. 134.18-135.2])
Then the apostles answered and said: 'Lord, we wish to know the deficiency of the aeons and their Pleroma,[13] and how we are held fast in this dwelling-place, or how we came to this place, or in what manner we shall come out, or how we possess (p. 135) the [authority] of frankness,[14] [or] why the powers strive against us.'[15]

(*Beginning of Jesus' speech in response* [p. 135.3-8])
Then a voice came to them out of the light, saying: 'It is you yourselves who bear witness that I have (already) said all these things to you. [But be]cause of your unbelief I will speak yet again.'

(*First answer of Jesus* [pp.135.8-136.15])
'Concerning [the deficiency] of the aeons - this [is] the deficiency: when the disobedience and the foolishness of the Mother[16] came to light against the command of the majesty of the Father, she wished to raise up aeons. And when she spoke, the Authades[17] <came> on the scene. But when she left behind a part (of herself), the Authades seized it, and so it became a deficiency. This is the deficiency of the aeons. Now when the Authades had taken a part, he sowed it, and appointed powers and authorities over it. And he enclosed it in the dead aeons. And all the powers of the world rejoiced that they had been begotten. But they (p. 136) do not know [him] who [is] pre-existent, since they are strangers to him. Rather this is the one to whom power was given. And they served him and praised him. But he, the Authades, became proud because of the praise of the powers. He became a jealous one.[18] And he wished to create an image in [place of an image] and a form in place of a form. He charged the powers in his authority to mould dead bodies. And they came into being in unlikeness, after the outward appearance.'[19]

(*Second answer of Jesus*[20] [pp. 136.16-137.4])
'Concerning the Pleroma, it is I. And I was sent in the body because of the seed which had fallen. And I came to their dead moulding. But they did not recognise me. They thought that I was a mortal man. And I spoke with him who is mine. But he listened to me even as you who have listened to me today. And I gave him the authority to enter into the inheritance of his fatherhood. And I took (p. 137) [him (?)[21] . . .]. They [became] filled [with . . .] .. through his salvation. And since he was a deficiency, because of this he became a *pleroma*.'

(Third answer of Jesus [p. 137.4-9])
'As to the fact that you are held fast, (it is) because you are mine. If you strip off what is devoted to corruption,[22] then you will become luminaries[23] in the midst of mortal men.'

(Fourth answer of Jesus [p. 137.10-13])
'As to the fact that it is you who must strive with the powers,[24] (that is so) because they have no rest like you, because they do not wish that you be saved.'

(Renewed question of the apostles and answer of Jesus [pp. 137.13-138.3])
Then the apostles worshipped once again, saying: 'Lord, teach us in what way we shall fight with the archons, since the archons are superior to us!' Then [a vo]ice cried out to them from him who had appeared, saying: 'As for you, you are to combat them in this way - for the archons fight with the inner man[25] - [but] you are to fight them in this way: come together and teach salvation in the world with a promise.[26] And gird yourselves with the power of my Father![27] And make your prayer known,[28] and so he, the Father, will help you, as he has (already) helped you when he sent me. (p. 138) Be not af[raid (?)[29] ...] as I have already s[ai]d to you when I was in the body.'

(End of the appearance of Jesus [p. 138.3-7])
Then there came lightning and thunder from heaven, and he who had appeared to them in that place was carried off into heaven.

(Discussion on the way and audition [pp. 138.7-139.4])
Then the apostles gave thanks to the Lord in all kinds of praise and returned to Jerusalem. But as they went up, they were talking with one another on the way about the light which had appeared. And a discussion developed about the Lord, and they said: 'If even our Lord suffered, how much more then we!' Peter answered, saying: 'He suffered for [our] sakes, and it is necessary that [we] also should suffer - because of our smallness.'

Then a voice came to them, saying: 'I have said to you many times that it is necessary for you to suffer[30] (and that in the words:) it is necessary for you to be brought into synagogues and (before) governors, so that you may suffer.[31] And he who does not suffer [will (?)] also not[32] (p. 139) [ ] [ ] my Father[33] [ ], that he [ ] ... [ ].'

(Summary[34] [p. 139.4-9])
But the apostles [re]joiced gr[ea]tly, and went up to Jerusalem. And they went up to the Temple and (there) taught salvation in the name of [the]

Lord Jesus Christ. And they healed [a] multitude.

(Words of Peter to his fellow-disciples [p. 139.9-13])
But Peter opened his mouth and said to his (fellow) disciples: '[Truly] our Lord Jesus when he was in the body gave us signs of all things. For he himself came down.'

(Speech of Peter. Part 1: rehearsal of the kerygma concerning Jesus[35] [pp. 139.13-140.1])
'My brethren, listen to my voice!' And he was filled with Holy Spirit and spoke thus: 'Our luminary Jesus [came] down and was hanged (on the cross). And he wore a crown of thorns, and was clothed with a purple robe.[36] And he was [hang]ed upon the tree and buried in a grave. And he rose up from the dead.'

(Speech of Peter. Part 2: interpretation of the kerygma [p. 139.21-28])
'My brethren, Jesus is a stranger to this suffering! But it is upon us that suffering has come because of the transgression of the Mother (Eve). And because of this he did all things in the same manner among us. For the Lord Jesus, the Son of the glory of the immeasurable Father, he is the originator of our life.'[37]

(Speech of Peter. part 3: paraenetic consequences [pp. 139.28-140.1])
'My brethren, let us not listen to these lawless ones and walk in (p. 140) [. . .].'[38]

(Prayer, miracles and separation of the apostles [p. 140.1-13])
[Pe]ter as[sembled the ot]her (apostles) and said[: 'Our Lord] Je[sus] Christ, the originator of our revival, give to us a spirit of understanding, that we also may work miracles!'

Then Pet[er] and the others saw and were filled with Holy Spirit. And each one of them accomplished healings. And they separated, that they might proclaim the Lord Jesus.

(Common prayer [140.13-15])[39]
And (before that) they gathered with one another and greeted one another, say[ing]: 'Amen'.

(Christophany[40] [p. 140.15-23])
Then Jesus appeared to them, saying to them: 'Peace be with you [all] and with everyone who believes in my name. And when you go, may joy, grace and power be yours. Be not faint-hearted! See, I am with you for ever.'

(Conclusion of Ep.Pet.Phil. [p. 140.23-27])
Then the apostles separated to 'the four words'[41] that they might preach.
And they went in the power of Jesus in peace.

Notes to Translation

The Letter of Peter, which he sent to Philip

1. Since Ep.Pet.Phil. with respect to its framework is not predominantly orientated to Luke's double work, we cannot regard Acts 8:1, 5-40 as the background here.
2. Cf. the difference from Lk. 24:27-49 and Acts 1:4-8.
3. For this designation cf. in the NT Jn. 20:28 and 1 Jn. 5:20, and in addition Ign. *Rom.* 3.3; *Sm.* 1.1; 10.1; *Trall.* 7.1.
4. Cf. Mk. 11:1 par.; Lk. 21:37; Acts 1:12 and often.
5. Cf. Jn. 1:5; Jas. 1:17.
6. Cf. Rom. 1:23; 1 Tim. 1:17.
7. Cf. Acts 3:13, 26; 4:27, 30.
8. Cf. Jn. 8:12; 12:35f.
9. Cf. *inter alia* Jn. 1:4; 11:25; 14:6.
10. Cf. 1 Tim. 6:16.
11. For this epiphany scene, cf. Mk. 9:1-13 par. and Acts 9:3ff.
12. Cf. Mt. 28:20.
13. ΠΛΗΡΩΜΑ: so also at pp. 136.16 and 137.4.
14. Cf. Acts 2:29; 4:13, 29, 31; 28:31.
15. Cf. Eph. 6:12.
16. It is a question of the figure of Sophia; cf. the corresponding parallels in Iren. *adv. Haer.* I 29.4; Ap.John; Soph.Jes.Chr. or Hyp.Arch. and Orig.World.
17. A name or designation of the Demiurge as in Ap.John BG, p. 46.1 par., and Hyp.Arch. p. 92.27; 94.17.
18. Cf. Exod. 20:5.
19. Cf. Gen. 1:26f.
20. In this section a certain proximity to many statements in the Johannine prologue is striking. It is however questionable whether there is any direct literary relationship.
21. Possible restoration of the lacuna: 'And I took [him up to my Father.] They [were] filled [with re]pose through his salvation.'
22. Cf. Col. 3:8-10; Eph. 4:22-24.
23. Cf. Mt. 5:16; Phil. 2:15.
24. Cf. Eph. 6:12.
25. Cf. Rom. 7:22; 2 Cor. 4:16.
26. Cf. Mt. 28:19f.; Acts 1:8.
27. Cf. 1 Thess. 5:8; Eph. 6:11-17; 1 Pet. 1:13.
28. Cf. Mk. 11:24 par.; Lk. 11:9f. par.; Jn. 16:23f.; Phil. 4:6.
29. We may think of something similar to Lk. 12:4 par. as the content of the lacuna.
30. Cf. Jn. 16:1-4; Acts 9:16.
31. Cf. Mk. 13:9-13 par.; Lk. 12:11 par.; Acts 5:41.
32. The conclusion, which stood in the lacuna, could have contained thoughts such as are known for example from Mk. 8:34ff. or Acts 14.22b.
33. In the following lacunae, in terms of content, we must think of Lk. 12:8f. par., in addition to the passages mentioned in notes 4 and 5.

34. Details in this section recall corresponding parts in Acts, cf. 1:12; 3:1-10, 11-26; 4:18; 5:26.

35. On this section of Peter's speech cf. Acts 2:22-24; 5:30-31a; 10:39f.

36. Cf. Mk. 15:1, 7-20 par.; Jn. 19:2f., 5.

37. Cf. Acts 3:15; 5:31.

38. Possible restoration of the lacuna: '[fear before them all]'.

39. Rudiments of a piece of liturgy; cf. Rom. 16:16; 1 Pet. 5:14.

40. On the whole section cf. Jn. 20:19-23 and Mt. 28:20.

41. So far as there is no textual corruption, this could be a circumlocution for the four points of the compass. The 'four words' would then be 'east', 'west', 'north' and 'south'. For the separation of the apostles for the purpose of worldwide preaching, cf. *inter alia* Act. Thom. 1 and Euseb. H.E. III 1.

IX. Other Gnostic Gospels and Related Literature

Henri-Charles Puech †; revised by Beate Blatz

Preliminary note

Wilhelm Schneemelcher

The contribution by H.-Ch. Puech under the title of this section in the previous edition (NTApo³ I, 231-362) was without doubt a particularly important part of the reworking of the collection at that time. There was, and still is, probably no such expert and comprehensive survey of the widely scattered material as this work by Puech. One disadvantage was that the pattern usually followed in the other parts of the book (introduction and translation) could not be adhered to. This departure from the rule was also connected with the fact that at the time of the revision of NTApo³ the texts from the Nag Hammadi discovery were still not so readily available that they could be presented in full.

The problem of a classification of the various texts in terms of their genre could also not be examined in detail at that time. Puech described many of the works he discusses as 'typically gnostic gospels'. This description rests on the observation that certain formal elements are common to these texts (dialogue, revelation discourse, etc.), and that they are intended to convey a glad and redeeming knowledge, in other words 'Gospel'.[1]

Puech also examined and presented texts which are described as 'gospel' in the Church tradition, but which strictly cannot be placed under the head of this *Gattung*. Their *Gattung* has to be investigated and defined in each separate case, so far as the meagre tradition allows.

This question of the genre of texts (i.e. the literary *Gattungen*) has been raised afresh through the progressive opening up of the texts from Nag Hammadi. The Coptic gnostic library is now available in a facsimile edition, and to some extent critical editions of the individual works have been published. An English translation of the complete material facilitates access,[2] and also makes it possible to investigate the question of the *Gattung*.

This, however, made it necessary to include in their full text those works from the Nag Hammadi discovery which in form and content could be reckoned to the literature presented in this volume, and arrange them in the order in which they logically had their place. Other sections of Puech's contribution could be omitted entirely, since the texts discussed there clearly do not belong to the category of New Testament apocrypha.

There remains a major part of Puech's work which ought not to be discarded, because even today it offers abundant information (above all for texts which do not derive from Nag Hammadi) which is important for research into our literature, whether from the point of view of literary history or from that of the history of religions. One may certainly argue about the acceptance of some works into this survey. There are probably also some texts considered which even on a very wide definition of the term 'New Testament apocrypha' do not directly belong here (e.g. Pistis Sophia, the Books of Jeu). But these texts too offer important insights for the whole problem of the apocrypha, and especially for the formation of gospels in Church and Gnosis.

Since H.-Ch. Puech at an early stage in the preparation of this work found himself no longer in a position to collaborate,[3] the 'residue' presented in the following pages has been revised by Beate Blatz and the editor, and completed by a few references to the literature. Gregor Ahn has contributed information about the literature for some sections. In these supplements completeness could not be achieved, nor should it be expected.

In order to bring the whole context of Puech's contribution once again before the eyes of users of this edition, all the titles have been included (in each case with the necessary references).

I have to thank C. Colpe, H.-J. Klimheit and H.-M. Schenke for help and advice in the shaping of this part.

Notes

IX. Other Gnostic Gospels and Related Literature

1. On the special problems of the 'dialogue gospels', see above, pp. 228 ff.
2. *The Facsimile Edition of the Nag Hammadi Codices*, published under the auspices of the Department of Antiquities of the Arab Republic of Egypt in conjunction with UNESCO, 12 vols., 1972ff. *The Coptic Gnostic Library*, ed. with English translation, introduction and notes, published under the auspices of the Institute for Antiquity and Christianity (the volumes appear in the series Nag Hammadi Studies, ed. M. Krause, J.M. Robinson, F. Wisse; cf. the survey in NHS vol. XXVI 1984 - NHC III 5 - pp. viiif.). *The Nag Hammadi Library in English*. Trans. by Members of the Coptic Gnostic Library Project of the Institute for Antiquity and Christianity (Director: J.M. Robinson), Leiden etc., 1977 (3rd rev. ed. 1988). Bibliography: D.M. Scholer, *Nag Hammadi Bibliography 1948-1969*, NHS 1, Leiden 1971. This bibliography is continued as 'Bibliographia Gnostica' in *Novum Testamentum* from vol. 13, 1971.
3. H.-Ch. Puech died in Paris on 11 January 1986.

A. Gospels under general titles

1. The Gospel of the Four Heavenly Regions

1. Literature: O. Braun, *De sancta Nicaena Synodo*. Syrische Texte des Maruta von Maipherkat, (Kirchengeschichtliche Studien IV 3), 1898. A. Harnack, *Der Ketzerkatalog des Bischofs Maruta von Maipherkat*, (TU 19.1b), 1899. F. Haase, *Altchristliche Kirchengeschichte nach orientalischen Quellen*, 1925.

2. Attestation: Maruta, bishop of Maiperkat (d. before 420), mentions a *Gospel of the Four Heavenly Regions or of the Four Corners of the World* in his work *De sancta synodo Nicaena*;[1] there he writes in the catalogue of heresies, in his note about the Simonians: 'And they (those godless men) made for themselves a gospel, (dividing it into four volumes, and called it) the Book of the regions of the world.' Arabic version and Latin translation by Abraham Ecchellensis:[2] *Sibi autem perfidi isti evangelium effinxerunt, quod in quattuor tomos secantes librum quattuor angulorum et cardinum mundi appellarunt.*

Maruta's notice is not of great value. Nevertheless Harnack[3] and Haase[4] are inclined to consider 'trustworthy' what is there said about the Gospel of the Four Regions. It might, in fact, be a question of one of the works which according to Const. *Apost.* VI 16 were current 'under the name of Christ and his disciples', and which were alleged to have been composed by Simon Magus and his followers. The title recalls the famous theory of Irenaeus (*adv. Haer*. III 11.8) on the fourfold Gospel: 'It cannot be admitted that there are either more or less than four Gospels. For since there are four regions of the world (*quattuor regiones mundi*, τέσσαρα κλίματα τοῦ κόσμου) in which we live, and four winds from the four cardinal points (*quattuor principales spiritus*, τέσσαρα καθολικὰ πνεύματα and since on the other hand the Church is spread over all the earth, and the Gospel and the Spirit of life are the pillar and foundation of the Church, it follows that this Church has four pillars, which from every part breathe out incorruptibility and quicken men to life.' Perhaps also we may recall certain passages of Pistis Sophia, e.g. c. 136, p. 232.14-16 (Jesus with his disciples turns to face the four corners of the world), or p. 254.10-27 (the twelve apostles going in threes to the four quarters of heaven, and preaching the Gospel of the kingdom in the whole world). However that may be, the title of the document and its division into four books, each corresponding to one of the four cardinal points, seem to indicate that the apocryphon ascribed to the Simonians claimed to be a universal Gospel, if not *the* universal Gospel. We know nothing more, nor can we guess anything further; whether the book ever existed at all remains doubtful.

Notes

A. Gospels under general titles

1. The Gospel of the Four Heavenly Regions

1. O. Braun, *op. cit.* p. 47; A. Harnack, *op. cit.* p. 7; F. Haase, *op. cit.* p. 324.
2. Mansi II, col. 1057b, and Harnack, *op. cit.* p. 15.
3. p. 7, note 2.
4. p. 324, note 2.

2. The Gospel of Perfection

1. Literature: A. Harnack, *Gesch. d. altchristl. Lit.* I 1, ²1958, 156, 167f.

2. Attestation: *The Gospel of Perfection* is mentioned by Epiphanius in his *Panarion* (26.2.5; I,p. 277. 13-17 Holl; tr. Williams, NHS 35, p. 84). The document is also mentioned in Filastrius of Brescia (*Haer.* 33.7, p. 18. 18 Marx), but this is dependent on Epiphanius, as the immediate context shows. The two heresiologues are content to adduce the title of the work (εὐαγγέλιον τελειώσεως *evangelium consummationis*), and both condemn it. Epiphanius gives as its authors the 'Gnostics', Filastrius the Nicolaitans (discussed in Epiph. *Pan.* 25) - whom he confuses with the *Gnostici*.

3. Content: Harnack (*Litg.* I, 167f.) and Hennecke (NTApo², p. 69) propose (not without reservations) to explain title and content with the aid of a Naassene saying quoted by Hippolytus (*Ref.* V 6.6; V 8.38, cf. X 9): 'The beginning of perfection (ἀρχὴ τελειώσεως) is the knowledge of man, the knowledge of God is complete perfection (ἀπηρτισμένη τελείωσις).' This proposal is debatable. One might also appeal to Irenaeus (*adv. Haer.* I 30.14) and conjecture that the gospel related to the 'future consummation' (*consummationem futuram*), which is to take place when all the spiritual 'seed of light' dispersed in the world is finally gathered together (*quando tota humectatio spiritus luminis colligatur*).

This theme of the σύλλεξις recurs in other gnostic gospels, notably the Gospel of Eve (see below pp. 358ff.) and the Gospel of Philip (see above, pp. 179ff.). By concentration, by focussing himself upon himself, the Gnostic regains knowledge and possession of himself, recovers his perfection and his state of being saved: on each such occasion, a morsel or part of the spiritual substance now scattered among the elect (the men of the superior race, who are 'born from above') is recovered, and at the same time is detached from its admixture of matter and brought back to the transcendent place of its origin; thus the greater part of this 'light-substance' is progressively restored. When in the course of time the process of collection is complete, the final 'consummation' will take place: the visible world will pass away, the perfecting of the σύλλεξις will be brought to a close, and the universal salvation of the 'spiritual race' will be finally assured. It is possible that our document described the manner, theoretical and practical, of this process. In more general and less specific terms, it must have been either a gospel teaching an ideal of perfection and the means of attaining thereto, or a gospel destined for the 'perfect', the τέλειοι, i.e. the πνευματικοί, the 'elect', or a gospel perfect in itself, the supreme Gospel containing in itself the sum total of revelation or of *gnosis*. However, owing to the paucity of our sources, all hypotheses can only be inadequate.

4. Date: Harnack dates the gospel to the 2nd century.

3. The Gospel of Truth

This work, which created quite a sensation at the time of its discovery, does not belong to the 'gospel' *Gattung*, despite its title. It is rather a meditation or a homily, at the centre of which however stands the redeeming and liberating 'gospel of truth', the word of knowledge.

Literature: *Facsimile Edition:* Codex I, 1977, pp. 16.31-43.24; Codex XII, 1973, pp. 53.19-60.30.
Edition: Harold W. Attridge (ed.), *Nag Hammadi Codex I (The Jung Codex)*, I: 'Introduction, Texts, Translations, Indices',(Coptic Gnostic Library, NHS 22), 1985, pp. 55-122; II: 'Notes',(NHS 23), 1985, pp. 39-135.
Translations: German: H-.M. Schenke, in W.C. van Unnik, *Evangelien aus dem Nilsand* 1960, pp. 174-185; W.C. Till in ZNW 50, 1959, 165-185. French: J.E. Ménard, NHS 2, 1972. English: *The NH Library in English* 1977, pp. 37-49 (rev. ed. 1988, pp. 40-51).
Bibliography: in NHS XXII, 55-59.

B. Gospels under the name of an Old Testament figure

The Gospel of Eve

1. Literature: A. Harnack, *Gesch. d. altchristl. Lit.* I 1, ²1958, 156; 166ff.; O. Bardenhewer, *Gesch. d. altkirchl. Lit.* ²1913 (1962), 347; 352.

2. Attestation: Epiphanius mentions a Gospel of Eve (Εὐαγγέλον Εὔας) in connection with the Gospel of Perfection, and ascribes its fabrication to the Gnostics (*Pan.* 26.2.6; I, pp.277.17-278.6 Holl; tr. Williams, NHS 35, p. 84).

3. Extant remains: The only certain quotation from the Gospel of Eve is found in Epiphanius:

I stood upon a high mountain and saw a tall man, and another of short stature, and heard as it were a sound of thunder and went nearer in order to hear. Then he spoke to me and said: I am thou and thou art I, and where thou art there am I, and I am sown in all things; and whence thou wilt, thou gatherest me, but when thou gatherest me, then gatherest thou thyself.

(Pan. 26.3.1; I, p. 278.8-13)

It is much less certain that, as is commonly supposed,[1] a second extract from the Gospel of Eve is preserved by Epiphanius:

I saw a tree which bore twelve fruits in the year, and he said to me: This is the Tree of Life.

(Pan. 26.5.1; I, 281.17-19)

4. Content: The first passage quoted in Epiphanius appears to belong to the beginning of the document. It is however very difficult to make any precise statements about the identity of the speaker and the mythical interlocutor. Eve herself could be the narrator of the vision, but it could just as well be some anonymous seer. Several interpretations may likewise be offered for the two figures who appear in the vision. They may represent 'the Urmensch and his dwarfish earthly likeness',[2] or the Urmensch and the Son of Man,[3] or it may be a question of 'God the Father and Barbelo, who is stunted because the power has been taken from her'.[4] Perhaps also the two figures are in reality one, seen at one and the same time under two different aspects, as is frequently the case in narratives of this type (cf. e.g. the beginning of the Apocryphon of John or appearances of Jesus Christ or other beings, divine or demonic, in manifold embodiments). All that is certain is that the Gospel of Eve belongs to the revelation documents, hence to the apocalyptic literature. It is constructed after the widespread pattern of the 'vision report' and employs the usual motifs of this kind of literature: the setting of the scene upon a mountain, the appearance of a figure of very great or gigantic stature, an address by this figure to the seer. The revealer, or divine being, discloses to his interlocutor his identity with him, by an almost stereotyped formula (ἐγὼ σὺ καὶ σὺ ἐγώ) which is often employed in gnostic, Hermetic, magic or alchemical texts.[5] This identity implies that the one is everywhere and always present to the other, and that there is a consubstantiality between them. 'To gather oneself' (ἑαυτὸν συλλέγειν), i.e. to gather the substance of one's spiritual 'light-nature' which is dispersed in the body and in matter, to recover and save one's 'ego' by disengaging it from the diversity of the world and restoring it to its original unity, is equivalent to saying that the one at the same time gathers and saves the substance, or a part of the substance, of the other, which is likewise scattered, dispersed and imprisoned in the world. There is a collaboration between the Saviour and the saved. Here again the theory and the language are gnostic.[6] They recur in Manicheism.[7]

On the other hand a reference in Epiphanius *(Pan.* 26.2.6; I, 278. 1-2 Holl: αὐτῆς [sc. Εὔας] δῆθεν ὡς εὑρούσης τὸ βρῶμα τῆς γνώσεως ἐξ ἀποκαλύψεως τοῦ λαλήσαντος αὐτῇ ὄφεως suggests that the writing had for its subject the discovery by Eve, in consequence of a revelation received from the mouth of the serpent, of the 'food' or 'fruit of Gnosis', the saving knowledge.[8]

It would then set forth the gnostic doctrine of salvation thus revealed. The encounter with the serpent and the latter's speech were probably reported either by Eve herself or by the narrator, who would have learned of it in the course of his vision. Since it contained the announcement made by Eve, or at least to Eve, of this 'good tidings' which is Gnosis, the true knowledge, and perhaps also because it took the form of a dialogue with a redeemer (Christ himself?), the work would in a sense be taken as a kind of 'gospel', transmitted by Eve, or with her as the central figure. The rather peculiar title would be much better explained in this way than on the assumption that Eve was a witness to the earthly life and teaching of Christ. The Armenian Infancy Gospel (chap. IX) relates how Eve was present with Joseph at the first suckling of Jesus, and testified to the virgin birth, so that this interpretation would not be entirely arbitrary. In the present case, however, it seems excluded.

The context of the second quotation adds that the 'Gnostics' read these lines *in apocrypha* (ἐν ἀποκρύφοις) and saw in them a symbolic reference to menstrual blood. But it is more probably a case of a very free quotation of Rev. 22:2 (K. Holl in his edition of the *Panarion*, I, 281, note to line 17). Even if it be maintained that ἀπόκρυφα here indicates an esoteric writing of gnostic origin, it would seem that the passage ought rather to be connected with 'The Great Questions of Mary' (below p. 390f), where we find a theory of menstrual blood, based on allegorical interpretation of other biblical passages, which is analogous to that which our quotation is held to presuppose (Epiph. *Pan.* 26.8.7 and 9.2).

Harnack (*Litg.* I, 166 and 168) believed it possible to find traces of the Gospel of Eve in the Pistis Sophia (c. 96) and among the Peratae (Hippol. *Ref.* V 16.8 and 13-14), but the evidence on which he relies admits of several opinions. On the other hand one may agree with him in the assumption (*op. cit.* II 1.539) that the work was written in the 2nd century.

Notes

B. Gospels under the name of an Old Testament figure

1. E.g. Harnack, *Litg.* I, 166; Bardenhewer, *Litg.* I², 347.
2. Hennecke, NTApo², p. 69; cf. perhaps a picture in Cubiculum I of the *hypogaeum* of the Aurelii, in C. Cecchelli, *Monumenti cristiani-eretici di Roma*, Rome 1949, pl. II right.
3. Holl in his edition of the *Panarion*, I, 278, note to line 8.
4. H. Leisegang, *Die Gnosis*⁴, Leipzig 1955, p. 190.
5. Cf. Reitzenstein, *Poimandres*, pp. 236-244; A. Dieterich, *Mithrasliturgie*³, pp. 97, 240; K. Holl in his edition of the *Panarion* I, 278, note to line 11; A.J. Festugière, *Corpus Hermeticum* I, 68, note 33.
6. Cf. Epiphanius, *Pan.* 26.10.9; Gospel of Philip, in Epiph. *Pan.* 26.13.2 (see above, p. 180); L. Fendt, *Gnostische Mysterien*, Munich 1922, pp. 4-32, 76f.; H. Jonas, *Gnosis und spätantiker Geist I*, Göttingen 1934, ²1954, pp. 139f.; R. Bultmann, ZNW 24, 1925, 118f.; id. *Das Evangelium des Johannes*¹¹, Göttingen 1950, p. 41 n. 2.
7. Cf. SB Berlin 1933, p. 308, and 1934, pp. 877 and 891.
8. Cf. Iren, *adv. Haer.* 30.15; ps.-Tertullian, *adv. Omnes Haer.* 2; Filastrius 1; Epiphanius *Pan.* 37.3.1: Ophites; Hippol. *Ref.* V 16.8: Peratae.

C. Gospels current, directly or indirectly, under the name of Jesus, and similar works

1. The Sophia Jesu Christi

This document, handed down in Codex III from Nag Hammadi, is a secondary reworking of a religio-philosophical document, the 'Letter of Eugnostos', which was also found at Nag Hammadi (Codex III, pp. 70.1-78.23; Codex V, pp. 7.24-9.11; Codex III, pp. 81.2-90.13). Through this reworking the text was converted into a dialogue between Jesus and his disciples. The work is also contained in Pap. Berolin. 8502, as well as in NH Codex III. In our collection it is not necessary to deal further with this text.

Literature: *Facsimile edition:* Codex III, 1978, pp. 90.14-119.18.

Edition: Die gnostischen Schriften des koptischen Papyrus Berolinensis 8502, hg., übersetzt und bearb. von Walter C. Till, 2nd ed. revised by H.-M. Schenke TU 60, 1972, pp. 194-295.

English translation: NH Library in English pp. 206-228 (rev. ed. 1988, pp. 220-243).

2. The Dialogue of the Redeemer

See above, pp. 300ff.

3. The Pistis Sophia

1. Literature: *Editions:* M.G. Schwartze, *Pistis Sophia: opus gnosticum Valentino adiudicatum e codice manuscripto coptico Londinensi descriptum.* Latine vertit M.G. Schwartze. Edidit J.H. Petermann. Berlin 1851/1853. C. Schmidt, *Pistis Sophia,* Coptica 2, Copenhagen 1925. *Pistis Sophia.* Text ed. by C. Schmidt, transl. and notes by Violet MacDermot, (The Coptic Gnostic Library = NHS 9), 1978.

Translations: German: (Schmidt-Till), *Koptisch-gnostische Schriften I. Die Pistis Sophia; die beiden Bücher des Jeu; Unbekanntes altgnostisches Werk,* ed. Carl Schmidt, (GCS 13, 1905); 3rd ed. rev. Walter Till,(GCS 45), 1959. Carl Schmidt, *Pistis Sophia. Ein gnostisches Originalwerk des 3. Jahrhunderts aus dem Koptischen übersetzt,* Leipzig 1925. French: E. Amélineau, *Pistis Sophia, ouvrage gnostique de Valentin, traduit du Copte en français avec une introduction,* Paris 1895. English: Violet MacDermot, NHS 9 (see above).

Bibliography: Schmidt-Till, vols. IX-XV; Erbetta I, 368f.; Schmidt-Mac Dermot, pp. 772-775.

2. Extant remains: The work, or more precisely group of works, traditionally known by this name is contained in a Coptic version (almost pure Sahidic, slightly influenced by Fayyumic) in a parchment manuscript of the second half of the 4th century,[1] the Codex Askewianus. Bought in a London bookshop in

1773 by the English collector Dr. A. Askew, it passed in 1785 to the British Museum, where it is now preserved as Ms. Add. 5114. Attention was first drawn to it in 1778 by C.G. Woide, under the title 'Pistis Sophia', and the text of the codex was published, with a Latin translation, in the posthumous work of M.G. Schwartze. Carl Schmidt was much occupied with this work, and also published an edition of the text, taken over (with some corrections) in NHS 9. For translations, see the details above.

3. Character and content: following the analysis of K.R. Köstlin,[2] the results of which were adopted and more precisely stated by C. Schmidt, it is today almost unanimously agreed that the four sections of the manuscript must be divided into two distinct groups. The first three sections correspond to the three books of one and the same work, probably composed between 250 and 300: the first book (pp. 1-81 of the Schmidt-Till translation) has neither superscription nor colophon; the second (pp. 82-162) has at the beginning the title (added later) 'The second book (τόμος) of the Pistis Sophia', but is designated at the end as 'A part (μέρος) of the books (or rolls:τεύχη) of the Saviour (σωτήρ)'; the third (pp. 164.20-231.9), separated from the second by an independent fragment, the end of a lost book, is likewise entitled in the colophon 'A part (μέρος) of the books (or rolls:τεύχη) of the Saviour (σωτήρ)'. On the other hand the fourth section (232.1-254.8), which has no title, is in reality a distinct work, composed in the *first* half of the 3rd century and thus older than those which precede it. Accordingly only the work contained in the first three books merits the name 'Pistis Sophia'.

Again, this is only a late title, added subsequently on one page of the manuscript, and strictly speaking is appropriate only to that part of the treatise which extends from the beginning to p. 118.36. It would seem better to give preference to the more primitive but less significant and rather technical title 'Books (Rolls) of the Saviour' (τὰ τεύχη τοῦ σωτῆρος). Pistis Sophia is moreover a title the meaning of which was long in dispute. K.R. Koestlin (*op. cit.* p. 9) explained it in relation to the main theme of the first part of the work: Sophia, fallen and repentant, expresses her hope of deliverance from the chaos into which she has fallen, her faith in her salvation. For Renan,[3] Pistis (perhaps read πιστή) Sophia was to be translated 'the faithful Wisdom'. R. Eisler[4] thinks that Sophia is here regarded as Wisdom, present at the side of God and intervening as Fidelity, Confidence and Faith in the work of creation. As Carl Schmidt has shown,[5] the true explanation seems to be supplied by a passage in the Sophia Jesu Christi (above, p. 361: BG 102.15-103.9 = Nag Hammadi Codex III 106.16-23), which Schmidt however wrongly ascribes to the Apocryphon of John: 'The Son of Man agreed (συμφωνεῖν) with Sophia, his consort (σύζυγος) and revealed himself in a [great light] as bisexual. His male nature (μέν) is called 'the Saviour (σωτήρ), the begetter of all things', but (δέ) his female 'Sophia, mother of all' (παγγενέτειρα), whom some call Pistis.' The same appears in the Epistle of Eugnostos, the probable source of the Sophia Jesu Christi (above, p. 361; pp. 81.21-82.6 in Codex III from Nag Hammadi), which further states that Pistis Sophia is at once the name of the consort of the Saviour and the female designation of the sixth of the emanations manifested by him.

Several authors have proposed to identify the Pistis Sophia proper, or parts thereof, with the 'little Questions of Mary', an apocryphon mentioned by Epiphanius (*Pan.* 26. 8.1-3) in connection with the Gnostics (see below, pp. 390 f.), but this hypothesis appears untenable.[6] Nor can we admit the view of Liechtenhan,[7] for whom Book I of Pistis Sophia might once have been called 'the Gospel of Philip' (see above, pp. 179 ff.), and Book II the 'Questions of Mary'; in the latter case it would not be a question either of the 'little' or of the 'great Questions of Mary' mentioned by Epiphanius.

All critics agree in regarding Egypt as the land of origin of the two writings of the Codex Askewianus. The attempt, made at the beginning, to claim them as the work of Valentinus or a Valentinian author has long been abandoned. They are much more probably to be ascribed to the 'Gnostics' (of Epiphanius), although it is not possible to determine more precisely whether they were Sethians or, as Schmidt for a time supposed, Severians.[8] That in these writings we have to do with translations of Greek originals seems certain; the suggestion that they were directly composed in Coptic[9] is exposed to objections and arguments of fact which appear to be decisive.[10]

The Pistis Sophia and the separate work which follows it in the manuscript have both the form of a gospel of the common gnostic type: they profess to contain the esoteric teaching revealed by the risen Christ to his disciples in response to their questions and in the form of a dialogue.

The first book of the Pistis Sophia begins as follows:

But (δέ) it came to pass, after Jesus was risen from the dead, that he spent 11 years discoursing with his disciples (μαθηταί), and taught them only as far as the places (τόποι) of the first commandment and as far as the places (τόποι) of the first mystery (μυστήριον) ... which is the last mystery (μυστήριον), i.e. the twenty-fourth.

(Pistis Sophia c. 1, Schmidt-Till 1.2-6, 12f.)

The supreme mystery, of which the disciples as yet are entirely ignorant, is to be revealed to them in the course of the twelfth and last year of the Saviour's sojourn among his followers between the resurrection and the final ascension on the 15th of the moon in the month of Tobe or Tybi (January). This date is perhaps to be connected with that on which, according to Clement of Alexandria (*Strom.* I, 21.146.2), some of the Basilidian Gnostics celebrated annually the baptism of Jesus (τὴν πεντεκαιδεκάτην τοῦ Τυβὶ μηνός: the 15th Tybi). The scenery here employed (action set upon a mountain, appearance of the Revealer in luminous and supernatural form, the terror of the spectators, the salutation, the promise of a direct and comprehensive revelation of the truth) is so characteristic, so completely typical, that despite its length this second introduction must be cited in full:

Now it came to pass, that the disciples (μαθηταί) were sitting together on the Mount of Olives, speaking these words and rejoicing greatly [lit. with a great joy], and being very glad and saying to one another: Blessed (μακάριοι) are we above (παρά) all men on earth, since the Saviour (σωτήρ) has revealed these things to us, and we have received the fulness (πλήρωμα) and complete perfection - this they were saying to one another, while Jesus sat a little way apart from them.

But (δέ) it came to pass on the 15th of the moon in the month Tybi, which is the day on which the moon becomes full, on that day now, when the sun was come out upon its path (βάσις), there came forth behind it a great power (δύναμις) of light, gleaming very bright, and the light that was in it was beyond measure. For (γάρ) it came out of the Light of lights, and it came out of the last mystery (μυστήριον), which is the 24th mystery (μυστήριον) from within outwards - those (= the 24 mysteries) which are in the orders (τάξεις) of the second space (χώρημα) of the first mystery (μυστήριον). But (δέ) that power of light descended upon Jesus and surrounded him entirely, while he sat apart from his disciples (μαθηταί), and he shone exceedingly, and the light that was upon him was beyond measure. And the disciples (μαθηταί) did not see Jesus because of the great light in which he was, or (ἤ) which was upon him, for (γάρ) their eyes were darkened because of the great light in which he was, but (ἀλλά) they saw only the light, which sent forth many beams (-ἀκτῖνες) of light. And the beams (-ἀκτῖνες) of light were not like unto one another, and the light was of different kinds, and it was of different form (τύπος) from below upwards, since one [sc. beam] was more excellent than the other [...] in a great and boundless splendour of light; it extended from beneath the earth as far as the heaven. - And when the disciples (μαθηταί) saw that light, they were in great fear and agitation.

Now it came to pass, when that power of light descended upon Jesus, it gradually surrounded him wholly; then (τότε) Jesus rose up or (ἤ) flew into the heights, since he was become exceeding shining in an immeasurable light. And the disciples (μαθηταί) followed him with their eyes, and none of them spoke, until he reached the heaven, but (ἀλλά) they were all in great silence (σιγή). This now came to pass on the 15th of the moon, on the day on which it becomes full in the month Tybi.

Now it came to pass, when Jesus went up into the heaven, after three hours, all the powers of heaven were troubled, and they all trembled together, they and all their aeons (αἰῶνες) and all their places (τόποι) and all their orders (τάξεις), and the whole earth was moved, and all that dwell upon it. And all men in the world (κόσμος) were troubled, and the disciples (μαθηταί) also, and all thought: Perhaps the world (κόσμος) will be rolled up. And all the powers that are in the heaven ceased not from their agitation, they and the whole world (κόσμος), and they were all moved one against the other from the third hour of the 15th of the moon <in the month> Tybi until the ninth hour of the following day. And all the angels (ἄγγελοι) and their archangels (ἀρχάγγελοι) and all the powers of the height all praised (ὑμνεύειν) the Inmost of the Inmost, so that (ὥστε) the whole world (κόσμος) heard their voice, without ceasing until the ninth hour of the following day.

But (δέ) the disciples (μαθηταί) sat together, in fear, and they were exceedingly troubled; but (δέ) they were afraid because of the great earthquake which took place, and wept with one another, saying: What then (ἄρα) will happen? Perhaps the Saviour (σωτήρ) will destroy all places (τόποι).

While they now said this and wept to one another, then the heavens opened, about the ninth hour of the following day, and they saw Jesus descend, shining very bright, and the light in which he was was beyond measure. For (γάρ) he shone more than at the hour when he ascended up to the heavens, so that (ὥστε) the (κόσμος) could not describe the light that was upon him, and it sent forth many beams (–ἀκτῖνες) of light, and its beams (–ἀκτῖνες) were beyond number, and its light was not like one to the other, but (ἀλλά) it was of different kind and of different form (τύπος), since some [sc. beams] surpassed the others countless times; and the whole light was together, it was of three different kinds, and one surpassed the others countless times; the second, which was in the midst, was superior to the first, which was beneath; and the third, which was above them all, was superior to both those which were beneath; and the first beam, which was beneath them all, was like the light which came upon Jesus before he ascended into the heavens, and was like only to itself in its light. And the three lights were of different kinds of light, and they were of different form (τύπος), whereby some surpassed others countless times.

But (δέ) it came to pass, when the disciples (μαθηταί) saw this, they were exceedingly afraid, and were troubled. Jesus now, the merciful and kind-hearted, when he saw that his disciples (μαθηταί) were greatly troubled [lit. troubled with a great troubling], spoke to them, saying: Be of good cheer; it is I, be not afraid [cf. Mt. 14:27, Mk. 6:50].

Now it came to pass, when the disciples (μαθηταί) heard these words, they said: O Lord, if it be thou, draw to thyself thy glorious light, that we may be able to stand, else are our eyes darkened and we are troubled, and also the whole world (κόσμος) is troubled because of the great light that is in thee.

Then (τότε) Jesus drew to himself the splendour of his light; and when this had come to pass all the disciples (μαθηταί) took courage, stood before Jesus, and all fell down together and worshipped him, rejoicing with great joy; they said to him: Rabbi, whither didst thou go, or (ἤ) what is thy service (διακονία) to which thou didst go, or (ἤ) why rather were all these upheavals and earthquakes which have taken place?

Then (τότε) spoke Jesus, the merciful, to them: Rejoice and be glad [cf. Mt. 5:12] from this hour on, for I went to the places (τόποι) out of which I came. From henceforth will I speak with you openly (παρρησία) from the beginning (ἀρχή) of the truth (ἀλήθεια) unto its completion, and I will speak with you face to face without parable [παραβολή: cf. Jn. 16:25]; I will not hide from you from this hour anything of the things of the height and of the things of the place (τόπος of the truth (ἀλήθεια). For (γάρ) to me is given by the Ineffable and by the first Mystery (μυσ–τήριον) of all mysteries [μυστήρια) the power (ἐξουσία: cf. Mt. 28:18], to speak with you from the beginning (ἀρχή) to the fulfilment (πλήρωμα) and from within to without, and from without to within. Hear now, that I may tell you all things.

(Pistis Sophia c. 2-6; Schmidt-Till 3.8-6.5)

Jesus begins by relating the journey which he has just accomplished through the aeons, in the course of which he has met Pistis Sophia 'quite alone', distressed and mourning', 'beneath the thirteenth aeon'. At the request of Mary he recounts at length the adventures and the lamentations of this being, who has fallen from the thirteenth aeon into matter (ὕλη), and whom he has finally restored to her original abode. Then follows a dialogue on other themes: the mysteries of light, especially the most sublime among them, those of the Ineffable and of the first mystery; the origin of sin and evil in the world of men; the necessity of repentance; the punishments which await the sinner after death.

The revelations by Jesus are interrupted by questions from the disciples and the holy women, to which the Saviour replies, each of his answers being followed by demonstrations of joy or of adoration, which mark the gratitude of those present. Sometimes also one of the disciples or one of the women supplies the explanation; Jesus encourages them to speak and inspires them, illuminating the 'man of light' who dwells within each. The following intervene in turn and on several occasions: Mary the mother of Jesus, Mary Magdalene, Philip, Peter, Martha, John, Andrew, Thomas, Matthew, James, Salome. A prominent place is reserved for Mary Magdalene and for John, 'the maiden' (παρθένος), of whom the Saviour declares:

But (ἀλλά) Mary Magdalene and John, the maiden (παρθένος), will surpass all my disciples (μαθηταί) and all men who shall receive mysteries (μυστήρια) in the Ineffable, they will be on my right hand and on my left, and I am they and they are I, and they will be equal with you in all things, save (ἀλλὰ πλήν) that your thrones (θρόνοι) will surpass theirs, and my own throne (θρόνος) will surpass yours and those of all men who shall find the word of the Ineffable.

(Pistis Sophia c. 96; Schmidt-Till 148.25-33)

It has been reckoned[11] that of the forty-six questions here put to Jesus thirty-nine fall to the lot of Mary Magdalene.

The content of the Pistis Sophia is too varied and extensive to be summarised here or evaluated in detail. As an example the following passage, already discussed by Hennecke,[12] Leisegang[13] and Marmorstein,[14] may be selected:

But (δέ) Mary answered and said: My Lord, concerning the word which thy power prophesied (προφητεύειν) through David [*Ps. 84:11f. LXX*]: 'Grace and Truth met one another, Righteousness (δικαιοσύνη) and Peace (εἰρήνη) kissed each other. Truth sprouted forth from the earth, and Righteousness (δικαιοσύνη) looked down from heaven', thy power prophesied (προφητεύειν) this word at this time concerning thee. When thou wast small, before the Spirit (πνεῦμα) was come upon thee, thou wast in a vineyard with Joseph. The Spirit (πνεῦμα) came out of the height and came to me in my house, in thy likeness, and I knew him not, and I thought that it was thou. And the Spirit (πνεῦμα) said to me: Where is Jesus my brother, that I may meet him (ἀπαντᾶν)? And when he said this to me, I was at a loss (ἀπορεῖν), and thought it was a spectre (φάντασμα), to tempt (πειράζειν) me. But (δέ) I took him and bound him to the foot of the bed which was in my house, until I could go out to you in the field, you and Joseph, and found you in the vineyard, while Joseph was fencing the vineyard. Now it came to pass, when thou didst hear me speak the word to Joseph, thou didst understand (νοεῖν) the word, and didst rejoice and say: Where is he, that I may see him, else I await him in this place (τόπος)? But (δέ) it came to pass, when Joseph heard thee say these words, he was perturbed, and we went off at once, entered into the house, and found the Spirit (πνεῦμα) bound to the bed. And we looked on thee and on him, and found thee like unto him; and he that was bound to the bed was set free, he embraced thee, and kissed thee, and thou also didst kiss him, and ye became one.

(Pistis Sophia c. 61; Schmidt-Till 77.33-78.20)

In the second treatise of the Codex Askewianus, contained in the fourth and last section of the manuscript, we have to do likewise with a gospel in dialogue form, but the episodes here narrated are set at a time and in a framework different from those of the previous work. Here the action takes place on the day after the resurrection, and in the first instance on the shore of the ocean:

Now it came to pass, when our Lord Jesus was crucified (σταυροῦν) and on the third day was risen from the dead [*cf. Synoptics, Acts, 1 Cor. 15:4*], then his disciples (μαθηταί) gathered round him, and entreated him, saying: Our Lord, have mercy upon us, for we have forsaken father and mother and the whole world (κόσμος) and have followed thee [*cf. Mt. 10:37; 19:27, 29; Mk. 10:28f.; Lk. 14:26; 18:28f.; Apocryphon Jacobi (above,*

367

pp. 285 ff.) *4:25-28 of NH Codex I; the Books of Jeu c. 2 (258. 5-9 Schmidt-Till) and c. 44 (306. 3-6)*].

Then (τότε) Jesus stood with his disciples (μαθηταί) by the water of the ocean (ὠκεανός) and called aloud (ἐπικαλεῖσθαι) this prayer (προσευχή), saying: Hearken to me, my Father, thou Father of all Fatherhood, thou boundless (ἀπέραντος) Light: αεηιουω·ϊαω·αωϊ· ωϊα·ψινωθερ·θερνωψ·νωψιτερ·ζαγουρη·παγουρη·νεθμομαωθ· νεψιομαωθμαραχαχθα·θωβαρραβαυ·θαρναχαχαν·ζοροκοθορα· ϊεου·σαβαωθ.''

But (δέ) while Jesus was saying this, Thomas, Andrew, James and Simon the Canaanite (Κανανίτης) were in the west, with their faces turned towards the east, but (δέ) Philip and Bartholomew were in the south (with their faces) turned towards the north, but (δέ) the other disciples (μαθηταί) and the women disciples (μαθητρίαι) stood behind Jesus. But (δέ) Jesus stood beside the altar (θυσιαστήριον).

And Jesus cried out, turning towards the four corners of the world (κόσμος) with his disciples (μαθηταί), who were all clothed in linen garments, and said: „ϊαω·ϊαω·ϊαω . This is its interpretation (ἑρμηνεία): Iota, since the All is gone forth - Alpha, since it will turn back again - Omega, since the perfection of all perfections will take place.

But (δέ) when Jesus had said this, he said: „ϊαφθα·ϊαφθα·μουναηρ· μουναηρ·ερμανουηρ·ερμανουηρ i.e. Thou Father of all Fatherhood of the Infinite (ἀπέραντα), hearken unto me for my disciples' (μαθηταί) sake; whom I have brought before thee, that they may believe (πιστεύειν) on all the words of thy truth (ἀλήθεια), and grant all whereof I cry to Thee, for I know the name of the Father of the treasure (–θησαυρός) of light.

(Pistis Sophia c. 136: Schmidt-Till 232.1-233.5)

The scene changes in the course of the narrative, and the action is set successively in an 'aëry' region on the way of the Midst (p. 233.29-30), in an 'air' of very strong light (p. 242.6), on the mount of Galilee (p. 243.12), and in *Amente* (p. 253.36f.).

Whatever the external frame, the speeches of Jesus, which give the writing its unity, all centre on the same theme. As K.R. Köstlin has put it (*Theol. Jahrbücher* 13, 1854, 6): 'One might describe the whole precisely . . . as a treatise περὶ μετανοίας(in the gnostic sense).' Jesus, here also called Aberamentho,[15] relates to his disciples the story of the archons of destiny, and sets forth the terrible punishments which they inflict upon men. To calm the fears of his audience, he celebrates before them the mysteries which purify from sin; but here only the lesser mysteries, of which the manuscript, here defective, describes only the first, the baptism of water. The revelation then continues and concludes with an exposition of the fate which awaits the soul of the sinner after death.

As in the Pistis Sophia, the disciples and the holy women intervene in turn, either in groups or as individuals, to ask questions of the Saviour. The following appear in succession: Mary, Salome, Peter, Andrew, Thomas, Bartholomew, Thomas (a second time), John and once again Mary.

4. Date: the document is dated to the 3rd century.

Notes

C. Gospels current, directly or indirectly, under the name of Jesus, and similar works

3. The Pistis Sophia

1. According to Carl Schmidt, who had originally opted for the 5th century; for an earlier date cf. L.Th. Lefort, 'La littérature égyptienne aux derniers siècles avant l'invasion arabe', *Chronique d'Egypte* 6, 1931, 321.
2. 'Das gnostische System des Buches Pistis Sophia', *Theol. Jahrbücher* 13, 1854, 1-104 and 137-196.
3. *Marc-Aurèle*[12], Paris, 1905, p. 120, note 3.
4. 'Pistis Sophia und Barbelo', *Angelos* 3, 1930, 93-110.
5. *Pistis Sophia*, Leipzig 1925, pp. xxif., and 'Die Urschrift der Pistis Sophia', ZNW 24, 1925, 235.
6. References in H. Leisegang, Pauly-Wissowa 1 Reihe, 40 Halbbd., 1950, cols. 1820.62-1821.11.
7. 'Untersuchungen zur kopt. -gnost. Literatur', *Zeitschr. f. wissenschaftl. Theol.* 44, 1901, 236-253.
8. Cf. however the reservations of E. de Faye, *Gnostiques et Gnosticisme*[2], Paris 1925, pp. 273-275.
9. So F. Granger, JTS 5, 1904, 401; F.C. Burkitt, 'Pistis Sophia', JTS 23, 1921/2, 271-280; id. 'Pistis Sophia again', JTS 26, 1924/5, 391-399; id. 'Pistis Sophia and the Coptic Language', JTS 27, 1925/6, 148-157.
10. C. Schmidt, *Pistis Sophia*, Copenhagen 1925, p. xxii; id. 'Die Urschrift der Pistis Sophia', ZNW 24, 1925, 218-240; R. Eisler, 'Pistis Sophia and Barbelo', *Angelos* 3, 1930, 110.
11. C. Schmidt, *Koptisch-gnostische Schriften* 1, Leipzig 1905, xv; H. Leisegang, *Die Gnosis*[4], Leipzig 1955, p. 353.
12. NTApo[2], pp. 102f.
13. 'Der Bruder des Erlösers', *Angelos* 2, 1925, 24-33.
14. 'Ein Wort über den Bruder des Erlösers', *Angelos* 2, 1926, 155f.
15. On this name see S. Eitrem, *Papyri Osloenses* I, Oslo 1925, 34 and 55; F.C. Burkitt, *Church and Gnosis*, Cambridge 1932, pp. 39 and 82f.; Campbell Bonner, *Studies in Magical Amulets*, Ann Arbor 1950, p. 203.

4. The two Books of Jeu

Literature: *Editions:* C. Schmidt, *Gnostische Schriften in koptischer Sprache aus dem Codex Brucianus,*(TU 8, 1892). (Schmidt-MacDermot), *The Books of Jeu and the Untitled Text in the Bruce Codex.* Text. ed. by Carl Schmidt. Translation and notes by Violet MacDermot, (The Coptic Gnostic Library = NHS 13), 1978.

Translations: German: (Schmidt-Till), *Koptisch-gnostische Schriften I. Die Pistis Sophia; Die beiden Bucher des Jeu; Unbekanntes altgnostisches Werk,* ed. Carl Schmidt, (GCS 13), 1905; 3rd ed. rev. Walter Till, (GCS 45), 1954. English: Schmidt-MacDermot, NHS 13.

Bibliography: Schmidt-Till pp. IX-XV; Erbetta I, 317; Schmidt-MacDermot, pp. 319-321.

This work, like an anonymous dogmatic treatise which follows it, is contained in the Codex Brucianus, the date of which is much disputed (9th or 10th cent.? 7th, 6th, 5th or 4th cent.? 3rd cent.?). The manuscript was bought in 1769 in Thebes, or more probably in Medinet Habu, by the Scottish traveller James Bruce, and since 1848 has been in the Bodleian Library, Oxford, as Bruce Ms 96. The treatise begins with the words:

This is the book of the knowledges (γνώσεις) of the invisible (ἀόρατος) God through the medium of the hidden mysteries (μυστήρια) which show the way to the chosen race (γένος), (leading) into rest to the life of the Father . . .

(Schmidt-Till 257.5-8)

The title is implicitly mentioned towards the end of the first part (301.27), and is given in a colophon to this part (302): 'the book of the great κατὰ μυστήριον λόγος'.

Despite the objections of E. Preuschen[1] and R. Liechtenhan[2] it is now generally admitted, as a result of the work of Carl Schmidt,[3] that the document thus described and transmitted is identical with the 'two books of Jeu' twice mentioned in the Pistis Sophia (158.18f., and 228.35). The text is written in Coptic (Sahidic), and shows only at the beginning some dialectic peculiarities which in Till's opinion betray an influence from Subachmimic. There is no doubt, however, that we have to do with the translation of a Greek original, probably composed in Egypt in the first half or at the beginning of the 3rd century. The writing, which especially in its second part is closely related to those of the Codex Askewianus, must derive from the same milieu: a circle of 'Gnostics' (in the narrow sense) or Barbelognostics with Encratite tendencies.

'The two books of Jeu' or 'The great λόγος κατὰ μυστήριον ' appears in its present form (perhaps artificially imposed) as a gospel of the gnostic type; otherwise it would be more readily compared with a didactic treatise in the form of a revelation. This work also professes to record the conversations of Jesus with his disciples and the holy women, either with all the apostles (ἀπόστολοι), 'Matthew and John, Philip and Bartholomew and James', as it is precisely stated on p. 258.26f., or with the 'Twelve' or 'twelve disciples (μαθηταί))' and the female disciples (μαθητρίαι), as it is put elsewhere (p. 303.3-6; cf. p. 308.4f.). As in the Gospel of Thomas (above, pp. 110ff.), in Manicheism and elsewhere, Jesus is designated as 'the living', i.e. as the 'risen' or as the 'life-giving'.[4] The revelations which he imparts to his disciples in response to their questions (here very few in number) are introduced in the following terms:

Jesus, the living one, answered and said to his apostles (ἀπόστολοι): Blessed is he who has crucified the world (κόσμος), and has not allowed the world (κόσμος) to crucify him [cf. Gal. 6:14]. The apostles (ἀπόστολοι) answered with one voice, saying: Lord, teach us the way to crucify the world (κόσμος), that it may not crucify us, and we perish and lose our life. Jesus, the living one, answered and said: He who has crucified the world (κόσμος) is he who has found my word, and has fulfilled it after the will of him who sent me [cf. Mt. 10:40 etc.] The apostles (ἀπόστολοι) answered, saying: Speak to us, Lord, that we may hear thee. We have followed thee with all our heart, have left father and mother, have left vineyard and field, have left our goods (κτῆσις), have left the king's glory and have followed thee, that thou mightest teach us the life of thy Father who hath sent thee [cf. Mt. 10:37; 19:27, 29; Lk. 14:26; 18:28-30; Apocryphon Jacobi (above, pp. 285ff.) 4.25-28 of NH Codex I; the second document of the Codex Askewianus, p. 232.4-6 Schmidt-Till]. Jesus, the living one answered and said: This is the life of my Father, that ye receive your soul (ψυχή) from the race (γένος) of reason (νοῦς), and it cease to be earthly (χοϊκός) and become wise (νοερός) through that which I say unto you in the course of my words, that ye may complete it and be delivered before the archon (ἄρχων) of this aeon (ἀιών) [cf. Jn. 12:31 etc.] and his snares, which have no end. But (δέ) you are my disciples (μαθηταί), make haste to receive my word carefully to yourselves, that ye may know it, that the archon (ἄρχων) of this aeon (ἀιών) may not strive with you, he who hath found none of his commands in me [cf. Jn. 14:31], and that ye yourselves, O my apostles (ἀπόστολοι), may fulfil my word in relation to me, and I myself may make you free, and ye may become whole through a freedom (–ἐλεύθερος) wherein is no blemish. As the Spirit (πνεῦμα) of the Comforter (παράκλητος) is whole, so shall ye also become whole through the freedom of the Spirit (πνεῦμα) of the holy Comforter (παράκληος) [cf. Jn. 14:16, 26; 15:26; 16:7]. All the apostles (ἀπόστολοι) answered with one voice, Matthew and John, Philip and Bartholomew and James, saying: Lord Jesus, thou living one, whose goodness (–ἀγαθός) is spread abroad upon those who have found his wisdom (σοφία) and his form in which he shines - O Light, that is in the light which has illumined our heart until we received the light of life - O true word (λόγος), which through knowledge (γνῶσις) teaches us the hidden knowledge of the Lord Jesus, the living one. Jesus, the living one, answered and said: Blessed is the man who knoweth this, and has brought the heaven down, and carried the earth and sent it to heaven, and he became the Midst, for it [*sc.* the Midst] is nothing. The apostles (ἀπόστολοι) answered, saying: Jesus, thou living one, O Lord, explain to us in what way one may bring down the heaven, for (γάρ) we have followed thee, that thou mightest teach us the true light.

(c. 1-3; Schmidt-Till 257.17-259.8)

In the first part of the work the answer of Jesus consists essentially in revealing how the Father projected from his bosom Jeu ('Ιεου) the 'true God', and in what manner there issued from him in turn twenty-eight emanations, whose form, mystic name and number (ψῆφος) are noted each time with great precision. In the second part Jesus bestows upon those present 'the three baptisms' (with water, with fire and with the Holy Spirit), and then the 'mystery' destined to remove from them the 'wickedness (κακία) of the archons', which must be followed by 'the mystery (μυστήριον) of the spiritual unction' (χρῖσμα πνευματικόν). Then is described the ascension which will lead the souls of the disciples, thus purified, initiated and saved, through the aeons of the transcendent world to the place of 'the great invisible (ἀόρατος) God', 'the great virginal Spirit' (παρθενικὸν πνεῦμα) and the twenty-four 'emanations (προβολαί) of the invisible God'. Here also are imparted the secret names of the aeons, their several numbers (ψῆφος), the 'seals' (σφραγίδες) and 'passwords', the formulae (ἀπολογίαι) which allow free passage through each of their spheres, one after the other, and ensure escape from their grasp and power.

The esoteric character of such teaching is so evident that it is unnecessary to enter into detail. Note should be taken, however, of the typical expressions employed by Jesus to instruct or admonish the disciples, the initiates, to keep his revelations secret and to transmit or divulge them only to the elite, i.e. to those only who are worthy to receive them and capable of understanding them:

These mysteries (μυστήρια) which I shall give you, preserve, and give them to no man except (εἰ μήτι) he be worthy of them. Give them not to father nor (οὐδέ) to mother, (οὐδέ) or brother or (οὐδέ) to sister or (οὐδέ) to kinsman (συγγενής), neither (οὐδέ) for food nor (οὐδέ) for drink, nor (οὐδέ) for woman-kind, neither (οὐδέ) for gold nor (οὐδέ) for silver, (nor (οὐδέ) for anything at all of this world (κόσμος). Preserve them, and give them to no one whatsoever for the sake of the good of this whole world (κόσμος).

(c. 43; Schmidt-Till 304.6-13)

The two formulae, or double formula: to keep hidden, securely and in secret (ἀσφαλῶς, ἐν ἀσφαλείᾳ ἔχειν), the teaching of the Master received orally or in writing; to preserve the tradition (παράδοσις) and impart it only to those who by initiation are worthy of it (ἄξιοι, *digni*) - these are almost technical in the language of the occult sciences and apocalyptic literature of the first centuries of our era;[5] but a still closer connection can be established between this passage and the epilogue of the Apocryphon of John (below, p. 387).

Notes

4. The Two Books of Jeu

1. ThLZ 7, 1894, cols. 184f.
2. 'Untersuchungen zur koptisch-gnost. Literatur', *Ztschr. f. wissenschaftl. Theol.* 44, 1901, 236-253.
3. 'Die in dem koptisch-gnostischen Codex Brucianus enthaltenen 'beiden Bücher Jeu' in ihrem Verhaltnis zu der Pistis Sophia', *Ztschr. f. wissenschaftl. Theol.* 37, 1894, 555-585.
4. Cf. Rev. 1:18; Irenaeus, *adv. Haer.* I 21.3; the anonymous work in the Codex Brucianus, p. 362.11 Schmidt-Till (264 = pp. 290-291 Schmidt-MacDermot); Acts of Thomas c. 60, c. 129, c. 169; E. Waldschmidt and W. Lentz, *Die Stellung Jesu in Manichäismus, Abh, d. preuss. Akad. d. Wissensch.* 1926, No. 4, p. 41; F.J. Dölger, *Ichthys* I², Münster 1928, 6*-8*; M. Kropp, *Ausgewählte koptische Zaubertexte* III, Brussels 1930, 64.
5. Cf. A.J. Festugière, *L'idéal religieux des Grecs et l'Évangile*, Paris 1932, p. 305, note 6; id. *La Révélation d'Hermès Trismégiste* I, Paris 1944, 309-354, esp. p. 345 note 6, and p. 352.

D. Gospels attributed to the Apostles as a group

1. The Gospel of the Twelve (or: of the Twelve Apostles)

Origen (*in Luc. hom.* I, p. 5.2-4 Rauer) mentions, immediately after the Gospel according to the Egyptians (above, pp. 209ff.) and before the Gospels of Basilides, Thomas and Matthias (below, pp. 397ff., above, pp. 110ff., below, pp. 382ff.), a heterodox writing entitled 'the Gospel of the Twelve (τὸ ἐπιγράμμε–νον τῶν Δώδεκα εὐαγγέλιον) 'or, according to Jerome's translation (adduced by Rauer *ad loc.*), 'the Gospel according to the Twelve Apostles' (*aliud* (*sc. evangelium*) *iuxta Duodecim Apostolos*). Echoes of this testimony are to be found in Ambrose (*Expositio euangelii Lucae* I 2, p. 10.18 Schenkl: *euangelium, quod duodecim scripsisse dicuntur*), Jerome (*Comm. in Mt.* Prol., PL XXVI 17A: *duodecim apostolorum euangelium*), Philip of Side (*Hist. eccl.* in TU .5 2, 1888, 169, No. 4), the Venerable Bede (*In Lucae euangelium expositio* I, Prol., PL XCII 307C), and in Theophylact (*Enarratio in Evangelium Lucae*, Prol., PG CXXIII 692A: το ἐπιγραφόμενον τῶν Δώδεκα).

The context in which Origen sets the work might lead one to think of a gnostic gospel. On the basis of a wrongly interpreted passage in Jerome (*Dial. adv. Pelag.* III 2) an abortive attempt was made to link the Gospel of the Twelve with the Gospel of the Hebrews, but the majority of critics today are inclined to identify it with the Gospel of the Ebionites (fragments collected in Preuschen, *Antilegomena*[2], pp. 9-12, or Klostermann, *Apokrypha* II[3], pp. 12-15; cf. Vielhauer, above, pp. 166ff.); according to Bardenhewer (*Litg.* I[2], 519), the complete title would have been Εὐαγγέλιον τῶν δώδεκα(or ἀποστόλων διὰ Ματθαίου).[1] The document consequently has probably nothing to do with Gnosticism, or at most is to be connected with gnosticising Jewish Christianity. The contrary opinion of A. Schmidtke (*Neue Fragmente und Untersuchungen zu den judenchristlichen Evangelien* = TU 37 1, Leipzig, 1911, pp. 170-174), who saw in it a gentile Christian gnostic gospel, has been criticised and refuted by H. Waitz.

The question, however, remains open whether there may not have existed, under the same or a similar title, another work, or perhaps even several distinct works, whose gnostic origin and character would be less in dispute.

Note

D. Gospels attributed to the Apostles as a group

1. The Gospel of the Twelve (or of the Twelve Apostles)

1. On the whole question cf. Bardenhewer *Litg.* I[2], 518-521; H. Waitz, 'Das Evangelium der zwölf Apostel (Ebionitenevangelium)', ZNW 13, 1912, 338-348; above pp. 134ff.

2. The (Kukean) Gospel of the Twelve

Marûtâ of Maiperkat reports in his catalogue of Heresies,[1] on the subject of the Kukeans (Qûqâjê) of the region of Edessa: 'With the names of the Twelve Apostles [they imagine] for themselves twelve Evangelists. Also they corrupt [the New Testament], but not the Old.' Abraham Ecchellensis writes[2] with reference to the same sect, whom he calls 'Phocalites': 'They have done away with the New Testament and forged for themselves another. On the twelve apostles they impose barbarous names, but they retain the Old Testament intact.'

For Harnack (*op. cit.* p. 11) and Zahn (*Forschungen zur Gesch. d. ntl. Kanons* VI, 279, note 1), this referred to a work called 'the Gospel of the Twelve Apostles', which was no other than the gospel of the same title in use among the Ebionites. Appealing to certain ritual practices ascribed to the sect in Marûtâ's notice (strict and scrupulous purification observances, abstinence from pork, abhorrence of all unclean contact, etc.), Harnack in fact held the Kukeans to be 'Jewish-Christian Gnostics' who lived in Edessa alongside the Bardesanites, who would represent a 'pagan-Christian' Gnostic group. On the other hand, apart from the Syrian recension of the text of Marûtâ published by I.E. Rahmani (*Studia Syriaca* IV, Rome 1909, 78) and the version of Abraham Ecchellensis, where they are more or less brought into relation with the Samaritans, the Kukeans are either mentioned only in association with the Marcionites, the Valentinians and the Bardesanites,[3] or are said to have separated themselves by a schism from the Valentinians,[4] or finally are accused of professing a system of Gnosis which in certain features recalls Bardesanism but was crudely mythical and even pagan in character.[5]

In the circumstances, one might be inclined to prefer the view of Schmidtke (*Neue Fragmente und Untersuchungen*, TU 37.1, 1911, pp. 173f.), who proposed linking the name of the sect with that of the 'Koddiani' (Epiphanius, *Pan.* 26.3.6-7), and thus identified the Qûqâjê with 'Gentile Christians strongly influenced by Parsism'; this would involve regarding their 'Gospel of the Twelve Apostles' as a gnostic production, and distinguishing it from that of the Ebionites. On the other hand Waitz (ZNW 14, 1913, 46ff.) has produced evidence that the reference in Marûtâ's catalogue concerns not a gospel but the gnostic system of the Qûqâjê, and affords no proof of the gentile Christian character of the 'Gospel of the Twelve'.

Notes

2. The (Kukean) Gospel of the Twelve

1. O.Braun, *De sancta synodo Nicaeana*, Münster 1898, p. 49; Harnack, TU 19. 1b, 1899 p.10.
2. Mansi, *Conc.* II, 1058E; Harnack, *op. cit.* p. 16; F. Haase, *Altchristliche Kirchengeschichte nach orientalischen Quellen*, Leipzig 1925, p. 322.
3. Ephraem, *adv. Haer. Hymn.* 22.2f., CSCO 169, pp. 78f., and 170, pp. 77f.; beside the

Sabbatians, however, *Hymn.* 2.6, CSCO 169, p. 7, and 170, p. 8; cf. also 24.16, CSCO 169, p. 95, and 170, p. 89, and the Testament of Ephraem in *Journal Asiatique*, 9 Série, 18, 1901, 298.

4. James of Edessa, *Ep. XIII*, to John the Stylite of Litharba; Syr. text: W. Wright, *Journal of sacred Literature and Biblical Record* 10, 1876, 24; French trans.: F. Nau, *Revue de l'Orient chrétien* 10, 1905, 278f.; German trans.: A. Rücker, BKV 61, pp. 13f.

5. Theodore bar Konai, *Liber scholiorum* XI: H. Pognon, *Inscriptions mandaïtes des coupes de Khouabir*, Paris 1898, pp. 144 and 209-212, or CSCO, Script. syri., ser. II, tom. 66, pp. 333f., ed. A. Scher.

3. The Memoria Apostolorum

A work of this title (Tradition, Statement, History or Memoirs of the Apostles? υπομνημα ?) is mentioned about 440 by Turribius of Astorga in his letter to the bishops Idacius and Ceponius (c. 5, PL LIV 694D), among the apocryphal literature common to the Manicheans and the Priscillianists, beside the Acts of Andrew, John, Thomas and others (see vol. II: XIII). The notice is somewhat vague:

'From these [*sc.* the Acts and apocryphal books] the Manicheans and Priscillianists, or whatever sect is akin to them, strive to establish all their false doctrine; and principally from that most blasphemous book which is called the *Memoria Apostolorum*, in which to the great authority of their perversity they falsely claim a doctrine of the Lord, who destroyed the whole law of the Old Testament and all that was divinely revealed to the blessed Moses concerning the diversity of creature and Creator; besides the other blasphemies of this same book, to recount which is vexatious.'

There is every reason to believe[1] that Turribius borrowed everything he knew and here says from an earlier document, which is in any case our primary source on this question: the *Consultatio* or *Commonitorium de errore Priscillianistarum et Origenistarum* composed, probably in 414, by Paulus Orosius (ed. Schepss, CSEL 18, 1889). It is there said of Priscillian:

And this very thing [*sc.* his dualistic doctrine of the eternity of hell, from which the 'prince of the world' has come forth] he establishes from a certain book entitled *Memoria Apostolorum*, wherein the Saviour appears to be questioned by the disciples in secret, and to show from the Gospel parable which has 'The sower went forth to sow' [*Mt. 13:3*] that he was not a good sower, asserting that if he had been good he would not have been neglectful, or cast seed 'by the wayside' or 'on stony places' or 'in untilled soil' [*Mt. 13:4f.*]; wishing it to be understood that the sower is he who scatters captive souls in diverse bodies as he wills. In which book also many things are said about the prince of dampness and the prince of fire, which is meant to signify that it is by art and not by the power of God that all good things are done in the world. For it says that there is a certain virgin of light whom God, when he wishes to give rain to men, shows to the prince of dampness, who since he desires to take

376

possession of her perspires in his excitement and makes rain, and when he is deprived of her causes peals of thunder by his roaring.

(Orosius c. 2, p. 154.4-18 Schepss; corrections on the basis of a manuscript in Milan: G. Mercati, 'Note di letteratura biblica e cristiana antica' = *Studi e Testi* 5, Rome 1901, 136.)

Here it is certainly a question of a gospel, gnostic both in form and in content. Jesus is presented as conversing in secret (*secreto*) with his disciples, revealing his teaching in answer to their questions, and in particular supplying the esoteric interpretation of a parable. The doctrinal content of the book was anti-biblical and dualistic, and contained a cosmogony which introduced certain mythical beings (among others, the archons of water and of fire). More precisely, the figure of the 'Virgin of light' (παρθένος τοῦ φωτός, Ιδēl) and the erotic myth relating to the production of rain appear also in other accounts of the opinions which Priscillian and his disciples were accused of holding (First Priscillianist Tractate of Würzburg, p. 24.13-17 Schepss; ps.-Jerome, *Indiculus de haer.* 6, I 287f. Oehler, *Corpus haereseologicum*); but they belong also to the common stock of the Nicolaitans, Borborians, 'Gnostics' (cf. e.g. Epiph. *Pan.* 25.2. 4) and Manicheans (Acta Archelai IX 1-4; Titus of Bostra, *c. Manich.* II 56 ed. P. de Lagarde; Ephraem, *Hymn. contra haer.* 50.5f.: CSCO 169, pp. 196f. and 170, pp. 172f.).[2]

The gnostic origin of the Memoria Apostolorum seems therefore beyond question.[3] Lipsius indeed has maintained that this apocryphon is 'a specifically Manichean writing' (Aa I, 74 note 1). The attempt has been made[4] to identify the Memoria with the gnostic gospel (?) referred to in Irenaeus (*adv. Haer.* I 25.5 = Theod. Cyr., *Haer. fab. comp.* I 5): 'In their writings [*sc.* of the Carpocratians or the Gnostics] it is written, and they themselves thus explain: saying that Jesus spoke in secret (*in mysterio*) and apart to his disciples and apostles, and that they requested that they might transmit these things to those who were worthy and agreed with them.' Since the relationship is far from clear, this is too bold. P. Alfaric[5] also goes too far in his assertion that the Memoria Apostolorum is identical with the gospel which according to Theodor Abû Qurra and al-Biruni was in use among the Manichees (see below no.4), and ultimately with the Gospel of the Twelve Apostles (above, pp.374f.) here itself identified with the Gospel of Ebionites.

All that is certain is that the writing was not a narrative about the apostles or, as A. Dufourcq writes (*op. cit.* IV, 162), 'a pretended history of Christ and the apostles', and that it has nothing to do with the apocryphal Acts of the collection attributed to Leucius.[6] It was a work of the ordinary type of Gnostic gospels and professed to relate either the secret conversations of Jesus with the apostles or, perhaps more exactly, the recollections of these conversations preserved and reported by the apostles themselves. The date of its composition - before the middle of the 4th century - cannot be exactly determined.

Notes

3. The Memoria Apostolorum

1. Cf. E.-Ch. Babut, *Priscillien et la Priscillanisme*, Paris 1909, p. 239.
2. Cf. F.C. Baur, *Das manichäische Religionssystem*, Tübingen 1831, pp. 214-225; F. Cumont, *Recherches sur le Manichéisme* I, Brussels 1908, 54-68; K. Holl, edition of the *Panarion* of Epiphanius, III 60, note to line 12. Cf. also Henry Chadwick, *Priscillian of Avila. The Occult and the Charismatic in the Early Church*, 1976, pp. 194f.
3. A. Dufourcq, *Étude sur les Gesta Martyrum romains* IV, Paris 1910, 162, note 3.
4. G. Schepss, note to p. 154, line 5, of his edition of *Priscilliani quae supersunt*; J.A. Davids, *De Orosio et Sancto Augustino Priscillianistarum adversariis commentatio*, Dissertation Nimwegen, The Hague 1930, p. 239.
5. *Les écritures manichéennes* II, Paris 1919, 173-177.
6. Lipsius Aa I, 74, note 1, against the view of Zahn, *Acta Johannis*, p. 204, note 1.

4. The (Manichean) Gospel of the Twelve Apostles

In the second part of the 8th century, Theodor Abû Qurra, Melchite bishop of Harran (Carrhae), writes in par. 24 of his Tractate on the Creator and the true Religion: 'I separated myself from these, and there met me people of the Manicheans. These are they who are called the Zanãdiqa, and they said: Thou must attach thyself to the (true) Christians and give heed to the word of their gospel. For the true Gospel is in our possession, which the twelve apostles have written, and there is no religion other than that which we possess, and there are no Christians apart from us. No one understands the interpretation of the Gospel save Mani, our Lord.'[1]

It is possible that the work here mentioned is a 'Gospel of the Twelve Apostles', but is it, as P. Alfaric holds,[2] a question of the Ebionite gospel of this name? One will hesitate also to ascribe to it, with the same scholar (p. 175), two extracts from a writing of Mani (The book of the 'Mysteries' or 'Secrets') quoted by al-Biruni:

The apostles asked Jesus about the life of inanimate nature, whereupon he said: If that which is inanimate is separated from the living element which is commingled with it, and appears alone by itself, it is again inanimate and is not capable of living, whilst the living element which has left it, retaining its vital energy unimpaired, never dies.

(India I, 48, trans. E. Sachau)

Since the apostles knew that the souls are immortal, and that in their migrations they array themselves in every form, that they are shaped in every animal, and are cast in the mould of every figure, they asked

378

Messiah what would be the end of those souls which did not receive the truth nor learn the origin of their existence. Whereupon he said: Any weak soul which has not received all that belongs to her of the truth perishes without any rest or bliss.

(India I, 54-55 Sachau; German trans. in A. Adam, *Texte zum Manichäismus*, (Kleine Texte 175), Berlin 1954, p. 10)

Perhaps we may here adduce a little-known testimony from Shenute of Atripe (d. 466), who reproaches the heretics for having said that there are 'twelve Gospels' (Coptic text in C. Wessely, *Studien zur Paläographie und Papyruskunde* IX, Leipzig 1909, 143). The heretics in question must in fact have been Manicheans.[3] But it would be unwise to attach much value to an apparently analogous account in al-Jaqûbî (in Kessler, *Mani* I, Berlin 1889, 206 and 329), who names among the books composed by Mani 'twelve gospels', 'of which' he adds, 'he [Mani] named each after one of the letters of the alphabet, and in which he expounded the prayer and what must be employed for the freeing of the spirit'. 'Twelve' is here an error for 'twenty-two'; from the context, it is evidently a reference to Mani's 'Living Gospel', which was divided into twenty-two chapters or sections, corresponding to the twenty-two letters of the Syriac alphabet (below, pp. 401ff.).

Notes

4. The (Manichean) Gospel of the Twelve Apostles

1. Translation from German of G. Graf, 'Des Theodor Abû Kurra Traktat über den Schöpfer und die wahre Religion', *Beiträge zur Geschichte der Philosophie des Mittelalters* XIV 1, Münster, 1913, 27.
2. *Les écritures manichéennes* II, 173 and 177.
3. Cf. W.E. Crum, *Journal of Egyptian Archaeology* 19, 1933, 198.

5. The Gospel of the Seventy

The only testimony we possess is that of al-Biruni: 'Everyone of the sects of Marcion, and of Bardesanes, has a special Gospel, which in some parts differs from the Gospels we have mentioned [*sc.* the orthodox Gospels previously discussed]. Also the Manicheans have a Gospel of their own, the contents of which from the first to the last are opposed to the doctrines of the Christians; but the Manicheans consider them as their religious law, and believe that it is the correct Gospel, that its contents are really that which Messiah thought and taught, that every other Gospel is false, and its followers are liars against Messiah. Of this Gospel there is a copy, called 'The Gospel of the Seventy', which is attributed to one *Balamis* (var.: *Iklamis*), and in the beginning of which it is stated, that Salam ben Abdallah ben Salam wrote it down as he heard it from Salman Alfarisi. He, however, who looks into it, will see at once that it is a forgery; it is not acknowledged by Christians and others' (Kitab al-Ahar al-baqiya; English translation from E. Sachau, *The Chronology of Ancient Nations*, London 1879, p. 27; partial German translation in K. Kessler, *Mani* I, Berlin 1889, 207f.).

The interpretation of such a testimony is exceptionally difficult. Kessler (*Mani*, p. 208) thinks it refers to Mani's 'Living Gospel' (below, pp. 401ff.). But in that case the writing al-Biruni mentions in the sequel, which he apparently considers a very different recension of the Manichean Gospel, must have been an independent work, a late apocryphon which, although perhaps placed under the authority of Clement of Rome (Iklamis), could not be dated earlier than the first half of the 7th century. Salman of Fars and 'Abd allah b. Salman, the Jew of Medina whose (fictitious?) son is alleged to have written the work at the dictation of the former, were contemporaries of Mohamed, with whom they are brought into relation by traditions more or less legendary. P. Alfaric, however, advances another interpretation.[1] The gospel in question would, in his view, be the Gospel of the Twelve Apostles. In his own words:

'The exemplar which Salman ben Abdallah transcribed . . . is here mentioned only because he did not confine himself to the reproduction of the text previously described. In Biruni's view, it was not a slavish 'copy', but an adaptation. It is for that reason that it bears a separate title: the Gospel of the Seventy. Instead of purporting to be the work of the *twelve* apostles, it professes to be that of the *seventy* disciples of Christ, to whom the Gnostics appealed. Just as the Gospel of the Twelve Apostles is said to have been composed by Matthew, so that of the seventy is derived from Balamis. In place of the latter name, which occurs in no list of disciples in the Christian literature of the early centuries, one manuscript offers that of Iklamis, the Arabic form of the name of the most famous among them, Clement of Rome. This last ascription seems very natural. Clement of Rome in fact enjoyed a very great popularity in gnostic circles, and particularly those in which the Gospel of the Twelve Apostles was current. The Homilies and Recognitions which have come down to us under his name show, despite numerous catholic revisions, the evident marks of Ebionite origin . . . It can be readily understood that in the same circles, and later among the Manicheans, there should have been a Gospel of Clement.' Alfaric's argument is however open to question in several of its details, and his theory can scarcely be said to carry conviction.

The same reserve is necessary in regard to another conjecture by this scholar, who thinks that we possess a fragment of the Gospel of the Seventy in a Uighur text, perhaps translated from Syriac, which was discovered at Bulayīq in the north of Turfan:

. . . my son, thy way is (evil?) Hear now the (command) of God. Go not upon this way. For if thou dost go without hearing, thou shalt fall into the great ditch (or: fire?). If thou ask Why?, the Adversary lies in wait for thee, he thinks to destroy thee utterly.

18th saying: This is good (to hear?): thus says Zavtai the Apostle [Zebedee, Zabdai in the Syriac list of the seventy disciples?]: Thou art, O Son of man, like the cow which lowed from afar after her calf, which had gone astray. When the calf . . . heard the voice of its mother, it came running quickly (?) . . . to meet its mother, it became free from suffering. So also thy (?) which . . . afar will (?) quickly (?) with great joy.

19th saying: This is bad (to hear?): thus says Luke the Apostle: Son of man, wash thy hands clean; before the evil (one?) have no fear; think pure thoughts; what thou dost possess of love for God, carry fully into effect. . . .

(A. von le Coq, *Ein christliches und ein manichäisches Manuskriptfragment*, SB Berlin 1909, pp. 1205-1208)

Note

5.The Gospel of the Seventy

1. *Les écritures manichéennes* II, Paris, 177-180.

6. Other 'Gospels of the Twelve Apostles'

The 'gospel' published by J. Rendel Harris from a Syriac manuscript of the 8th (?) century (*The Gospel of the Twelve Apostles, with the Apocalypses of each of them, edited from the Syriac ms. with a translation and introduction*, Cambridge 1900), and said to have been translated from Hebrew into Greek and from Greek into Syriac, does not belong in this section of the New Testament apocrypha. This document has nothing to do with the Gospel of the Twelve, and is shown by the doctrines which it contains to be a forgery of very late date (cf. E. Nestle, ThLZ, 1900, 557-559).

The pretended Gospel of the Twelve Apostles published by E. Revillout (PO II 2, Paris 1904, pp. 117-198) is only a collection of sixteen independent Coptic fragments, likewise of late date, arbitrarily grouped under a fictitious title (cf. A. Baumstark, 'Les apocryphes coptes', *Rev. Bibl.* NS 3, 1906, 245-265; P. Ladeuze, 'Apocryphes evangéliques coptes: Pseudo-Gamaliel, Évangile de Barthélemy', RHE 7, 1906, 245-268).

E. Gospels under the name of an Apostle

1. The Gospel of Philip

See above, pp. 179ff.

2. The Gospel of Thomas

See above, pp. 110ff.

3. The Book of Thomas the Athlete

See above, pp. 232ff. (= The Book of Thomas)

4. The Gospel according to Matthias. The Traditions of Matthias

1. Literature: O. Bardenhewer, *Gesch. d. altkirchl. Lit. I*, [2]1913, 529f. A. Harnack, *Gesch. d.altchristl. Lit. I*, [2]1958 17f.; II 1, [2]1958, 595-598. Th. Zahn, *Gesch. d. ntl. Kanons II 2*, 1890, 751-761. Erbetta I, 288ff.

2. Attestation: a Gospel according to Matthias or of Matthias (τὸ εὐαγγέλιον κατὰ Ματθίαν , *Euangelium secundum Matthiam, Euangelium nomine Matthiae*) stands beside the Gospel according to Thomas on the list of heterodox works drawn up by Origen (*in Luc. hom.* I, p. 5.14 Rauer) and Eusebius of Caesarea (H.E. III 25.6). It is also mentioned by Ambrose (*Expositio euangelii Lucae* I 2, p. 11.1 Schenkl), Jerome (*Comm. in Mt.* prol., PL XXVI 17A), the Venerable Bede (*In Luc. evang. expos.* I, prol., PL XCII 307C), the so-called Decretum Gelasianum 3.1 (TU 38. 4, p. 11), and the 7th-century Byzantine Index known as 'The Index of the sixty books' (above, pp. 42f.). On the other hand we know of 'Traditions' (παραδόσεις) ascribed to Matthias or current under his name; these were probably recorded in a separate document.

Three quotations from these 'Traditions' are preserved by Clement of Alexandria (see below). A further passage from Clement's *Stromateis* can probably also be assigned to the Traditions, following a suggestion by Zahn (*op. cit.* p. 752): a parallel to Luke 19:1-10, in which the tax-collector is named not Zacchaeus but Matthias (see below).[1]

3. Extant remains:

1. The beginning thereof [*sc. of the knowledge of the truth*] is to wonder
at things, as Plato says in the Theaetetus and Matthias in the Traditions
when he warns 'Wonder at what is present' (θαύμασον τὰ παρόντα),
establishing this as the first step to the knowledge of things beyond (τῆς
ἐπέκεινα γνώσεως).

BAC 148: 58 (§1)

(Clem. Alex. Strom. II 9.45.4; II 137.1-3 Staehlin)

2. They (the Gnostics) say that Matthias also taught as follows: 'To strive
with the flesh and misuse it (σαρκὶ μάχεσθαι καὶ παραχρῆσθαι),
without yielding to it in any way to unbridled lust, but to increase the soul
through faith and knowledge (διὰ πίστεως καὶ γνώσεως).'

BAC 148: 59 (§2)

(Clem. Alex. Strom. III 4.26.3; II 208.7-9 Staehlin = Euseb. H.E. III 29.4,
where the Syriac version has the variant Tholmai instead of Matthias)

3. They say that Matthias the apostle in the Traditions explains at every
turn: 'If the neighbour of one of the chosen (ἐκλεκτοῦ) sin, then has the
elect sinned; for if he had so conducted himself as the Word (ὁ λόγος)
commends, the neighbour would have had such awe at his way of life that
he would not have fallen into sin.'

BAC 148: 59 (§3)

(Clem. Alex. Strom. VII 13.82.1; III 58.20-23 Staehlin)

4. (?) Zacchaeus then (but some say Matthias), a chief tax-gatherer,
when he heard that the Lord had seen fit to be with him, (said) 'Behold,
the half of my goods I give in alms, O Lord; and if I have extorted
anything from any man, I restore it fourfold.' Whereupon the Saviour
also said 'The Son of man is come today, and has found that which was
lost.'

BAC 148: 59 (§4)

(Clem. Alex. Strom. IV 6.35.2; II 263.30-264.3 Staehlin)

4. Content: apart from the second, these citations have manifestly no marked
gnostic character. The word *gnosis* indeed appears in the first and second
fragments, but in the first it belongs to the context, where it has been
introduced by Clement, and in the second, where it is linked with πίστις, it need
not strictly speaking have the specific technical sense. The theory presupposed
by the first fragment, which makes of admiration or astonishment (θαῦμα) the
first step or first stage in the progressive advance to contemplation or to the
supreme knowledge, is more or less commonplace, a Topos of ancient philosophy (cf. for example, in addition to Plato, *Theaetetus* 155 D, to which Clement
appeals, *Epinomis* 986 C-D; Aristotle, *Metaph.* A 2, 982b; Plotinus, *Enn* III 8.10).
At most one might observe that it occurs in gnostic writings, or works read by
Gnostics: in the Corpus Hermeticum (IV 2; XIV 4; cf. Asclepius 13) and in the
Gospel of Thomas (Logion 2, see above p. 117 = POx 654, lines 6-9: 'Let him
who seeks, not cease seeking until he finds, and when he finds, he will be
troubled, and when he has been troubled, he will marvel').

383

Nevertheless, it should be noted that Clement (*Strom* II. 9.45.5, more fully in V 14.96.3) quotes a saying which corresponds to logion 2 of the Gospel of Thomas, and compares it with our fragment 1 of the Traditions; now of this logion he says expressly that it derived from the Gospel of the Hebrews. The editor of the sayings collection current under the name of Thomas seems therefore to have taken it from the Gospel according to the Hebrews; thus it need not necessarily be of gnostic origin. Further, the precept cited by Clement from the Traditions of Matthias ('Wonder at what is present') recalls logion 5 of the Gospel of Thomas (see above, p. 118 =POx 654. 27-31; Manichean Kephalaia LXV, p. 163.28f.): 'Know what is in thy sight, and what is hidden from thee will be revealed to thee. For there is nothing hidden which will not be manifest.' Perhaps this logion also derives from the Gospel according to the Hebrews, and thus proves nothing for the gnostic origin of the Traditions.

In the third fragment of the Traditions ἐκλεκτός (elect) is indeed probably a gnostic term (Valentinian or Basilidian: cf. Clem Alex. *Strom.* VI 6.53.4); but it might here just as well be a synonym for 'Christian' (cf. 1 Pet. 2:9). In the second fragment the interpretation of παραχρῆσθαι remains ambiguous. The verb means either (construed, as in our passage, with the dative) 'to make a bad use of', 'to misuse', or (with the genitive or accusative) 'to make little of', 'to despise'. If we take it in the first sense, the maxim would recommend carnal freedom, and in particular sexual licence. It would then conform to the libertine doctrines ascribed, among other Gnostics, to the Basilidians (Agrippa Castor, in Euseb. H.E. IV 7.7; Irenaeus, *adv. Haer.* I 24.5.; Clem. Alex. *Strom.* III 1.1-3, 4; Epiphanius, *Pan.* 24.3.7; Filastrius, *Haer.* 32.7) and the Nicolaitans, who according to Clement of Alexandria (*Strom.* II 20.118.2f.; III 4.26.3 = Euseb. H.E. III 29.2) appealed precisely to the text of the Traditions of Matthias now in question.

But the fact that Gnostics employed this text and understood it in such a way proves neither the gnostic origin of the passage nor the correctness of such an interpretation, the more so since Clement himself considers it a misuse. Just as he recognises (*Strom.* III 3.3-4) that the libertinism of the Basilidians of his own time was a deviation from the original and strictly moral doctrine of the founder of the sect, so he maintains in the texts mentioned that the Nicolaitans had falsely interpreted a saying of Nicolaus in such a way as to favour their ethical licentiousness, whereas Nicolaus himself understood it in an ascetic sense, as a command to despise the things of the flesh and abstain therefrom. The ambiguity therefore remains. To declare, as for example do Bardenhewer (*Litg.* I², 530) and A. de Santos Otero (Santos, p. 58), that the Traditions of Matthias, of which our four fragments are, with varying degrees of certainty, the only known extracts, derive from gnostic circles, is to go beyond the evidence; it is only possible, or at most probable.

Finally, Clement of Alexandria and Hippolytus of Rome speak of a certain secret tradition inherited from Matthias by the Basilidians. The first testimony is somewhat obscure. Clement (*Strom.* VII 17.108.1; III, 76.20-24 Staehlin), quoting examples of heresies which bear the name of their founders, writes: 'Of the sects, some are called from a (personal) name, as that of Valentinus and of Marcion and of Basilides, even if they boast to present the doctrine of Matthias; for as there was (only) one doctrine of all the apostles, so (there is only) the (one) tradition.' Hippolytus (*Ref.* VII 20.1; 286.1-6 Marcovich) is more precise and much more instructive: 'Basilides and Isidore, the true son and disciple of Basilides, say that Matthias spake to them secret words (λογοι αποκρυφοι) which he heard from the Saviour when he was taught in private (cf. VII 20.5; 287.25f.: 'something of the secret words of Matthias'). Let us see, then, how manifestly Basilides and Isidore also and all their crew calumniate not simply Matthias only but also even the Saviour Himself.' Probably these secret teachings, transmitted presumably under the name of Matthias, should be linked with the traditions vouched for by the same apostle.

The problem is thus to know whether or not these alleged Traditions are identical with the Gospel of Matthias mentioned in other sources. The most widely different solutions have been proposed. Harnack (*Litg.* II 1, 595-598) believed that two distinct works were involved. On the contrary, Zahn (*Gesch. d. ntl. Kanons* II, 751-761), Bardenhewer (*Litg.* I², 529f.), James (p. 12) and G. Bonaccorsi (*Vangeli Apocrifi* I, Florence 1948, xvif. and 23-31) decide more or less confidently for their identity. Others, like O. Stählin ('Die altchristliche griechische Literatur', in W.C. Christ, *Gesch. der griech. Literatur*, II Teil, 2 Hälfte, ⁶Munich 1924, 1192 note 3) or J. Tixeront (*Précis de Patrologie*, Paris 1928, p. 83), would incline rather towards distinguishing the works. Finally, some (e.g. A. Puech, *Histoire de la littérature grecque chrétienne* I, Paris 1928, 169) are content to express their hesitation.

Zahn and Bardenhewer draw their chief argument from fragment 4: its parallelism with Lk. 19:1-10 proves that the Traditions contained accounts after the fashion of the Gospels. But still we should require to be certain that the fragment really did belong to the παραδόσεις. It would perhaps be tempting to recall the gnostic tradition reported by the Pistis Sophia (c. 42f.; p. 44.19-45.19 Schmidt-Till), according to which Jesus after his resurrection entrusted to Matthew - or rather, as Zahn conjectures (II 758f.) to Matthias - as well as to Philip and to Thomas the task of reporting all his acts and recording all his words. If we accept Zahn's suggestion (approved by Bardenhewer, *Litg.* I², 530, but rejected by Harnack, *Litg* II 1, 597f.), then Matthias would appear as the author of a gospel, or better still of a gospel parallel to those of Philip and of Thomas (now rediscovered: above, pp. 179ff. and 110ff.), which like the latter of these may have contained sayings or 'secret words' of Jesus, transmitted in secret 'Traditions'. This would agree fairly well with the testimony of Hippolytus, but remains nevertheless uncertain.

5. Dating: the Gospel or Traditions of Matthias could only have been composed before the beginning of the 3rd century. There seems to be nothing against Bardenhewer's dating (*Litg.* I², 530), which is followed by Altaner (p. 52): the first decade or the first half of the 2nd century. We must probably also assume, with the same scholars, that the apocryphon originated in Alexandria, or at any rate in Egypt.

Note

E. Gospels under the name of an Apostle

4. The Gospel according to Matthias. The Traditions of Matthias

1. It would be hazardous to link with these citations, as Klostermann suggests, with great reserves (*Apokrypha* II, KlT 8, [3]Berlin 1929, 18), a passage from Haimo of Auxerre, *in Hebr*. 13:4 (PL CXVII 930 A): 'Hence the blessed Matthew [1. Matthias?] the Apostle says in a certain place that lawful wedlock and the bed undefiled (Heb. 13:4) have in a sense something vile, in the mingling of seed, but that they do not have the stain of sin.'

5. The Gospel of Judas

1. **Attestation:** the most important and oldest source here is Irenaeus (*adv. Haer.* I 31.1 = Theodoret of Cyrus, *Haereticorum fabularum compendium* I 15, PG LXXXIII 368 B): certain gnostic sectaries possessed in addition to other works of their own composition, a 'gospel' under the name of the traitor Judas (*Iudae euangelium*, εὐαγγέλιον 'Ιούδα); these sectaries are elswhere identified with the Cainites, and reckoned among the 'Gnostics' of Epiphanius, the Nicolaitans, Ophites, Sethians, or Carpocratians. The existence and title of the document (εὐαγγέλιον τοῦ 'Ιούδα) are also attested by Epiphanius (*Pan.* 38.1.5; II, 63.13f. Holl).

2. **Content:** it would be rash to ascribe to the Gospel of Judas a quotation derived by Epiphanius from a Cainite book (*Pan.* 38.2.4; II, 64.17-19 Holl: 'This is the angel who blinded Moses, and these are the angels who hid the people about Korah and Dathan and Abiram, and carried them off'). Still less reason is there for ascribing to this gospel a formula reproduced by Irenaeus (I 31.2) and Epiphanius 38.2.2),which accompanied the sexual rite practised by the sect for the attainment of the 'perfect gnosis'. As to the subject and content of the apocryphon, we are reduced to simple conjecture, supported at best by some characteristics of Cainite doctrine as it is known from the notices of the heresiologues. It is possible, but far from certain, that this 'gospel' contained a passion story setting forth the 'mystery of the betrayal' (*proditionis mysterium*, μυστήριον προδοσίας) and explaining how Judas by his treachery made possible the salvation of all mankind: either he forestalled the destruction of the truth proclaimed by Christ, or he thwarted the designs of the evil powers, the archons, who wished to prevent the crucifixion since they knew that it would deprive them of their feeble power and bring salvation to men (ps.-Tertullian, *adv. Omn. Haer.* 2; Epiphanius, *Pan.* 38.3.3-5; Filastrius, *Haer.* 34; Augustine, *de Haer.* 18; ps.-Jerome, *Indiculus de haer.* 8; cf. Bauer, *Leben Jesu*, p. 176). However that may be, the work was probably in substance an exposition of the secret doctrine (licentious and violently antinomian in character) ostensibly

revealed by Judas, a summary of the Truth or of the superior and perfect Gnosis which he was supposed to possess by virtue of a revelation (Irenaeus, I 31.1.; Epiph. *Pan.* 38.1.5; Filastrius, *Haer.* 34).

3. Dating: the Gospel of Judas was of course composed before 180, the date at which it is mentioned for the first time by Irenaeus in *adv. Haer.* If it is in fact a Cainite work, and if this sect - assuming that it was an independent gnostic group - was constituted in part, as has sometimes been asserted,[1] in dependence on the doctrine of Marcion, the apocryphon can scarcely have been composed before the middle of the 2nd century. This would, however, be to build on weak arguments. At most we may be inclined to suspect a date between 130 and 170 or thereabouts.

Note

5. The Gospel of Judas

1. E.g. E. de Faye, *Gnostiques et Gnosticisme,*[2] Paris 1925, p. 371.

6. The Apocryphon of John

We may forego any detailed discussion of this text, which has come down to us in four manuscripts (and two recensions), because it is a gnostic revelation document which has been only secondarily transformed into a conversation between Jesus and John. It is in any case predominantly a monologue, a discourse in which gnostic ideas are presented. Even though this document is of very great importance for the history of Gnosis, it still does not belong in this collection.

Facsimile Edition: Codex II, 1974, pp. 1.1-32.9; Codex III, 1976, pp.1.1-40.11; Codex IV, 1975, pp.1.1-49.28.

Editions: Die gnostischen Schriften des koptischen Papyrus Berolinensis 8502, hg., übersetzt und bearb. von W.C. Till, (TU 60), 2nd ed. revised by H.-M. Schenke, 1972, pp. 78-195. M. Krause and P. Labib, *Die drei Versionen des Apokryphon des Johannes im Koptischen Museum zu Alt-Kairo,* (Abh. Dt. Arch. Inst. Kairo, Kopt. Reihe Bd. 1), 1962.

English translation: The Nag Hammadi Library in English, pp. 98-116 (rev. ed. 1988, pp. 104-123).

7. Fragments of a Dialogue between John and Jesus

1. Literature: W.E. Crum, 'Coptic Anecdota', JTS 44, 1943, 176-182. Paul E. Kahle jr., *Bala'izah. Coptic Texts from Deir el Bala'izah in Upper Egypt*, I, London 1954, 473-477.

2. Extant remains: only fragments of the document survive. In the first part of his article W.E. Crum published, under the title 'A gnostic Fragment', a parchment leaf (paginated 41 and 42) found at Deir el-Bala'izah (probably the ancient monastery of Apa Apollo) to the west of Assiut, and two other fragments belonging to the same manuscript. Kahle published the text afresh, with an improved translation. The manuscript is written in Sahidic, with some archaic forms.

3. Content and character: the gnostic character of the work, of which only these fragments survive, is beyond doubt. The biblical themes treated (Adam, paradise, Abel and Cain, Noah, etc.) and also the terminology and ideas (five trees, five powers, etc.) point clearly to the realm of Gnosis. Many parallels can be adduced from the Nag Hammadi documents.

To judge from what remains, the document could have been a 'revelation', an ἀποκάλυψις, in which John himself ostensibly relates the secret revelations which he received from the Saviour in the course of a conversation with him. The apocryphon probably consisted of a series of questions posed by the apostle, to each of which Christ replies. For this reason and also because of the themes treated, it must be brought into close connection with the Apocryphon of John; it is not however to be identified with it, or regarded as a special version of this document. On the other hand it has no connection with the various other apocrypha ('Apocalypse', 'Mysteries of John', etc.) current under the name of the same apostle.

4. Dating: Crum dates the manuscript to the 5th or 4th century, Kahle to the 4th. Nothing can be said with regard to the age of the Greek *Vorlage* of the Coptic translation.

5. Translation:
' ...] the body (σῶμα) [...] naked [...] without sin [...] the spiritual (? λογικός) power, ere it (she) had been revealed, its (her) name was not this, but its (her) name was Σιγή. For (ἐπειδή) all they that (were) in the heavenly paradise (παράδεισος) were sealed in silence. But such as shall partake thereof (paradise, or the tree of knowledge?) will become spiritual (?λογικός), having known all; they shall seal the five powers in silence. Lo, I have explained (ἑρμηνεύειν) unto thee, O Johannes, concerning Adam and paradise (παράδεισος) and the five trees, in an intelligible allegory (σύμβολον νοερόν).' When I, Johannes, heard these (things), I said: 'I have made a good beginning (ἄρχεσθαι, ἀρχή);

388

I have completed knowledge (γνῶσις) and a hidden mystery (μυστήριον) [cf. Rom. 15:14; 1 Cor. 13:2] and allegories (σύμβολον) of truth, having been encouraged (προτρέπειν) by thy love (ἀγάπη). Now I desire further to ask thee that thou wouldst explain (ἑρμηνεύειν) unto me in thy will concerning Cain and Abel: according to what fashion (τύπος) did Cain slay Abel? And not this only, but he was asked by him (that) spoke with him, saying, Where is Abel, thy brother? But Cain denied (ἀρνεῖσθαι), saying, Am (μή) I the keeper . . . ' [Gen. 4:9].

' . . .] of the fullness (πλήρωμα) he (or: it) being completed. Lo, I have explained (ἑρμηνεύειν) unto thee, O Johannes, concerning Noah and [his?] ark (κίβωτος) and [. . . '

' . . .] Now I desire further to [ask Thee what Thou wouldst] explain (ἑρμηνεύειν) [unto me] concerning Melchizedek. Is it not (μή) said [concerning him]: being without [father, being without] mother, his generation (γενεά) [was not mentioned], having no beginning (ἀρχή)[of days], having no end of life, [being] like to the Son of God, being a priest for ever [Heb. 7:3]?. It is also said concerning him . . . [. . . '

(Papyrus from Deir el-Bala'izah: Oxford, Bodl. Ms. Copt. d54, ed. P.E. Kahle, *Bala'izah*, pp. 473-477. By permission of the Trustees of the Griffith Institute, Oxford)

8. The Apocryphon of James (Apocryphon Jacobi)

See above, pp. 285ff. (= Letter of James)

9. The Gospel of Bartholomew

See below, pp. 537ff.

F. Gospels under the names of holy women

1. The Questions of Mary

Among their extensive apocryphal literature the 'Gnostics' properly so called possessed, according to Epiphanius (*Pan.* 26.8.1; I, 284. 11f. Holl), certain books entitled 'Questions of Mary' (ἐρωτήσεις Μαρίας), in which Jesus is represented as the revealer of the obscene practices (αἰσχρουργία) which constituted the rites of redemption peculiar to the sect. The same Father tells us more exactly (*Pan.* 26.8.2f; I, 284.17-24 Holl) that two distinct works were described by this title: the 'Little Questions' (μικραὶ ἐρωτήσεις) and the 'Great Questions' (μεγάλαι ἐρωτήσεις) of Mary; of the latter he supplies moreover two brief quotations, interpolated into the analysis of one of its episodes:

For in the Questions of Mary which are called 'Great' (for there are also 'Little' (Questions) forged by them), they assert that he [*sc. Jesus*] gave her [*sc. Mary*] a revelation, taking her aside to the mountain and praying; and he brought forth from his side a woman and began to unite with her, and so, forsooth, taking his effluent, he showed that 'we must so do, that we may live'; and how when Mary fell to the ground abashed, he raised her up again and said to her: 'Why didst thou doubt, O thou of little faith?' (Epiphanius, *Pan.* 26.8.2-3; I, 284.17-24 Holl; for the last phrase cf. Mt. 14:31 and Apocryphon Johannis p. 21.14-18, p. 83 Till)

It would therefore appear that the 'Great Questions of Mary' belonged to the ordinary type of gnostic gospel: it was a revelation, an ἀποκάλυψις; a secret teaching of Christ was therein imparted to a privileged hearer, and no doubt, as the title suggests, in the form of a dialogue composed of questions and answers. The action - or at least one of its episodes - took place upon a mountain (the Mount of Olives?). The other character is here probably, as in other works of the same kind, Mary Magdalene rather than Mary the mother of the Lord or Mary Salome. The procedure here ascribed to Jesus is influenced by Gen. 2:21f. (Eve, the woman, the 'mother of all living', produced from the side or from a rib of Adam, the first man). The following actions (sexual union, gathering and offering of the seed, etc.) are intended to serve as the model and first example, the prototype, for the eucharistic rites actually in use among the Nicolaitans, the Borborians and other licentious Gnostics in Egypt (Epiphanius, *Pan.* 25.3.2; 26.4.1-8; 8.4-9.9; 10.8f.; Pistis Sophia c. 147; Second Book of Jeu, c. 43). Later the Manicheans also were accused of practising them.[1]

The character of the Little Questions of Mary remains more enigmatic. It has often been suggested that they are to be identified with the Pistis Sophia (above, pp. 361ff.) or, more exactly, with the first three books of that work.[2] This hypothesis finds its chief support in the fact that in the Pistis Sophia of the forty-six questions addressed by the disciples to Jesus thirty-nine are placed in the mouth of Mary Magdalene.[3] It has - it seems rightly - been criticised and rejected by Liechtenhan[4] and Bardenhewer.[5] Even Schmidt himself [6] has abandoned it. Nor is there any ground for identifying the *Little Questions of Mary* with *The Gospel of Mary* to which we next turn.

Notes

F. Gospels under the names of holy women

1. The Questions of Mary

1. On the whole subject see L. Fendt, *Gnostische Mysterien*, Munich 1922, pp. 3-29.
2. E. Renan, *Marc Aurèle*, [12]Paris 1905, p. 120, note 3; Harnack, *Über das gnostische Buch Pistis Sophia*, TU 7. 2, 1891, pp. 107-109; id. *Litg.* I, 172 and II 2, 194f.; C. Schmidt, *Gnostische Schriften in koptischer Sprache*, TU 8. 1-2, 1892, p. 597; E. de Faye, *Gnostiques et Gnosticisme*, [2]Paris 1925, p. 288, note 2; more vaguely, H. Leisegang, *Die Gnosis*, [4]Leipzig 1955, p. 353; cf. Pauly-Wissowa, 1 Reihe, 40 Halbbd., 1950, cols. 1820.62-1821.11.
3. Leisegang, *op. cit.* p. 353.
4. 'Untersuchungen zur koptisch-gnostischen Literatur', *Zeitschr. f. wissenschaftl. Theol.* 44, 1901, 240.
5. *Litg.* I[2], 355, note 2.
6. *Koptisch-gnostische Schriften*, 1. Bd., Leipzig 1905, p. xviii.

2. The Gospel of Mary

1. Literature: *Editions:* W.C. Till, *Die gnostischen Schriften des koptischen Papyrus Berolinensis 8502*, hg., übers. u. bearb., TU 60, 2nd ed. rev. by H. -M. Schenke, 1972, pp. 24-32 and 62-79. G.W. MacRae and R. McL. Wilson, 'The Gospel according to Mary. BG 1: 7. 1-19. 5', in D.M. Parrott (ed.), *Nag Hammadi Codices V 2-5; VI with Pap. Berol. 8502, 1 and 4* (NH Studies 11, Leiden 1979), pp. 453-471.

Translations: Till, TU 60 (see above); *The Nag Hammadi Library in English*, pp. 471-474 (rev. ed. 1988, pp. 523-527).

Studies: C. Schmidt, 'Ein vorirenäisches gnostisches Originalwerk in koptischer Sprache', SbPAW 1896, 839-847. R. Liechtenhan, 'Die pseudepigraphe Literatur der Gnostiker', ZNW 3, 1902, 228. C. Schmidt, *Gespräche Jesu mit seinen Jüngern*, TU 43, 1919, p. 239. id. *Pistis Sophia*, 1925, lxxxiii-xc (with translation of some passages). G. Quispel, 'Das Hebräerevangelium im gnostischen Evangelium nach Maria', *Vig.Chr.* 11, 1957,139-144. R.M. Grant, *Gnosticism: A Source Book of Heretical Writings from the Early Christian Period*, New York 1961, 65-68. R.McL. Wilson, *Gnosis and the New Testament*, Philadelphia 1968, pp. 101-103. Anne Pasquier, 'L'eschatologie dans l'Evangile selon Marie; étude des notions de nature et d'image', in B. Barc (ed.), *Colloque international sur les Textes de Nag Hammadi*, (BCNH,. Études 1), Quebec/ Leuven 1981, pp. 390-404. Further references in Scholer, *NH Bibliography* and in NHS 11, p. 453.

2. Extant remains: (a) Part of the text is preserved in a Coptic (Sahidic) translation at the beginning of the Papyrus Berolinensis 8502 (5th cent.) pp. 7.1-19.5 = pp. 62-79 Till. The first six pages and also pages 11 to 14 are missing. Of this writing therefore, which in the original state of the manuscript extended to 18 pages only, ten are lost and only eight - or very little more - remain. The title of the work is given in the colophon (p. 19.3-5; p. 79 Till): *peuaggelion kata marihamm* (written *mariham* in the body of the text).

(b) The text of the final pages (pp. 17.5-21 and 18.5-19.5 of the Coptic MS) is preserved in Greek, i.e. in the language of the original, in Papyrus No. 463 (beginning of 3rd cent.) of the John Rylands collection in Manchester. This is a single leaf (numbered 21 on the recto and 22 on the verso) of the papyrus codex brought from Oxyrhynchus and acquired in 1917. Here also the title is indicated at the end: τὸ εὐαγγέλιον κατὰ Μαριάμ (this is the consistent spelling of the name in the Greek fragments: Lührmann [see below], p. 330). The Greek version differs at some points from the Coptic, and must have been a little longer.

The papyrus was examined and published by C.H. Roberts (*Catalogue of the Greek and Latin Papyri in the John Rylands Library*, III, Manchester 1938, 18-23), and in a new edition, with some notes, by G.P. Carratelli in *La Parola del Passato*, fasc. 2.,1946, pp. 266f.; cf. further G. Kapsamenos, Τὸ κατὰ Μαριὰμ ἀπόκρυφον Εὐαγγέλιον (P. Ryl. III 463), ᾽Αθηνᾶ 49, 1939, pp. 177-186.

A further Greek papyrus fragment from the 3rd century, found in Egypt, (*Oxyrhynchus Papyri* L, London 1983, 12-14; POx 3525) offers a text which with some variations corresponds to pp. 9.1-10.14 of the Coptic version (Till, pp. 66ff.); see D. Lührmann, 'Die griechischen Fragmente des Mariaevangeliums POx 3525 und PRyl 463', *Nov. Test.* 30, 1988, 321-338.

3. Content: the document consists of two different parts. The first, the beginning of which is lost, reproduces - like the Sophia Jesu Christi, the Dialogue of the Redeemer, the Letter of Peter to Philip and the Pistis Sophia - a dialogue between the risen Jesus and his disciples (see above, pp. 300ff.; 342ff.; 361ff.). Christ is here described exclusively as 'Saviour' - cf. Irenaeus, *adv. Haer.* I 1.3 - or 'the Blessed'. The Saviour answers questions put to him, and describes the future destiny of matter; then, in reply to Peter, he gives instruction on the nature of sin ('the sin of the world'). Finally he takes leave of his hearers:

When the Blessed One (μακάριος) had said this, he saluted (ἀσπάζεσθαι) them all saying: 'Peace (εἰρήνη) (be) unto you [*Lk. 24:36; Jn. 20:19, 21, 26; 1 Pet. 5:14*]. Receive you my peace (εἰρήνη [*cf. Jn.14:27*]. Beware that no one lead you astray (πλανᾶν) [*Mt. 24:5; Mk. 13:5*] with the words: 'See here!' or 'See there!' [*Mt. 24:23; Mk. 13:21; Lk. 17:21, 23*]. For (γάρ) the Son of man is within you [*cf. Lk. 17:21*]. Follow after him! Those who seek him shall find him [*cf. Mt. 7:7*]. Go then and preach the Gospel (εὐαγγέλιον) of the kingdom [*cf. Mt. 4:23; 9:35; 28:19*]. I have issued no command (ὅρος) save (παρά) that which I appointed you. Nor (οὐδέ) have I given any law (νόμος) like the lawgiver (νομοθέτης), that (μήποτε) ye may not be constrained thereby.' When he had said this, he went his way.

(PBerol. pp. 8.12-9.5; pp. 65-67 Till)

Thereupon the disciples are in great perplexity:

But (δέ) they were grieved (λυπεῖσθαι) and wept sore, saying: 'How shall we go to the heathen (ἔθνος) and preach the Gospel (εὐαγγέλιον) of the kingdom of the Son of Man? If he was not spared at all, how shall we be spared?'

(PBerol. p. 9.5-12; p. 67 Till)

Here Mary intervenes (Mary Magdalene, as is almost the rule in gnostic literature), to comfort the disciples and draw them out of their indecision:

Then (τότε) arose Mary, saluted (ἀσπάζεσθαι) them all, and spake to her brethren: 'Weep not, be not sorrowful (λυπεῖσθαι), neither (οὐδέ) be ye undecided, for (γάρ) his grace (χάρις) will be with you all and will protect you (σκεπάζειν). Let us rather (μᾶλλον δέ) praise his greatness, for he hath made us ready, and made us to be men.'

(PBerol. p. 9.12-20; p. 67 Till)

Then follows the apparent conclusion:

When Mary said this, she turned their mind to good (ἀγαθόν), and they began (ἄρχεσθαι) to discuss (γυμνάζεσθαι) the words of the [Saviour].

(PBerol. p. 9.20-24; p. 67 Till)

The second part (pp. 10.1-19.2 of PBerol.) begins with a question from Peter, who asks Mary to impart to him and the other disciples the revelations which she separately has received from the Saviour, who loved her above all other women. Mary consents, and relates an appearance of the Lord in a vision (ὅραμα), in which the Saviour in reply to her question informed her that what sees the vision is neither the soul (ψυχή) nor the spirit (πνεῦμα) but the understanding (νοῦς), which is in the middle between the two. In addition he described (probably, since four pages are here missing) how a soul journeying through the planetary spheres converses with four hostile powers (ἐξουσίαι), from which it frees itself in order to attain to rest (ἀνάπαυσις) 'at the time (χρόνος) of the season (καιρός) of the Aeon (αἰών) in silence'. The passage is thus of a different kind from that of the preceding pages; it is related to the gnostic gospels which, like the Apocryphon of John or the Gospel of Eve (above, pp. 387 and 358ff.), take the form of an account of a vision in the course of which the seer and the Revealer or Saviour exchange questions and answers.

393

Mary's testimony meets with unbelief from Andrew and Peter:

When Mary had said this, she was silent, so that (ὥστε) (thus) the Saviour (σωτήρ) had spoken with her up to this point. But (δέ) Andrew answered and said to the brethren: 'Tell me, what think ye with regard to what she says? I at least (μέν) do not believe (πιστεύειν) that the Saviour (σωτήρ) said this. For (γάρ) certainly these doctrines have other meanings.' Peter in answer spoke with reference to things of this kind, and asked them [*sc. the disciples*] about the Saviour (σωτήρ): 'Did he then (μήτι) speak privily with a woman rather than with us, and not openly? Shall we turn about and all hearken unto her? Has he preferred her over against us?'

(PBerol. p. 17.7-22; p. 75 Till = PRyl. lines 2-17)

The attitude of Andrew and Peter here corresponds more or less to that ascribed to them in the Pistis Sophia, where the former (c. 100) is rebuked for his lack of insight, while reference is made twice over (c. 36 and 72) to Peter's hostility towards women and in particular towards Mary Magdalene. Again, in the last logion of the Gospel of Thomas (see above, p. 129) Peter is made to say to the other disciples: ('Let Mary (*Mariham*) go out from among us, because women are not worthy of the Life.')

This distrust reduces Mary to despair; Levi (the son of Alphaeus, likewise mentioned with Simon Peter and Andrew in the Gospel of Peter 14 (60)?) comes to her defence:

Then (τότε) Mary wept and said to Peter: 'My brother Peter, what dost thou then believe? Dost thou believe that I imagined this myself in my heart, or (ἤ) that I would lie about the Saviour (σωτήρ)?' Levi answered (and) said to Peter: 'Peter, thou hast ever been of a hasty temper. Now I see how thou dost exercise thyself (γυμνάζεσθαι) against the woman like the adversaries (ἀντικείμενος). But (δέ) if the Saviour (σωτήρ) hath made her worthy (ἄξιος), who then (δέ) art thou, that thou reject her? Certainly (πάντως) the Saviour (σωτήρ) knows her surely (ἀσφαλῶς) enough. Therefore did he love her more than us. Let us rather (μᾶλλον) be ashamed, put on the perfect (τέλειος) Man, [form ourselves (?)] as (κατ]ά) he charged us, and proclaim the Gospel (εὐαγγέλιον), without requiring any further command (ὅρος) or (οὐδέ) any further law (νόμος) beyond (παρά) that which the Saviour (σωτήρ) said (Gr.: neither limiting [ὁρίζειν] nor legislating [νομοθετεῖν] as the Saviour said).'

(PBerol. p. 18.1-21; p. 77 Till = PRyl. lines 18-31)

We are thus brought to the conclusion of the whole work:

> But [when Levi had said this,] they set about (ἄρχεσθαι) going to preach and to proclaim (Gr.: When he had thus spoken, Levi went away and began to preach).
>
> (PBerol. pp. 18.21-19. 2; pp. 77-79 Till = PRyl. lines 31-33)

The work therefore seems to have been put together from two small, originally independent writings (cf. W.C. Till, TU 60, p. 26), which have been more or less artificially united by the introduction, at the end of the first part, of Mary Magdalene, whose intervention is supposed to restore courage to the disciples. There is in fact a contrast between the dominant role which she plays in the second part and the modest place which she assumes in the first, or seems to have had in the work which lies behind it. At any rate the title 'Gospel of Mary' is strictly appropriate only to the second part of our present apocryphon.

The language and the different themes of the writing leave no doubt of its gnostic character and origin. It is however difficult, if not impossible, to ascribe it to any particular gnostic school. On the other hand we may date it fairly certainly in the 2nd century.

3. The 'Genna Marias'

The apocryphal document *Genna Marias* (Birth, Genealogy or Descent of Mary?) may be included here, or mentioned by way of an appendix. It belonged to the numerous writings produced or read by the 'Gnostics' properly so called, and of its existence, its title and part of its contents we know only from a passage in the account devoted to these sectaries by Epiphanius (*Pan.* 26. 12.1 -4; I, 290.19-291.13 Holl):

> Among them [*sc. the Gnostics*] an immense number of other forged writings are tolerated. For they say that there is a certain book, the 'Genna Marias', and when they suggest terrible and destructive things they say these are there. It was for this reason, they say, that Zacharias was slain in the Temple [*cf. Mt. 23:35; Lk. 11:51*], because, they say, he had seen a vision, and when he wished to tell the vision his mouth was stopped up [*cf. Lk. 1:22*] from fear. For he saw, they say, at the hour of the incense-offering as he was burning incense, a man standing, they say, having the form of an ass [*cf. Lk. 1:9-12*]. And when he came out, they say, and wished to say 'Woe unto you! Whom do ye worship?', he who appeared to him within in the Temple stopped up his mouth, that he could not speak [*cf. Lk. 1:20*]. But when his mouth was opened, that he might speak [*cf. Lk. 1:64*], then he revealed it to them, and they slew him. And so, they

say, died Zacharias. For it was to this end that the priest was charged by the Law-giver himself, they say, to wear bells [cf. Exod. 28:33-35], in order that whenever he entered in to do priestly service he who was worshipped, hearing the sound, might hide himself, that the likeness of his form might not be discovered.

(Epiphanius, *Pan.* 26.12.1-4; I, 290.19-291.13 Holl)

This section has been specially examined by A. Berendts.[1] It may be enough to note: that the identification of the Zacharias here in question with the father of John the Baptist occurs also in the Protevangelium of James 23f. and in Origen (*Comm.* ser. 25 in Mt.);[2] that the semblance ascribed to the figure who appeared to Zacharias in the Temple in the form of an ass (or with an ass's head?) conforms not only with the conception formed of the God of the Jews by certain pagan circles and by the polemic of antiquity,[3] but also with a conception of the same God, or of the planetary archon identified with him, which was common among the 'Gnostics', the Ophites, and other sectaries (Origen, *c. Cels.* VI 30, vol.II, p. 100.19-22: Θαφαβαώθ, Θαρθαραώθ , or 'Ονοήλ;vol. VI 37 p. 106.19 and 23; VII 40, p. 191.6 and 10; Epiphanius, *Pan.* 26.10.6, I, 287.15: Σαβαώθ; Apocryphon of John, pp. 122.19f. Till: Eloaios = Elohim; a Coptic Gnostic fragment in C. Schmidt-Till, *Koptisch-gnostische Schriften* p. 384. 8-10: *eio* = Τυφῶν; for magical gems and amulets cf. Campbell Bonner, *Studies in Magical Amulets*, Ann Arbor 1950, pp. 130-132); and more generally that if the 'Genna' thereby manifests a violent hostility towards Judaism, the title of the work appears to confirm the interest taken by the Gnostics in Mary the mother of Jesus.

The document is perhaps, as A. Meyer suggests (NTApo[2], p. 82), to be ascribed to the middle of the 2nd century.

Notes

3. The 'Genna Marias'

1. *Studien über Zacharias-Apokryphen und Zacharias-Legenden*, Leipzig 1895, pp.32-37.
2. Cf. Zahn, *Gesch. d. ntl. Kanons* II 2, 695 and 776, note 2.
3. Cf. among others A. Jacoby, 'Der angebliche Eselskult der Juden und Christen', *Archiv f. Religionswissensch.* 25, 1927, 265-282.

G. Gospels attributed to an arch-heretic

1. The Gospel of Cerinthus

We cannot well speak (as does e.g. Quasten I, 128) of a *Gospel of Cerinthus*, nor can we appeal to Epiphanius (*Pan.* 51.7.3; II, 257.6f Holl) in support of the claim that the Cerinthians, or Merinthians, composed an independent gospel of their own. As Epiphanius himself indicates elsewhere (*Pan.* 28.5.1, I, 317.10 f. Holl; 30.14.2, I, 351.9f.), the gospel used by Cerinthus, and also by Carpocrates, was in fact identical with that of the Ebionites and apparently only a truncated version of Matthew; Bardy calls it a 'judaizing rather than Gnostic' gospel ('Cérinthe', in *Rev. Bibl.* 30, 1921, 373). The heresiological tradition reckons the Cerinthians among the Gnostics, and occasionally treats them as akin to the Carpocratians; but some scholars have been led to consider them rather as Judaisers,[1] while others point to the confusion, notably in Epiphanius, between certain Jewish Christians, arbitrarily associated with a legendary Cerinthus, and the adherents of a Gnostic of the same name whose historical existence is much more probable and who worked in Asia Minor.[2]

Notes

G. Gospels attributed to an arch-heretic

1. The Gospel of Cerinthus

1. A. Wurm, 'Cerinth - ein Gnostiker oder Judaist?', *Theol. Quartalschr* 86, 1904, 20-38.
2. Cf. C. Schmidt-J. Wajnberg, *Gespräche Jesu mit seinen Jüngern nach der Auferstehung*, (TU 43), 1919, pp. 403-453.

2. The Gospel of Basilides

Among the non-canonical gospels which 'many' have 'undertaken' to write - or taken the liberty of writing - (Gospels of the Egyptians, of the Twelve, of Thomas, Matthias, etc.), Origen mentions (*in Luc. hom.* I, p. 5. 5-7 Rauer) that Basilides also had had the audacity to compose a work of this kind, a *Gospel according to Basilides* (κατὰ Βασιλείδην εὐαγγέλιον). This testimony is thus translated by Jerome (*op. cit.* p. 5.4-6): *Ausus fuit et Basilides scribere euangelium et suo illud nomine titulare.* Ambrose in his turn reproduces it (*Expositio euangelii Lucae* i. 2; p. 10. 19f. Schenkl): *Ausus est etiam Basilides euangelium scribere, quod dicitur secundum Basilidem.* Elsewhere (*Comm. in Mt.*, prol., PL XXVI 17A) Jerome mentions, beside a Gospel of Apelles, the *euangelium Basilidis.* Cf. further the Venerable Bede, *In Lucae euangelium expositio* I, prol., PL XCII 307 C. An echo of Origen's testimony occurs in a fragment of Philip of Side's history of the Church (TU 5 .2, 1888, p. 169, No. 4).

It is very difficult to frame any conception of the form and content of this 'gospel', assuming that it really was an original and independent work. Hilgenfeld[1] conjectured that it was a gospel related to that of Luke. Windisch[2] saw in it a redaction of Luke, which would thus represent a counterpart to Marcion's Gospel (below, p. 399). According to Zahn[3] it was on the contrary a kind of Gospel-harmony, in which passages from the four canonical Gospels were arranged in a tendentious fashion.

This view was followed by Buonaiuti:[4] 'The Gospel of Basilides was very probably a patchwork derived from the canonical Gospels.' Hennecke for his part (NTApo[2] p. 68) thought that the work made use of Matthew, as well as of a number of esoteric traditions. He writes: 'But according to the text of the title this [sc. the Gospel of Basilides] cannot have been merely an abbreviated older Gospel (Luke, in fact, according to Windisch, ZNW 1906, pp. 236-246), it also very probably contained (despite Windisch pp. 239, 245) in a variant form (Clem. Alex. III. 1. 1) the independent saying Mt. 19:11f. (on its use among the early Christians cf. W. Bauer in Ntl. Studien für Georg Heinrici 1914, pp. 235ff.), and in addition (over and above the Synoptic character of the language) possibly some accounts which rested upon the familiar alleged relationship of Basilides to Matthias (Hippol. Ref. VII. 20. 1 [above, p. 384f.] and to Glaucias, an interpreter of Peter (Clem. Alex. VII. 17. 106. 4).' Hendrix again came to the conclusion: 'This 'Gospel according to Basilides' must have shown some relationship with the writing of the same name κατὰ Λουκᾶν which lies before us, and must have agreed at many points with our Fourth Gospel, since indeed at different places in Basilides' doctrine a passage from the last-named writing may already be adduced. To reconstruct the content is no longer possible. We may only here and there conjecture what may have stood therein.'[5]

To judge from the list of Gospel passages quoted or employed in the extant parts of Basilides Ἐξηγητικά - i.e. his commentary 'in 24 books on the Gospel' (his own gospel?) (Agrippa Castor, in Euseb. H.E. IV 7.7; Clem. Alex. Strom. IV 12.81, who gives extracts from Book 23) - the use of Matthew beside Luke appears probable. In a fragment of Book 13 (Acta Archelai LXVII 5) the parable of the rich man and Lazarus (peculiar to Luke 16:19-31) is expounded; the expression natura sine radice might perhaps by inspired by Lk. 8:13 (cf. Mt. 13:21; Mk. 4:6 and 17). Another passage, quoted by Clement of Alexandria (Strom. III 1.1), makes use of Mt. 19:11-12 (peculiar to Matthew!). A saying of Basilides reported by Epiphanius (Pan. 24.5.2; I, 262.8-10 Holl), which Holl believes to be derived from the Ἐξηγητικά, appeals to Mt. 7:6:

We are the men, but all the others are swine and dogs. And for this cause he said: 'Cast not the pearls before the swine, neither give that which is holy to the dogs.'

From the context, the passage may have been a comment on Mt. 10:33. Much less certain is Bardenhewer's conjecture (Litg. I[2], 349) that the Basilidian theory of the μετενσωμάτωσις based on Rom. 7:9-10 and summarised by Origen in his Commentary on Romans (V 1; PG XIV 1015 A/B; add VI 8, 1083 A/B), also belonged to the Ἐξηγητικά.

In short, it must be said that all conjectures concerning the Gospel of Basilides remain uncertain.

Notes

2. The Gospel of Basilides

1. *Historische-kritische Einleitung in das Neue Testament*, Leipzig 1875, pp. 46f.; *Zeitschr. f. wissensch. Theol.* 21, 1878, 234, note; *Die Ketzergeschichte des Urchristentums*, Leipzig 1884, p. 201.
2. 'Das Evangelium des Basilides', ZNW 7, 1906, 236-246.
3. 'Basilides und die kirchliche Bibel', in *Gesch. d. ntl. Kanons* I, 763-774.
4. *Frammenti gnostici*, Rome 1923, p. 10 (ET London 1924, p. 6).
5. *De Alexandrijnsche Haeresiarch Basilides. Een Bijdrage tot de Geschiedenis der Gnosis*, Amsterdam 1926, p. 82.

3. The Gospel of Marcion

We need not discuss in detail the so-called 'gospel' of Marcion, since this was not an independent work of this type but - as is today almost unanimously agreed - an 'expurgated' Gospel of Luke. Marcion on the basis of his own theological position reworked this Gospel in such a way as, in his view, to restore the original unadulterated text. But he had no intention of creating a new apocryphal gospel.

Literature: A. von Harnack, *Marcion. Das Evangelium vom fremden Gott*, ²1924, especially pp.177*-255* (still fundamental; for criticism of Harnack's conception cf. B. Aland, 'Marcion. Versuch einer neuen Interpretation', ZThK 70, 1973, 420-447). A. Pott, 'Marcions Evangelientext', ZKG 42, 1923, 202-223. J. Knox, *Marcion and the New Testament*, Chicago 1942. A.F.J. Klijn, *A Survey of the Researches into the Western Text of the Gospels and Acts* (Diss. Utrecht), 1949. E.C. Blackman, *Marcion and his Influence*, London 1948. G. Bardy, Marcion, *Dict. de la Bible*, Suppl. V, 1957, cols. 862-877. On the significance of Marcion for the history of the canon, see above, pp. 23 f.

4. The Gospel of Apelles

According to Jerome (*Comm. in Mt.*, prol., PL XXVI 17A), whom the Venerable Bede copies (*in Luc. ev. expos.* I, prol., PL XCII 307 C), Apelles, at first a disciple of Marcion, composed a gospel which bore his name (*Apellis euangelium*). Jerome mentions it after the Gospels of the Egyptians, of Thomas, Matthias and Bartholomew, of the Twelve Apostles and of Basilides. But in fact, as Bardenhewer notes (*Litg.* I², 374, note 1), Jerome when he wrote this passage had under his eyes Origen's first *Homily on Luke*. Such a gospel is mentioned neither in the Greek text of this homily nor in Jerome's own Latin translation (p. 5.1-15 Rauer), nor in a text of Ambrose (*Expositio euangelii Lucae* I 2, pp. 10f. Schenkl) which follows Origen very closely. The testimony of Jerome, who here adds to his source, may therefore rest on his own invention or on an error. If it did exist, the Gospel of Apelles would seem to have been only 'a further elaboration or a new redaction of the Gospel of Marcion'.[1]

In a later work Harnack[2] advanced a more radical theory: 'We cannot believe Jerome's statement that Apelles had a gospel of his own; pseudo-Tertullian attests the Marcionite canon for A. The lost sheep and Lk. 8:20 were cited by him (Tert., *de carne* 7; the same chapter presupposes that A. rejected John), and the Infancy Narrative was lacking. Certainly A. quoted (in Epiphanius, *Haer.* 44. 2. 6) the saying: 'Be good money changers' as standing in the Gospel: but that proves nothing. However, there is nothing against the view that A. altered Marcion's gospel just as much as other disciples. Hippolytus (*Ref.* VII. 38.2) expresses himself too generally when he says of A. that he took out of the Gospels and the Apostolos whatever pleased him.'

In this sense we may adduce the following testimony of Origen (*Epist. ad quosdam amicos Alexandrinos*, in Rufinus, *De adulteratione librorum Origenis*, PG XVII 625 C): 'You see with what a purging he hath cleansed our disputation, such a purging indeed as that with which Marcion cleansed the Gospels and the apostle, or his successor Apelles after him. For just as they overturned the truth of the scriptures, so he also, subtracting the things that were truly spoken, inserted for our condemnation things that are false.'

Notes

4. The Gospel of Apelles

1. Bardenhewer, *Litg.* I², 374, who refers to Harnack, *De Apellis gnosi monarchica*, Leipzig 1874, pp. 74f.
2. *Marcion*, ²Leipzig 1924, p. 190, note 1. Cf. also p. 418*, note 1.

5. The Gospel of Bardesanes

Like Marcion, or beside Marcion, Bardesanes of Edessa is accused here and there in the heresiological tradition of having composed or possessed for his own use a special gospel. But the testimonies are so slight that nothing can be derived from them. On this subject cf. W. Bauer, (*Rechtgläubigkeit und Ketzerei im ältesten Christentum*, ²1964, pp. 35-37; ET *Orthodoxy and Heresy*, Philadelphia 1971, pp. 29-32), who is inclined to assimilate the gospel in question to the Syriac Diatessaron.

6. The Gospel of Mani*

Here several questions must be distinguished:

(a) It is certain that the Manichees made use of the four canonical Gospels: very numerous exact quotations occur in their literature, especially (as is to be expected) in those works which were read in or emanated from their Western communities.[1] Mani himself in one of his works, the *Shaburakan*, employed and cited at length Mt. 25:31-46, as is proved by two extant fragments of the original text (Turfan fragments M 475 and M 477, in *Abh. d. pr. Akad. d. Wissensch.* 1904, *Anhang, Phil.-hist. Abh., Abh.* II, 11-15), and he knew also other New Testament texts.[2] Like many of his disciples however he seems to have used especially the Syriac version of Tatian's Diatessaron.[3]

(b) On the other hand, the Manichees received into the volume of their scriptures a certain number of apocryphal gospels borrowed from Christian or Gnostic literature: the Gospel of Peter (above, pp. 216ff.), the Gospel of Philip (above, pp. 179ff.), the Gospel of Thomas (above, pp. 110ff.); probably the Memoria Apostolorum, the Gospel of the Twelve Apostles, the Gospel of the Seventy (disciples) (see above, pp. 374ff.); perhaps also the Genna Marias (above, pp. 395f.), or a similar work, and the Infancy of the Lord.[4]

From the remains of accounts of the passion and the resurrection preserved in the Turfan fragments M 132 and M 18 it can be established that canonical and extra-canonical Gospels were employed, and also a Gospel harmony identical with, or rather similar to, the Diatessaron.

The first fragment (*Abh. d. pr. Akad. d. Wissensch.* 1904. *Anhang, Phil.-hist. Abh., Abh.* II, 36f., ed. F.W.K. Müller), the remains of a writing which cannot be more exactly identified, relating to the trial of Jesus before Pilate and the mockery, contains and combines quotations from the Gospels, especially that of John:

Jesus ... when he ... governor (ἡγεμών : [*cf. Mt. 27:2*]) and Pilate ... asked: '[I am not] in the house of Jacob and in the race of Israel' ... gave answer to Pilate: 'My dominion is not of this world' [*Jn. 18:36*], nevertheless through the pressure of the Jews bound ... [sent] to King Herod [*cf. Lk. 23:6-16; Diatessaron; Ev. Petri 1-5*] ... clothing [a crown of thorns] set upon his head [*Jn. 19:2; cf. Mt. 27:27f.; Mk. 15:17*] ... with a reed they smote him on the cheek [*Mt. 27:30; Mk. 15:19; Diatess.; Ev. Petri 9*], spat (?) upon his eyes [*cf. Ev. Petri 9*] and cried: 'Our sovereign Messiah!' [*Jn. 19:3; Mt. 27:29; Mk. 15:18*]. - Moreover three times - came, and three times they fell down [*cf. Jn. 19:4-16?*].

> (Turfan fragment M 132; *Abh. d. pr. Akad.* 1904,
> *Anhang, Phil.-hist. Abh., Abh.* II, 36f.)

The second fragment (*Abh. d. pr. Akad.* 1904, *Anhang, Phil.-hist. Abh.* II, 34-36), of which it is expressly said in the superscription that it belonged to a cycle of crucifixion hymns, was interpreted by Alfaric[5] as part of Mani's 'living

Gospel' (below, pp. 404ff.); F.C. Burkitt[6] called it a fragment of a 'controversial writing' which combined different extracts from Christian works, perhaps in order to 'show inconsistencies in the orthodox account of the Passion'. In reality, as H.H. Schaeder has shown,[7] we have here a quotation drawn from a Gospel harmony which in addition to the four canonical Gospels made use of an apocryphal gospel. The beginning of the fragment is in fact influenced by the Gospel of Peter (45-48):

'[In] truth [he] is the Son of God.' And Pilate thus replied: 'I have no part in the blood of this Son of God.' The centurions and soldiers (*qatriyonan va istratiyotan*) received at that time from Pilate a command, namely: 'Keep this secret!' and the Jews gave promises (?) [*cf. Ev. Petri 45-48*] . . . But he [*it? the gospel commented on?*] shows that on the Sunday, at the beginning of cock-crow, Maryam, Salōm [*Salome*] [and] Maryam came among many other women; they brought sweet-smelling herbs and nard [*cf. Mk. 16:1*]. They had come near to the grave . . . the angel . . . See the greatness (the glory), as did Maryam, Salōm and Arsani'ah [*Arsinoe; cf. Copt. Manich. Psalter, pp. 192.24 and 194.22*], when the two angels spoke to them: 'Seek not the living among the dead! [*Lk. 24:5*]. Think on Jesus' words, how he taught you in Galilee: 'Me will they deliver up and crucify; on the third day will I rise again from the dead' [*Lk. 24:6f.*] On this (?) afternoon go to Galilee, and bear the news to Simon and the others' [*cf. Mk. 16:7*] . . .

(Turfan fragment M 18; *Abh. d. pr. Akad.* 1904, *Anhang, Phil.-hist. Abh., Abh.* II, 34-36)

(*c*) A special place must be reserved for the logia or agrapha which are found in fairly large numbers here and there in Manichean works, but have for the most part hitherto remained unobserved. Several of them are certainly drawn from apocryphal gospels, but in other cases borrowing from sources of this kind is no more than probable, and of some we cannot say whence they derive, or might derive.

Two sayings of Jesus, one concerning the essential immortality of the living substance, the other about the doom of the soul which remains a stranger to the truth, are quoted by Mani in two passages of his Book of Mysteries (or Secrets) preserved by al-Biruni (*India* I, 48 and 54f., trans. Sachau). They are represented as pronounced in reply to a question of the apostles, and have been reproduced above (pp. 378 f.). Whether they come, as Alfaric (*Écrit. manich.* II, 175) has suggested, from the Gospel of the Twelve is doubtful.

On the other hand, the following four sayings, culled from the Manichean literature, certainly have as their source the Gospel of Thomas, or at least occur in that gospel:

(He said): 'The grey-haired old men, the little children instruct them. They that are six years old instruct them that are sixty years old.'

(Coptic Psalm-book II, 192.2f. ed. C.R.C. Allberry ; cf. Evang. Thom., logion 4: above p. 117)

On this mystery [*sc. of Light and Darkness*], which to the sects (δόγμα) is hidden, the Saviour (Σωτήρ) gave a hint to his disciples: 'Know what is before your face, and what is hidden from you will be revealed to you' [*cf. Mt. 10:26f.; Mk. 4:21f.; Lk. 8:16f. and 12:2f.*].

(*Kephalaia* LXV; I, 163.26-29 ed. C. Schmidt- A. Böhlig ;cf. Ev. Thom., logion 5: above p. 118)

. . . that I may redeem you from death and annihilation. I will give you what ye have not seen with the eye, nor heard with the ears, nor grasped with the hand [*cf. 1 Cor. 2:9*]. He who . . . on the sinners . . . . '

(Turfan fragment M 789; *Abh. d. pr. Akad.* 1904, *Anhang,Phil.-hist. Abh., Abh.* II, 68; cf. M 551, *ibid.* pp. 67f. ; Ev. Thom., logion 17: above, p. 119)

'Maryam, Maryam, know me: do not touch me. Stem the tears of thy eyes and know me that I am thy master. Only touch me not, for I have not yet seen the face of my Father [*cf. Jn. 20:15-17*]. Thy God was not stolen away, according to (κατά) the thoughts of thy littleness; thy God did not die, rather he mastered death. I am not the gardener (κηπουρός) [*cf. Jn. 20:15*]. I have given, I have received the . . ., I appeared (?) [not] to thee until I saw thy tears and thy grief . . . for (?) me. Cast this sadness away from thee and do this service (λειτουργία): be a messenger for me to these wandering orphans (ὀρφανός). Make haste rejoicing, and go unto the Eleven. Thou shalt find them gathered together on the bank of the Jordan. The traitor (προδότης) persuaded (πείθειν) them to be fishermen as they were at first and to lay down their nets with which they caught men unto life [*cf. Mt. 4:18f.; Jn. 21:2-8?*]. Say to them: 'Arise, let us go, it is your brother that calls you.' If they scorn my brotherhood, say to them: 'It is your Master.' If they disregard (ἀμελεῖν) my mastership, say to them: 'It is your Lord.' Use all skill (τέχνη) and advice until thou hast brought the sheep to the shepherd. If thou seest that their wits are gone, draw Simon Peter unto thee; say to him 'Remember what I uttered between thee and me. Remember what I said between thee and me in the Mount of Olives: I have something to say, I have none to whom to say it.''

(Coptic Psalm-book II, p. 187.2-29 Allberry ; cf. Ev. Thom., logion 38: above, p. 123)

The Manichean Psalter, however, contains some other logia which are missing from the Gospel of Thomas, and which with two exceptions appear here for the first time:

It is Jesus, who giveth repentance (μετάνοια) unto him that repents (μετανοεῖν). He stands in our midst, he winks unto us secretly, saying: 'Repent (μετανοεῖν), that I may forgive you your sins' [*cf. Lk. 17:3f.?*].
(Psalm CCXXXIX; II, 39.19-22 Allberry)

He [*sc. Jesus*] is not far from us, my brethren, even as he said in his preaching: 'I am near to you, like the clothing of your body (σῶμα)' [*cf. Origen, in Jerem. hom. XVIII 9; p. 163.24-27 Klostermann: 'And it is promised through the prophets (Jer. 13:11?), saying: I will be nearer to them than the tunic to their skin'*).
(Psalm CCXXXIX; II, 39.23f. Allberry)

I gave myself up to death trusting in the . . . divine word: 'He that dies shall live, he that humbles himself shall be exalted' [*cf. Mt. 16:25; 23:12 and par.*].
(Psalm CCLXXIII; II, 93.10f. Allberry)

. . . according to (κατά) thy word which thou [*sc. Jesus*] didst utter: 'Where (?) thy (?) mind (νοῦς) . . . ' [*cf. perhaps the Gospel of Mary (above, pp. 393.), p. 10.13-16: 'He (Jesus) answered and said to me (Mary): 'Well for thee, that thou didst not flinch at the sight of me, for where the mind (νοῦς) is, there is thy countenance''*] (= treasure; [*cf. Mt. 6:21, Lk. 12:34*]).
(Psalm CCLXXIV; II, 94.24f. Allberry)

As the Saviour (σωτήρ) hath said: 'Where your heart is, there will your treasure be' [*cf. Mt. 6:21, Lk. 12:34*].
(*Kephalaia LXXXIX* vol. I, 223.3-4 Böhlig; cf. *Kephal. XCI* vol. I, 234.8-9)

A man called down unto the world (κόσμος), saying: 'Blessed is he that shall know (νοεῖν) his soul' [*cf. Epist. Fundam. in Augustine, c. Felic I 16: 'But the love of the Holy Spirit shall open the inmost places of your heart, that with your own eyes ye may see your souls'*).
(Psalms of Thomas XIII; II, 219.19f. Allberry)

d) Up to this point we have considered only the 'gospel', or more exactly the different gospels, read, used and commented on by Mani and his adherents. But by 'Gospel of Mani' we ought, strictly speaking, to understand a work by the founder of Manicheism, the original gospel composed by Mani himself.[8] This work, generally entitled 'The Living Gospel' but also called, here and there, 'the Gospel of the Living', 'the Great Gospel', or simply 'the Gospel' (Gr. το ζων εὐαγγέλιον, τὸ εὐαγγέλιον), is one of the four, five or seven canonical works of the master, the 'Enlightener', and as such appears regularly - most often at the head of the list - in the different canons of the scriptures transmitted either by the Manichees themselves, by their opponents, or by neutral witnesses (*Homilies*, pp. 25.2 and 94.18f.; cf. p. 43.16; Kephalaia, Introduction, p. 5.23 and c. CXLVIII, SB Berlin 1933, p. 35; Coptic Psalm-book II, p. 46.21 and 139.56; Chinese Manichean catechism or 'Compendium of the Religion of the Buddha of Light, Mani', trans. G. Haloun-W.B. Henning, *Asia Major*, New Series, III, part II, 1952, 194: 'the first: the great *ying-lun*, interpreted 'book of wisdom' which thoroughly understands the roots and origins of the entire doctrine' = unpublished translation by P. Pelliot-P. Demieville: 'Ière classe: ta-ying-louen, en traduction: Livre sacré de la connaissance qui pénètre l'origine de toutes choses, ou (mot à mot) des dix mille dharma'; *Acta Archelai* c. LXII 6; Cyril of Jerusalem, *Cat.* VI 22; Epiphanius, *Pan.* 66.2.9; Timotheus of Constantinople, *de Recept. Haer.*, PG LXXXVI 1, 21 C; first or little Greek abjuration-formula, PG C 1321 B; second or great Greek abjuration-formula, PG I 1465 D; Germanus of Constantinople, *de Haer. et Syn.* 4, PG XCVIII 44 A; al-Râzî, reproduced by al-Biruni, in *Isis 5*, 1923, 31 (J. Ruska) = al-'Awfi, Jawâmi'al-Hikâyât, p. 41 ed. Nizâmu'd-Din; al-Ja'qûbî, in Kessler, *Mani*, p. 329; al-Biruni, *Chronol.*, p. 190 Sachau).

'Living', the epithet applied to this gospel, is frequently employed in the language of Manicheism, and was inherited from Gnosticism (cf. for example, 'the living Spirit', 'the living soul', 'Jesus, the Living One', perhaps also - see H.H. Schaeder, *Urform und Fortbildungen des manichäischen Systems*, p. 88, note 1 - Mani haija, Μανιχαῖος , Mani 'the living'). The term might imply that the document was presented and considered as of divine origin or nature, as emanating from the higher world of Light, Truth and Life (cf. the tradition or legend reported by Mirkhond (in Kessler, *Mani*, p. 379), according to which, to prove his prophetic claims, Mani produced a book, the 'Gospel', and said: 'This book has come down from heaven'). It means in any case that the work brought to its readers a message of regenerating truth, which could bring about and accomplish their spiritual resurrection and thus procure for them salvation: this 'Gospel of Life' or 'Living Gospel' is above all a 'life-giving Gospel' (τὸ νεκροποιὸν εὐαγγέλιον, ὅπερ ζῶν καλοῦσι : in these words it is rejected in the second Greek abjuration-formula, PG I 1465 D).

The work was divided into twenty-two books or λογοι, corresponding to the twenty-two letters of the Syriac alphabet, each section being designated in succession by one of these letters (Epiphanius, *Pan.* 66.13.3-5. where this arrangement is wrongly attributed to the Book of Mysteries; al-Ja'qubi, in Kessler, *Mani*, pp. 206 and 329: 'twelve [read: two and twenty] gospels, of which he named each gospel after one of the letters of the alphabet'; al-Biruni, *Chronol.* p. 207 tr. Sachau, or in Kessler, p. 206 and pp. 317f.). The 'Living Gospel' is also compared in the Coptic Psalm-book (Psalm CCXLI, p. 46.20) to an antidote (ἀντίδοτος) composed 'of twenty-two ingredients (μῖγμα)', and in the fourth of the Homilies, also translated into Coptic (p. 94.18-19), it is called 'the Great Gospel from Alpha to Omega' (i.e. corresponding to the original 'from Alaph to Tau'). This arrangement is confirmed and illustrated by two fragments from Turfan. One of these, S 1, published by C. Salemann ('Ein Bruchstück manichäischen Schrifttums im Asiatischen Museum', *Mémoires de l'Academié Impériale des Sciences de Saint-Pétersbourg*, 8ème série, VI, no.6 p..1-7), contains three successive references (lines 4-6; *op. cit.* pp. 2 and 4f.):

'The Gospel alaph is taught'
'The Gospel tau is taught'
'The Gospel of the 22 is taught'

As for fragment M 17, published by F.W.K. Müller ('Handschriften-Reste in Estrangelo - Schrift aus Turfan, Chinesisch-Turkistan', II Teil, *Abh. d. pr. Akad. d. Wissensch.* 1904, *Anhang, Phil.-hist. Abh., Abh.* II, 25-27), it bears a superscription which in the light of the preceding document apparently ought to be interpreted:

'The Gospel arab (alaph) is taught.'

That a section or a book corresponded to each of these letters seems also to be confirmed by one of the volumes (still unpublished) of the Manichean library discovered in 1930 in the Fayyum, where reference is made (SB Berlin 1933, pp. 30 and 37) to 'the third Logos of the Living Gospel' and (A. Böhlig, *Wissenschaftliche Zeitschrift der Martin-Luther-Universität, Halle-Wittenberg* 6, 1957, 485) to 'the first' or 'the ninth Logos'.

It is very difficult to form any very precise or exact idea of the content of the work. If we may believe Photius, or pseudo-Photius (*c. Manich.* I 12, PG CII 36 A), it contained a falsified account of the life or of certain acts of Jesus (' . . . in which certain destructive and ill-omened acts of Christ our God are invented by a disposition hostile to God'). Peter of Sicily on the contrary (*Hist. Manich.* 11, PG CIV 1257 C) affirms that it did not touch on any such subject. The impression left by a testimony of much greater value - that of al-Biruni, who had the writing in his hands - is that it was a gospel of a special kind, and one of which the form and content contrasted strongly with those of the canonical Gospels received by the Christians. Al-Biruni writes in fact (A. Adam, *Texte zum Manichäismus*, (KLT 175), 1954, p. 1): 'The adherents of Mani have a gospel of a special kind, which from beginning to end contains the opposite of what the Christians hold. And they confess what stands therein, and declare that it is the genuine Gospel, and its demands that to which the Messiah held and which he brought; everything outside this gospel is invalid, and its adherents [*sc.* of the Church's Gospel] speak lies about the Messiah.'

The little that we know about the subjects there treated allows us to suppose that the writing was either, perhaps, a gospel of the gnostic type or a commentary on the Gospel of Jesus designed to correct or supplant it, or more probably a work of didactic and dogmatic character expounding the Manichean system as a whole or at least some of its principal points. The first book was devoted to the description of the Kingdom of Light which regularly opens every exposition of the doctrinal myth. We read in fact in al-Murtada ('Das volle Meer', text and German trans. in Kessler, *Mani*, pp. 349 and 354): 'Mani declares in his 'Gospel' and in the 'Shaburakan' that the King of the world of Light dwells in the navel of his earth. He declares further, in the section 'alif of his Gospel and in the first part of the Shaburakan, that he (the God of the world of Light) is present on his whole earth (i.e. not only in its inmost part), from without as from within; he has no limits, save on the side where his earth abuts on that of his enemy [*the Kingdom of Darkness*].'

Elsewhere, according to the Kephalaia (LXI,vol. I, 153.29-31), an episode belonging to a later part of the same myth was dealt with: the swallowing and absorption of water, one of the five 'elements of light', by the archons of matter or of darkness. As the work continued a further theme - according to the witness of al-Ja'qubi (*Chronicle* I, p. 181 Houtsma; German trans. in Kessler, *Mani*, pp. 206 and 329) - was that of prayer and of 'what must be employed for the liberation of the spirit'. In another passage Jesus was praised and blessed before the Father, the supreme God, as is attested by the allusion in a Turfan fragment, T II D 173c, composed in Uighur (A. von Le Coq, 'Turkische Manichaica aus Chotscho III,' *Abh. d. pr. Akad. d. Wissensch.* 1922, No. 2, p. 12): 'And the disciples, thus speaking (their) doubts, said to their teacher: "On what ground does one in the great Gospel-book praise and bless first the Moon-god (Jesus) and only thereafter the great princely king of the Gods, the God Zarwan?"' Finally we learn from al-Biruni (*Chronol.* p. 207 Sachau; pp. 206 and 318 Kessler) that Mani, no doubt to authenticate his gospel and guarantee its authority as superior to any other, affirmed therein that he was 'the Paraclete announced by Messiah [Jn. 14:16f.; 14:26; 16:7-15], and the seal of the prophets'. Unfortunately we can derive nothing from the Turfan fragment M 733 (*Abh. d. pr. Akad. d. Wissensch.* 1904, *Anhang, Phil.-hist. Abh., Abh.* II, 31), in which a quotation is announced: 'And in the gospel alaph of the Living he (Mani) says . . . ' The quotation has not survived.

The only text from this work which has come down to us direct is supplied by the combination of two Turfan fragments which in part coincide and more or less complete each other (cf. E. Waldschmidt and W. Lentz, *Abh. d. pr. Akad. d. Wissensch.* 1926, No. 4, pp. 22f.): fragments M 172 and M 17. The first (*Abh. d. pr. Akad. d. Wissensch.* 1904, *Anhang, Phil.-hist. Abh., Abh.* II, 100-103; 1926, No. 4, p. 23) bears the subscription: 'The argument of the living Gospel of the eye and the ear is brought to an end, and the fruit of the truth is taught.' The second (*Abh. d. pr. Akad.* 1904, *loc. cit.* pp. 25-27) preserves the superscription: 'The gospel 'alaph is taught.' The passage may be approximately restored as follows:

Praised is, and praised may he be, the dear son of Love, the life-giver Jesus, the chief of all these gifts. Praised is and praised shall be the Virgin of Light, the chief of all excellences. Praised is and praised shall be the holy religion (the pure totality of the holy religion) through the power of the Father, through the blessing of the Mother and through the goodness of the Son (Jesus). Salvation and blessing upon the sons of salvation and upon the speakers and the hearers of the renowned word (or: of the commandment of the Holy Ghost)! Praise and glory be to the Father and to the Son and to the elect Breath, the Holy Spirit, and to the creative (or: holy) Elements! The word (argument) of the 'living gospel' of the eye and ear is taught, and the fruit of truth is presented. The Blessed shall receive this offering ... ; the wise shall know; the strong shall put on good things to him that knoweth ... For all is, and all that is and shall be exists through his power.

Then after a considerable interval:

I, Mani, the emissary of Jesus the friend, in the love of the Father, of God the renowned (holy), every ... was from him ...

On the other hand, it is only with great hesitation and with express reserves that we can attach to the Living Gospel several sayings or teachings of Mani quoted in the second part of the long Turfan fragment M 801 (W. Henning, 'Ein manichäisches Bet- und Beichtbuch', *Abh. d. pr. Akad. d. Wissensch.* 1936, No. 10, pp. 18-41; on the source of the quotations cf. pp. 13f):

... as he taught in the scripture: 'Whosoever strives to come to that world of peace, he must from henceforth collect his soul (himself) in the sign of the gods of paradise.'

(M 801 §§ 476-481; p. 32)

As he taught: 'He who sees himself only on the outside, not within, becomes small himself and makes others small.'

(M 801 §§ 547-551; p. 34)

... he will have compassion on his own soul, and will weep and lament, pray and implore, and beg remission of his sins.

(M 801 §§ 594-599; p. 36)

As he taught: 'Where love is little, all acts are imperfect' [*cf. 1 Cor. 13:13*]
(M 801 §§ 628-630; p. 37)

As he taught in the scripture: 'What profit is it to a righteous man, who says: 'I have power in my members', when by eye, ear and the other senses ('members') he creates corruption?'

(M 801 §§ 650-656; pp. 37f.;
cf. also *Abh. d. pr. Akad.* 1904,
Anhang, Phil.-hist. Abh., Abh. II, 99f.)

As he taught: 'At every time shall ye come together for the remission and begging of pardon (?) for sins; forgive, and seek pardon from one another; he who does not forgive, to him it is not forgiven' [*cf. Mt. 6:15; 18:35; Ecclus. 28:2*].

(M 801 §§ 738-741; p. 40)

No doubt we shall be in a better position to know the structure and content of the work when one of the Coptic Manichean writings found in the Fayyum in 1930 has been published. Thirty-one pages of it have been acquired by the Berlin Museum and two hundred and fifty by the Chester Beatty collection in London.[9] If we may depend upon the remains of the superscriptions which it has so far been possible to read or to communicate ('the σύναξις (assembly? homily?)... of the ninth σύναξις ', 'The first λόγος of the first Logos of the living gospel', 'The second σύναξις' or 'the third σύναξις of the third λόγος of the living gospel'), it may be presumed that we have here a kind of commentary or else homilies (?) on the Gospel of Mani, which we owe to one of his disciples.

The Living Gospel has often been confused, or there has been a tendency to confuse it, with a work of Mani famous in the Persian tradition under the name of *Ertenk* (Erzeng) and entitled in Parthian *Ardhang*.[10] Schaeder indeed went so far as to declare that *Ardhang* (derived from Old Persian *arta-Θa^{n}ha* - 'message of truth') was the Persian (and not Parthian!) equivalent of εὐαγγέλιον. But it is today no longer doubtful that in reality we have here two distinct works.

The *Ardhang* was a picture-book, a kind of *Tafelband*, a collection of drawings and pictures, intended to illustrate in concrete form the essential aspects of the dualistic doctrine, perhaps as an accessory or appendix to the Living Gospel. This is shown by the following among other proofs: the title Εἰκών given to it in Greek and in Coptic; the reference to it furnished in the Chinese 'Compendium of the religion of the Buddha of Light, Mani' (*Asia Major*, New Series, vol. III, part 2, 1952, p.195), at the end of a list of the seven canonical scriptures which begins with a mention of the 'Great Gospel' ('one drawing: *ta-men-ho-yi*, [the great *men-ho-yi*], interpreted 'the drawing of the great two principles''); and finally the allusions to its content made by Ephraem (C.W. Mitchell, *Ephraim's Prose Refutations of Mani, Marcion and Bardaisan* I, London-Oxford 1912, xciii) and the Kephalaia (c. XCII, p. 235.1-17). There was even a commentary to the illustrations collected in this album, the *Ardhang Wifras*, of which fragments have been discovered in Parthian.

On the whole subject cf. E. Waldschmidt-W. Lentz, *Abh. d. pr. Akad. d. Wissensch.* 1926, No. 4, p. 23. C. Schmidt-H.J. Polotsky, SB Berlin 1933, p. 45, note 3. - H.J. Polotsky, *Manichäische Homilien*, Stuttgart 1934, p. 18, note a; id. 'Abriss des manichäischen Systems', Pauly-Wissowa, Supp. VI, Stuttgart 1934, col. 244.65-68. W.B. Henning, *Bull.* SOAS 11, 1943, 71 and 12, 1947, 310, note 4; id. *Asia Major*, New Series, vol.III, part 2, 1952, pp.209-210.

Notes

6. The Gospel of Mani

* The following section on the Gospel of Mani is reprinted without change, although new discoveries and investigations in the interval, relating specifically to this text, need to be listed. But Puech's contribution, as a brief account of the complicated situation, is still important, and the evaluation of new finds and also the new interpretations are not so far advanced that this section could really be replaced and reshaped. Reference is made to some new investigations in an appendix (*W. Schn.*)

1. Cf. for example P. Alfaric, *L'évolution intellectuelle de saint Augustin*, Paris 1918, pp. 193-213; id. *Les écritures manichéennes* II, Paris 1919, 161-169; *A Manichean Psalm-book*, Part II, ed. C.R.C. Allberry, Stuttgart 1938, pp. 47*f.: 'Scriptural Quotations and References'; for the Manicheism of Central Asia see E. Waldschmidt and W. Lentz, 'Die Stellung Jesu im Manichäismus', *Abh. d. pr. Akad. d. Wissensch.* 1926, No. 4, pp. 20-40.
2. Cf. F.C. Burkitt, *The Religion of the Manichees*, Cambridge 1925, pp. 86-91: 'Mani and the Gospels'.
3. H.H. Schaeder, 'Urform und Fortbildungen des manichäischen Systems', *Vorträge der Bibliothek Warburg*, 1924-1925, Leipzig-Berlin 1927, p. 72; A. Baumstark, *Or. Chr.* 3 Serie, 10, 264f., and 3 Serie, 12, 169-191; Curt Peters, 'Das Diatessaron Tatians' = *Orientalia Christiana Analecta* 123, Rome 1939, pp. 125-132.
4. Cf. P. Alfaric, *Les écritures manichéennes* II, 169-185.
5. *Écrit. manich.* II, 38.
6. *The Religion of the Manichees*, p. 88.
7. *Urform und Fortbildungen des manichäischen Systems*, p. 74, note 3.
8. Cf. K. Kessler, *Mani* I, Berlin 1889, 205-212; P. Alfaric, *Les écritures manichéennes* II, Paris 1919, 34-43; C. Schmidt-H.J. Polotsky, 'Ein Mani-fund in Ägypten', SB Berlin 1933, pp. 29, 31, 35-37; H.-Ch. Puech, art. 'Evangelium (Lebendiges)' in F. König, *Religionswissenschaftliches Wörterbuch*, Freiburg 1956, cols. 237f.
9. C. Schmidt-H.J. Polotsky, 'Ein Mani-Fund in Ägypten', SB Berlin 1933, pp. 30 and 34; C. Schmidt, *Neue Originalquellen des Manichäismus aus Ägypten*, Stuttgart 1933, pp. 12f.; A. Böhlig, 'Synaxis = Homilia?' *Wissenschaftl. Zeitschr. d. Martin-Luther-Univers. Halle-Wittenberg* 6, 1957, 485f.
10. K. Kessler, *Mani*, pp. 209-212; P. Alfaric, *Les écritures manichéennes* II, 40-43; H.H. Schaeder, *Gnomon* 9, 1933, 347.

Appendix

Wilhelm Schneemelcher

a) The relations set out by Puech (above, pp. 401 ff.) between Manichean texts and Tatian's Diatessaron and apocryphal gospels (above all the Gospel of Peter) are confirmed through the opening up of the hitherto unpublished Turfan texts. After M. Boyce published a catalogue of this collection in 1960,[1] W. Sundermann has occupied himself with the deciphering, edition and evaluation of these texts. We may refer here only to an essay which is important for our purposes: 'Christliche Evangelientexte in der Überlieferung der iranisch-manichäischen Literatur' (in *Mitt. des Inst. für Orientforschung* 14, Berlin 1968, pp. 386-405).[2] Sundermann here sets out a number of Parthian, Persian and Sogdian fragments from the Turfan stock in Berlin. One fragment (M 4570) is part of a Parthian version of the Diatessaron. The text belongs to the passion narrative. Other pieces are parts of the 'crucifixion hymns', while in others the exact origin cannot be given.

Sundermann's essay shows very clearly that important insights into the reception of the Gospel tradition in Manicheism are still to be expected from the further opening-up of the Turfan material. This relates to the canonical Gospels as well as the Diatessaron or the apocryphal gospels.

b) H.J. Klimkeit in 1989 published a collection: *Hymnen und Gebete der Religion des Lichts. Iranische und türkische liturgische Texte der Manichäer Zentralasiens*, (Abh. Rhein. - Westf. Akademie der Wiss. 79). Among these liturgical texts there are some which confirm the influence of apocryphal traditions and also the use of the Diatessaron. Klimkeit has also been able to improve the reading and translation of the fragments already known, in some cases considerably (e.g. M 132 and M 18, see above, pp. 401 f.). In any case we shall still have to give much attention to these hymns from the point of view of the continuance of the apocrypha in Manicheism.

c) In 1970 A. Henrichs and L. Koenen published a report about a Greek parchment codex in the Cologne papyrus collection with a biography of Mani.[3] This preliminary account was followed in 1975-1982 by the provisional edition of this text, and in 1988 by a critical edition.[4] This discovery of the Cologne Mani Codex (abbreviated CMC) has rightly aroused considerable attention. It provides us with important new information about the life and theology of Mani.[5]

In their preliminary report Henrichs and Koenen already entered into detail regarding the 'Fragment from Mani's Living Gospel' contained in CMC[6], and also drew upon the two Turfan fragments M 17 and M 172 (see above, pp. 407 f.). In this section of the CMC (p. 65.23ff.) it is a question of the prologue of Mani's gospel. The text runs:

[Again] he wrote [and] (p. 66) said in the gospel of his most holy hope: 'I, Mani, apostle of Jesus Christ through the will of God, the Father of truth, of whom I too am born; who lives and abides to all eternity, existing before all and also abiding after all. All things that came into being and shall come into being exist through his power. From this same one I was born; I am also from his will. From him all that is true was revealed to me; and I am from his truth. [The eternal truth which he revealed to me] I have seen. Truth (p. 67) I showed to my fellow travellers, peace I proclaimed to the children of peace. Hope I preached to the immortal race. I chose (my) elect and I showed the way which leads to the height to those who ascend in accordance with this truth. Hope I preached, and this revelation I revealed; this immortal gospel I have written, in which I have included and set forth the highest mysteries and the greatest works, the greatest and most exalted forms of the most mighty works [which surpass all measure]. What [he revealed], that I showed (p. 68) to those who [live] from the vision full of truth, which I have seen, and from the most glorious revelation that was revealed to me'.

(Ed. L. Koenen and C. Römer, pp. 44-47)

We cannot give here an exhaustive interpretation of this, the most extensive fragment of the 'Gospel of Mani' that we possess. Since only very little is known about this work (cf. above, pp. 404 ff.), the prologue which has been found naturally means a considerable enrichment of our knowledge, even though one must be very cautious about any far-reaching conclusions. One thing however seems to be clear: This work does indeed bear the title 'Gospel', but scarcely belongs to the familiar *Gattung* so described. Mani appears here to have summarised his teaching. For this outline of his doctrine he chose the term 'gospel' which was known to him, not however as the description of a literary *Gattung* but as a characterisation of its content: life-giving good tidings.

It may be that in the composition of his 'gospel' Mani made use of pericopae from the canonical Gospels, or a gospel harmony or apocryphal gospels, as is attested in other texts. But of that nothing can be said in view of the meagre witnesses.

The significance of this 'gospel' for the Manicheans is also clear from the fact that this work was evidently used liturgically.[7] In literary terms we may reckon this text even less to the *Gattung* of the apocryphal gospels than many gnostic texts which called themselves 'gospels'.

Notes

Appendix

1. M. Boyce, *A Catalogue of the Iranian Manuscripts in Manichean Script in the German Turfan Collection*, Berlin 1960.
2. I thank H.J. Klimkeit for making this essay available to me.
3. *Zeitschrift fur Papyrologie und Epigraphik*, (ZPE), 5, 1970, pp. 97-216.
4. ZPE 19, 1975, pp. 1-85; 32, 1978, pp. 87-199; 44, 1981, pp. 201-318; 48, 1982, pp. 1-59. *Der Kölner Mani-Kodex. Über das Werden seines Lebens*. Kritische Edition aufgrund der von A. Henrichs und L. Koenen besorgten Erstedition hrsg. und übers. von L. Koenen und C. Römer, Papyrologica Coloniensia 14, 1988.
5. Cf. the literature adduced in ZPE 32, 1978, pp. 88-91 and in the critical edition.
6. ZPE 5, 1970, pp. 189ff.
7. Cf. Henrichs-Koenen, ZPE 5, 1970, p. 196.

H. Gospels under the Names of their Users

Two distinct works are known under the name of 'Gospel of the Egyptians':

a) A gospel of this description is attested by Clement of Alexandria, but only very little of it has survived (see above, pp. 209 ff.).

b) Two codices of the Nag Hammadi discovery each contain an exemplar of a work with the title 'The Holy Book of the Great Invisible Spirit', which is also described in the colophon as 'The Gospel of the Egyptians'. This work has nothing to do with the gospel mentioned under a). It is a dogmatic treatise, and therefore need not be discussed in detail here.

Literature: *Facsimile Edition:* Cod. III, 1976, pp. 40.12-44.28; 49.1-69.20; Cod. IV, 1975, pp. 55.20-60.30.

Edition: A. Böhlig and F. Wisse, *Nag Hammadi Codices III 2 and IV 2*, NHS 4, Leiden 1975.

German translation: H.-M. Schenke, NTS 16, 1969/70, pp. 196-208.

English translation: The Nag Hammadi Library in English 195-205 (rev. ed. 1988, pp. 209-219)

X. Infancy Gospels

Oscar Cullmann

General introduction

The Gospels of Mark and John say nothing of the childhood of Jesus. The oldest gospel tradition records only those incidents in his life of which the disciples, or at least some of them, could be regarded as witnesses. Thus the first event in Mark is the appearance of John as a necessary preliminary for the baptism of Jesus. Although the Gospel of John in its prologue goes back beyond this historical 'beginning' (Mk 1:1) to the absolute beginning of everything, the real story of Jesus similarly commences with John the Baptist (see also Acts 1:22).

Moreover, in the earliest period it was not the birth and childhood of Jesus which were of theological interest but primarily his death and resurrection and secondly his words and works. It is therefore not surprising that Christmas was not observed until the 4th century, while at first, but also comparatively late, and moreover among the Gnostics, it was his *baptism* which was commemorated as his appearing upon earth.[1]

But the need to go back beyond the information attested in general by the apostles to the youth, infancy and birth of Jesus was felt much earlier, and already comes to expression in two of our canonical Gospels, Matthew and Luke. Of course, the material to be found there must have circulated for a long time in the tradition in an oral and, to a certain extent, also in a written form before it was incorporated into these Gospels. The following are the narratives in question: (1) promise and account of the birth of the Baptist, Lk. 1:5-25, 57-80; (2) promise of the birth of Jesus, Lk. 1:26-38; (3) birth of Jesus, Lk. 2:1-20; (4) circumcision, presentation in the Temple, Symeon and Anna, Lk. 2:21-38; (5) the child Jesus in the Temple, Lk. 2:41-52; (6) promise and account of the birth of Jesus, Mt. 1:18-25; (7) the Magi, Mt. 2:1-12; (8) murder of the Holy Innocents at Bethlehem, flight into Egypt, and return to Nazareth, Mt. 2:13-23.

Since the motives for the fixation of this material are partly the same as those which gave rise to the apocryphal infancy gospels, but on the other hand operate in a fundamentally different way in the special circumstances of an earlier stage of development, a brief discussion is necessary of, firstly, the motives which produced the canonical infancy narratives, and, secondly, the motives for the further development of the material into the apocryphal infancy gospels.

1. The reasons for the formation of the infancy narratives in Matthew and Luke:

a) It is in accord with natural curiosity if in time the early Christians wished to learn something of that part of the life of Jesus concerning which the oldest tradition is silent. Whenever biographical literature shows gaps, legend generally springs up, in the absence of reliable information, to supply the deficiency. It is to be noted, however, that the stories about Jesus' birth and infancy in Matthew and Luke are few. They actually deal only with the nativity itself and the events directly connected with it. Of the long period between the return to Nazareth and the baptism of Jesus Matthew says nothing, and Luke, apart from the statement, 'the child grew and became strong' (2:40), which refers only to his normal human development during this time, has only the story of Jesus at the age of twelve in the Temple; a story which has extra-biblical parallels and acted as a powerful stimulus for the creation of the apocryphal infancy narratives. Even the canonical birth stories betray legendary motives which have parallels in extra-biblical literature, especially in India, Egypt and Persia (for India see especially G.A. van den Bergh van Eysinga, *Indische Einflüsse auf evangelische Erzählungen*, ²1909; for Egypt, E. Norden, *Die Geburt des Kindes*, 1924; for Persia, T.K. Cheyne, *Bible Problems*, 1904. For a critical examination cf. Th. Boslooper, 'Jesus' Virgin Birth and Non-Christian 'Parallels'', *Religion in Life* 26, 1956-57, 87-97).

b) So far as the canonical infancy stories are concerned, the purely narrative interest, while undoubtedly already present, is quite secondary to the theological interest which was the chief impulse to their formation. Consequently, in contrast to the apocryphal gospels, they reveal a certain sobriety and above all a close connection with Christology, even where they employ extraneous material. Thus the nativity story, for which there are already two different and independent versions in Matthew and Luke, is told in terms of a theological proposition in primitive Christian belief, namely that God has revealed himself in Christ so directly that unity of will and being must be assumed. While the great majority of New Testament writers are content with the fact as such, the two birth stories seek to answer the question of the nature of this unity by means of conception by the Holy Spirit and the virgin birth, and are therefore obliged to view Joseph's paternity as adoptive.

This solution leads to a certain tension with another concern, probably already to the forefront of theological interest, to emphasise the christological affinity of Jesus with the Old Testament. This affinity also must be proved by means of the stories of his birth. This is done on the one hand in the two divergent genealogies (Mt. 1:1ff.; Lk. 3.23ff.), in which, in order to establish the Davidic descent of Jesus, already contained in an old confessional formula (Rom. 1:3), the line of his ancestors has to be traced back.

On the other hand there was the concern, especially in the face of Jewish polemic (Jn 7:41f.), to remove the difficulty that Jesus came from Nazareth, whereas according to prophecy Bethlehem was to be his place of origin. Thus Matthew's nativity story is concerned to show that Jesus' parents fled from his birthplace Bethlehem only because of Herod's persecution, and on their return from Egypt did not go there but to Nazareth (Mt. 2:22f.). Conversely Luke's story seeks to show that it was only because of the census that Jesus of Nazareth was born in Bethlehem.

Behind the story of the wise men from the east there lies the theological idea of Christ's universal kingdom, and the same theological tendency governs the story of the flight of his parents, which brings the child Jesus into Egypt.

Luke's Christmas story, in which Jesus first sees the light of day amidst poverty and in the company of poor shepherds, is an example of the third evangelist's theological emphasis on the ideal of poverty. The stories of the presentation of the infant Jesus in the Temple, of the coming of Symeon and Anna, and of Jesus' presence in the Temple at the age of twelve are intended to point to the fulfilment of the priesthood in Christ.

Finally, the connection made by Luke between the nativity story of Jesus and that of John, the latter of which originally was probably already fixed in the quite independent tradition of the later Baptist sect, is intended to transpose to the time of the births of the fore-runner and of him who came after him the association of John the Baptist with the appearance of Jesus, which was regarded in Christian tradition from the outset as 'the beginning of the Gospel' (Mk. 1:1). In this way the true relation between John and Jesus was to be brought out, in opposition to the misrepresentations of the Baptist sect, which saw in John the Messiah. On the other hand, in this later combination of two originally independent traditions there are already to be seen tendencies important for the development of the apocryphal infancy gospels: first the typical linking of different legends into larger cycles, effected by secondary connective elements; and then above all the endeavour to make interesting in themselves figures which in the original gospel tradition are significant only through their function in relation to the person of Jesus Christ.

Literature on the New Testament infancy narratives: G. Erdmann, *Die Vorgeschichten des Lukas- und Matthäusevangeliums* (FRLANT, NF 48), 1932. M. Dibelius, 'Jungfrauensohn und Krippenkind' (1932), in id. *Botschaft und Geschichte* I, 1953, 1-78. M.S. Enslin, 'The Christian Stories of the Nativity', JBL 59, 1940, 317-338. E. Burrows, *The Gospel of the Infancy and other Biblical Essays*, 1945. R.E. Brown, *The Birth of the Messiah*, London 1977; id. 'Gospel Infancy Narrative Research from 1976 to 1986: Part I (Matthew)', *Catholic Biblical Quarterly* 43, 1986, 468-483; Part II (Luke), *ibid.* 660-680. R. Laurentin, *Les Evangiles de l'enfance du Christ. Vérité de Noël au-delà des mythes. Exégese et sémiotique. Historicité et théologie*, Paris 1982.

Cf. also the commentaries on Mt. and Lk. (above all: for Mt., U. Luz, EKK, 1985; W.D. Davies and D.C. Allison, ICC, 1988; for Lk., J.A. Fitzmyer, The Anchor Bible, [2]1986).

2. The motives for the further development of the infancy stories in the apocrypha:

a) In the further development of the birth and infancy stories in later days the narrative interests become predominant, although theological interests are still present. The tendency to draw upon extraneous legends, already discernible in the infancy narratives of Matthew and Luke, is greatly increased. The further we move in time from the beginnings, the more unrestrained becomes the application to Jesus of what is recounted about the birth and infancy of sons of gods and children of supernatural origin. Here the traditions preserved in the (infancy) Gospel of Thomas, about the impudent boy Jesus who in marvellous fashion plays the most audacious tricks, go a very long way. The formation of the canon, which took place about the middle of the 2nd century, was able to check only to a slight degree the legendary accretions which grew up around the childhood of Jesus, in so far as in Matthew and Luke, as we have seen, nothing is reported about this whole period in his life. In Matthew's infancy narrative itself the flight into Egypt, which is only mentioned and not narrated, supplies rich soil for the growth of fantasy and the borrowing of extraneous material. And so here full rein is given to the laws which govern the formation of legend.

The narrative interest now concentrates in particular on those figures and events which in the primitive tradition remained on the periphery, and played a part only in so far as they had to do directly with the work of Christ. They acquire a value of their own and, quite independently of the story of Jesus itself, become the vehicles of legendary motifs. This is especially the case with Mary and Joseph. It is true that Matthew and Luke also are interested in the parents of Jesus, but only for the purpose of showing his connection with Israel and the royal house of David. Now in contrast Mary and Joseph become leading characters, whose history has an interest of its own. Details are supplied about Mary's parents, her own miraculous birth is recounted, and her perpetual virginity is affirmed (in the framework of the older tradition, concerned as it is solely with Jesus, this is unknown and indeed excluded). Joseph the carpenter gets a biography of his own. In the apocryphal gospels which employ all this material, the Protevangelium Jacobi for the legends about Mary and the History of Joseph the Carpenter for those about Joseph (see below, chapter XI, pp. 470 ff.), it is only subsequently that a loose connection with Jesus is restored.

b) Despite this, however, apologetic and theological considerations are also at work. The very problems which were caused by the formation of the divergent infancy narratives in the canonical Gospels still awaited a solution. Already in Matthew and Luke the story of a birth without a human father raises difficulties in the face of the older demonstration of Davidic descent through Joseph. Matthew at the end of the genealogy (1:16) and Luke at the beginning (3:23) found a formula which allowed an adoptive view of the paternity of Joseph, and consequently of the Davidic sonship of Jesus. This solution clearly could not satisfy everybody. So another solution was proposed, that Mary also was descended from David. This tradition, already widespread in the 2nd century (Justin), found a firm foothold in the legend of Mary (Protev. James 10).

An answer had also to be given to Jewish attacks based on the older accounts of the virgin birth. The Jews had spread abroad the idea that Jesus was the illegitimate child of a soldier called Panthera (NTApoHdb, pp. 47ff.; H. Strack, *Jesus, die Häretiker u. die Christen nach den ältest. jüd. Angaben*, 1910; cf. also below, pp. 424 f.,484, 501 f.). In the face of such slanders, at which Matthew already seems to hint, the virgin birth through Mary had to be demonstrated more palpably by means of a special narrative. The discreet allusions in Matthew and Luke no longer sufficed.

Again, the assertion of Mary's perpetual virginity had to be reconciled with the fact that in the primitive tradition Jesus had brothers. In contrast to the later catholic explanation that these brothers were cousins, Joseph was now made out to be a widower, and they were his sons by a former marriage.

On the other hand it was also necessary to rebut gnostic and docetic views which denied the reality of the body of Jesus, by emphasising the reality of his birth, although at the same time it was already maintained that Mary remained inviolate.

c) It is in particular the Gnostics who appear to have been interested in infancy stories, and to have encouraged the collection of all this kind of material. They were always on the look-out for details in the life of Jesus upon which to hang the speculations which they attributed to Christ. Besides the appearances of the risen Jesus to his disciples it was especially stories like that of the twelve-year-old Jesus in the Temple, and all the legends which attached to them, which provided a suitable framework for gnostic gospels. This was the genesis of the development of gnostic infancy narratives (see 3 below, p. 453 ff.).

d) Throughout the Middle Ages the growth of legends about the birth and childhood of Jesus and what preceded them continued apace in ever-increasing profusion. New collections of such material were continually being made, its dubious nature partially disguised by borrowings from the canonical Gospels. Despite this, opposition was aroused against this whole type of literature, especially in the West, where Jerome assailed it with particular zeal, so that it was condemned by the Popes Damasus and Innocent I. The Decretum Gelasianum lists by name a series of infancy gospels which are to be rejected. Later, in the 16th century under Pius V, the office of St Joachim, the father of Mary according to the Protevangelium of James, was even removed from the Roman breviary, and the text of the Presentation of Mary in the Temple was suppressed, although both were later restored.

Despite every effort, it was not possible completely to uproot this popular material, especially in its widely disseminated form in the Latin pseudo-Matthew. Attempts were made only to give it a more acceptable form through excisions and alterations. Luther, who had become a monk at the summons of St Anne, mother of Mary according to the Protevangelium of James, later came out strongly against the apocryphal infancy gospels.

In fact these writings, in antiquity, in the Middle Ages and in the Renaissance, exercised a stronger influence on literature and art than the Bible itself. Poets like Prudentius in antiquity, the nun Roswitha in the Middle Ages, and many others have sung the praises of Mary (see R. Reinisch, *D. Pseudo-Evangelien von Jesu u. Marias Kindheit in d. roman. u. german. Lit.* 1879). Early Christian and mediaeval art showed a special interest in the infancy gospels, in the miracles performed by the child Jesus, his birth in the cave, and above all in Mary spinning for the Temple curtain. In the 9th century Leo III caused the whole story of Joachim and Anne to be portrayed in St Paul's church in Rome (see E. Hennecke, *Altchristl. Malerei u. altchristl. Lit.* 1896; J.E. Weis-Liebersdorf, *Christus- u. Apostelbilder. Der Einfluss der Apokryphen auf die ältesten Kunsttypen*, 1902). The artists of the Renaissance continued this tradition unbroken (see B. Kleinschmidt, *Die heil. Anna. Ihre Verehrung in Geschichte, Kunst und Volkstum*, 1930; on the whole question see also C. Cecchelli, *Mater Christi*, vols. I-IV, 1946-1954; cf. also above, p. 65).

Literature: *Complete editions of the apocryphal infancy gospels:* Tischendorf, Ea, 1876, pp. 1-209. C. Michel and P. Peeters, *Evangiles apocryphes*, Texts et documents pour l'étude historique du Christianisme dir. par H. Hemmer et P. Lejay, I[2], 1924; II, 1914 (text and French trans.). de Santos[6], pp. 118-366 (text and Spanish trans.; bibliographical supplement pp. xvif.)

Translations: Moraldi I, 433-352. Erbetta I 2, 3-227. Starowieyski I, 175-406.

Literature on the infancy gospels in general: NTApoHdb, pp. 95-142 (E. Hennecke and A. Meyer). W. Bauer, *Leben Jesu*, pp. 4-100. K.L. Schmidt, *Kanonische und apokryphe Evangelien und Apostelgeschichten*, AThANT 5, 1944. Vielhauer, *Lit. gesch.* pp. 665-679. H. Köster, 'Überlieferung und Geschichte der frühchristlichen Evangelien-literatur', ANRW 25 2, 1984, 1463-1542.

3. Short survey of the texts referred to or translated:

a) The basis for all the vast later literature constituting the apocryphal infancy gospels is the so-called Protevangelium of James, probably of the 2nd century, particularly for the birth, childhood and motherhood of Mary, and the Gospel of Thomas, not much later in its original form, for the miracles of the child Jesus. These two are therefore translated here in full, with a divergent passage of some length from the Syriac version of the Gospel of Thomas.

b) From the older gnostic infancy traditions are given a fragment from the Gnostic Justin and two extracts from the Pistis Sophia.

c) The exceedingly numerous later infancy gospels are almost entirely compilations made from earlier writings, with the occasional incorporation of new sources or new material. Leaving aside the translations into Syriac, Latin, Armenian, Coptic etc. of the original text, more or less expanded, of the older apocryphal infancy gospels, the most notable of these later gospels, of which some important extracts are here translated, are the following: the Arabic infancy gospel, which goes back to a Syriac text and in addition to the material already known contains all kinds of legends about the holy family's sojourn in Egypt; the Latin Gospel of pseudo-Matthew, mistakenly regarded by Jerome as a translation of the Hebrew Matthew; a later Latin gospel (Arundel-Hereford MS), which incorporates an otherwise unknown and probably older source into the material generally known; and finally a portion from an Arabic Life of John the Baptist, probably translated from the Greek.

Notes

X. Infancy Gospels

General introduction

1. Literature on the history of the Christmas festival: H. Usener, *Das Weihnachtsfest*, ²1911. O. Cullmann, *Der Ursprung des Weihnachtsfestes*, ²1960 ('The Origin of Christmas', *The Early Church*, ed. A.J.B. Higgins, 1956, pp. 17-36). L. Fendt, 'Der heutige Stand der Forschung über das Geburtsfest Jesu am 25.XII und uber Epiphanias', ThLZ 78, 1953, cols.1-10 .A.Strobel, 'Jahrespunkt-Spekulationen und frühchristliches FestjahrThLZ 87, 1962, cols. 183-194. C. Andresen, *Die Kirchen der alten Christenheit*, 1971, pp. 361-366.

1. The Protevangelium of James

1. Transmission, editions and literature: as with similar apocrypha, the tradition of this work is very manifold. 'Theological interests and popular piety saw to it that the text of these writings could not be stabilised to the same extent as the text of the canonical Gospels' (Köster, ANRW 25/2, 1483). This statement, intended with reference to many apocryphal gospels, applies in a special way to the Protevangelium of James. Since the work was evidently accepted very early into 'liturgical' collective manuscripts, it has survived in a large number of manuscripts and many versions. A brief survey will bring to view the most important branches of this tradition.

a) The edition of the Greek text by Tischendorf (Ea, pp. 1-50) was for a long time the standard edition, which also formed the basis for later editions (E. Amman, *Le Protévangile de Jacques et ses remaniements latins*, Paris 1910; C. Michel, *Evangiles apocryphes I*, ²1924, 1-51; de Santos⁶ pp. 120-170). The discovery of some papyrus fragments (PSI 6 and PGrenfell II 8: cf. E. de Strycker, *La forme la plus ancienne du Protévangile de Jacques. Recherches sur le Papyrus Bodmer 5 avec une édition critique du texte et une traduction annotée*, SHG 33, 1961, pp. 34f.) and also of two palimpsest leaves (cf. de Strycker, *op. cit.* p. 35) made no difference to that.

It was only with the discovery of the Papyrus Bodmer 5 (edition: M. Testuz, *Papyrus Bodmer V. Nativité de Marie*, 1958; the papyrus is probably to be dated to the 4th cent. rather than to the 3rd, as by Testuz) that a new phase began in research into the Greek tradition. In 1961 E. de Strycker published his great investigation (for title, see above), in which he wrought the printed Greek texts and the versions into a text which was intended to present 'the most ancient form'. In the process the significance of PBodmer 5 was certainly rated very high, but it was not overestimated. Thus de Strycker was able on the one hand to correct many errors in Testuz' edition, and on the other to show that some development of the text had already preceded the Bodmer papyrus. 'The redaction of the Bodmer Papyrus is the result of an early and unintelligent abridgement' (*op. cit.* p. 391).¹

This 'provisional' edition by de Strycker is at present probably the best edition and also the appropriate basis for work on the Protevangelium Jacobi. E. de Strycker himself has in the interval published a list of the 140 Greek manuscripts so far taken up by him ('Die griechischen Handschriften des Protevangeliums Jacobi', in D. Harlfinger (ed.), *Griechische Kodikologie und Textüberlieferung*, 1980, pp. 577-612). Here he has evaluated in particular the work of A. Ehrhardt, *Überlieferung und Bestand der homiletischen und hagiographischen Literatur der griechischen Kirche von den Anfängen bis zum Ende des 16.Jh.* (first part in three volumes: TU 50; 51; 52, 1938-1952). For the Protevangelium is handed down above all in hagiographical manuscripts. By classifying this mass of material into several families, de Strycker has laid a solid foundation for further work.

b) The *Syriac* translation, of which we have four manuscripts (in part, however, fragmentary), probably originated in the 5th century. It can claim a great significance, alongside PBodmer, since here we have a text older that the 6th century, even if the quality of the text is not so good as that of PBodmer 5. On this version cf. de Strycker, *La forme*, pp. 35f., 353-355.

c) The *Georgian* version is preserved in a palimpsest of the 7th century (c. IX.1-XVIII.2) and another codex from the year 983: G. Garitte, 'Le 'Protévangile de Jacques' en géorgien', *Muséon* 70, 1957, 233-265; J.N. Birdsall, 'A Second Georgian Recension of the Protevangelium Jacobi', *Muséon* 83, 1970, 49-72.

d) We knew of a *Latin* translation through extracts included in other works (cf. de Strycker, *La forme*, pp. 39-41 and 363-371; J.A. de Aldama, 'Fragmentos de una versión latina del Protevangelio de Santiago y una nueva adaptación de sus primeros capitulos', *Biblica* 43, 1962, 57-74).

In the meantime there is now a manuscript of the 9th century, which contains c. VIII.1-XXV.2 (with lacunae): E. de Strycker, 'Une ancienne version latine du Protévangile de Jacques avec des extraits de la Vulgate de Matthieu 1-2 et Luc 1-2', *Anal. Boll.* 83, 1965, 365-402. Cf. also J. Gijsel, 'Het Protevangelium Jacobi in het Latijn', *L'antiquité classique* 50, 1981, 351-366.

In connection with the Latin version we may also mention the *Irish* tradition, which indeed presupposes a Latin version. Cf. on this M. McNamara, *The Apocrypha in the Irish Church*, Dublin 1975.

e) An *Armenian* version is preserved in two complete manuscripts (15/16th and 13/14th cent.); in addition there is a fragmentary manuscript of the 12/13th cent. The translation possibly originated in the 6th or 7th century. Cf. on this de Strycker, *La forme*, pp. 37 and 355-359; as an appendix to de Strycker, H. Quecke has translated into Latin the three texts handed down (pp. 441-473).

f) One *Arabic* version has so far been published from a 10th-century manuscript: G. Garitte, ''Protevangelii Jacobi' versio arabica antiquior', *Muséon* 86, 1973, 377-396. The translation appears to have been made directly from a Greek *Vorlage*. Cf. also G. Graf, *Geschichte der christlichen arabischen Literatur I*, 1944, 224-225.

g) Of a *Coptic* version (Sahidic) there are only two fragments (10th and 11th cent.). Cf. de Strycker, *La forme*, pp. 38f. and 363.

h) An *Ethiopic* translation, which is however more a paraphrase, is available in M. Chaine's edition (CSCO, ser. aeth. I, vol. VII, 1909). Cf. on this de Strycker, *La forme*, pp. 38 and 361-363.

i) The Protevangelium must have enjoyed especial popularity in the *Slavonic* area. A. de Santos Otero lists 169 Church Slavonic manuscripts of this work: *Die handschriftliche Überlieferung der altslavische Apokryphen II*, PTS 23, 1981, 4-32. There is still no investigation of this extensive material in regard to its value for the history of the tradition.

This brief survey shows how widely the Protevangelium circulated in the eastern area of the Church. In the West it evidently did not gain such prevalence. Here on the one hand its early condemnation hindered its dissemination, while on the other the material in this work was at an early date incorporated into the Latin Gospel of pseudo-Matthew (see below, pp. 457 ff.).

It has probably also now become clear that the constitution of a secure 'original text' will be a very difficult matter. This task still awaits a solution.

The most important *editions* of the text have been listed above.

Literature: *Translations:* James, pp. 38-49 (English); de Santos[6], pp. 130-170 (Spanish); Moraldi I, 57-90 (Italian); Erbetta, I/ 2. 7-43 (Italian).

Detailed bibliographies: in de Santos, Moraldi and Erbetta.

Older literature: in A. Meyer, NTApoHdb pp. 106ff. and NTApo[2], pp. 84f. H.R. Smid, *Protevangelium Jacobi. A Commentary.* Trans. by G.E. van Baaren-Pape, (Apocrypha Novi Testamenti I), Assen 1965. Fr. Manns, *Essais sur le Judéo-Christianisme,* (Studium Biblicum Franciscanum Analecta 12), Jerusalem 1977, pp. 69-144. A. Fuchs, *Konkordanz zum Protevangelium des Jacobus,* (Studien zum NT und seiner Umwelt B 3), Linz 1978. Vielhauer, *Lit. gesch.* pp. 667-672. H. Köster in ANRW 25/2, 1483f.

2. Title and contents: the familiar designation 'Protevangelium' is not old. It is to Postel and Neander that it owes its established position. PBodmer 5 has 'Birth of Mary. Revelation of James', the later Greek manuscripts mostly 'Story', 'History' or 'Account' and then, either with or without mention of James, give the contents, which they usually describe as 'Birth of Saint Mary, Mother of God'. The Syriac translation bears the title 'Birth of our Lord and our Lady Mary'. Origen mentions our document as 'Book of James' (on the title cf. de Strycker, *La forme*, pp. 208-216).

Although it reaches the birth of Jesus and recounts it, it is really much more an account of the miraculous birth of Mary, the daughter of the wealthy Joachim and his wife Anne, her upbringing in the Temple and her virginity, which is not impaired by the widower Joseph, to whom she is entrusted by lot, and by the birth of Jesus. Chapters 22-24 recount the murder of Zacharias, who is identified with the father of the Baptist.[2]

3. Author and date: according to his own testimony the author purports to be James, who wrote the book after the death of Herod (the Great; or Herod Agrippa, as the necessity for the author's flight might suggest). By this James is probably meant the Lord's brother, who according to the Protev. was Joseph's son by a former marriage. This appears to have been the most widespread assumption, although the Greek Fathers, probably because of their reservations with regard to the content, speak of 'a certain James'. The Decretum Gelasianum, which condemns the writing, appears to know it under the name of James the younger (cf. Mk. 15:40).

In reality the book cannot have been written before 150. It presupposes the canonical infancy stories, is certainly not to be regarded as their source, scarcely goes back to a written source common to both, and probably - apart perhaps from isolated passages - was not originally composed in Hebrew. Certainly it makes very free use of the stories familiar from Mt. and Lk., probably to some extent following oral tradition (birth of Jesus in a cave at Bethlehem). The formation of the canon thus cannot yet have reached a conclusion. Since Origen certainly, and Clement of Alexandria probably, knew our document, and Justin shows very close contacts with its ideas (birth in the cave, Davidic descent of Mary), we may probably go back, so far as its roots are concerned, to the second half of the 2nd century, although we must regard several chapters as later additions (see below). We cannot deduce a Jewish-Christian origin for the author from the content. On the contrary, ignorance of the geography of Palestine and of Jewish customs (expulsion of Joachim for childlessness, upbringing of Mary in the Temple) could point rather to a non-Jew.

4. Unity of the work: the basic document appears to have used materials already shaped, of varying provenance, and combined them together, as is indicated by divers discrepancies which the manuscripts attempt to harmonise. In particular this popular work must already have undergone supplementary expansion at an early date. In the impressive description of the cessation of nature at the moment of Jesus' birth, found in the text previously known, Joseph suddenly speaks in the first person (18.2). It was always a very natural conjecture that this passage, deriving from another source, was only later incorporated into our narrative. This seems to be confirmed by the fact that it is missing from P. Bodmer 5. The late manuscripts (at 20.2) also have a prayer of Salome (probably added only secondarily to the midwife as a witness to the virginity of Mary) as well as some unimportant details not known to P. Bodmer 5. Although the text of the papyrus sometimes appears to show later abbreviations, such passages also do not actually belong to the original text. But certainly P. Bodmer 5 itself already shows very clear traces of later expansion of a basic document which probably consisted of chapters 1-20, the narrative of the birth and childhood of Mary and also the birth of Jesus. Thus it can be shown that the murder of Zacharias reported in chapters 22-24 probably did not yet belong to the book in the time of Origen, for although he cites the work in connection with a reference to Joseph's first marriage, he gives at another point a version completely different from what is reported in chapters 22ff. of the reason for Zacharias' death (see A. Berendts, *Studien über Zacharias-Apokryphen und Zacharias-Legenden*, 1895; id. *Die handschriftliche Überlieferung der Zacharias- und Johannes-Apokryphen*, (TU 26.3), 1904). The story is thus a later addition to the Protev., on the analogy of the combination of the John and Jesus traditions known from Luke. The question whether the entire middle section (chapters 17-21) about the birth of Jesus was only added later to the Mary narrative proper, a view which has in its favour the difference of motif, cannot be resolved with any certainty, since here there is in any case a closer connection (on the problem of the unity of the Protev. Jac. cf. especially the thorough investigations of E. de Strycker)

5. Literary style and theological character: the work has great merit, especially in comparison with the later infancy gospels. The borrowing of legendary details (with the exception of the story of the midwife) is comparatively restrained. The whole presentation is impressive and extremely graphic, and is evidence of a sober, sincere and poetic mind. If the author has used sources from oral and literary Christian tradition, and especially much material from the Old Testament, in particular the story of Samuel, he has yet understood how to combine them into an artistic whole. Only where apologetic requires it does he not hesitate to retain crude and even distasteful features.

The whole was written for the glorification of Mary. Not only are Jewish calumnies (see above, p. 417) by implication vigorously refuted, but all the future themes of Mariology are already propounded: the 'immaculate conception' of the mother of Jesus is not indeed yet taught, but her birth, in itself miraculous, is recorded. The virgin birth of Jesus, in contrast to the more unbiassed views of Tertullian and Origen, is already understood as implying Mary's perpetual virginity. This is harmonised with the existence of brothers of Jesus in the primitive tradition by postulating an earlier marriage of Joseph, an explanation which was accepted as plausible down to the time of Jerome. Yet this very assumption provoked Jerome, who wished to have the brothers of Jesus regarded as his cousins, into a sharp polemic against the Protev. of James, which was then taken up by the popes. In the Eastern Church the book was popular from the beginning: first above all among the Ebionites, but also among the Greek Fathers, and in the Syrian, Coptic and Armenian churches it was highly valued because of its praise of the ideal of virginity.

On the one hand we see, then, that devotion to Mary had already made considerable advances even at the comparatively early date when the book was written, and that features which in the primitive tradition are reserved for Jesus are transferred to Mary. On the other hand, both in East and West the Protev., although never regarded as canonical and indeed even condemned in the West, had a powerful influence on the development of Mariology. Apart from its importance for catholic devotion and art, its doctrinal importance in the narrower sense in connection with recent developments of catholicism cannot be sufficiently emphasised.

The following translation is based on the editions of Tischendorf and de Strycker, with special consideration of PBodmer 5. Naturally we cannot list the numerous variants, which de Strycker presents in his (provisional) edition. Square brackets [ ] indicate textual variants (especially differences between Tischendorf and PBodmer 5). Round brackets ( ) indicate explanatory supplements.

Notes

1. The Protevangelium of James

1. A further papyrus fragment (6th cent.) with a few lines from chapter 25 was published in 1983: POx 3524 (*The Oxyrhynchos Papyri*, L, London 1983, 8-12; references also there to two other unpublished papyrus fragments).
2. On the question of the *Gattung* to which the Protevangelium Jacobi should be assigned, Vielhauer notes: 'In terms of *Gattung* the Protevangelium of James does not belong to the gospels; it also does not itself make this claim. It is only traditionally discussed in the context of the gospels because it has for its subject persons and events of NT pre-history. In terms of *Gattung* it is a collection of personal legends, a garland of legends' (*Lit. gesch.* 672). For a somewhat different view of things cf. Köster, ANRW 25 2, 1483f.

The Birth of Mary
(The History of James)

BAC
148:
130-70

1. 1. In the 'Histories of the Twelve Tribes of Israel' Joachim was a very rich (man), and he brought all his gifts for the Lord twofold; for he said in himself: What I bring in excess, shall be for the whole people, and what I bring for forgiveness shall be for the Lord, for a propitiation for me.

2. Now the great day of the Lord drew near and the children of Israel were bringing their gifts. Then they stood before him, and Reubel [Reuben] also, who said: 'It is not fitting for you to offer your gifts first, because you have begotten no offspring in Israel.' 3. Then Joachim became very sad, and went to the record of the twelve tribes of the people [and said]: 'I will search in the record of the twelve tribes of Israel, whether I am the only one who has not begotten offspring in Israel.' And he searched and found of all the righteous that they had raised up offspring in Israel. And he remembered the patriarch Abraham that in his last days God gave him a son, Isaac. 4. And Joachim was very sad, and did not show himself to his wife, but betook himself into the wilderness; there he pitched his tent and fasted *forty days and forty nights*;[1] and he said to himself; 'I shall not go down either for food or for drink until the Lord my God visits me; prayer shall be my *food* and drink.'[2]

2. 1. Meanwhile Anna his wife uttered a twofold lamentation and gave voice to a twofold bewailing: 'I will bewail my widowhood, and bewail my childlessness.'

2. Now the great day of the Lord grew near, and Euthine [Judith] her maidservant said to her: 'How long do you humble your soul, for the great day of the Lord is near, and you ought not to mourn. But take this headband, which the mistress of the work gave me; it is not fitting for me to wear it, because I am your slave and it bears a royal mark.'

3. But Anna said: 'Away from me! That I will never do. It is the Lord who has greatly humbled me. Who knows whether a deceiver did not give it to you, and you have come to make me share in your sin!' Euthine [Judith] answered: 'Why should I curse you because you have not listened to me? The Lord God has *shut up your womb*,[3] to give you no fruit in Israel.'

4. And Anna was very sad; but she put off her mourning-garments, cleansed her head, put on her bridal garments, and about the ninth hour went into her garden to walk there. And she saw a laurel tree and sat down beneath it and [after she had rested] implored the Lord, saying: 'O God of our fathers, bless me and hear my prayer, as thou didst bless the womb of Sarah [our mother Sarah] and gavest her a son, Isaac.'[4]

3. 1. And Anna sighed towards heaven, and saw a nest of sparrows in the laurel tree and immediately she made lamentation within herself:

'Woe to me, who begot me,

What womb brought me forth?

For I was born as a curse [before them all and] before the children of Israel,

And I was reproached, and they mocked me and thrust me out of the Temple of the Lord.

2. Woe, is me, to what am I likened?

I am not likened to the birds of the heaven;

for even the birds of the heaven are fruitful before thee, O Lord.

Woe is me, to what am I likened?

I am not likened to the unreasoning animals;

for even the unreasoning animals are fruitful before thee, O Lord.

Woe is to me, to what am I likened?

I am not likened to the beasts of the earth;

for even the beasts of the earth are fruitful before thee, O Lord.

3. Woe is me, to what am I likened?

I am not likened to these waters;

for even these waters gush forth merrily, and their fish praise thee, O Lord.

Woe is me, to what am I likened?

I am not likened to this earth;

for even this earth *brings forth its fruit in its season*[5] and praises thee, O Lord.'

4. 1. And *behold an angel of the Lord came to her*[6] and said: 'Anna, Anna, *the Lord has heard your prayer. You shall conceive and bear,*[7] and your offspring shall be spoken of in the whole world.' And Anna said: '*As the Lord my God lives,*[8] if I bear a child, whether male or female, I will *bring it as a gift to the Lord my God,*[9] and it shall *serve him all the days of its life.*'[10]

2. And behold there came two messengers, who said to her: 'Behold, Joachim your husband is coming with his flocks; for an angel of the Lord came down to him and said to him: 'Joachim, Joachim, the Lord God has *heard your prayer.*[11] Go down; behold, your wife Anna has conceived [*shall conceive*].''[12] 3. And immediately Joachim went down and called his herdsmen and said: 'Bring me ten lambs without blemish and without spot; they shall belong to the Lord my God. And bring me twelve [tender] calves, and the twelve calves shall be for the priests and the elders, and a hundred kids, and the hundred kids shall be for the whole people.' 4. And behold Joachim came with his flocks, and Anna stood at the gate and saw Joachim coming and ran immediately and hung on his neck, saying: 'Now I know that the Lord God has richly blessed me [thee]; for behold

the widow is no longer a widow, and I, who was childless,[13] have conceived [shall conceive].'

And Joachim rested the first day in his house.

5. 1. But the next day he offered his gifts, saying in himself: 'If the Lord God is gracious to me the frontlet of the priest[14] will make it clear to me.'

And Joachim offered his gifts, and observed the priest's frontlet when he went up to the altar of the Lord; and he saw no sin in himself. And Joachim said: 'Now I know that the Lord God is gracious to me and has forgiven all my sins.' And *he went down* from the Temple of the Lord *justified, and went to his house.*[15]

2. And her six months [her months] were fulfilled, as (the angel) had said: in the seventh [ninth] month Anna brought forth. And she said to the midwife: 'What have I brought forth?' And the midwife said: 'A female.' And Anna said: '*My soul*[16] is magnified this day.' And she laid it down. And when the days were fulfilled, Anna purified herself from her childbed and gave suck to the child, and called her name Mary.

6. 1. Day by day the child *waxed strong;*[17] when she was six months old her mother stood her on the ground to try if she could stand. And she walked seven steps and came to her mother's bosom. And she took her up, saying: '*As the Lord my God lives,*[18] you shall walk no more upon this ground until I take you into the Temple of the Lord.' And she made a sanctuary in her bedchamber, and did not permit anything common or unclean to pass through it. And she summoned the undefiled daughters of the Hebrews, and they cared for her amusement.

2. On the child's first birthday Joachim made a *great feast,*[19] and invited the chief priests and the priests and the scribes and the elders and the whole people of Israel. And Joachim brought the child to the priests, and they blessed her, saying: 'O God of our fathers, bless this child and give her a name renowned for ever *among all generations.*'[20] And all the people said: 'So be it, [so be it] Amen.' And they brought her to the chief priests, and they blessed her, saying: 'O God of the heavenly heights, look upon this child and bless her with a supreme and unsurpassable blessing.' And her mother carried her into the sanctuary of her bedchamber and gave her suck. And Anna sang this song to the Lord God:[21]

'I will sing a [holy] song to the Lord my God,

for he has visited me and *taken away from me the reproach*[22] of my enemies.[23]

And the Lord gave me the *fruit of righteousness,*[24] unique and manifold before him.

Who will proclaim to the sons of Reubel [Reuben] that Anna gives suck?[25]

[Hearken, hearken, you twelve tribes of Israel: Anna gives suck]'.

And she laid the child down to rest in the bedchamber with its

428

sanctuary, and went out and served them. When the feast was ended they went down rejoicing and glorified the God of Israel.

7. 1. The months passed, and the child grew. When she was two years old, Joachim said to Anna: 'Let us bring her up to the Temple of the Lord,[26] that we may fulfil the promise which we made, lest the Lord send (some evil) upon us and our gift become unacceptable.' And Anna replied: 'Let us wait until the third year,[27] that the child may not long after her father and mother.' And Joachim said: 'Very well.'

2. And when the child was three years old, Joachim said: 'Let us call the undefiled daughters of the Hebrews, and let each one take a lamp, and let these be burning, in order that the child may not turn back and her heart be enticed away from the Temple of the Lord.' And he did so until they went up to the Temple of the Lord. And the priest took her and kissed her and blessed her, saying: 'The Lord has magnified your name among all generations; because of you the Lord at the end of the days[28] will manifest his redemption to the children of Israel.'

3. And he placed her on the third step of the altar, and the Lord God put grace upon the child, and she danced for joy with her feet, and *the whole house of Israel loved her.*[29]

8. 1. And her parents went down wondering, praising and glorifying the almighty God because the child did not *turn back*[30] [to them]. And Mary was in the Temple nurtured like a dove and received food from the hand of an angel.

2. When she was twelve years old, there took place a council of the priests, saying: 'Behold, Mary has become twelve years old in the Temple of the Lord. What then shall we do with her, that she may not pollute the sanctuary of the Lord [our God]?' And they [the priests] said to the high priest [to him]: 'You stand at the altar of the Lord; enter (the sanctuary) and pray concerning her, and what the Lord shall reveal to you will do.'

3. And the high priest took the vestment with the twelve bells and went into the Holy of Holies and prayed concerning her. And behold, an angel of the Lord (suddenly) stood before him and said to him: 'Zacharias, Zacharias, go out and assemble[31] the widowers of the people, [who *shall each bring a rod*[32]], and to whomsoever the Lord shall give a (miraculous) sign, his wife she shall be.' And the heralds went forth and spread out through all the surrounding country of Judaea; the trumpet of the Lord sounded, and all ran to it.

9. 1. And Joseph threw down his axe and went out to meet them. And when they were gathered together, they took the rods and went to the high priest. The priest took the rods from them and *entered*[33] the Temple and prayed. When he had finished the prayer he took the rods, and went out (again) and gave them to them: but there was no sign on them. Joseph received the last rod, and behold, a dove came out of the rod and flew on

to Joseph's head.[34] And the priest said to Joseph: 'Joseph, to you has fallen the good fortune to receive the virgin of the Lord; take her under your care.'

2. (But) Joseph answered him: 'I (already) have sons and am old, but she is a girl. I fear lest I should become a laughing-stock to the children of Israel.' And the priest said to Joseph: 'Fear the Lord thy God, and remember all that God did to Dathan, Abiram and Korah, how the earth was rent open and they were all swallowed up because of their rebellion.[35] And now fear, Joseph, lest this happen (also) in your house.' And Joseph was afraid, and took her under his care. And Joseph said to her: 'Mary, I have received you from the Temple of the Lord, and now I leave you in my house and go away to build [my] buildings; (afterwards) I will come (again) to you; the Lord will watch over you.'

10. 1. Now there was a council of the priests, who resolved: 'Let us make a veil for the Temple of the Lord.' And the priest said: 'Call to me the pure virgins of the tribe of David.' And the officers departed and searched, and they found seven (such) virgins. And the priest remembered the child Mary, that she was of the tribe of David and was pure before God. And the officers went and fetched her.

2. Then they brought them into the Temple of the Lord, and the priest said: 'Cast me lots, who shall weave the gold, the amiant, the linen, the silk, the hyacinth-blue, the scarlet and the pure purple.'[36] And to Mary fell the lot of the 'pure purple' and 'scarlet'. And she took them and went away to her house. At that time *Zacharias became dumb*,[37] and Samuel took his place until Zacharias was able to speak (again). But Mary took the scarlet and spun it.

11. 1. And she took the pitcher and went forth to draw water, and behold, a voice said: *'Hail, thou that art highly favoured, the Lord is with thee, blessed art thou among women.'*[38] And she looked around on the right and on the left to see whence this voice came. And trembling she went to her house and put down the pitcher and took the purple and sat down on her seat and drew out (the thread).

2. And behold an angel of the Lord (suddenly) stood before her and said: *'Do not fear, Mary; for you have found grace* before the Lord of all things *and shall conceive of his Word.'*[39] When she heard this she doubted in herself and said: 'Shall I conceive of the Lord, the living God, [and bear] as every woman bears?'

3. *And the angel of the Lord came and said to her*: 'Not so, Mary; for *a power* of the Lord *shall overshadow you; wherefore also that holy thing which is born of you shall be called the Son of the Highest.*[40] *And you shall call his name Jesus; for he shall save his people from their sins.'*[41] And Mary said: *'Behold, (I am) the handmaid of the Lord before him: be it to me according to your word.'*[42]

12. 1. And she made (ready) the purple and the scarlet and brought (them) to the priest. And the priest took (them), and blessed (Mary) and said: 'Mary, the Lord God has magnified your name, and *you shall be blessed among all generations of the earth.*'[43]

2. And Mary rejoiced, and went to Elizabeth her kinswoman,[44] and knocked on the door. *When Elizabeth heard it,*[45] she put down the scarlet, and ran to the door and opened it, [and when she saw Mary[, she blessed her and said: '*Whence is this to me, that the mother of my Lord should come to me?*[46] *For behold, that which is in me leaped*[47] and blessed thee.' But Mary forgot the mysteries which the [arch[angel Gabriel had told her, and raised a sigh towards heaven and said: 'Who am I, [Lord], that all the women [generations] of the earth count me blessed?'[48]

3. And she remained *three months with Elizabeth.*[49] Day by day her womb grew, and Mary was afraid and went *into her house and hid herself*[50] from the children of Israel. And Mary was sixteen years old when all these mysterious things happened [to her].

13. 1. Now when she was in her sixth month, behold, Joseph came from his building and entered his house and found her with child. And he smote his face, threw himself down on sackcloth, and wept bitterly, saying: 'With what countenance shall I look towards the Lord my God? What prayer shall I offer for her [for this maiden]? For I received her as a virgin out of the Temple of the Lord my God and have not protected her. Who has deceived me? Who has done this evil in my house and defiled her (the virgin)? Has the story [of Adam] been repeated in me? for as Adam was (absent) in the hour of his prayer and *the serpent came and found Eve alone and deceived her*[51] and defiled her, so also has it happened to me.'

2. And Joseph stood up from the sackcloth and called her [Mary] and said to her: 'You who are cared for by God, why have you done this and forgotten the Lord your God? Why have you humiliated your soul, you who were brought up in the Holy of Holies and received food from the hand of an angel?'

3. But she wept bitterly, saying: 'I am pure, and know not a man.'[52] And Joseph said to her: 'Whence then is this in your womb?' And she said: '*As the Lord my God lives,*[53] I do not know whence it has come to me.'

14. 1. And Joseph feared greatly and parted from her, pondering what he should do with her. And Joseph said: 'If I conceal her sin, I shall be found opposing the law of the Lord. If I expose her to the children of Israel, I fear lest that which is in her may have sprung from the angels and I should be found *delivering up innocent blood* to the judgment of death.[54] What then shall I do with her? *I will put her away secretly.*'[55] And the night came upon him.

2. And behold, *an angel of the Lord appeared to him in a dream, saying:* 'Do not fear *because of this child. For that which is in her is of the Holy Spirit. She shall bear* [to you] *a son, and you shall call his name Jesus; for he shall save his people from* their sins.'[56] And *Joseph arose from sleep* and glorified the God of Israel who had bestowed his [this] grace upon him, and he kept watch over her [the maiden].[57]

15. 1. And Annas the scribe came to him and said to him: 'Joseph, why did you not appear in our assembly?' And Joseph said to him: 'I was weary from the journey, and I rested the first day.' And Annas turned and saw that Mary was with child.

2. And he went hastily to the priest and said to him: 'Joseph, for whom you are a witness, has grievously transgressed.' And the high priest said: 'In what way?' And he said: 'The virgin whom he received from the Temple of the Lord, he has defiled, and has stolen marriage with her, and has not disclosed it to the children of Israel.' And the high priest said to him: 'Joseph has done this?' And [Annas] said to him: 'Send officers, and you will find the virgin with child.' And the officers went and found her as he had said, and brought her to the Temple. And she stood before the court. And the priest said to her: 'Mary, why have you done this? Why have you humiliated your soul and forgotten the Lord your God, you who were brought up in the Holy of Holies, and received food from the hand of angels and heard their hymns of praise and danced before them? Why have you done this?' But she wept bitterly, saying: '*As the Lord my God lives*,[58] I am pure before him and I know not a man.' And the high priest said: 'Joseph, why have you done this?' And Joseph said: '*As the Lord my God lives* [and Christ lives and the witness of his truth], I am pure concerning her.' And the high priest said: 'Do not give false witness, but speak the truth. You have stolen marriage with her [consummated your marriage in secret], and have not disclosed it to the children of Israel, and have not *bowed* your head *under the mighty hand*[59] in order that your seed might be blessed.' And Joseph was silent.

16. 1. And the high priest said: 'Give back the virgin whom you received from the Temple of the Lord.' And Joseph wept bitterly. And the high priest said: 'I will give you the water of the conviction of the Lord to drink and it will make manifest your sins before your eyes.'[60]

2. And the high priest took (it) and gave (it) to Joseph to drink and sent him into the wilderness [into the hill-country]; and he came (back) whole. And he made Mary also drink, and sent her into the wilderness [into the hill-country]; and she (also) returned whole. And all the people marvelled, because (the water) had not revealed any sin in them. And the high priest said: 'If the Lord God has not made manifest your sins, neither do I condemn you.'[61] And he released them. And Joseph took Mary and departed to his house, rejoicing and glorifying the God of Israel.

17. 1. *Now there went out a decree from* the king *Augustus that all* (inhabitants) of Bethlehem in Judaea *should be enrolled.*[62] And Joseph said: 'I shall enroll my sons, but what shall I do with this child? How shall I enroll her? As my wife? I am ashamed to do that. Or as my daughter? But all the children of Israel know that she is not my daughter. The day of the Lord itself will do as [t]he [Lord] wills.'

2. And he saddled his ass [his she-ass] and sat her on it; his son led it, and Samuel [Joseph] followed. And they drew near to the third mile(stone). And Joseph turned round and saw her sad, and said within himself: 'Perhaps that which is within her is paining her.' And again Joseph turned round and saw her laughing. And he said to her: 'Mary, why is it that I see your face at one time laughing and at another sad?' And she said to him: 'Joseph, I see with my eyes *two peoples*,[63] one weeping and lamenting and one rejoicing and exulting.'

3. And they came half the way, and Mary said to him: 'Joseph, take me down from the ass [from the she-ass], for the child within me presses me, to come forth.' And he took her down there and said to her: 'Where shall I take you and hide your shame? For the place is desert.'

18. 1. And he found a cave there and brought her into it, and left her in the care of his sons and went out to seek for a Hebrew midwife in the region of Bethlehem.

2. [Now I, Joseph, was walking about, and (yet) I did not walk. And I looked up to the vault of heaven, and saw it standing still, and I looked up to the air, and saw the air in amazement, and the birds of heaven remain motionless. And I looked at the earth, and saw a dish placed there and workmen lying round it, with their hands in the dish. But those who chewed did not chew, and those who lifted up anything lifted up nothing, and those who put something to their mouth put nothing (to their mouth), but all had their faces turned upwards. And behold, sheep were being driven and (yet) they did not come forward, but stood still; and the shepherd raised his hand to strike them [with his staff], but his hand remained up. And I looked at the flow of the river, and saw the mouths of the kids over it and they did not drink. And then all at once everything went on its course (again).]

(P. Bodmer)

19. 1. And he found one who was just coming down from the hill-country, and he took her with him, and said to the midwife: 'Mary is betrothed to me; but she conceived of the Holy Spirit after she had been brought up in the Temple of the Lord.'

(Tischendorf)

And behold, a woman came down from the hill-country and said to me: 'Man, where are you going?' And I said: 'I seek a Hebrew midwife.' And she answered me: 'Are you from Israel?' And I said to her: 'Yes.' And she said: 'And who is she who brings forth in the cave?'

And I said: 'My betrothed.' And she said to me: 'Is she not your wife?' And I said to her: 'She is Mary, who was brought up in the Temple of the Lord, and I received her by lot as my wife. And (yet) she is not my wife, but she has conceived of the Holy Spirit.' And the midwife said to him: 'Is this true?' And Joseph said to her: 'Come and see.'

And the midwife went with him. 2. And they went to the place of the cave, and behold, *a* dark [*bright*] *cloud overshadowed*[64] the cave. And the midwife said: 'My soul is magnified to-day, *for my eyes have seen wonderful things; for salvation is born to Israel.*'[65] And immediately the cloud disappeared from the cave, and a great light appeared in the cave,[66] so that our eyes could not bear it. A short time afterwards that light withdrew until the child appeared, and it went and took the breast of its mother Mary. And the midwife cried: 'How great is this day for me, that I have seen this new sight.' 3. And the midwife came out of the cave, and Salome met her. And she said to her: 'Salome, Salome, I have a new sight to tell you; a virgin has brought forth, a thing which her nature does not allow.' And Salome said: *'As the Lord my God lives,*[67] *unless I put (forward) my finger*[68] and test her condition, I will not believe that a virgin has brought forth.'

20. 1. And Salome went in and made her ready	1. And the midwife went in and said to Mary: 'Make yourself ready, for there is no small contention concerning you.' [And when Mary heard this, she made herself ready.]

And Salome put forward her finger

And Salome put forward her finger to test her condition. And she cried out, saying:

'Woe for my wickedness and my unbelief; for

'I have tempted the living God; and behold, my hand falls away from me, consumed by fire!'

2. And she prayed to the Lord.	2. And Salome bowed her knees before the Lord, saying: 'O God of my fathers, remember me; for I am the seed of Abraham, Isaac and Jacob; do not make me a public

example to the children of Israel, but restore me to the poor. For thou knowest, Lord, that in thy name I perform my duties and from thee I have received my hire.'

3. And behold, an angel of the Lord stood [before Salome] and said to her: 'Salome, God the Lord has heard your prayer. Stretch out your hand to the child and touch him (take him in your arms), so will healing and joy be yours.' And full of joy Salome came to the child, touched him, [and said: I will worship him, for (in him) a great king has been born to Israel.'] And Salome was healed at once [as she had requested], and she went out of the cave [justified[69]]. And behold, an angel of the Lord [a voice] cried: 'Salome, Salome, tell [not] what marvel you have seen, before the child comes to Jerusalem.'

21. 1. And behold, Joseph prepared to go forth to Judaea. And there took place a great tumult in Bethlehem of Judaea. For there came *wise men* saying: '*Where is the* [*new-born*] *king of the Jews? For we have seen his star in the east and have come to worship him.*' 2. When Herod heard this he was troubled and sent officers [to the wise men],

and sent for them and they told him about the star.

and sent for *the high priests* and questioned them: 'How is it written concerning the Messiah? *Where is he born?*' They said to him: '*In Bethlehem of Judaea; for so it is written.*'[70] And he let them go. And he questioned the wise men[71] and said to them: 'What sign did you see concerning the new-born king?' And the wise men said: '*We saw* how an indescribably greater *star* shone among these stars and dimmed them, so that they no longer shone; and so we knew that a king was born for Israel. *And we have come to worship him.*'[72] And Herod said: '*Go and seek, and when you have found him, tell me, that I also may come to worship him.*'[73]

3. And behold, they saw stars in the east, and they went before them

3. And the wise men *went forth. And behold, the star which they had seen in the east, went before them,*

until they came to the cave. And *it stood* over the head of the child [the cave].[74] And the wise men *saw the young child with Mary his mother*, and they took out of their bag gifts, *gold, and frankincense and myrrh*.[75]

4. And being warned by the angel that *they should not* go into Judaea, *they went to their own country by another way*.[76]

22. 1. But when *Herod* perceived *that he had been tricked by the wise men he was angry and sent* his murderers and commanded them *to kill all the children who were two years old and under*.[77]

2. When Mary heard that the children were being killed, she was afraid and took the child and *wrapped him in swaddling clothes and laid him in an ox-manger*.[78]

3. But Elizabeth, when she heard that John was sought for, took him and went up into the hill-country. And she looked around (to see) where she could hide him, and there was no hiding-place. And Elizabeth groaned aloud and said: 'O mountain of God, receive me, a mother, with my child.' For Elizabeth could not go up (further) for fear. And immediately the mountain was rent asunder and received her. And that mountain made a light to gleam for her; for an angel of the Lord was with them and protected them.

23. 1. Now Herod was searching for John, and sent officers to Zacharias at the altar to ask him: 'Where have you hidden your son?' And he answered and said to them: 'I am a minister of God and attend continually upon his Temple. How should I know where my son is?'

2. And the officers departed and told all this to Herod. Then Herod was angry and said: 'Is his son to be king over Israel?' And he sent the officers to him again with the command: 'Tell the truth. Where is your son? You know that your blood is under my hand.' And the officers departed and told him [all] this.

3. And Zacharias said: 'I am a martyr of God. Take my blood! But my spirit the Lord will receive,[79] for you shed innocent blood in the forecourt of the Temple of the Lord.'[80] And about the dawning of the day Zacharias was slain. And the children of Israel did not know that he had been slain.

24. 1. Rather, at the hour of the salutation the priests were departing, but the blessing of Zacharias did not meet them according to custom. And the priests stood *waiting for Zacharias*, to greet him with prayer and to glorify God the Most High.

2. But when he *delayed to come*,[81] they were all afraid. But one of them took courage and went into the sanctuary. And he saw beside the altar of the Lord[82] congealed blood; and a voice said: 'Zacharias has been slain, and his blood shall not be wiped away until his avenger comes.' And when he heard these words, he was afraid, and went out and told the priests what he had seen [and heard].

3. And they heard and saw what had happened. and the panel-work of the ceiling of the Temple wailed, and they *rent* their clothes *from the top to the bottom.*[83] And they did not find his body, but they found his blood turned into stone. And they were afraid, and went out and told [all the people]: 'Zacharias has been slain.' And all the tribes of the people heard it and mourned him and lamented[84] three days and three nights.

4. And after the three days the priests took counsel whom they should appoint in his [Zacharias'] stead. And the lot fell upon *Symeon*. Now it was he to whom *it had been revealed by the Holy Spirit that he should not see death until he had seen the Christ in the flesh.*[85]

25. 1. Now I, James, who wrote this history, when a tumult arose in Jerusalem on the death of Herod, withdrew into the wilderness until the tumult in Jerusalem ceased. And I will praise the Lord, who gave me the wisdom to write this history. Grace shall be with all those who fear the Lord.

[Nativity of Mary. Apocalypse of James. Peace be to him who wrote and to him who reads!]

Notes

The Birth of Mary

1. Mt. 4:2 (Lk. 4:2); cf. Exod. 24:18; 34:28; 1 Kings 19:8.
2. Jn. 4:34.
3. Cf. 1 Sam. 1:6.
4. Gen. 21:1-3.
5. Cf. Ps. 1:3.
6. Cf. Lk. 2:9; Acts 12:7.
7. Lk. 1:13; Gen. 16:11; Jud. 13:3, 5, 7; 1 Sam 1:20.
8. Jud. 8:19; cf. 1 Sam. 1:26.
9. 1 Sam. 1:11.
10. 1 Sam. 2:11; 1:28.
11. Lk. 1:13; See n. 7.
12. Cf. Lk. 1:31.
13. Cf. Isa. 54:1.
14. Exod. 28:36-38.
15. Cf. Lk. 18:14.
16. Cf. Lk. 1:46.
17. Cf. Lk. 2:40.
18. See above, note 8.
19. Cf. Gen. 21:8.
20. Cf. Lk. 1:48.
21. Cf. 1 Sam. 2:1.
22. Gen. 30:23; cf. Lk. 1:25.
23. Cf. Pss. 42:10; 102:8.
24. Cf. Prov. 11:30; 13:2; Am. 6:12; Jas. 3:18.
25. Gen. 21:7.
26. Cf. 1 Sam. 1:21ff.
27. Cf. 1 Sam. 1:22.

28. Cf. 1 Pet. 1:20.
29. Cf. 1 Sam. 18:16.
30. Cf. Gen 19:26.
31. Cf. Num. 17:16-24 (1-9).
32. Num. 17:17(2).
33. Num. 17:23(8).
34. Cf. Mt. 3:16.
35. Num. 16:1, 31-33.
36. Cf. Exod. 35:25; 26:31, 36; 36:35, 37; 2 Chron. 3:14.
37. Cf. Lk. 1:20-22, 64.
38. Lk. 1:28, 42; cf. Jud. 6:12.
39. Lk. 1:30f.
40. Lk. 1:35, 32.
41. Mt. 1:21; Lk. 1:31.
42. Lk. 1:38.
43. Gen. 12:2f.; Lk. 1:42, 48.
44. Lk. 1:39, 36.
45. Lk. 1:41.
46. Lk. 1:43.
47. Lk. 1:44, 41.
48. Lk. 1:48.
49. Lk. 1:56.
50. Lk. 1:56, 24.
51. Gen. 3:13; 2 Cor. 11:3; 1 Tim. 2:14.
52. Lk. 1:34.
53. See above, note 8.
54. Cf. Mt. 27:4.
55. Mt. 1:19.
56. Mt. 1:20f.
57. Mt. 1:24.
58. See above, note 8.
59. Cf. 1 Pet. 5:6.
60. Num. 5:11-31.
61. Cf. Jn. 8:11.
62. Lk. 2:1; Mt. 2:1.
63. Gen. 25:23; cf. Lk. 2:34.
64. Cf. Mt. 17:5.
65. Cf. Lk. 2:30, 32.
66. Isa. 9:2.
67. See above, note 8.
68. Jn. 20:25.
69. Lk. 18:14.
70. Mt. 2:1-5.
71. Mt. 2:7.
72. Mt. 2:2.
73. Mt. 2:8.
74. Mt. 2:9.
75. Mt. 2:11.
76. Mt. 2:12.
77. Mt. 2:16.
78. Lk. 2:7.
79. Cf. Acts 7:59; Lk. 23:46.

80. Cf. 2 Chron. 24:20-22; Mt. 23:35.
81. Cf. Lk. 1:21.
82. Mt. 23:35.
83. Cf. Mt. 27:51.
84. Cf. Zech. 12:10, 12-14.
85. Lk. 2:25f.

2. The Infancy Story of Thomas

1. Transmission, texts and literature: the history of the tradition of this infancy narrative is very complicated, and cannot at the moment be set out unambiguously. The Greek texts, i.e. the versions in the original language, are handed down only in late manuscripts. The numerous versions can contribute to the establishing of the oldest text, but are naturally also influenced by many later tendencies. The attempt by P. Peeters to trace back the different versions of the infancy story of Thomas to a Syriac basic form, which he thought to be specially well represented in a late manuscript (Cod. Vat. Syr. 159, 17th cent.), is untenable (P. Peeters, *Evangiles apocryphes*, vol. II, 1914; for criticism see A. de Santos Otero, *Das kirchenslavische Evangelium des Thomas*, PTS 6, 1967, pp. 148ff.).

Despite the great advance marked by the investigation of the Church Slavonic tradition of this text by de Santos, provision of the 'Urtext', i.e. the version of the 2nd century, is not yet possible. 'A final critical edition is still awaited. But even if such an edition should succeed in reconstructing a text underlying the later manuscripts and translations, the question still remains whether the original infancy gospel can be reconstructed at all, and whether any statements about the date of composition will be possible. For as the 'Epistula Apostolorum' shows, the individual narratives, in this gospel often only loosely strung together, were already freely circulating in the second century' (H. Köster, ANRW 25/2, 1484).[1] This means, however, that the transmission of this text in manuscripts and versions was also partly determined by its literary genre. Since it is a ca_e of 'collected material, which in literary terms is only meagrely held together' (Vielhauer, *Lit. gesch.* p. 674), slight alterations in compass and content could easily be made in the course of transmission.

On the other hand - as the Church Slavonic texts show - there is also a certain stability to be seen in the individual strands of tradition, so that the effort to recover the oldest version is perfectly reasonable. But these questions cannot be discussed in detail here. It must suffice to adduce the different witnesses in a brief survey[2].

a) The *Greek* texts were divided by Tischendorf into two recensions and edited separately. Recension A (Ea, pp. 140-157) is the version contained in two manuscripts (Bologna Univ. 2702 and Dresden 1187, 15/16th cent.). To these may be added the Codex Athous Vatopedi 37, a non-menological hagiographic collection (14th cent.), in which chapters 1-14 are handed down, but which has so far not been evaluated. The fragments in the manuscripts in Paris (Bibl. Nat. gr. 239, 15th cent.) and Vienna (Phil. gr.144, in the meantime lost) were reckoned by Tischendorf to Recension A, but in view of the similarities to the Church

Slavonic version this is probably to be corrected (cf. de Santos, *op. cit.* p. 152).

The version published by A. Delatte also (Greek manuscript no. 355 of the National Library in Athens, from the 15th cent.: *Anecdota Atheniensia I*, Paris-Liege 1927, 264-271) - as comparison with the Latin and the Church Slavonic texts shows - cannot be regarded as evidence for Recension A. The version in Cod. Vat. Palat. 364, to which de Santos draws attention (*Überlieferung* II, p.50 note), seems to belong with this text of Delatte.

Recension B (Ea, pp. 158-163) is a shorter form of the infancy gospel. Tischendorf edited it after a manuscript of the 14/15th century discovered by him in the monastery on Sinai.[3]

This survey shows that the Greek tradition of the infancy gospel of Thomas is thoroughly inadequate and also very far from uniform. After the investigations of de Santos one must say even more: the text edited by Tischendorf as Recension A and widely recognised as a *textus receptus* 'is to be regarded as a later reworking which originated only after the 11th century, and in which essential elements of the old Greek apocryphon have been lost' (de Santos, *op. cit.* p. 158). This statement is however only possible because alongside the meagre Greek tradition we have a series of versions at our disposal.

b) A *Syriac* version is extant in three manuscripts: 1. Cod. Brit. Mus. Add. 14464 (6th cent.), edited with English translation by W. Wright, *Contributions to the Apocryphal Literature of the New Testament*, London 1865 (reprinted in E.A.W. Budge, *The History of the Blessed Virgin Mary etc.* I, London 1899, 217-222). 2. A manuscript from Sinai in the Göttingen University Library (cf. A. Meyer, NTApo[2], p. 94). 3. From the 17th century comes the Cod. Vat. Syr. 159, which Peeters adduced above all as proof of the dependence of all versions of the infancy gospel upon the Syriac text form (cf. above, p. 439). This hypothesis is untenable, but despite this considerable importance attaches to the Syriac version.

c) The *Latin* version was published by Tischendorf (Ea, pp. 164-180) from a Vatican manuscript (Vat. Reg. 648) and a palimpsest in Vienna (5th/6th cent.). On the Vienna manuscript cf. G. Philippart in *Anal.Boll.* 90, 1972, 391-411. There is still no rigorous investigation of the Latin tradition. The proximity which can be established to the Syriac and Church Slavonic versions, as well as to the Greek version published by Delatte, makes this branch of the tradition important.

d) The old *Georgian* version, which stands close to the Syriac, but has so far scarcely been noticed in the West, is now available in a Latin translation: G. Garitte, 'Le fragment géorgien de l'Évangile de Thomas', RHE 61, 1956, 513-520.

e) The *Church Slavonic* tradition of this apocryphon, which is represented by fifteen manuscripts, is particularly important (cf. de Santos, *Überlieferung* II, 49-54). These manuscripts all go back to an old Bulgarian translation originating at the latest in the 11th century. A. de Santos Otero has convincingly reconstructed the Greek *Vorlage* of this old Bulgarian version (*Kirchenslav. Evangelium*, pp. 159-171), and summarises his conclusions thus: 'This Greek *Vorlage*, which in essentials coincides with the old versions of the infancy gospel (the Syriac, Latin and Georgian) and the Greek text of Ms no. 355 of the Athens National Library

(Delatte), bears witness to the existence of an old Greek version of the Infancy Gospel of Thomas which proves to be far more complete and considerably older than the Greek Redactions A and B made known by Tischendorf' (*op. cit.* p. 185).

With this, not only are completely new insights gained for the history of the transmission of this work, but also the problem of the 'gnostic' character of the infancy story of Thomas is posed afresh. Thus for example the more detailed version of chapter 6 (see below, pp. 445 and n.9.) appears to be more original than the shorter one in Recension A. This longer version, however, shows clearly gnostic tendencies, which however cannot yet be precisely determined.[4]

f) Finally it may be noted that this apocryphon is also extant in an *Ethiopic* version (ed. S. Grébaut in *Patrologia Orientalis* XII 4, 1919, 625-642; cf. id. in *Rev. de l'Orient Chrétien* 16, 1911, 255-265; 356-367; cf. also V. Arras - L. van Rompay in *Anal.Boll.* 93, 1975, 133-146). Attention must also be paid in any investigation of the transmission to the continuance in later works (Arabic infancy gospel, Armenian infancy document) of traditions which occur in this writing.

This survey of the extant material confirms the statement that the Infancy Gospel of Thomas had a very complicated tradition, and that despite the pioneering work of de Santos many questions still remain open. In any case we cannot at present reconstruct any original form of this work. In the present volume we must therefore content ourselves with a compromise: the *textus receptus* of Tischendorf (Recension A) is presented in translation, supplemented in the apparatus by references to variants which point to an older and better version. It must be emphasised that here we cannot aspire to completeness.

Literature: Tischendorf's edition of the text (Ea, pp. 140-180) is still important even today, and is taken up by the later editors: C. Michel, *Évangiles apocryphes* I, [2]1924, 161-189; de Santos[6], pp. 276-300.

Translations: James, pp. 49-64 (English); de Santos[6], pp. 279-297 (Spanish); Moraldi I, 247-279 (Italian); Erbetta I 2, 78-101 (Italian).

Detailed bibliographies: in de Santos, Moraldi and Erbetta.

Older literature: in A. Meyer, NTApoHdb pp. 132f. M.R. James, 'The Gospel of Thomas', JTS 30, 1928, 51-54. J. Carney, 'The Irish Gospel of Thomas. Text, Translation and Notes', *Eriu* 18, 1958, 1-43. S. Gero, 'The Infancy Gospel of Thomas: A Study of the Textual and Literary Problems', *Nov.Test.* 13, 1971, 46-80. M. McNamara, 'Notes on the Irish Gospel of Thomas', *Irish Theol. Quarterly* 38, 1971, 42-46. J. Noret, 'Pour une édition de l'Évangile d'enfance de Thomas', *Anal.Boll.* 90, 1972, 412. A. Fuchs-F. Weissengruber, *Konkordanz zum Thomasevangelium, Version A und B*, unter Mitarbeit von Ch. Eckmair, Studien zum NT und seiner Umwelt B 4, Linz 1978.

2. Title and contents: the manuscripts speak of 'Infancy of the Lord Jesus' (Syriac version), or are entitled 'Account of the Infancy of the Lord, by Thomas the Israelite philosopher' (Greek MS A), or again 'Book of the holy apostle Thomas concerning the life of the Lord in his Infancy' (Greek MS B; see below, p. 449, note 1).

The gospel contains stories of miracles wrought by the child Jesus between the ages of five and twelve years. It ends with the narrative of the twelve-year-old Jesus in the Temple, which is taken from Luke.

3. Date and author: direct relationships with the gnostic Gospel of Thomas, which has now become known in a Coptic version (see above, pp. 110ff.), cannot be traced, although one is tempted to see in the instructions of the boy Jesus concerning the allegorical significance of the alphabet a narrative starting-point for gnostic speculations. The choice of Thomas (who is now called an apostle, now an 'Israelite philosopher') as the author may be connected with the tradition of Thomas's apostolate in India. Perhaps it is also no accident that it is precisely for the material here employed that parallels in Indian legends are particularly to be taken into account (see above, p. 415).

According to Irenaeus (*adv. Haer.* I 13.1) the Marcosians had a document containing a passage of our Gospel of Thomas (chapter 6). It thus probably belongs towards the end of the 2nd century. That the author was of gentile Christian origin may be assumed with certainty, since his work betrays no knowledge of things Jewish.

4. Character of the material, literary style and theological tendencies of the document: it was not the youth of Jesus between the age of twelve and his coming to be baptised at the Jordan at the age of thirty that was the chief interest for legend, but rather the years before the incident reported by Luke, when Jesus was twelve years old. For the intention is precisely to present the boy Jesus as an infant prodigy. All the miracles he was later to perform are here anticipated in a particularly blatant fashion. There is, however, a great difference between these miracles and those reported in the canonical Gospels. Here the extraneous material is simply imported into the story of Jesus, without the slightest attempt to make it fit, even remotely, the portrait of Christ. If the name of Jesus did not stand alongside the description 'child' or 'boy', one could not possibly hit upon the idea that these stories of the capricious divine boy were intended to supplement the tradition about him. Parallels from the legends of Krishna and Buddha, as well as all kinds of fables, can here be adduced in particular quantity. The cruder and more startling the miracle, the greater the pleasure the compiler finds in it, without the slightest scruple about the questionable nature of the material. In this respect there is a vast difference also between the Gospel of Thomas and the Protevangelium of James.

Not only the miracle-worker but also Christ the teacher must be foreshadowed in the child. What Luke relates relatively soberly about the twelve-year-old Jesus in the temple is here exaggerated into the grotesque. The boy not only possesses all the wisdom of the age, but baffles all human teachers by profound and often obscure pronouncements. In particular the longer version of chapter 6 (see above, p. 441) shows how the boy Jesus becomes the gnostic Revealer. He proclaims gnostic speculations, and already possesses all divine wisdom in its fullest range; in contrast to Luke 2:40, he has no need whatever of 'growth in wisdom'. The book displays the docetic tendency which ultimately lies at the root of most of the infancy gospels. Although lacking in good taste, restraint and discretion, it must be admitted that the man who collected these legends and composed the Gospel of Thomas was endowed with a gift of vivid story-telling, especially when he depicts scenes from everyday childhood.

5. Dissemination of the Gospel of Thomas: on the one hand, readers were attracted from the start by its popular material, free from any theological bias, and the gospel enjoyed wide popularity, as the numerous translations and its use in later gospels testify. To be sure, it also caused offence, above all through its all too crude emphasis on the miraculous, often quite devoid of ethical feeling. (Perhaps there is a certain reaction to this in the History of Joseph the Carpenter, which specially stresses the meekness of the child Jesus: Morenz, TU 56, pp.1; 43 , see below, pp. 484f.). Moreover the whole attempt to remove from the boy Jesus the necessity for a purely human development would have appeared questionable in some quarters. Where this literature was rejected, a contributory factor was probably the feeling that on the one hand the true humanity of Jesus finds expression in the fact that his growing-up took place in seclusion, and on the other that the devil would have no inkling of the coming of the Son of God.

Despite all mistrust, the Gospel of Thomas triumphed again and again. It spread far and wide not only through its translation into other languages, but also through the fact that it was combined in major popular collections with material from the favourite Protev. of James and all kinds of popular legends about the sojourn of the child Jesus in Egypt (see pp. 460ff.).

The following translation presents Tischendorf's Recension A. In the notes a selection is offered of variants from the Church Slavonic version (= Slav.) which de Santos has set out (see above), in order to reveal something of the problems of the tradition. Occasionally reference is also made to agreements between Slav. and the text of the Cod. Paris. Bibl. Nat. gr. 355 (see above) published by Delatte (= Del.).

Notes

2. The Infancy Story of Thomas

1. S. Gero (*Nov.Test.* 13, 1971, 46ff.) has expressed views similar to those of Köster. He thinks that the oral traditions collected in the infancy story of Thomas would not have undergone fixation in writing before the 5th century (*op. cit.* p. 56, note 1). This is a hypothesis which at present cannot be confirmed.
2. There is a survey of the whole material, which is, however, partly governed by the hypothesis mentioned above, in Gero, pp. 48-56.
3. Noret (*Anal.Boll.* 90, 1972, 412) gives notice in a short communication of the plan for a new edition, and also enumerates a series of manuscripts in which this work is contained but which were previously unknown. Further details are lacking.
4. Cf. also Gero, *op. cit.* pp. 73-80, whose statements, however, are not all convincing.

BAC
148:
279-97

**The account of Thomas the Israelite philosopher
concerning the childhood of the Lord[1]**

1. I, Thomas the Israelite,[2] tell and make known to you all, brethren from among the Gentiles, all the works of the childhood of our Lord Jesus Christ and his mighty deeds, which he did when he was born in our land.[3] The beginning is as follows.

2. 1. When this boy Jesus was five years old he was playing at the ford of a brook, and he gathered together into pools the water that flowed by, and made it at once clean, and commanded it by his word alone.

2. He made soft clay and fashioned from it twelve sparrows. And it was the sabbath when he did this. And there were also many other children playing with him.

3. Now when a certain Jew saw what Jesus was doing in his play on the sabbath, he at once went and told his father Joseph: 'See, your child is at the brook, and he has taken clay and fashioned twelve birds and has profaned the sabbath.'

4. And when Joseph came to the place and saw (it), he cried out to him, saying: 'Why do you do on the sabbath what ought not to be done?' But Jesus clapped his hands and cried to the sparrows: 'Off with you!'[4] And the sparrows took flight and went away chirping.

5. The Jews were amazed when they saw this, and went away and told their elders what they had seen Jesus do.

3. 1. But the son of Annas the scribe was standing there with Joseph; and he took a branch of a willow and (with it) dispersed the water which Jesus had gathered together.

2. When Jesus saw what he had done he was enraged and said to him: 'You insolent,[5] godless dunderhead, what harm did the pools and the water do to you? See, now you also shall wither like a tree and shall bear neither leaves nor root nor fruit.'

3. And immediately that lad withered up completely; and Jesus departed and went into Joseph's house. But the parents of him that was withered took him away, bewailing his youth, and brought him to Joseph and reproached him: 'What a child you have, who does such things.'

4. 1. After this again he went through the village, and a lad ran and knocked against his shoulder. Jesus was exasperated and said to him: 'You shall not go further on your way', and the child immediately fell down and died. But some, who saw what took place, said: 'From where does this child spring, since his every word is an accomplished deed?'

2. And the parents of the dead child came to Joseph and blamed him and said: 'Since you have such a child, you cannot dwell with us in the village; or else teach him to bless and not to curse.[6] For he is slaying our children.'

5. 1. And Joseph called the child aside and admonished him saying: 'Why do you do such things that these people (must) suffer and hate us and persecute us?' But Jesus replied: 'I know that these words are not yours;[7] nevertheless for your sake I will be silent. But they shall bear their punishment.' And immediately those who had accused him became blind.

2. And those who saw it were greatly afraid and perplexed, and said concerning him: 'Every word he speaks, whether good or evil, was a deed and became a marvel.' And when Joseph saw that Jesus had so done, he arose and took him by the ear and pulled it hard. 3. And the child was angry and said to him: 'It is sufficient for you to seek and not to find, and most unwisely have you acted. Do you not know that I am yours? Do not vex me.'[8]

6. 1. Now a certain teacher, Zacchaeus by name, who was standing there, heard in part Jesus saying these things to his father, and marvelled greatly that, being a child, he said such things.

2. And after a few days he came near to Joseph and said to him: 'You have a clever child, and he has understanding. Come, hand him over to me that he may learn letters, and I will teach him with the letters all knowledge, and to salute all the older people and honour them as grandfathers and fathers, and to love those of his own age.'[9]

3. And he told him all the letters from Alpha to Omega clearly, with much questioning. But he looked at Zacchaeus the teacher and said to him: 'How do you, who do not know the Alpha according to its nature, teach others the Beta? Hypocrite, first if you know it, teach the Alpha, and then we shall believe you concerning the Beta.' Then he began to question the teacher about the first letter, and he was unable to answer him.

4. And in the hearing of many the child said to Zacchaeus: 'Hear, teacher, the arrangement of the first letter, and pay heed to this, how it has lines and a middle mark which goes through the pair of lines which you see, (how these lines) converge, rise, turn in the dance, three signs of the same kind, subject to and supporting one another, of equal proportions; here you have the lines of the Alpha.'

7. 1. Now when Zacchaeus the teacher heard so many such allegorical descriptions of the first letter being expounded, he was perplexed at such a reply and such great teaching and said to those who were present: 'Woe is me, I am forced into a quandary, wretch that I am; I have brought shame to myself in drawing to myself this child.

2. Take him away, therefore, I beseech you, brother Joseph. I cannot endure the severity of his look, I cannot make out his speech at all. This child is not earth-born; he can tame even fire. Perhaps he was begotten even before the creation of the world. What belly bore him, what womb nurtured him I do not know. Woe is me, my friend, he stupefies me, I

cannot follow his understanding. I have deceived myself, thrice wretched man that I am! I strove to get a disciple, and have found myself with a teacher.

3. My friends, I think of my shame, that I, an old man, have been overcome by a child. I can only despair and die because of this child, for I cannot in this hour look him in the face. And when all say that I have been overcome by a small child, what have I to say? And what can I tell concerning the lines of the first letter of which he spoke to me? I do not know, my friends, for I know neither beginning nor end of it.

4. Therefore I ask you, brother Joseph, take him away to your house. He is something great, a god or an angel or what I should say I do not know.'

8. 1. And while the Jews were trying to console Zacchaeus, the child laughed aloud and said: 'Now let that which is yours bear fruit, and let the blind in heart see. I have come from above to curse them and call them to the things above, as he commanded who sent me for your sakes.'[10]

2. And when the child had ceased speaking, immediately all those were healed who had fallen under his curse. And no one after that dared to provoke him, lest he should curse him, and he should be maimed.

9. 1. Now after some days Jesus was playing on a roof in the upper storey, and one of the children who were playing with him fell down from the roof and died. And when the other children saw it they fled, and Jesus remained alone.

2. And the parents of him that was dead came and accused him of having thrown him down. And Jesus replied: 'I did not throw him down.' But they continued to revile him.

3. Then Jesus leaped down from the roof and stood by the body of the child, and cried with a loud voice: 'Zenon' - for that was his name - 'arise and tell me, did I throw you down?' And he arose at once and said: 'No, Lord, you did not throw me down, but raised me up.' And when they saw it they were amazed. And the parents of the child glorified God for the miracle that had happened and worshipped Jesus.

10. 1. After a few days a young man was cleaving wood in a corner and the axe fell and split the sole of his foot, and he bled so much that he was about to die.

2. And when a clamour arose and a concourse of people took place, the child Jesus also ran there, and forced his way through the crowd, and took the injured foot, and it was healed immediately. And he said to the young man! 'Arise now, cleave the wood and remember me.' And when the crowd saw what happened, they worshipped the child, saying: 'Truly the spirit of God[11] dwells in this child.'

11. 1. When he was six years old, his mother gave him a pitcher and sent him to draw water and bring it into the house.

2. But in the crowd he stumbled, and the pitcher was broken. But Jesus spread out the garment he was wearing, filled it with water and brought it to his mother. And when his mother saw the miracle, she kissed him, and kept within herself[12] the mysteries which she had seen him do.

12. 1. Again, in the time of sowing the child went out with his father to sow wheat in their land. And as his father sowed, the child Jesus also sowed one corn of wheat.[13]

2. And when he had reaped it and threshed it, he brought in a hundred measures[14], and he called all the poor of the village to the threshing-floor and gave them the wheat, and Joseph took the residue of the wheat. He was eight years old when he worked this miracle.

13. 1. His father was a carpenter and made at that time[15] ploughs and yokes. And he received an order from a rich man to make a bed for him. But when one beam was shorter than its corresponding one and they did not know what to do, the child Jesus said to his father Joseph: 'Put down the two pieces of wood and make them even from the middle to one end.'

2. And Joseph did as the child told him. And Jesus stood at the other end and took hold of the shorter piece of wood, and stretching it made it equal with the other. And his father Joseph saw it and was amazed, and he embraced the child and kissed him, saying: 'Happy am I that God has given me this child.'

14. 1. And when Joseph saw the understanding of the child and his age, that he was growing to maturity, he resolved again that he should not remain ignorant of letters; and he took him and handed him over to another teacher. And the teacher said to Joseph: 'First I will teach him Greek, and then Hebrew.'[16] For the teacher knew the child's knowledge and was afraid of him. Nevertheless he wrote the alphabet and practised it with him for a long time; but he gave him no answer.

2. And Jesus said to him: 'If you are indeed a teacher, and if you know the letters well, tell me the meaning of the Alpha, and I will tell you that of the Beta.' And the teacher was annoyed and struck him on the head. And the child was hurt and cursed him, and he immediately fainted and fell to the ground on his face.

3. And the child returned to Joseph's house. But Joseph was grieved and commanded his mother: 'Do not let him go outside the door, for all those who provoke him die.'

15. 1. And after some time yet another teacher, a good friend of Joseph, said to him: 'Bring the child to me to the school. Perhaps I by persuasion can teach him the letters.' And Joseph said to him: 'If you have the courage, brother, take him with you.' And he took him with fear and anxiety, but the child went gladly.

2. And he went boldly into the school and found a book lying on the reading-desk[17] and took it, but did not read the letters in it, but opened his

mouth and spoke by the Holy Spirit and taught the law to those that stood by. And a large crowd assembled and stood there listening to him,[18] wondering at the grace of his teaching and the readiness of his words,[19] that although an infant he made such utterances.

3. But when Joseph heard it, he was afraid and ran to the school, wondering whether this teacher also was without skill (might be maimed?).[20] But the teacher said to Joseph: 'Know, brother, that I took the child as a disciple; but he is full of great grace and wisdom; and now I beg you, brother, take him to your house.'

4. And when the child heard this, he at once smiled on him and said: 'Since you have spoken well and have testified rightly, for your sake shall he also that was smitten be healed.' And immediately the other teacher was healed. And Joseph took the child and went away to his house.

16. 1. Joseph sent his son James to bind wood and take it into his house, and the child Jesus followed him. And while James was gathering the sticks, a viper bit the hand of James.

2. And as he lay stretched out and about to die, Jesus came near and breathed upon the bite, and immediately the pain ceased, and the creature burst, and at once James became well.

17. 1. And after these things in the neighbourhood of Joseph a little sick child[21] died, and his mother wept bitterly.[22] And Jesus heard that great mourning and tumult[23] arose, and he ran quickly, and finding the child dead, he touched[24] his breast and said: 'I say to you,[25] do not die but live and be with your mother.'[26] And immediately he looked up and laughed. And he said to the woman: 'Take him and give him[27] milk and remember me.'

2. And when the people standing round saw it, they marvelled and said[28] 'Truly, this child is either a god or an angel of God, for every word of his is an accomplished deed.' And Jesus departed from there and played with other children.

18. 1. After some time a house was being built and a great disturbance arose, and Jesus arose and went there. And seeing a man lying dead he took his hand and said: 'I say to you, man, arise,[29] do your work.' And immediately he arose and worshipped him.

2. And when the people saw it, they were amazed and said: 'This child is from heaven, for he has saved many souls from death, and is able to save them all his life long.'

19. 1. And when he was twelve years old his parents went according to the custom to Jerusalem to the feast of the passover with their company, and after the passover they returned to go to their house. And while they were returning the child Jesus went back to Jerusalem. But his parents supposed that he was in the company.

2. And when they had gone a day's journey, they sought him among

their kinsfolk, and when they did not find him, they were troubled, and returned again to the city seeking him. And after the third day they found him in the Temple sitting among the teachers, listening to the law and asking them questions. And all paid attention to him and marvelled how he, a child, put to silence the elders and teachers of the people, expounding the sections of the law and the sayings of the prophets.

3. And his mother Mary came near and said to him: 'Why have you done this to us, child? Behold, we have sought you sorrowing.' Jesus said to them: 'Why do you seek me? Do you not know that I must be in my Father's house?'[30]

4. But the scribes and Pharisees said: 'Are you the mother of this child?' And she said: 'I am.' And they said to her: 'Blessed are you among women, because the Lord has blessed the fruit of your womb.[31] For such glory and such excellence and wisdom we have never seen nor heard.'

5. And Jesus arose and followed his mother and was subject to his parents; but his mother kept (in her heart) all that had taken place. And Jesus increased in wisdom and stature and grace.[32] To him be glory for ever and ever. Amen.

Notes

The account of Thomas the Israelite philosopher concerning the childhood of the Lord

1. The original title probably ran: 'The Childhood of our Lord (and God and Saviour) Jesus Christ'. Cf. de Santos, pp. 37f.
2. *Slav.:* + 'the elect'.
3. *Slav.:* + 'called Bethlehem and in the town of Nazareth'; similarly *Del.*
4. *Slav.:* + 'and think of me, you who live'; similarly *Del.* Cf de Santos, pp.45f., note 22.
5. *Slav.* has instead of 'insolent': 'sodomite'; similarly *Del.* and *Lat.*
6. Cf. Rom. 12:14
7. *Slav.:* 'I know that these words are not mine which I have spoken.' Similarly *Del.* and Latin-Syriac variant: 'If the words of my father were not wise, he would not know how to teach children.' And again he said: 'If these children were born in wedlock, they would not be accursed. Such will see no torment.'
8. *Slav.:* 'It is enough for you to seek me and not to find me, you rogue, for in fact you do not know whether I belong to you. However, I am not aggrieved, for I am yours and come to you.' Cf. the detailed note by de Santos ad loc. (pp. 62ff.).
9. *Slav.* deviates particularly widely from Greek A here. After 6.2 there follows:
3. And Joseph was very angry with the child and said to the teacher: 'And who can instruct him? Do you think, my brother, that he is perhaps a small cross?' 4. When the boy Jesus heard how his father said this, he burst into laughter and said to Zacchaeus: 'It is all true, teacher, what my father has said (to you). I am the Lord here, but you are an alien. To me alone has power been given, for I existed formerly and exist also now. I have been born among you and dwell among you. You do not know who I am. But I know whence you come and who you are, when you were born and how many years your life will endure.

Truly I tell you, teacher, when you were born, I was there, and before your birth I was already there. If you wish to be a perfect teacher, then listen to me, and I will teach you a wisdom which no one knows except me and him who sent me to you to instruct you. I am actually your teacher, while you rank as my own teacher, for I know how old you are, and I also know exactly how long your life will yet endure. When you once see my cross, of which my father has spoken to you, then you will believe that all that I say to you is the truth. I am the Lord, but you are an alien, for I remain for ever still the same.' 5. And the Jews who were there and listening were filled with astonishment and said: 'O strange and unheard-of wonder! This child is no five-year-old who speaks such utterances as we have never heard from any high priest or scribe or Pharisee!' Then Jesus answered and said to them: 'You do indeed marvel, but you do not believe what I have said to you. But I know exactly when you and your fathers were born. I proclaim to you something (more) that is unheard of: I know as well as the one who sent me to you when the world was created.' When the Jews heard him speak thus, they were afraid, and could give him no answer. Then the boy came and played and leaped about and laughed at them and said: 'I know that you are not very capable of amazement, and not very intelligent, for the splendour has been conferred on me the child for solace.' VIa 1 Then the teacher said to his father Joseph: 'Come, bring me this child to the school, and I will teach him the letters.' Joseph took Jesus by the hand and brought him to the school. And the teacher began the instruction with confidence in inspiring words, and wrote out the alphabet for him. Then he began to expound it, reading out several times what he had written down. But the child remained silent, and for a long time paid no attention. Then the teacher grew indignant and struck him on the head. The child answered him: 'You are behaving unworthily; am I to instruct you, or is it rather you who instruct me? For I can already do the letters which you instil into me. Many condemn you, because these (letters) in me are like sounding brass or a tinkling cymbal, which neither reproduce an intelligible sound nor the splendour of wisdom nor the power of the soul and the understanding.' The child remained still a while, and then recited the whole alphabet in detail from A to T. Then he glared angrily at the teacher and said to him: 'Why do you teach others the Beta, you who do not know the Alpha according to its nature? You hypocrite! If you know (it), teach me first the Alpha, then I will believe you with regard to the Beta.'

And then he began to expound to the teacher the nature of the first letter.

From here on *Slav.* once again largely agrees with chapter 6.4 of Form A (see above). On this text cf. de Santos, pp. 69ff. There is probably no question that in *Slav.* we have an older form which shows stronger gnostic tendencies.

10. *Slav.:* 'Let the unfruitful bear fruit, let the blind see, and let the deaf hear with the understanding of their hearts, that I am come from above to redeem the lowly and call them into the heights, as he who sent me has commanded.' De Santos (pp. 105ff.) lists several parallels from *Del.* and the versions, which together with *Slav.* allow us to deduce a better text than Form A. Cf. the variants from the Syriac text, p. 452 below.

11. Instead of 'spirit of God', *Slav.* writes 'God'.

12. Lk. 2:19, 51.

13. *Slav.:* 'a bushel of corn'.

14. Cf. Lk. 16:7.

15. *Syr.* and *Lat.* instead of 'at that time': only. *Slav.* abbreviates.

16. *Slav.:* 'What letters shall I teach him?' Joseph said: 'First the Greek, then the Hebrew'. This reading is confirmed by *Del.* Cf. de Santos, p. 124, note.

17. Cf. Lk. 4:16f.

18. *Slav.:* + 'and begged him to speak further'.

19. Cf. Lk. 4:22.

20. An obscure passage which cannot be explained even with the help of *Slav.* and other versions.
21. Cf. Mk. 5:22ff.; Lk. 7:11ff.
22. Cf. Mk. 5:38; Lk. 7:13.
23. Mk. 5:38.
24. Lk. 7:14.
25. Lk. 7:14.
26. Cf. Lk. 7:15.
27. Cf. Mk. 5:43; Lk. 8:55.
28. Cf. Lk. 7:16.
29. Cf. Lk. 7:14; Mk. 5:41.
30. Lk. 2:41-52.
31. Lk. 1:42.
32. Lk. 2:51f.

Variant of the Syriac Gospel of Thomas to chapters 6-8
(The Boy Jesus and Zacchaeus the Teacher)

But a teacher, whose name was Zacchaeus, heard him speaking with his father, and said: 'O wicked boy!' And he said to Joseph his father: 'Till when wilt thou not choose to hand over this boy, that he may learn to be fond of children of his years, and may honour old age?' Joseph answered and said: 'And who is able to teach a boy like this? Does he think (dost thou think) that he is equal to a small cross?' Jesus answered and said to the teacher: 'These words which thou hast spoken, and these names, I am strange to them; for I am apart from you, though I dwell among you. Honour in the flesh I have not. Thou art by the law, and in the law thou abidest. For when thou wast born, I was. But thou thinkest that thou art my father. Thou shalt learn from me a doctrine, which another man knows not and is not able to learn. And (as for) the cross of which thou hast spoken, he shall bear it, whose it is. For when I am greatly exalted, I shall lay aside whatever mixture I have of your race. For thou dost not know whence thou art; for I alone know truly when ye were born, and how long time ye have to remain here.' But when they heard, they were astonished, and cried out and said: 'O wonderful sight and hearing! Words like these we have never heard man speak, neither the priests, nor the scribes, nor the Pharisees. Whence was this (one) born, who is five years old, and speaks such words? Man hath never seen the like of this.' Jesus answered and said to them: 'Ye wonder at what I have said to you, that I know when ye were; and yet I have something more to say to you.' But they, when they heard, were silent, and were not able to speak. And Zacchaeus the teacher said to Joseph: 'I will teach him whatever is proper for him to learn.' And he made him go into the school. And he, going in, was silent. But Zacchaeus the scribe began to tell him (the letters) from Alaph, and was repeating to him many times the whole alphabet. And he says to him that he should answer and say after him; but he was silent. Then the scribe became angry, and struck him with his hand upon his head. And Jesus said: 'A smith's anvil, being beaten, can learn, and it has no feeling; but I am able to say those things, which are spoken by you, with knowledge and understanding.' The scribe answered and said: 'This (child) is something great. He is either God, or an angel, or - what I should say I know not.' Then the boy Jesus laughed and said: 'Let those in whom there is no fruit, produce fruit; and let the blinded see the fruit of life of the Judge.'

(Trans. W. Wright, *Contributions to the Apocryphal Literature*, 1865, pp. 7-9; cf. also the Latin translation. Cf. also the Church Slavonic version of the Gospel of Thomas: de Santos, pp. 65ff. and above, pp. 449f., note 9).

Story from the Arabic Infancy Gospel and the Paris Manuscript of the Gospel of Thomas (The Child Jesus and the Dyer)

One day, when Jesus was running about and playing with some children, he passed by the workshop of a dyer called Salem. They had in the workshop many cloths which he had to dye. The Lord Jesus went into the dyer's workshop, took all these cloths and put them into a cauldron full of indigo. When Salem came and saw that the cloths were spoiled, he began to cry aloud and asked the Lord Jesus, saying: 'What have you done to me, son of Mary? You have ruined my reputation in the eyes of all the people of the city; for everyone orders a suitable colour for himself, but you have come and spoiled everything.' And the Lord Jesus replied: 'I will change for you the colour of any cloth which you wish to be changed', and he immediately began to take the cloths out of the cauldron, each of them dyed in the colour the dyer wished, until he had taken them all out. When the Jews saw this miracle and wonder, they praised God.

From the Arabic Infancy Gospel c. 37 (Ea, pp. 200-201); cf. the Greek fragment Paris *Bibl. nat. gr.* 239 (see above) and the expanded form in the Armenian Infancy Gospel c. 21; see P. Peeters, *Évang. apocr.* II, 1914, 232-246. On this story cf. H. -G. Gaffron, *Studien zum koptischen Philippusevangelium* (Diss. Ev. Theol. Bonn), 1969, pp. 137ff., 324ff., and Vielhauer. *Lit. gesch.* p. 673.

3. Gnostic Legends

Perhaps infancy gospels were written by Gnostics at an early date. Certainly such material did not originate with them. But in order to be able to derive their speculations from Jesus himself, they needed as a framework a setting in his life which could be fitted into the older gospel tradition, but without being controlled by its content. Besides the resurrection appearances during the forty days, there was available the whole childhood of Jesus left untouched by the older Gospels. We have seen how fruitful in this respect were the themes of Jesus at the age of twelve in the Temple and of his education. What they required, however, was a child Jesus who was only a child in appearance, but had in fact no need of development, since he possessed the full revelation in its entirety, and already had unlimited power to perform miracles.

The tendency to Docetism behind all the legends of the infancy met this need, and at the same time was greatly strengthened by it. The statements of heresiologists, and the fragments given below, show that legends in which the child Jesus stands in permanent union with the Spirit and the source of all revelation from the very beginning, and even before his baptism, were especially the ones to be adopted and developed.

Docetism, further, was bound to affect the way in which the birth of Jesus was told. The tendency is to eliminate all traces of a normal, human origin in the story of the birth of Jesus of the virgin Mary. Thus the Gnostics early wrote a 'Prehistory (Genna) of Mary', mentioned by Epiphanius (*Haer.* 26.12), which shows that the material of the Protevangelium of James was used in gnostic circles. The apocryphal expansions of the original nativity stories all betray a more or less marked docetic tendency (see the Christian interpolation in theAscension of Isaiah, c. 11.5ff., and especially the fragment of the Arundel MS given under 4).

As time went on, the narrative element in the gnostic writings faded more and more into the background. The few infancy legends still provided are completely subordinated to the scheme of the teaching of the heavenly beings. Increasingly it is regarded as sufficient to supply a merely introductory reference to the familiar framework or to mention (in the title) the traditional authority for all gnostic statements about the infancy: Thomas.

Story of the Gnostic Justin concerning the sending of the angel Baruch to the twelve-year-old shepherd boy Jesus

The following story is to be found in Hippolytus' description (*Ref.* V 26.29f.) of the system of the Gnostic Justin and is closely connected with his speculations concerning the heavenly beings. The angel of Elohim, Baruch, is sent to the earth to deliver men.

Lastly in the days of King Herod Baruch is again sent down as an emissary of Elohim. When he came to Nazareth, he found Jesus (there), the son of Joseph and Mary, as a twelve-year-old boy tending sheep, and told him from the beginning everything which had happened from the time of Edem and Elohim, and what was to happen in the future, and said: 'All the prophets before you[1] allowed themselves to be seized. Take heed, Jesus, son of man, that you do not allow yourself to be seized, but proclaim this word to men, and tell them what concerns God and the good, and ascend to the good and seat yourself there[2] by the side of Elohim the father of us all.' And Jesus obeyed the angel and said: 'Lord, all this will I do', and he preached.

(Hippol. Ref.V.26.29f., Mankovich p.208.149ff.)

Legends from the Pistis Sophia (3rd century)
Translated after Carl Schmidt-W. Till, *Koptisch-gnostische Schriften I*, GCS 45,[2]1954.

Concerning the communication of heavenly powers by the child Jesus to the Baptist and Mary

'And when I set out for the world, I came to the midst of the Archons of the Sphere and had the form of Gabriel, the angel of the Aeons, and the Archons of the Aeons did not recognise me, but they thought that I was the angel Gabriel. Now it happened that, when I had come to the midst of the Archons of the Aeons, I looked down upon the world of mankind at the command of the first Mystery. I found Elizabeth, the mother of John the Baptist, before she had conceived him, and I sowed in her a power-which I had taken from the little Jao, the Good, who was in the midst, that he might be able to proclaim before me, and prepare my way and baptise with water of the forgiveness of sins.'

(Pistis Sophia c. 7, Schmidt-Till, pp. 7.26-8.2;
cf. Schmidt-MacDermot, NHS 9, 12 [= p. 25])

Jesus again continued in his speech and said: 'Now it happened afterwards, when at the command of the first Mystery I looked down upon the world of mankind and found Mary, who is called 'my mother' according to the material body, that I spoke with her in the form of Gabriel, and when she had turned upwards towards me, I thrust into her the first power, which I had taken from Barbelo, that is, the body which I have borne on high. And in the place of the soul I thrust into her the power which I have taken from the great Sabaoth the Good, who dwells in the place of the right.'

(Pistis Sophia c. 8, Schmidt-Till, pp. 8.27-9.2;
Schmidt-MacDermot, 13 [= p. 27])

Concerning the union of the child Jesus with the Spirit

[Mary declares to the risen Jesus]: 'When you were small, before the Spirit had come upon you, while you were with Joseph in a vineyard, the Spirit came from on high and came to me in my house, resembling you, and I did not recognise him, and I thought that it was you. And the Spirit said to me: 'Where is Jesus, my brother, that I may meet him?' When he said this to me, I was perplexed and thought that it was a ghost come to tempt me. And I seized him and bound him to the foot of the bed which is in my house, until I went out to you both, to you and Joseph in the field and found you in the vineyard, while Joseph was fencing in the vineyard. Now it came to pass that, when you heard me speak the word to Joseph, you understood the word, and were glad and said: 'Where is he, that I may see him? for I await him in this place.' And it came to pass that, when Joseph heard you say these words, he was perplexed, and we went up together, entered the house, and found the Spirit bound to the bed. And we looked at you and him and found that you resembled him, and when he who was bound to the bed was freed, he embraced you and kissed you, and you kissed him and you both became one.'

(Pistis Sophia c. 61, Schmidt-Till, pp. 78.1-78.20;
Schmidt-MacDermot, 121 [= p. 243])

Notes

3. Gnostic Legends

Story of the Gnostic Justin concerning the sending of the angel Baruch to the twelve-year-old shepherd boy Jesus

1. Cf. Jn. 10:8.
2. Cf. Ps. 110:1.

4. Later Infancy Gospels

It is in accord with the natural law of the growth of legend if on the one hand ever new stories about the childhood of Jesus grouped around the two older ones, the Protev. Jac. and the Infancy Gospel of Thomas. If the tendency towards expansion of the material dominates the development, yet on the other hand the concern to eliminate legends that were lacking in taste or dogmatically offensive makes for abbreviation. Both tendencies are to be seen, and operate already in the old translations mentioned, which at one and the same time present enlarged or shortened versions. In addition to these translations, there now come into being deliberate combinations of the two older sources with one another, in which the canonical narratives and all kinds of new legendary material are also used: above all stories of the flight into Egypt and Jesus' sojourn there, about which there was perhaps already a separate older written source. The lines between expanded or shortened translations and compilations of this kind cannot always be sharply drawn. On the whole question of the complicated literary-historical relationships see the discussion by Paul Peeters in the introduction to his selection of later infancy stories (*Evang. apocr*. II, 1ff.). He assumes, of course, that ultimately all extant redactions of this kind go back to a Syriac basic form, which according to him is to be placed before the 5th century - a thesis which cannot be proved.

Among these compilations special reference should be made to the *Arabic infancy gospel* already mentioned, today extant in several manuscripts (Florence, Laur. orient. 32; Vat. syr. 159) and probably a translation from the Syriac. It combines the three cycles: birth of Jesus, miracles in Egypt (in which Mary plays a dominant role), and miracles of the boy Jesus, most of which are taken from the (infancy) Gospel of Thomas. Thanks to this translation into Arabic the legends also became known among the Muslims. At any rate Mohammed was familiar with this tradition, and adopted many of the legends into the Koran (see NTApoHdb, pp. 165ff.). The infancy stories also probably reached India in this form.

The first edition of the Arabic infancy gospel was made by H. Sike, *Evangelium infantiae vel liber apocryphus de Infantia Salvatoris*, 1697, who, however, could rely only on a single manuscript, now lost (reprinted, as well as elsewhere, in Thilo, pp. 66-131); the text is available in Ea, pp. 181-209 (Latin); Peeters, *Évang. apocr.* II, 1-65 (French); A de Santos Otero, pp. 309-338, ⁶pp. 301-332 (Spanish); extracts in F. Amiot, pp. 93-107 (French; German ed. pp. 77-89); *Il Vangelo arabo dell'Infanzia, secondo il ms. Laurenziano Orientale (n.387)*, ed. Mario E. Provera, Jerusalem 1973 (Arabic and Italian). The major part of the document is also contained in a 'History of the Blessed Virgin Mary and the History of the Likeness of Christ' discovered and edited by E.A.W. Budge (2 vols., London 1899; MS of the 13th/14th cent.), which is specially important for the probably Syriac archetype. See in general for the problems posed by the transmission of this work P. Peeters, *Évang. apocr.* II, i-xxix (supplemented in *Anal. Boll.* 41, 1923, 132-134) and G. Graf, *Geschichte d. christl. arab. Literatur I*, Studi e Testi 118, 1944, 225-227. Cf. further the bibliographical note in U. Monneret de Villard, *Le leggende orientali sui magi evangelici* (Studi e Testi 163), 1952, p. 73, note 1, and the literature in de Santos Otero, pp. 308f. and xxiv, ⁶pp. 302f. and xvii.

In similar fashion the *Armenian infancy gospel*, which probably also rests upon a Syriac base (Peeters, *Évang. apocr.* II, xxixff.), fuses together the whole material including the Protevangelium Jacobi (see above, pp. 421ff.), but with considerable expansion. The Magi are here royal brothers: Melqon rules over Persia, Balthasar over India, and Gaspar over Arabia. First edition by Isaias Daietsi (Venice 1898), according to two MSS of the Mechitarist library in Venice; there are other MSS in Vienna and in the Edschmiadsin monastery. The text is available in Peeters, *Évang. apocr.* II, 69-286 (French); extracts in F. Amiot, pp. 81-93 (French; German ed., pp. 65-77) and de Santos Otero, pp. 359-365, ⁶pp. 353-359 (Spanish). On the whole subject see also Peeters, *Évang. apocr.* II, pp. xxix-l.

From a later period there is also a *Coptic* literature about the birth of Mary. Its content is used in addresses by Cyril of Jerusalem, Demetrius of Alexandria, Cyril of Alexandria and others (see F. Robinson, *Coptic Apocryphal Gospels*, 1896; E.A.W. Budge, *Miscellaneous Coptic Texts*, 1915). Here we should also mention the gnostic-tinged Ethiopic 'Miracles of Jesus' (ed. with French translation by S. Grébaut, PO XII. 4, 1919), which in the 6th-9th miracles brings together the most varied traditions about the childhood and youth of Jesus.

The further development of the infancy legends in the West merits particular interest. We have seen that we possess only fragments of the Latin translation of the Protev. Jac., but that its content must have been known (Prudentius used it, and before him Zeno of Verona in the 4th cent.). Of the (infancy) Gospel of Thomas there is a Latin MS as early as the 5th or 6th century. Admittedly opposition was aroused specifically in the West against this whole literature, first and foremost by Jerome, and that on theological grounds (sons of Joseph by a former marriage); but there was also displeasure at the bad taste of many of the legends (story of the midwife). Popes then condemned the books (see above, p. 418). Since, however, the material in the rejected writings continued to enjoy great popularity among Church people, it became necessary in course of time to bring it together in a refined form in a new collection, renouncing certain all too crude miracles. This was done in the so-called *pseudo-Matthew*, which was written probably about the 8th or 9th century for the glorification of Mary as queen of the virgins. It is almost ironic that this work, in which the story of Joseph's first marriage still retains its place, was actually put out as a translation prepared by Jerome. This is connected with the fact that it was identified with the Hebrew Matthew of which Jerome had spoken. On the other hand Jerome, at the request of the bishops Chromatius and Heliodorus, had translated into Latin an allegedly Aramaic book entitled 'Tobias'. In connection with this a spurious correspondence was forged, in which Jerome is asked by these same bishops to translate the Hebrew Matthew.

There is a large number of MSS for this pseudo-Matthew, of which Tischendorf used four for his edition in Ea, pp. 51-112 (three from the 14th cent., one from the 15th). The text may be found in Thilo (pp. 339-499); E. Amman, *Le Protévangile de Jacques*, 1910, pp. 272-339 (text and French); C. Michel, *Évang. apocr.* I, 54-159 (text and French); Bonaccorsi I (text and Italian); de Santos Otero, pp. 179-242, [6]pp. 173-236 (text and Spanish); extracts also in F. Amiot; cf. also J. Gijsel, *Die unmittelbare Textuberlieferung des sog. pseudo-Matthäus*, Proc. Royal Acad. Belgium 43, 1981, No. 96, Brussels 1981. The extraordinary importance of the work consists in the fact that in this form the legends from the older infancy gospels now really became the common property of the people, and were able to exercise an enormous influence on literature and art (see above, p. 418). Pseudo-Matthew also, however, underwent a shorter 'improved' edition, the 'Story of the Birth of Mary', first to eliminate Joseph's first marriage, now prohibited as heretical, and some other offensive details, and secondly by pruning to make the material less tedious. This edition also was provided with the fictitious correspondence of Jerome. Through its inclusion in the *Golden Legend* of Jacob of Voragine (1298) it gained a very wide circulation throughout the world.

In addition to this main stream, infancy legends flowed and developed in subsidiary channels of all kinds, and hitherto unknown texts are constantly coming to light. Of interest is a *Latin infancy gospel* edited in 1927 (M.R. James, *Latin Infancy Gospels*, 1927; cf. on this J.A. Robinson, JTS 1928, 205-207; M.J. Lagrange, *Rev. Bibl.* 1928, 544-557; B. Capelle, *Rev. Bén.* 1929, 79ff.; S. Ferri, *Studi Mediolatini e Volgari* I, 1955, 119-125; J. Gijsel, 'Les Evangiles latins de l'Enfance de M.R. James', *Anal.Boll.* 94, 1976, 289-302), which is attested by two MSS: the Hereford MS (Library of the Chapter of Hereford 0.3.9; 13th cent.) and the Arundel MS (Brit. Mus. 404; 14th cent.). They diverge widely from one another. On the one hand they come close to the text of the Protev. Jac., but on the other they contain much from pseudo-Matthew and in addition a number of peculiar features. Symeon, a son of Joseph, is named as the authority cited. Since in particular the story of the birth of Jesus, which we give in translation, shows a strongly docetic character, James has raised the question whether perhaps we have here a source comparable with the docetic Gospel of Peter (see above, pp. 216ff.). However, to reach any certainty the MSS would have to be minutely compared with the whole of the rest of the material. Extracts are to be found in Bonaccorsi I, 232-259 (text and Italian); de Santos Otero, pp. 260-275, [6]pp. 254-269 (text and Spanish).

We also give a translation of an infancy narrative from a Life of John the Baptist, which became known comparatively late. Written in Arabic with Syriac letters ('Garshuni'), it purports according to his own testimony to have been composed by the Egyptian bishop Serapion (probably in Greek) between 385 and 395, and is extant in two MSS of the Mingana collection (Ming. Syr. 22: 16th cent., and Ming. Syr. 183: 18th cent.); edited by A. Mingana himself: 'Woodbrooke Studies. Edition and Translation of Christian Documents in Syriac and Garshuni by A. Mingana, with Introduction by Rendel Harris', BJRL, Manchester 1927, 329ff.

A) Extracts from the Arabic Infancy Gospel

a) Legends of the child Jesus in Egypt

17. . . . the woman took sweet-smelling water to wash the Lord Jesus; when she had washed him, she kept that water with which she had done that, and poured some of it upon a girl who lived there and whose body was white with leprosy, and washed her with it. Immediately the girl was cleansed of the leprosy. And the inhabitants of that town said: 'There is no doubt that Joseph and Mary and this child are gods, not men.' And when they prepared to depart from them, that girl who had suffered from leprosy came to them, and asked them to take her with them as a companion.

(Ea, pp. 188f.)

23. From there Joseph and the lady Mary departed and came to a desert place, and when they heard that it was infested with raids by robbers, they decided to pass through this region by night. But behold, on the way they saw two robbers lying on the road, and with them a crowd of robbers, who belonged to them, likewise sleeping. Now those two robbers, into whose hands they had fallen, were Titus and Dumachus. And Titus said to Dumachus: 'I ask you to let these (people) go free, and in such a way that our companions do not observe them.' But Dumachus refused and Titus said again: 'Take from me forty drachmae and have them as a pledge.' At the same time he reached him the girdle which he wore round him, that he might hold his tongue and not speak. When the noble lady Mary saw that this robber had shown kindness to them, she said to him: 'The Lord God will uphold you with his right hand and grant you forgiveness of sins.' And the Lord Jesus answered and said to his mother: 'In thirty years, mother, the Jews will crucify me in Jerusalem, and those two robbers will be fastened to the cross with me, Titus on my right hand and Dumachus on my left,[1] and after that day Titus will go before me into paradise.' And she said: 'God preserve you from that,[2] my son.' And they departed from there to the city of idols; and when they drew near to it, they had been changed into sandhills.

(Ea, pp. 192f.)

24. From there they went to that sycamore tree which today is called Matarea, and the Lord Jesus made to gush forth in Matarea a spring, in which the lady Mary washed his shirt. And from the sweat of the Lord Jesus which she wrang out there, balsam appeared in that place.

(Ea, p. 193)

b) The children who were changed into goats

40. One day the Lord Jesus went out into the street and saw children who had come together to play. He followed them, but the children hid themselves from him. Now when the Lord Jesus came to the door of a house and saw women standing there, he asked them where those children had gone. They replied that no one was there; and the Lord Jesus said: 'Who are those whom you see in the furnace?' 'They are three-year-old goats', they answered. And the Lord Jesus said: 'Come out to your shepherd, you goats.' Then the children in the form of goats came out and began to skip round him. When those women saw this, they were seized with wonder and fear, and speedily fell down before the Lord Jesus and implored him, saying: 'O our Lord Jesus, son of Mary, truly you are the good shepherd[3] of Israel, have mercy on your handmaids who stand before you and have never doubted: for you have come, our Lord, to heal and not to destroy.'[4] The Lord Jesus answered and said: 'The children of Israel are like the Ethiopians among the peoples.' And the women said: 'You, Lord, know everything, and nothing is hidden from you; but now we beg and implore you of your mercy to restore to their former state these children, your servants.' So the Lord Jesus said: 'Come, children, let us go and play.' And immediately in the presence of these women the goats were changed into children.

(Ea, pp. 202f.; cf. also the Syriac 'History of the Virgin': E.A.W. Budge, *History of the Virgin*, 1899; cf. also Church Slavonic Gospel of Thomas XXII: de Santos pp. 145f.).

B) Extracts from the Gospel of Pseudo-Matthew

a) Ox and ass at the manger
(first mention)

14. On the third day after the birth of our Lord Jesus Christ holy Mary went out from the cave, and went into the stable and put her child in a manger,[1] and an ox and an ass worshipped him. Then was fulfilled that which was said through the prophet Isaiah: 'The ox knows his owner and the ass his master's crib.'[2] Thus the beasts, ox and ass, with him between them, unceasingly worshipped him. Then was fulfilled that which was said through the prophet Habakkuk: 'Between two beasts are you known.'[3] And Joseph remained in the same place with Mary for three days.

(Ea, p. 80)

b) Legends of the child Jesus in Egypt

18. 1. When they came to a cave and wished to rest (in it), holy Mary dismounted and sat down with the child Jesus in her lap. And on the journey there were with Joseph three boys and with Mary some maidens. And behold, suddenly many dragons came out of the cave. When the boys saw them they cried out in terror. Then Jesus got down from his mother's lap, and stood on his feet before the dragons; thereupon they worshipped Jesus, and then went back from them. Then was fulfilled that which was spoken through the prophet David: 'Praise the Lord, you dragons from the earth, you dragons and all deeps.'[4]

2. And the child Jesus himself went before the dragons and commanded them not to harm anyone. But Mary and Joseph had great fear lest the child should be hurt by the dragons. And Jesus said to them: 'Have no fear, and do not think that I am a child; for I have always been and even now am perfect; all wild beasts must be docile before me.'[5]

19. 1. Likewise lions and leopards worshipped him and accompanied them in the desert. Wherever Joseph and holy Mary went, they went before them, showing (them) the way and lowering their heads (in worship); they showed their servitude by wagging their tails and honoured him with great reverence. But when Mary saw the lions and leopards and all kinds of wild beasts surrounding them, she was at first gripped by violent fear. But the child Jesus looked at her face with a happy countenance, and said: 'Do not fear, mother; for they do not come to harm you, but they hasten to obey you and me.' With these words he removed all fear from her heart.

2. And the lions went along with them, and with the oxen and asses and the beasts of burden which carried what they needed, and they harmed no

462

one, although they remained (with them). Rather they were docile among the sheep and rams which they had brought with them from Judaea and had with them. They walked among wolves without fear, and neither was harmed by the other. Then was fulfilled that which was said through the prophet: 'The wolves pasture with the lambs: lions and oxen eat straw together.'⁶ And the lions guided on their journey the two oxen and the wagon in which they carried what they needed.

20. 1. Now on the third day of their journey, as they went on, it happened that blessed Mary was wearied by the too great heat of the sun in the desert, and seeing a palm-tree, she said to Joseph: 'I should like to rest a little in the shade of this tree.' And Joseph led her quickly to the palm and let her dismount from her animal. And when blessed Mary had sat down, she looked up at the top of the palm-tree and saw that it was full of fruits, and said to Joseph: 'I wish someone could fetch some of these fruits of the palm-tree.' And Joseph said to her: 'I wonder that you say this; for you see how high this palm-tree is, and (I wonder) that you even think about eating of the fruits of the palm. I think rather of the lack of water, which already fails us in the skins, and we have nothing with which we can refresh ourselves and the animals.'

2. Then the child Jesus, who was sitting with a happy countenance in his mother's lap, said to the palm: 'Bend down your branches, O tree, and refresh my mother with your fruit.' And immediately at this command the palm bent its head down to the feet of blessed Mary, and they gathered from it fruits with which they all refreshed themselves. But after they had gathered all its fruits, it remained bent down and waited to raise itself again at the command of him at whose command it had bent down. Then Jesus said to it: 'Raise yourself, O palm, and be strong, and join my trees which are in the paradise of my Father. And open beneath your roots a vein of water which is hidden in the earth, and let the waters flow so that we may quench our thirst from it.' And immediately it raised itself, and there began to gush out by its root a fountain of water very clear, fresh, and completely bright. And when they saw the fountain of water, they rejoiced greatly, and quenched their thirst, and also all the beasts of burden and all the animals, and gave thanks to God.

21. On the next day, when they went on from there, and at the hour when they set out, Jesus turned to the palm and said to it: 'O palm, I give you this privilege, that one of your branches be carried by my angels and be planted in the paradise of my Father. This blessing I will confer on you, that to all who shall be victorious in a contest it shall be said: 'you have won the palm of victory'.' When he said this, behold, an angel of the Lord⁷ appeared, standing above the palm-tree, and took one of its branches and flew to heaven with the branch in his hand. When they saw this, they fell on their faces and were as dead men. And Jesus spoke to them saying:

'Why does fear grip your hearts? Do you not know that this palm, which I have caused to be carried to paradise, will stand ready for all the saints in the place of blessedness, as it has for us in the place of solitude?' And they were filled with joy, and were all strengthened and arose.

22. 1. Now when they were journeying on, Joseph said to Jesus: 'Lord, we are being roasted by this heat; if you agree, let us go alongside the sea, that we may be able to rest in the coastal towns.' Jesus said to him: 'Do not fear, Joseph; I will shorten your journey: what you were intending to traverse in the space of thirty days, you will complete in one day.' And while they were speaking, behold they perceived already the mountains of Egypt and began to see its cities.

2. And happy and rejoicing they came to the region of Hermopolis, and entered an Egyptian city called Sotinen. And since there was in it no one they knew whom they could have asked for hospitality, they entered a temple which was called the 'capitol of Egypt'. In this temple stood 365 idols, to which on appointed days divine honour was paid in idolatrous rites. The Egyptians of this city entered the Capitol, in which the priests admonished them, to offer sacrifice on so many appointed days according to the honour of their deity.

23. But it came to pass that, when blessed Mary entered the temple with the child, all the idols fell to the ground, so that they all lay on their faces completely overturned and shattered. Thus they openly showed that they were nothing. Then was fulfilled what was said through the prophet Isaiah: 'Behold, the Lord shall come upon a swift cloud and shall enter into Egypt, and all (the idols) prepared by the hands of the Egyptians shall be removed before his face.'[8]

24. When this was told to Affrodosius, the governor of that city, he came to the temple with his whole army. And when the high priests of the temple saw that Affrodosius (Affrodosio) went to the temple with his whole army, they expected immediately to see his vengeance upon those because of whom the gods were destroyed. But when he entered the temple and saw all the idols lying prostrate on their faces, he went up to blessed Mary, who was carrying the Lord in her bosom, and worshipped him, and said to his whole army and to all his friends: 'If he were not the God of our gods, our gods would not have fallen on their faces before him, and they would not lie stretched out in his presence. Thus they silently confess him as their Lord. And if we do not with prudence do all that we see our gods do, we shall perhaps be in danger of angering him and of all being destroyed, as happened to Pharaoh, king of the Egyptians, who was drowned in the sea with his whole army, because he did not believe such great wonders.' Then all the people of the city believed in the Lord God through Jesus Christ.

25. After a short time the angel said to Joseph: 'Return to the land of Judah; they are dead who sought the child's life.' [9]

(Ea, pp. 85-93)

§§ 62-76,
89-96:
BAC
148; 254
71

C) Extract from the Latin Infancy Gospel in the Arundel Manuscript

The midwife's account of the birth in the cave

BAC
148;
260-62

73. When therefore the hour drew nearer, the might of God manifested itself. And the maiden (Mary) stood looking up to heaven, and became as a grape vine (?).[17] For now the end of the events of salvation was far advanced. And when the light had come forth, Mary worshipped him whom she saw that she had brought forth. And the child himself shone brightly round about like the sun, and was pure and most beautiful to behold, since he alone appeared as peace spreading peace everywhere. And in that hour when he was born there was heard a voice of many invisible beings saying with one accord 'Amen'.[2] And the light itself which was born increased and darkened the light of the sun with the brightness of its shining. And this cave was filled with bright light together with a most sweet odour. This light was born just as dew descends on the earth from heaven. For its odour is more fragrant than any aroma of ointments.

74. And I stood there stupefied and amazed, and fear seized me. For I was looking upon the intense brightness of the light which was born. But the light itself, gradually withdrawing, became like a child, and in a moment became a child as children are customarily born. And I took courage and bent down and touched him, and took him up in my hands with great fear, and was seized with terror because he had no weight like other children who are born. And I looked at him and there was no defilement in him, but he was in all his body shining as in the dew of the most high God, light to carry, radiant to behold. And while I wondered greatly because he did not cry as new-born babes are accustomed to cry, and while I held him and looked at his face, he smiled at me with the most sweet smile, and opened his eyes and looked sharply on me. And suddenly there came forth from his eyes a great light like a brilliant flash of lightning.

(From the Latin text, ed. M.R. James, *Latin Infancy Gospels*, 1927, pp. 68, 70)

D) Extract from the Life of John according to Serapion

The Child Jesus and John

(While the child Jesus is living with his parents in Egypt, the child John wanders through the desert with his mother Elizabeth.)

After five years the pious and blessed old mother Elizabeth passed away, and the holy John sat weeping over her, as he did not know how to shroud her and bury her, because on the day of her death he was only seven years and six months old. And Herod also died the same day as the blessed Elizabeth.

The Lord Jesus Christ who with his eyes sees heaven and earth saw his kinsman John sitting and weeping near his mother, and he also began to weep for a long time, without anyone knowing the cause of his weeping. When the mother of Jesus saw him weeping she said to him: 'Why are you weeping? Did the old man Joseph or any other one chide you?' And the mouth that was full of life answered: 'No, O my mother, the real reason is that your kinswoman,[1] the old Elizabeth, has left my beloved John an orphan. He is now weeping over her body which is lying in the mountain.'[2]

When the Virgin heard this she began to weep over her kinswoman, and Jesus said to her: 'Do not weep, O my Virgin mother, you will see her in this very hour.' And while he was still speaking with his mother, behold a luminous cloud came down and placed itself between them. And Jesus said: 'Call Salome and let us take her with us.' And they mounted the cloud which flew with them to the wilderness of 'Ain Kārim and to the spot where lay the body of the blessed Elizabeth, and where the holy John was sitting.

The Saviour said then to the cloud: 'Leave us here at this side of the spot.' And it immediately went, reached that spot, and departed. Its noise, however, reached the ears of Mar John, who, seized with fear, left the body of his mother. A voice reached him immediately and said to him: 'Do not be afraid, O John. I am Jesus Christ, your master. I am your kinsman Jesus, and I came to you with my beloved mother in order to attend to the business of the burial of the blessed Elizabeth, your happy mother, because she is my mother's kinswoman.' When the blessed and holy John heard this, he turned back, and Christ the Lord and his virgin mother embraced him. Then the Saviour said to his virgin mother: 'Arise, you and Salome, and wash the body.' And they washed the body of the blessed Elizabeth in the spring from which she used to draw water for herself and her son. Then the holy virgin Mart Mary got hold of the blessed (John) and wept over him, and cursed Herod on account of the numerous crimes which he had committed. Then Michael and Gabriel came down from heaven and dug a grave; and the Saviour said to them: 'Go and bring the soul of Zacharias, and the soul of the priest Symeon, in order that they may sing while you bury the body.' And Michael brought immediately the souls of Zacharias[3] and Symeon[4] who shrouded the body of Elizabeth and sang for a long time over it. . . .

And Jesus Christ and his mother stayed near the blessed and the holy John seven days, and condoled with him at the death of his mother, and taught him how to live in the desert.[5] And the day of the death of the blessed Elizabeth was the 15th of February.

Then Jesus Christ said to his mother: 'Let us now go to the place where I may proceed with my work.' The Virgin Mary wept immediately over the loneliness of John, who was very young, and said: 'We will take him with us, since he is an orphan without anyone.' But Jesus said to her: 'This is not the will of my Father who is in the heavens. He shall remain in the wilderness till the day of his showing unto Israel. Instead of a desert full of wild beasts,[6] he will walk in a desert full of angels and prophets, as if they were multitudes of people. Here is also Gabriel,[7] the head of the angels, whom I have appointed to protect him and to grant to him power from heaven. Further, I shall render the water of this spring of water as sweet and delicious to him as the milk he sucked from his mother. Who took care of him in his childhood? Is it not I, O my mother, who love him more than all the world? Zacharias also loved him, and I have ordered him to come and inquire after him, because although his body is buried in the earth, his soul is alive. . . . '

These words the Christ our Lord spoke to his mother, while John was in the desert. And they mounted the cloud, and John looked at them and wept, and Mart Mary wept also bitterly over him, saying: 'Woe is me, O John, because you are alone in the desert without anyone. Where is Zacharias, your father, and where is Elizabeth, your mother? Let them come and weep with me today.'

And Jesus Christ said to her: 'Do not weep over this child, O my mother. I shall not forget him.' And while he was uttering these words, behold the clouds lifted them up and brought them to Nazareth. And he fulfilled there everything pertaining to humanity except sin.[8]

(Translation of A. Mingana in BJRL, Manchester, 11, 1927, pp. 446-449)

Notes

4. Later Infancy Gospels

A) Extracts from the Arabic Infancy Gospel

1. Cf. Mk. 15:27.
2. Cf. Mt. 16:22.
3. Jn. 10:11.
4. Cf. Jn. 3:17.

B) Extracts from the Gospel of Pseudo-Matthew

1. Lk. 2:7.
2. Isa. 1:3.
3. Cf. Hab. 3:2 LXX.
4. Ps. 148:7.
5. Cf. Mk. 1:13.
6. Isa. 11:6f.
7. Lk. 2:9f.
8. Isa. 19:1.
9. Mt. 2:20.

C) Extract from the Latin Infancy Gospel in the Arundel Manuscript

1. Robinson alters *vinea* to *nivea*: 'and became snow white'.
2. Cf. Rev. 5:14.

D) Extract from the Life of John according to Serapion

1. Lk. 1:36.
2. Lk. 1:39.
3. Lk. 1:5.
4. Lk. 2:25.
5. Mk. 1:4.
6. Cf. Mk. 1:13.
7. Lk. 1:19, 26.
8. Cf. Hebr. 4:15.

XI. The Relatives of Jesus

Wolfgang A. Bienert

1. General:

Literature: Th. Zahn, *Brüder und Vettern Jesu* (Forschungen zur Geschichte des ntl. Kanons u.d. altkirchl. Lit. 6), 1900, pp. 225-364. W. Bauer, *Das Leben Jesu im Zeitalter der neutestamentlichen Apokryphen*, 1909 (= Darmstadt 1967). J. Blinzler, *Die Brüder und Schwestern Jesu*, (Stuttgarter Bibelstudien 21), ²1967. G.W. Lathrop, ''Who Shall Describe His Origin?' Tradition and Redaction in Mark 6, 1-6a', Diss. Nijmegen 1969. E. Gräßer, 'Jesus in Nazareth (Mc 6,1-6a). Bemerkungen zur Redaktion und Theologie des Markus', in W. Eltester (ed.), *Jesus in Nazareth*, (BZNW 40), 1972, pp. 1-37. J.D. Crossan, 'Mark and the Relatives of Jesus', *Nov.Test.* 15, 1973, 81-113. J. Lambrecht, 'The Relatives of Jesus in Mark', *Nov.Test.* 16, 1974, 241-258. L. Oberlinner, *Historische Überlieferung und christologische Aussage. Zur Frage der 'Brüder Jesu' in der Synopse*, (Forschung z. Bibel 19), 1975 (Lit.). J. Gilles, *Les 'frères et soeurs' de Jésus*, Paris 1979. R. Pesch, *Das Markusevangelium. 1.Teil*, (Herders Theol. Komm. z. NT II 1), 1976, esp. pp. 322-324; supplements in 3rd ed. 1980, pp. 453-462 and 4th ed. 1984, p. 479.

In Protestant research, since the fundamental works of Zahn and Bauer, the point of departure has generally been that the references to brothers and sisters of Jesus in the NT (e.g. Mk 3:31f.; 6:3 etc.) are historically reliable and mean bodily siblings. On the Catholic side, on the other hand, it has long been maintained (cf. in particular J. Blinzler) that here it is not a question of bodily siblings but simply of relatives of some more distant degree - half-brothers and sisters or cousins of Jesus. This view was already stoutly upheld in the early Church, especially in defence of the virginity of Mary (cf. for example Jerome, *adv. Helvidium*, PL 23, on which see Blinzler pp. 141ff.). But recently the conviction is more and more gaining ground, in Catholic research also, that an 'unbiassed exegesis' allows only the affirmation 'that in Mk 6:3 the names of four bodily brothers of Jesus and the existence of bodily sisters are attested' (R. Pesch, *Markusevangelium* I, 1976, 324; cf. also L. Oberlinner and the supplements in the 3rd and 4th editions (1980 or 1984) of Pesch's commentary on Mark).

It can, however, be observed how particular theological interpretations of the Christ event and of the person of Jesus, developed out of the confession of him as Son of God and Son of David, are already superimposed on the historical background in the NT. Traditions are supplemented (cf. the family tree of Jesus, see below, pp. 486 ff.) or embellished and expanded by legends, the historical foundations of which can often only be discovered with difficulty. This holds already for the synoptic Gospels, as recent exegetical research has shown. Hence in our search for historically reliable information we must constantly take into account the different theological interests of the respective authors. Above all we ought not to attempt out of hand to harmonise the various reports about the family of Jesus. Rather it seems more correct first to scrutinise the different documents individually - so far as possible in chronological order - and examine their statements critically for themselves in each case, before we set about constructing relationships. Special difficulties arise from the fact that names like Mary, Joseph, James and so on occur fairly frequently in the NT writings and beyond, so that it is easy to fall into confusion. The question of the earthly relatives of Jesus is however at the same time of eminent theological importance, for it may preserve the story of Jesus from being transformed into an unhistorical myth.

The oldest information about the relatives of Jesus appears in Paul. This is the more significant in that the apostle himself reveals no special interest in the 'Christ after the flesh' (cf. 2 Cor. 5:16). It is, however, part of his basic conviction that Christ, the Son of God, was born of a woman and belonged to the community of the Jewish people (Gal. 4:4). Paul does not speak of a 'virgin', nor does he mention the name of Jesus' mother. Also historically significant is his reference to James the Lord's brother (Gal. 1:19). Paul himself met James (Gal. 2:9), who clearly occupied a leading position in the Jerusalem community (Gal. 2:12). According to 1 Cor. 15:7 he was one of the first witnesses of the resurrection of Jesus. Along with Kephas/Peter he is the only person mentioned by name in this context. These two things together account for the special position of James in the primitive Church. Finally Paul refers, on the basis of tradition handed down to him, to the fact that Jesus Christ, the Son of God, was according to the flesh of the seed of David (Rom. 1:3f.). Whether this confession of Jesus as the promised Messiah of Israel can be used historically and biographically cannot be said with any certainty. Paul does not pursue this question. He contents himself with holding fast to this traditional faith, in which the connection with the history of the people of Israel finds expression.

Paul thus mentions three elements which play an essential role in the question of the relatives of Jesus: a) his human birth, b) his incorporation into the Jewish people, which is underlined by the title Messiah, and c) the existence of bodily brothers (cf. 1 Cor. 9:5), which because of its mention by Paul must be treated as historically reliable. All three elements did indeed undergo expansion and alteration in time to come - particularly through the influence of the Gospel traditions - but remain essentially uncontested. The severest change, under the influence of Mariology and the Immanuel promise (Isa. 7:14; Mt. 1:23), affected the conception of the human birth of Jesus. It developed into the doctrine of the virgin birth. It is, however, striking that even Paul never speaks of Jesus' human father. For this there are probably above all theological reasons; Paul thereby emphasises Jesus' divine sonship. In later times the Davidic sonship is anchored in the history of Israel, and beyond that in world history, by the drawing-up of genealogical tables. The mention of James the Lord's brother or of the 'brothers of the Lord', of whom Paul writes that some of them were married (1 Cor. 9:5), nevertheless raises the question of the relatives of Jesus in the wider sense.

In Mk. 6:3 it is reported that the inhabitants of Nazareth, Jesus' native town, asked: 'Is this not the carpenter [perhaps the original reading ran: 'the carpenter's son', cf. the parallel Mt. 13:55], the son of Mary and brother of James, Joses [in Mt. 'Joseph'], Judas and Simon? And are not his sisters here with us?' Here for the first time we learn the names of *four* brothers, and in addition hear of sisters of Jesus (so also Mt. 13:56). Again, in the passage about his true relatives (Mk. 3:20-35), there is mention at the end of brothers and sisters (Mk. 3:32-34). In the parallel in Matthew, however (12:46-50), there is only an indirect reference to sisters in the final sentence. There it is said: Whoever does the will of God, 'he is my brother and sister and mother' (Mk. 3:34/Mt. 12:50). The whole pericope in Mk. appears to have been shaped on the basis of this verse. It is striking that Luke nowhere mentions sisters of Jesus, and the same applies to John. It is equally striking that Mark - like Paul - does not name a human father for Jesus, if we once disregard the manuscript variant at Mk. 6:3. But that too names no name. Of the brothers of Jesus, apart from James, only Judas is mentioned by name in a later context (Euseb. H.E. III 20 = Hegesippus; cf. III 32.5). The two New Testament letters circulating under their names were also ascribed to them, although the authenticity of this ascription is already doubted by Eusebius (H.E. II 23.24f.).

The legend tradition also knows the names of *two* sisters, in addition to those of the four brothers. In the 'History of Joseph the Carpenter' (*c.* 400) they are called in c. 2 Lysia and Lydia (S. Morenz, p. 2; according to Tischendorf, Ea, pp. 122ff.: Assia and Lydia). Epiphanius (*Ancor.* 60; *Pan.* 78.8) calls them Mary or Anna and Salome. The name of the second brother varies in the tradition between Joses, Joseph and Josetos (History of Joseph c. 2; according to Tischendorf, *loc. cit.* 'Justus').

The statements about the brothers of Jesus in the Gospel of John are peculiarly contradictory. In Jn. 7:3-5 it is said that they urged Jesus to show himself to the world, although they did not themselves believe in him. The rejection of Jesus by his family, or at least an originally critical and distant attitude on their part towards him, accordingly seems to be historical (cf. Mk. 3:21, 31f.). The only curious thing is that in the crucifixion scene (Jn. 19:25-27) Jesus links his mother with 'the disciple whom he loved' as mother and son, as if she had no other sons. For that matter, John is the only one to report that the mother of Jesus was present at the crucifixion. In Acts 1:14 it is then said that the mother and brothers of Jesus very soon stood in close contact with the apostles. In the Gospel of the Nazareans it is his mother and brothers who call upon Jesus to have himself baptised by John the Baptist for the forgiveness of sins, which Jesus interestingly declines (Jerome, *adv. Pelag.* III 2; see above, p. 160). Interest in the earthly relatives of Jesus was particularly widespread in the Jewish-Christian traditions. This shows itself in a special way in regard to the person of James the Lord's brother. In association with gnostic tendencies, however, the human and earthly becomes at the same time the counterpart of the pneumatic.

2. James the Lord's brother:

Literature (supplementary): F. Sieffert, art. 'Jakobus im NT', RE³ 8, 1900, pp. 574-581. H. Frhr. von Campenhausen, 'Die Nachfolge des Jakobus. Zur Frage eines urchristlichen 'Kalifats'', ZKG 63, 1950/51, 133-144 = id. *Aus der Frühzeit des Christentums*, 1963, pp. 134-151. A. Böhlig, 'Zum Martyrium des Jakobus', *Nov.Test.* 5, 1962, 207-213 (slightly revised in *Mysterion und Wahrheit*, Leiden 1968, pp. 112-118). K. Beyschlag, 'Das Jakobusmartyrium und seine Verwandten in der frühchristlichen Literatur', ZNW 56, 1965, 149-178. H.-M. Schenke, 'Der Jakobusbrief aus dem Codex Jung', OLZ 66, 1971, 117-130. W.-P. Funk, *Die zweite Apokalypse des Jakobus aus Nag-Hammadi-Codex V*, (TU 119), 1976 (cf. above, pp. 327-341). G. Strecker, 'Judenchristentum und Gnosis', in *Altes Testament - Frühjudentum - Gnosis*, ed. K.-W. Tröger, 1980, pp. 261-282; id. *Das Judenchristentum in den Pseudoklementinen*, (TU 70²), ²1981 (Lit.). W. Pratscher, *Der Herrenbruder Jakobus und die Jakobustradition*, (FRLANT 139), 1987. E. Ruckstuhl, TRE XVI, 1987.

'James, to whom the ancients because of the excellence of his virtue gave the surname 'the Just'' (Euseb. H.E. II 1.2-5; cf. already Hegesippus ap. Euseb. H.E. II 23.4-18. The epithet also occurs in gnostic writings: Gos. Thom. = NHC II 2, log. 12; 1 Apoc. Jas. p. 32, see above p. 322; 2 Apoc. Jas. p. 44, see above, p. 333), is in Paul (Gal. 1:19) and later above all in Hegesippus called 'the brother of the Lord' (Euseb. H.E. II 32.6; IV 22.4; cf. III 10.11; III 32.4; also Josephus, *Ant.* XX 9.1, see below, p. 489). If Eusebius himself adds the qualification 'so-called' (H.E. I 12.5; II 1.2; VII 19), this gives expression to the fact that in the interval the conviction of Mary's perpetual virginity has widely prevailed within the Church. The possibility that after her 'first son' (Lk. 2:7) Mary could also have had other children, as the New Testament witnesses suggest to the unbiased reader, now appears no longer feasible. The way was prepared for this development above all by the Protev. Jacobi (cf. 8.3; 9.2; 17.1f.; 18.1), which originated in the middle of the 2nd century. The apocryphal traditions link directly on to it (Ps.-Mt. 8.8; 18.1; History of Joseph 2.3). Origen refers also to the Gospel of Peter (*Comm. in Mt.* X 17), but we can no longer verify this statement. From the time of Clement of Alexandria, Hippolytus and Origen the view that with the brothers (and sisters) of Jesus mentioned in the NT it is a question of children of Joseph by an earlier marriage, i.e. of half-brothers and sisters, appears in nearly all Church fathers (references in Blinzler, pp. 131ff.). In gnostic texts moreover the common fatherhood becomes a special problem. Thus in 2 Apoc. Jas. it is said that James and Jesus were foster- brothers and at the same time cousins (p. 50; see above p. 335, and on this Funk, p. 122). It is expressly emphasised that they did not have the same father ('Your father is not my father', p. 51). But behind this there is at the same time the gnostic conviction that the one derives from the heavenly Father, whereas the other has his being from the Demiurge. 1 Apoc. Jas. speaks of a purely spiritual brotherhood between the two. There Christ says to James: 'Not for nothing have I called you 'my brother', although you are not my brother materially' (NHC V 3, 24.12-18). Tertullian in contrast had still emphasised, with an express anti-gnostic or anti-docetic tendency, that in the case of the brothers of Jesus it is a question of bodily brothers and children of Mary. He wished in this way to underscore the reality of the incarnation of Christ (*De carne Christi 7; adv. Marc.* IV 19; cf. Blinzler, pp. 139f.). A literal understanding of the references to the brothers of Jesus nevertheless increasingly ranked either as simplistic or as Judaistic.

In the early Jerusalem community James played a prominent role. He was one of the 'pillars' (Gal. 2:9), and had a decisive influence over Peter and Barnabas (cf. Gal. 2:12f.). In Acts he appears as a leading authority, who is concerned above all to preserve the Jewish heritage in the Church (15:13-22). Paul too submits to his guidance (21:18-26). James indeed is no opponent of the gentile mission, but expects that the converted heathen should at least in specific matters adhere to the Jewish law (*ibid.*). After the death of James the son of Zebedee and the departure of Peter (cf. Acts 12:1-17), the Lord's brother appears to have been the sole controlling leader of the Jerusalem community. In later witnesses he is therefore described as its first bishop (Euseb. H.E. II 1.2; Ps.-Clem. *Recog.* I 43; 66.2; 70.3 and often; cf. G. Strecker, *Pseudoklementinen*, p. 235, with further evidence from Clement of Alexandria, Epiphanius, etc.). It is worthy of note that Hegesippus calls him so only indirectly (Euseb. H.E. IV 22.4), whereas in the Ps.-Clementines he is even described as ἐπίσκοπος ἐπισκόπων (*Ep. Clem.* 1.1; cf. *Recog.* I 68.2). This indicates that the designation 'bishop' is secondary. By the fact that Hegesippus describes his successor Symeon as 'second bishop' (Euseb. H.E. IV 22.4), however, the points are set. Symeon according to Hegesippus' information (cf. Euseb. H.E. III 11) was a cousin of Jesus, and indeed a son of Clopas (cf. Lk. 24:18; Jn. 19:25), who was a brother of Jesus' father Joseph. Eusebius mentions later (H.E. VII 19) that James' episcopal throne was still preserved in his day. It is however improbable that James was already a bishop in the sense of the monarchic episcopate (cf. H. von Campenhausen). Nevertheless it is worthy of note that in the Jerusalem community relatives of Jesus evidently played a leading role for a long time. Hegesippus reports of Symeon that he suffered as a martyr by crucifixion in the time of the Emperor Trajan, at the age of 120 years (Euseb. H.E. III 32.6).

The special position of James in the primitive Church was not only due to his kinship with Jesus. He was also one of the earliest witnesses of the resurrection (cf. 1 Cor. 15:7), and one to whom - according to the Gospel of the Hebrews - the risen Jesus appeared personally. According to this, Jesus 'took the bread . . . and gave it to James the Just and said to him: My brother, eat thy bread, for the Son of man is risen from among them that sleep' (Jerome, *Vir. ill.*2; see above, p. 178). Personal revelations by the Redeemer, moreover, form the background for the gnostic tradition in which James appears as a mediator of Christian Gnosis, as in the two apocalypses handed down under his name (see above, pp. 313ff.). In the Coptic Gospel of Thomas also (above, pp. 110ff.) James the Just is exalted as the one 'for whom heaven and earth were made' (see above, p. 119). In Hippolytus (*Ref.* V 7.1; X 9.3) it is said of the Naassenes that they traced their teachings back to James the Lord's brother, who transmitted them to Mariamne. Hippolytus, however, considers this a slander. In the Epistula Jacobi (NHC I 2), which was perhaps addressed to Cerinthus (Schenke, OLZ 1971, 119f.), it is presumably James the apostle who is meant and not the Lord's brother, for the author counts himself among the twelve (p. 1.24f. = Schenke, p. 120; cf. above, p.291). The connection between Gnosticism and Jewish Christianity which is recognisable here shows itself in another way in the so-called Pseudo-Clementines, in which the relations between James, Peter and Clement of Rome, as well as between Rome and Jerusalem, are developed in novelistic fashion. Here the episcopal conception of the Church is already presupposed. The fact that the Lord's brother from the beginning is distinguished from the apostles, however closely he may be connected with them, also speaks for the view that the Nag Hammadi Epistula Jacobi means the apostle and not the Lord's brother. In this connection an exposition of Is. 17:6 by Eusebius is interesting. The bishop of Caesarea there interprets the fourteen fruits left remaining at the olive harvest as the twelve apostles, supplemented by Paul, the 'celebrated apostle', and James, the Lord's brother and first bishop of the Jerusalem community (*Comm. in Jes.* 17.5 = Ziegler, GCS 1975, p. 116.16-25).

About the martyrdom of James we have various accounts, some of them very extensive, the value of which as sources is, however, in dispute. Some descriptions show typical features and contacts with the early Christian martyr literature (cf. A. Böhlig and especially K. Beyschlag, who however does not discuss in detail the text handled by Böhlig), which makes investigation of the historical background difficult.

We find the oldest report of James' end in the Jewish historian Josephus (*Ant.* XX 9.1; cf. below, p. 489). According to this the high priest Ananus the younger, in the period after the death of the procurator Festus (cf. Acts 25f.) and before the entry into office of his successor Albinus, i.e. in the year 62, induced the Sanhedrin to condemn and stone James along with a few others for violation of the law. Complaints about this proceeding then led to the deposition of Ananus by King Agrippa. This passage is sometimes regarded as a Christian interpolation, but this assumption is not convincing. It is otherwise with the remark which in Origen and Eusebius is likewise ascribed to Josephus - although without any precise statement of the passage - and in which it is said, with reference to the siege of Jerusalem by Vespasian: 'This fate befell the Jews in retribution for James the Just, the brother of Jesus, the so-called Christ; for although he was most righteous, the Jews slew him' (Euseb. H.E. II 23.20; cf. Origen, *c. Cels.* I 47; II 13; *Comm. in Mt.* X 17). The passage is missing in our Josephus tradition.

The same tendency appears in the Christian tradition of this martyrdom in book V of the 'memoirs' of Hegesippus from the period about 180. The description of the end of James given by this champion of orthodoxy, who came from the East - but, because of his sometimes 'quixotic statements about things Jewish', scarcely from Judaism (Vielhauer, *Lit. gesch.* p. 776; against Euseb. H.E. IV 22.8) - differs not insignificantly from the statements of Josephus. It has moreover a strongly stylised effect and is decked out in legendary fashion - linking up with elements from the life and passion of Jesus, the journeys of Paul, the martyrdom of Stephen etc. (cf. K. Beyschlag) - and is also not free from factual errors and absurdities. The text handed on by Eusebius (H.E. II 23.4-18; cf. 22.4) is as follows:

'The Lord's brother, James, took over the (leadership of the) church along with the apostles. From the days of the Lord until our own he was called by all 'the Just', for there were many who bore the name of James. This man was holy from his mother's womb. Wine and intoxicating liquors he did not drink, nor did he eat animal food [cf. Lev. 10:9; Num. 6:3]. A razor never came upon his head, he did not anoint himself with oil, and he never used a bath [Num. 6:5]. To him alone it was permitted to enter the sanctuary. For he never wore woollen clothing, but linen. He used to go alone into the Temple, and was found continually upon his knees entreating forgiveness for the people, so that his knees became hard like those of a camel because he was always bending them, worshipping God and begging forgiveness for the people. Because of the exceeding greatness of his righteousness he was called 'the Just' and 'Oblias', which is in Greek (περιοχὴ τοῦ λαοῦ = a rampart for the people; cf. Micah 4:8), and righteousness, as the prophets show concerning him (cf. Is. 3:10).

Now some of the seven sects in the (Jewish) people, of whom I have written above in my 'memoirs' [cf. Euseb. H.E. IV 22.7], asked him: 'What is the door of Jesus?' And he answered that this was the Saviour [cf. Jn 10:7]. From which some believed that Jesus is the Christ (= the Messiah). But the aforesaid sects did not believe either in the resurrection or that he will come to requite each according to his works. But as many as believed did so because of James. Now when many of the leaders (of the people) also believed, there was a tumult among the Jews and scribes and Pharisees, who said that the whole people was in danger of expecting Jesus as the Christ (= the Messiah). They therefore went together to James and said to him: 'We entreat you, restrain the people, for they have been led astray after Jesus, as if he were the Christ. We entreat you to persuade all who come to the day of the passover concerning Jesus, for we all have confidence in you. For we and all the people bear you witness that you are righteous, and no respecter of persons. Therefore persuade the people not to be led astray concerning Jesus. For indeed the whole people and all of us have confidence in you. Stand therefore upon the pinnacle of the Temple, that up there you may be clearly visible, and your words may be easily heard by all the people. For because of the passover all the tribes have come together, with the Gentiles also.'

So the scribes and Pharisees mentioned stood James upon the pinnacle of the Temple, and cried out to him and said: 'O just man, to whom we all owe confidence! Since the people is going astray after Jesus, the crucified, declare to us, what is the door of Jesus?' And he answered with a loud voice: 'Why do you ask me about the Son of man? He sits in heaven at the right hand of the great power, and is about to come on the clouds of heaven' [cf. Mt. 26:64; Mk. 14:62]. But when many burst into excited jubilation at the testimony of James and cried: 'Hosanna to the Son of David!' - then these same scribes and Pharisees said to one another: 'We have done ill in affording such a testimony to Jesus. But let us go up and cast him down, that in fear they may not believe him.' And they cried out: 'Oh, oh, even the Just has gone astray!' And they fulfilled the scripture that is written in Isaiah: 'Let us do away with the just, for he is troublesome to us! Wherefore they shall eat the fruit of their works' [Is. 3:10]. So they went up and cast down the Just, and said to one another: 'Let us stone James the Just.' And they began to stone him, since he did not die when he fell. But turning about he fell on his knees and said: 'I entreat thee, Lord, God, Father, forgive them; for they know not what they do' (cf. Lk 23:34; Acts 7:59f.).

But while they were still stoning him, one of the priests of the sons of Rechab, a descendant of the Rechabites whom the prophet Jeremiah mentions (Jer. 35:2ff.), cried out, saying: 'Stop! What are you doing? The Just is praying for you.' Then one of them, a fuller, took the club with which he beat out the clothes and brought it down on the Just's head. And so he suffered martyrdom. And they buried him on the spot near the Temple. This man was for both Jews and Greeks a true witness that Jesus is the Christ. And straightway Vespasian laid siege to them.'

This story, by which perhaps Clement of Alexandria is already influenced (*Hypotyp.* VII = Euseb. H.E. II 1.5), as Epiphanius certainly is (*Pan.* 78), shows many improbable features. Among them are the peculiar juxtaposition of the various Jewish sects, in which Hegesippus had a special interest (Euseb. H.E. IV 22.5-6), the stylised portrait of James as a saint, Nazirite and ascetic, a man of prayer who alone might enter the sanctuary (the Holy of Holies?), but also the singular linking-together of the fall from the Temple, the stoning (without any judicial process) and the slaying by the fuller. This is clearly a Christian martyr legend, shot through with motifs from the Old Testament (Is. 3:10; cf. Ps. 34:16) and the New (Jesus, Stephen; cf. also Jas. 5:16), so that there is considerable doubt as to the historical value of the information given. It is however a testimony to the veneration which James enjoyed in certain - probably Jewish-Christian - circles.

We may compare two fairly long parallels, which are based on older sources. The one is in one of the source documents of the Pseudo-Clementines, the so-called AJ II source (G. Strecker, *Pseudo-Klementinen*, pp. 221-254), which possibly originated about 150. There (*Recog.* I 43-71) there is mention of James 'who was appointed bishop by the Lord' (*Recog.* I 43.3), and of discussions with different groups in Judaism (53ff.: Samaritans, Pharisees, Sadducees), which finally develop into a public dispute between Gamaliel, James and Caiaphas the high priest. Then suddenly a 'hostile man' appears (*Recog.* I 70.1,8; 71.3: cf. 73.4), who seizes a billet of wood from the altar and strikes James with it, so that he falls from the Temple steps and lies as dead. There is no reference to stoning. Instead this *homo inimicus* is revealed to be Paul, the enemy of the Christians, who has received from the high priest Caiaphas the commission to persecute all who believe in Jesus (cf. Acts 9.1ff.). But this throws the usual chronology in regard to the death of James into complete confusion.

The other parallel is in 2 Apoc. Jas. (above, pp. 327ff.). There James delivers a long revelation-speech from the fifth, the 'beautiful' step of the Temple. It is written down by a certain Marim, and a report about it is given by a priest to Theudas, the father of James (p.44.11ff.; above, p. 333) - according to p. 50 James is foster-brother and cousin to Jesus (see above, p. 335). Then follows at the end of the text an account, originally probably independent, of the martyrdom of James (p.61.15ff.; above, p. 339; see on this Funk, pp. 172ff.; on the structure of the document, pp. 192ff., cf. also A. Böhlig). This shows many surprising agreements with Hegesippus, particularly in the stoning scene, using Is. 3:10 LXX (Euseb. H.E. II 23.15; see above, pp. 476f.), while the apocalypse itself is at many points related to the tradition in the Ps.-Clementines. In contrast to Hegesippus, the death-scene in the apocalypse from Nag Hammadi is expanded by a long prayer (pp. 62.16-63.29; above, pp. 339f.). It is, however, remarkable that the description of the stoning procedure is 'partly reminiscent of the Talmudic regulations for execution of the sentence' (Funk, p. 176; cf. p. 177 and note 1, where references are given to Sanh. VI 4 and SifreDt 17.7 §151). This leads to a connection between the notice in Josephus and the description of Hegesippus, via the Apocalypse of James. The fall from the Temple steps probably also belongs to the historical core. Details of the description on the other hand are either decked out in legendary fashion or rest on roving motifs of legendary tradition, e.g. in the interpretation of Ps. 118 (cf. K. Beyschlag, p. 167, note 32 and elsewhere). The text of the martyrdom in 2 Apoc. Jas. 61f. runs in Funk's translation (above, p. 339):

And they rose up, saying: 'Well then, let us kill this man, that he may be removed from our midst! For he will be of no use to us at all.' And they were there, and they found him standing by the pinnacle of the Temple, beside the mighty cornerstone. And they decided to cast him down from the height, and they cast him down.

But [when] they [looked upon him], they observed [that he was still alive (?). Then] they arose (?) [and went down,] (*p. 62*) seized him and [abused] him, dragging him on the ground. They stretched him out, rolled a stone on his abdomen, and trampled him with their feet, saying: '(O you) who have gone astray!' Again they raised him up, since he was (still) alive, made him dig a hole, and made him stand in it. When they had covered him up to his abdomen, they stoned him in this manner'.

Then after a brief introduction a long prayer follows (cf. on it Funk, pp. 211ff.), with the final note: 'After he had spoken (the prayer), [he] was silent' (p. 63.30; above 340).

The author of this martyrdom description starts out from two fixed points: the fall and the widespread tradition of the stoning, in which, taking over the Talmudic regulations, he inserts the detail of the 'first stone' but otherwise presents a violent and merciless picture. 'Almost every sentence reflects the tendency to bestow superhuman features on the portrait of James and so make his person the more heroic' (Funk, p. 178).

Epiphanius finally reports that the Ebionites in particular had a special liking for James. On the one hand they appealed to the apostolic authority of James (*Pan.* 30.23), which very probably refers to the Lord's brother, and on the other they valued the document 'Ascent of James' ('Αναβαθμὸς 'Ιακώβου, *Pan.* 30.16), a work no longer extant but one which, if we set out from Epiphanius' report, must have stood indirectly in some connection with the Ps.-Clementines (cf. G. Strecker, *Pseudoklementinen*, pp. 251ff.). In it Paul was attacked as an opponent of circumcision, the sabbath and the Law, but James also according to it rejected the Temple cult.

3. Mary the mother of Jesus:

Literature: a) *Sources:* S. Alvarez Campos (ed.),*Corpus Marianum patristicum*, 4 vols., Burgos 1970-1976. D. Casagrande (ed.), *Enchiridion Marianum biblicum patristicum*, Rome 1974. W. Delius (ed.), *Texte zur Geschichte der Marienverehrung und Marienverkundigung in der Alten Kirche*, (Kl.Texte 178), 2nd revised and enlarged edition ed. H.-U. Rosenbaum, 1973.

b) *Aids*: G.M. Besutti, *Bibliographia Mariana* 1948-1977, 6 vols., Rome 1950-1980. *Lexikon der Marienkunde*, ed. K. Algermissen *et al.* (only vol. I, A-E), 1967. W. Beinert/H.Petri (eds.), *Handbuch der Marienkunde*, 1984.

c)*Presentations*: O. Zöckler, art. 'Maria, die Mutter des Herrn', RE[3] XII, 1903, 309-326. E. Cothenet, 'Marie dans les apocryphes', in *Maria. Études sur la sainte Vierge*, ed. H. du Manoir, VI, Paris 1961, 71-156 (Lit.). H. von Campenhausen, 'Die Jungfrauengeburt in der Theologie der Alten Kirche', SHAWPhil 1962.3 = id. *Urchristliches und Altchristliches*, 1979, pp. 63-161. W. Delius, *Geschichte der Marienverehrung*, 1963. H. Räisänen, *Die Mutter Jesu im NT*, Helsinki 1969. R. Laurentin, 'Mythe et dogme dans les apocryphes', in *Acta congr. mariologici-mariani in Lusitania a.1967 celebr.* IV, Rome 1970, 14-29. J.A. de Aldama, *María en la patristica des los siglos I y II*, (BAC 300), Madrid 1970. B. Bagatti, 'La verginità di Maria negli apocrifi del II-III secolo', in *Marianum* 33, 1971, 281-292. J. McHugh, *The Mother of Jesus in the New Testament*, London 1975 (bibliography pp. 475-498). G. Söll, 'Mariologie', HbDG III 4, 1978 (Lit.). P. Grelot/F. Fernandez, art. 'Marie (Vierge) I-II', in *Dict. Spir.* X 1, 1980, 409-440. R.E. Brown *et al.* (eds.), *Mary in the New Testament*, Philadelphia 1978 (German ed. 1981). R. Mahoney, 'Die Mutter Jesu im NT', in *Die Frau im Urchristentum*, ed. G. Dautzenberg,(QD 95), 1983, pp. 92-116. P. Plank, ''Gottesgebärerin und Immerjungfrau'. Altchristliche Quellen ostkirchlicher Marienverehrung', in *Mariologische Studien* VI, ed. H. Petri, 1984, 59-76.

The number of contributions to research on Mary and the beginnings of Mariology stands in inverse relationship to what we possess in the way of historically reliable tradition about the mother of Jesus. Later dogmatic decisions about the 'mother of God' and the 'perpetual virgin' - the terms are attested from the 4th century on - have overlaid the original picture and made it almost unrecognisable. In any attempt to recover this original picture - at least in its basic features - it must here also be noted, as recent research has strongly emphasised, that even our oldest sources already reflect the theological interests of their respective authors.

In the oldest documents of the NT, the letters of Paul, the mother of Jesus is not mentioned by name. It is however presupposed that Jesus - like any man - had a human mother (Gal. 4:4; Gal. 1:19; 1 Cor. 9:5). The earliest testimony that the mother of Jesus was called Mary is found in Mark (Mk. 6:3). This is at the same time the only passage in which the evangelist mentions her name. The name is missing in an earlier scene, connected with it in terms of content, which is concerned with Jesus' 'true kinsfolk' (Mk. 3:20f., 31-35). In contrast to the latter scene, clearly shaped by Mark, the rather casual reference to the mother, brothers and sisters of Jesus, with mention of their names (Mk. 6:3), has the effect of a remnant of early tradition. On the other hand, other passages in the Gospels (e.g. Jn. 2:1-12; 7:3ff.) also lead us to suspect that the mother and brothers of Jesus initially took up a critical stance towards his public ministry, even if they later adhered to the community (Acts 1:14). Later traditions attempted in some measure to correct this picture, above all by the addition of the infancy narratives, in which Mary emerges from this shadow and gains a positive significance, while at the same time her importance for the history of salvation is given a stronger emphasis. This holds first of all for Matthew who, apart from the parallels to Mark (cf. Mt. 12:46-50; 13:53-58; by name only in 13:55), mentions Mary only in the infancy story (chapters 1-2). The genealogy at the beginning ends with the sentence: 'Jacob begot Joseph, the husband of Mary; of her was born Jesus, who is called Christ' (1:16). The genealogy relates to Joseph, who however does not appear as the bodily father of Jesus. For Mary becomes pregnant through the operation of the Holy Spirit (1:18, 20). In this way Matthew sees here the fulfilment of the promise of Is. 7:14 (= Mt. 1:23), in which Davidic sonship (cf. Rom. 1:3f.) and virginal conception corresponding to the tradition of the Greek Old Testament are bound together.

Matthew's christological interest is clear: Jesus is the promised 'God with us' whom Mary brings into the world. The historical anchoring of the Davidic sonship is achieved through the genealogy of Joseph, while the promise of Is. 7:14 is fulfilled in Mary. Matthew has no further interest in the person of Mary. In the whole of the infancy narrative she remains completely passive, and is further mentioned only in 2:11 - rather in passing. The express statement (1:25) that up to the birth of Jesus Joseph refrained from sexual intercourse with Mary remains worthy of note. This at least leaves open the existence of further children from this marriage, and hence of bodily siblings of Jesus (cf. Mt. 13:53ff.).

In Luke the mother of Jesus is mentioned by name only one other time, outside the birth and infancy stories, at the beginning of Acts (1:14). In the Gospel of Luke there are in addition two other passages in which there is reference to her. In connection with the question of Jesus' true kindred (Lk. 8:19-21, par. Mk. 3:31-35/Mt. 12:46-50), it is striking not only that - as in Matthew - there is no reference to sisters of Jesus, but also that altogether there is an avoidance of any impression that there was any conflict between Jesus and his

480

relatives. Jesus' saying is transformed into a universalised statement, which ultimately confirms yet again the picture which Luke has drawn of Mary in the infancy story. For Mary in her hearing and keeping of the divine message is positively the ideal of true discipleship (cf. 8:21 with 2:19; 2:51). It is also striking that in the parallels to Mk. 6:3f. (Lk. 4:22, 24; Mt. 13:55, 57) the mother and siblings of Jesus are not mentioned at all. Instead, Luke makes the people in Nazareth ask: 'Is this not Joseph's son?' This fits with the remark in Lk. 3:23: 'He was thought to be the son of Joseph', which is an indirect allusion to the virginal conception. The second mention of the mother of Jesus outside the infancy stories is Lucan special material. A woman from the crowd cries out to Jesus: 'Blessed is the womb that bore you, and the breasts which you sucked.' And Jesus answers: 'Blessed rather are those who hear the word of God and keep it' (Lk. 11:27f.). He thus confirms once more the picture of true discipleship which Mary, according to Luke, so admirably fulfils. The prophecy of blessings in the Magnificat (Lk. 1:48) is for the first time fulfilled. At the same time Luke thus gives a hint of the beginnings of veneration of Mary, at the centre of which stand the conception and birth of Jesus.

Luke emphasises Mary's virginity more strongly than Matthew (Lk. 1:27). The relation to Is. 7:14 is rather indirect (cf. 1:31). Instead, the structure of the story, the annunciation of conception and birth by the angel Gabriel, Mary's response referring to her inviolate virginity (1:34), the reference to the operation of the Holy Spirit, the drawing in of Mary's 'kinswoman' Elizabeth (1:35f.; she appears in the NT only in this context), and finally - as, for the moment, the high point - the Magnificat (1:46-55), all give to the whole event a very plastic and dramatic character, which brings the Virgin Mary into the foreground, whereas the christological theme recedes in comparison. Joseph, the affianced husband (1:27; 2:5; cf. Mt. 1:18), also plays only a subordinate role, although in Luke too the Davidic sonship is linked with his genealogy (3:23). Even in the story of the twelve-year-old Jesus (2:41-52) Mary is the speaker (2:48; cf. 2:51). The reference to the birth of the 'first-born' son (2:7) makes it clear, however, that Luke, like Matthew, evidently understood the brothers of Jesus as bodily brothers and children of Mary. It is only the Protevangelium Jacobi, to which we owe the information about Joachim and Anna, Mary's parents (see above, pp. 421ff.), that for the first time emphatically vouches for Mary's perpetual virginity. This is done in a completely different way in the gnostic Gospel of Philip, where it is said (NHC II 3, p. 55.23ff. = §17; cf. above, p. 190): 'Some said: 'Mary conceived by the Holy Spirit.' They are in error. They do not know what they are saying. When did a woman ever conceive by a woman? ['Spirit' in semitic languages is feminine]. Mary is a virgin whom the powers did not defile . . . This virgin whom the powers did not defile is childless. The powers defiled (themselves).' This corresponds with the Valentinian idea, that Christ passed without contact through the virgin womb 'like water through a pipe' (Iren. adv. Haer. I 7.2). The gnostic emphasis on the virginity corresponds with a docetic Christology, according to which Christ descended direct from heaven. The Protevangelium Jacobi on the other hand is concerned with a real birth, in which the virginity of Mary in wonderful fashion remained intact, as the midwife summoned to the spot testifies. We first find the anti-docetic emphasis on the real birth in association with the doctrine of the birth of Jesus from the Virgin Mary in Ignatius of Antioch (c. 110; cf. *Smyrn.* 1.1; *Eph.* 19.1; also *Eph.* 7.2; 18.2; *Trall.* 9.1). It was to become a fundamental element in the Church tradition. On the Jewish side, the doctrine of the virgin birth met with violent criticism. It was understood as a taking-over of Greek mythology. The Christians ought - in their view - to say rather that Jesus was in origin a man like any other man. The reference to messianic prophecy was incorrect; for the reference there was to a young woman (νεᾶνις) and not to a virgin (παρθένος) (Justin, *Dial.* 67.1ff.; cf. 43.8). Justin himself in his argumentation relies on this reading (*Apol.* I 32.9-35.1 and often) - the usual one in the Greek translations of the OT in general.

The Gospel of John draws a portrait of the mother of Jesus independent of this tradition. Here it is striking that her name is not mentioned. She remains as anonymous as the disciple 'whom Jesus loved' (Jn. 13:23; 19:26 and often). This already makes it clear that the author is not concerned to convey historical details. Closer examination of the scenes in which the mother of Jesus appears confirms this impression. There are only two passages, which are however of decisive importance for the Christology of John's Gospel, for they mark the beginning and the end of Jesus' public activity. At the beginning stands the wedding at Cana (2:1-12), in which Mary has a hand in preparing for the first manifestation of the Son of God. As his bodily mother she is the guarantor of the real incarnation of the Logos (Jn. 1:14), and her behaviour at the wedding at the same time gives expression to her complete humanity and her earthly limitations. The second time, we find her beneath the cross of Jesus (Jn. 19:25-27). Here too the author's concern is evidently with the anti-docetic proof (cf. 19:34) that Jesus on the cross, at the point of death, is a real man who before his death also fulfils the natural obligations of a son towards his mother. Similarly Ignatius of Antioch laid claim to Mary as guarantor in the face of a docetic Christology (cf. Ign. *Eph.*7.2). It is difficult to say to what extent the scenes portrayed by John relate to historical facts. The Synoptics report nothing about the presence of Jesus' mother at the crucifixion. All the same, this scene not only permanently enriched iconography but in combination with the Lucan legacy it gave a strong impulse to Mariology as a whole.

The combination of various statements about Mary in the NT made it possible for later exegetes (e.g. Jerome against Helvidius) to preserve the virginity of Jesus' mother either by treating the siblings of Jesus as Joseph's children by his first marriage - here the legendary tradition had a powerful influence - or by regarding them as cousins, i.e. as children of a relative who was likewise called Mary. For Jerome it was according to Jn. 19:25 a question of a sister of Mary who was also called Mary, which however raises problems. It is more probable that the text speaks of four women, the sister of Mary remaining nameless (perhaps this was Salome; cf. Mk. 15:40). The basis for the view recently advocated by J. Blinzler is the peculiar circumstance that in Mk. 15:40 (cf. 15:47; 16:1) a Mary is mentioned who is described as the mother of 'James the younger' and Joses. In the parallel in Matthew (27:56, 61; 28:1) the children are named James and

Joseph, and their mother is called 'the other Mary'. Since in Mk. 6:3 (par.) the two brothers of Jesus first mentioned are likewise named James and Joses (or Joseph), the two statements could be combined in such a way that the so-called 'other Mary' is possibly the mother of all these children. Jn. 19:25 speaks of the fact that in addition to the mother of Jesus another Mary, the wife (or daughter; see the Sahidic version) of a certain Clopas, also stood beneath the cross of Jesus. According to Hegesippus, Clopas was an 'uncle of the Lord' (Euseb. H.E. IV 22.4), and indeed a brother of Joseph (cf. Euseb. H.E. III 11). The children of this Mary would then in fact be cousins (or children of the female cousin) of Jesus. One could, however, also argue otherwise, and see in the mother of 'James the younger' and Joses the mother of Jesus himself (so in addition to Helvidius both Gregory of Nyssa and John Chrysostom; cf. Th. Zahn p. 340, note 3), especially since Jn. 19:25 attests their presence beneath the cross. It is in any case probable that James the Lord's brother was a younger brother of Jesus. We should then perhaps have in Mk. 15:40 the remains of a very old tradition about the mother of Jesus in connection with the passion story, which however neither Mark nor Matthew was able to fit into his conception, while Jn. 19:25 with its reference to the mother of Jesus beneath the cross would have preserved a piece of authentic tradition. For Mark and Matthew, however, it is beyond doubt a question of different women with the name of Mary. The description 'mother of James the younger' clearly serves to distinguish this James from other bearers of this name, by no means uncommon in the time of Jesus, and also to distinguish him from the James mentioned in Mk. 6:3. The expression 'the other Mary' used by Matthew underlines the difference still more clearly.

4. Joseph, the father of Jesus:

Literature (supplementary): S. Morenz, *Die Geschichte von Joseph dem Zimmermann*,(TU 56), 1951. L.Th. Lefort, 'A propos de l 'Histoire de Joseph le Charpentier'', *Le Muséon* 66, 1953, 201-222. G.-M. Bertrand, *Saint Joseph dans les écrits des Pères*, Paris-Montreal 1966. G. Giamberardini, *S. Joseph dans la tradition copte (CJos 17)*, Montreal 1969. M. Motté, ''Mann des Glaubens'. Die Gestalt Josephs nach dem NT', *Bibel und Leben* 11, 1970, 176-189. *Saint Joseph durant les quinze premiers siècles de l'Église (CJos 19)*, Montreal 1971. P. Grelot/G.-M. Bertrand, art. 'Joseph (saint), époux de Marie I-II', *Dict. Spir.* VIII, 1974, 1289-1308 (Lit.). Cf. the series: *Estudios Josefinos*, Madrid 1947ff. and *Cahiers de Joséphologie*, Montreal 1953ff. (= *CJos*).

The historically reliable statements about Joseph, the father of Jesus, are almost even more meagre that those about Mary. Paul and also Mark do not mention him. Evidently they already felt it a problem to ascribe to the Son of God an earthly human father. In Mk. 6:3 the people of Nazareth call Jesus 'the carpenter'. In the parallel in Mt. 13:55 he is called 'son of the carpenter' (Lk. 4:22 writes 'son of Joseph'), which possibly reflects the historical situation. This is moreover the oldest passage in which Jesus' father is described as a carpenter. The legendary tradition (Protev. Jacobi 9.1, 3; 31.1; History of Joseph; Infancy

Gospel of Thomas, etc.) developed this feature further, and from there it passed later into pictorial representations. According to the information in the Infancy Gospel of Thomas (c. 13; above, p. 447; cf. also Justin, *Dial.* 88.8), Joseph could make only ploughs and yokes. Although Lk. 3:23 emphasises that Jesus was only thought to be a son of Joseph, immediately thereafter the Davidic sonship is given a foundation in Joseph's genealogy (Lk. 3:23-38; cf. Mt. 1:10; Lk. 1:27; 2:4; see below, pp. 486f.). And while in the infancy narratives in Mt. 1:18 and Lk. 1:35 - and even more in the Protev. Jacobi (c. 13f.) - Joseph's fatherhood is contested in the interests of Mary's virginity, the Gospel of John can describe Jesus without more ado as 'son of Joseph from Nazareth' (1:45). In Jn. 6:42 the Jews ask: 'Is this not Joseph's son, whose father and mother we know?' They thus indirectly give expression - in the author's anti-docetic interest - to the fact that in this Jesus the 'bread from heaven' has quite really become a man.

The peculiar marriage-like relationship between Joseph and Mary, as it developed in the further tradition, gave rise to new problems. It is probably also the reason for the story, attested by the pagan anti-Christian author Celsus (about 178) and probably deriving from Jewish polemic, of Joseph the deceived husband, who puts away his young wife - her name is not mentioned - because of her adultery (Origen, *c. Cels.* I 28). According to this the real father of Jesus was a soldier named Panthera (cf. *c. Cels.* I 32f.; 69) and his mother a poor working girl who finally brought her child into the world in some obscure place.

In contrast to Luke's infancy narrative, in which Mary stands at the centre of events, Joseph in Matthew plays the decisive role. It is he to whom the angel of the Lord three times appears in a dream (1:20; 2:13, 19), and who obediently follows the divine instructions. He takes to himself his wife, pregnant of the Holy Ghost, and does not put her away. He gives his son the name Jesus (1:24f.), and thereby recognises him as his son. Later he journeys to Egypt with his wife and the child, threatened by Herod (2:13f.), and only returns after the king's death, finally settling in Nazareth (2:23). He does all this, according to Matthew's theological conception, in order that God's plan of salvation may be fulfilled. In Luke, the family already lives in Nazareth (2:4) and travels for the census to Bethlehem, in order that Jesus may be born there, and then returns again to Nazareth. Joseph is last mentioned in connection with the story of the twelve-year-old Jesus (2:41-52) and then disappears completely from the story. Whether he died before Jesus' public emergence, as is often conjectured, cannot be determined with any certainty. There may also be theological reasons for the fact that he is not mentioned in Mk. 6:3.

The Protev. Jacobi portrays Joseph as an elderly widower who already has children (9.2), and to whom Mary is entrusted as a young girl. The siblings of Jesus are thus here understood as older half-brothers and sisters, which does not fully harmonise with the other information in the NT Gospels. While the Protev. Jac. brings Mary into the foreground, the History of Joseph the Carpenter concerns itself with the fate of Joseph. This is a document which presumably originated in Egypt about 400, and was perhaps originally composed in Greek. It consists essentially of a speech by Jesus about the life and death of his father, which he delivered to his disciples on the Mount of Olives shortly before his death. The work is preserved complete in Coptic only in Bohairic (also in Latin and Arabic), and partly also in Sahidic (Morenz; Lefort; cf. P. de Lagarde, *Aegyptiaca*, 1883). In chapters 1-11, which in part show contacts with the Protev. Jac., there is reference by name to four brothers and two sisters of Jesus, who however appear as children of Joseph's first marriage with a woman not further identified (c. 2. In antiquity this woman was occasionally called Salome; cf. Zahn, p. 341, note 2). Joseph, who died at the age of 111, had married at the age of 40 and became a widower at 89, before he married Mary. In c. 11 it is reported that the two sons Josetos (Joses) and Simon as well as the daughters Lydia and Lysia (cf. c. 2) had married, while 'James the younger' (cf. Mk. 15:40 and often) remained at home. In c. 12-32 there is then a detailed account of the sickness and death of Joseph, and finally there is a discussion between Jesus and the apostles as to why Jesus' father had to die, when Enoch and Elijah for example attained immortality. The answer is that these two must also die before they can inherit eternal life. Morenz in his commentary points to numerous contacts in details with Egyptian religion, while H. Eberding ('Der Nil in der liturgischen Frömmigkeit des Christlichen Ostens', *Or. Christ.* 37, 1953, 56-88) denies in particular the connection with the Osiris cult affirmed by Morenz.

Somewhere about the same time - presumably also in Egypt - there came into being the description of Mary's passing (*Transitus Mariae*), which is extant in many languages (Greek, Latin, Syriac, Coptic, Arabic and - as the most recent editions show - also Ethiopic and Georgian; cf. on this B. Altaner/A. Stuiber, *Patrologie*, [8]1978, pp. 139f. and 576). The narrative begins with the Ascension of Jesus (cf. Acts 1:14; on the whole, see M. Jugie, *La mort et l'assomption de la S. Vierge*, ST 114, 1944) and portrays the relationship between Mary and the apostles. The main part is taken up by Mary's death and burial, in which despite many differences in the several versions Mary is ultimately carried off bodily into paradise. It is interesting that Epiphanius (*Pan.* 78.11) turns aside questions about the death and burial of Mary - as well as the question whether John took her with him to Asia.

In gnostic traditions Mary and Joseph do not play any prominent role. For the gnostics Mary Magdalene was of greater significance than the mother of Jesus (cf. for example the Gospel of Mary, above pp. 391ff.). There was however occasionally some intersection of the various Mary traditions.

5. The genealogy of Jesus: further relatives:

Literature (supplementary): W. Reichardt, *Die Briefe des Sextus Julius Africanus an Aristides und Origenes*, (TU 34).3, 1909. M.D. Johnson, *The Purpose of the Biblical Genealogies with Special Reference to the Setting of the Genealogies of Jesus*, Cambridge 1969. Chr. Burger, *Jesus als Davidssohn*, (FRLANT 98), 1970. A. Vögtle, 'Die Genealogie Mt 1,2-16 und die matthäische Kindheitsgeschichte, *Bibl. Zeitschr.* 8, 1964, 45-58, 239-262; 9, 1965, 32-49 = id. *Das Evangelium und die Evangelien*, 1971, pp. 57-102. H. Stegemann, "Die des Uria'. Zur Bedeutung der Frauennamen in der Genealogie von Matthäus 1,1-17', *Tradition und Glaube* (FS K.G. Kuhn), 1971, pp. 246-276. H. Merkel, *Die Widersprüche zwischen den Evangelien*, (WUNT 13), 1971. E.L. Abel, 'The Genealogies of Jesus 'Ho Christos'', *NT Stud.* 20, 1973/74, 203-210. R.E. Brown, *The Birth of the Messiah: A Commentary on the Infancy Narratives in Matthew and Luke*, New York/London 1977/78 (supplementary bibliographical report: CBQ 48, 1986, 468-483 and 660-680). E. Lerle, 'Die Ahnensverzeichnisse Jesu', ZNW 72, 1981, 112-117. R. Warns, 'Apokryphe Erzählung von der Hebamme Salome', *Studien z. spätantiken u. frühchr. Kunst u. Kultur d. Orients*, ed. G. Koch, (Göttinger Orientforschungen II 6), 1982, pp. 56-71.

The differences and contradictions between the two genealogies of Jesus presented in Mt. 1:1-17 and Lk. 3:23-38 already required a convincing explanation at an early date, and various solutions were advanced. Since Christ was at the same time priest and king, possibly Matthew set out the royal line of ancestors, Luke the priestly, or Matthew offers the genealogy of Joseph, but Luke that of Mary. Since the virgin birth through Mary ruled out any bodily relationship of Jesus with David through the family of Joseph, Mary must herself be of Davidic descent. The genealogies in the NT, which relate expressly to Joseph, would then merely indicate legal membership of his family (cf. Ignatius, *Eph.* 18.2 and often; Justin, *Dial.* 43, 45, 101, 120; Protev. Jac. 10.1; Tertullian, *adv. Marc.* III 17, 20 and often; Origen, *c. Cels.* I 39; II. 32; Euseb. H.E. I 7.17).

One of the oldest attempts at harmonisation of the statements in Matthew and Luke occurs in Sextus Julius Africanus (c. 160-240) in his letter to Aristides (in Euseb. H.E. I 7.2-16; *Dem. ev.* VII 3.18; cf. Reichardt). He relates the line of ancestors in Matthew to the legal or royal descent, that in Luke to the physical. For in Matthew the series runs: David, Solomon and then goes on to Jacob and Joseph; Luke on the other hand names David, Nathan and finally Eli and Joseph. Julius Africanus solves the problem of the different grandfathers of Joseph by the assumption of levirate marriage (Deut. 25:5f.). According to this, Melchi of the line of Nathan (Lk. 3:24) married the widow of Matthan of the line of Solomon (Mt. 1:15), and begot Eli. The latter died childless. Thereupon Matthan's son Jacob married his widowed sister-in-law and begot Joseph, who was accordingly Jacob's bodily son but legally Eli's son. Africanus evidently did not read the Matthat and Levi mentioned in Lk. 3:24 in the manuscript he used. He refers for his statements to the relatives of the Lord, who once put together the family tree. He is himself, however, quite clear that he has only put forward an attempt at a solution. The basis for the genealogy was no doubt genealogical tables from the OT (cf. 1 Chron. 2:1-15; 3:5-24; Ruth 4:12, 18-22), but also probably family traditions, although this does not mean that a convincing family tree for Jesus can be constructed.

A special problem is posed by the statement in Epiphanius (*Pan.* 78.7.5) that Jacob, Jesus' grandfather, had the surname 'Panther'. According to Eusebius (*Ecl. Proph.* III 10) this statement was made with slanderous and defamatory intent (cf. also Celsus in Origen, *c. Cels.* I 32f., 69). How far Jewish traditions played a part here, as is often assumed, is a debated question (cf. J. Maier [see below, p. 489] pp. 260-267).

Modern research renounces any attempt to harmonise the sometimes contradictory statements in the genealogies of Jesus. Instead it stresses their character as theological statements, which is already discernible in the basic outline in each case. Luke traces the descent of Jesus back to Adam, and thereby points to the universality of God's saving activity from the beginning of creation. Matthew remains within the historical framework of the election of Israel, which began with Abraham. But for him too it is a matter of the blessing of Israel for the nations, which is expressed in the promise made to Abraham and was fulfilled in Christ. The two genealogies clearly go beyond the historical establishing of Christ's Davidic sonship (cf. Rom. 1:3f. and elsewhere). How much they are conceived, even in details, as theological statements is shown for example by H. Stegemann's investigation of the four non-Israelite women in Jesus' genealogy in Matthew. E. Lerle attempts a consistently christological interpretation of the two genealogies.

The fact remains, however, that both genealogies relate to Joseph, since people were evidently of the opinion that he was the natural father of Jesus. The conviction that Jesus was the bodily son of Joseph and Mary was for a long time still firmly held by the so-called 'Ebionite' Jewish Christians. For this reason, and because they rejected the doctrine of the pre-existence of Christ, they very soon ranked in the early Church as heretics (Irenaeus, *adv. Haer.* III 21.1; V 1.3; Euseb. H.E. III 27.2; VI 17; cf. Justin, *Dial.* 48). The christological confession of Chalcedon, however, holds fast the two things, that Christ was true God from all eternity, but also true man, woven into history and into human relationships - which means also family relationships.

Eusebius reports from the work of Hegesippus already mentioned (cf. H.E. III 12; 19f; III 32.4-6) about bodily relatives of Jesus in the time of Domitian (down to the time of Trajan), who were denounced because of their descent from the house of David. These were grandsons of the Lord's brother Jude, whose names are given at another point as Jacob and Zoker (Zahn, p. 240). About them Hegesippus writes (Euseb. H.E. III 20.1-6): 'There were still living of the family of the Lord the grandsons of Jude, who was called his brother according to the flesh. These were denounced as being of the house of David. The *evocatus* [= a veteran soldier] brought them to the Emperor Domitian, for like Herod he was fearful of the coming of Christ. He asked them if they were of David's race, and they confessed that they were. (2) Then he asked them how much property they had, and what riches they possessed. They both answered that they had only 9000 denarii, of which half belonged to each of them. And this, they said, they had not in the form of money but in the value of a plot of land of only 39 *plethra* [yokes: about 10 acres]. From this they raised their taxes and supported themselves by their own labour. (3) Then [so Eusebius continues, following Hegesippus] they showed him their hands and, to prove that they did toil themselves, the hardness of their bodies and the calluses which from constant labour had formed upon their hands. (4) When they were asked about Christ and his kingdom, of what kind it was and where and when it was to appear, they answered that it was not of this world or earthly, but heavenly and angelic, and would come (only) at the end of the world, when (Christ) would come in glory to judge the living and the dead and reward each according to his works. (5) At this, Domitian did not condemn them in any way, but despised them as simple folk and let them go free; he also by an edict commanded the persecution of the Church to cease. (6) Thus set at liberty, they became leaders of the churches, as being at once confessors and of the Lord's family. And peace having come, they continued alive until the time of Trajan' (cf. the verbatim quotation from Hegesippus in Euseb. H.E. III 32.6).

In addition to Anna and Joachim, who appear as Mary's parents in the Protev. Jacobi, Elizabeth the mother of John the Baptist, who in Lk. 1:36 is described as a kinswoman of Mary, Clopas the brother of Joseph and uncle of Jesus, whose son Symeon took over the leadership of the Jerusalem community after the death of James the Lord's brother, and others, Salome also probably belongs among the relatives of Jesus. If we combine the statements of Mk. 15:40; 16:1 about the three women at the tomb of Jesus with Mt. 27:56 and Jn. 19:25, she would have been a sister of Jesus' mother and also the mother of the sons of Zebedee (James and John) (cf. Zahn, p. 341). Epiphanius mentions in addition a sister of Jesus named Salome (*Pan.* 78.8; *Ancor.* 60). The name of the other sister, who is also named in this passage, varies however between Anna and Maria, and in the History of Joseph the two sisters are called Lydia and Lysia! In the Protev. Jacobi also a certain Salome appears (c. 19f.), who expresses doubt about the virginity of Mary after Jesus' birth. This scene is recalled by four Paris Coptic fragments, recently edited afresh and translated by R. Warns (first published in E. Revillout, 'La sage-femme Salomé d'après un apocryphe copte', *Journ. Asiatique* 10, ser. 5, 1905, 409-461). There, however, Salome is the woman to whom Joseph speaks during his search for a midwife. The co-ordination of the Salome traditions with the relatives of Jesus is extremely difficult, in view of the very diverse traditions - including those in gnostic (Gos. Thom. log. 61b) and Manichean (Thomas-Psalm 16) texts; the more especially since evidently different persons of this name are intended, and occasionally they are confused with one another.

XII. The Work and Sufferings of Jesus

1. The Witness of Josephus (*Testimonium Flavianum*)
Wolfgang A. Bienert

Literature: the older literature, arranged according to defenders of its authenticity (A. Harnack, F. Dornseiff and others), opponents (B. Niese, W. Bauer, E. Schürer, E. Norden, H. Conzelmann and others) and adherents of an interpolation theory (J.C.L. Gieseler, J. Klausner, W. Bienert, F. Scheidweiler, P. Winter, S.G.F. Brandon and others), is listed in P. Winter, 'Excursus II - Josephus on Jesus and James', in E. Schürer, *History of the Jewish People in the Age of Jesus Christ (175 B.C. - A.D. 135)*, rev. version ed. G. Vermes/F. Millar/M. Black, I, Edinburgh 1973, 428-441 (esp. pp. 428-430); cf. id. 'Josephus on Jesus', *Journ. Hist. Stud.* 1, 1968, 289-302. See further: S. Pines, *An Arabic Version of the Testimonium Flavianum and its Implications*, Jerusalem 1971. A.-M. Dubarle, 'Le témoignage de Josèphe sur Jésus d'après la tradition indirecte', *Rev. Bibl.* 80, 1973, 481-513. D.S. Wallace-Hadrill, 'Eusebius of Caesarea and the 'Testimonium Flavianum'', *Journ. Eccles. Hist.* 25, 1974, 353-362. E. Bammel, 'Zum Testimonium Flavianum', in *Josephus-Studien* (FS O. Michel), ed. O. Betz, K. Hacker, M. Hengel, 1974, pp. 2-22 (with supplements in id. *Judaica. Kleine Schriften I*, 1986, 179-189). J. Maier, *Jesus von Nazareth in der talmudischen Überlieferung*, (EdF 82,) 1978.

Jesus is mentioned at two places in the *Jewish Antiquities* of Flavius Josephus, which was published about 93/94. In Book XX 9.1 (§200, ed. B. Niese III, 260f.) it is said in the context of the change of the Roman procurators from Festus to Albinus, i.e. at the year 62, that Ananus the younger (the high priest) was a bold and reckless man, and an adherent of the sect of the Sadducees, 'who are savage in matters of judgment above all the Jews. Thinking he had a suitable opportunity, since Festus had (just) died and Albinus was still on his way, he called the Sanhedrin to judgment and brought before it the brother of Jesus the so-called Christ, James by name, and some others, and accusing them of transgression of the law handed them over to be stoned.'

The text of Josephus is already handed on in Eusebius (H.E. II 23.22), and in terms of content was known to Origen (*c. Cels.* I 47; II 13; *Comm. in Mt* X 17, ed. E. Klostermann, p. 22). The changed word-order in Eusebius - τοῦ Χριστοῦ λεγομένου - could also be translated 'who is called Christ'. But for Josephus the formulation 'the so-called Christ' may be more accurate, since it gives stronger expression to his distance from the Christian faith. There is then, however, little reason for denying this note to Josephus, or considering it a Christian interpolation. For the rest, the reference to James the Lord's brother is of interest (see above pp. 473ff.).

In contrast, the authenticity of the other passage in the *Antiquities*, Book XVIII 3.3 (§§ 63-64, ed. Niese III, 130f.), the so-called 'Testimonium Flavianum', is much debated:

At that time lived Jesus, a wise man, if indeed one may call him a man. For he was a doer of incredible deeds and a teacher of men, who with joy received the truth. And he attracted many Jews, and many also of the Greek sort. This was the Christ. And although Pilate at the instance of our leading men punished him with crucifixion, those who loved him at first did not cease loving him. For he appeared to them on the third day living again, as the divine prophets had prophesied this and a thousand other wonderful things about him. And even to this day the tribe of the Christians which is named after him has not vanished away.

This text too was already known to Eusebius as the witness of Josephus (H.E. I 11.7-8; *Dem. ev*. III 5. 105f.). It is, however, striking that Origen evidently still does not know it, for he expressly denies to Josephus faith in 'Jesus the Christ' (*c. Cels*. I 47). The sentence 'this was the Christ' is in any case only comprehensible as the confession of a Christian, so that at least the assumption of a Christian interpolation lies close at hand. The fact that all manuscripts of the *Antiquities* contain it is no contradiction of this, for none of them originated before the 11th century. The authenticity of this passage is therefore - so far as I can see - today no longer defended. Instead of complete rejection, however, the view generally advocated is that the text has been worked over. But there is so far no consensus among scholars as to the nature and extent of the Christian redaction. In the effort to reconstruct the original text of Josephus, recourse has been had in various ways to the Christian-influenced Old Russian version of Josephus' *Jewish War* (R. Eisler, 1929, W. Bienert 1936; cf. F. Scheidweiler, ZNW 1950/51, 155-178). The version of Eusebius must have been influenced by the forerunners of this tradition, yet its value for the restoration of the original text is small. Among more recent attempts at reconstruction, that of E. Bammel merits special attention, because he makes do with extremely few conjectures. He would alter the text at three places only, in order in this way to recover 'the oldest surviving literary denunciation of the Christians' (p. 21f.). He writes: 'If we replace ἀγαπ- by ἀπατ-, delete the ἦν , and make the very probable change of ἐπηγάγετο into ἀπηγάγετο, the text can stand as it is transmitted' (p. 20). In terms of content, the difference would be considerable. The original text would then have raised the accusation of the deception and leading-astray of the people by the alleged Christ, and the Christian redaction would have converted it into the opposite with a minimum of interference with the text. But apart from the fact that this reconstruction of the original text is almost too ingenious, there is no other evidence that Josephus had so negative an opinion of the first Christians (in the alteration of ἐπηγάγετο into ἀπηγάγετο which is attested in the manuscript tradition of the text in Eusebius, we could for example have a later intervention, in the interest of anti-Christian polemic). The largely positive reception of his writings by the early Christian tradition rather speaks against it.

Another way of getting nearer to the original text of Josephus may possibly result from S. Pines' reference to a note in the Christian Arabic historian Agapius (10th cent.). In his *Kitāb al-'Unwān* he writes: ' . . . that at the time there was a man who was called Jesûa', showed a good way of life, and was known as virtuous (or: learned), and had many people from the Jews and from other nations as disciples. Pilate had condemned him to crucifixion and to death, but those who had become his disciples did not give up his discipleship (or: teaching), and related that he had appeared to them three days after the crucifixion and was alive, and therefore was perhaps the Messiah, with reference to whom the prophets said wonderful things' (translation after J. Maier, pp. 42f.).

Should this testimony actually reflect the original text of Josephus - the tradition history of this relatively late witness is extremely difficult to elucidate - the result would be an essentially more positive picture from the Jewish author of Jesus and his disciples, although the distance from Christianity would not be obliterated. In addition, the other mention of Jesus already cited, which is generally treated as authentic, speaks for a neutral to benevolent assessment of Christianity on the part of Josephus. On the other side there still remains the critical reserve not only with regard to the Christian doctrine of the resurrection of Jesus, but also with regard to the affirmation of Messiahship with its politically suspect consequences, which Josephus must have felt disquieting. This too fits very well with the other ideas of this Jewish friend of Rome. The description of the Christians as a tribe (φῦλον; cf. Justin, *Dial.* 119.4) corresponds moreover with the situation of Judaism about A.D. 100, when it was separating itself from religious splinter groups.

2. The Abgar Legend
H.J.W.Drijvers

Literature: on the Abgar legend: R.A.Lipsius, *Die edessenische Abgar-Sage*, 1880; L.-J. Tixeront, *Les origines de l'église d'Édesse et la légende d'Abgar. Étude critique*, Paris 1888; E. von Dobschütz, *Christusbilder. Untersuchungen zur christlichen Legende*,(TU 18), 1899; J.B. Aufhauser, *Antike Jesus-Zeugnisse*, Kl.Texte 126, 1913, pp. 17-31; Bardenhewer I², 1913, 590-596; Quasten I, 140-143; Yassa 'Abd al-Masih, BIFAO 45, 1947, 65-80; 54, 1954, 13-43; R. Peppermüller, 'Griechische Papyrusfragmente der Doctrina Addai', *Vig.Chr.* 25, 1971, 289-301; A. de Santos,⁴ pp. 662-669, ⁶pp. 656-663 (lit.); G. Phillips, *The Doctrine of Addai, the Apostle*, London 1876 (reprint G. Howard, *The Teaching of Addai*, Scholars Press, Chico 1981); H.J.W. Drijvers, 'Addai und Mani. Christentum und Manichäismus im dritten Jahrhundert in Syrien', *Or. Chr. A.* 221, Rome 1983, 171-185; id. 'Jews and Christians at Edessa', JJS 36, 1985, 88-102; id. 'Facts and Problems in Early Syriac-Speaking Christianity', *The Second Century* 2, 1982, 157-175 = *East of Antioch. Studies in Early Syriac Christianity*, London 1984, VI. A. Desreumaux, 'La doctrine d'Addaï, l'image du Christ et les monophysites', in F. Boespflug - N. Lossky, *Nicée II 787-1987*, Paris 1987, pp. 73-79.

1. Content - introduction: the exchange of letters between Jesus and King Abgar V Ukama of Edessa (4 B.C.-A.D. 7; 13-50 A.D.) forms the core of the Abgar legend. The king has heard of the miraculous healings of Jesus and invites him by letter to Edessa, that he may on the one hand cure Abgar from his sickness and on the other protect himself from the hostility of the Jews. In his reply, Jesus felicitates the king, because he has believed without having seen him. He cannot however accept the invitation, because after the fulfilment of his earthly task he will be taken up to his heavenly Father who sent him. Then he will send to Abgar one of his disciples, who will heal the king and bring life to him and to his people. After the ascension of Jesus, Judas Thomas sends the apostle Addai, called Thaddaeus by Eusebius, to Edessa, where he heals Abgar and wins the city for Christianity.

2. Attestation and tradition: Eusebius is the first to mention this legendary story (H.E. I 13; II 1.6-8), and firmly emphasises that he had these letters and the story of the apostle Thaddaeus and his appearance in Edessa from the archives of the city; he has incorporated a literal translation from the Syriac at this appropriate point in his *Church History* (I 13.5,22; II 1.6ff.). Ephraem Syrus (d. 373) does indeed mention the apostle Addai, when he extols the conversion of the city, but he is silent about the correspondence. The western pilgrim Egeria, who visited Edessa in 384 (P. Devos, AB 85, 1967, 381-400), admired the palace of Abgar and was told about the letters by the bishop of Edessa (*Peregrinatio Egeriae* 17.1; 19, SC 296, 1982). It is remarkable that Egeria treats Thomas as the apostle of Edessa and does not mention the names Thaddaeus or Addai at all, although she reports in detail about the correspondence. The bishop told Egeria that King

Abgar and others after him brought Jesus' letter to the gate when a siege threatened. When the letter was read there, the enemy immediately dispersed. Hence the Edessenes later fixed a transcript of the letter to the city gates, to protect the city from its enemies. This use of Jesus' letter to Abgar is based on the closing line, which pronounces the impregnability of the city in the face of its enemies but is missing from the text of Eusebius. This last line appears, however, in extant Greek papyrus fragments of the letter (R. Peppermüller, 'Griechische Papyrusfragmente der Doctrina Addai', *Vig.Chr.* 25, 1971, 289-301) and also in the Syriac *Doctrina Addai* (G. Phillips, *The Doctrine of Addai, the Apostle*, London 1876).

The material known from Eusebius, the exchange of letters between Jesus and King Abgar, the subsequent sending of the apostle Addai to Edessa, Addai's preaching and the conversion of the city, all appears again in the *Doctrina Addai*, but here considerably expanded by a detailed account of the apostle's preaching and the conversion of the heathen priests (Drijvers, *Cults and Beliefs at Edessa*, Leiden 1980) and of the Jews (Drijvers, 'Jews and Christians at Edessa', JJS 1985, 88-102). In addition, the legend of the discovery of the cross by Protonice, the wife of Claudius, and the anti-Jewish correspondence between Abgar and the Emperor Tiberius have found admission into the *Doctrina Addai*. Some indications suggest that this recension of the *Doctrina Addai* first came into being at the beginning of the 5th century (cf. A. Desreumaux, 'La Doctrine d'Addai. Essai de classement des témoins syriaques et grecs', *Augustinianum* 23, 1983, 181-186). This form of the legend of the discovery of the cross is known at the earliest at the beginning of the 5th century (M. van Esbroeck, *Bedi Kartlisa* 37, 1979, 102-132) and an allusion to a rebellion in Spain and the war which followed is historically comprehensible only after the invasion of the Goths (409). Comparison of the Eusebius text, the papyrus fragments and the Syriac text of the *Doctrina Addai* leads to the conclusion that these three witnesses probably go back to a common Syriac source, which was also translated into Greek. The text of the Greek papyri cannot be completely traced back to the text of Eusebius, so that we must reckon with the existence of a Greek version independent of Eusebius (Peppermüller, *Vig. Chr.* 25, 1971, 299ff.). The tradition history of the Abgar legend is thus more complicated than E. von Dobschütz in his time assumed ('Der Briefwechsel zwischen Abgar und Jesus', ZWTh 43, 1900, 422-486). It is to be assumed that this original version of the Abgar legend contained the correspondence, with the famous last line of the letter of Jesus to Abgar, in which Jesus promises: 'Your city will be blessed, and the enemy will no longer prevail over it.' This closing line then provided the occasion for Jesus' letter to Abgar being also transmitted separately, in inscriptions[1], on papyrus leaves, and on ostraca.[2] Here it was often a question of use as an amulet.

The Abgar legend enjoyed the widest circulation, in the Syriac, Armenian, Greek, Latin, Arabic, Persian, Slavonic and Coptic linguistic areas. The Latin translation of Eusebius' *Church History* by Rufinus (402-3) greatly furthered the spread of the legend in the West. In the East the Armenian version in particular, which goes back to the Syriac, is of great importance; it was incorporated into his *Church History* about 700 by pseudo-Moses of Chorene (BHO 9.24, pp. 1040,

1041, 1141-1147; cf. M. van Esbroeck, 'Le roi Sanatrouk et l'apôtre Thaddée', REA 1972, 266ff.). In the Greek tradition the legend is linked with the name of Thaddaeus and was further developed - right down to the Acts of Thaddaeus, deriving from the 6th century (ed. R.A. Lipsius, Aa I, 273-278; cf. Fr. Halkin, BHG 2, ²1957, pp. 264-266). It is no mistake to assume that the Abgar legend in Eusebius' version played the godfather for the life and work of Thaddaeus, so that almost the entire tradition stood under the name of Thaddaeus, one of the Seventy or one of the Twelve. The legend of Thaddaeus as one of the Twelve (cf. Mt. 10:3) belongs to the region around Hamidiya on the Syrian coast and to Beirut and Arwad, and has nothing whatever to do with Edessa. Eusebius also knew that, so that he makes the apostle, who in the Syriac tradition is called Addai and thus bore a name which Eusebius certainly read in his *Vorlage*, into Thaddaeus, one of the Seventy, because Addai as the name of an apostle was completely unknown to him. The later tradition confused with one another Thaddaeus (one of the Seventy) and Thaddaeus (one of the Twelve), which has made the tradition history of the legend extremely complicated.

3. Aim and origin: the key to the solution of the riddle of the Abgar legend lies in the name of the apostle of Edessa and in the structure and significant elements of the correspondence, which become comprehensible within the frame of local religious history and show its propagandist character. The legend is a historical fiction, but not pure fantasy, for it received its form and development in a historical situation at the end of the 3rd century, in which Manicheism was the most dangerous rival to orthodoxy. The name of the apostle Addai, the correspondence, the special relationship between the apostle and King Abgar, and the motif of the portrait of Jesus which Hanan the scribe painted in Jerusalem and brought to King Abgar, could provide further support for this thesis (for detailed discussion see Drijvers, 'Addai und Mani. Christentum und Manichäismus im dritten Jahrhundert in Syrien', *Or. Chr. A.* 221, Rome 1983, 171-185; id. 'Facts and Problems in Early Syriac-Speaking Christianity', *The Second Century* 2, 1982, 157-175 = id. *East of Antioch. Studies in Early Syriac Christianity*, London 1984, no. VI). An apostle of Jesus with the name of Addai is completely unknown before the time of Eusebius. The name was so strange to the church historian that he transformed it into Thaddaeus, one of the Seventy, although the semitic name Addai occurs in Greek as Adda(s), Addaios or Addai (see H. Wuthnow, *Die semitischen Menschennamen in griechischen Inschriften und Papyri des vorderen Orients*, 1930, p. 12). In the Manichean tradition Addai or Adda is one of the best-known missionaries, who belongs to the inner circle around Mani himself; his greatest activity was set in the Syrian area, and he possessed the same miraculous power of healing as Mani himself. The traditions about the two men named Addai thus show a certain analogy, which points to the conclusion that the Christian Addai is a borrowing from Manicheism. The connection between Jesus and Abgar is established through an exchange of letters. Eusebius knows two letters, the *Doctrina Addai* only one and a reply from Jesus to Abgar, which is written out word for word by Hanan and is thus a form of dictation. The alternative of letter or reply by word of mouth makes no substantial difference: Hanan brings what Jesus dictated, and its literal setting-down in writing differs only in nuance from a letter. The original form of the legend probably knew two letters. The transformation of a letter of Jesus into an oral but written answer can be explained on dogmatic grounds: Christ wrote nothing (Augustine, *c. Faustum* 28.4; Jerome, *in Ez*. 44.29; Decretum Gelasianum, ed. von Dobschütz 1912, 5.8.1, 2). The Manicheans claimed to possess letters from Jesus (Augustine, *c. Faustum* 28.4), and Mani too wrote many letters to communities and to private persons. The letter-collection was part of the Manichean canon, and the Cologne Mani Codex preserves fragments of a letter from Mani to his community in Edessa (CMC 64.8-65.18; cf. Koenen-Römer, *Der Kölner Mani-Kodex* (critical ed. 1988), pp. 42ff.), in which Mani is manifested as the Paraclete. As is well known, the Apostle of Light regarded himself as the promised Paraclete prophesied in Jn. 16:7-8. It is precisely the Paraclete saying and Mani's self-designation as a physician from the land of Babylon which can advance understanding of Abgar's correspondence with Jesus. Abgar's letter to Jesus: "Abgar Ukama to Jesus, the good physician, who has appeared in the township of Jerusalem ..." finds an exact parallel in Mani's self-designation "I am a physician from the land of Babylon", which he uses in addressing the Sassanid king Shapur. It is precisely the miraculous healing power of Jesus and Mani which brings the kings, Abgar and Shapur, to acknowledge their supernatural origin! The answer of Jesus to Abgar is even more instructive. The beginning is a variant of the familiar words of Jesus to Thomas in Jn. 20.29, which is not elsewhere attested. Jesus' promise to send a disciple is a variant of the Paraclete saying in Jn. 16:7-8, which played a central role in Mani's consciousness of revelation and established *par excellence* the connection with the Christian tradition. Addai, the promised apostle, in this way takes up a position of rivalry to Mani! This is an ingenious piece of propaganda: a *Christian* apostle in rivalry with Mani, whose best-known apostle was actually called Addai! If the Paraclete saying is the basis and core of the letter of reply, then it is not out of the question to interpret the words about the blessing of Edessa also in this context. The appearance of the Paraclete is at the same time the judgment over the princes of this world (Jn. 16:11). Probably the enemy who is no longer to prevail over Edessa was originally not a political foe, but was intended to be Satan. This also makes comprehensible the use of the letter as an amulet, which is early attested. The political interpretation and application of the word of blessing would then be a later re-interpretation. Jesus' letter in reply to Abgar is thus a pointed version of the Paraclete saying, directed against Manich-ean claims and the Manichean mission in Edessa. The apparent anomaly in the course of the narrative, that Judas Thomas sends Addai to Edessa, whereas Jesus had promised that he himself would send one of his disciples, also finds a solution within the framework of the interpretation advocated here. The relation of Judas Thomas to Addai is comparable to the relation of Mani's heavenly twin or companion to the Apostle of Light himself. Mani's heavenly twin (Syr. *toma-tauma*) clothes him with miraculous healing power and charges him to proclaim the message of the truth, exactly the same task for which Judas Thomas sends Addai to Edessa! When King Abgar after his healing becomes the special patron of Addai and promoter of the Gospel and the Church, this shows a certain resemblance to the role of Shapur, who was likewise the patron of Mani and his message.

The final motif in the Abgar legend, which can provide a further basis for its anti-Manichean purpose, is the portrait of Christ painted by Hanan and brought by him to King Abgar. It stands quite isolated in the *Doctrina Addai*, and Eusebius does not mention it, for which there may be dogmatic reasons: images were repugnant to this Church Father (H.E. VII 18; *Epist. ad Constantiam Aug.*, PG 20. 1545; see also S. Runciman, 'Some Remarks on the Image of Edessa', CHJ 3, 1929-30, 238-252; K. Schäferdiek, 'Zu Verfasserschaft und Situation der Epistula ad Constantiam De Imagine Christi', ZKG 91, 1980, 177-186). It has often been assumed that at the moment when the motif of the portrait of Christ was brought into the legend the letter motif had been dropped. But the alternative letter or portrait holds only for the later development of the legend; the motif of the portrait is traceable only from the 6th century on (von Dobschütz, *Christusbilder*, pp. 105ff., esp. p. 115; Averil Cameron, 'The History of the Image of Edessa: The Telling of a Story', *Harvard Ukrainian Studies* 7, 1983, 80-94). There are therefore no decisive reasons against the assumption that the portrait of Christ also belonged to the original version of the Abgar legend, especially since it has no connection whatsoever with the Edessa icon later so famous. In the Abgar legend the portrait of Jesus serves as a pictorial affirmation of the report written out by Hanan and of Jesus' letter of reply. It is a supplement to the written word. The portrait of Mani had an essential function in Manichean worship and in the mission. It was set up on the *bema*, from which the Apostle of Light exercised the function of the Paraclete, particularly the forgiveness of sins. Eusebius saw a portrait of Mani which was worshipped by Manicheans, as he relates in his letter to the Empress Constantia. The portrait of Jesus in the Abgar legend could therefore best be evaluated as a Christian pendant to the portrait of Mani. It is gifted to Abgar by Hanan, who also brings to him the message of Jesus, as the portrait of Mani and the proclamation of the Paraclete go together.

The Abgar legend is a document of Christian propaganda which originated in a historical situation in Edessa at the end of the 3rd century, in which the Manichean version of the Christian faith and the Manichean mission were sharply threatening orthodoxy, which formed only a minority. Even in the time of Ephraem Syrus (*Hymn. c. Haer.* 22.5.6) the orthodox minority was called the group of the Palutians, after Palut, who is mentioned at the end of the *Doctrina Addai* as the successor of Aggai, the successor of Addai. This finding of the Abgar legend is fully in agreement with the historical reports of the beginnings of Christianity in Edessa, as the *Chronicon Edessum* relates them: Marcion, Bardaisan and Mani dominated the scene, and orthodoxy was a late-comer (see also W. Bauer, *Rechtgläubigkeit und Ketzerei im ältesten Christentum*, [2]1964, pp. 6-48; ET *Orthodoxy and Heresy*, 1971, pp. 1-43). There is therefore no justification for postulating, on the basis of the Abgar legend, a Christian King Abgar, whether Abgar V or Abgar VIII the Great (177-212), in whose time Bardaisan lived, as has recently been affirmed yet again by E. Kirsten (RAC IV, 569-70), J.J. Gunther (*Le Muséon* 93, 1980, 129ff.) and I. Shahid (*Rome and the*

Arabs. A Prolegomenon to the Study of Byzantium and the Arabs, Washington 1984, pp. 109-112).

The *oldest form* of the Abgar legend, here presented, is contained in the *Church History* of Eusebius (ed. E. Schwartz 1908; appended there, in Th. Mommsen's edition, is Rufinus' Latin translation of 402/3, which is particularly important in our case because it greatly furthered the dissemination of the legend in the West). The Church Father first gives a brief report, then adduces the documents, and then returns to his narrative. After a brief summary of the content (I 13.1-4), Eusebius introduces the text of the two letters in the following sentences (I 13.5):

For this there is a written testimony, taken from the public records of the city of Edessa, which at that time was governed by a king. For in the public registers there, which contain both the events of the past and also the transactions concerning Abgar, these also are found preserved from his time even until now. But there is nothing like hearing the letters themselves, which we have taken from the archives and translated literally from the Syriac tongue in the following manner.

Copy of letter written by the toparch Abgar to Jesus, and sent to him at Jerusalem by the hand of Ananias the courier:

Abgar Uchama the toparch to Jesus the good Saviour, who has appeared in the city of Jerusalem, greeting. I have heard of thee and of thy healings, that they are done by thee without drugs and herbs. For as it is said, thou dost make blind men see again and lame walk, and dost cleanse lepers, and cast out unclean spirits and demons, and heal those tormented by long disease, and raise the dead.[3] And when I heard all these things about thee, then I concluded that either thou art God come down from heaven to do them, or thou art the son of God, who doest these things. Therefore now I write and beseech thee to visit me, and heal the affliction which I have. Moreover I have heard that the Jews murmur against thee,[4] and wish to do thee injury. Now I have a city, small indeed but noble, which is sufficient for both.

The reply sent by Jesus, by the hand of Ananias the courier, to the toparch Abgar:

Blessed art thou, who hast believed in me without having seen me.[5] For it is written concerning me, that they who have seen me will not believe in me, and that they who have not seen me shall believe and live.[6] But concerning what thou hast written to me, that I should come to thee, it is necessary that I fulfil here all for which I was sent, and after this fulfilment be taken up again unto him who sent me. And when I am taken up, I will send to thee one of my disciples, that he may heal thine affliction and give life to thee and them that are with thee[7].

To these letters there was also appended in the Syriac tongue the following:

After the ascension of Jesus, Judas who is also called Thomas sent to him the apostle Thaddaeus, one of the seventy.[8] He came and dwelt with Tobias the son of Tobias. When the news concerning him was heard, it was reported to Abgar: 'An apostle of Jesus has come hither, as he wrote to thee.' Thaddaeus then began in the power of God to heal every disease and infirmity,[9] so that all were amazed. But when Abgar heard the great deeds and wonders which he wrought, and how he healed, he began to suspect that this was the very man of whom Jesus had written, saying: When I am taken up again, I will send to thee one of my disciples, who will heal thine affliction. He therefore sent for Tobias, with whom he stayed, and said: 'I have heard that a powerful man has come and is staying in thy house. Bring him to me.' Tobias came to Thaddaeus, and said to him: 'The toparch Abgar sent for me, and bade me bring thee to him, that thou mightest heal him.' And Thaddaeus said: 'I am going, since I have been sent with power to him.'

On the following day Tobias rose up early, and taking Thaddaeus with him went to Abgar. But as he went up, his chief men were present standing, and suddenly as he entered a great vision appeared to Abgar in the face of the apostle Thaddaeus. Seeing it, Abgar did obeisance to Thaddaeus, and all who stood around were amazed; for they had not seen the vision,[10] which appeared to Abgar alone. He asked Thaddaeus: 'Art thou truly a disciple of Jesus, the Son of God, who hath said[11s] to me 'I will send thee one of my disciples, who will heal thee and give thee life'?' And Thaddaeus said: 'Because thou hast greatly believed in him who sent me, therefore was I sent to thee; moreover, if thou believe in him the petitions of thy heart shall be granted, as thou dost believe.' And Abgar said to him: 'So much did I believe in him that I would have taken a force and destroyed the Jews who crucified him, had I not been prevented because of the Roman sovereignty'. And Thaddaeus said: 'Our Lord has fulfilled the will of his Father, and having fulfilled it was taken up again to his Father.' Abgar said to him: 'I too believe in him and in his Father.' And Thaddaeus said: 'Therefore do I lay my hand upon thee in his name.' And when he had done this, immediately he was healed of the disease and the affliction which he had. And Abgar was astonished that, even as he had heard concerning Jesus, so in very deed had he received through his disciple Thaddaeus, who healed him without drugs and herbs, and not him only but also Abdus the son of Abdus, who had the podagra. He also came and fell at his feet, and was healed though prayer and the laying on of hands. And many others of their fellow citizens did he heal, doing great and wonderful things and proclaiming the word of God.

Thereafter Abgar said: 'Thaddaeus, thou dost do these things by the power of God, and we for our part are filled with wonder. But I pray thee further, tell me about the coming of Jesus, how it came to pass, and about his power, and in what manner of power he did those things whereof I have heard.' And Thaddaeus said: 'Now shall I be silent, since I was sent to proclaim the word; but tomorrow assemble me all thy citizens, and before them will I preach, and sow in them the word of life, both concerning the coming of Jesus, how it came to pass, and concerning his mission, and for what reason he was sent by the Father; and concerning his power and works, and the mysteries which he declared in the world, and in what manner of power he did these things; and concerning his new preaching, and his lowliness and humiliation, and how he humbled himself and laid aside his deity and made it small, and was crucified and descended into hell, and burst asunder the barrier which had remained unbroken from eternity, and raised up the dead; alone he descended, but with a great multitude did he ascend up to his Father.'

Then Abgar commanded that on the (following) morning his citizens should assemble to hear the preaching of Thaddaeus, and thereafter he ordered unminted gold to be given him. But he would not receive it, saying: 'If we have left our own,[12] how shall we take what belongs to others?'

This took place in the year 340.[13]

The whole is brought to a conclusion by the words of Eusebius:
This story, literally translated and for good reason from the Syriac tongue, may here find its appropriate place.

Notes

XII. The Work and Sufferings of Jesus

2. The Abgar Legend

1. M. v. Oppenheim and F. Hiller von Gaertringen, *Höhleninschrift von Edessa mit dem Briefe Jesu an Abgar*, SBA, 1914, pp. 817-828; door inscription in Ephesus, see Hiller, p. 823. Inscription from Pontus, *Studia Pontica III*, 1910, No. 210, 226.
2. Survey of the material then known in E. von Dobschutz, *Christusbilder*, TU 18, 1899, pp. 102-105; 158⁺-259⁺; 130⁺⁺-156⁺⁺; see also ZWTh 43, 1900, 422-486; further S. Grébaut, 'Les relations entre Abgar et Jésus', ROC 21, 1918-1919, 73ff. 190ff. 253ff. F. Nau, 'Une inscription grecque d'Edesse: La lettre de N.S.J.-C. à Abgar', ROC 21, 1918-1919, 217ff.; Ch. Picard, 'Un texte nouveau de la correspondance entre Abgar et Jésus-Christ gravé sur une porte de ville a Philippes (Macédoine)', BCH 44, 1920, 41-69; H.P. Blok, 'Die koptischen Abgarbriefe des Leidener Museums', *Ac.Or.* 5, 1927, 238-251; L. Casson-L.E. Hettich, 'Excavations at Nessana II', 1950, 143-147; Yassa 'Abd al-Masih, 'An Unedited Bohairic Letter of Abgar', BIFAO 45, 1947, 65-80; 54, 1954, 13-43; S. Giversen, '*Ad Abgarum*. The Sahidic Version of the Letter to Abgar on a Wooden Tablet', *Ac.Or.* 24, 1959, 71-82; R. Peppermüller, 'Griechische Papyrusfragmente der Doctrina Addai', *Vig.Chr.* 25, 1971, 289-301, esp. p. 291, note 14, with all the new discoveries.
3. Cf. Mt. 11:5.; Lk. 7:22.
4. Cf. Jn. 6:41.
5. Cf. Jn. 20:29.
6. Cf. Isa. 6:9; 52:15; also Mt. 13:14ff.; Jn. 12:39f.; Acts 28:25ff.: an anti-Jewish element in the correspondence!
7. Cf. Jn.16:5-15, esp. 7-s8
8. Cf. Lk. 10:1.
9. Cf. Mt. 4:23; 10.1.
10. Cf. Acts 9:3-7.
11. Of communication by letter as in 1 Cor. 6:5; 7:6; 11:22 and often in Paul.
12. Cf. Mt. 19:27; Lk. 5:11, 28.
13. = 28/29 A.D.

3. The Gospel of Nicodemus
Acts of Pilate and Christ's Descent into Hell

Felix Scheidweiler †[1]

Introduction: Justin in his *First Apology* refers twice (c. 35 and 48) to documents of the trial of Jesus before Pilate. The same author in c. 34, however, and in the same terms, invites us to examine the schedules of the census under Quirinius, which certainly did not exist. This prompts the suspicion that Justin's reference to the *acta* of Pilate rests solely on the fact that he assumed that such documents must have existed. A second point is this: barely 50 years after the composition of Justin's *Apology*, Tertullian speaks in chapters 5 and 21 of his *Apologeticus* about a dispatch from Pilate to Tiberius, which contained such a detailed account of the miracles of Jesus that Tertullian believed he could regard Pilate as a Christian by conviction. He must thus have known an apocryphal Christian document under Pilate's name, which must have stood in some relation not indeed to the *acta* of the trial mentioned by Justin, but probably to the Letter of Pilate presented on pp. 527. Now Eusebius in the second chapter of the second book of his *Church History*, referring to Tertullian, comments at length on this forged letter of Pilate; but he makes no reference to Christian Acts of Pilate, although some mention of them would have been natural. This is all the more striking in that he knows pagan Acts (anti-Christian), which were fabricated under the persecutor Maximin and which at his command had to be read in the schools and committed to memory (H.E. I 9 and IX 5.1).

Accordingly the prevailing view today is that Christian Acts of Pilate were first devised and published as a counterblast to the pagan Acts just mentioned, and that previously there had been nothing of the sort. Justin's testimony is thereby set aside. Justin however also adduces these Acts to attest the miracles of Jesus, and so the question arises whether he could have assumed of purely conjectural documents that in them mention was made of the miracles. In the canonical Gospels, miracles are not once mentioned during the proceedings before Pilate. Moreover it can be shown with some probability from the Acts now before us that the work which lies behind them must have originated very early. In chapter 2 it is asserted by the mass of the Jews that Jesus was born of fornication. Some devout Jews seek to refute this by referring to the fact that they had been present (probably as witnesses to the marriage) when Mary was married to Joseph. If this reference means anything at all, then the thought behind it must be that if Mary before her marriage had entered into relations with anyone else, then even if the consequences were not yet visible in her bodily constitution there would at least have been a rumour in circulation about it, and in that case Joseph would have renounced the marriage. In this way, then, the mother of Jesus is defended against the reproach of premarital intercourse. When Celsus about 178 wrote his polemic against the Christians, the charge the Jews brought against Mary had already become adultery. This more extreme form of the Panthera story must, however, have been preceded by the milder charge of premarital relationships. Possibly it was already current when the list of Jesus' ancestors in the Gospel of Matthew was compiled, for the original concluding sentence, preserved in the Sinaitic Syriac, seems directed against it: 'Joseph, to whom Mary was betrothed as a virgin, begat Jesus.' If this is not the case, and the slanderous gossip was derived perhaps from Mt. 1:18, the conclusion drawn by a Jew who did not believe in the overshadowing by the Holy Spirit would be that Mary was guilty of premarital relationships, not of adultery. Our Acts of Pilate thus presuppose the earlier form of the Panthera story.

The situation is similar in regard to the account of the ascension of Jesus. Anyone who reads chapters 13 and 14 in succession has the impression that the message brought by the Galileans Phineas, Addas and Angaeus about the ascension follows in time immediately upon the report of the watchers at the grave about the resurrection. No one would think of an interval here of forty days. Now these forty days admittedly appear in our editions at a later point. At the end of the fifteenth chapter Jesus advises Joseph of Arimathaea, whom he has delivered from the prison into which the Jews had thrown him, to remain for forty days in hiding in his house in Arimathaea. But here an important MS, the only Greek MS also to contain the prologue, reads four days instead of forty; and this seems to me the original reading. Joseph is naturally to remain in hiding until the danger for him is past. Here there is no thought of the possibility that the Jews might seek him in his house in Arimathaea. Thus he is in danger only if he shows himself in Jerusalem, and this danger is removed at the moment when the three Galileans bring to the city the news of the ascension; for this news makes the Jews so despondent that they dare no longer proceed against the adherents of Jesus.

But when could this news arrive? The author, who here sticks exclusively to Matthew, naturally assumes that Jesus' disciples, on hearing the news of the resurrection from the women, set out for Galilee immediately on the Sunday morning, to meet their Lord on a mountain there - here it is called Mamilch or something similar. Being active young men, they will have covered the distance in barely two and a half days, for they were in haste. Josephus reckons three days from Sogane, which lay fairly far to the north of Galilee, to Jerusalem, but here the people in question were already advanced in years (*Life* c. 52). By a forced march Sebaste (roughly in the middle of Samaria) could be reached from Jerusalem in one day (Jos. *Ant.* 15.8.5), and Galilee thus in two days. We can therefore fix the Tuesday morning for the meeting of Jesus with the disciples, and the ascension which followed. The three Galileans, who on the way to Jerusalem became by chance witnesses of this farewell scene, will have arrived in Jerusalem in the course of the Thursday afternoon, for they too were in haste to bring their news, but not too late, for they left again on the same day. For Joseph of Arimathaea the days during which he must remain hidden extended from Sunday - for Jesus appeared to him on Saturday night - to Wednesday inclusive. If he actually set out for Jerusalem as early as the Thursday, he will scarcely have arrived there earlier than the Galileans.[2] Thus the calculation agrees with the four days of his concealment. If the Galileans had observed the ascension only on the fortieth day, they would have reached Jerusalem at the earliest on the forty-second day, and Joseph would have had to remain in hiding for at least forty-one days.

This disregard of the forty days which the risen Jesus spent on earth, according to the canonical Acts, is naturally a point in favour of the early composition of the *Grundschrift* of the Acts of Pilate, unless we ascribe its authorship to an Ebionite. For this there is something to be said. We have already seen that the author adheres solely to Matthew respecting the resurrection and ascension. Now according to Epiphanius the Gospel of the Ebionites was a revision of this very Gospel. Further, the only alternative suggested for illegitimate birth is that Joseph was actually the father of Jesus. We shall consider this a matter of course, since it is Jews who here give their verdict; but that for a mediaeval writer it was not a matter of course is shown by the author of the second Greek version, who makes the Jews who speak in favour of Jesus actually say that Joseph under the guise of marriage simply took Mary into his protection. Among the Ebionites, however, one group long held fast to the physical descent of Jesus from Joseph. Be that as it may, the possibility that apocryphal Acts of Pilate were already available to Justin cannot seriously be disputed.

With Epiphanius we have really firm ground beneath our feet. When he wrote in 375 or 376 against the Quartodecimans (*Haer.* 50.1), he mentioned that these people believed that with the aid of the Acts of Pilate they could determine exactly the date of the passion, namely that it was the eighth day before the Kalends of April. This is precisely what we read in our Acts of Pilate. At this time, therefore, the *Grundschrift* at any rate was in existence, but possibly already in an expanded version as compared with the original. The versions now before us are further adaptations of the text used by Epiphanius.[3] The older of the extant Greek versions (A) goes back, according to the statements in the prologue, to the year 425. We have it also in Latin, Coptic, Syriac,[4] Armenian and Old Slavonic translations, and it was still not expanded by the addition of the second part of the Gospel of Nicodemus, the 'Descensus Christi ad inferos'. The addition is thoroughly out of keeping, since the work is complete and does not admit of any expansion.

The second Greek version (B) describes the mother of Jesus six times in close succession as θεοτοκός, and thus presupposes the Council of Ephesus, but may indeed be considerably later. To discover in it, with Bardenhewer (*Litg.* I[2], p. 545, note 3), the original recension, is impossible. B is a redaction of A. The changes made are in part by no means skilful.[5] In particular it is expanded where A left biblical material unconsidered, thus especially in chapters 10 and 11, which deal with the crucifixion and death of Jesus. Here Simon of Cyrene, who bore the cross, is introduced; the three words of Jesus on the cross in A are augmented by a further two; reference is made to the breaking of the legs of the robbers crucified with Jesus, and to the thrusting of the lance into his side, etc. Also added is a lamentation for Jesus, in which one after the other his mother, Mary Magdalene and Joseph of Arimathaea give expression to their grief. Joseph's visit to Pilate to ask for the body of Jesus is developed into an extended scene. Thus these two chapters in B take up more than three times as much room as in A. But at other points we find abbreviation, particularly in the final chapter, which is reduced to less than a seventh of its extent in A. The abbreviation admittedly gives the redactor the opportunity to add the Descensus. The conclusion of A shows the Jews resolved to reject the divinity and resurrection of Jesus; but previously they were at one time undecided. There were influential witnesses in Jesus' favour, and Deut. 19:15 was quoted: '*At the mouth of two or three witnesses shall a matter be decided.*'

Immediately after this B breaks off, and thus it is possible for Joseph of Arimathaea to intervene and bring the story round to the sons (here still nameless) of the aged Symeon, who shared in Christ's descent into hell and were raised again with the Lord. In this way the Descensus could be appended, but to begin with the expansion remains without result. There is no indication that the description of Christ's descent to Hell exercised any influence upon the Jews. A substantially older fragment has thus been simply added, without the redactor noticing that the real theme of the Acts of Pilate had not yet been brought to a close. This situation becomes different only in the Latin redactions, but these will be dealt with later. First of all there now follows the oldest version in each case of the Acts of Pilate proper and of the Descensus.

Editions and literature: the standard work is still the edition of the Greek and Latin texts by Tischendorf, Ea, pp. 210-486; the following translation is based on Tischendorf, Ea, pp. 210-286 and 323-332. On the Syriac version see below, p. 533 n.3. The Coptic version was published (after a papyrus in Turin and fragments in Paris) by E. Revillout, *Les apocryphes coptes II, Acta Pilati*, PO IX 2, 1913. The Turin fragments, already used by Tischendorf, have recently been edited and translated by M. Vandoni and T. Orlandi (*Vangelo di Nicodemo*, vols. I-II, Milan-Varese 1966); see further J.W. Barns, 'Bodleian Fragments of a Sa'idic Version of Acta Pilati', *Coptic Studies in Honor of W.E. Crum* II, Boston 1950, 245-250. The Armenian version has been edited by F.C. Conybeare with a re-translation into Greek or Latin: *Acta Pilati, Studia biblica et ecclesiastica* 4, 1896; this version agrees largely with Rescension A; cf. further S. Der Nersessian, 'Homily on the Raising of Lazarus and the Harrowing of Hell', *Biblical and Patristic Studies in Memory of R.P. Casey*, Freiburg 1963, pp. 219-234. On the Georgian version, the oldest witness of which (Ms. Sinai georg. No.78) derives from the year 1031, see G. Garitte, *Catalogue des mss. géorgiens littéraires du Mont Sinaï*, Louvain 1956, pp. 225ff. On the Old Slavonic version see A. Vaillant, *L'Évangile de Nicodème*, Geneva-Paris 1968, and A. de Santos Otero, *Die handschriftliche Überlieferung der altslavischen Apokryphen II*, Berlin-New York 1981, 61-98. On the Latin *Acta Pilati* cf. G. Philippart, 'Fragments palimpsestes latins du Vindobonensis 563', *An.Boll.* 90, 1972, 391-411; H. Kim, *The Gospel of Nicodemus, Gesta Salvatoris*, edited from the Codex Einsidlensis ms. 326, Toronto 1973; D. Werner, *Pylatus, Untersuchungen zur metrischen lateinischen Pilatuslegende und kritische Textausgabe*, 1972; W. Speyer, 'Neue Pilatus-Apokryphen', *Vig. Chr.* 32, 1978, 53-59. On the mediaeval German translations see A. Masser, *Dat Ewangelium Nicodemi van deme lidende vnses Heren Ihesu Christi*, 1978, and A. Masser-M. Siller, *Das Evangelium Nicodemi in spätmittelaltlicher deutscher Prosa*, 1987. On Old French translations see A.E. Ford, *L'Évangile de Nicodème. Les versions courtes en* *ancien français et en prose*, Geneva 1973. A Middle English version, which derives from Old French sources, has been published by B. Lindstrom, *A Late Middle English Version of The Gospel of Nicodemus*, Uppsala 1974 (with two Old French versions). On the Irish versions which developed from Latin sources see M. McNamara, *The Apocrypha in the Irish Church*, Dublin 1975, pp. 68-75. James, pp. 94-146 gives a good conspectus of the different recensions. Santos[6] pp. 388-529 (Ciclo de Pilato, pp. 466ff.: Escritos complementarios).

Further Literature: R.A. Lipsius, *Die Pilatusakten*, 1871 (2nd ed. 1886); E. v. Dobschütz, 'Der Process Jesu nach den Acta Pilati', ZNW 3, 1902, 89-114; Th. Mommsen, 'Die Pilatus-Akten', ZNW 3, 1902, 198-205; A. Stülcken, 'Pilatusakten', NTApoHdb 143-153; J. Kroll, *Gott und Holle. Der Mythos vom Descensuskampfe*, 1932, pp. 83ff.; P. Vannutelli, *Actorum Pilati textus synoptici*, Rome 1938; S.P. Brock, 'A Fragment of the Acta Pilati in Christian Palestinian Aramaic, JTS 22, 1971, 157-158; M. Craveri, *I Vangeli apocrifi*, Turin 1969, pp. 299-377; L. Moraldi I, 519-654; M. Starowieyski I, 461-493; R.McL. Wilson, art. 'Apokryphen', TRE III, 337; M. Erbetta I 2, 231-288.

Acts of Pilate

Prologue: I, Ananias, an officer of the guard, being learned in the law, came to know our Lord Jesus Christ from the sacred scriptures, which I approached with faith, and was accounted worthy of holy baptism. And having searched for the reports made at that period in the time of our Lord Jesus Christ <and for that>[1] which the Jews committed to writing under Pontius Pilate, I found these acts in the Hebrew language and according to God's good pleasure I translated them into Greek for the information of all those who call upon the name of our Lord Jesus Christ, in the eighteenth year of the reign of our Emperor Flavius Theodosius and in the fifth year of the 'Nobility' of Flavius Valentinianus, in the ninth indiction.[2]

Therefore all you who read this and copy it out, remember me and pray for me that God may be gracious to me and forgive my sins which I have sinned against him. Peace be to those who read and hear it, and to their servants. Amen.

In the nineteenth year of the reign of the Roman Emperor Tiberius, when Herod was king of Galilee, in the nineteenth year of his rule, on the eighth day before the Kalends of April, that is, the 25th of March, in the consulate of Rufus and Rubellio, in the fourth year of the two hundred and second Olympiad, when Joseph Caiaphas was high priest of the Jews.[3]

What Nicodemus after the passion of the Lord upon the cross recorded and delivered concerning the conduct of the chief priests and the rest of the Jews - and the same Nicodemus drew up his records in the Hebrew language - runs approximately as follows:[4]

I. The chief priests and scribes assembled in council, Annas and Caiaphas, Semes, Dathaes and Gamaliel, Judas, Levi and Nephthalim, Alexander and Jairus and the rest of the Jews, and came to Pilate accusing Jesus of many deeds. They said: 'We know that this man is the son of Joseph the carpenter and was born of Mary; but he says he is the Son of God and a king. Moreover he pollutes the sabbath and wishes to destroy the law of our fathers.' Pilate said: 'And what things does he do that he wishes to destroy it?' The Jews say: 'We have a law that we should not heal anyone on the sabbath. But this man with his evil deeds has healed on the sabbath the lame, the bent, the withered, the blind, the paralytic, and the possessed.' Pilate asked them: 'With what evil deeds?' They answered him: 'He is a sorcerer, and by Beelzebub the prince of the devils he casts out evil spirits, and all are subject to him.' Pilate said to them: 'This is not to cast out demons by an unclean spirit, but by the god Asclepius.'

2. The Jews said to Pilate: 'We beseech your excellency to place him before your judgment-seat and to try him.' And Pilate called them to him and said: 'Tell me! How can I, a governor, examine a king?' They answered: 'We do not say that he is a king, but he says he is.' And Pilate summoned his messenger and said to him: 'Let Jesus be brought with gentleness.' So the messenger went out, and when he perceived him, he did him reverence, and taking the kerchief which was in his hand, he spread it upon the ground, and said to him: 'Lord, walk on this and go in, for the governor calls you.' But when the Jews saw what the messenger had done, they cried out against Pilate and said: 'Why did you not order him to come in by a herald, but by a messenger? For as soon as he saw him the messenger reverenced him, and spread out his kerchief on the ground, and made him walk on it like a king.'

3. Then Pilate called for the messenger and said to him: 'Why have you done this, and spread your kerchief on the ground and made Jesus walk on it?' The messenger answered him: 'Lord governor, when you sent me to Jerusalem to Alexander, I saw him sitting on an ass, and the children of the Hebrews held branches in their hands and cried out; and others spread their garments before him, saying: 'Save now, thou that art in the highest! Blessed is he that comes in the name of the Lord!''

4. The Jews cried out to the messenger: 'The children of the Hebrews cried out in Hebrew; how do you know it in Greek?' The messenger replied: 'I asked one of the Jews, and said: What is it that they cry out in Hebrew? And he interpreted it to me.' Pilate said to them: 'And what did they cry out in Hebrew?' The Jews answered: 'Hosanna membrome baruchamma adonai.'[5] Pilate asked again: 'And the Hosanna and the rest, how is it translated?' The Jews replied: 'Save now, thou that art in

the highest. Blessed is he that comes in the name of the Lord.' Pilate said to them: 'If you testify to the words of the children, what sin has the messenger committed?' And they were silent. The governor said to the messenger: 'Go out and bring him in in whatever way you wish.' And the messenger went out and did as before and said to Jesus: 'Enter, the governor calls you.'

5. Now when Jesus entered in, and the standard-bearers were holding the standards, the images of the emperor on the standards bowed and did reverence to Jesus. And when the Jews saw the behaviour of the standards, how they bowed down and did reverence to Jesus, they cried out loudly against the standard-bearers. But Pilate said to them: 'Do you not marvel how the images bowed and did reverence to Jesus?' The Jews said to Pilate: 'We saw how the standard-bearers lowered them and reverenced him.' And the governor summoned the standard-bearers and asked him: 'Why did you do this?' They answered: 'We are Greeks and servers of temples, and how could we reverence him? We held the images; but they bowed down of their own accord and reverenced him.'

6. Then Pilate said to the rulers of the synagogue and the elders of the people: 'Choose strong men to carry the standards, and let us see whether the images bow by themselves.' So the elders of the Jews took twelve strong men and made them carry the standards by sixes, and they were placed before the judgment-seat of the governor. And Pilate said to the messenger: 'Take him out of the praetorium and bring him in again in whatever way you wish.' And Jesus left the praetorium with the messenger. And Pilate summoned those who before carried the images, and said to them: 'I have sworn by the safety of Caesar that, if the standards do not bow down when Jesus enters, I will cut off your heads.' And the governor commanded Jesus to enter in the second time. And the messenger did as before and besought Jesus to walk upon his kerchief. He walked upon it and entered in. And when he had entered in, the standards bowed down again and did reverence to Jesus.

II. When Pilate saw this he was afraid, and sought to rise from the judgment-seat. And while he was still thinking of rising up, *his wife sent to him saying: Have nothing to do with this righteous man. For I have suffered many things because of him* by night [Mt. 27:19]. And Pilate summoned all the Jews, and stood up and said to them: 'You know that my wife fears God and favours rather the customs of the Jews, with you.' They answered him: 'Yes, we know it.' Pilate said to them: 'See, my wife sent to me saying: Have nothing to do with this righteous man. For I have suffered many things because of him by night.' The Jews answered Pilate: 'Did we not tell you that he is a sorcerer? Behold, he has sent a dream to your wife.' 2. And Pilate called Jesus to him and said to him: 'What do these men testify against you? Do you have nothing to say?' Jesus answered: 'If they had no power, they would say nothing; for each man has power over his own mouth, to speak good and evil. They shall see (to it).'

3. Then the elders of the Jews answered and said to Jesus: 'What should we see? Firstly, that you were born of fornication; secondly, that your birth meant the death of the children in Bethlehem; thirdly, that your father Joseph and your mother Mary fled into Egypt because they counted for nothing among the people.' 4. Then declared some of the Jews that stood by, devout men: 'We deny that he came of fornication, for we know that Joseph was betrothed to Mary, and he was not born of fornication.' Pilate then said to the Jews who said that he came of fornication: 'Your statement is not true; for there was a betrothal, as your own fellow countrymen say.' Annas and Caiaphas say to Pilate: 'We, the whole multitude, cry out that he was born of fornication, and we are not believed; these are proselytes and disciples of his.' And Pilate called to him Annas and Caiaphas and said to them: 'What are proselytes?' They answered: 'They were born children of Greeks, and now have become Jews.' Then said those who said that he was not born of fornication, namely Lazarus, Asterius, Antonius, Jacob, Amnes, Zeras, Samuel, Isaac, Phineës, Crispus, Agrippa, and Judas: 'We are not proselytes, but are children of Jews and speak the truth; for we were present at the betrothal of Joseph and Mary.'

5. And Pilate called to him these twelve men who denied that he was born of fornication, and said to them: 'I put you on your oath, by the safety of Caesar, that your statement is true, that he was not born of fornication.' They said to Pilate: 'We have a law, not to swear, because it is a sin. But let *them* swear by the safety of Caesar that it is not as we have said, and we will be worthy of death.' Pilate said to Annas and Caiaphas: 'Do you not answer these things?' And Annas and Caiaphas said to Pilate: 'These twelve men are believed (who say) that he was not born of fornication. But we, the whole multitude, cry out that he was born of fornication, and is a sorcerer, and claims to be the Son of God and a king, and we are not believed.' 6. And Pilate sent out the whole multitude, except the twelve men who denied that he was born of fornication, and commanded Jesus to be set apart. And he asked them: 'For what cause do they wish to kill him?' They answered Pilate: 'They are incensed because he heals on the sabbath.' Pilate said: 'For a good work do they wish to kill him?' They answered him: 'Yes.'

III. And Pilate was filled with anger and went out of the praetorium and said to them: 'I call the sun to witness that I find no fault in this man.'

The Jews *answered and said* to the governor: '*If this man were not* an evildoer, *we would not have handed him over to you*' [Jn. 18:30]. *And Pilate said: 'Take him yourselves and judge him by your own law.' The Jews* said to Pilate: '*It is not lawful for us to put any man to death*' [Jn. 18:31]. Pilate said: 'Has God forbidden you to slay, but allowed me?'

2. *And Pilate entered the praetorium again and called Jesus* apart *and asked him: 'Are you the king of the Jews?' Jesus answered* Pilate: '*Do you say this of your own accord, or did others say it to you about me?' Pilate answered* Jesus: '*Am I a Jew? Your own nation and the chief priests have handed you over to me. What have you done?' Jesus answered: 'My kingship is not of this world*; for *if my kingship were of this world, my servants would fight, that I might not be handed over to the Jews. But now is my kingship not from here.' Pilate said to him: 'So you are a king?' Jesus answered him: 'You say that I am a king. For for this cause I was born and have come*, that *every one who is of the truth* should hear my voice.' *Pilate said* to him: '*What is truth?*' [Jn. 18:33-38]. Jesus answered him: 'Truth is from heaven.' Pilate said: 'Is there not truth upon earth?' Jesus said to Pilate: 'You see how those who speak the truth are judged by those who have authority on earth.'

IV. And Pilate left Jesus in the praetorium and *went out to the Jews and said to them: 'I find no fault in him*' [Jn. 18:38]. The Jews said to him: 'He said: *I am able to destroy* this *temple and build* it *in three days*' [Mt. 26:61]. Pilate said: 'What Temple?' The Jews said: 'That which Solomon built in forty-six years; but this man says he will destroy it and build it in three days.' Pilate said to them: '*I am innocent of the blood of this* righteous *man; see to it yourselves.*' The Jews replied: '*His blood be on us and on our children*' [Mt. 27:24f.]. 2. And Pilate called to him the elders and the priests and the Levites and said to them secretly: 'Do not act thus; for nothing of which you have accused him deserves death. For your accusation concerns healing and profanation of the sabbath.' The elders and the priests and the Levites answered: 'If a man blasphemed against Caesar, is he worthy of death or not?' Pilate said: 'He is worthy of death.' The Jews said to Pilate: 'If a man has blasphemed against Caesar, he is worthy of death, but this man blasphemed against God.'

3. Then the governor commanded the Jews to go out from the praetorium, and he called Jesus to him and said to him: 'What shall I do with you?' Jesus answered Pilate: 'As it was given to you.' Pilate said: 'How was it given?' Jesus said: 'Moses and the prophets foretold my death and resurrection.' The Jews had been eavesdropping and heard, and they said to Pilate: 'What further need have you to hear of this blasphemy?' Pilate said to the Jews: 'If this word is blasphemy, *take him*,

bring him into your synagogue *and judge him according to your law*' [Jn. 18:31]. The Jews answered Pilate: 'It is contained in our law, that if a man sins against a man, he must receive forty strokes save one, but he who blasphemes against God must be stoned.'

4. Pilate said to them: 'Take him yourselves and punish him as you wish.' The Jews said to Pilate: 'We wish him to be crucified.' Pilate said: 'He does not deserve to be crucified.' 5. The governor looked at the multitudes of the Jews standing around, and when he saw many of the Jews weeping, he said: 'Not all the multitude wishes him to die.' But the elders of the Jews said: 'For this purpose has the whole multitude of us come, that he should die.' Pilate said to the Jews: 'Why should he die?' The Jews said: 'Because he called himself the Son of God and a king.'

V. Now Nicodemus, a Jew, stood before the governor, and said: 'I beseech you, honourable[6] (governor), to allow me a few words.' Pilate said: 'Speak.' Nicodemus said: 'I said to the elders and the priests and the Levites and to all the multitude in the synagogue: What do you intend (to do) with this man? This man does many signs and wonders, which no one has done nor will do. Let him alone and contrive no evil against him. If the signs which he does are from God, they will stand; if they are from men, they will come to nothing [Acts 5:38f.]. For Moses also, when he was sent by God into Egypt, did many signs which God commanded him to do before Pharaoh, king of Egypt. And there were there servants of Pharaoh, Jannes and Jambres, and they also did signs not a few which Moses did, and the Egyptians held them as gods, Jannes and Jambres. And since the signs which they did were not from God, they perished themselves and those who believed them. And now let this man go, for he does not deserve death.'

2. The Jews said to Nicodemus: 'You became his disciple and speak on his behalf.' Nicodemus answered them: 'Has the governor also become his disciple, and speaks on his behalf? Did not Caesar appoint him to this high office?' Then the Jews raged and gnashed their teeth against Nicodemus. Pilate said to them: 'Why do you gnash your teeth against him, when you hear the truth?' The Jews said to Nicodemus: 'Receive his truth and his portion.' Nicodemus said: 'Amen, may it be as you have said.'

VI. Then one of the Jews hastened forward and asked the governor that he might speak a word. The governor said: 'If you wish to say anything, say it.' And the Jew said: 'For thirty-eight years I lay on a bed in anguish of pains, and when Jesus came many demoniacs and those lying sick of diverse diseases were healed by him. And certain young men took pity on me and carried me with my bed and brought me to him. And when Jesus saw me he had compassion, and spoke a word to me: *Take up your bed and walk.* And I took up my bed and walked' [Mk. 2:1ff.; Jn. 5:1ff.]. The Jews said to Pilate: 'Ask him what day it was on which he was healed.' He that was healed said: 'On a sabbath.' The Jews said: 'Did we not inform you so, that on the sabbath he heals and casts out demons?'

2. And another Jew hastened forward and said: 'I was born blind; I heard any man's voice, but did not see his face. And as Jesus passed by I cried with a loud voice: *Have mercy on me, Son of David.* And he took pity on me and put his hands on my eyes and I saw immediately' [Mk. 10:46ff.]. And another Jew hastened forward and said: 'I was bowed, and he made me straight with a word.' And another said: 'I was a leper, and he healed me with a word.'

VII. And a woman called Bernice [Latin: Veronica] crying out from a distance said: 'I had an issue of blood and I touched the hem of his garment, and the issue of blood, which had lasted twelve years, ceased' [Mk. 5:25ff.]. The Jews said: 'We have a law not to permit a woman to give testimony.'

VIII. And others, a multitude of men and women, cried out: 'This man is a prophet, and the demons are subject to him.' Pilate said to those who said the demons were subject to him: 'Why are your teachers also not subject to him?' They said to Pilate: 'We do not know.' Others said: 'Lazarus who was dead he raised up out of the tomb after four days.' Then the governor began to tremble and said to all the multitude of the Jews: 'Why do you wish to shed innocent blood?'

IX. And he called to him Nicodemus and the twelve men who said he was not born of fornication and said to them: 'What shall I do? The people are becoming rebellious.' They answered him: 'We do not know. You yourself must see to it.' Again Pilate called all the multitude of the Jews and said: 'You know the custom that at the feast of unleavened bread a prisoner is released to you. I have in the prison one condemned for murder, called Barabbas, and this Jesus who stands before you, in whom I find no fault. *Whom do you wish me to release to you?*' But they cried out: '*Barabbas.*' *Pilate said: 'Then what shall I do with Jesus who is called Christ?*' The Jews cried out: '*Let him be crucified*' [Mt. 27:15ff.]. But some of the Jews answered: '*You are not Caesar's friend if you release this man* [Jn. 19:12], for he called himself the Son of God and a king. You wish him therefore to be king and not Caesar.'

2. And Pilate was angry and said to the Jews: 'Your nation is always seditious and in rebellion against your benefactors.' The Jews asked: 'What benefactors?' Pilate answered: 'As I have heard, your God brought you out of Egypt out of hard slavery, and led you safe through the sea as if it had been dry land, and in the wilderness nourished you and gave

you manna and quails, and gave you water to drink from a rock, and gave you the law. And despite all this you provoked the anger of your God: you wanted a molten calf and angered your God, and he wished to destroy you; and Moses made supplication for you, and you were not put to death. And now you accuse me of hating the emperor.' 3. And he rose up from the judgment-seat and sought to go out. And the Jews cried out: 'We know as king Caesar alone and not Jesus. For indeed the wise men brought him gifts from the east, as if he were a king. And when Herod heard from the wise men that a king was born, he sought to slay him. But when his father Joseph knew that, he took him and his mother, and they fled into Egypt. And when Herod heard it, he destroyed the children of the Hebrews who were born in Bethlehem.'

4. When Pilate heard these words, he was afraid. And he silenced the multitudes, because they were crying out, and said to them: 'So this is he whom Herod sought?' The Jews replied: 'Yes, this is he.' *And* Pilate *took water and washed his hands* before the sun *and said: 'I am innocent of the blood of this* righteous *man. You see to it.'* Again the Jews cried out: '*His blood be on us and on our children*' [Mt. 27:24f.]. 5. Then Pilate commanded the curtain to be drawn[7] before the judgment-seat on which he sat, and said to Jesus: 'Your nation has convicted you of claiming to be a king. Therefore I have decreed that you should first be scourged according to the law of the pious emperors, and then hanged on the cross in the garden where you were seized. And let Dysmas and Gestas, the two malefactors, be crucified with you.'

X. And Jesus went out from the praetorium, and the two malefactors with him. And when they came to the place, they stripped him and girded him with a linen cloth and put a crown of thorns on his head. Likewise they hanged up also the two malefactors.[8] *But Jesus said: 'Father, forgive them, for they know not what they do'* [Lk. 23:34]. And the soldiers parted his garments among them. And *the people* stood *looking* at him. And the chief priests *and the rulers* with them *scoffed at him, saying: 'He saved others, let him save himself. If he is the Son of God, let him come down from the cross.'* And the soldiers also mocked him, coming and offering him vinegar with gall, and they said: '*If you are the king of the Jews, save yourself*' [Lk. 23:35ff.]. And Pilate after the sentence commmanded the crime brought against him to be written as a title in Greek, Latin and Hebrew, according to the accusation of the Jews that he was king of the Jews [Jn. 19:19f.].

2. *One of the malefactors who were crucified* said to him: 'If you are the Christ, *save yourself and us.'* But Dysmas answering rebuked him: '*Do you not at all fear God, since you are in the same condemnation? And we indeed justly. For we are receiving the due reward of our deeds. But*

this man has done nothing wrong.' And he said to Jesus: 'Lord, *remember me* in your kingdom.' *And* Jesus said to him: '*Truly, I say to you, today you will be with me in paradise*' [Lk. 23:39ff.].

XI. And *it was about the sixth hour, and there was darkness* over the land *until the ninth hour*, for the sun was darkened. And *the curtain of the Temple was torn in two. And Jesus cried with a loud voice*: 'Father, baddach ephkid rouel',[9] which means: '*Into thy hands I commit my spirit.*' And having said this he gave up the ghost. *And when the centurion saw what had happened, he praised God, saying: 'This man was righteous.' And all the multitudes who had come to this sight*, when they saw what had taken place, *beat* their *breasts and returned* [Lk. 23:44-48].

2. But the centurion reported to the governor what had happened. And when the governor and his wife heard, they were greatly grieved, and they neither ate nor drank on that day. And Pilate sent for the Jews and said to them: 'Did you see what happened?' But they answered: 'There was an eclipse of the sun in the usual way.' 3. And his acquaintances had stood far off and the women who had come with him from Galilee, and saw these things. *But a* certain *man* named *Joseph, a member of the council, from the town of Arimathaea*, who also was waiting *for the kingdom of God, this man went to Pilate and asked for the body of Jesus. And he took it down, and wrapped it in a clean linen cloth, and placed it in a rock-hewn tomb*, in which *no one had ever yet been laid* [Lk. 23:50-53].

XII. When the Jews heard that Joseph had asked for the body, they sought for him and the twelve men who said that Jesus was not born of fornication, and for Nicodemus and for many others, who had come forward before Pilate and made known his good works. But they all hid themselves, and only Nicodemus was seen by them, because he was a ruler of the Jews. And Nicodemus said to them: 'How did you enter into the synagogue?' The Jews answered him: 'How did you enter into the synagogue? You are an accomplice of his, and his portion shall be with you in the world to come.' Nicodemus said: 'Amen, amen.' Likewise also Joseph came forth [from his concealment?] and said to them: 'Why are you angry with me, because I asked for the body of Jesus? See, I have placed it in my new tomb, having wrapped it in clean linen, and I rolled a stone before the door of the cave. And you have not done well with the righteous one, for you did not repent of having crucified him, but also pierced him with a spear.'

Then the Jews seized Joseph and commanded him to be secured until the first day of the week. They said to him: 'Know that the hour forbids us to do anything against you, because the sabbath dawns. But know also that you will not even be counted worthy of burial, but we shall give your flesh to the birds of the heaven.' Joseph answered: 'This word is like that of the boastful Goliath, who insulted the living God and the holy David. For God said by the prophet: *Vengeance is mine, I will repay, says the Lord* [Rom. 12:19; cf. Deut. 32:35]. And now he who is uncircumcised in the flesh, but circumcised in heart, took water and washed his hands before the sun, saying: I am innocent of the blood of this righteous man. You see to it. And you answered Pilate: *His blood be on us and on our children* [Mt. 27:25]. And now I fear lest the wrath of God come upon you and your children, as you said.' When the Jews heard these words, they were embittered in their hearts, and laid hold on Joseph and seized him and shut him in a building without a window, and guards remained at the door. And they sealed the door of the place where Joseph was shut up.

2. And on the sabbath the rulers of the synagogue and the priests and the Levites ordered that all should present themselves in the synagogue on the first day of the week. And the whole multitude rose up early and took counsel in the synagogue by what death they should kill him. And when the council was in session they commanded him to be brought with great dishonour. And when they opened the door they did not find him. And all the people were astonished and filled with consternation because they found the seals undamaged, and Caiaphas had the key. And they dared no longer to lay hands on those who had spoken before Pilate on behalf of Jesus.

XIII. And while they still sat in the synagogue and marvelled because of Joseph, there came some of the guard which the Jews had asked from Pilate to guard the tomb of Jesus, lest his disciples should come and steal him. And they told the rulers of the synagogue and the priests and the Levites what had happened: how there was a great earthquake. 'And we saw an angel descend from heaven, and *he rolled away the stone* from the mouth of the cave, *and sat upon it*, and he shone *like snow and like lightning*. And we were in great fear, and lay *like dead men* [Mt. 28:2-4]. And we heard the voice of the angel speaking to the women who waited at the tomb: *Do not be afraid. I know that you seek Jesus who was crucified. He is not here. He has risen, as he said: Come and see the place where* the Lord *lay. And go quickly and tell his disciples that he has risen from the dead* and is in Galilee' [Mt. 28:5-7].

2. The Jews asked: 'To what women did he speak?' The members of the guard answered: 'We do not know who they were.' The Jews said: 'At what hour was it?' The members of the guard answered: 'At midnight.' The Jews said: 'And why did you not seize the women?' The members of the guard said: 'We were like dead men through fear, and gave up hope of seeing the light of day; how could we then have seized them?' The Jews said: 'As the Lord lives, we do not believe you.' The members of the

guard said to the Jews: 'So many signs you saw in that man and you did not believe; and how can you believe us? You rightly swore: As the Lord lives. For he *does* live.' Again the members of the guard said: 'We have heard that you shut up him who asked for the body of Jesus, and sealed the door, and that when you opened it you did not find him. Therefore give us Joseph and we will give you Jesus.' The Jews said: 'Joseph has gone to his own city.' And the members of the guard said to the Jews: 'And Jesus has risen, as we heard from the angel, and is in Galilee.' 3. And when the Jews heard these words, they feared greatly and said: '(Take heed) lest this report be heard and all incline to Jesus.' And the Jews took counsel, and offered *much money and gave it to the soldiers of the guard, saying*: 'Say that when you were sleeping *his disciples* came *by night* and *stole him. And if this is heard by the governor, we will persuade* him *and keep you out of trouble*' [Mt. 28:12-14].

XIV. Now Phineës a priest and Adas a teacher and Angaeus a Levite came from Galilee to Jerusalem, and told the rulers of the synagogue and the priests and the Levites: 'We saw Jesus and his disciples sitting upon the mountain which is called Mamilch. And he said to his disciples: *Go into all the world and preach the gospel to the whole creation. He who believes and is baptised will be saved; but he who does not believe will be condemned. And these signs will accompany those who believe: in my name they will cast out demons; they will speak in new tongues; they will pick up serpents; and if they drink any deadly thing, it will not hurt them; they will lay their hands on the sick, and they will recover* [Mk. 16:16-18]. And while Jesus was still speaking to his disciples, we saw him taken up into heaven.'

2. Then the elders and the priests and the Levites said: 'Give glory to the God of Israel, and confess before him if you indeed heard and saw what you have described.' Those who told them said: 'As the Lord God of our fathers Abraham, Isaac and Jacob lives, we heard these things and saw him taken up to heaven.' The elders and the priests and the Levites said to them: 'Did you come to tell us this, or did you come to offer prayer to God?' They answered: 'To offer prayer to God.' The elders and the chief priests and the Levites said to them: 'If you came to offer prayer to God, to what purpose is this idle tale which you have babbled before all the people?' Phineës the priest and Adas the teacher and Angaeus the Levite said to the rulers of the synagogue and priests and Levites: 'If the words which we spoke <concerning what we heard> and saw are sin, see, we stand before you. Do with us as it seems good in your eyes.' And they took the law and adjured them to tell this no more to any one. And they gave them to eat and drink, and sent them out of the city, having given them money and three men to accompany them, and ordered

them to depart as far as Galilee; and they went away in peace.

3. But when those men had departed to Galilee, the chief priests and the rulers of the synagogue and the elders assembled in the synagogue, and shut the gate, and raised a great lamentation, saying: 'Why has this sign happened to Israel?' But Annas and Caiaphas said: 'Why are you troubled? Why do you weep? Do you not know that his disciples gave much money to the guards of the tomb, <took away his body[10]> and taught them to say that an angel descended from heaven and rolled away the stone from the door of the tomb?' But the priests and the elders replied: 'Let it be that his disciples stole his body. But how did the soul enter again into the body, so that Jesus now waits in Galilee?' (But they, unable to give an answer, came with difficulty to say: 'It is not lawful for us to believe the uncircumcised.'[11])

XV. And Nicodemus stood up and stood before the council and said: 'What you say is right. You know, people of the Lord, that the men who came from Galilee fear God and are men of substance, that they hate covetousness,[12] and are men of peace. And they have declared on oath: We saw Jesus on the mountain Mamilch with his disciples. He taught them what you have heard from them. And we saw him (they said) taken up into heaven. And no one asked them in what manner he was taken up. Just as the holy scriptures tell us that Elijah also was taken up into heaven, and Elisha cried with a loud voice, and Elijah cast his sheepskin cloak upon Elisha, and Elisha cast his cloak upon the Jordan, and crossed over and went to Jericho. And the sons of the prophets met him and said: Elisha, where is your master Elijah? And he said that he was taken up into heaven. But they said to Elisha: Has perhaps a spirit caught him up *and cast him on one of the mountains*? But let us take our servants with us and search for him. And they persuaded Elisha, and he went with them. *And they searched* for him *for three days and did not find him*, and they knew that he had been taken up [2 Kings 2]. And now listen to me, and let us send to every mountain of Israel and see whether the Christ was taken up by a spirit and cast upon a mountain.' And this proposal pleased them all. And they sent to every mountain of Israel, and searched for Jesus and did not find him. But they found Joseph in Arimathaea and no one dared to seize him.

2. And they told the elders and the priests and the Levites: 'We went about to every mountain of Israel, and did not find Jesus. But Joseph we found in Arimathaea.' And when they heard about Joseph, they rejoiced and gave glory to the God of Israel. And the rulers of the synagogue and the priests and the Levites took counsel how they should meet with Joseph, and they took a roll of papyrus and wrote to Joseph these words. 'Peace be with you. We know that we have sinned against

God and against you, and we have prayed to the God of Israel that you should condescend to come to your fathers and your children, because we are all troubled. For when we opened the door we did not find you. We know that we devised an evil plan against you; but the Lord helped you, and the Lord himself has brought to nothing our plan against you, honoured father Joseph.'

3. And they chose from all Israel seven men who were friends of Joseph, whom also Joseph himself acknowledged as friends, and the rulers of the synagogue and the priests and the Levites said to them: 'See! If he receives our letter and reads it, know that he will come with you to us. But if he does not read it, know that he is angry with us, and salute him in peace and return to us.' And they blessed the men and dismissed them. And the men came to Joseph and greeted him with reverence, and said to him: 'Peace be with you!' He replied: 'Peace be with you and all Israel!' And they gave him the roll of the letter. Joseph took it and read it and kissed the letter, and blessed God and said: 'Blessed be God, who has delivered the Israelites from shedding innocent blood. And blessed be the Lord, who sent his angel and sheltered me under his wings.' And he set a table before them, and they ate and drank and lay down there. 4. And they rose up early in the morning and prayed. And Joseph saddled his she-ass and went with the men, and they came to the holy city Jerusalem. And all the people met Joseph and cried: 'Peace be to your entering in!' And he said to all the people: 'Peace be with you!' And all kissed him, and prayed with Joseph, and were beside themselves with joy at seeing him. And Nicodemus received him into his house and made a great feast, and called the elders and the priests and the Levites to his house, and they made merry, eating and drinking with Joseph. And after singing a hymn each one went to his house; but Joseph remained in the house of Nicodemus.

5. And on the next day, which was the preparation, the rulers of the synagogue and the priests and the Levites rose up early and came to the house of Nicodemus. Nicodemus met them and said: 'Peace be with you!' They answered: 'Peace be with you and with Joseph and with all your house and with all the house of Joseph!' And he brought them into his house. And the whole council sat down, and Joseph sat between Annas and Caiaphas. And no one dared to speak a word to him. And Joseph said: 'Why have you called me?' And they beckoned to Nicodemus to speak to Joseph. Nicodemus opened his mouth and said to Joseph: 'Father, you know that the honourable teachers and the priests and the Levites wish information from you.' Joseph answered: 'Ask me.' And Annas and Caiaphas took the law and adjured Joseph, saying: 'Give glory to the God of Israel and make confession to him. For Achan also, when

adjured by the prophet Joshua, did not commit perjury, but told him everything and concealed nothing from him [Joshua 7]. So do you also not conceal from us a single word.' Joseph answered: 'I will not conceal anything from you.' And they said to him: 'We were very angry because you asked for the body of Jesus, and wrapped it in a clean linen cloth, and placed it in a tomb. And for this reason we secured you in a house with no window, and locked and sealed the door, and guards watched where you were shut up. And on the first day of the week we opened it, and did not find you, and were much troubled, and all the people of God were amazed until yesterday. And now tell us what happened to you.'

6. And Joseph said: 'On the day of preparation about the tenth hour you shut me in, and I remained the whole sabbath. And at midnight as I stood and prayed, the house where you shut me in was raised up by the four corners, and I saw as it were a lightning flash in my eyes. Full of fear I fell to the ground. and someone took me by the hand and raised me up from the place where I had fallen, and something moist like water flowed from my head to my feet, and the smell of fragrant oil reached my nostrils. And he wiped my face and kissed me and said to me: Do not fear, Joseph. Open your eyes and see who it is who speaks with you. I looked up and saw Jesus. Trembling, I thought it was a phantom, and I said the (ten) commandments. And he said them with me. Now as you well know, a phantom immediately flees if it meets anyone and hears the commandments. And when I saw that he said them with me, I said to him: Rabbi Elijah! He said: I am not Elijah. And I said to him: Who are you, Lord? He replied: I am Jesus, whose body you asked for from Pilate, whom you clothed in clean linen, on whose face you placed a cloth, and whom you placed in your new cave,and you rolled a great stone to the door of the cave. And I asked him who spoke to me: Show me the place where I laid you. And he took me and showed me the place where I laid him. And the linen cloth lay there, and the cloth that was upon his face. Then I recognised that it was Jesus. And he took me by the hand and placed me in the middle of my house, with the doors shut, and led me to my bed and said to me: Peace be with you! Then he kissed me and said to me: Do not go out of your house for four days. For see, I go to my brethren in Galilee.'

XVI. And when the rulers of the synagogue and the priests and the Levites heard these words from Joseph, they became as dead men and fell to the ground and fasted until the ninth hour. And Nicodemus and Joseph comforted Annas and Caiaphas and the priests and Levites, saying: 'Get up and stand on your feet, and taste bread and strengthen your souls. For tomorrow is the sabbath of the Lord.' And they rose up and prayed to God, and ate and drank, and went each to his own house.

2. And on the sabbath our teachers and the priests and the Levites sat and questioned one another saying: 'What is this wrath which has come upon us? For we know his father and his mother.' Levi the teacher said: 'I know that his parents fear God and do not withhold their prayers and pay tithes three times a year. And when Jesus was born, his parents brought him to this place, and gave God sacrifices and burnt offerings. And the great teacher Symeon took him in his arms and said: *Lord, now lettest thou thy servant depart in peace, according to thy word; for mine eyes have seen thy salvation which thou hast prepared in the presence of all peoples, a light for revelation to the Gentiles, and for glory to thy people Israel. And Symeon blessed them and said to Mary his mother*: I give you good tidings concerning this child. And Mary said: Good, my lord? And Symeon said to her: Good. *Behold, this child is set for the fall and rising of many in Israel, and for a sign that is spoken against and a sword will pierce through your own soul also, that thoughts out of many hearts may be revealed*' [Lk. 2:28-35].

3. They said to Levi the teacher: 'How do you know this?' Levi answered them: 'Do you not know that I learned the law from him?' The council said to him: 'We wish to see your father.' And they sent for his father. And when they questioned him, he said to them: 'Why did you not believe my son? The blessed and righteous Symeon taught him the law.' The council said: 'Rabbi Levi, is the word true which you have spoken?' He answered: 'It is true.' Then the rulers of the synagogue and the priests and the Levites said among themselves: 'Come, let us send to Galilee to the three men who came and told us of his teaching and of his being taken up, and let them tell us how they saw him taken up.' And this word pleased them all. And they sent the three men who before had gone to Galilee with them, and said to them: 'Say to Rabbi Adas and Rabbi Phineës and Rabbi Angaeus: Peace be with you and all who are with you. Since an important inquiry is taking place in the council, we were sent to you to call you to this holy place Jerusalem.'

4. And the men went to Galilee and found them sitting and studying the law, and greeted them in peace. And the men who were in Galilee said to those who had come to them: 'Peace be to all Israel.' They answered: 'Peace be with you.' And again they said to them: 'Why have you come?' Those who had been sent replied: 'The council calls you to the holy city Jerusalem.' When the men heard that they were sought by the council, they prayed to God and sat down at table with the men and ate and drank, and then arose and came in peace to Jerusalem.

5. And on the next day the council sat in the synagogue and questioned them, saying: 'Did you indeed see Jesus sitting on the mountain Mamilch, teaching his eleven disciples? And did you see him

taken up?' And the men answered them and said: 'As we saw him taken up, so we have told you'.

6. Annas said: 'Separate them from one another, and let us see if their accounts agree.' And they separated them from one another. And they called Adas first and asked him: 'How did you see Jesus taken up?' Adas answered: 'As he sat on the mountain Mamilch and taught his disciples, we saw that a cloud overshadowed him and his disciples. And the cloud carried him up to heaven, and his disciples lay on their faces on the ground.' Then they called Phineës the priest and asked him also: 'How did you see Jesus taken up?' And he said the same thing. And again they asked Angaeus, and he said the same thing. Then the members of the council said: '*At the mouth of two or three witnesses shall every matter be established*' [Deut. 19:15]. Abuthem the teacher said: 'It is written in the law: *Enoch walked with God, and was not, for God took him*' [Gen. 5:24]. Jairus the teacher said: 'Also we have heard of the death of the holy Moses, and we do not know how he died.[13] For it is written in the law of the Lord: And Moses died as the mouth of the Lord determined, and no man knew *of his sepulchre to this day*' [Deut. 34:5f.]. And Rabbi Levi said: 'Why did Rabbi Symeon say, when he saw Jesus: *Behold, this (child) is set for the fall and rising of many in Israel, and for a sign that is spoken against?*' [Lk. 2:34]. And Rabbi Isaac said: 'It is written in the law: *Behold, I send my messenger before your face. He will go before you to guard you in every good way. In him[14] my name is named*' [Exod. 23:20f.].

7. Then Annas and Caiaphas said: 'You have rightly said what is written in the law of Moses, that no one knows the death of Enoch and no one has named the death of Moses. But Jesus had to give account before Pilate; we saw how he received blows and spitting on his face, that the soldiers put a crown of thorns upon him, that he was scourged and condemned by Pilate and then was crucified at the place of a skull; he was given vinegar and gall to drink, and Longinus the soldier pierced his side with a spear. Our honourable father Joseph asked for his body; and, he says, he rose again. And the three teachers declare: We saw him taken up into heaven.[15] And Rabbi Levi spoke and testified to the words of Rabbi Symeon: *Behold, this child is set for the fall and rising of many in Israel, and for a sign that is spoken against* (Lk. 2:34).' And all the teachers said to all the people of the Lord: 'If this is from the Lord, and it is marvellous in your eyes, you shall surely know, O house of Jacob, that it is written: Cursed is every one who hangs on a tree [Deut. 21:23]. And another passage of scripture teaches: *The gods who did not make the heaven and the earth shall perish* [Jer. 10:11].' And the priests and the Levites said to one another: 'If Jesus is remembered after fifty years,[16] he

will reign for ever and create for himself a new people.' Then the rulers of the synagogue and the priests and the Levites admonished all Israel: 'Cursed is the man who shall worship the work of man's hand, and cursed is the man who shall worship created things alongside the creator.' And the people answered: 'Amen, amen.'

8. And all the people praised the Lord God and sang: 'Blessed be the Lord who has given rest to the people of Israel according to all his promises. Not one word remains unfulfilled of all the good which he promised to his servant Moses. May the Lord our God be with us as he was with our fathers. May he not forsake us. May he not let the will die in us,[17] to turn our heart to him, and walk in all his ways, and keep his commandments and law which he gave to our fathers. And the Lord shall be king over all the earth on that day. And there shall be one God and his name shall be one, our Lord and king. He shall save us. There is none like thee, O Lord. Great art thou, O Lord, and great is thy name. Heal us, O Lord, in thy power, and we shall be healed. Save us, Lord, and we shall be saved. For we are thy portion and inheritance. The Lord will not forsake his people for his great name's sake, for the Lord has begun to make us his people.' After this hymn of praise they all departed, every man to his house, glorifying God. For his is the glory for ever and ever. Amen.

Christ's descent into Hell

I (XVII). Joseph said: 'Why then do you marvel at the resurrection of Jesus? It is not this that is marvellous, but rather that he was not raised alone, but raised up many other dead men who appeared to many in Jerusalem. And if you do not know the others, yet Symeon, who took Jesus in his arms, and his two sons, whom he raised up, you do know. For we buried them a little while ago. And now their sepulchres are to be seen opened and empty but they themselves are alive and dwelling in Arimathaea.' They therefore sent men, and they found their tombs opened and empty. Joseph said: 'Let us go to Arimathaea and find them.'

2. Then arose the chief priests Annas and Caiaphas, and Joseph and Nicodemus and Gamaliel and others with them, and went to Arimathaea and found the men of whom Joseph spoke. So they offered prayer, and greeted one another. Then they went with them to Jerusalem, and they brought them into the synagogue, and secured the doors, and the chief priests placed the Old Testament of the Jews in the midst and said to them: 'We wish you to swear by the God of Israel and by Adonai and so speak the truth, how you arose and who raised you from the dead.'

3. When the men who had arisen heard that, they signed their faces with the sign of the cross, and said to the chief priests: 'Give us paper and

ink and pen.' So they brought these things. And they sat down and wrote as follows:

II (XVIII). 'O Lord Jesus Christ, the resurrection and the life of the world, give us grace that we may tell of thy resurrection and of thy miracles which thou didst perform in Hades. We, then, were in Hades with all who have died since the beginning of the world. And at the hour of midnight there rose upon the darkness there something like the light of the sun and shone, and light fell upon us all, and we saw one another. And immediately our father Abraham, along with the patriarchs and the prophets, was filled with joy, and they said to one another: This shining comes from a great light. The prophet Isaiah, who was present there, said: This shining comes from the Father and the Son and the Holy Spirit. This I prophesied when I was still living: The land of Zabulon and the land of Nephthalim, the people that sit in darkness saw a great light [9:1, 2].

2. Then there came into the midst another, an anchorite from the wilderness. The patriarchs asked him: Who are you? He replied: I am John, the last of the prophets, who made straight the ways of the Son of God, and preached repentance to the people for the forgiveness of sins. And the Son of God came to me, and when I saw him afar off, I said to the people: *Behold, the Lamb of God, who takes away the sin of the world* [Jn. 1:29]. And with my hand I baptised him in the river Jordan, and I saw the Holy Spirit like a dove coming upon him, and heard also the voice of God the Father speaking thus: *This is my beloved Son, in whom I am well pleased* [Mt. 3:16f.]. And for this reason he sent me to you, to preach that the only begotten Son of God comes here, in order that whoever believes in him should be saved, and whoever does not believe in him should be condemned. Therefore I say to you all: When you see him, all of you worship him. For now only have you opportunity for repentance because you worshipped idols in the vain world above and sinned. At another time it is impossible.

III (XIX). Now when John was thus teaching those who were in Hades, the first-created, the first father Adam heard, and said to his son Seth: My son, I wish you to tell the forefathers of the race of men and the prophets where I sent you when I fell into mortal sickness. And Seth said: Prophets and patriarchs, listen. My father Adam, the first-created, when he fell into mortal sickness, sent me to the very gate of paradise to pray to God that he might lead me by an angel to the tree of mercy, that I might take oil and anoint my father, and he arise from his sickness. This also I did. And after my prayer an angel of the Lord came and asked me: What do you desire, Seth? Do you desire, because of the sickness of your father, the oil that raises up the sick, or the tree from which flows such oil? This cannot be found now. Therefore go and tell your father that after the completion of 5,500 years from the creation of the world, the only-begotten Son of God shall become man and shall descend below the earth. And he shall anoint him with that oil. And he shall arise and wash him and his descendants with water and the Holy Spirit. And then he shall be healed of every disease. But this is impossible now. When the patriarchs and prophets heard this, they rejoiced greatly.

IV (XX). And while they were all so joyful, Satan the heir of darkness came and said to Hades: O insatiable devourer of all, listen to my words. There is one of the race of the Jews, Jesus by name, who calls himself the Son of God. But he is (only) a man, and at our instigation the Jews crucified him. And now that he is dead, be prepared that we may secure him here. For I know that he is (only) a man, and I heard him saying: *My soul is very sorrowful, even to death* (Mt. 26:38). He did me much mischief in the world above while he lived among mortal men. For wherever he found my servants, he cast them out, and all those whom I had made to be maimed or blind or lame or leprous or the like, he healed with only a word, and many whom I had made ready to be buried he also with only a word made alive again.

2. Hades said: Is he so powerful that he does such things with only a word? And if he is of such power, are you able to withstand him? It seems to me that no one will be able to withstand such as he is. But whereas you say that you heard how he feared death, he said this to mock and laugh at you, being determined to seize you with a strong hand. And woe, woe to you for all eternity. Satan answered: O all-devouring and insatiable Hades, did you fear so greatly when you heard about our common enemy? I did not fear him, but worked upon the Jews, and they crucified him and gave him gall and vinegar to drink. Therefore prepare yourself to get him firmly into your power when he comes.

3. Hades answered: O heir of darkness, son of perdition, devil, you have just told me that many whom you made ready to be buried he made alive again with only a word. If then he freed others from the grave, how and with what power will he be overcome by us? I a short time ago swallowed up a certain dead man called Lazarus, and soon afterwards one of the living snatched him up forcibly from my entrails with only a word. And I think it is the one of whom you speak. If, therefore, we receive him here, I fear lest we run the risk of losing the others also. For, behold, I see that all those whom I have swallowed up from the beginning of the world are disquieted. I have pain in the stomach. Lazarus who was snatched from me before seems to me no good sign. For not like a dead man, but like an eagle he flew away from me, so quickly did the earth cast him out. Therefore I adjure you by your gifts and

mine, do not bring him here. For I believe that he comes here to raise all the dead. And I tell you this: by the darkness which surrounds us, if you bring him here, none of the dead will be left for me.

V (XXI). While Satan and Hades were speaking thus to one another, a loud voice like thunder sounded: *Lift up your gates, O rulers, and be lifted up, O everlasting doors, and the King of glory shall come in* [Ps. 23:7 LXX]. When Hades heard this, he said to Satan: Go out, if you can, and withstand him. So Satan went out. Then Hades said to his demons: Make fast well and strongly the gates of brass and the bars of iron, and hold my locks, and stand upright and watch every point. For if he comes in, woe will seize us.

2. When the forefathers heard that, they all began to mock him, saying: O all-devouring and insatiable one, open, that the King of glory may come in. The prophet David said: Do you not know, blind one, that when I lived in the world, I prophesied that word: *Lift up your gates, O rulers*? [Ps. 23:7]. Isaiah said: I foresaw this by the Holy Spirit and wrote: *The dead shall arise, and those who are in the tombs shall be raised up, and those who are under the earth shall rejoice* [26:19]. *O death, where is thy sting? O Hades, where is thy victory?* [1 Cor. 15:55, taken as referring to Isa. 25:8].

3. Again the voice sounded: Lift up the gates. When Hades heard the voice the second time, he answered as if he did not know it and said: *Who is this King of glory?* The angels of the Lord said: *The Lord strong and mighty, the Lord mighty in battle* [Ps. 23:8 LXX]. And immediately at this answer the gates of brass were broken in pieces and the bars of iron were crushed and all the dead who were bound were loosed from their chains, and we with them. And the King of glory entered in like a man, and all the dark places of Hades were illumined.

VI (XXII). Hades at once cried out: We are defeated, woe to us. But who are you, who have such authority and power? And who are you, who without sin have come here, you who appear small and can do great things, who are humble and exalted, slave and master, soldier and king, and have authority over the dead and the living? You were nailed to the cross, and laid in the sepulchre, and now you have become free and have destroyed all our power. Are you Jesus, of whom the chief ruler Satan said to us that through the cross and death you would inherit the whole world?

2. Then the King of glory seized the chief ruler Satan by the head and handed him over to the angels, saying: Bind with iron fetters his hands and his feet and his neck and his mouth. Then he gave him to Hades and said: Take him and hold him fast until my second coming.

VII (XXIII). And Hades took Satan and said to him: O Beelzebub, heir of fire and torment, enemy of the saints, through what necessity did you contrive that the King of glory should be crucified, so that he should come here and strip us naked? Turn and see that not one dead man is left in me, but that all which you gained through the tree of knowledge you have lost through the tree of the cross. All your joy is changed into sorrow. You wished to kill the King of glory, but have killed yourself. For since I have received you to hold you fast, you shall learn by experience what evils I shall inflict upon you. O arch-devil, the beginning of death, the root of sin, the summit of all evil, what evil did you find in Jesus that you went about to destroy him? How did you dare to commit such a great wickedness? How were you bent on bringing down such a man into this darkness, through whom you have been deprived of all who have died since the beginning?

VIII (XXIV). While Hades was thus speaking with Satan, the King of glory stretched out his right hand, and took hold of our forefather Adam and raised him up. Then he turned also to the rest and said: Come with me, all you who have suffered death through the tree which this man touched. For behold, I raise you all up again through the tree of the cross. With that he put them all out. And our forefather Adam was seen to be full of joy, and said: I give thanks to thy majesty, O Lord, because thou hast brought me up from the lowest (depth of) Hades. Likewise also all the prophets and the saints said: We give thee thanks, O Christ, Saviour of the world, because thou hast brought up our life from destruction.

2. When they had said this, the Saviour blessed Adam with the sign of the cross on his forehead. And he did this also to the patriarchs and prophets and martyrs and forefathers, and he took them and leaped up out of Hades. And as he went the holy fathers sang praises, following him and saying: *Blessed be he who comes in the name of the Lord.* Alleluia [Ps. 118:26]. To him be the glory of all the saints.

IX (XXV). Thus he went into paradise holding our forefather Adam by the hand, and he handed him over and all the righteous to Michael the archangel. And as they were entering the gate of paradise, two old men met them. The holy fathers asked them: Who are you, who have not seen death nor gone down into Hades, but dwell in paradise with your bodies and souls? One of them answered: I am Enoch, who pleased God and was removed here by him. And this is Elijah the Tishbite. We shall live until the end of the world. But then we shall be sent by God to withstand Antichrist and to be killed by him. And after three days we shall rise again and be caught up in clouds to meet the Lord.

X (XXVI). While they were saying this there came another, a humble man, carrying a cross on his shoulder. The holy fathers asked him: Who are you, who have the appearance of a robber, and what is the cross you carry on your shoulder? He answered: I was, as you say, a robber and a thief in the world, and therefore the Jews took me and delivered me to the death of the cross together with our Lord Jesus Christ. When, therefore, he hung on the cross, I saw the wonders which happened and believed in him. And I appealed to him and said: Lord, when you reign as king, do not forget me. And immediately he said to me: *Truly, truly, today, I say to you, you shall be with me in paradise* [Lk. 23:43]. So I came into paradise carrying my cross, and found Michael the archangel, and said to him: Our Lord Jesus Christ, who was crucified, has sent me here. Lead me, therefore, to the gate of Eden. And when the flaming sword saw the sign of the cross, it opened to me and I went in. Then the archangel said to me: Wait a short while. For Adam also, the forefather of the race of men, comes with the righteous, that they also may enter in. And now that I have seen you, I have come to meet you. When the saints heard this, they all cried with a loud voice: Great is our Lord, and great is his power.

XI (XXVII). All this we saw and heard, we two brothers who also were sent by Michael the archangel and were appointed to preach the resurrection of the Lord, but first to go to the Jordan and be baptised. There also we went and were baptised with other dead who had risen again. Then we went to Jerusalem also and celebrated the passover of the resurrection. But now we depart, since we cannot remain here. *And the love of God* the Father and *the grace of* our *Lord Jesus Christ and the fellowship of the Holy Spirit* be with you all [2 Cor. 13:13].' When they had written this and had sealed the books, they gave one to the chief priests and the other to Joseph and Nicodemus. And they immediately vanished. To the glory of our Lord Jesus Christ. Amen.

The Latin version of the Descensus and the rest of the Pilate literature

I. The first Latin form of the Descensus (Ea, pp. 389-416) does not differ materially from the Greek, apart from the conclusion. The sons of Symeon are given the names Karinus and Leucius, which are somehow connected with Leukios Charinos, the alleged author of the Acts of John. In the speech of John the admonition to repentance, which as addressed to the righteous is inappropriate, is omitted. But otherwise the speeches are greatly expanded, and not to their advantage, so that we get the impression that the author is fascinated by his phraseology. To turn to the conclusion, in the Greek Descensus there is no description of the effect produced on the Jews by the disclosures of the sons of Symeon. But here the Jews go home in great distress, beating their breasts in fear and trembling. But Joseph of Arimathaea and Nicodemus inform Pilate of what they have heard, and he orders everything to be recorded and stored in the archives. Then he summons the chief priests and scribes of the Jews, and adjures them to tell him truthfully whether Jesus is really the promised Messiah. And behind closed doors they recount to him how in the first book of the Seventy the archangel Michael revealed to Seth that 5,500 years would pass before the advent of the Messiah, and how the same number emerges from a correct interpretation of the measurements of the ark of Noah, and how these 5,500 years have now run their full course. And they say that they have hitherto told no one this, and ask Pilate urgently not to make it known. Pilate laid up this information also in his archives. Moreover, he sent the following account to the Roman emperor Claudius:[1]

Pontius Pilate to his Emperor Claudius, greeting. There happened recently something which I myself brought to light. The Jews through envy have punished themselves and their posterity with a fearful judgment. For their fathers had received the promise that God would send them from heaven his holy one, who would rightly be called their king and whom God had promised to send to earth by a virgin. But when he came to Judaea when I was governor, and they saw that he restored sight to the blind, cleansed lepers, healed paralytics, expelled evil spirits from men, and even raised the dead, and commanded the winds, and walked dry-shod upon the waves of the sea, and did many other miracles, and all the people of the Jews acknowledged him to be the Son of God, the chief priests were moved by envy against him, and they seized him and delivered him to me, and bringing forward lie after lie they accused him of being a sorcerer and transgressing their law. And I believed this was so, and ordered him to be scourged, and handed him over to their will. And they crucified him, and set guards at his tomb. But he rose again on the third day, while my soldiers kept watch. But the Jews were so carried away by their wickedness that they gave money to my soldiers, saying: 'Say that his disciples stole his body.' But although they took the money, they were unable to keep silent about what had happened. For they testified that he had arisen, and that they had seen it, and that they had received money from the Jews. I have reported this lest anyone should lie about the matter and you should think that the lies of the Jews should be believed.

(Ea, pp. 423-416)

II. More peculiar, and more interesting, is the second Latin recension (Ea, pp. 417-432). It begins with an account by the three Galilaean rabbis who had witnessed the ascension of Jesus:

When we came from Galilee to Jordan, there met us a great multitude of men clothed in white, who had died before this time. Among them we saw also Karinus and Leucius, and when they came up to us we kissed

527

one another, for they were dear friends of ours, and asked them: 'Tell us, friends and brethren, what is this soul and flesh? And who are these with whom you go? And how is it that you, who died, remain in the body?'

2. They answered: 'We rose with Christ from hell, and he himself raised us from the dead. And from this you may know that the gates of death and darkness are destroyed, and the souls of the saints are set free and have ascended to heaven with Christ the Lord. But we have also been commanded by the Lord himself to walk on the banks and hills of Jordan for a set time, without being visible to all and speaking with all, except for those with whom he permits it. And even now we should not have been able to speak to you nor to be seen by you, unless we had been permitted by the Holy Spirit.' 3. Then Caiaphas and Annas said to the council: 'Now shall it be made plain concerning all that these men have testified, formerly and later. If it is true that Karinus and Leucius remain alive in the body, and if we can see them with our eyes, then the testimony of these men is true in all points. If we find them, they will explain everything to us. If not, then know that all is false.

(Ea, pp. 417-419)

It is next established that the graves of Karinus and Leucius are really empty. The narrative continues:

5. Then all the council was greatly troubled and distressed, and they said to one another: 'What shall we do?' Annas and Caiaphas said: 'Let us have recourse to the place where they are reported to be, and send to them men from among those of rank, to implore them: perhaps they will condescend to come to us.' Then they directed to them Nicodemus and Joseph and the three Galilaean rabbis who had seen them, who were to entreat them to condescend to come to them. They set forth and wandered through all the region of Jordan and the mountains, but did not find them and returned home again.

6. And, behold, there suddenly appeared a very great multitude coming down from Mount Amalech, about 12,000 men, who had risen with the Lord.

(Ea, pp. 419f.)

Karinus and Leucius are not in this multitude, but those who were sent are ordered to seek them in their house. They are found engaged in prayer, and they are ready immediately to go with them. In the synagogue the priests put the books of the Law in their hands, and adjure them by the God Heloi and by the God Adonai, and by the Law and the prophets, to declare how they arose from the dead.

8. Then Karinus and Leucius beckoned to them with their hands to give them paper and ink. This they did because the Holy Spirit did not allow them to speak with them. They gave each of them a papyrus roll and separated them one from the other in different cells. And they made with their fingers the sign of the cross of Christ and began each one to write on his roll. And when they had finished, they cried out as with the one voice each from his cell: 'Amen'. Then they rose, and Karinus gave his roll to Annas and Leucius to Caiaphas; and they saluted one another and went out and returned to their sepulchres.

(Ea, p. 421)

What they wrote is not essentially different from the account in the two other recensions. Only the order of events is changed. At the beginning the cry rings out: 'Open your gates, O princes, open the everlasting doors. The King of glory, Christ the Lord, shall come in.' The dialogue between Satan and Hades precedes Seth's account of his fruitless mission to paradise. Then follows the reference of Isaiah to his word about the people who sit in darkness, and the coming of John the Baptist, whose call to repentance is here omitted. After David and Jeremiah have pointed to their prophecies, great joy reigns among the saints, but Satan is gripped by fear and tries to flee, but is prevented by Hades and his minions. Then chapter VII continues:

And again the voice of the Son of the most high Father sounded, like great thunder: *'Open your gates, O princes; open, ye everlasting doors. The King of glory shall come in.'* Then Satan and Hades cried out: *'Who is this King of glory?'* And the Lord's voice answered them: *'The Lord strong and mighty, the Lord mighty in battle'* [Ps. 23:7f. LXX]. 2. After this voice there came a man who had the appearance of a robber, carrying a cross on his shoulder and crying without: 'Open to me that I may enter in.' Satan opened the gate to him a little and brought him in to the house, and shut the gate after him. And all the saints saw him shining brightly, and said to him immediately: 'Your appearance is that of a robber. Tell us, what is the burden you bear on your back?' He answered humbly: 'Truly, I was a robber, and the Jews hanged me on a cross with my Lord Jesus Christ, the Son of the most high Father. I come thus as his forerunner, but he himself comes immediately after me.' 3. Then the holy David was enraged against Satan, and cried aloud: 'Open your gates, most foul one, that the King of glory may come in.' Likewise also all the saints rose up against Satan and tried to seize him and tear him in pieces. And again the cry rang out within: *'Open your gates, O princes, open, ye everlasting doors. The King of glory shall come in.'* Again at this clear voice Hades and Satan asked: *'Who is this King of glory?'* And that wonderful voice replied: *'The Lord of hosts, he is the King of glory'* [Ps. 23:9f. LXX].

(Ea, pp. 428f.)

529

Now the gates of the underworld are shattered, Christ enters in, chains Satan and hands him over to Hades. At the bidding of the saints he sets up his cross in the midst of Hades as the sign of his victory. The journey to paradise and the meeting with Enoch and Elijah are omitted. The account ends in chapter X:

Then we all went out with the Lord, and left Satan and Hades in Tartarus. And to us and many others it was commanded that we should rise again with our bodies to testify in the world to the resurrection of our Lord Jesus Christ and the things which happened in Hades. Beloved brethren, this is what we saw and do testify, being adjured by you. And our testimony is confirmed by him who died for us and rose again.

(Ea, p. 432)

The last chapter (XI) reads:

But when the roll (*of Karinus*) was completely read through, all who heard it fell on their faces weeping bitterly and relentlessly beating their breasts, and cried out repeatedly: 'Woe to us! Why has this happened to us wretched men?' Pilate fled, Annas and Caiaphas fled, the priests and Levites fled, and all the people of the Jews, lamenting and saying: 'Woe to us miserable men! We have shed innocent blood.' Therefore for three days and three nights they tasted no bread or water at all, and none of them returned to the synagogue. But on the third day the council asssembled again, and the second roll, that of Leucius, was read, and there was found in it neither more nor less, not even to a single letter, than what was contained in the writing of Karinus. Then the synagogue was filled with dismay, and they all mourned for forty days and forty nights, and expected destruction and punishment from God. But he, the gracious and merciful one, did not destroy them immediately, but gave them generously an opportunity for repentance. But they were not found worthy to turn to the Lord.

These, beloved brethren, are the testimonies of Karinus and Leucius, concerning Christ the Son of God and his holy acts in Hades. To him let us all give praise and glory always and for ever. Amen.

(Ea, pp. 431f.)

III. Most of the remaining Pilate literature is much later. It includes a forged letter of Pilate to Tiberius (Ea, pp. 433f.), a harsh reply from the emperor (cf. Santos[6], pp. 467ff.), a letter of Pilate to Herod and one from Herod to Pilate (cf. Santos[6], pp. 479ff.). More interesting are the accounts of Pilate's end. Comparatively old is the Paradosis, i.e. the handing over of Pilate (Ea, pp. 449-455), which is appended to the Anaphora (report) (Ea, pp. 435-449). Anaphora and Paradosis have been described as an appendix to the Acts of Pilate. Since the Anaphora is identical in content with the letter of Pilate to Claudius translated on

p. 527, only more detailed (the earthquake at the death of Jesus and the darkness receive special emphasis), I confine myself to the Paradosis.

When the report (of Pilate) reached Rome and was read to Caesar, while not a few stood by, all were amazed that it was because of the lawless conduct of Pilate that the darkness and the earthquake had come upon the whole world; and Caesar, filled with anger, sent soldiers with orders to bring Pilate in chains.

2. And when he had been brought to Rome and Caesar heard that Pilate was there, he sat down in the temple of the gods in the presence of the whole senate and the whole army and all the great ones of his empire. And he commanded Pilate to come forward and said to him: 'How could you dare to do such a thing, you most impious one, when you had seen such great signs concerning that man? By your wicked daring you have destroyed the whole world.'

3. Pilate answered: 'Almighty Caesar, I am innocent of these things; it is the multitude of the Jews who are the guilty instigators.' Caesar asked: 'Who are they?' Pilate said: 'Herod, Archelaus, Philip, Annas and Caiaphas and all the multitude of the Jews.' Caesar said: 'Why did you follow their advice?' Pilate said: 'This nation is rebellious and refractory, and does not submit to your power.' Caesar said: 'As soon as they handed him over to you, you should have kept him secure and sent him to me, and not have followed them and crucified such a man who was righteous and did such wonderful signs as you have mentioned in your report. For it is clear from these signs that Jesus was the Christ, the king of the Jews.'

4. And when Caesar said this and named the name of Christ, all the gods fell down, where Caesar sat with the senate, and became as dust. And all the people who stood by Caesar trembled by reason of the naming of the name and the fall of their gods, and gripped by fear they all went away, each to his own house, marvelling at what had taken place. And Caesar commanded that Pilate should be kept in custody, in order that he might learn the truth about Jesus.

5. On the next day Caesar sat on the Capitol with all the senate with the intention of questioning Pilate. And Caesar said: 'Speak the truth, you most impious man, for through your godless behaviour against Jesus, even here the working of your crime was shown in the overthrowing of the gods. Tell me now: Who is that crucified one, that his name destroyed all the gods?' Pilate answered: 'Truly, the charges made against him are true. For I myself was convinced by his deeds that he is greater than all the gods whom we worship.' Caesar said: 'Why then did you treat him with such wickedness, although you knew him? In doing this you must have wished to harm my kingdom.' Pilate answered: 'I did it because of the unlawful insubordination of the lawless and godless Jews.'

6. Then Caesar, filled with anger, took counsel with all the senate and his forces, and ordered the following decree to be recorded against the Jews: 'To Licianus, chief governor of the East, greeting! At the present time the Jews who live in Jerusalem and the neighbouring towns have committed a lawless crime in forcing Pilate to crucify Jesus who was acknowledged as God. Because of this crime of theirs the world was darkened and dragged down to ruin. Therefore by this decree proceed there with all speed with a strong body of troops and take them prisoner. Obey, and advance against them, and dispersing them among all the nations enslave them, and expel them from Judaea, making the nation so insignificant that it is no longer to be seen anywhere, since they are men full of evil.'

7. When this decree arrived in the East, Licianus carried out its terrible instructions and destroyed the whole Jewish nation, and those who were left in Judaea he scattered as slaves among the nations, so that Caesar was pleased when he learned of the actions of Licianus against the Jews in the East.

8. And again Caesar questioned Pilate, and commanded an officer called Albius to behead him, saying: 'As this man raised his hand against the righteous man called Christ, so shall he fall in the same way, and find no deliverance.' 9. And when Pilate came to the place of execution, he prayed silently: 'Lord, do not destroy me with the wicked Hebrews, for it was through the lawless nation of the Jews that I raised my hand against you, because they plotted a revolt against me. You know that I acted in ignorance. Therefore do not condemn me because of this sin, but pardon me, Lord, and your servant Procla who stands with me in this hour of my death, whom you made to prophesy that you must be nailed to the cross. Do not condemn her also because of my sin, but pardon us and number us among your righteous ones.' 10. And behold, when Pilate had finished his prayer, there sounded a voice from heaven: 'All generations and families of the gentiles shall call you blessed, because in your governorship all was fulfilled which the prophets foretold about me. And you yourself shall appear as my witness at my second coming, when I shall judge the twelve tribes of Israel and those who have not confessed my name.' And the prefect cut off Pilate's head, and behold, an angel of the Lord received it. And when Procla his wife saw the angel coming and receiving his head, she was filled with joy, and immediately gave up the ghost, and was buried with her husband.

Here we have Pilate regarded as a saint, as in the Coptic Church. The other accounts of his death have a totally different complexion: *Mors Pilati* (Ea, pp. 456-458), *Cura sanitatis Tiberii, Vindicta Salvatoris* (Ea, pp. 471-486). In all three Tiberius is very sick. He hears of the wonder-working physician Jesus and hopes to be healed by him. But his emissary Volusianus learns from Pilate that Jesus is no longer alive. But he meets Veronica, whose handkerchief had imprinted on it the wonder-working picture of Jesus, and takes her with him to Rome. So Tiberius is healed. Now punishment overtakes Pilate. In the *Mors Pilati* he protects himself from Caesar's anger for a long time by wearing the seamless robe of Jesus. But this becomes known, and Caesar forces him to commit suicide. (In the *Vindicta Salvatoris* Volusianus has already imprisoned him in Damascus, in the *Cura sanitatis Tiberii* he is sent into exile.) His body is thrown into the Tiber. There it attracts the evil spirits, which rage so fiercely that all who live near are terrified. Then the body is taken out of the Tiber and sunk in the Rhone. There also the raging of the evil spirits is repeated, so that the inhabitants of Vienne, which is interpreted via gehennae (way to hell), in allusion to Pilate, also wish to be rid of him. He then comes to the region of Lausanne, and after being removed from there also, finally finds a resting-place in a well surrounded by mountains, i.e in an Alpine lake near the mountain named after him. There the rumbling of the spirits ceases to annoy.[2]

Notes

3. The Gospel of Nicodemus: Introduction

1. Revised and supplemented by A. de Santos Otero.
2. Arimathaea is 19 miles distant from Jerusalem.
3. Some years ago G.C. O'Ceallaigh (HTR 56, 1963, 21-58) opposed this view, familiar among scholars. He sees in the extant text of the Gospel of Nicodemus not a later reworking of the *Acta Pilati* mentioned by Epiphanius and other writers, but actually the original text of this apocryphon. For this assertion, however, he offers no evidence. His argument only makes it appear probable that the version of this gospel which has come down to us did not originate before 555.
4. The Syriac translation was discovered by the Syrian Catholic Patriarch Ignatius Ephraim II Rahmani, under the title 'Hypomnemata of our Lord', in two MSS, one in Mosul, the other at Mardin in Media. He published them with a Latin translation in *Studia Syriaca*, fasc. II, 1908. This translation was rendered into German, under the title 'Neue Pilatusakten', by Jaroslav Sedlácek in the *Sitzungsberichte der Kgl. Böhm. G. d. W.* 1908, No. 11.

What leads me to discuss in greater detail just this Syriac version is the assertion, made by Rahmani and repeated by Jaroslav Sedlácek, that the Greek original of this version presented an older and more original text than A. But this is by no means the case. The prologue of Ananias stands at the end, and in it the certainly original date is wanting. The Syriac translator thus undertook abridgments, and these abbreviations relate often to such charming thoughts as that Pilate's wife inclined to the Jewish faith, and to lively scenes like XIII 2. Moreover there are some thoroughly unskilful additions. In II 2 Jesus makes no reply to Pilate's questions. Whereupon Pilate says: *'Dost thou not speak? Dost thou not know that I have power to crucify thee, and to set thee free?'* Jesus said to him: 'If thou hadst the power, yet is this power *given* thee only *from above* [Jn. 19:10f.]. For every man has the power in his mouth to speak good and evil. Yet the Jews have their lips and bring accusations.' The addition from Jn. 19:10f. does not fit the context. According to II 4 the whole Jewish people was present at the wedding of Joseph and Mary. The conclusion of II 5 runs: 'And Pilate called Annas and Caiaphas and said to them: How do you defend yourselves against these? Those twelve said to him: We speak the truth when we say that it was not of adultery that he came, that man of whom all the people cry out that he was born of adultery. These are liars, and say he was a magician and made himself Son of God and a king; they do not merit any confidence.' Compare the two texts! The ascension naturally takes place on the Mount of Olives, and the command to baptise (in the name of Father, Son and Holy Spirit!), omitted probably deliberately in the original text, is added, while the words derived from the spurious ending of Mark on the other hand are omitted. On further Pilate literature in Syriac see S.P. Brock, 'A Syriac Version of the Letters of Lentulus and Pilate', *Orientalia christiana periodica* 35, 1969, 45-62.

5. This holds also for the insertion of the Mount of Olives (in Galilee!) instead of the mountain Mamilch. A. Resch admittedly has conjectured (*Ausserkanonische Parallel-texte zu den Evangelien*, TU X 1, 1893f., pp. 381ff.) that Galilee in the Acts of Pilate, but also in Mt. 28:16, indicates the environs of Jerusalem, so that by the mountain in Galilee it is actually the Mount of Olives that is meant. Nevertheless, even if we may put the Hebrew *galil(ah)* for *g:lilah, gilgal* (region, district), there is no support for such a form in connection with Jerusalem, and no New Testament passage knows anything of a Galilee standing in relation to the Mount of Olives, while statements like that in the Itinerary of Antonius of Cremona, compiled about 1330 (*Prope montem Oliveti est mons collateralis, qui olim dictus est mons offensionis, eo scilicet quod rex Salamon quondam posuit ibi ydolum Moloch adorans illud. In eodem monte offensionis est locus, qui vocatur Galilaea, ubi apparuit Christus discipulis suis*), are suspect since they are probably the result of an effort to harmonise the divergent accounts of Mt. and Lk. That communication between Galilee and Jerusalem in the Acts of Pilate presupposes only a matter of hours, as Resch declares, is false. Cf. the discussion of the four days (above, p. 502).

Acts of Pilate

1. The Latin translation has 'et, *quae Iudaei vulgarunt'*.
2. The ninth indiction extended from 1 September, 425, to 1 September, 426. Theodosius II ascended the throne on 1 May, 408. Thus it was not the seventeenth year of his reign, as in the only Greek MS which contains the prologue, which fell in the ninth indiction, but the eighteenth, as in the Latin version. Valentinianus III became Augustus in 425, but previously bore the title Nobilissimus, which he probably received, according to Gutschmid, on 8 February, 421. Thus the fifth year of his 'Nobility' fell in the ninth indiction. So the Coptic version, whereas the Greek MS gives the sixth. The Latin reads *Valentiniano Augusto*. For new proposals for amendment to reconcile these sharply divergent statements, see I. Cazzaniga, 'Osservazioni critiche al testo del 'prologo' del Vangelo di Nicodemo', *Rendiconti del Istituto Lombardo - Accademia di Scienze e Lettere* 102, Milan 1968, 535-548.
3. Manuscripts and versions vary between the fifteenth, eighteenth and nine-teenth year of the reign of Tiberius. The year of the Olympiad (202.4 = 32/33) supports the nineteenth, which is also given in the Armenian version of the Chronicle of Eusebius. Eusebius dates the reign of Herod Antipas from the two thousand and forty-eighth year of Abraham = A.D. 14. Rufus and Rubellio are C. Fufius Geminus and L. Rubellius Geminus, the consuls of the year 29. This would correspond to the fifteenth year of Tiberius, the date of the crucifixion according to the oldest Christian chronology, based on Lk. 3:1.

4. I read: Ὅσα μετὰ τὸν σταυρὸν καὶ τὸ πάθος τοῦ κυρίου ἱστορήσας Νικόδημος παρέδωκεν (πεπραγμένα) τοῖς ἀρχιερεῦσιν καὶ τοῖς ἄλλοις Ἰουδαίοις – συνέταξεν δέ ὁ αὐτὸς Νικόδημος γράμμασιν ἑβραϊκοῖς– <ὧδέ πως ἔχει>. The last three words are found in Monac. 192(A): πεπραγμένα is supplied from Paris. 929(E) and the versions (*quae summi sacerdotes . . . fecerunt, acta principibus . . .*).

5. Correctly: *hōši'āh-nā' bimrōmin; barūch habbā' <b:šem> 'adonāi* .

6. The remarkable vocative εὐσεβή is protected by the vocative ἀσεβή in the (Infancy) Gospel of Thomas (Ea, pp. 142, 158). Tischendorf translates the εὐσεβής of the Coptic by *colende praesul* (Ea, p. 235 has *praeses*), taking εὐσεβής as passive. I have followed him. The *pie* of the Syriac (Rahmani) Sedllácek translates by 'merciful'.

7. The author has no knowledge of how trials were actually conducted. For him the tribunal (βῆμα judgment-seat) was in the praetorium; in actual fact it was never set up there, but 'under the open sky or in a covered space accessible to the public' (Mommsen, ZNW 3, 1902, 201), which the praetorium is not (except in the Acts of Pilate). Correctly Jn. 19:13. A curtain was drawn only at non-public trials; when the public was admitted, as at the pronouncement of the verdict, it was removed. Here the opposite takes place: the tribunal is visible during the trial, and the curtain is drawn before it for the pronouncement of sentence.

8. Coptic and Armenian add: 'Dysmas on the right, Gestas on the left'.

9. Correctly: *b:jād:chā aphkidh ruachi*.

10. Supplied from the versions (Coptic: *discipuli magnam pecuniae vim dederunt militibus, abstulerunt corpus Jesu atque illos ita edocuerunt*).

11. What Annas and Caiaphas say makes no sense. Since the beginning of the speech of Nicodemus: 'What you say is right', relates to the preceding utterance of the priests and elders, I have bracketed the last sentence of c. 14.

12. As men of substance and hating covetousness they could not be bribed by the disciples of Jesus.

13. The correct reading is οἴδαμεν, the object (αὐτόν), referring to Μωϋσέως θάνατον

14. αὐτῇ wrongly, in agreement with the preceding ὁδῷ. It should be αὐτῷ (i.e. ἀγγέλῳ). We have here an attempt to make clear the conclusion of Exod. 23:21 τὸ γὰρ ὄνομά μου ἐστὶν ἐπ' αὐτῷ='my own being operates in the angel' by substituting κέκληται for ἐστίν

15. With *ascendentem in coelum*, that is, at this point, one of the two recensions of the Latin translation ends, followed by the Latin recension A of the Descensus. The other follows the Greek text a little further, taking over Levi's quotation of the words of Symeon, but remoulding the rest in a way impossible to the spirit of the Acts of Pilate: 'Then the teacher Didas said to all the congregation: 'If everything which these men have testified came to pass in Jesus, it is of God, and let it not be marvellous in your eyes.' The rulers of the synagogue and the priests and the Levites said one to another: 'It is contained in our law: His name shall be blessed for ever. His place endures before the sun and his seat before the moon, and in him shall all the tribes of the earth be blessed, and all nations shall serve him; and kings shall come from afar to worship and magnify him'' (after

Ps. 71 LXX). The Latin recension B of the Descensus is attached to this conclusion.

16. Greek: Εἰ ἕως τοῦ Σώμμου τοῦ λεγομένου 'Ιωβὴλ τὸ μνημόσυνον αὐτοῦ; Coptic: *Usque ad Sum et eum quem vocabant Jobel memoria eius permanet.* 'Ιωβήλ is the year of jubilee following 7 x 7 years; in Σώμμου or *Sum* a graecised form of *šānāh* (Hebrew = year) could lie concealed.

17. In the Greek μὴ ἀπολέσῃ ἡμᾶς καὶ μὴ ἀπολέσῃ ἡμᾶς τοῦ κλῖναι καρδίαν ἡμῶν πρὸς αὐτόν the double ἀπολέσῃ is hardly correct. The second ἀπολέσῃ, although with a quite unusual meaning, must be retained, for the first ἀπολίπῃ is to be substituted. One MS has ἐγκαταλίπῃς, the Coptic *ne derelinquas.*

The Latin version of the Descensus and the rest of the Pilate literature

1. The report is included in the original Greek in the Acts of Peter and Paul §40-§42 (Aa I, 196f.). In the translation I have taken the Greek text into account. The incorrect substitution of Claudius for Tiberius is explained by R.A. Lipsius as due to the fact that the dispute between Peter and Simon Magus, in which this report was read, took place in the original legend under Claudius, who consequently became the recipient of the letter.

2. Further literature on this cycle of themes: M. Martins, 'O Evangelho de Nicodemo e as Cartas de Abgar e de Pilato nos 'Autos dos Apostolos'', *Itinerarium* 1, 1955, 846-853. P. Winter, 'A Letter from Pontius Pilate', *Nov.Test.* 7, 1964, 37-43. W. Speyer, 'Der Tod der Salome', JbAC 10, 1967, 176-180. M. Craveri, *I Vangeli apocrifi*, Turin 1969, pp. 380-422. L. Moraldi I, 693-746. A. Micha, 'Une rédaction de la 'Vengeance de notre Seigneur'', in *Mélanges offerts à R. Lejeune* II, Gembloux 1969, 1291-1298. E. Cerulli, 'Tiberius and Pontius Pilate in Ethiopian Tradition and Poetry', *Proc. British Acad.* 59, 1973, 141-158. M. Starowieyski I, 461-493. M. Erbetta I 2, 367-406. See also below on the 'Gospel of Gamaliel' (pp. 558f.).

4. The Gospel of Bartholomew*

Felix Scheidweiler † Wilhelm Schneemelcher

Introduction

Wilhelm Schneemelcher

In his *Commentary on Matthew* Jerome mentions among other apocryphal writings an *Evangelium iuxta Bartholomaeum* (PL XXVI 17f). It is uncertain whether this reference is derived from a secondary source (perhaps Origen), or is due to personal knowledge of Jerome himself. The Decretum Gelasianum also mentions among apocryphal works which are to be rejected *Evangelia nomine Bartholomaei* (cf. above, p. 38; should *evangelium* be read?). Further references to such a work are to be found in pseudo-Dionysius Areopagita (PG III 1000 B) and in Epiphanius the monk (PG CXX 213 B-D). A short quotation in the so-called Book of Hierotheos refers to a Gospel of Bartholomew (cf. F.S. Marsh in JTS 23, 1922, 400f.; on this book see Baumstark, *Gesch. d. syr. Lit.*, p. 167). The statement by the Venerable Bede (PL XCII 307) comes from Jerome. 'We learn from Heinrich von Herford (ed. Potthast) that Ludwig the Bavarian was acquainted with the gospel of Bartholomew (comparison with Mt. and thus perhaps only in reference to Euseb., H.E. V. 10, 3)' (E. Hennecke, ZKG 45, 1927, 311, note 1). No other allusions have yet been found. The late and sparse testimony, while not a proof of the lateness of the apocryphon, could well be explained in that way.

There exists a whole series of texts associated with the name of the apostle Bartholomew. These are firstly the so-called Questions of Bartholomew in Greek, Latin and Slavonic; also a Coptic text called 'Book of the Resurrection of Jesus Christ, by Bartholomew the apostle'; and in addition an abundance of Coptic fragments in various libraries, some of which have been assigned to the Gospel of Bartholomew. These Coptic fragments clearly contain late texts, which hardly date from before the 5th-7th centuries. Nevertheless, a brief discussion of them is worthwhile, because these legendary narratives are in some respects descendants of older versions, and because their subject-matter provides a typical illustration of the principles of the development of apocryphal literature both in Egypt and elsewhere. The popular character, typical of these texts, never allows development to cease. This complicates considerably the question of the contents and structure of the original Gospel of Bartholomew, and the history of research on the apocryphon has produced a variety of hypotheses. In particular it was long disputed whether a distinction should not be drawn between an Apocalypse of Bartholomew and a Gospel of Bartholomew, a view which was found to be untenable. Moreover, the problem of a 'Gospel of Gamaliel' has been connected with that of the Gospel of Bartholomew, because some of the fragments have been assigned to the Gospel of Gamaliel. Some mention must be made of this question. First (a) will be given an abstract of the Greek, Latin and Slavonic Questions of Bartholomew, and then (b) a brief account of the Coptic texts. For introduction to the problem of the tradition reference may be made, among others, to A. Wilmart - E. Tisserant, 'Fragments grecs et latins de l'Évangile de Barthélemy' (*Rev. Bibl.* 10, 1913, 161ff.). Further literature below.

A number of references are made in the literature to the gnostic ideas in the Gospel of Bartholomew (e.g. A. Baumstark, *Rev. Bibl* 3, 1906, 249ff.). Ancient Egyptian types of thought have also been pointed out (so, among others, by E.A.W. Budge, *Coptic Apocrypha*, pp. lxiff.). Now it is true that in these late witnesses of Coptic popular religion many ideas do appear which are found earlier in ancient Egyptian religion. But this does not prove much. The whole complex of relationships must be kept constantly in mind, and the problem of the survival of ancient Egyptian conceptions in the Coptic Church is very much more intricate than a mere comparison of ideas and words would suggest (cf. W. Schneemelcher, 'Der Sermo 'De anima et corpore'', in *Festschrift für G. Dehn*, 1957, p. 130, note 37). The question of Gnosticism in the Gospel of Bartholomew deserves serious consideration. In fact many parallels to the gnostic gospels, in content and not only in form, can be adduced (cf. the survey by H.-Ch. Puech, pp. 354ff. above; But statements about the 'gnostic' character of the Gospel of Bartholomew are only possible when we can say exactly what this gospel looked like, and we are still far from being able to do that. As regards dependence on gnostic ideas, the same principle applies as for dependence on ancient Egyptian types of thought.

Note

4. The Gospel of Bartholomew

* Revised and supplemented by A. de Santos Otero.

a) The Questions of Bartholomew

(Felix Scheidweiler †)

The document entitled in the manuscripts 'Questions of Bartholomew' is extant in five recensions, two Greek ones in Vindobonensis Gr. historicus 67 (G) and in Hierosl. sabaiticus 13 (H), two Latin ones in Vaticanus Reginensis 1050 (R) and in Casanatensis 1880 (C), and a Slavonic one in two manuscripts,[1] one at Petersburg (P) and one in Vienna (Vindob. slav. 125 = V). The complete text is preserved only in C, but in a very corrupt form full of extensive interpolations, especially towards the end. The most valuable recension seems to be H, but it contains barely a third of the text. R contains still less, comprising but three fragments. What is essential in the textual variants is given in the notes to the translation that follows. The translation sometimes follows one recension, sometimes another. In one place I have found it necessary to place the shorter form of H alongside the longer one of CPV.

Right at the beginning it is clear that even C is not without value. The reading of H and V, 'after the resurrection', is impossible, in view of the saying of Jesus: 'Before I have laid aside this body of flesh'. We therefore have to choose between P 'before the resurrection' and C '*Antequam pateretur*'. C undoubtedly is to be preferred. Bartholomew I 7 in H says: εἶδόν σε ἀφανῆ γεγονότα ἀπὸ τοῦ σταυροῦ, φωνῆς δὲ μόνον ἤκουον ἐν τοῖς καταχθονίοις, as against C: '*Vidi te inparabilem* (!, *inapparabilem*?) *factum de cruce, voces tantum audiebam in abissum*' and PV: 'I saw you disappear on the cross, but I heard voices in the underworld.' Here the reading of H must be accepted, and σε must be understood as 'your voice', referring to φωνῆς. By φωνή can only be meant the cry of Jesus which follows in I 19:"Εασόν με εἰσελθεῖν εἰς σεαυτόν· πρὸ γὰρ σοῦ ἐγὼ πλαστός εἰμι, which is also found in C, although this in other respects agrees with the expanded form: '*Dimitte me ingredere in te ipsum, quia a* (read *ante*) *te plasmatus sum.*'

That Jesus spoke thus must, of course, be restored. The reason for the omission is obvious. But P and V have altered the text (this section is missing in G) because the cry is meaningless on the lips of Hades. P reads: 'Allow me, do not oppose me; for I was created before you', V: 'Allow me, interpose yourself; for I was created before you', which completely fails to fit the preceding question of Hades: 'Where are we to hide ourselves from the face of the great king?' and besides would convey the remarkable information that Hades had been created before Satan. H therefore here preserves the original text. Christ was the first thing created by God. G seems to protest against this in an interpolation in IV 28: τὸ γὰρ υἱὸν αὐτοῦ πρὸ τοῦ τοὺς οὐρανοὺς καὶ τὴν γῆν (καὶ) ἡμᾶς (i.e. the angels) πλασθῆναι εἶχεν (to be read instead of εἶχον).

Also remarkable in this connection is the prayer of Jesus in IV 70 with the twice repeated address to God: δόξα σοι, κύριε. But the cry of Jesus must be addressed to Satan. In IV 25 Satan says of himself: Εἰ θέλεις μαθεῖν τὸ ὄνομά μου, πρῶτον ἐλεγόμην Σαταναήλ, ὃ ἑρμηνεύεται ἐξάγγελος θεοῦ. ὅτε δὲ ἀπέγνων (so Bonwetsch instead of ἀγνωὸν) ἀντίτυπον τοῦ θεοῦ, ἐκλήθη τὸ ὄνομά μου Σατανᾶς. ὅ ἐστιν ἄγγελος ταρταροῦχος. This is reminiscent of the teaching of the Bogomils according to Cosmas: Christus is the elder son of God, Satan (ael) is the younger. No chronological conclusions can be deduced from this, but the lack of any influence of the gospel of Nicodemus may be significant. Doubtless H has abbreviated, so that its version is scarcely to be understood without comparing it with the complete form, and we can hardly assume that Satan granted Jesus admittance merely on the strength of his claim to have been created before him. But this is not sufficient to justify the view that H omits the expansions of the complete form derived from the Gospel of Nicodemus. There appears to be no objection to assigning the original form of the Gospel of Bartholomew, which lay before H, to the 3rd century.

Literature: A. Vassiliev, *Quaestiones sancti Bartholomaei apostoli: Anecdota Graeco-Byzantina* I, 1893. N. Bonwetsch, *Die apokryphen Fragen des Bartholomäus*: Gött. Gel. Nachr. 1897 (Editions of G and PV in both these works). André Wilmart-Eug. Tisserant, 'Fragments Grecs et Latins de l'Évangile de Barthélemy', *Rev. Bibl.* 1913, 161ff. (H and R). Umberto Moricca, 'Un nuovo testo dell' evangelo di Bartolomeo', *Rev. Bibl.* 1921, 481ff.; 1922, 20ff. (C). Felix Haase, 'Zur Rekonstruktion des Bartholomäusevangeliums', ZNW 1915, 93ff. Jos. Kroll, *Gott und Hölle. Der Mythos vom Descensuskampfe*, 1932, pp. 71ff. de Santos[4], pp. 536-572, [6]pp. 530-566. M. Craveri, *I Vangeli apocrifi*, Turin 1969, pp. 423-444. L. Moraldi, I, 749-800. A.F.L. Beeston, 'The Quaestiones Bartholomaei', JTS 25, 1974, 124-127. R.McL. Wilson, art. Apokryphen II, TRE III 336. M. Starowieyski, I 494-519. M. Erbetta, I/2 288-319.

Note

a) The Questions of Bartholomew

1. On further Slavonic manuscripts see A. de Santos Otero, *Die handschriftliche Überlieferung der altslavischen Apokryphen* II, PTS 23, 1981, 58-59.

I 1. In the time before the passion[1] of our Lord Christ all the apostles were gathered together. And they asked and besought him: Lord, show us the secrets of the heaven. 2. But Jesus answered: I can reveal nothing to you before I have put off this body of flesh. 3. But when he had suffered and risen again, all the apostles at the sight of him did not dare to ask him, because his appearance was not as it was before, but revealed the fulness of his godhead. 4. But Bartholomew went up to him and said: Lord, I wish to speak to you. 5. Jesus answered him: Beloved Bartholomew, I know what you wish to say. Ask then, and I will tell you all you wish to know. And I myself will make known to you what you do not say. 6. Bartholomew said to him: Lord, when you went to be hanged on the cross, I followed you at a distance and saw how you were hanged on the cross and how the angels descended from heaven and worshipped you. 7. And when darkness came, I looked and saw that you had vanished from the cross; only I heard your voice[2] in the underworld, and suddenly there a great wailing and gnashing of teeth arose. Tell me, Lord, where you went from the cross. 8. And Jesus answered: Blessed are you, Bartholomew, my beloved, because you saw this mystery. And now I will tell you everything you ask me. 9. When I vanished from the cross, I went to the underworld to bring up Adam and all the patriarchs, Abraham, Isaac and Jacob. The archangel Michael had asked me to do this.[3]

H:10. Then Bartholomew said: What voice was heard? Jesus answered: Hades said to Beliar: As I perceive, God has come here. 16/17. Beliar answered Hades: Look carefully, who it is who <has come here>, whether, as it seems to me, it is Elias or Enoch or one of the prophets. But Hades answered Beliar: The 6,000 years are not yet accomplished. From where then can these have come? I have the record of the number in my hands. 18. <And Beliar said to Hades>: Do not fear. Secure your gates and make strong your bars. Consider, God does not come down upon the earth. 19. Hades answered: I pay no heed to your fine words. I have gripes in my belly and my entrails rumble. It cannot but be that God has come down. Woe is me! Where shall I flee before the face of the mighty great God? <And I cried>: Allow me to enter into you. For I was created before you. 20. Then I entered in and scourged him and bound him with chains that cannot be loosed.

CPV:10. When I descended with my angels to the underworld, in order to dash in pieces the iron bars and shatter the portals of the underworld, Hades said to the devil: I perceive that God has come down upon the earth. 11. And the angels cried to the mighty ones: Open your gates, you princes, for the King of glory has come down to the underworld. 12. Hades asked: Who is the King of glory who has come down to us? 13. And when I had descended 500 steps, Hades began to tremble violently and said; I believe that God has come down. His strong breath goes before him. I cannot bear it. 14. But the devil said to him: Do not submit, but make yourself strong. God has not come down. 15. But when I had descended 500 steps more, the strong angels cried out: Open, doors of your prince! Swing open, you gates! For see: the King of glory has come down. And again Hades said: Woe is me! I feel the breath of God. And yet you say: God has not come down upon the earth. 16. Beelzebub replied: Why are you afraid? It is a prophet, and you think it is God. The prophet has made himself like God. We will take him and bring him to those who think to ascend into heaven. 17. And Hades said: Which of the prophets is it? Tell me. Is it Enoch the scribe of righteousness?[4] But

God has not allowed him to come down upon the earth before the end of the 6,000 years. Do you say that it is Elias the avenger? But he does not come down before the end. What am I to do, for the destruction is from God? For already our end is at hand. For I have the number <of the years> in my hands. 18. But when the devil perceived that the Word of the Father had come down upon the earth, he said: Do not fear, Hades; we will make fast the gates and make strong our bars. For God himself does not come down upon the earth. 19. And Hades said: Where shall we hide ourselves from the face of God, the great king? Permit me, do not resist; for I was created before you.[5] 20. And thereupon they dashed in pieces the gates of brass and he ('I'?)[6] shattered the iron bars. And I went in and smote him with a hundred blows and bound him with fetters that cannot be loosed.

And I brought out all the patriarchs and came again to the cross. 21. And Bartholomew said to him: Lord, I saw you again hanging on the cross and all the dead[7] arising and worshipping you. Tell me, Lord, who was he whom the angels carried in their arms, that exceedingly large man? And what did you say to him that he groaned so deeply? 22. It was Adam, the first created, for whose sake I came down from heaven upon the earth. And I said to him: I was hanged upon the cross for your sake and for the sake of your children. And when he heard that, he groaned and said: So you were pleased to do, O Lord.

23. Again Bartholomew, said: Lord, I also saw the angels ascending before Adam and singing praises. 24. But one of the angels, greater than the others, would not go up. He had in his hand a fiery sword and looked at you[8] 25. And all the angels besought him to go up with them; but he would not. But when you commanded him, I saw a flame issuing out of his hands, which reached as far as the city of Jerusalem. 26. And Jesus said to him: Blessed are you, Bartholomew my beloved, because you saw

these mysteries. This was one of the avenging angels who stand before my Father's throne. He sent this angel to me. 27. And for this reason he would not go up, because he wished to destroy the power of the world. But when I commanded him to go up, a flame issued from his hand, and after he had rent the veil of the Temple, he divided it into two parts as a testimony to the children of Israel for my passion, because they crucified me.

28. And when he had said this, he said to the apostles: Wait for me in this place, for today a sacrifice is offered in paradise, that I may receive it after my arrival. 29. And Bartholomew said to him: Lord, what sacrifice is offered in paradise? Jesus answered: That souls of the righteous, when they leave the body, go to paradise, and unless I am present there they cannot enter. 30. Bartholomew asked: Lord, how many souls leave the world every day? Jesus answered: Thirty thousand. 31. And again Bartholomew asked: Lord, when you lived among us, did you receive the sacrifices in paradise? 32. Jesus answered: Verily, I say to you, my beloved, even when I taught among you, I sat at the right hand of the Father and received the sacrifices in paradise. 33. And Bartholomew said: Lord, if 30,000 souls leave this world daily, how many are admitted in paradise? Jesus answered: Only three.[9] 34. Bartholomew again asked: Lord, how many souls are born into the world every day? Jesus answered: Only one over and above those who leave the world.

35. And when he had said this, he gave them the peace and vanished from their sight.

II 1. Now the apostles were in the place Chritir[10] with Mary. 2. And Bartholomew came to Peter and Andrew and John, and said to them: Let us ask Mary, her who is highly favoured, how she conceived the incomprehensible or how she carried him who cannot be carried or how she bore so much greatness. But they hesitated to ask her. 3. Therefore Bartholomew said to Peter: Father Peter, do you as the chief one go to her and ask her. But Peter said to John: You are a chaste youth and blameless; you must ask her. 4. And as they all were doubtful and pondered the matter to and fro, Bartholomew came to her with a cheerful countenance and said: You who are highly favoured, tabernacle of the Most High,[11] unblemished, we, all the apostles ask you, but they have sent me to you. Tell us how you conceived the incomprehensible, or how you carried him who cannot be carried or how you bore so much greatness. 5. But Mary answered: Do not ask me concerning this mystery. If I begin to tell you, fire will come out of my mouth and consume the whole earth. 6. But they asked her still more urgently. And since she did not wish to deny the apostles a hearing, she said: Let us stand up in prayer. 7. And the apostles stood behind Mary. And she said to Peter: Peter, chief of the apostles, the greatest pillar, do you stand behind me? Did not our Lord[12] say: *The head of the man is Christ, but the head of the woman is the man*? Therefore stand in front of me to pray. 8. But they said to her: In you the Lord set his tabernacle and was pleased to contained by you. Therefore you now[13] have more right than we to lead in prayer. 9. But she answered them: You are shining stars, as the prophet said: *I lifted up my eyes to the hills, from which comes my help* [Ps. 120:1 LXX]. You, then, are the hills and you must pray. 10. The apostles said to her: You ought to pray as the mother of the heavenly king. 11. Mary said to them: In your likeness God formed the sparrows and sent them to the four corners of the world.[14] 12. But they answered her: He whom the seven heavens scarcely contain was pleased to be contained in you.

13. Then Mary stood up before them, and spread out her hands to heaven and began to pray thus:[15] O God exceeding great and all-wise, king of the ages, indescribable, ineffable, who didst create the breadths of the heavens by the word and arrange the vault of heaven in harmony,[16] who didst give form to disorderly[17] matter and didst bring together that which was separated, who didst part the gloom of the darkness from the light, who didst make the waters to flow from the same source, before whom the beings of the air tremble and the creatures of the earth fear, who didst give to the earth its place and didst not wish it to perish, in bestowing upon it abundant rain and caring for the nourishment of all things, the eternal Word (Logos) of the Father. The seven heavens could scarcely contain thee, but thou wast pleased to be contained in me, without causing me pain, thou who art the perfect Word (Logos) of the Father, through whom everything was created. Glorify thine exceedingly great name, and allow me to speak before thy holy apostles. 14. And when she had ended the prayer, she began to say to them: Let us sit down on the ground. Come, Peter chief of the apostles, sit on my right hand and put your left hand under my shoulder. And you, Andrew, do the same on my left hand. And you, chaste John, hold my breast. And you, Bartholomew, place your knees on my shoulders and press close my back so that, when I begin to speak, my limbs are not loosed.

15. And when they had done that, she began: When I lived in the Temple of God and received my food from the hand of an angel,[18] one day there appeared to me one in the form of an angel; but his face was indescribable and in his hand he had neither bread nor cup, as had the angel who came to me before. 16. And immediately the veil of the Temple was rent and there was a violent earthquake, and I fell to the earth, for I could not bear the sight of him. 17. But he took me with his hand and raised me up. And I looked toward heaven; and there came a cloud of dew on my face and sprinkled me from head to foot, and he wiped me with his

robe. 18. Then he said to me: Hail, you who are highly favoured, the chosen vessel[19] And then he struck the right side of his garment and there came forth an exceedingly large loaf, and he placed it upon the altar of the Temple, and first ate of it himself and then gave to me also. 19. And again he struck his garment, on the left side, and I looked and saw a cup full of wine. And he placed it upon the altar of the Temple, and drank from it first himself and gave it also to me. And I looked and saw that the bread did not diminish and the cup was full as before. 20. Then he said: Three years more, and I will send my word and you shall conceive my son, and through him the whole world shall be saved. But you will bring salvation to the world. Peace be with you, favoured one, and my peace shall be with you for ever. 21. And when he had said this, he vanished from my eyes and the Temple was as before.

22. As she was saying this, fire came from her mouth, and the world was on the point of being burned up. Then came Jesus quickly and said to Mary: Say no more, or today my whole creation will come to an end. And the apostles were seized with fear lest God should be angry with them.

III 1. And he went with them to the mountain Mauria[20] and sat down in their midst. 2. But they hesitated to question him, because they were afraid. 3. And Jesus answered and said: Ask me what you wish, so that I can teach you and show you. For there are still seven days, and then I ascend to my Father and shall no more appear to you in this form. But they, hesitating, said to him: Lord, show us the abyss, as you promised us. 5. He answered: It is not good for you to see the abyss. But if you wish it, I will keep my promise. Come, follow me and see. 6. And he led them to a place called Cherubim,[21] that is, place of truth. 7. And he beckoned to the angels of the west. And the earth was rolled up like a papyrus roll, and the abyss was exposed to their eyes. 8. When the apostles saw it, they fell on their faces. 9. But Jesus said to them: Did I not say to you that it was not good for you to see the abyss? And he again beckoned to the angels, and the abyss was covered up.

IV 1. And he took them and brought them to the mount of Olives. 2. And Peter said to Mary: You who are favoured, ask the Lord to reveal to us all that is in the heavens. And Mary answered Peter: O rock hewn above,[22] did not the Lord build his Church upon you? You therefore should be the first to go and ask him. 4. Peter said again: You were made the tabernacle of the most high God. You ask him. 5. Mary said: You are the image of Adam. Was not he formed first and then Eve? Look at the sun. It shines like Adam. Look at the moon. It is full of clay, because Eve transgressed the commandment. For God placed Adam in the east and Eve in the west, and he commanded the two lights to shine, so that the sun with its fiery chariot should shine on Adam in the east, and the moon in the west should shed on Eve its milk-white light. But she defiled the commandment of the Lord, and therefore the moon became soiled, and its light does not gleam. Since, therefore, you are the likeness of Adam, you ought to ask him. But in me the Lord took up his abode, that I might restore the dignity of women.

6. Now when they came to the top of the mountain, the Lord parted from them for a little while. Then Peter said to Mary: You made good the transgression of Eve, changing her shame into joy. So you ought to ask. 7. But when Jesus appeared again, Bartholomew said to him: Lord, show us the adversary of men, that we may see his form, or what his work is, or where he comes from, or what power he has that he did not even spare you, but caused you to be hanged on the cross. 8. And Jesus looked at him and said: O bold[23] heart! You ask for that which you cannot look upon. 9. But Bartholomew was frightened, and he fell at Jesus' feet and began to say: O lamp never extinguished, Lord Jesus Christ, everlasting one, who gave grace for the whole world to those who love you, and gave everlasting light through your appearing on earth, who at the command of the Father gave up your life above[24] and completed your work, who changed the dejection of Adam into joy and overcame the sorrow of Eve with gracious countenance by your birth from a virgin mother, do not be angry with me, and grant me the right to ask. 10. When he said this, Jesus raised him up and asked him: Bartholomew, do you wish to see the adversary of men? I tell you that, when you see him, not only you but the apostles with you, and Mary will fall on your faces and will be like the dead. 11. But they all said to him: Lord, we wish to see him. 12. And he led them down from the mount of Olives, and threatened the angels of the underworld, and beckoned to Michael to sound his mighty trumpet in the height of heaven. Then the earth was shaken and Beliar came up, held by 660[25] angels and bound with fiery chains.

13. He was 1600 yards long and 40 yards broad. His face was like a lightning of fire, and his eyes like sparks,[26] and from his nostrils came a stinking smoke. His mouth was like a cleft of rock[27] and a single one of his wings was 80 yards long. 14. As soon as the apostles saw him, they fell to the ground on their faces and became like dead men. 15. But Jesus came near and raised up the apostles, and gave them the spirit of power. Then he said to Bartholomew: Come near to him, Bartholomew, and place your feet on his neck; then he will tell you what his work is, and how he deceives men. 16. And Jesus stood at a distance with the apostles. 17. And Bartholomew raised his voice and said: O womb more spacious than a city! O womb wider than the span of heaven! O womb that contained him whom the seven heavens do not contain. You contained him without pain

and held in your bosom him who changed his being into the smallest of things.[28] O womb that bore, concealed in (your) body, the Christ who has been made visible to many. O womb that became more spacious than the whole creation.[29] 18. And Bartholomew was afraid, and said: Lord Jesus, give me a hem of your garment, that I may venture to approach him. 19. Jesus answered him: You cannot have a hem of my garment, for it is not the garment which I wore before I was crucified. 20. And Bartholomew said: Lord, I fear lest, as he did not spare your angels, he will swallow me up also. 21. Jesus answered: Were not all things made by my word and according to the plan of my Father? The spirits were made subject to Solomon himself. Go therefore, since you have been commanded to do so in my name, and ask him what you wish.

22. And Bartholomew went and trod upon his neck, and pressed down his face to the earth as far as his ears. 23. And Bartholomew asked him: Tell me who you are and what is your name. He replied: Ease me a little, and I will tell you who I am and how I came into this condition and what my work is and how great my power is. 24. Bartholomew eased him and asked him: Tell me all you have done and all you do. 25. Beliar answered and said: If you wish to know my name, I was first called Satanael, which means 'angel of God'. But when I rejected the image of God, I was called Satan, which means 'angel of hell'. 26. And again Bartholomew asked him: Reveal everything to me, and conceal nothing from me. 27. And he replied: I swear to you by the mighty glory of God that even if I wished, I can conceal nothing from you; for he who can convict me stands near me. For if I had the power, I would destroy you as I hurled one of you to destruction.[30] 28. I was the first angel to be created. For when God made the heavens, he took a handful of fire and formed me first, 29. Michael second,[31] the captain of the hosts above, Gabriel third, Uriel fourth, Raphael fifth, Nathanael sixth and 6000 other angels, whose names I cannot tell. There are rod-bearers (lictors) of God, and these scourge me seven times a day and seven times a night and never leave me alone and break in pieces all my power. These are the avenging angels, who stand by God's throne. All these belong to the first-created angels. 30. And after them was the whole number of the angels created: 100 myriads for the first heaven, and the same number for the second, third, fourth, fifth, sixth and seventh heavens. Outside the seven heavens there is the first sphere (the firmament); and there dwell the angels of power who influence men. 31. There are also four angels who are set over the winds. The first rules over Boreas. He is called Chairum,[32] and he has in his hand a fiery rod, and restrains the great moisture which this wind has, so that the earth should not dry up. 32. And the angel who rules over Aparktias[33] is called Oertha. He has a torch of fire in his hand, and holds it to him and to his sides and

warms his coldness so that he does not freeze the earth. 33. And the angel of the south wind is called Kerkutha, and he breaks his violence so as not to shake the earth. 34. And the angel who is set over the south-west wind is called Naoutha. He has a rod of ice in his hand and puts it at his mouth, and quenches the fire which comes from his mouth. And if the angel did not quench it at his mouth, it would set the whole world on fire. 35. And another angel rules over the sea, and makes it rough with the waves.[34] 36. I will not tell you more, for he who stands near me does not permit it.

37. Then Bartholomew asked him: How do you chastise the souls of men? 38. Beliar answered: Am I to describe to you the punishment of the hypocrites, the slanderers, the jesters, the covetous, the adulterers, the sorcerers, the soothsayers, and of those who believe in us, and of all behind whom I stand? 39. Bartholomew said to him: I wish you to be brief. 40. And he gnashed his teeth together, and there came up from the abyss a wheel with a sword flashing fire, which had pipes. 41. And I asked him: What is the sword? 42. He answered: It is the sword for the gluttonous. They are put into this pipe, because in their gluttony they turn to every kind of sin. Into the second pipe come the slanderers, because they secretly slander their neighbours. Into the third pipe come the hypocrites and the rest whom I trip up with my machinations. 43. And Bartholomew said: Do you do this by yourself? 44. Satan replied: If I were able to go out by myself, I would destroy the whole world in three days, but neither I nor any of the 600 goes out. We have other swift servants whom we command. We equip them with a many-barbed hook, and send them out to hunt, and they catch men's souls for us, enticing them with the sweetness of various allurements, that is, drunkenness, laughter, slandering, hypocrisy, pleasures, fornications, and the other devices in their treasury which weaken men.[35] 45. I will tell you also the rest of the names of the angels. The angel of the hail is called Mermeoth. He holds the hail on his head, and my servants adjure him and send him wherever they wish. And other angels rule over the snow,[36] and others over the thunder, and others over the lightning, and when a spirit wishes to go forth from among us, either over land or over water, these angels send out fiery stones and set our limbs on fire. 46. Bartholomew said: Be silent, dragon of the abyss. 47. And Beliar said: I will tell you much about the angels. Those who run together through the heavenly and earthly regions are Mermeoth, Onomatath, Duth, Melioth, Charuth, Graphathas, Hoethra, Nephonos, and Chalkatura. Together they fly through the regions of heaven, of earth, and the underworld . . .

48. Bartholomew interrupted him and said: Be silent and powerless, so that I can entreat my Lord. 49. And Bartholomew fell on his face, and scattered earth on his head, and began: O Lord Jesus Christ, the great and

glorious name. All the choirs of the angels praise you, Lord; and I also, who am unworthy in my lips,[37] praise you, Lord. Hear me, your servant, and as you called me from the custom-house[38] and did not allow me to remain to the end in my former manner of life, hear me, Lord Jesus Christ, and have mercy on the sinners. 50. When he had so prayed, the Lord said to him: Stand up, turn to him that groans. I will declare the rest to you. 51. And Bartholomew raised up Satan, and said to him: Go to your place with your angels,[39] but the Lord has mercy on all his world. 52. But the devil said: Allow me to tell you how I was cast down here, and how God made man. 53. I wandered to and fro in the world, and God said to Michael: Bring me earth from the four ends of the world and water out of the four rivers of paradise. And when Michael had brought them to him, he formed Adam in the east, and gave form to the shapeless earth, and stretched sinews and veins, and united everything into a harmonious whole. And he showed him reverence for his own sake, because he was his image. And Michael also worshipped him. 54. And when I came from the ends of the world, Michael said to me: Worship the image of God which he has made in his own likeness. But I said: I am fire of fire, I was the first angel to be formed, and shall I worship clay and matter? 55. And Michael said to me: Worship, lest God be angry with you. I answered: God will not be angry with me, but I will set up my throne over against his throne, and shall be as he is [Isa. 14:14f.].[40] Then God was angry with me and cast me down, after he had commanded the windows of heaven to be opened.

56. When I was thrown down, he asked the 600 angels that stood under me, whether they would worship (Adam). They replied: As we saw our leader do, we also will not worship him who is less than ourselves. 57. After our fall upon the earth we lay for forty years in deep sleep, and when the sun shone seven times more brightly than fire, I awoke. And when I looked around, I saw the 600 under me overcome by deep sleep. 58. And I awoke my son Salpsan, and took counsel with him how I could deceive the man on whose account I had been cast out of heaven. 59. And I devised the following plan. I took a bowl in my hand, and scraped the sweat from my breast and my armpits, and washed myself in the spring of water from which the four rivers flow.[41] And Eve drank of it, and desire came upon her. For if she had not drunk of that water, I should not have been able to deceive her. 60. Then Bartholomew commanded him to go into Hades. 61. And he himself came to Jesus, and fell at his feet, and began with tears to speak thus: Abba, Father, who cannot be discovered by us, Word of the Father, whom the seven heavens hardly contained, but who were pleased to be contained easily and without pain in the body of the Virgin, without the Virgin knowing that she carried you, while you by your thought ordained everything as it should be, you who give us our daily bread[42]

without our asking for it. 62. You who wore a crown of thorns, in order to prepare for us repentant sinners the precious heavenly crown, who hung upon the cross <and were given gall and vinegar to drink>, in order to give us to drink the wine of contrition, and were pierced in the side with the spear, in order to satisfy us with your body and blood. 63. You who gave names to the four rivers, to the first Phison because of the faith (πίστις!), which you preached after your appearance on earth, to the second Geon, because man was formed of earth (γῆ !), to the third Tigris, that by you we might be shown the consubstantial Trinity (τριάς!) in heaven, and to the fourth Euphrates, because by your coming on earth you made every soul to rejoice (εὐφραίνειν !) through the message of immortality. 64. My God, great Father and King, save, Lord, the sinners.

65. When Bartholomew had uttered his prayer, Jesus said to him: Bartholomew, the Father named me Christ, that I might come down on earth and anoint (χρίειν !) with the oil of life everyone who came to me. And he called me Jesus, that I might heal (ἰᾶσθαι !) every sin of the ignorant and give to men the truth of God.[43] 66. And again Bartholomew said to him: Lord, may I reveal these mysteries to every man? 67. Jesus answered him: Bartholomew, my beloved, entrust them to all who are faithful and can keep them for themselves. For there are some who are worthy[44] of them; but there are also others to whom they ought not to be entrusted, for they are boasters, drunkards, proud, merciless, idolaters, seducers to fornication, slanderers, teachers of falsehood, and doers of all the works of the devil, and therefore they are not worthy that they should be entrusted to them. 68. These things are also to be kept secret because of those who cannot contain them. For all who can contain them shall have a share in them. As regards this, therefore, my beloved, I have spoken to you, for you are blessed and all who are akin to you in having this message entrusted to them, for all who contain it shall receive all they wish in all times[45] of my judgment. 69. At that time, I, Bartholomew, wrote this in my heart, and I took the hand of the friend of men, and began joyfully to speak thus: Glory be to thee, O Lord Jesus Christ, who givest to all thy grace which we have all perceived. Alleluia. Glory be to thee, O Lord, the life of sinners. Glory be to thee, O Lord, through whom death is put to shame. Glory be to thee, O Lord, the treasure of righteousness. We praise thee as God. 70. And when Bartholomew spoke thus, Jesus put off his mantle, and took the kerchief[46] from Bartholomew's neck and began joyfully to say: I am good to you. Alleluia. I am meek and kind to you. Alleluia. Glory be to thee, O Lord. For I give myself to all who desire me. Alleluia. Glory be to Thee, O Lord, world without end. Amen. Alleluia. 71. And when he had finished, the apostles kissed him, and he gave them the peace of love.

V 1. Bartholomew said to him: Tell us, Lord, which sin is more grievous than all other sins. 2. Jesus replied: Truly, I say to you that hypocrisy and slander are more grievous than all other sins. For because of them the prophet said in the Psalm [1:5]: *The ungodly shall not stand in the judgment nor sinners in the congregation of the righteous*, nor the godless in the judgment of my Father. *Truly, truly, I say to you, that every sin shall be forgiven every man, but the sin against the Holy Spirit shall not be forgiven* [Mt. 12:31]. 3. And Bartholomew said: What is the sin against the Holy Spirit? 4. Jesus answered: Everyone who decrees against any man who serves my Father has blasphemed against the Holy Spirit. For every man who serves God with reverence is worthy of the Holy Spirit, and he who speaks any evil against him shall not be forgiven. 5. Woe to him who swears by the head of God, even if he does not commit perjury, but speaks the truth.[47] For God, the Most High, has twelve heads. He is the truth, and in him is no lie and perjury. 6. Go, therefore, and preach to the whole world the word of truth, and you, Bartholomew, preach this (secret) word to everyone who wishes it, and all who believe in it shall have eternal life. 7. Bartholomew said: If any sins with lust of the flesh, how is he recompensed? 8. Jesus answered: It is good if he who is baptised preserves his baptism without blame. But the lust of the flesh will practise its allurement.[48] A single marriage belongs to chaste living. For truly I say to you: He who sins after the third marriage is unworthy of God. 9. But do you preach to all, that they must guard themselves from such things. For I do not depart from you and I give you the Holy Spirit. 10. And Bartholomew with the apostles glorified God before him exceedingly, saying: Glory be to thee, Holy Father, inextinguishable sun, incomprehensible, full of light. To thee be honour, to thee glory and worship world with end. Amen.

Notes

Translation

1. Following C (*antequam pateretur*); 'after the resurrection', H, V; 'before the resurrection' P.
2. φωνῆς δὲ μόνον ἤκουον H; *voces tantum audiebam* C; 'but I only heard voices' PV.
3. The last sentence is missing in the Slavonic versions.
4. Ethiopic Enoch 12:4 and 15:1.
5. C: *Dimitte me ingredere in te ipsum, quia a te plasmatus sum.*
6. The 'I?' comes from Bonwetsch. C makes this sentence passive, but continues: *Et ingressus dominus apprehendit eum*, etc.
7. So C. PV simply: 'the dead'; cf. Mt. 27:52f. In H the first sentence of 21 is missing.
8. The archangel Michael is meant. Paragraphs 25-28 are omitted in H, R has 25, the second part of 26 and 27 in the main. In C 26 is omitted altogether. G begins with §28.

9. So C; PV:10, H:50. G is strange. There Bartholomew asks in §30 about the number of souls admitted into paradise and receives the answer: Three. Then come 32f., where in my view we must read: (Κύριε, εἰ) τρισμύριαι (text τρεῖς μόνον) ψυχαὶ ἐξέρχονται καθ' ἑκάστην ἡμέραν, <πόσαι εἰσέρχονται εἰς τὸν παράδεισον;> λέγει αὐτῷ ὁ Ἰησοῦς· Μόλις αἱ [πεντήκοντα] τρεῖς, ἀγαπητέ μου. Πάλιν Β. λέγει· Καὶ πῶς τρεῖς μόνον εἰσέρχονται εἰς τὸν παράδεισον; λέγει αὐτῷ ὁ Ἰησοῦς· Αἱ μέντοι [πεντήκοντα] τρεῖς εἰσέρχονται εἰς τὸν παράδεισον ἤτοι ἀποτίθονται εἰς τὸν κόλπον Ἀβραάμ. αἱ δὲ λοιπαὶ ἴασιν εἰς τὸν τόπον τῆς ἀναστάσεως (place where they await the resurrection, [ὅτι οὐκ εἰσὶν αἱ τρεῖς ὡς αὐταὶ αἱ πεντήκοντα].

10. Chritir V, Ritor P, Χηλτουρά H, Χερουβίμ G; C gives no name.

11. G σκηνὴ περικομμένη (= κυρίου γενομένη?): 'become most high' PV.

12. Actually Paul, 1 Cor. 11:3.

13. συνιέναι, derived from νῦν ἰέναι?

14. In the Infancy Gospel of Thomas c. 2, p. 135 Tischendorf, p. 444. above.

15. I have omitted the supposedly original Hebrew at the beginning.

16. Following H; GPV are obscure; C has introduced changes.

17. διάτριτα is to be amended to ἀδιάκριτα.

18. According to the Protevangelium of James 8:1 (p. 429 above).

19. G has also καὶ χάρις ἀνέκλειπτε (ever favoured?), which is lacking in H and C.

20. So PV, Μαυρεῖ H, Mambre C.

21. So G, Χαιρουδῆκ H, Cherukt PV. This form is reminiscent of Ἀχερούσια λίμνη.

22. ἀκρότομος 'hewn above', because on it the Church shall be built.

23. So RC; σοὶ ἡ καρδία σκληρά H (PV), ὦ καρδία αὐστηρά G.

24. ὁ τὴν ἄνω οὐσίαν λόγῳ <καταλιπὼν> πατρὸς ἔργον ἐπιτελέσας? (ἐπιτελέσαι?).

25. This and the following numbers vary in the different traditions.

26. So PV, ξοφώδεις GH; nubiliosi C.

27. PV end here.

28. E. Kurtz has altered the meaningless ὡσιουθέν – into οὐσιωθέντα. I have added to it πρὸς βραχύν which comes later with εὐρυχωρότερα γεναμένη but does not fit in there.

29. The gnostic hymn to the μήτρα enlarged to cosmic proportions is out of place here. In H §17 reads: 'And seized by fear Bartholomew raised his voice and cried: 'Praised be the name of your immortal kingdom from henceforth for ever.' When Bartholomew had said this, Jesus permitted him: 'Go and tread upon the neck of Beliar.' And Bartholomew went quickly and trod upon his neck, and Beliar trembled.' At the beginning of §18 H makes Bartholomew not only fear, but weep. Then follows the same prayer as in G. - R has for §17 only: *Tunc tremuit Antichristus et furore repletus est.*

30. Judas.

31. Here G has the following insertion: 'For God had his Son, before heaven and earth and we were created. For when God wished to create all things, his Son spoke the word of creation, so that we also were created by the will of the Son and the decision [or 'with the consent'] of the Father.'

32. This and the following names of the angels are different in C.

33. Aparktis is also a north wind. E. Kurtz conjectures ἀπηλιώτου (east wind).

34. C: 'He breaks the might of the waves', which is more suitable.

35. For ὀλιγωρίας Bonwetsch tentatively suggests παλευτρίας, but this is too remote from the context. According to Kurtz, who cites Hesychius' explanation through ἀδημονεῖν, ὀλιγωρεῖν in 48 means something like 'become weak, powerless'.

My rendering of ὀλιγωρίας corresponds to this. Since 45-47 incl. breaks the connection and contradicts 36, I regard it as an interpolation.

36. χαλάζης is wrongly repeated, and some such word as above is necessary in the translation.

37. G has κήσας (or κήσε) ὄργανον, which I am unable to emend.

38. Transferred from Matthew to Bartholomew.

39. ἄθλων amended apparently by James to ἀγγέλων

40. Of the parallel accounts of the fall of Satan which Bonwetsch has collected, that from the Latin Book of Adam [c. 15] is important, since Satan's threat does not begin so abruptly as it does here: *si irascitur mihi (deus), ponam sedem meam super sidera caeli, et ero similis altissimo.*

41. Here he will have thrown the bowl with his sweat into the water and let it flow into paradise. C: *Accipiensque folia ficus in manibus meis extersi sudorem pectoris mei et sub alarum mearum et proieci secus decursus aquarum.*

42. τὰ ἑκούσια is a corruption of τὰ ἐπιούσια, which is formed on the model of ἄρτος ἐπιούσιος in the Lord's Prayer. James translates 'that which we need'.

43. The text is corrupt: τῶν ἀγνούντων ὑπὸ θεοῦ ἢ καὶ θείων ἄραι τοῖς ἀνθρώποις δωρήσομαι. In C among the mass of expansions the sentence *'dei veritatem ego omnibus donavi'* may come from the original text.

44. The text has ἀνάξιοι. But since the unworthy are mentioned subsequently, I have followed James, who translates 'For some there are that be worthy of them'.

45. ἐν τοῖς . . . κρίσεως μου. I supply καιροῖς.

46. The priest's stole, first used in this sense at the synod of Laodicea between 343 and 381. There the use of the kerchief is only permitted to clergy from the grade of deacon upwards, and so not to the subdeacon, reader, and singer.

47. This must be the meaning of the corrupt text: οὐαὶ τόν ὀμνύοντα κατὰ τῆς κεφαλῆς τοῦ θεοῦ, οὐδὲ τῷ ἐπιορκοῦντι κατ' αὐτοῦ ἀληθῶς. This is supported by the quotation of Mt. 5:36 in C at this point. James seems to alter οὐδέ into οὐαί, but this is insufficient, and it must have continued: οὐαὶ αὐτῷ εἴτε ἐπιορκοῦντι κατ' αὐτῆς εἴτε ἀληθῶς ὀμνύοντι. We must accept the change from the rare construction of οὐαί with acc. (Rev. 8:13) to the usual one with dat.

48. ἐραστής to be altered to ἐρατή or ἐραστή, 'desired'.

(b) Coptic Bartholomew Texts

(Wilhelm Schneemelcher)

1. The tradition: reference has already been made above (p. 537) to the fact that there is a series of Coptic texts which either themselves claim a connection with Bartholomew or are ascribed in modern research to a Gospel of Bartholomew. The problem with which we are concerned has not exactly been made any clearer by the abundance of hypotheses, and a detailed discussion of all the suggestions cannot be undertaken here. The texts are available in the following editions: 'The Book of the Resurrection of Jesus Christ by Bartholomew the Apostle' was published according to the Brit. Mus. Ms. Or. 6804 by E.A. Wallis Budge (*Coptic Apocrypha in the Dialect of Upper Egypt*, 1913, pp. 1-48 Coptic text; pp. 179-215 English translation). To this certainly belong various fragments in the National Library in Paris and one leaf in the Staatsbibliothek in Berlin, published by P. Lacau ('Fragments d'apocryphes coptes', in *Mémoires publieés par les* *membres de l'Institut français d'archéologie orientale du Caire* IX, 1904, 39-77, with French translation; English translation in Budge *op. cit.* 216-230). These leaves collected by Lacau present two recensions of this work, differing from one another, while the London MS represents a third recension. A part of the leaves which Lacau printed is also to be found in E. Revillout, *Les apocryphes coptes* I (= PO II 2, Paris 1904; reprinted 1946), 185-194.

Now in addition to these fragments, which clearly are related to the text of the London MS and in which Bartholomew appears as the narrator, so that they belong to the Coptic Bartholomew-literature, Revillout published a larger number of leaves (mostly from the Paris National Library, but partly from other libraries) which he declared to be the remains of a 'Gospel of the Twelve Apostles'. A. Baumstark (*Rev.Bibl.* 3, 1906, 245-265) and P. Ladeuze (RHE VII, 1906), 245-268) have already demonstrated that both association and title are completely arbitrary (cf. also the judgment of H.-Ch. Puech, above p. 381f.): the texts which Revillout collected are of very diverse origin and in part do not belong to any apocryphal gospel at all, but are the remains of a homiletic work. Only for particular pieces in Revillout's collection may we consider a connection with a writing of Bartholomew, as for others we may assume a relationship with a writing of Gamaliel.

F. Haase (ZNW 16, 1915, 93-112) endeavoured to bring a certain order into the mass of the fragments, which can indeed be achieved, above all with the aid of the London text, which was not known either to Lacau, to Revillout, or to Baumstark. James provides a survey of the fragments (James, pp. 147-152: 'Coptic Narratives of the Ministry and the Passion'); in an analysis of the 'Book of the Resurrection of Jesus Christ by Bartholomew the Apostle' he has further tried to summarise the text, so that the train of thought (so far as we can speak of such a thing at all) of the two (or three) recensions becomes clear (James, pp. 181-186). Haase distinguishes K^1 (= fragments in Lacau and Revillout) and K^2 (= British Museum MS), but it must be observed that K^1 is extant in two recensions; at any rate for some sections the tradition contains two versions slightly different from one another, while K^2 appears rather a paraphrase than a recension of K^1.

2. Content: the reconstruction of the two recensions of K^1, of which of course only individual leaves are extant, can be undertaken with some probability for those sections which present manifest parallels with K^2. On the other hand it is very difficult to adduce texts from the fragments, as parts of K^1, for the portions which are lacking in K^2. Nevertheless, reference may be made to a few leaves which may possibly be considered to belong to this group of writings:

(a) *The fragments* (K^1)
    (i) Revillout, No. 6 (pp. 157f.)
Jesus is sitting with his disciples at the last supper. Matthias brings a cock which he has killed, and reports how the Jews observed that the blood of his master (*sc.* Jesus) would be shed like that of the cock. Jesus recalls the cock to life again as an indication of his resurrection.

No cogent reasons can be produced for assigning this fragment to a document of Bartholomew. Since some pages are missing before the present beginning of the 'Book of the Resurrection', the possibility may be admitted that such a narrative of the last supper, developed in very legendary fashion, belonged to it - but no more. James (p. 150) refers to the Ethiopic 'Book of the Cock' and to other versions of the motif.

(ii) Revillout, No. 5 (pp. 156f.) and App. No. 1 (pp. 195f.)

In these two fragments the subject is the betrayal by Judas. The first relates that Judas' wife induced her husband to treachery. The second describes how the seven-month-old child of Joseph of Arimathaea, to whom Judas' wife served as nurse, besought his father to send the woman away since she and her husband had accepted the blood-money. To this is added a short description of the incidents at the crucifixion.

Connection with a Bartholomew-document is more than questionable. The second part of the second fragment especially points to a different relationship; in particular it is much more concise in its presentation. This argument is not, however, decisive, since similar summaries also occur in K^2.

(iii) Revillout, Nos. 7-9 (pp. 159-161)

These fragments have already been discussed above (pp. 103 ff.). They derive from the Strasbourg Papyrus and (against James, pp. 150 and 182) can hardly be linked with the 'Book' of Bartholomew.

(iv) Revillout, No. 12 (pp. 165ff.)

This tells of a man named Ananias, who hurries to the cross and cries out to the Jews that they ought to crucify him and not Christ. A voice from the cross promises him that his soul shall not enter into Amente, nor his body decay. The high priests seek to stone Ananias, but the attempt fails. In the fire into which he is then cast he remains three days and three nights unharmed. Finally he is slain with a spear, and Jesus takes his soul with him into heaven.

That this fragment belongs to the 'Book' of Bartholomew is probable because there is a reference to this incident at the present beginning of the London MS: 'After they had crucified the Saviour, they laid him in a grave; on the completion of the third day he rose up from the dead; he took the soul of the holy Apa Ananias with him into heaven' (fol. 1a; Budge p. 1).

(v) Lacau IV (pp. 39-77 = Revillout, pp. 185-194 and pp. 149f.; but Revillout gives a shorter text than Lacau; Lacau in his translation prints side by side the two extant versions of this passage).

The text begins with the conquest of hell and the deliverance of the children of Adam. Then follows the cursing of Judas. After a gap it is related how Death (who previously had remained with the body of Jesus at the grave) sends his son Pestilence to secure Amente (i.e. hell). But when Death with his six decans comes to Amente, he finds only three 'voices' left, Judas, Cain and Herod. All the rest have been set free by Christ. After a short transitional passage the narrative begins afresh: the holy women go to the grave - they are enumerated in detail - and Mary falls into conversation with Philogenes, the gardener, who relates the events at the resurrection of Jesus. Jesus himself now appears and speaks with Mary, whom he first favours with words of blessing and then charges to inform his disciples of his resurrection. Mary asks for Jesus' blessing, and receives the promise that she will be with Christ in his kingdom. Here the account suddenly changes to the first person: 'Believe me, my brethren, ye apostles, I Bartholomew, the apostle of the Son of God, saw the Son of God . . . ' (Lacau, p. 54). After the description of what Bartholomew saw, the promise to Mary is continued (have two different traditions grown together here?). Mary then goes to the apostles, who are celebrating the eucharist on the Mount of Olives.

Some pages are now missing. The text begins again with the bringing of Adam and Eve and their children before God. 'Believe me, O my brethren, ye apostles, I Bartholomew have never since my birth seen such a human form as was comparable with the form of Adam, save that of the Saviour' (Lacau, p. 59). The description of the figures of Adam and Eve is followed by their acquittal by God and by the angels' song of praise. All this is given by Bartholomew as an eye-witness account, and for this he is praised by the apostles, but for his part stresses his unworthiness. A new appearance follows: Christ takes the apostles with him into heaven, where they are blessed one after the other by God. This too is the account of Bartholomew! In a new scene Christ is sent by God to comfort the apostles. He finds them in Galilee, and bestows on them the Holy Spirit. Here the fragment breaks off. There can be no doubt that these long passages represent a recension, or two recensions, of the 'Book' of Bartholomew. There are corresponding passages in the London text, which is however more detailed.

Other fragments from Revillout's collection cannot be adduced here since there are no indications of any kind that they belong to the Bartholomew literature. Perhaps a palaeographic examination of the Coptic leaves bound up together in the Paris library may yet provide a more accurate indication of where other fragments belong. From the content it is not possible, at any rate for the present, to allocate any others.

(b) *The London Text* (K²)

Despite many gaps, the London MS presents a coherent account, although the beginning is missing. Budge conjectures that five leaves have been lost. An important point is that the title of the work can be inferred from the text; in fol. 23b (Budge, p. 46) we find: 'This is the Book of the Resurrection of Jesus Christ our Lord in joy and exultation'. Since in this text also Bartholomew frequently appears as the narrator - moreover it is reported that he committed these secrets to his son Thaddaeus (fol. 9a) - Budge has given the work the title: 'The Book of the Resurrection of Jesus Christ, by Bartholomew the Apostle'. Also interesting is the admonition not to let the book fall into the wrong hands, i.e. those of heretics or unbelievers (fol. 9a; cf. Puech, NTApo³, pp. 328f.).

In this recension the composition of the document is even less rigorously thought out. The different items are reported in broad array, and contradictions are not lacking: scenes in the underworld, a dialogue between Death and the corpse of Jesus, the descent of Christ into hell, the cursing of Judas, the freeing of the sons of Adam (save three, whose names however are not here mentioned), appearances of the risen Christ, the report of Philogenes, the promises to Mary,

556

the ascent of the Redeemer and his reception in heaven, Adam and Eve in heaven, the hymns of the angels, a new epiphany of Jesus, the blessing of the apostles by God, the death and raising up of Siophanes (the son of Thomas), the story of doubting Thomas, the return of Jesus to heaven and the eucharist of the apostles, who now separate and preach in the name of the holy and consubstantial (ὁμοούσιος !) Trinity. All this is strung together, without any real logical connection between the individual episodes. The delight in broad narrative is stronger than the literary concern to produce a finished work. If we compare the corresponding parts of the London MS with the fragments adduced above, the relationship becomes clear, but so also does the further development. Often indeed the London text seems to be a paraphrase of an older original. On the significance of this text for the angelology of the Coptic Church, see C. Detlef G. Müller, *Die Engellehre der koptischen Kirche*, Wiesbaden 1959, pp. 275-281; *id.* in *Kindlers Literaturlexikon*, I, 1964 (reprint 1981), 1383-1384. For a complete Italian translation - with restorations and variants from Recension K[1] - see Erbetta I 2, 301-319.

3. Assessment of the Coptic texts: as has been shown, the Coptic texts are not a unity but reflect a development of the material with which we are concerned. So long as we do not possess texts which represent an older stage than K[1], it must admittedly be difficult to establish exactly what is original and what expansion within the Coptic field. That this literature goes back to Greek antecedents is to be assumed. The 'Questions of Bartholomew' however, in the forms in which they have come down to us, are not the direct antecedents of the Coptic recensions. Certainly there are isolated parallels (cf. for example what is said about Adam in I 22 with fol. 11a f. in the London MS). More important is the general tenor: in both works the descent of Christ to hell, his resurrection and the deliverance of Adam, and finally the figure of Bartholomew stand in the foreground. But this is certainly not enough for precise statements about the connection between the tradition in Greek, Latin and Slavonic and the Coptic texts. We can only conjecture that both streams of tradition go back to a special Bartholomew-tradition of the 3rd or 4th centuries. Possibly there was at that time a shorter Gospel of Bartholomew, which was the starting-point for this literature. Even this primitive version, however, is probably not to be dated too early, since almost nothing at all is known from the first centuries about a special reverence for Bartholomew. Only in the Coptic Church does this apostle come to play a more prominent role. The Coptic texts are at any rate not older than the 5th-7th centuries, and for K[2] a still later date lies within the range of possibility.

The Coptic texts are, however, a particularly characteristic example of the growth of apocryphal literature, and especially of the survival of important cycles of narrative and motifs. In these late texts distinctive tendencies can scarcely be detected any longer. Isolated gnostic motifs may certainly be observed, but the general tendency of the versions before us is not to be described as gnostic.

5.The Gospel of Gamaliel

(*M.-A. van den Oudenrijn* †)[1]

This book is concerned with the events of Good Friday and the days which followed. The ostensible author is a contemporary of Christ, the Rabbi Gamaliel the Elder known from Acts (5:34; 22:3) and also from the Mishnah. The name 'Gospel' was bestowed on this document by Anton Baumstark (*Rev. Bibl.* 1906, 253) and Paulin Ladeuze (RHE, 1906, 245). The narrative was utilised by Heryâqos of Al-Bahnasâ, a bishop who is often mentioned elsewhere but cannot yet be more precisely identified, in a homily which in the Ethiopic version bears the title 'Lament of Mary' (*Lâha Mâryâm*), and so has come down to us. This Lament of Mary must have been a favourite work among the Copts.

Some Coptic fragments were published at the beginning of the century by Pierre Lacau ('Fragments d'apocryphes coptes', in *Mémoires publiées par les membres de l'Institut français d'archéologie orientale*, vol. IX, Cairo 1904) and E. Revillout (*Les apocryphes coptes*, I, PO II, 116-189, Paris 1904). There are several Arabic redactions, which in part have also appeared in print in Coptic-Arabic devotional books (Cairo 1902, 1927 and 1945; cf. Jean Simon, *Orientalia* 1940 (9), 159 and G. Giamberardini, *L'immacolata Concezione di Maria nella Chiesa Egiziana*, Cairo 1953, p. 31, note 3). A. Mingana published in 1928 an Arabic version from two Garshûni MSS in private hands (*Woodbrooke Studies* II, 211-240; Introduction, English translation and notes, *ib.* pp. 178-210 = BJRL 12, 1928, 411ff.). The Ethiopic version also, which is the most complete of all, was translated in the 14th century from an Arabic prototype. It was in its time very widely disseminated in Ethiopia, and was read in sections in Holy Week. Two fragments of this Ethiopic text had already been known since 1892 (cf. M.R. James, *The Apocryphal New Testament*, Oxford ⁵1953, p. 152), and were recognised by Felix Haase (*Literarkr. Untersuchungen zur orient.-apokr. Evangelienliteratur*, Leipzig 1913, pp. 20-21) as detached fragments of Gamaliel.

The title 'Lament of Mary' handed down in the Ethiopic MSS is no longer appropriate for the second half of the homily; in the second part of the narrative the Virgin is not mentioned at all. In one MS, admittedly late, we find a division of the booklet into eleven chapters. In the first five it is not always clearly evident where we have to do with the original Gamaliel-narrative (G) and where with the additions of the homilist (H), but by and large the following division may be close to the mark:

I.1-16 Exordium of the homily (H); I.17-35 first lament of the Virgin (H); I.36-44 Mary and the apostles (doubtful); I.45-55 second lament of the Virgin (H, but in verses 49-51 possibly G in a shortened form); I.56-59 John takes the place of Peter (G); I.60 to II.12 the Virgin betakes herself to Calvary (H); II.13-21 the Mother beneath the cross (G?); II.22-26 further laments of the Virgin (H); II.27-34 continuation of the narrative (G); II.35-38 Mary's parting words (H); II.39-41 earthquake and darkness at the death of Jesus (G); II.42-51 renewed lament of the Virgin (H); II.52-III.25 continuation of the narrative (G); III.26-40 insertion by the homilist (H); III.40-IV.4 continuation of the narrative (G);

IV.5-V.1 homiletic developments (H). From V.2 to XI.11 we have the Gamaliel narrative, only rarely interrupted by some rhetorical outbursts from the homilist (e.g. VIII.4). VI. 21-VII.9 Pilate believes in the resurrection of Jesus; VII.10-21 he cross-examines the soldiers who stood guard at the grave, and unmasks their falsehoods; VII.22-VIII.14 healing of the captain through contact with Jesus' grave-clothes; VIII.15-XI.5 raising up of a dead man in Jesus' grave; XI.6-11 explanation by the ostensible eye-witness Gamaliel. The final passage (XI.12-50) with the exchange of letters between Pilate and Herod is probably a later continuation of the Gamaliel story, which breaks off with XI.50.

The text as we now have it appears to be no older than the 5th or 6th century, but older elements may have been worked up in the narrative. The captain in Mt. 27:54 (Mk. 15:39), who plays a major role in the narrative, here bears no proper name. The document was evidently composed in Coptic by an orthodox Christian, who was, however, hostile to the Jews. His chief desires were first to confirm the fact of the resurrection of Jesus by alleged new arguments, and secondly to present Pilate, who in the Coptic Church is revered as a saint, so far as possible in a favourable light.[2]

Notes

5. The Gospel of Gamaliel

1. In connection with their criticism of the Coptic texts published by Revillout (cf. above, p. 554), Baumstark and Ladeuze drew attention to a lost Gospel of Gamaliel, of which we otherwise know nothing. Now Professor M.-A. van den Oudenrijn discovered in an Ethiopic MS a sermon in which this apocryphon has probably been worked up. The discoverer, who has since died, made a short account of this text available for NTApo[3], and it is here reprinted, supplemented by a fairly long note by A. de Santos Otero (*W. Schn.*).

2. After his outline printed above, M.-A. van den Oudenrijn published the Ethiopic original of the homily by the Coptic bishop Heryâqos, known as the 'Lament of Mary', in which are incorporated extensive fragments of the presumed 'Gospel of Gamaliel', in an excellent edition with introduction, German translation and commentary (*Gamaliel: Äthiopische Texte zur Pilatusliteratur*, (Spicilegium Friburgense 4), Freiburg (Switzerland) 1959).

The result of this investigation confirms in essentials the assessment of the 'Gospel of Gamaliel' given by van den Oudenrijn himself shortly before in the contribution reprinted above, and at the same time makes clear the extremely complicated tradition-history of this apocryphon, from its origin in the Coptic milieu down to the remains which have come down to us, through several translations and reworkings, in the Ethiopic homily mentioned. As a result the important question of the identity of this document, which has occupied scholars since the discovery of the first Coptic fragments at the beginning of this century, is largely resolved. Similarly the question of the position of this 'gospel' within the manifold extant Pilate literature seems also to be resolved. It is certainly not the debris of a Greek archetype, such as the Gospel of Nicodemus or that of Peter, but an original Coptic reworking of material already extant in Greek models, with an emphatic edifying and apologetic tendency. One of the salient features of the 'Gospel of Gamaliel' is in this connection its concern to exonerate Pilate the governor from responsibility for the crucifixion of Jesus. This tendency can of course also be found outside the Coptic sphere of influence, but nowhere is it so pronounced as in this document and in the 'Martyrium Pilati', also published by van den Oudenrijn (*op. cit.* pp. 112-180) and likewise ascribed to Gamaliel, in which the Roman governor, in unison with Coptic-Ethiopic hagiography, is made into a Christian martyr (for further details on this see E. Cerulli, 'Tiberius and Pontius Pilate in Ethiopian Tradition and Poetry', *Proc. British Acad.* 59, 1973, 141-158).

On the basis of this and similar observations (cf. van den Oudenrijn, *op. cit.* pp. xlff.), this gospel may be reckoned to the abundant Pilate literature, in the origin of which the Acts of Pilate (= Gospel of Nicodemus), which has come down to us in Greek, directly or indirectly played the godfather. Examples of such imitations of apocrypha are by no means rare in Coptic literature, particularly in the area of the so-called 'Later Acts of Apostles', where we find numerous reworkings, adaptations and paraphrases of the Greek models alongside genuine translations from the Greek (cf. on this vol. II, chapter XVI). The fact that in their Coptic *Vorlage* the apostolic Acts already formed a closed corpus explains why the several writings show a relatively settled textual tradition in the extant Coptic, Arabic and Ethiopic versions. For the apocryphal gospels - apart from the gnostic area - there was no such corpus in Coptic literature, which resulted *inter alia* in the discordant and problematic textual tradition of the 'Gospel of Gamaliel', to which we have already referred.

After van den Oudenrijn's edition of the 'Lament of Mary', extracts from it in Italian appeared in Moraldi (I, 661-680) and a complete translation in Erbetta (I/2, 346-366) *(de Santos Otero)*.

Reviews

JTS 25 (1923-24) 184-89
422-25

TS 21 (1960) 292-94
26 (1965) 116-18

TQ 139 (1959) 340-41
144 (1964) 233-34

TRu 6 (1960-61) 84-85
30? (1964) 278-79

JBL 83 (1964) 316-17
428-31
85 (1966) 524-25

R. McL. Wilson, JTS 40,1 (1989) 217-219
[German 5th ed].

J. K. Elliott, NovT 31/2 (1989) 186-189
[German 5th ed].

R. I. Pervo. Sec Cent. 8/3 (1991) 184-186
[German 5th ed].

A. Y. Collins, CBQ 55/1 (1993) 180-82.

J. K. Elliott, NovT 34/4 (1992) 406-9.

J. A. Fitzmyer, TS 53/2 (1992) 342-43.

PAUL D. SANSONE, O.F.M.

910716B   29.95 (21.95)